Brief Contents

Writing
from Sources

NINTH EDITION

Brenda Spatt

The City University of New York

bedford/st.martin's
Macmillan Learning

Boston | New York

For Bedford/St. Martin's

Vice President, Editorial, Macmillan Higher Education Humanities: Edwin Hill
Editorial Director, English and Music: Karen S. Henry
Senior Publisher for Composition, Business and Technical Writing, Developmental Writing:
Leasa Burton
Executive Editor: Molly Parke
Senior Developmental Editor: Rachel Goldberg
Editorial Assistant: Jennifer Prince
Production Editor: Lidia MacDonald-Carr
Production Supervisor: Robert Cherry
Marketing Manager: Emily Rowin
Permissions Editor: Angela Boehler
Text Permissions Manager: Kalina Ingham
Senior Art Director: Anna Palchik
Cover Design: William Boardman
Cover Images: (notebooks, papers, books) urfinguss/Getty Images; (phone) jpgfactory/
Getty Images; (laptop) RaStudio/Getty Images
Project Management: Graphic World, Inc.
Cartographer: Mapping Specialists, Ltd.
Composition: Graphic World, Inc.
Printing and Binding: RR Donnelley and Sons

Manufactured in the United States of America.

0 9 8 7 6
f e d c b

For information, write: Bedford/St. Martin's, 75 Arlington Street, Boston, MA 02116
(617-399-4000)

ISBN 978-1-319-08576-6

Acknowledgments
Text acknowledgments and copyrights appear at the back of the book on pages 537–42, which constitute an extension of the copyright page. Art acknowledgments and copyrights appear on the same page as the art selections they cover. It is a violation of the law to reproduce these selections by any means whatsoever without the written permission of the copyright holder.

To the Instructor

A warm greeting to all those who have used my book or are now considering adopting it.

While preparing this ninth edition, I have been pondering the difference between *Writing from Sources* and other textbooks about writing research essays. What defines my book is its method. As a young instructor at the City University of New York in a time of open admissions, I needed to find a more effective way of teaching the dreaded basic composition course. My students were keen to learn, but without the educational foundations that make the process easy. They lacked the tools that students at many other colleges took for granted: wide vocabulary, the habit of reading, facility in writing. What I learned in that pre-Internet decade was that it was folly to send these students to the library to do research before they had been taught how to examine a source, to understand it, to write about it, and, eventually, to incorporate that source, with others, into essays of their own. To my mind, research textbooks that started the semester in the library were putting the end-product cart before the acquisition-of-skills horse. Hence, the slow, cumulative process that distinguishes *Writing from Sources*.

As users know, if you follow the sequence of chapters, exercises, and assignments more or less as they are presented in the book, your students will gradually become equipped to make that trip to the library or to Google Scholar and become proper researchers. Such skills as summary, quotation, and paraphrase need to be learned incrementally, through practice, and *Writing from Sources* provides more than enough material for your students to gain that practice. Few instructors ever assign all 38 exercises in any given semester. But the range of choices allows them to adapt the sequence to the specific needs of their classes and to provide variety for themselves so that their teaching won't get stale. Similarly, each assignment and exercise offers one to three readings so that you have a variety of options from semester to semester. In effect, the only sine qua non about *Writing from Sources* is the sequence; everything else is your choice.

A great deal has changed in the 35 years since the first edition, from the inexorable rise of technology with its opportunities and distractions, to the gradual loss of interest in reading texts of any length, to the barrage of Internet sources of dubious value, to the increasing focus on college as a provider of professional training rather than a liberal arts education. These changes have presented formidable challenges to the teaching of composition, with the research essay now regarded by many students as an almost arcane obstacle to be surmounted. Again, I believe that "slow learning," like the "slow food" movement, is helpful in making these challenges less daunting.

But *Writing from Sources* has also changed as its constituency has changed. Readings are shorter, less dense and abstract, and are often accompanied by marginal glosses against which students can check their understanding of the text. This doesn't mean that the readings have been dumbed down; the authors remain noted academics, authorities in their fields, and journalists writing for respected periodicals. The clusters of readings on two topics in the eighth edition—*the college experience* and *social media*—proved to be very popular and have been retained and refreshed, together with a new, smaller group of readings on *gender differences*. As a preliminary, or even an alternative, to sending your students off to do research, you can easily assign a mini-research essay by choosing several readings from one of the clusters (see p. 564). Wherever possible—given that you can't avoid the printed word for long in a textbook on writing—material from other media is introduced, especially in the second half of the book.

To give you some insight into how *Writing from Sources* can work in the classroom, we have asked Cliff Toliver, of Missouri Southern State University, to provide a section of the Instructor's Manual called "WFS in the Classroom." Cliff has used the textbook for over twenty years and has tried numerous permutations of exercises and combinations of assignments. He particularly values the incremental approach, asking his students to review previous chapters as necessary and making sure that skills practiced at the beginning of the term are retained throughout. For instructors who would like to look at a model sequence as a starting point, Cliff has included a sample syllabus. He also discusses ways to use exercises as group activities.

Here is a summary of the changes that you'll find in the ninth edition of *Writing from Sources*:

- Over 50 new readings from authors such as Jonathan Safran Foer, Steven Pinker, Sherry Turkle, Dinesh D'Souza, Kwame Anthony Appiah, and Hanna Rosin.
- New "Background" notes on many of the earlier readings, to help students adjust to academic writing.
- Expanded treatment of "thesis" throughout the book.
- Expanded references to visuals and other media, with more suggestions for including pictures, videos, and audio recordings in essays.
- Revised prefaces to the four main sections of the book, connecting writing in college with writing in the professions.
- Marginal annotations provided for many model readings and bibliographies and for the "horror film" research essay in Chapter 11.

- Three thematic clusters—the college experience, social media, and gender differences—all containing new readings suitable for use in comparison or multiple-source assignments.

- Updated coverage of databases for research and an all-new Chapter 12, with a more precise and current presentation of MLA and APA documentation for a variety of sources.

- A completely revised Instructor's Manual, with suggestions about how to use every reading and every assignment in the book.

- "WFS in the Classroom," a new section of the Instructor's Manual that provides a model for creating your own syllabus and ideas for devising group activities to make full use of the exercises.

Acknowledgments

Many instructors participated in the preparation of this ninth edition by sharing their responses to and experiences of the previous edition. I want to thank Dianna Baldwin, Michigan State University; Brandon Belcher, Guilford Technical Community College; Deborah Carmichael, Michigan State University; James Crooks, Shasta College; Lara Gary, Sacramento City College; Hayley Haugen, Ohio University Southern; Nina Haydel, Rider University; Karen Jensen, The University of Texas at San Antonio; Gail Levy, Leeward Community College; Brooke Lopez, The University of Texas at San Antonio; Tanya Millner-Harlee, Manchester Community College; Lyle Morgan, Pittsburg State University; Paula Priamos, California State University at San Bernardino; Dixie Shaw-Tillmon, The University of Texas at San Antonio; Greg Thomas, Morgan Community College; and William Waters, University of Houston–Downtown.

Three instructors also undertook to review the vast range of readings that were initially considered for inclusion in the new edition and helped us to choose texts that would be most likely to appeal to your students and sustain their interest as they worked on their assignments: Elizabeth Johnston, Monroe Community College; C. Cole Osborne, Guilford Technical Community College; and Cliff Toliver, Missouri Southern State University. I am particularly indebted to Cliff for his advice, encouragement, and insight into what would and would not work in the classroom. And I have appreciated the efforts of Erica Appel, Jennifer Prince, and everyone at Bedford/St Martin's, but especially the contributions of my excellent editor, Rachel Goldberg, who not only deftly guided the book through the editorial and production processes, but also assumed responsibility for preparing the new, improved, and easier-than-ever-to-use Chapter 12 on Methods of Documentation.

I do hope that you and your students will find using the ninth edition of *Writing from Sources* both productive and enjoyable.

Get the Most Out of Your Course with *Writing from Sources*

Bedford/St. Martin's offers resources and format choices that help you and your students get even more out of your book and course. To learn more or to order any of the following products, contact your Bedford/St. Martin's sales representative, e-mail sales support (**sales_support@bfwpub.com**), or visit the Web site at **macmillanhighered.com/writingfromsources/catalog**.

Choose from Alternative Formats of *Writing from Sources*

Bedford/St. Martin's offers a range of affordable formats, allowing students to choose the one that works best for them. For details, visit **macmillanhighered .com/writingfromsources/catalog**.

- *Paperback* To order the paperback edition, use ISBN 978-1-4576-7453-2.
- *Other popular e-book formats* For details, visit **macmillanhighered .com/ebooks**.

Select Value Packages

Add value to your text by packaging one of the following resources with *Writing from Sources*. To learn more about package options for any of the following products, contact your Bedford/St. Martin's sales representative or visit **macmillanhighered.com/writingfromsources/catalog**.

Writer's Help 2.0 is a powerful online writing resource that helps students find answers whether they are searching for writing advice on their own or as part of an assignment.

- **Smart search.** Built on research with more than 1,600 student writers, the smart search in *Writer's Help 2.0* provides reliable results even when students use novice terms, such as *flow* and *unstuck*.
- **Trusted content from our best-selling handbooks.** Choose *Writer's Help 2.0 for Hacker Handbooks* or *Writer's Help 2.0 for Lunsford Handbooks* and ensure that students have clear advice and examples for all of their writing questions.
- **Adaptive exercises that engage students.** *Writer's Help 2.0* includes LearningCurve, game-like online quizzing that adapts to what students already know and helps them focus on what they need to learn.

Student access is packaged with *Writing from Sources* at **a significant discount.** Order ISBN 978-1-319-06283-5 for *Writer's Help 2.0 for Hacker Handbooks* or ISBN 978-1-319-06282-8 for *Writer's Help 2.0 for Lunsford Handbooks* to ensure your students have easy access to online writing support. Students who rent a book or buy a used book can purchase access to *Writer's Help 2.0* at **macmillanhighered .com/writershelp2.**

Instructors may request free access by registering as an instructor at **macmillanhighered.com/writershelp2.** For technical support, visit **macmillan highered.com/getsupport.**

Portfolio Keeping, **Third Edition, by Nedra Reynolds and Elizabeth Davis,** provides all the information students need to use the portfolio method successfully in a writing course. *Portfolio Teaching,* a companion guide for instructors, provides the practical information instructors and writing program administrators need to use the portfolio method successfully in a writing course. To order *Portfolio Keeping* packaged with this text, contact your sale representative for a package ISBN.

Instructor Resources

macmillanhighered.com/writingfromsources/catalog

You have a lot to do in your course. Bedford/St. Martin's wants to make it easy for you to find the support you need—and to get it quickly.

The Instructor's Manual for Writing from Sources is available as a PDF that can be downloaded from the Bedford/St. Martin's online catalog at the URL above. In addition to chapter overviews and teaching tips, the instructor's manual includes sample syllabi and possible responses for exercises and assignments.

Teaching Central offers the entire list of Bedford/St. Martin's print and online professional resources in one place. You'll find landmark reference works, sourcebooks on pedagogical issues, award-winning collections, and practical advice for the classroom—all free for instructors. Visit **macmillanhighered. com/teachingcentral**.

Join Our Community! The Macmillan English Community is now Bedford/ St. Martin's home for professional resources, featuring Bedford *Bits,* our popular blog site offering new ideas for the composition classroom and for composition teachers. Connect and converse with a growing team of Bedford authors and top scholars who blog on *Bits*: Andrea Lunsford, Nancy Sommers, Steve Bernhardt, Traci Gardner, Barclay Barrios, Jack Solomon, Susan Bernstein, Elizabeth Wardle, Doug Downs, Liz Losh, Jonathan Alexander, and Donna Winchell.

In addition, you'll find an expanding collection of additional resources that support your teaching.

- Sign up for webinars
- Download resources from our professional resource series
- Start a discussion
- Ask a question
- Follow your favorite members
- Review projects in the pipeline

Visit **community.macmillan.com** to join the conversation with your fellow teachers.

To the Student

Every day, as you talk, write, and work, you use sources. Much of your knowledge and many of your ideas originate outside yourself. You have learned from your school classes and from observing the world around you, from reading, from watching television and movies, from the Internet, and from a multitude of other experiences. Most of the time, you don't consciously think about where you got the information; you simply write and make decisions using what you know.

Sources in College

In college, your contact with sources intensifies. Each class, each book, bombards you with new facts and ideas. Your academic success depends on how well you understand and retain what you read and hear in your courses, distinguish between the more important and the less important, relate new facts and ideas to what you already have learned, and, especially, communicate your findings to others.

Most college writing contains material taken from sources as well as your own ideas. Depending on the individual course and assignment, a college paper may emphasize your own conclusions, supported by your research, or it may emphasize the research itself, showing that you have assembled and mastered a certain body of information. Either way, the paper will contain something of others and something of you. If 20 students in your class are all assigned the same topic, the other 19 papers will all be somewhat different from yours.

Sources in the Professional World

College writing assignments help you to consolidate what you have learned in your classes and expand your capacity for constructive thinking and clear communication. These are not merely academic skills; in most careers, success depends on these abilities. You will listen to the *opinions* of your boss your colleagues, and your customers; read the *case histories* of your clients or patients; study the marketing *reports* of your salespeople or the product *specifications* of your suppliers; or perhaps even grade the *papers* of your students! Whatever your job, the decisions that you make and the actions that you take will depend on your ability to understand and evaluate what your sources are saying (whether orally or in writing), to recognize any important pattern or theme, and to form conclusions. As you build on other people's ideas, you will be expected to remember which facts and opinions came from which sources and give appropriate credit. Chances are that you will also be expected to draft a memo, a letter, a report, or a case history that will summarize your information and understanding and present and support your conclusions.

To help you see the connection between college and professional writing, here are some typical essay topics for various college courses, each followed by a parallel writing assignment that you might have to do on the job. Notice that all of the pairs of assignments call for many of the same skills: the writer must consult a variety of sources, present what he or she has learned from those sources, and interpret that knowledge in the light of experience.

ACADEMIC ASSIGNMENT	PROFESSIONAL ASSIGNMENT	SOURCES
For a *political science* course, you choose a law now being debated in Congress or the state legislature and argue for its passage.	As a *lobbyist, consumer advocate,* or *public relations expert,* you prepare a pamphlet to arouse public interest in your agency's after-school program.	debates *Congressional Record* editorials periodical articles your opinions
For a *health sciences* course, you summarize present knowledge about the appropriate circumstances for prescribing tranquilizers and suggest some safeguards for their use.	As a *member of a medical research team,* you draft a report summarizing present knowledge about a new medication for diabetes and suggesting likely directions for your team's research.	books journal articles government and pharmaceutical industry reports online abstracts
For a *psychology* course, you analyze the positive and negative effects of peer-group pressure.	As a *social worker* attached to a halfway house for adolescents, you write a case history of three boys, determining whether they are to be sent to separate homes or kept in the same facility.	textbooks journal articles case studies interviews Web sites personal experience photographs

(continued)

ACADEMIC ASSIGNMENT	PROFESSIONAL ASSIGNMENT	SOURCES
For a *business management* course, you decide which department or service of your college should be eliminated if the budget were cut by 3 percent next year; you defend your choice.	As an *assistant to a management consultant*, you draft a memo recommending measures to save a manufacturing company that is in severe financial trouble.	ledgers interviews newspaper articles journal articles financial reports Dow Jones news charts

For a *sociology* or *history* course, you compare reactions to unemployment in the 1990s with reactions to unemployment in the 1930s.	As a *staff member in the social-services agency* of a small city, you prepare a report on the consequences that would result from closing a major factory.	newspaper
		    articles
		magazine
		    articles
		books
		interviews
		statistics
		Web sites
		charts

For a *physical education* course, you classify the ways in which a team can react to a losing streak and recommend some ways in which coaches can maintain team morale.	As a *member of a special committee of physical-education teachers*, you help plan an action paper that will improve your district's performance in interscholastic sports.	textbooks
		articles
		observation and
		    personal
		    experience
		Web sites

For an *anthropology* course, you contrast the system of punishment used by a tribe that you have studied with the penal code used in your hometown or college town.	As *assistant to the head of the local correction agency*, you prepare a report comparing the success of eight minimum-security prisons around the country.	textbooks
		lectures
		articles
		statistics and
		    other data
		observation
		    and personal
		    experience
		charts and graphs

For a *physics* course, you write a definition of "black holes" and explain why theories about them were fully developed in the second half of the twentieth century—not earlier, not later.	As a *physicist* working for a university research team, you write a grant application based on an imminent breakthrough in your field.	books journal articles online abstracts e-mail Web sites

ACADEMIC ASSIGNMENT	PROFESSIONAL ASSIGNMENT	SOURCES
For a *nutrition* course, you explain why adolescents prefer junk food.	As a *dietician* at the cafeteria of a local high school, you write a memo that accounts for the increasing waste of food and recommend changes in the menus.	textbooks articles interviews observation Web sites e-mail
For an *engineering* course, you describe changes and improvements in techniques of American coal mining over the last hundred years.	As a *mining engineer*, you write a report determining whether it is cost-effective for your company to take over the derelict mine that you were sent to survey.	books articles observation and experience e-mail Web sites photographs

Writing from Sources will help you learn the basic procedures that are common to all kinds of academic and professional writing and will provide enough practice in these skills to enable you to write from sources confidently and successfully. Here are the basic skills.

1. *Choosing a topic:*
   - deciding what you are actually writing about
   - interpreting the requests of your instructor, boss, or client, and determining the scope and limits of the assignment
   - making the project manageable
2. *Finding sources and acquiring information:*
   - deciding how much supporting information you are going to need (if any) and locating it
   - evaluating sources and determining which are most suitable and trustworthy for your purpose
   - taking notes on your sources and on your own responses to them
   - judging when you have sufficient information
3. *Determining your main idea:*
   - determining your intention in writing this assignment and your expected conclusions
   - redefining the scope and objective in the light of what you have learned from your sources
   - establishing a thesis

4. *Presenting your sources:*
   - using summary, paraphrase, and quotation
   - deciding when and how much to use each skill

5. *Organizing your material:*
   - deciding what must be included and what may be eliminated
   - arranging your evidence in the most efficient and convincing way so that your reader will reach the same conclusions as you
   - calling attention to common patterns and ideas that will reinforce your thesis
   - making sure that your presentation has a beginning, a middle, and an end, and that the stages are in logical order

6. *Writing your assignment:*
   - breaking down the mass of information into easily understood units or paragraphs
   - constructing each paragraph so that it will advance your main idea
   - providing examples and details in each paragraph that will support your argument
   - writing an introduction and, as needed, a conclusion
   - if appropriate, choosing visual and audio materials to supplement your essay

7. *Giving credit to your sources:*
   - ensuring that your reader knows who is responsible for which idea
   - distinguishing between the evidence of your sources and your own interpretation and evaluation
   - judging the relative reliability and usefulness of each source and giving it appropriate emphasis

This list of skills may seem overwhelming right now. But remember: you will be learning these procedures *gradually*. In Parts I and II, you will learn how to get the most out of what you read and how to use the skills of summary, quotation, and paraphrase to present accurate accounts of your sources. In Part III, you will begin to apply these skills as you prepare an essay based on a single reading and then a synthesis essay drawing on a group of sources. Finally, in Part IV, you will begin the complex process of research.

The best way to gain confidence and facility in writing from sources is to master each skill so that it becomes automatic, like riding a bicycle or driving a car. To help you break down the task into workable units, each procedure will first be illustrated with a variety of models and then followed by exercises to give you as much practice as you need before going on to the next step. As you begin to write essays for other courses, you can concentrate more and more on *what* you are writing rather than on *how* to write from sources, for these methods will have become natural and automatic.

A Note about Documentation and Academic Writing

Colleges are academic institutions that expect you to understand and maintain generally accepted standards of scholarship. Simply put, this means that you don't cheat when you take examinations and you don't plagiarize when you prepare your written assignments. By academic standards, plagiarism violates the very principles and the body of knowledge that you've come to college to learn. Plagiarism means stealing and presenting the words or ideas of someone else as your own.

To make sure that you don't inadvertently abuse the rules that define academic integrity, *Writing from Sources* asks you to devote a great deal of time and attention to learning how to *document your sources,* giving appropriate credit to each of the authors whose ideas or words you use when you write your essay. As well as using summary, quotation, and paraphrase to present your sources, you'll also learn to ensure that your reader knows who these sources are and where and when they were published, along with which material in your essay is theirs and which material is yours. This is called attribution—giving a person or an organization credit for being the author of a text or the source of an idea.

There are complex systems of documentation that make the attribution of sources absolutely clear, and you will probably be asked to use two or three of them during your time at college.

- The **MLA** (Modern Language Association) and **APA** (American Psychological Association) systems both use names and page numbers in parentheses at the end of material obtained from sources.

- The **footnote/endnote** system, as outlined in *The Chicago Manual of Style,* places information about sources at the bottom of the page or at the end of the essay, keyed by a set of numbers.

In Chapter 11, you can see two research papers, one using the MLA system and the other using the APA system. Every system of documentation requires the inclusion of a bibliography, which usually comprises all the works mentioned (or "cited") in the essay, article, or book. Different disciplines require different forms of documentation, and your instructor will generally tell you which one to use. For a detailed account of MLA and APA documentation and sample citations, consult Chapter 12.

As you look through the readings in *Writing from Sources,* you will notice that some of the authors use documentation—most often endnotes—to cite their sources, and some do not. That's because some of the authors were writing for an academic audience and some were not. Most nonfiction books, as well as articles in newspapers and popular magazines, are intended to provide information and commentary for a general audience. The authors are expected to include the names of their sources (and, as appropriate, the name of the specific book or article being cited), but they aren't required to include formal documentation. Not so for the authors you'll find in this book whose work was published in scholarly journals or by academic presses. When you prepare research papers for your courses, you may use popular sources, academic sources, or a combination of both, depending on your assignment. But as a student in an academic institution, you'll always be expected to provide full documentation for all your sources.

Contents

College experience cluster; Men and women cluster; Social media
cluster. See p. 564 for a full list of the thematic reading clusters.

PART II
WRITING ABOUT SOURCES   73

Presenting Your Sources to Your Reader   74

6 Synthesizing Sources for the Multiple-Source Essay   240

PART IV
WRITING FROM RESEARCH   301

9   Writing the Research Essay   397

Part I

READING FOR RESEARCH

Research Starts with Reading

Whether in the university or at the office, academic and professional writers rely on sources to develop and present their ideas. You may be a staff writer in an advertising agency, preparing a campaign for a new product based on the opinion of a focus group of consumers, or you may be a sociologist at a university analyzing theories about what makes a successful advertising campaign by reviewing company sales reports as well as articles in scholarly journals. In these—and virtually all—cases of nonfiction writing, you are expected to integrate your own ideas with the ideas and words of other people. We call this process research.

Chapter 1 shows you some of the ways that authors put together their ideas into a finished work. As you read each text, you will be encouraged to ask questions about the writer's meaning and methods, and to answer those questions. First, you'll learn the habit of noting down what interests and puzzles you about a text; that process is called annotation. As your questions become more complex, you will focus on identifying the text's main idea, or thesis, and the strategies the author uses to present and support that thesis. Eventually, you will understand what the author wants to say, and how and why he or she is trying to say it, including logical techniques of argumentation, such as the presentation of evidence. Soon, you will have the opportunity to work with a range of sources and begin to apply these methods to your own research.

·1·

Reading Sources

Before class began, I happened to walk around the room and I glanced at some of the books lying open on the desks. Not one book had a mark in it! Not one underlining! Every page was absolutely clean! These twenty-five students all owned the book, and they'd all read it. They all knew that there'd be an exam at the end of the week; and yet not one of them had had the sense to make a marginal note!

Teacher of an English honors class

Why was this teacher so horrified? The students had fulfilled their part of the college contract by reading the book and coming to class. Why write anything down, they might argue, when the ideas are already printed on the page. All you have to do is read the assignment and, later on, review by skimming it again. Sometimes it pays to underline or highlight an important point, but only in very long chapters, so that you don't have to read every word all over again.

Not true! Reading is hard work. Actively responding to what you are reading and thinking about an author's ideas requires concentration.

As with any job, reading becomes more rewarding if you have a product to show for your efforts. In active reading, this product is *notes*: the result of a mental dialogue between your mind and the author's.

Underlining

Underlining is used for selection and emphasis. When you underline, you are choosing between what is important (and worth rereading) and what you can skip on later readings. Underlining text on a first reading is usually hard, since you don't yet know which material is crucial to the work's main ideas.

Guidelines for Effective Reading

- As you read and reread, note which ideas make you react.
- Pause frequently—not to take a break but to think about and re-spond to what you have read. If the reading has been difficult, these pauses will provide time for you to ask yourself questions.
- **Working with sources on paper:** Have a pen or pencil in your hand so that you can make lines, checks, and comments in and around what you are reading. You may even want to use several colors to help you distinguish between different ideas or themes as they recur. Of course, if you don't own the book or periodical, make a copy of key pages or take notes on separate paper. If you underline or write in a library copy, you are committing an act of vandalism, like writing graffiti on a wall.
- **Working with sources on the computer:** For electronic material, print out key pages and work with a hard copy. Or if the material can be downloaded into a file, type comments and questions into the text [using brackets to indicate your own work].

Pointless underlining: Too often, underlining just indicates that the eyes have run over the lines. Pages are underlined or highlighted so completely that there is hardly anything left over. Everything has been chosen for emphasis.

Productive underlining: Underlining requires selection. Some points are worth remembering and reviewing, and some are not. You probably would want to underline:

- important generalizations and topic sentences
- examples that have helped you understand a difficult idea
- transitional points, where the argument changes

You can also *circle* and *bracket* words and phrases that seem worth rereading and remembering. Or put *checks in the margin*. However you choose to mark the text, deciding what to mark helps you to learn.

Annotating

Annotation refers to the comments you write in the margins when you interpret, evaluate, or question the author's meaning, define a word or phrase, or clarify a point.

You are annotating when you jot down short explanations, summaries, or definitions in the margin. You are also annotating when you note an idea of your own: a question or counterargument, perhaps, or a point for comparison. Sometimes you will need to look up an unfamiliar word and put a brief definition into a marginal note. Not every reading deserves to be annotated. Since the process takes time and concentration, save your marginal notes for material that is especially difficult or stimulating.

Annotating: *Land of Desire*

Here is an example of a passage that has been annotated on the second reading. Difficult words have been defined; a few ideas have been summarized; and some problems and questions have been raised.

from LAND OF DESIRE: MERCHANTS, POWER, AND THE RISE OF A NEW AMERICAN CULTURE
William Leach

A finalist in 1993 for the National Book Award for nonfiction, Land of Desire *is concerned with America's development as a consumer culture. William Leach is a professor of history at Columbia University.*

Background: As you can see at the end of this reading, the author is using notes to give credit to his sources. Footnotes and endnotes are systems that academic authors use to document their sources. *Documentation means providing evidence to prove that a statement is true.* Later, you will learn how to use various systems of documentation. Meanwhile, when you're reading an academic text, it shouldn't be necessary to annotate the notes. See page xiv–xv for an Introduction to Documentation and Academic Writing.

Topic: *When and why did we start to tip waiters in restaurants?*

why quotes?

entrust: customers are precious possessions

all European

1

service grew faster than manufacturing industry (same in recent years)

Did they speak English? Who trained them?

sweatshops = long hours/low wages

To make customers feel welcome, merchants trained workers to treat them as @special people@ and as @guests.@ The numbers of service workers, including those entrusted with the care of customers, rose five-fold between 1870 and 1910, at two-and-a-half times the rate of increase of industrial workers. Among them were the restaurant and hotel employees hired to wait on tables in exchange for wages and "tips," nearly all recent immigrants, mostly poor Germans and Austrians, but also Italians, Greeks, and Swiss, who suffered nerve-wracking seven-day weeks, eleven-hour days, low wages, and the sometimes terrible heat of the kitchens. Neglected by major unions until just before World War I, they endured sweated conditions equal in their misery only to those of the garment and textile workers of the day.[83]

depends on luck, not good service

tastes and manners of the upper classes

"American Plan"—based on middle-class culture

waiter portrayed as victim

cliché

statement of theme expressed in par. 2

all these quotation marks are distracting

all an illusion

Tipping was supposed to encourage waiters and waitresses to (tolerate) these conditions in exchange for possible windfalls from customers. Tipping was an unusual practice in the United States before 1890 (although common in the luxurious and (aristocratic) European hotels), when the prevailing "American Plan" entailed serving meals at fixed times, no frills, no tipping, and little or no follow-up service. After 1900 the European system of culinary service expanded very quickly in the United States, introduced first to the (fancy) establishments and then, year by year, to the more popularly priced places. By 1913 some European tourists were even expressing "outrage" at the extent of tipping in the United States.[84] Its effect on workers was (extremely) mixed. On the one hand, it helped keep wages low, increased the frenzy and tension of waiting, and lengthened the hours. "The tipping business is a great evil," wrote an old, retired waiter in the 1940s. "It gives the waiter an inferiority complex—makes him feel he is at the mercy of the customers all the time."[85] On the other hand, some waiters were stirred by the "speculative excitement" of tipping, the risk and (chance). *chance = luck, not opportunity*

For customers, however, tipping was intended to have only one effect—to make them feel at home and in the (lap of luxury). On the backs of an ever-growing sweated workforce, it aristocratized consumption, integrating upper-class patterns of comfort into the middle-class lifestyle. Tips rewarded waiters and waitresses for making the customer "feel like 'somebody,'" as one restaurant owner put it. Such a "feeling," he wrote, "depends" on the "service of the waiter," who ushers us to "our table" and "anticipates our every want or whim." "Courteous service is a valuable asset to the restaurateur. There is a curious little twist to most of us: We enjoy the luxurious feeling of affluence, of being 'somebody,' of having our wishes catered to."[86]

2

barely endure

meals at any time; more choice in return for higher prices

middle class attracted by upper-class style

Hours were longer because of tipping or because of greater service?

3

tipping as a marketing device

it's the customer who has the inferiority complex

83. Matthew Josephson, *The History of the Hotel and Restaurant Employees and Bartenders International Union, AFL-CIO* (New York, 1955), pp. 4–5, 84–95.
84. Barger, *Distribution's Place*, pp. 4, 92–93. Also, on the earlier "American plan," see Josephson, pp. 4–5.
85. Quoted in Josephson, p. 90.
86. W. L. Dodd, "Service, Sanitation, and Quality," *The American Restaurant* (August 1920): 37.

As the marginal comments demonstrate, annotation works by reminding you of ideas that you have thought about and understood. Some marginal notes provide a shorter version of the major ideas of the passage. Others remind you of places where you disagreed with the author, looked at the ideas in a new way, or thought of fresh evidence. Your marginal notes can even suggest the topic for an essay of your own—for example, *Is tipping a fair way to pay for service? Is a good restaurant meal or a night out based on an illusion of luxury?*

You can also make marginal comments about pictures or graphics that accompany a text. In "The Weight of the World," published in *Atlantic* in 2003, Don Peck uses maps to support his analysis of the increase in obesity worldwide. In fact, the maps are more thought-provoking—and therefore worth annotating—than is Peck's text. Here's what an annotated excerpt from the text and some of the maps might look like:

17% rise in 23 years

What determines ideal weight? Does it vary according to environment or only by sex and age?

The United States contains more fat people—by a large margin—than any other nation. Sixty-four percent of American adults are overweight, versus 47 percent in 1980. Some nine million Americans are now "morbidly obese," meaning roughly a hundred pounds or more overweight, and weight-related conditions cause about 300,000 premature deaths a year in this country—more than anything else except smoking.

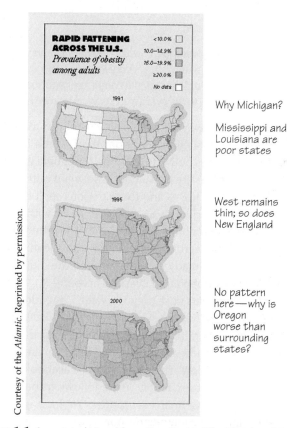

Why Michigan?

Mississippi and Louisiana are poor states

West remains thin; so does New England

No pattern here—why is Oregon worse than surrounding states?

Courtesy of the *Atlantic*. Reprinted by permission.

Figure 1-1 Annotated Visual from Don Peck's "The Weight of the World"

Important! When you write marginal notes, *try always to use your own words* instead of copying or abbreviating a phrase from the text. Expressing it yourself will help you to understand and remember the point—and make it easier to present the source when you are writing your own essay.

EXERCISE 1: Annotating a Passage

A.   As your instructor indicates, read either the excerpt from Evgeny Morozov's *To Save Everything, Click Here* or the excerpt from Stephen Gundle's *Glamour*.

B.   Then reread the passage carefully, underlining and circling key ideas and inserting annotations in the margins. Remember to include the photograph and its caption in the Gundle excerpt in your marginal comments.

from TO SAVE EVERYTHING, CLICK HERE
Evgeny Morozov

The author of two books, Evgeny Morozov has written for a variety of publications, including the New Republic *and* Slate. *He frequently explores the dangers that technology, particularly the Web, may pose to the social order.*

Topic: Luddites were 19th century textile workers who feared — and even destroyed — new machinery intended to make the industry more productive. Today, the term has negative connotations. Should those who choose not to participate in social media be regarded as Luddites?

Think of it this way: all of us have a right not to have a cell phone or a Facebook profile. But that right means little in a society where almost everyone has both those things, for people without cell phones or Facebook profiles are presumed to be weird outliers with their own reasons for staying low — and those reasons can't be good, can they? Law enforcement agencies already view those without cell phones as potential terrorists or drug dealers — this, if anything, turns your "right" to keep away from certain technologies into a joke. A similar set of interpretations has already emerged around the digital refuseniks who stubbornly resist opening a Facebook account. 1

If just a few years ago, they were seen as Luddites or, at best, as deeply spiritual individuals who didn't want to bother with the hassle of social networking, today such people are portrayed as suspicious creeps who either have no social life to report or are hiding some dark past from public view. This suspicion of Facebook holdouts permeates our public culture deeply. Thus, following the Aurora shootings in June 2012, the German newspaper *Der Tagesspiegel* pointed out that neither James Holmes, the Aurora gunman, nor the Norwegian mass murderer Anders Behring Breivik had Facebook accounts, implying that the absence of any Facebook activity might itself indicate that a person has problems. The same sentiment was echoed by Slate's columnist Farhad Manjoo, who suggested, "If you are going out 2 with someone and they don't have a Facebook profile, you should be suspicious."

259. The German newspaper *Der Tagesspiegel:* Katrin Schulze, "Machen sich Facebook-Ver-weigerer verdächtig?," *Der Tagesspiegel,* July 24, 2012, http:/www.tagesspiegel.de/weltspiegel/nach-dem-attentat-von-denver-kein-facebook-profil-kein-job-angebot/6911648-2.html.

239. "If you are going out with someone": quoted in Kashmir Hill, "You Don't Need a Facebook Account to Be Considered 'Normal' (but It Helps)," Forbes.com, August 13, 2012, http://www.forbes.com/sites/kashmirhill/2012/08/13/you-dont-need-a-facebook-account-to-be-considered-normal-but-it-helps.

from GLAMOUR
Stephen Gundle

Stephen Gundle has taught at universities in Great Britain and France, and has written and coedited several books about the film industry and its relationship to popular and political culture.

Topic: *Historically, a courtesan occupied the highest place in the spectrum of women who exchanged sex for money. What social function did courtesans serve?*

Courtesans were the glamour queens of the nineteenth century. They were flamboyant women who, through determination and luck, rose to become icons of beauty and leaders of fashion. They occupied an important place in the social and commercial life of several capitals and they loom large in the art and literature of the period. They were figures of luxury who led extraordinarily opulent lifestyles. Typically, they were young women of lowly or foreign origins who possessed charm, beauty, and steely determination. At one level, they were high-class prostitutes, but they were also much more than this. They were a category with specific features and functions that mediated the complex social and cultural passage from aristocratic to bourgeois society. The courtesans were all distinctive individuals with particular histories and influences. In some instances they were versatile figures, like the actress and writer Mary Robinson, who enjoyed a number of high-profile liaisons from which she drew profit; in others, like the most famous courtesan of the Regency, Harriet Wilson, they were commodities available to the men who frequented the Rotten Row promenade, the theatre and the opera, and Brighton. After the Regency, courtesans played a limited role in London life, but they

© British Library Board / Robana / Art Resource, NY

Figure 1-2 "Perdita Dolly the tall, and the bird of Paradise, preparing to receive company." Image from the *Rambler's Magazine*.

prospered elsewhere, and most especially in Paris, where they became part of the city's attractions. They were a feature of the developing consumer economy and of the dream world that it fuelled. As professionals of performance and masquerade, they pioneered the modern idea of sex appeal as an organized tease. By this means, they reinforced the role of sex in glamour and established a connection that would never be broken.

Annotating: "A Question of Degree"

The next step is to apply annotating skills to a full-length essay. Written by Blanche Blank, who was a professor of education at Hunter College of the City University of New York, "A Question of Degree" is 17 paragraphs long. Here is what the first two paragraphs look like with basic annotations about the meaning of words and phrases:

everyone believes it

Perhaps we should rethink an idea fast becoming an <u>undisputed premise</u> of American life: that a college degree is a (necessary) (and perhaps even a (sufficient)) precondition for success. I do not wish to quarrel with the assumptions made about the benefits of orthodox education. I want only to expose its (false god:) the four-year, all-purpose, degree-granting college, aimed at the so-called college-age population and by now almost universally accepted as the stepping-stone to "<u>meaningful</u>" and "<u>better</u>" jobs.

1

necessary vs. sufficient?

= false idol

quotes mean B.B. doesn't agree

What is wrong with the current (college/work cycle) can be seen in the following (anomalies:) we are selling college to the youth of America as a take-off pad for the (material) good life. College is literally (advertised and packaged) as a means for getting more money through "better" jobs at the same time that Harvard graduates are taking jobs as taxi drivers. This situation is a (perversion) of the true spirit of a university, a perversion of a humane social ethic and, at bottom, a (patent) fraud. To take the last point first, the economy simply is not geared to guaranteeing these presumptive "better" jobs; the colleges are not geared to training for such jobs; and the ethical propriety of the entire enterprise is very questionable. We are by (definition) (rather than by (analysis) establishing two kinds of work: work labeled "better" because it has a degree requirement tagged to it and non-degree work, which, through this logic, becomes automatically "low level."

= inconsistencies

high salary + expensive possessions

2

college leads to work

presented to the public

= corruption

= obvious

colleges can't deliver what they promise

definition = by saying so

analysis = by observing what's right and real

Asking Questions

As you read actively and try to understand what you read, you will start asking questions about the text. Sometimes you will want to write your answers down; sometimes answering your questions in your head is enough.

As the questions in the following box suggest, to understand what you read, your mind has to sweep back and forth between each sentence on the page and the larger context of the whole paragraph or essay. You can misunderstand the author's meaning if you interpret ideas out of context, ignoring the way in which they fit into the work as a whole.

Context means the overall framework in which a word, passage, or idea occurs.

Understanding takes time and careful reading. Being a fast reader is not necessarily an advantage. In fact, it is usually on the second reading, when you begin to grasp the overall meaning and structure of the work, that questions begin to pop into your head and you begin to read more effectively.

| | Asking Questions as You Read |

- What is the meaning of this word?
- How should I understand that phrase?
- Where do I have difficulty understanding the text? Why? Which passages are easy for me? Why?
- What does this passage remind me of?
- What is the topic sentence of the paragraph?
- What is the connection between these two points?
- What is the transitional word telling me?
- This concept is difficult: how would I express it in my own words?
- Is this point a digression from the main idea, or does it fit in with what I've already read?
- Can the whole page be summarized briefly?
- What point is the writer trying to make?

Asking Questions: "A Question of Degree"

Now, read "A Question of Degree," and answer the questions asked in the margins. These questions go beyond the simple definitions of the previous annotation, asking *why* and *how*. Your answers can be brief, but *use your own words*.

Some of the sample questions may seem very subtle to you, and you may wonder whether you would have thought of all of them yourself. But they are model questions, to show you what you *could* ask if you wanted to gain an especially thorough understanding of the essay.

When you're sure of the answers to these questions, you're sure of the author's meaning. Then, compare your answers with those on pages 16–21.

A QUESTION OF DEGREE

Blanche D. Blank

Topic: *Are college degrees really necessary and important?*

Perhaps we should rethink an idea fast becoming an undisputed   1
premise of American life: that a college degree is a necessary (and
perhaps even a sufficient) precondition for success. I do not wish to
quarrel with the assumptions made about the benefits of orthodox

A. In what context can a college degree be a false god?

B. Why does Blank put "meaningful" and "better" in quotation marks?

C. What conclusion can be drawn from the "Harvard graduates" sentence?

D. How many perversions does Blank mention? Can you distinguish between them?

E. In the last two sentences, what are the two types of "fraud" that are described?

F. What is the "practical curriculum"?

G. What is the danger to the universities?

H. What groups have suffered as a result of "compulsory" college?

I. What is Blank's contribution to "our 'equal opportunity' policy"?

J. What does "legitimacy" mean in this context?

education. I want only to expose its false god: the four-year, all-purpose, degree-granting college, aimed at the so-called college-age population and by now almost universally accepted as the stepping-stone to "meaningful" and "better" jobs.

What is wrong with the current college/work cycle can be seen in the following anomalies: we are selling college to the youth of America as a take-off pad for the material good life. College is literally advertised and packaged as a means for getting more money through "better" jobs at the same time that Harvard graduates are taking jobs as taxi drivers. This situation is a perversion of the true spirit of a university, a perversion of a humane social ethic and, at bottom, a patent fraud. To take the last point first, the economy simply is not geared to guaranteeing these presumptive "better" jobs; the colleges are not geared to training for such jobs; and the ethical propriety of the entire enterprise is very questionable. We are by definition (rather than by analysis) establishing two kinds of work: work labeled "better" because it has a degree requirement tagged to it and nondegree work, which, through this logic, becomes automatically "low level."

This process is also destroying our universities. The "practical curriculum" must become paramount; the students must become prisoners; the colleges must become servants of big business and big government. Under these conditions the university can no longer be an independent source of scientific and philosophic truth-seeking and moral criticism.

Finally, and most important, we are destroying the spirit of youth by making college compulsory at adolescence when it may be least congruent with emotional and physical needs; and we are denying college as an optional and continuing experience later in life, when it might be most congruent with intellectual and recreational needs.

Let me propose an important step to reverse these trends and thus help restore freedom and dignity to both our colleges and our workplaces. We should outlaw employment discrimination based on college degrees. This would simply be another facet of our "equal opportunity" policy and would add college degrees to sex, age, race, religion and ethnic group as inherently unfair bases for employment selection.

People would, wherever possible, demonstrate their capacities on the job. Where that proved impractical, outside tests could still serve. The medical boards, bar exams, mechanical, mathematical and verbal aptitude tests might still be used by various enterprises. The burden of proof of their legitimacy, however, would remain with

2

3

4

5

6

the using agencies. So too would the costs. Where the colleges were best equipped to impart a necessary skill they would do so, but only where it would be natural to the main thrust of a university endeavor.

The need for this rethinking and for this type of legislation may best be illustrated by a case study. Joe V. is a typical liberal-arts graduate, fired by imaginative art and literature. He took a job with a large New York City bank, where he had the opportunity to enter the "assistant manager training program." The trainees rotated among different bank departments to gain technical know-how and experience and also received classroom instruction, including some sessions on "how to write a business letter." The program was virtually restricted to college graduates. At the end of the line, the trainees became assistant bank managers: a position consisting largely of giving simple advice to bank customers and a modest amount of supervision of employees. Joe searched for some connection between his job and the training program, on the one hand, and his college-whetted appetites and skills on the other. He found none.

7

K. What point(s) does the example of Joe help to prove?

In giving Joe preference for the training program, the bank had bypassed a few enthusiastic aspirants already dedicated to a banking career and daily demonstrating their competence in closely related jobs. After questioning his superiors about the system, Joe could only conclude that the "top brass" had some very diffuse and not-too-well-researched or even well-thought-out conceptions about college men. The executives admitted that a college degree did not of itself ensure the motivation or the verbal or social skills needed. Nor were they clear about what skills were most desirable for their increasingly diverse branches. Yet, they clung to the college prerequisite.

8

L. What are the colleges' reasons for cooperating with business?

Business allows the colleges to act as recruiting, screening and training agencies for them because it saves money and time. Why colleges allow themselves to act as servicing agents may not be as apparent. One reason may be that colleges are increasingly becoming conventional bureaucracies. It is inevitable, therefore, that they should respond to the first and unchallenged law of bureaucracy: Expand! The more that colleges can persuade outside institutions to restrict employment in favor of their clientele, the stronger is the college's hold and attraction. This rationale becomes even clearer when we understand that the budgets of public universities hang on the number of students "serviced." Seen from this perspective, then, it is perhaps easier to understand why such matters as "university independence," or "the propriety" of using the public bankroll to support enterprises that are expected to make private profits, can be

9

M. What is the conflict of interest?

dismissed. Conflict of interest is difficult to discern when the interests involved are your own....

What is equally questionable is whether a college degree, as such, is proper evidence that those new skills that are truly needed will be delivered. A friend who works for the Manpower Training Program feels that there is a clear divide between actual job needs and college-degree equirements. One of her chief frustrations is the knowledge that many persons with the ability to do paraprofessional mental-health work are lost to jobs they could hold with pleasure and profit because the training program also requires a two-year associate arts degree.

Obviously, society can and does manipulate job status. I hope that we can manipulate it in favor of the greatest number of people. More energy should be spent in trying to upgrade the dignity of all socially useful work and to eliminate the use of human beings for any work that proves to be truly destructive of the human spirit. Outlawing the use of degrees as prerequisites for virtually every job that our media portray as "better" should carry us a long step toward a healthier society. Among other things, there is far more evidence that work can make college meaningful than that college can make work meaningful.

N. What does this sentence mean?

O. Is Blank recommending that everyone go to work before attending college?

My concern about this degree/work cycle might be far less acute, however, if everyone caught up in the system were having a good time. But we seem to be generating a college population that oscillates between apathy and hostility. One of the major reasons for this joylessness in our university life is that the students see themselves as prisoners of economic necessity. They have bought the media messages about better jobs, and so they do their time. But the promised land of "better" jobs is, on the one hand, not materializing; and on the other hand the student is by now socialized to find such "better" jobs distasteful even if they were to materialize.

P. What does "prisoners of economic necessity" mean?

One of the major improvements that could result from the proposed legislation against degree requirements for employment would be a new stocktaking on the part of all our educational agencies. Compulsory schools, for example, would understand that the basic skills for work and family life in our society would have to be compressed into those years of schooling.

Q. What are the "compulsory schools," and how would their role change if Blank's proposal were adopted?

Colleges and universities, on the other hand, might be encouraged to be as unrestricted, as continuous and as open as possible. They would be released from the pressures of ensuring economic survival through a practical curriculum. They might best be modeled after museums. Hours would be extensive, fees minimal, and services available to anyone ready to comply with course-by-course

10

11

12

13

14

R. What role does Blank envisage for the university in a healthier society?

demands. Colleges under these circumstances would have a clearly understood focus, which might well be the traditional one of serving as a gathering place for those persons who want to search for philosophic and scientific "truths."

S. What are the "strange and gratuitous practices" of the universities? What purpose do they serve?

This proposal should help our universities rid themselves of some (strange and gratuitous practices.) For example, the university would no longer have to organize itself into hierarchical levels: B.A., M.A., Ph.D. There would simply be courses of greater and lesser complexity in each of the disciplines. In this way graduate education might be more rationally understood and accepted for what it is — more education.   15

The new freedom might also relieve colleges of the growing practice of instituting extensive "work programs," "internships" and "independent study" programs. The very names of these enterprises are tacit admissions that the campus itself is not necessary for many genuinely educational experiences. But, along with "external degree" programs, they seem to pronounce that whatever one has learned in life by whatever diverse and interesting routes cannot be recognized as increasing one's dignity, worth, usefulness or self-enjoyment until it is converted into degree credits.   16

T. What, according to Blank, would be a "rational order of priorities"?

The legislation I propose would offer a more (rational order of priorities.) It would help recapture the genuine and variegated dignity of the workplace along with the genuine and more specialized dignity of the university. It should help restore to people of all ages and inclinations a sense of their own basic worth and offer them as many roads as possible to reach Rome.   17

Answering Questions: "A Question of Degree"

Paragraph One

A. In what context can a college degree be a false god?

A. Colleges are worshiped by students who believe that the degree will magically ensure a good career and a better life. Blank suggests that college degrees no longer have magic powers.

B. Why does Blank put "meaningful" and "better" in quotation marks?

B. Blank doesn't believe the adjectives are applicable; she is using quotation marks to show her disagreement with the idea that some jobs should be seen as better or more meaningful than others.

Paragraph Two

C. What conclusion can be drawn from the "Harvard graduates" sentence?

C. If Harvard graduates are driving taxis, a degree does not ensure a high-level job.

D. How many perversions does Blank mention? Can you distinguish between them?

D. When degrees are regarded as vocational qualifications, the university's proper purpose is perverted; society's conception of proper qualifications for employment and advancement is perverted; and, by implication, young people's belief in the reliability of rewards promised by society is perverted.

E. In the last two sentences, what are the two types of "fraud" that are described?

E. One kind of fraud is the deception practiced on young college students who won't get the good jobs they expect. A second type of fraud is practiced on workers without degrees, whose efforts and successes are undervalued because of the division into "better" and "worse" jobs.

Paragraph Three

F. What is the "practical curriculum"?

F. "Practical curriculum" refers to courses that will train college students for specific jobs; the term is probably being contrasted with "liberal arts."

G. What is the danger to the universities?

G. The emphasis on vocational training perverts the universities' traditional pursuit of knowledge for its own sake, as it makes financing and curriculum very closely connected with the economic needs of the businesses and professions for which students will be trained.

Paragraph Four

H. What groups have suffered as a result of "compulsory" college?

H. Blank has so far referred to four groups: students in college; workers who have never been to college; members of universities, both staff and students, interested in a liberal arts curriculum; and older people who might want to return to college after a working career.

Paragraph Five

I. What is Blank's contribution to "our 'equal opportunity' policy"?

I. Blank suggests that a college degree does not indicate suitability for employment and, therefore, that requiring it should be classed as discriminatory, along with sex, age, etc.

Paragraph Six

J. What does "legitimacy" mean in this context?

J. If certain professions choose to test the qualifications of aspirants, professional organizations should prove that examinations are necessary and that the results will measure the applicant's suitability for the job. These organizations should be responsible for the arrangements and the financing; at present, colleges serve as a "free" testing service.

Paragraphs Seven and Eight

K. What point(s) does the example of Joe help to prove?

K. Joe's experience supports Blank's argument that college training is not often needed in order to perform most kinds of work. Joe's expectations that his college education would prepare him for work were also pitched too high, as Blank has suggested, while the experience of other bank employees who were passed over in favor of Joe exemplifies the plight of those workers without college degrees, whose experience is not sufficiently valued.

Paragraph Nine

L. What are the colleges' reasons for cooperating with business?

L. Colleges are competing for students in order to increase their enrollment; they, therefore, want to be able to assure applicants that many companies prefer to hire their graduates. Having become overorganized, with many levels of authority, the bureaucratic universities regard enrollment as an end in itself.

M. What is the conflict of interest?

M. The interests of an institution funded by the public might be said to be in conflict with the interests of a private, profit-making company.

Paragraph Eleven

N. What does this sentence mean?

N. Instead of discriminating between kinds of workers and kinds of work, we should distinguish between work that benefits everyone, and should therefore be considered admirable, and work that is degrading and should, if possible, not be performed by people.

O. Is Blank recommending that everyone go to work before attending college?

O. Although Blank is not insisting that working is preferable to or should have priority over a college education, she implies that most people gain more significant knowledge from the work experience than from college.

Paragraph Twelve

P. What does "prisoners of economic necessity" mean?

P. Young people who believe that a degree will get them better jobs have no choice but to spend a four-year term in college, whether or not they are intellectually and temperamentally suited to the experience.

Paragraph Thirteen

Q. What are the "compulsory schools," and how would their role change if Blank's proposal were adopted?

Q. Compulsory schools are grade and high schools, which students must attend up to a set age. If students were not automatically expected to go on to college, the lower schools would have to offer a more comprehensive and complete education than they do now.

Paragraph Fourteen

R. What role does Blank envisage for the university in a healthier society?

R. Blank sees the colleges in a role quite apart from the mainstream of life. Colleges would be easily accessible centers of learning, to which people could go for intellectual inquiry and stimulation in their spare time.

Paragraph Fifteen

S. What are the "strange and gratuitous practices" of the universities? What purpose do they serve?

S. The universities divide the process of education into a series of clearly defined levels of attainment. Blank finds these divisions "gratuitous" or unnecessary, perhaps because they are "hierarchical" and distinguish between those of greater or lesser achievement and status.

Paragraph Seventeen

T. What, according to Blank, would be a "rational order of priorities"?

T. Blank's first priority is the self-respect of the average member of society, who currently may be disappointed and frustrated at not being valued for his or her work. Another priority is restoration of the university to its purely intellectual role.

EXERCISE 2: Understanding What You Read

A. Read "The Last Thanksgiving of my Childhood," by Jonathan Safran Foer, twice.

B. On the second reading, answer the questions in the margins. You will notice that some of the "questions" resemble instructions, very much like examination questions, directing you to explain, define, or in other ways analyze the reading. *Answer in complete sentences*, and use your own words as much as you can.

"THE LAST THANKSGIVING OF MY CHILDHOOD"
Jonathan Safran Foer

An award-winning author, Jonathan Safran Foer has published three novels as well as Eating Animals, *a world of nonfiction that explores his lifelong interest in vegetarianism.*

Topic: *What does Thanksgiving mean to Americans?*

A. In what way is the "unlikely pairing of histories" at the Thanksgiving celebration especially American?

Throughout my childhood, we celebrated Thanksgiving at my uncle and aunt's house. My uncle, my mother's younger brother, was the first person on that side of the family to be born on this side of the Atlantic. My aunt can trace her lineage back to the *Mayflower*. That unlikely pairing of histories was no small part of what made those Thanksgivings so special, and memorable, and, in the very best sense of the word, American. 1

B. From whose point of view does Foer describe the scene at his uncle and aunt's home: himself as a child or himself, now, as an adult?

We would arrive around two o'clock. The cousins would play football on the sloping sliver of a front yard until my little brother got hurt, at which point we would head up to the attic to play football on the various video game systems. Two floors beneath us, Maverick salivated at the stove's window, my father talked politics and cholesterol, the Detroit Lions played their hearts out on an unwatched TV, and my 2

C. What is the significance of his grandmother thinking "in the language of her dead relatives"?

E. The family members were "supposed to" put popcorn kernels on the table. Do you think that they did? Does it matter?

G. Kugel is a Jewish dish. Why is it "incongruous"?

I. Why was "our own anguish" not suitable for Thanksgiving conversation?

J. Why does Foer use the exaggerated word "starving"?

K. Between paragraph 3 and paragraph 4, the reading changes. In what way?

L. What's the difference between "celebrating America" and celebrating "American ideals"?

M. Define "jingoism." Can you connect the reference to "crimes that made America possible" with the suppressed anguish mentioned in the previous paragraph?

O. What is the effect of Foer's disclaimers (sentences 2 to 4) that we cannot expect every meal to be like Thanksgiving?

grandmother, surrounded by her family, thought in the language of her dead relatives.

Two dozen or so mismatched chairs circumscribed four tables of slightly different heights and widths, pushed together and covered in matching cloths. No one was fooled into thinking this setup was perfect, but it was. My aunt placed a small pile of popcorn kernels on each plate, which, in the course of the meal, we were supposed to transfer to the table as symbols of things we were thankful for. Dishes came out continuously; some went clockwise, some counter, some zigzagged down the length of the table: sweet potato casserole, home-made rolls, green beans with almonds, cranberry concoctions, yams, buttery mashed potatoes, my grandmother's wildly incongruous kugel, trays of gherkins and olives and marinated mushrooms, and a cartoonishly large turkey that had been put in the oven when last year's was taken out. We talked and talked: about the Orioles and Redskins, changes in the neighborhood, our accomplishments, and the anguish of others (our own anguish was off-limits), and all the while, my grandmother would go from grandchild to grandchild, making sure no one was starving.

Thanksgiving is the holiday that encompasses all others. All of them, from Martin Luther King Day to Arbor Day to Christmas to Valentine's Day, are in one way or another about being thankful. But Thanksgiving is freed from any particular thing we are thankful for. We aren't celebrating the Pilgrims, but what the Pilgrims celebrated. (The Pilgrims weren't even a feature of the holiday until the late nineteenth century.) Thanksgiving is an American holiday, but there's nothing specifically American about it—we aren't celebrating America, but American ideals. Its openness makes it available to anyone who feels like expressing thanks, and points beyond the crimes that made America possible, and the commercialization, kitsch, and jingoism that have been heaved onto the shoulders of the holiday.

Thanksgiving is the meal we aspire for other meals to resemble. Of course most of us can't (and wouldn't want to) cook all day every day, and of course such food would be fatal if consumed with regularity, and how many of us really want to be surrounded by our extended families every single night? (It can be challenge enough to have to eat with myself.) But it's nice to imagine all meals being so deliberate. Of the thousand-or-so meals we eat every year, Thanksgiving dinner is the one that we try most earnestly to get right. It holds the hope of

3

D. Put the second sentence of this paragraph in your own words. Was the "setup" perfect, or wasn't it?

F. Foer is creating an impression of excess. Why?

H. The description of the turkey—the first reference to eating meat—is presented almost as a joke. Why?

4

5

N. What's the significance of the word "aspire"? How does it support Foer's point about the symbolic role of Thanksgiving in American life?

P. Notice the repetition of "good"—even italicized. How does Foer take us from "good eating" to "good thinking"?

R. The last sentence of paragraph 6 might sum up Foer's theme. Express it in your own words.

T. Foer poses a question about the morality of eating turkey at Thanksgiving. What broader themes has he raised in this reading?

being a *good* meal, whose ingredients, efforts, setting, and consuming are expressions of the best in us. More than any other meal, it is about good eating and good thinking.

And more than any other food, the Thanksgiving turkey embodies the paradoxes of eating animals: what we do to living turkeys is just about as bad as anything humans have ever done to any animal in the history of the world. Yet what we do with their dead bodies can feel so powerfully good and right. The Thanksgiving turkey is the flesh of competing instincts—of remembering and forgetting.

I'm writing these final words a few days before Thanksgiving. I live in New York now and only rarely—at least according to my grandmother—get back to DC. No one who was young is young anymore. Some of those who transferred kernels to the table are gone. And there are new family members. (*I* am now *we*.) As if the musical chairs I played at birthday parties were preparation for all of this ending and beginning.

This will be the first year we celebrate in my home, the first time I will prepare the food, and the first Thanksgiving meal at which my son will be old enough to eat the food the rest of us eat. If this entire book could be decanted into a single question—not something easy, loaded, or asked in bad faith, but a question that fully captured the problem of eating and not eating animals—it might be this: Should we serve turkey at Thanksgiving?

6

Q. A paradox is a statement that seems self-contradictory. Does the cartoon help you to understand the paradox of eating turkey at Thanksgiving?

7

S. What is the effect of Foer's switch to the present time in paragraph 7? Consider, also, the title of the reading.

8

© Mike Twohy The New Yorker Collection/ The Cartoon Bank

Figure 1-3 *"It's worth a try."*

Questioning the Author

Asking questions about a text helps you to understand the meaning of words, sentences, and paragraphs. Still, having done so, you may not yet fully understand the meaning of the text itself: the author's *reason* for writing it, the *validity* and *persuasiveness* of the ideas. Has the author's point been made? Was it worth making?

To analyze an author's *intention*, you need to use some standard vocabulary: thesis, bias, and tone.

Thesis

Do not confuse the words "topic" and "thesis."

A topic means a subject: *what is being discussed or written about. It is often a question to answer.*

A thesis means a statement of intention and purpose, expressing the central idea of an essay that the author undertakes to support and validate.

- The thesis should be a *statement*, not a question. The author is not just raising a question for exploration but attempting to *answer that question*.

These are topics, not theses.
> **Topic:** Who should go to college?
>
> **Topic:** How can students succeed in college?
>
> **Thesis:** Only students who will make the fullest use of their education should go to college.

- The thesis should be *broad* enough and *arguable* enough to be worth defending. It should not be an obvious truth.

Who would disagree? It's hardly worth arguing.
> **Too obvious:** Poorly prepared students can find college work difficult.

Too specific to sustain an essay.
> **Too narrow:** Some of the students in my history course found the second assignment too difficult.

Solves the problem of how students can succeed in college.
> **Thesis:** To help unprepared students succeed, colleges should provide a full range of support services.

Answers question—who should go to college?—by *defining* that group.
> **Thesis:** Since college can be difficult for poorly prepared students, admission should depend on the applicant's meeting certain standards of achievement.

■ The thesis should define the *scope* and *limits* of the essay. The author should stay within the boundaries of the thesis and not digress into other topics. Which of the following statements correctly corresponds to the scope of "A Question of Degree"?

Too narrow: Employment discrimination arises from an overemphasis on college degrees.

Too broad: College is wasted on the young.

A good thesis, which is often complex, cannot always be expressed in a short sentence.   **Thesis:** Regarding the college degree as a prerequisite for a good job and a better life can only discourage a fair and efficient system of employment and subvert the true purpose of higher education.

The author's general purpose in writing is to present a thesis clearly and support it convincingly. The thesis will vary according to the nature of the topic and what the author intends to do with it.

What Is a Thesis?

A thesis will be a broad statement, worth defending, that defines the scope and limits of the essay.

1. The thesis will be a substantial generalization that can stand by itself. It should answer, not ask, a question.
2. The thesis will be *broad* enough and *arguable* enough to be worth defending. It will not be an obvious truth.
3. The thesis will define the *scope* and *limits* of the essay. The author should stay within the boundaries of the thesis and not digress into other topics.

Intention

If thesis denotes *what* the essay is about, intention suggests *how* the thesis will be developed. Take, for example, **the topic of *college drinking***. In this group of four theses, notice how the author's intention changes with each one.

1. Students have ample opportunity to drink to excess on our campus.

   The author's intention is to **explain** why it's easy to get drunk at her college—probably by citing *facts* and *statistics* such as the number of bars near campus and the rules on liquor in dormitories, as well as *anecdotes* and *examples*. With a thesis like this one, the reader can't easily tell whether the author approves of, disapproves of, or is indifferent toward the drinking.

2. The behavior of students who drink to excess can represent a cry for help.

    Here, the author has made an interesting observation and undertakes to **analyze** or **interpret** it. Developing a theory about the habits of college drinkers and what they signify requires a more complex level of inquiry and speculation than does exploring how easy it is to get access to alcoholic beverages. Such a theory might also be supported by *anecdotes* and *examples*, as well as by the "hard" evidence of *facts* and *statistics*, but that evidence will have to be correctly interpreted if the reader is to be convinced. While the thesis might be controversial—you can disagree with it—the author intends to do something other than merely defend one side of the issue.

3. Students who drink to excess should be expelled.

    No question here that the author will be engaged in **persuasion**, defending a thesis that represents a particular point of view. Doing so may or may not include the explanation and analysis mentioned above, but it will certainly require presenting a *line of reasoning* for the reader to follow.

4. Because the deficiencies of their colleges cause many students to drink to excess, colleges ought to provide a better environment for learning.

    This thesis combines elements from all three of the previous examples. Do many students drink to excess? **Explain and demonstrate.** Why do they drink to excess? **Analyze and interpret.** What should be done about this problem? ("Deficiencies" indicates that this writer isn't going to be neutral about this issue.) **Argue and persuade.**

Developing a Thesis

Authors can develop a thesis in several ways, depending on their intention. A complex thesis involves several methods of approach, usually including:

- explanation
- analysis and interpretation
- argument and persuasion

Recognizing Intention

You can often determine an author's intention just by reading the first few paragraphs of an essay and asking some questions. Look at the following examples:

Botstein's thesis is clear and upfront: his intention is to persuade his readers that high schools should be abolished. He starts by alluding to the worthless values prevalent in schools.

A. The national outpouring after the Littleton shootings has forced us to confront something we have suspected for a long time: the American high school is obsolete and should be abolished. In the last month, high school students present and past have come forward with stories about cliques and the artificial intensity of a world defined by insiders and outsiders, in which the insiders hold sway because of superficial definitions of good looks and attractiveness, popularity and sports prowess.

LEON BOTSTEIN, from "Let Teenagers Try Adulthood"

Jekanowski is citing statistics to explain and demonstrate one aspect of his thesis about the need for time-saving products.

B. With today's hectic lifestyles, time-saving products are increasingly in demand. Perhaps one of the most obvious examples is fast food. The rate of growth in consumer expenditures on fast food has led most other segments of the food-away-from-home market for much of the last two decades. Since 1982, the amount consumers spent at fast food outlets grew at an annual rate of 6.8 percent (through 1997) compared with a 4.7 percent growth in table service restaurant expenditures. The proportion of away-from-home food expenditures on fast food increased from 29.3 to 34.2 percent between 1982 and 1997, while the restaurant proportion decreased from 41 to 35.7 percent.

MARK D. JEKANOWSKI, from "Causes and Consequences of Fast Food Sales Growth"

Bok's likely intention is to analyze and interpret this aspect of Roman behavior. We can't tell yet what her thesis will be.

C. No people before or since have so revelled in displays of mortal combat as did the Romans during the last two centuries BC and the first three centuries thereafter, nor derived such pleasure from spectacles in which slaves and convicts were exposed to wild beasts and killed in front of cheering spectators. According to Nicolaus of Damascus, writing in the first decade AD, Romans even regaled themselves with lethal violence at private banquets; he describes dinner guests relishing the spectacles of gladiators fighting to the death:

> Hosts would invite their friends to dinner not merely for other entertainment, but that they might witness two or three pairs of contestants in a gladiatorial combat; on these occasions, when sated with dining and drink, they called in the gladiators. No sooner did one have his throat cut than the masters applauded with delight at this feat.

SISSELA BOK, from *Mayhem: Violence as Public Entertainment*

Bias

Because authors often have strong feelings about proving their point, they may be less than objective in their choice of methods, evidence, and words. A work can lose credibility if the author's bias leads him or her to omit or distort evidence.

Bias means a preconceived preference or prejudice.

If you think you detect bias at a specific point in a text, consider the entire text. Determine whether the presentation is *balanced* and all relevant points are given a fair hearing, or whether the author consistently gives unreasonable weight to one side of the issue.

Knowing something about the author's background may help you to determine whether he or she has an ax to grind. In a previous example, we can't be sure whether Mark D. Jekanowski is extolling fast food or merely recording its growth in popularity. Knowing that, at the time of writing, he was an agricultural economist with the U.S. Department of Agriculture might reassure you about his objectivity. Does that impression change when you learn from a Google search that he subsequently became a senior consultant, with responsibilities including research on consumer demand, for a consulting firm specializing in agribusiness? (See pp. 354–355 and 361–362 for more information about detecting bias in sources.)

Tone

Most academic authors write in a measured, straightforward style; serious subjects call for a serious tone. But, outside of academia, there are many exceptions. Some writers use *humor* to win over their readers. Others will try *irony* to make a point, so that readers, unsure whether the author means what she says, have to question apparently obvious assumptions.

In describing how snobbery works, Joseph Epstein establishes a light, almost flippant tone, poking fun at himself as well as others:

> Nearly every human being deserves respect, but the question is, how much? And who does the calculations? By one's own reckoning, it is safe to say that a great deal of respect is owed. By the world's reckoning, the estimate is, somehow, almost inevitably likely to be lower. Journals kept by the young tend to give off a strong whiff of depression, chiefly because the world doesn't yet recognize the youthful journal keeper's genius, however unproven it may be. Sometimes one feels one isn't getting the consideration (another euphemism for deference) one deserves as a veteran, senior man or woman, someone whose mettle has been established. Awaiting a decision from an editor that

takes longer than I think it ought, I find myself mumbling about the ignorance of people who don't understand that I am much too important to be kept waiting so long.

JOSEPH EPSTEIN, from Snobbery: The American Version

Sometimes the tone of a work is *strident and overbearing,* which can be a clue to the possibility of bias: the author is so eager to make his case that he may be willing to cut corners to do so. Such a work may be a *polemic*—an argument that aggressively courts controversy. Here, for example, is a passage filled with sweeping generalizations in which the author is rejecting what he says is a common form of American patriotism:

Many of our superpatriots love this country because it is considered a land of opportunity, a place where people can succeed if they have the right stuff. But individual success usually comes by prevailing over others. And when it comes to the really big prizes in a competitive, money-driven society, almost all of us are losers or simply noncontestants. Room at the top is limited to a select few, mostly those who have been supremely advantaged in family income and social standing from early in life. Even if the U.S. economy does reward the go-getters who sally forth with exceptional capacity and energy, is the quality of life to be measured by the ability of tireless careerists to excel over others? Even if it were easy to become a multimillionaire in America, what is so great about that? Why should one's ability to make large sums of money be reason to love one's country? What is admirable about a patriotism based on the cash nexus?

MICHAEL PARENTI, from Superpatriotism

In another example of immoderate tone, Waller Newell's anger at the misappropriation of the song "Imagine" spills over into his prose:

I am rarely at a loss for words, and like most political junkies I enjoy a good rant, especially after a dose of the television and newspaper opinion makers who can be counted on to make my blood boil—and stir my appetite for more reasoned polemics. But I must confess my stupefaction at how, in the painful months after 9/11, in schools, church basements, and community centers across the land, children's sweet voices swelled in repeated performances of John Lennon's 1970s ballad. That decent people truly believe this song is an appropriate tribute to the victims, that it contains some profound lesson for these trying times, sums up more completely than any other single example how much we desperately need some better guides for manly reflection.

WALLER NEWELL, from The Code of Man

Audience

The author's perception of the likely audience for the work may affect the tone. Writing for a general audience reading a popular magazine will be different from writing for an audience of specialists reading a scholarly journal, and writing for an audience inclined to agree with a thesis will probably be less challenging than writing for its opponents. The author has to make assumptions about the readers, and the style of the essay changes accordingly. (For more information on audience, see pp. 355–357.) Identifying an essay's characteristic tone and probable audience can help you to judge how well the author carries out her intention and supports her thesis.

Questioning the Author: "Why Is There Peace?"

Read through "Why Is There Peace?" by Steven Pinker, looking at the marginal annotations as you read. Some of the comments are concerned with basic points about the author's meaning; others are more general comments about thesis, method, intention, and tone. Notice how some of them try to sum up what the author has said so far. Others point to a transitional place where the author is turning from one idea to another. Familiarize yourself with this advanced process of annotation, which resembles carrying on a dialogue with the author. What other questions could you ask?

WHY IS THERE PEACE?

Steven Pinker

Holder of a prestigious professorship at Harvard, Steven Pinker is an experimental psychologist. His books include How the Mind Works, The Stuff of Thought, *and, most recently,* The Better Angels of Our Nature.

Background: This material was originally presented as a lecture given at the TED Conference in Monterey, California, in 2007. That audio version, titled "The Surprising Decline in Violence," can be found at https://www.ted.com/talks/steven_pinker_on_the_myth_of_violence. In essay form, it appears in the anthology *The Compassionate Instinct*.

Topic: *Is the world more or less violent than it was thousands of years ago?*

historical
examples

1st generalization
set up (and then
knocked down):
modernity exacer-
bates violence

Over the past century, violent images from World War II concentration camps, Cambodia, Rwanda, Darfur, Iraq, and many other times and places have been seared into our collective consciousness. These images have led to a common belief that technology, centralized nation-states, and modern values have brought about unprecedented violence.

1

Our seemingly troubled times are routinely contrasted with idyllic images of hunter-gatherer societies, which allegedly lived in a state of harmony with nature and each other. The doctrine of the noble savage — the idea that humans are peaceable by nature and corrupted by modern institutions — pops up frequently in the writing of public intellectuals like, for example, Spanish philosopher José Ortega y Gasset, who argued that "war is not an instinct but an invention."

But now that social scientists have started to count bodies in different historical periods, they have discovered that the romantic theory gets it backward: Far from causing us to become more violent, something in modernity and its cultural institutions has made us nobler. In fact, our ancestors were far more violent than we are today. Indeed, violence has been in decline over long stretches of history, and today we are probably living in the most peaceful moment of our species' time on earth.

A history of violence

In the decade of Darfur and Iraq, that statement might seem hallucinatory or even obscene. But if we consider the evidence, we find that the decline of violence is a fractal phenomenon: We can see the decline over millennia, centuries, decades, and years. When the archeologist Lawrence Keeley examined casualty rates among contemporary hunter-gatherers — which is the best picture we have of how people might have lived 10,000 years ago — he discovered that the likelihood that a man would die at the hands of another man ranged from a high of 60 percent in one tribe to 15 percent at the most peaceable end. In contrast, the chance that a European or American man would be killed by another man was less than one percent during the 20th century, a period of time that includes both world wars. If the death rate of tribal warfare had prevailed in the 20th century, there would have been two billion deaths rather than 100 million, horrible as that is.

Ancient texts reveal a stunning lack of regard for human life. In the Bible, the supposed source of all our moral values, the Hebrews are urged by God to slaughter every last resident of an invaded city. "Go and completely destroy those wicked people, the Amalekites," reads a typical passage in the book of Samuel. "Make war on them until you have wiped them out." The Bible also prescribes death by stoning as the penalty for a long list of nonviolent infractions, including idolatry, blasphemy, homosexuality, adultery, disrespecting one's parents, and picking up sticks on the Sabbath. The Hebrews, of course, were no more murderous than other tribes; one also finds frequent boasts of torture and genocide in the early histories of the Hindus, Christians, Muslims, and Chinese.

Margin notes: "seemingly" / "allegedly" = not true. 2nd generalization set up (and knocked down): humans are peaceful creatures. "But" = turn in the argument. Pinker's thesis (opposite of paragraph one). "hallucination" contrasted with "evidence". authority provides statistics. argument is based on contrast. how much of present-day violence is still tribal? "supposed" questions the role of religion as a force for peace. textual evidence: violence was part of primitive morality.

2. doctrine = beliefs held and enforced by authority (e.g., church, government). authority cited.
3. statistics can determine which theory is right. what's the difference between "noble" and "peaceable"? does "probably" mean that Pinker isn't sure?
4. horrific examples. "fractal" suggests solid evidence is available over the whole curve of history. a subset of the world's population — what about Asia, Africa? is this statement valid, given the omission of 2/3 of the world?
5. no mention of the New Testament

a narrower defini-
tion of violence:
"socially sanc-
tioned" = enforced
by government
authority

examples of
disproportionate
judicial violence
as a deterrent
to enforce good
behavior

nonjudicial
violence:
statistics for
Europe only

expands the
territory being
considered

contrast, again
how is "conflict"
defined"?

turn in the argu-
ment = what's
the basis for
the original
statement?

violence is memo-
rable, newsworthy

activists need to
believe the worst
so they can work
for improvement

our image of
ourselves has
become more
benign and we
are shocked by
any instance of
violence

But from the Middle Ages to modern times, we can see a steady reduction in socially sanctioned forms of violence. Many conventional histories
reveal that mutilation and torture were routine forms of punishment for
infractions that today would result in a fine. In Europe before the Enlightenment, crimes like shoplifting or blocking the king's driveway with your
oxcart might have resulted in your tongue being cut out, your hands being chopped off, and so on. Many of these punishments were administered
publicly, and cruelty was a popular form of entertainment.

We also have very good statistics for the history of one-on-one murder,
because for centuries many European municipalities have recorded causes
of death. When the criminologist Manuel Eisner scoured the records of
every village, city, county, and nation he could find, he discovered that
homicide rates in Europe had declined from 100 killings per 100,000 people
per year in the Middle Ages to less than one killing per 100,000 people in
modern Europe.

And since 1945 in Europe and the Americas, we've seen steep declines
in the number of deaths from interstate wars, ethnic riots, and military
coups, even in South America. Worldwide, the number of battle deaths has
fallen from 65,000 per conflict per year to less than 2,000 deaths in this decade. Since the end of the Cold War in the early 1990s, we have seen fewer
civil wars, a 90 percent reduction in the number of deaths by genocide, and
even a reversal in the 1960s-era uptick in violent crime.

Given these facts, why do so many people imagine that we live in
an age of violence and killing? The first reason, I believe, is that we have
better reporting. As political scientist James Payne once quipped, the
Associated Press is a better chronicler of wars across the globe than were
16th-century monks. There's also a cognitive illusion at work. Cognitive
psychologists know that the easier it is to recall an event, the more likely
we are to believe it will happen again. Gory war zone images from TV
are burned into memory, but we never see reports of many more people
dying in their beds of old age. And in the realms of opinion and advocacy,
no one ever attracted supporters and donors by saying that things just
seem to be getting better and better. Taken together, all these factors help
create an atmosphere of dread in the contemporary mind, one that does
not stand the test of reality.

Finally, there is the fact that our behavior often falls short of our
rising expectations. Violence has gone down in part because people got
sick of carnage and cruelty. That's a psychological process that seems to be
continuing, but it outpaces changes in behavior. So today some of us are
outraged — rightly so — if a murderer is executed in Texas by lethal injection

6

the public
becomes inured
to brutality

7

8
1945 = WWII

no sources cited
for the statistics

conflating
group violence
("conflicts")
with individual
violence ("crimes")

9

media at fault

our minds play
tricks

false emphasis

10
anticipates the
next paragraph

after a 15-year appeal process. We don't consider that a couple of hundred years ago a person could be burned at the stake for criticizing the king after a trial that lasted 10 minutes. Today we should look at capital punishment as evidence of how high our standards have risen, rather than how low our behavior can sink.

glass should be half-full

Expanding the circle

Why has violence declined? Social psychologists find that at least 80 percent of people have fantasized about killing someone they don't like. And modern humans still take pleasure in viewing violence, if we are to judge by the popularity of murder mysteries, Shakespearean dramas, the Saw movie franchise, Grand Theft Auto, and hockey.

Pinker turns from effect (violence in decline) to cause (why?)

11

violence still has a role to play in our fantasy lives—vicarious pleasure

What has changed, of course, is people's willingness to act on these fantasies. The sociologist Norbert Elias suggested that European modernity accelerated a "civilizing process" marked by increases in self-control, long-term planning, and sensitivity to the thoughts and feelings of others. These are precisely the functions that today's cognitive neuroscientists attribute to the prefrontal cortex. But this only raises the question of why humans have increasingly exercised that part of their brains. No one knows why our behavior has come under the control of the better angels of our nature, but there are four plausible suggestions.

appeal to authority

greater empathy and self-control

signals four causes (and four authorities)

12

1st time Pinker seems unsure of the answer

The first is that the 17th-century philosopher Thomas Hobbes got it right. Life in a state of nature is nasty, brutish, and short—not because of a primal thirst for blood but because of the inescapable logic of anarchy. Any beings with a modicum of self-interest may be tempted to invade their neighbors and steal their resources. The resulting fear of attack will tempt the neighbors to strike first in preemptive self-defense, which will in turn tempt the first group to strike against them preemptively, and so on. This danger can be defused by a policy of deterrence—don't strike first, retaliate if struck—but to guarantee its credibility, parties must avenge all insults and settle all scores, leading to cycles of bloody vendetta.

1. we're violent by nature because we need to survive

self-preservation requires vigilance and strict enforcement of punishment

13

These tragedies can be averted by a state with a monopoly on violence. States can inflict disinterested penalties that eliminate the incentives for aggression, thereby defusing anxieties about preemptive attack and obviating the need to maintain a hair-trigger propensity for retaliation. Indeed, Manuel Eisner attributes the decline in European homicide to the transition from knightly warrior societies to the centralized governments of early modernity. And today, violence continues to fester in zones of anarchy, such as frontier regions, failed states, collapsed empires, and territories contested by mafias, gangs, and other dealers of contraband.

justice enforced by the state takes the burden away from the individual and the tribe

14

the rule of law

the parts of the world that don't support Pinker's statistics

2. a higher standard of living moves us away from the need for violence and encourages empathy for others

James Payne suggests another possibility: that the critical variable in the indulgence of violence is an overarching sense that life is cheap. When pain and early death are everyday features of one's own life, one feels less compunction about inflicting them on others. As technology and economic efficiency lengthen and improve our lives, we place a higher value on life in general.

3. globalization of technology and cooperation increases well-being

A third theory, championed by journalist Robert Wright, invokes the logic of non-zero-sum games: scenarios in which two agents can each come out ahead if they cooperate, such as trading goods, dividing up labor, or sharing the peace dividend that comes from laying down their arms. As people acquire knowhow that they can share cheaply with others and develop technologies that allow them to spread their goods and ideas over larger territories at lower cost, their incentive to cooperate steadily increases, because other people become more valuable alive than dead.

people more useful than corpses

4. one's concern and empathy expand outward from one's immediate circle

Then there is the scenario sketched by philosopher Peter Singer. Evolution, he suggests, bequeathed people a small kernel of empathy, which by default they apply only within a narrow circle of friends and relations. Over the millennia, people's moral circles have expanded to encompass larger and larger polities: the clan, the tribe, the nation, both sexes, other races, and even animals. The circle may have been pushed outward by expanding networks of reciprocity, à la Wright, but it might also be inflated by the inexorable logic of the Golden Rule: The more one knows and thinks about other living things, the harder it is to privilege one's own interests over theirs. The empathy escalator may also be powered by cosmopolitanism, in which journalism, memoir, and realistic fiction make the inner lives of other people, and the precariousness of one's own lot in life, more palpable—the feeling that "there but for fortune go I."

empathy is culturally reinforced by religion (Golden Rule) and education

call to action

Whatever its causes, the decline of violence has profound implications. It is not a license for complacency: We enjoy the peace we find today because people in past generations were appalled by the violence in their time and worked to end it, and so we should work to end the appalling violence in our time. Nor it necessarily grounds for optimism about the immediate future, since the world has never before had national leaders who combine pre-modern sensibilities with modern weapons.

has the point actually been made?

Pinker doesn't explain how and why these leaders remain in the Dark Ages

recognition of the mechanism of his argument—cause and effect

But the phenomenon does force us to rethink our understanding of violence. Man's inhumanity to man has long been a subject for moralization. With the knowledge that something has driven it dramatically down, we can also treat it as a matter of cause and effect. Instead of asking, "Why is there war?" we might ask, "Why is there peace?" If our behavior has improved so much since the days of the Bible, we must be doing something right. And it would be nice to know what, exactly, it is.

ends on an uncertain note

15

16

17

18

19

Questioning the Author: Points to Consider

- What is the thesis?
- What method is the author using to support this thesis?
- For which audience is the author writing? the general public? peers?
- Is the presentation serious or flippant or ironic?
- Does the author have any special interest in the topic that might amount to bias?
- Does the author try to manipulate the reader in any way?
- Are you inclined to believe everything that you read?
- How well does the author support the thesis? Is the reader convinced?

EXERCISE 3: Examining Intention

A. Read the excerpt from *The Wisdom of Crowds,* by James Surowiecki, twice.

B. On the second reading, use the margins to ask questions and make comments about the meaning of the author's words and phrases and his thesis and intention.

from THE WISDOM OF CROWDS: WHY THE MANY ARE SMARTER THAN THE FEW AND HOW COLLECTIVE WISDOM SHAPES BUSINESS, ECONOMICS, AND SOCIETY

James Surowiecki

Originally a financial journalist, James Surowiecki is a staff writer for the New Yorker *and has been a columnist for* New York *magazine and a contributing editor for* Fortune *magazine.*

Background: You may want to supplement this reading with a 17-minute TED talk given by James Surowiecki in 2005. "The Power and the Danger of Online Crowds" discusses the role played by social media in the acquisition and dissemination of news worldwide. It can be found at www.ted.com/speakers/james_surowiecki

Topic: *Can large masses of people be trusted to regulate their group behavior?*

Culture also enables coordination in a different way, by establishing norms and conventions that regulate behavior. Some of these norms are explicit and bear the force of law. We drive on the right-hand side of the road because it's easier to have a rule that everyone follows rather than to have to play the guessing game with oncoming drivers. Bumping into a fellow pedestrian at the crosswalk is annoying, but smashing into an oncoming Mercedes-Benz is quite another thing. Most norms are long-standing, but it also seems possible to create new forms of behavior quickly, particularly if doing so solves a problem. The journalist Jonathan Rauch, for instance, relates this story about an experience [Thomas] Schelling had while teaching at Harvard: "Years ago, when he taught in a second-floor classroom at Harvard, he noticed that both of the building's two narrow stairwells — one at the front of the building, the other at the rear — were jammed during breaks with students laboriously jostling past one another in both directions. As an experiment, one day he asked his 10:00 AM class to begin taking the front stairway up and the back one down. 'It took about three days,' Schelling told me, 'before the nine o'clock class learned you should always come up the front stairs and the eleven o'clock class always came down the back stairs' — without, so far as Schelling knew, any explicit instruction from the ten o'clock class. 'I think they just forced the accommodation by changing the traffic pattern,' Schelling said." Here again, someone could have ordered the students to change their behavior, but a slight tweak allowed them to reach the good solution on their own, without forcing anyone to do anything.

Conventions obviously maintain order and stability. Just as important, though, they reduce the amount of cognitive work you have to put in to get through the day. Conventions allow us to deal with certain situations without thinking much about them, and when it comes to coordination problems in particular, they allow groups of disparate, unconnected people to organize themselves with relative ease and an absence of conflict.   2

Consider a practice that's so basic that we don't even think of it as a convention: first-come, first-served seating in public places. Whether on the subway or a bus or a movie theater, we assume that the appropriate way to distribute seats is according to when people arrive. A seat belongs, in some sense, to the person occupying it. (In fact, in some places — like movie theaters — as long as a person has established his or her ownership of a seat, he or she can leave it, at least for a little while, and be relatively sure no one will take it.)   3

This is not necessarily the best way to distribute seats. It takes no account, for instance, of how much a person wants to sit down. It doesn't ensure that people who would like to sit together will be able to. And it makes no allowances — in its hard and fast form — for mitigating   4 factors like age or illness. (In practice, of course, people do make allowances for these factors, but only in some places. People will give up a seat on the subway to an elderly person, but they're unlikely to do the same with a choice seat in a movie theater, or with a nice spot on the beach.) We could, in theory, take all these different preferences into account. But the amount of work it would require to figure out any ideal seating arrangement would far outweigh whatever benefit we would derive from a smarter allocation of seats. And, in any case, flawed as the first-come, first-served rule may be, it has a couple of advantages. To begin with, it's easy. When you get on a subway, you don't have to think strategically or worry about what anyone else is thinking. If there's an open seat and you want to sit down, you take it. Otherwise you stand. Coordination happens almost without anyone thinking about it. And the convention allows people to concentrate on other, presumably more important things. The rule doesn't need coercion to work, either. And since people get on and off the train randomly, everyone has as good a chance of finding a seat as anyone else.

Still, if sitting down really matters to you, there's no law preventing you from trying to circumvent the convention by, for instance, asking someone to give up his seat. So in the 1980s, the social psychologist Stanley Milgram decided to find out what would happen if you did just that. Milgram suggested to a class of graduate students that they ride the subway and simply ask people, in a courteous but direct manner, if they could have their seats. The students laughed the suggestion away, saying things like, "A person could get killed that way." But one student agreed to be the guinea pig. Remarkably, he found that half of the people he asked gave up their seats, even though he provided no reason for his request.

This was so surprising that a whole team of students fanned out on the subway, and Milgram himself joined in. They all reported similar results: about half the time, just asking convinced people to give up their seat. But they also discovered something else: the hard part of the process wasn't convincing the people, it was mustering the courage to ask them in the first place. The graduate students said that when they were standing in front of a subject, "they felt anxious, tense, and embarrassed." Much of the time, they couldn't even bring themselves to ask the question and they just moved on. Milgram himself described the whole experience as "wrenching." The norm of first-come, first-served was so ingrained that violating it required real labor.

The point of Milgram's experiment, in a sense, was that the most successful norms are not just externally established and maintained. The most successful norms are internalized. A person who has a seat on the subway doesn't have to defend it or assert her right to the seat because, for the people standing, it would be more arduous to contest that right.

Even if internalization is crucial to the smooth workings of conventions, it's also the case that external sanctions are often needed. Sometimes, as in the case of traffic rules, those sanctions are legal. But usually the sanctions are more informal, as Milgram discovered when he studied what happened when people tried to cut into a long waiting line. Once again, Milgram sent his intrepid graduate students out into the world, this time with instructions to jump lines at offtrack betting parlors and ticket counters. About half the time the students were able to cut the line without any problems. But in contrast to the subway — where, when people refused to give up their seat they generally just said no or even refused to answer — when people did try to stop the line cutting, their reaction was more vehement. Ten percent of the time they took some kind of physical action, sometimes going so far as to shove the intruder out of the way (though usually they just tapped or pulled on their shoulders). About 25 percent of the time they verbally protested and refused to let the jumper in. And 15 percent of the time the intruder just got dirty looks and hostile stares.

Interestingly, the responsibility for dealing with the intruder fell clearly on the shoulders of the person in front of whom the intruder had stepped. Everyone in line behind the intruder suffered when he cut the line, and people who were two or three places behind would sometimes speak up, but in general the person who was expected to act was the one who was closest to the newcomer. (Closest, but behind: people in front of the intruder rarely said anything.) Again, this was not a formal rule, but it made a kind of intuitive sense. Not only did the person immediately behind the intruder suffer most from the intrusion, but it was also easiest for him to make a fuss without disrupting the line as a whole.

That fear of disruption, it turns out, has a lot to do with why it's easier to cut a line, even in New York, than you might expect. Milgram, for one, argued that the biggest impediment to acting against line jumpers was the fear of losing one's place in line. The line is, like the first-come, first-served rule, a simple but effective mechanism for coordinating people, but its success depends upon everyone's willingness to respect the line's order. Paradoxically, this sometimes means letting people jump in front rather than risk wrecking the whole queue. That's why Milgram saw an ability to tolerate line jumpers as a sign of the resilience of a queue, rather than of its weakness.

A queue is, in fact, a good way of coordinating the behavior of   11
individuals who have gathered in a single location in search of goods
or a service. The best queues assemble everyone who's waiting into a
single line, with the person at the head of the line being served first.
The phalanx, which you often see in supermarkets, with each check-
out counter having its own line, is by contrast a recipe for frustration.
Not only do the other lines always seem shorter than the one you're
in — which there's a good chance they are, since the fact that you're in
this line, and not that one, makes it likely that this one is longer — but
studies of the way people perceive traffic speed suggest that you're
likely to do a bad job of estimating how fast your line is moving relative
to everyone else's. The phalanx also makes people feel responsible for
the speed with which they check out, since it's possible that if they'd
picked a different line, they would have done better. As with strategiz-
ing about the subway seat, this is too much work relative to the payoff.
The single-file queue does have the one disadvantage of being visually more intimidating than the phalanx (since everyone's packed into
a single line), but on average everyone will be served faster in a single
queue. If there's an intelligent way to wait in line, that's it. (One change
to convention that would make sense would be to allow people to sell
their places in line, since that would let the placeholders trade their
time for money — a good trade for them — and people with busy jobs
to trade money for time — also a good trade. But this would violate the
egalitarian ethos that governs the queue.)

At the beginning of this chapter, I suggested that in liberal societies   12
authority had only limited reach over the way citizens dealt with each
other. In authority's stead, certain conventions — voluntarily enforced,
as Milgram showed, by ordinary people — play an essential role in
helping large groups of people to coordinate their behavior with each
other without coercion, and without requiring too much thought or
labor. It would seem strange to deny that there is a wisdom in that
accomplishment, too.

Pages 92–93. Jonathan Rauch, "Seeing Around Corners," *Atlantic*
289 (April 2002): 35–48.

Pages 94–96. The subway and line-jumping studies, along with many of
Milgram's most interesting papers, are included in *The Individual in a Social
World,* edited by Stanley Milgram (New York: McGraw-Hill, 1992). Milgram's
description of how the subway study came about is from the Introduction
to that book (xix–xxxiii).

Using Evidence

The author presents a thesis and attempts to prove it; the reader decides whether the thesis is convincing. Whether the author is writing an explanatory, analytical, or persuasive essay, *the credibility of the thesis depends on the strength of the evidence and reasoning.* Why should you believe this thesis? Because the author offers solid evidence as proof, using a process of logical reasoning to persuade you.

Evidence

Evidence refers to any kind of *concrete information* that can support a thesis. Just as evidence is necessary for a criminal to be convicted in court—there, the thesis to be proved is that John Doe robbed Richard Roe—so authors are expected to cite evidence in supporting a thesis.

Evidence can take several forms. Most authors use more than one.

Facts and Statistics

Authors frequently offer *facts* and *statistics* to back up their thesis, especially when they are working in the social sciences. When Mark D. Jekanowski (see p. 27) assures the reader that "the proportion of away-from-home food expenditures on fast food increased from 29.3 to 34.2 percent between 1982 and 1997...," he is using statistics to support his thesis about the growing popularity of fast food.

To prove a thesis about **excessive drinking on a college campus**, an author might cite:

- the college's policy governing drinking in the dormitories (*facts*)
- the number of bars near the campus (*statistics*)
- the number of students who frequent those bars (*statistics*)
- the number of students who have sought help from college counselors for drinking problems (*statistics*)

and so on. Some of this evidence might be obtained from surveys that the author has carried out. Or to provide a broader context for the argument, the author might consult government Web sites or publications such as the *Chronicle of Higher Education* to find additional data about practices on campuses nationwide.

Surveys

Whatever the source, the data must be reliable. Surveys and polls, for example, depend on *generalizing from a representative sample*, based on an appropriate "population." In other words, they use limited evidence (the opinions of, say,

1,000 respondents) to predict the opinions of a much larger group—possibly the entire nation—by assuming that the opinions of the smaller group reflect proportionately the opinions of the larger. So, a 1989 poll surveying almost 4,000 people from three countries about the state of their national health care was able to conclude that 89 percent of all Americans regarded their health-care system as "fundamentally flawed." The author is using the responses of the 4,000 people surveyed to make larger claims about whole national groups. As you will see in Exercise 5, Tara Parker-Pope cites similar surveys in her article about the improvement in teenage behavior.

The same rules of samples and populations would apply to a survey cited as evidence in an essay on **college drinking**. How many people took part in the survey? If percentages are cited, what was the base population? If an author says that 60 percent of those students surveyed drank excessively, does that mean five, or fifteen, or fifty people? How many drinks were defined as "excessive," and was drinking measured by the day, by the week, or by the month?

Examples

An example is a *single representative instance* that serves to support a thesis. Blanche Blank (see pp. 14–16) uses the example of Joe V. to show her readers that college graduates are overqualified for many kinds of work. In the following passage from *Mapping Human History*, Steve Olson provides a series of examples to demonstrate the absurdity of ethnic enmities:

> Many of the harshest conflicts in the world today are between people who are indistinguishable. If someone took a roomful of Palestinians and Is-raelis from the Middle East, or of Serbs and Albanians from the Balkans, or of Catholics and Protestants from Ireland, or of Muslims and Hindus from north-ern India, or of Dayaks and Madurese from Indonesia, gave them all identical outfits and haircuts, and forbade them to speak or gesture, no one could dis-tinguish the members of the other group—at least not to the point of being willing to shoot them. The antagonists in these conflicts have different ethnici-ties, but they have been so closely linked biologically throughout history that they have not developed marked physical differences.
>
> Yet one of the most perverse dimensions of ethnic thinking is the "racial-ization" of culture—the tendency to think of another people as not just cultur-ally but genetically distinct. In the Yugoslavian war, the Croats caricatured their Serbian opponents as tall and blond, while the Serbs disparaged the darker hair and skin of the Croats—even though these traits are thoroughly intermixed between the two groups. During World War II the countries of Europe fiercely stereotyped the physical attributes of their enemies, despite a history of inter-marriage and migration that has scrambled physical characteristics through-out the continent. In Africa, the warring Tutsis and Hutus often call attention to the physical differences of their antagonists, but most observers have trouble

distinguishing individual members of the two groups solely on the basis of appearance.

Keep in mind, though, that because examples are only single instances of a broad and complex situation, they may provide only limited support for the thesis. Specific examples of students whose **drinking** resulted in academic, social, or emotional difficulties may catch your attention, but shouldn't by themselves persuade you that the problem is widespread or serious enough to require action. Rather, they should serve as supplements to more broad-based evidence.

Anecdotes

Anecdotes are stories—extended examples with a beginning, middle, and end—that illustrate the point an author wants to make. Here's the way Stephen L. Carter starts an essay on the topic of civility:

> Let us begin with a common and irritating occurrence. As you sit down to dinner with your family, the telephone rings. When you answer, you find that you are being offered a subscription to the local paper or invited to donate to the volunteer fire department. And although you may enjoy reading your local paper and admire the volunteers who keep the city from burning to the ground, if you are like me, a wave of frustration passes through you, and you face the serious temptation to say something rude....

And Carter continues to describe how his family deals with this dinnertime interruption. He has used an anecdote as a vivid way of introducing his point about the disappearance of common courtesy in daily life.

Like examples, anecdotes attract and interest the reader (and, for that reason, they are often placed at the beginning of essays). But they can take up a great deal of space. "Anecdotal evidence" is never enough to prove a thesis.

Appeal to Authority

Authors often support their theses by citing their own research or the work of acknowledged authorities. Data and examples have considerably more credibility when they are endorsed by sources with a reputation as *experts in the field*. An author needs to cite the evidence of such sources in reasonable detail and, if possible, convey the strength of their credentials. A thesis should not depend on nameless sources such as "1,000 doctors" or "authorities in the field." (Chapter 8 discusses how you can determine which sources are authoritative and which are not.) As you've seen, Steven Pinker cites authorities by name in "Why Is There Peace?" Notice also the way David Leonhardt cites sources by name in "Maybe Money Does Buy Happiness After All" (pp. 170–172). He identifies the scholar's field ("economist," "psychologist") and university ("University of Pennsylvania," "University of Southern California"); the reputation of the institutions help to validate the research that Leonhardt is presenting.

An author writing about **college drinking** is likely to find evidence in *published sources*—books, magazines, scholarly journals—and *reliable* Web sites. The source of that evidence must be acknowledged in the text, with documentation containing the author's name, the work, and the place and date of its publication. In this way, when you read the essay, you can determine whether the author is citing a reputable and appropriate source and, if you wish, locate that source and find out more about the topic.

Looking for Evidence

- Does the author use facts and/or statistics to support the thesis? If so, do they seem reliable?
- Does the author use examples and anecdotes? If so, are they the main or only evidence for the thesis?
- Are the sources for the evidence acknowledged?
- Do these sources seem credible?
- Are there some points that are not supported by evidence?
- Does the author seem biased?
- Based on the evidence provided, do you accept the author's thesis?

EXERCISE 4: Citing Evidence

A. Read "Two-Year Students Have Long Had Four-Year Dreams," by Stephen J. Handel, twice.

B. On your second reading, identify the kinds of evidence cited in the article.

C. Distinguish between *information* supported by evidence, *information* that isn't supported by evidence, and *opinions* offered by the author that derive from the evidence he cites. Is all the evidence equally convincing?

TWO-YEAR STUDENTS HAVE LONG HAD FOUR-YEAR DREAMS
Stephen J. Handel

Stephen J. Handel is presently in charge of undergraduate admissions at the University of California system. The author and coauthor of several books on transferring from community colleges, he was formerly executive director of the National Office of Community College Initiatives at the College Board. This article appeared in the *Chronicle of Higher Education.*

Topic: *What motivates students to attend community colleges — getting a good job or earning a college degree?*

Earning a four-year degree is the pre-eminent educational goal 1
for most incoming community-college students. A 2009 survey by the
U.S. Department of Education indicated that more than 80 percent
of all new, first-time community-college students sought bachelor's
degrees. The desire was especially strong among students from
groups traditionally underrepresented in higher education, such as
Latinos (85 percent), African-Americans (83 percent), and those in the
lowest income quartile (84 percent).

The desire to earn a four-year degree has a long history. Between 2
1966 and 1999, when the University of California at Los Angeles's
Cooperative Institutional Research Program surveyed the educational
aspirations of junior-college, and then community-college, students
separately from those entering four-year institutions, the proportion
of two-year-college students whose education goal was a bachelor's
degree (or higher) never dropped below 70 percent. Steven G. Brint
and Jerome Karabel, in their classic book, *The Diverted Dream* (1989),
quote survey results from the 1920s through the 1950s, all of which reported the intentions of two-year college students as largely directed
toward a bachelor's degree.

Despite their desire to earn a baccalaureate, however, few achieve 3
that goal. Data indicate that only about one-quarter to one-third
of students who wish to transfer actually succeed, despite the fact
that—as the clearinghouse data reflect—their chances of earning a
four-year degree after transfer are good.

Perversely, the low number of actual transfers is used to justify the 4
recalibration of student intentions toward pre-baccalaureate credentials. But higher-education observers like Richard Kahlenberg, writing
in the *Chronicle*, argue the opposite: "Some look at these numbers and
suggest community colleges should downplay the idea of transfer, but
it makes more sense to improve and strengthen transfer paths."

Few people seem concerned about the mismatch between what 5
community-college students intend to do and what they actually
achieve. A recently published monograph chastises community-college
leaders by noting that while community-college "students will readily
identify transfer and long-term academic goals, their ultimate goal is on
employment.... Unfortunately this simple fact is overlooked by most
community colleges." Even if we stipulate in the absence of evidence
that students are concerned only with jobs, it is unclear how their focus
on "transfer and academic goals" undermines that future.

It seems that the wreckage of the recent recession has left us 6
wondering whether the investment in a college degree will continue

to signal something other than a labor-market payoff, as reflected in a recent essay, "The Diploma's Vanishing Value," in the *Wall Street Journal*, by Jeffrey J. Selingo, the *Chronicle's* editor at large.

In response, there is insistence that the nation fill a growing number of jobs requiring pre-baccalaureate skills. This is accompanied by data showing that individuals earning associate degrees in certain fields will earn more initially than those who obtain baccalaureate degrees.   7

Embedded in this rhetorical handwringing is a nod to the cost-effectiveness of junior and community colleges, as if those institutions, around for a century, had only recently matured into something more than colleges that other people's kids attended.   8

Yet, despite the praise of politicians for the vocational aspects of a community-college credential, they have been unable or unwilling to provide the money to improve completion rates. A recent report from the Century Foundation, *Bridging the Higher Education Divide*, notes that between 1999 and 2009, per-student support at private research institutions went up $14,000, while public community colleges benefited from a per-student increase of just $1.   9

Of course, the pressure on college students to train for jobs has been around for a long time. Critics have complained since Harvard was founded that college learning yielded very little in the way of marketable skills. For a time in the late 20th century, however, Big Science, the cold war, and billowing middle-class incomes made the baccalaureate degree the accepted passport to *Mad Men* martinis and split-level suburban homes — assuming, of course, that you were not poor, a member of an ethnic minority group, or a person with a disability. Those folks went to community colleges to train for jobs, right?   10

Then, as now, we comforted ourselves with the notion that such students, assuming they were exceptionally qualified, could transfer to four-year institutions, perhaps even to elite universities. In reality, however, very few were admitted there. Researchers at the University of Southern California and the University of Arizona estimate the number of two-year transfer students attending any one of the country's 179 most elite private and public campuses at fewer than 200, on average.   11

In a nation galvanized around college completion, we label tragic those students attending four-year institutions, even nonselective ones, who fail to earn four-year degrees. We seem satisfied, however, with community-college students — working toward an identical goal — who similarly fail.   12

An enduring contribution of America's community colleges will continue to be the breadth of credentials they offer students of all   13 ages, including occupational certificates, industry-certified training programs, and associate degrees. But let's not forget that many new, first-time community-college students want something more.

They have always wanted more.   14

Interpreting Evidence

There are three major ways to describe how an author uses evidence and how you form conclusions from that evidence: *stating*, *implying*, and *inferring*. To illustrate these terms, here is an excerpt from "The Other Gender Gap," a 2004 *New York Times* article. Marshall Poe is asserting that, in recent years, various initiatives have encouraged girls to earn college, graduate, and professional degrees in ever greater numbers. In contrast, far fewer boys achieve comparable academic success: only 70 percent complete high school, 40 percent enter college, and 8 percent go to graduate school. According to Poe, the difference between boys' and girls' characteristic behavior in the classroom, as early as elementary school, might account for this disparity of achievement.

Statement: Girls' ability to focus on a task is one reason why they do well in school.

From kindergarten on, the education system rewards self-control, obedience, and concentration—qualities that, any teacher can tell you, are much more common among girls than boys, particularly at young ages. Boys fidget, fool around, fight, and worse. Thirty years ago teachers may have accommodated and managed this behavior, in part by devoting more attention to boys than to girls. But as girls have come to attract equal attention, as an inability to sit still has been medicalized, and as the options for curbing student misbehavior have been ever more curtailed, boys may have suffered. Boys make up three quarters of all children categorized as learning disabled today, and they are put in special education at a much higher rate (special education is often misused as a place to stick "problem kids," and children seldom switch from there to the college track). Shorter recess times, less physical education, and more time spent on rote learning (in order to meet testing standards) may have exacerbated the problems that boys tend to experience in the classroom. It is no wonder, then, that many boys disengage academically.

Statement: Three times as many boys as girls are considered learning disabled.

Statements

The two sentences in the margins of this excerpt are restatements of information presented in the article. The words are different; the point is the same. Although the author does not provide data to prove the validity of these two statements, it would be reasonable for you to include this information in an essay, provided that you acknowledge the author—Marshall Poe—and, if possible, document the source: the name of the article, the publication in which it appeared, and the date of its first appearance.

Implications

So far, we have been examining only what the article *explicitly* states. But most sources also inform you indirectly, by implying obvious conclusions that are not stated in so many words. (To *imply* means to suggest an idea not directly expressed in a statement.) The implications of a statement can be easily found within the statement itself; they just are not directly expressed.

Here, for example, is one of Poe's statements side by side with an implication derived from that statement that Poe himself does not make:

Poe's Statement	Implication
Shorter recess times, less physical education, and more time spent on rote learning (in order to meet testing standards) may have exacerbated the problems that boys tend to experience in the classroom.	Boys' poor educational performance might be improved if they had more outlets for their energy during the school day.

In effect, the emphasis is reversed: Poe states the *problem* (an excess of energy); the implication uses the information to suggest a *solution* (more opportunities to work off that energy).

Here is another implication that can be found in the excerpt from Poe:

Poe's Statement	Implication
Boys fidget, fool around, fight, and worse. Thirty years ago teachers may have accommodated and managed this behavior, in part by devoting more attention to boys than to girls. But as girls have come to attract equal attention, as an inability to sit still has been medicalized, and as the options for curbing student misbehavior have been ever more curtailed, boys may have suffered.	Classrooms today tend to be more rowdy than they used to be, and teachers may have more difficulty controlling their students, especially the boys.

Poe states that teachers may have fewer options for controlling the behavior of boys in the classroom. The implication takes the point a step further: teachers may have difficulty maintaining discipline. Poe almost, but doesn't quite, make this point. The focus has shifted from the boys—causing a problem—to the teachers—struggling to find a solution.

If included in an essay, implications like these would be presented just as you would present a source's statement: by acknowledging the author and documenting the work in which the information can be found. Here's what the citation in your text might look like:

In Marshall Poe's view, the fact that boys find it hard to sit still makes it difficult for them to focus on learning. He suggests that boys should be provided with more opportunities to let off steam during the school day.

More on methods of *documentation* can be found in later chapters, particularly Chapter 10.

Inferences

It is also acceptable to draw a conclusion that is *not* implicit in the source, as long as you reach that conclusion through reasoning based on sound evidence. To *infer* means to form a probable conclusion from a statement by reasoning. Unlike implication, inference requires the analysis of information—putting 2 and 2 together—for the hidden idea to be observed. When you express an implication, everything you need is in the text. When you form an inference, you may apply your own knowledge of the subject or experience of life. **The text implies; the reader infers.**

Throughout this excerpt, Poe focuses on the discomfort that boys feel in the classroom (contrasted, by implication, with the ease with which girls are able to learn). One can, therefore, safely infer, from everything that Poe describes, that *most boys don't like school*. Poe does not explicitly or even implicitly make this point; it can't be found in the text. But it is there for readers to infer if they care to do so.

Inferences tend to push the author's point a little further than anything that can be found in the text. Poe, for example, alludes to the possibility that, in the past, boys' energies might have been "accommodated and managed" by teachers who, previously, had enough time to focus on their pupils' individual needs. One can extend this point—infer from it—by suggesting that *more teachers and smaller classes might enable boys to have the individual attention they need to do well in school.* Again, this point isn't in the text; it can only be derived from the text, through inference, by the reader. And, like many inferences, this one uses "might" to convey a degree of doubt. An inference is usually a possibility or probability, not a certainty.

As with statements and implications, inferences require that the source be acknowledged and documented. But, for inferences, it becomes important to distinguish in your essay between what the author says and what you infer:

> Marshall Poe reminds us that, in the past, boys' energies might have been "accommodated and managed" by teachers who, previously, had enough time to focus on their pupils' individual needs. This supports my point that more teachers and smaller classrooms would give boys the individual attention they need to succeed academically.

Unsupported Inferences

Finally, it's always possible to push inference too far and end up with an assertion for which there is no basis in the source. Here are two examples of statements that are unsupported by Poe's article:

> Boisterous and inattentive behavior was considered natural for boys 30 years ago.
>
> > **Unsupported:** We're given no information about how society regarded boys' behavior 30 years ago; we're only told that teachers dealt with it differently.
>
> Women are likely to earn less than men, so girls have to perform better in school to get ahead.
>
> > **Unsupported:** We're given no information that links academic performance with higher salaries for women.

Differentiating among Statement, Implication, and Inference

Statement: The information is provided in the text even though the wording may be different.

Implication: The text suggests an idea that is not directly stated in the source.

Inference: Through reasoning, the reader can form a probable conclusion that is not suggested in the text.

EXERCISE 5: Drawing Inferences

A.   Read "The Kids Are More Than All Right," by Tara Parker-Pope, twice.

B.   On your second reading, decide, according to the information in the article, which of the following sentences are *stated*, are *implied*, can be *inferred*, or are *unsupported*.

1.   As they reach their twenties and thirties, today's teenagers will continue to avoid engaging in risky behavior.

2.   Over the past three decades, use of marijuana by high school seniors has decreased by 14.5%.

3.   The marketing of cigarettes to teenagers by tobacco manufacturers is now more limited, and therefore less successful, than it used to be.

4.   It is probable that the 6.6% of seniors who frequently smoke marijuana are also among the 20% who are smoking tobacco and the 40% who drink alcoholic beverages.

5.   The number of teenage boys who have had sex declined far more sharply than the number of teenage girls.

6.   Thirty years ago, drug use and teenage pregnancy rates were higher in the United States than in most other developed countries.

7.   A small proportion of reckless teenagers have been giving the entire generation a bad reputation.

8.   The government and the judiciary have probably played a role in the decline of teenage drinking and smoking.

9.   New technology has a big role to play in discouraging teenage misbehavior.

10.   The decline in the number of sexually active teenage boys has leveled off in the past decade and may well continue to do so.

THE KIDS ARE MORE THAN ALL RIGHT

Tara Parker-Pope

Tara Parker-Pope is a columnist for the New York Times *and the author of four books on health and social issues. This article appeared in the* New York Times.

Background: Notice that Tara Parker-Pope acknowledges and identifies all four of the sources of her evidence. But, unlike some of the previous readings, no notes accompany this article to indicate where the sources can be found. Documentation in the form of notes can generally be found only in academic books and scholarly journals. Newspapers, like the *New York Times*, and general interest magazines and periodicals, like the *New Yorker* and *Atlantic* (from which you'll find readings later in this book) do not provide separate documentation.

Topic: *Do teenagers engage in risky behavior as often as they did 30 years ago?*

Every few years, parents find new reasons to worry about their teenagers. And while there is no question that some kids continue to experiment with sex and substance abuse, the latest data points to something perhaps more surprising: the current generation is, well, a bit boring when it comes to bad behavior.

1

By several noteworthy measures, today's teenagers are growing increasingly conservative. While marijuana use has recently had an uptick, teenagers are smoking far less pot than their parents did at the same age. In 1980, about 60 percent of high-school seniors had tried marijuana and 9 percent smoked it daily. Among seniors today, according to the University of Michigan's Monitoring the Future survey, which has tracked teenage risk behaviors since 1975, 45.5 percent have tried the drug and 6.6 percent are smoking it frequently.

2

Adolescent use of alcohol, tobacco and most illegal drugs is also far lower than it was 30 years ago. In 1980, about a third of 12th graders had smoked in the past month; today that number has dropped to fewer than 1 in 5. Teenage alcohol use has reached historic lows. In 1980, 72 percent of high-school seniors said they had recently consumed alcohol, compared with just 40 percent in 2011. In 1981, about 43 percent of 12th graders had tried an illegal drug other than pot; in 2011 that number fell to 25 percent.

3

Today's teenagers are also far less likely to have sex or get pregnant compared with their parent's generation. In 1988, half of boys 15 to 17 had experienced sex; by 2010 that number fell to just 28 percent. The percentage of teenage girls having sex dropped, to 27 percent from 37.2 percent, according to the, latest data from the U.S. Centers for Disease Control and Prevention.

4

Health officials say drug use and teenage pregnancy rates are higher here than most other developed nations, but most trends are improving. What about TV shows like "Teen Mom" and "Gossip Girl" that suggest adolescence is dominated by sex and booze? "There is a lot more media hype around the kids who are raising hell," says Dr. John Santelli, president-elect for the Society for Adolescent Health and Medicine. "There are a lot of kids who are pretty responsible."

5

Nobody knows exactly why sex and drug use has declined among teenagers, but there are a number of compelling possibilities that may have contributed. The last three decades have included a rise in the drinking age to 21; a widespread fear of H.I.V.; and legal challenges that stymied tobacco marketing. And while cellphones and Facebook have created new ways for teenagers to stir up trouble, they may also help

6

parents monitor their children. Still, today's children have found ways to rebel (think energy drinks and sexting) that aren't tracked in national surveys. "The entire purpose of the teen years is to push the envelope," Ann Shoket, editor of Seventeen magazine, said. "The fact of the matter is every generation of teens freaks their parents out in some way."

Using Logical Reasoning

The structure of most texts used in research consists of a *logical progression of general points that lead to an overall thesis or conclusion*; each point may be followed by more concrete statements of supporting evidence. The sequence of general points is determined by logical reasoning. For instance, if you look out a window and observe that the street and sidewalk are wet and the sky is overcast, you would most likely conclude that it had rained recently. You didn't directly observe the rain, but you can infer from past experiences with the same evidence and apply this inference to a specific experience in the present. Although this may seem like a simpleminded illustration, it is typical of the reasoning we all engage in every day.

Or, to build on the preceding discussion of implication and inference (see pp. 47–49):

1. Observers typically note that young boys display more physical energy in the classroom than girls do. (*statement*)
2. They are restless and find it difficult to settle down to a task. (*statement*)
3. As a result, many perform poorly in the classroom. (*inference*)
4. To make it easier for boys to learn, we propose that short periods of physical activity be included in the daily schedule. (*conclusion*)

There are two types of reasoning in formal logic—*deductive reasoning* and *inductive reasoning*, each a distinct process for arriving at defensible conclusions based on evidence.

Deductive Reasoning

Deduction means reasoning from general statements to form a logical conclusion.

The classic format for deductive reasoning is the *syllogism*, which consists of a series of carefully limited statements, or premises, pursued to a circumscribed conclusion:

All reptiles are cold-blooded. (premise)
Iguanas are reptiles. (premise)
Therefore, iguanas are cold-blooded. (conclusion)

This is a line of reasoning based on classification, that is, the creation of a generalized category based on shared traits. Members of the group we call "reptiles" have cold-bloodedness in common—in fact, cold-bloodedness is a defining trait of reptiles. Iguanas are members of the group "reptiles," which means that they must also have that shared trait.

Notice that the opening premise of a syllogism is usually a statement that the reader will be willing to grant as true without explicit proof. For example, James Surowiecki, in *The Wisdom of Crowds* (p. 35), establishes a (presumably) shared *major premise*:

1. Cultural norms exist to make society run smoothly and to discourage friction among people living in crowded environments.

Surowiecki follows this major premise with a *secondary premise* and a *conclusion*:

2. Such norms encourage us to internalize the right way to behave.
3. In a well-run society, socially desirable behavior becomes automatic.

Later in the excerpt, Surowiecki uses two complementary syllogisms to explain how society deals with disruptions to its code:

1. For the social code to work, everyone must follow the rules.
2. Those who break the rules are regarded as disruptive.
3. Most people will take responsibility for enforcing the social code against those who disrupt it.

1. Sometimes, publicly defending the right way to behave causes greater disruption.
2. Individuals in a line may refrain from arguing with a queue-jumper.
3. Maintaining order in the line is more important than punishing those who break the code.

Deductive reasoning follows an almost mathematical rigor; provided the premises are accepted as true and the line of reasoning valid, the conclusion must necessarily be true.

Inductive Reasoning

Induction means reasoning from specific evidence to form a general conclusion.

The conclusions reached through inductive reasoning are always conditional to some extent—that is, there's always the possibility that some new evidence may be introduced to suggest a different conclusion. Given the available evidence, you may be perfectly justified in concluding that a wet street and an overcast sky always mean that it has rained; but suppose one day, observing these conditions, you turn on the radio and learn that a water main in the area has broken overnight. That overcast sky may be coincidental, and you should be prepared to revise your original conclusion based on the new information.

> *Inductive reasoning uses the available evidence to construct the most likely conclusion.*

Using Logic to Establish Common Ground with the Reader

Whether authors support their theses by explanation, interpretation, or persuasion—or all three—most of them use elements of inductive and deductive reasoning to prove their claims. The reader is encouraged to re-create the author's logic and view an issue as the author does. The core of the reasoning is usually *deductive*, consisting of a series of *premises* or *assumptions* that the reader shares—or can be persuaded to share—with the author. These premises often depend on *common cultural values*. That is why a thesis can lose its force over time as values change. One hundred years ago, authors could safely reason from the premise that heroism is defined by slaying the enemy in battle, or that engaging in sex before marriage warrants a girl's expulsion from polite society, or that whipping young children is an effective and acceptable punishment. Today, those statements would not have much credibility. In the same way, those who believe that the needs of the individual are all-important will reject Surowiecki's premise that cultural norms must prevail, as well as the statements that follow from that initial assumption.

To establish common ground with the reader, the author usually needs to spell out his or her assumptions and define them so precisely that they seem not only true but inevitable. For instance, few people would challenge a claim that cruelty to animals is wrong, but there is a wide range of opinion regarding exactly what constitutes cruelty, or whether certain specific activities (the use of animals in scientific research, for instance) are or are not cruel. If inflicting pain serves some larger purpose, is it still cruel, or does "cruelty" refer only to *unnecessary* or *unjustifiable* pain? Before contesting the ethics of medical research practices, the author would have to begin by establishing a premise—in this case, a definition of "cruelty"—that the reader will also find acceptable.

Using Logic for Persuasion

To be fully convincing, the reasoning that follows from your premises must be inductive as well as deductive. It must be supported by a range of evidence, which you present, analyze, and interpret for your reader.

Logical Flaws and Fallacies

Sometimes we find it difficult to accept an author's logic:

- The reasoning may be based on an initial premise that is unconvincing or that we don't share.
- The line of reasoning that connects one premise to the next may be flawed.
- The evidence itself may be misrepresented in some way.

Logical fallacies are breakdowns in reasoning; they occur when an author draws unjustifiable conclusions from the available evidence.

Begging the Question

Initial premises are generally expressed with confidence in the reader's agreement—remember, the author assumes that the reader will accept the opening premises without explicit proof. As you read, you should be careful to identify the assumptions an author uses in constructing a line of reasoning. For example, look at the following opening premise, from the second paragraph of an unsigned editorial attacking a proposed ban on tobacco products. The editorial appeared in the magazine *National Review* in 1994.

> Even though nine-tenths of smokers don't die of lung cancer, there are clearly health dangers in cigarettes, dangers so constantly warned about that smokers are clearly aware that these dangers are the price they pay for the enjoyment and relaxation they get from smoking.

The author claims here that because the health risks connected with smoking have been widely publicized, the decision to smoke is rational—that is, based on smokers' weighing their desire for "enjoyment and relaxation" against the potential health risks. You might grant that the dangers of smoking have been well documented and publicized, but does it necessarily follow that knowing the risks involved ensures a rational decision? If, as has also been widely demonstrated, cigarettes are addictive, then the decision to keep smoking may *not* be entirely rational.

The author here is committing a common logical lapse known as **begging—or evading—the question**. The assumption here—that smokers are making a rational decision—is false; yet we are expected to accept the point without question. The key word here is "clearly"—"smokers are clearly aware"—which may persuade the careless reader that the point has already been proved. When an author is begging the question, you often find language that preempts the issue and discourages scrutiny: "obviously," "everyone knows," or "it goes without saying."

Sometimes, the process of begging the question is more subtle. Here, an author arguing against euthanasia begins with a strong statement:

> Every human being has a natural inclination to continue living. Our reflexes and responses fit us to fight attackers, flee wild animals, and dodge out of the way of trucks. In our daily lives we exercise the caution and care necessary to protect ourselves. Our bodies are similarly structured for survival right down to the molecular level.... Euthanasia does violence to this natural goal of survival. It is literally acting against nature because all the processes of nature are bent towards the end of bodily survival.

By limiting his view of existence to purely bodily functions, J. Gay-Williams simplifies the complex issue of euthanasia. What he omits are the key functions of the mind, will, and emotions, which, some would say, can override the force of the instinct toward "bodily survival" and make the choice to die. The key here is the first sentence: "Every human being has a natural inclination to continue living." This broad assumption allows for no exceptions. *It begs the question by telling only part of the story.*

Post hoc ergo propter hoc

Post hoc ergo propter hoc means "after this, therefore because of this." This logical fallacy assumes that because one event precedes another, it must somehow cause the second event.

It is often true that one event causes a second, later event, as in the case of rain causing the wet street you observe the next morning. But if you make that reasoning a universal rule, you might, for instance, conclude that because swimsuits habitually appear in your local clothing stores in May, and summer follows in June, swimsuits somehow cause summer. It may be perfectly true that swimsuits appear in stores in May and that summer usually begins in June, but this argument fails to consider alternative explanations—in this case, that the approach of summer actually causes manufacturers to ship and retailers to display swimsuits in May, rather than the other way around; the swimsuits *anticipate*, rather than cause, summer.

False Dilemma

Most fallacies result from a tendency to oversimplify issues, to take shortcuts in dealing with complex and diverse ideas. With the **false dilemma**, an author limits the ground for disagreement by proceeding as if there are only two alternatives; everything else is ignored. Here is part of the argument presented by an author who supports laws allowing euthanasia:

> Reality dictates the necessity of such laws because, for some dying patients experiencing extreme suffering, a lethal prescription is the only way to end an

extended and agonizing death. Consider the terrible dilemma created when
so-called passive measures fail to bring about the hoped-for death. Are we to
stand helplessly by while a patient whose suicide we legally agreed to assist
continues to suffer and deteriorate—perhaps even more so than before? Or
do we have a moral imperative, perhaps even a legal responsibility, to not only
alleviate the further suffering we have brought about but to take action to
fulfill our original agreement [to withdraw life support]?

Barbara Dority has reduced the situation to a simple choice: passive doctor and patient in agony versus active doctor who brings an end to suffering, abides by morality, and keeps her promise. There are many possibilities
for intervention between these two extremes, but at least at this point in her
argument, the author does not acknowledge them. Through her language, she
also loads the dice: does one identify with the ineffectual doctor "stand[ing]
helplessly by" or with the heroic doctor with a "moral imperative" who knows
how to "take action" to "alleviate...suffering"?

Hasty Generalization

The tendency to oversimplify, to base claims on insufficient evidence, can
result in the **hasty generalization**. A convincing generalization will be
supported by strong evidence, not one or two examples. And when an author
does cite examples, consider whether they clearly support the claim. Gertrude
Himmelfarb, for example, builds her argument about the decline of morality
in our society by criticizing what she claims is an increasing tendency to be
nonjudgmental. She offers the following generalization:

> Most of us are uncomfortable with the idea of making moral judgments even
> in our private lives, let alone with the "intrusion," as we say, of moral judg-
> ments into public affairs.

To support her generalization, she observes that public officials, such as the
president's cabinet and the Surgeon General, tend to avoid using the word
"immoral." In one of her two examples, the Secretary of Health and Human
Services is quoted as saying:

> I don't like to put this in moral terms, but I do believe that having children out
> of wedlock is just wrong.

This last quotation, in itself, hardly strengthens Himmelfarb's initial point since
many would consider "wrong" a judgment equivalent to "immoral." Then, on
the basis of two examples, she reiterates her original claim:

> It is not only our political and cultural leaders who are prone to this failure of
> moral nerve. Everyone has been infected by it, to one degree or another.

The argument has moved around in a circle, from one hasty generalization to another.

Ad Hominem

An especially unpleasant kind of logical fallacy is the *ad hominem* [about the man] argument, a personal attack in which an author criticizes a prominent person who holds opposing views without considering whether the criticism is relevant to the issue. The ad hominem argument is often used in political campaigns and other well-publicized controversies.

Paul McHugh, for example, spends the first half of an argument against euthanasia demonstrating why he regards Dr. Jack Kevorkian, who facilitated a number of mercy killings, as "'certifiably' insane." McHugh compares him with other zealots who would do anything to advance their cause and finally cites "the potential for horror in an overvalued idea held by a person in high authority" such as Adolf Hitler. Certainly, the comparison is strained—Dr. Kevorkian was not "in high authority." Yet, even though McHugh now moves to a completely different basis for argument, the infamy generated by the association between Kevorkian and Hitler reverberates throughout the rest of the essay.

False Analogy

Analogy means the idea that if two things are alike in some ways they will be alike in most or all ways.

Authors often support their points by reasoning through analogies. They may compare a disputed idea or situation to some other, less controversial idea in order to reveal a parallel or an inconsistency. For instance, some might claim that the wide availability of *foreign-made consumer products* is analogous to an *infection* that threatens to destroy the health of the nation's economy. What similarities in the two situations are being exploited? What parallels can be drawn between them? In both cases, some entity (in the first case a nation, and in the second a human being) is "invaded" by something potentially harmful (such as a Chinese-made iPad or German-built car in the case of the nation, and a virus or bacterial infection in the case of the person). Analogies can provide vivid and persuasive images, but they are easily distorted when pushed too far.

In a **false analogy**, the two ideas or circumstances being compared are not actually comparable. To illustrate the pitfalls of false analogy, let's return to the editorial from the *National Review* on the proposed tobacco ban. Here's the entire paragraph:

> Even though nine-tenths of smokers don't die of lung cancer, there are clearly health dangers in cigarettes, dangers so constantly warned about that

smokers are clearly aware that these dangers are the price they pay for the enjoyment and relaxation they get from smoking. As mortals we make all kinds of trade-offs between health and living. We drive automobiles knowing that forty thousand people die in them in the U.S. each year; we cross busy streets, tolerate potentially explosive gas in our homes, swim in fast-moving rivers, use electricity though it kills thousands, and eat meat and other foods that may clog our arteries and give us heart attacks and strokes. All the ... demagoguery about the tobacco industry killing people could be applied with similar validity to the automobile industry, the electric utilities, aircraft manufacturers, the meat business, and more.

Here, the reader is asked to compare the health risks associated with smoking with those of parallel but comparatively uncontroversial activities, such as crossing a busy street. According to the author, the situations are comparable because both involve voluntarily engaging in activities known to be health risks. That similarity is used to suggest that laws *prohibiting* smoking would be logically inconsistent because we don't prohibit other risky activities like crossing streets. If potential health risks justify regulation, or even prohibition, then many modern activities should, by analogy, be regulated. Yet, in spite of the risks in crossing busy streets, no one ever suggests preventing people from doing so for their own good; smoking, however, is singled out for regulation and possible prohibition. The reader can further *infer* from this line of reasoning that, since we daily engage in all kinds of risky activities, individuals in all cases should be allowed to decide without government interference which risks to take.

To determine whether an analogy is false, one need only decide whether the differences in the two situations are more significant than the similarities. In this case, we need to consider:

- if the decision to smoke and the decision to cross a busy street are *genuinely* comparable; and

- if there may be sound reasons for regulating smoking, and equally sound reasons for *not* regulating crossing the street (except, of course, for providing red lights).

Most people could not live a normal life without crossing a busy street, but the same cannot be said of smoking. In addition, if a minimal amount of caution is exercised in crossing busy streets, most people will not be injured; when injuries do occur, they're the result of accidents or some other unexpected or unusual set of events. The same is true of the other "hazards" described in the editorial (driving automobiles, using gas appliances, and so on): injuries result from their *misuse*. By contrast, cigarettes pose a serious health threat when used exactly as intended by their manufacturers; no amount of caution will protect you from the risks associated with cigarettes.

Misrepresenting Evidence

You might also object to this rejection of the smoking ban on grounds that go beyond the logic of the reasoning to the ways the evidence is presented. The author states, for instance, that 9 in 10 smokers don't die of lung cancer, implying not only that a 10 percent death rate is insignificant but that death or lung cancer is the only potential health risk connected to smoking worth mentioning. The author then tells us that "forty thousand people die" in automobiles each year in the United States. But since that number isn't presented as a percentage of all drivers on the road over the course of the year, it doesn't really address the *comparable* level of risk—those 40,000 may represent fewer than 1 percent of all drivers, which would make driving considerably less risky than smoking. Misrepresenting the evidence in this way prods the careful reader to question the author's trustworthiness and credibility.

Analyzing an Author's Logic

1. What assumptions is the author making as the basis for the thesis? Is it reasonable to assume that the reader shares these assumptions?

2. Does the text provide a logical sequence of assertions that can be easily followed and that leads to a persuasive conclusion? Are there any convincing alternatives to the author's conclusion?

3. Is the reasoning primarily inductive (deriving generalizations from probabilities established by the author), or is it deductive (deriving specific conclusions from broad assertions that are tested and proved)?

4. Are appropriate and sufficient data and examples provided?

5. Are the sources of the evidence clearly indicated?

6. Has the author lapsed into any fallacies that distort the logic and support a false conclusion?

7. What inferences does the author make from the evidence provided? Are they reasonable, or does the author attempt to manipulate the reader's perception of the evidence to suit the purposes of the thesis?

EXERCISE 6: Analyzing an Author's Logic

A. As your instructor indicates, read either the excerpt from *The End of Sex*, by Donna Freitas, or the excerpt from *"Eye for an Eye: The Case for Revenge,"* by Thane Rosenbaum. Read the excerpt twice.

B.   On your second reading, make marginal comments about the logical processes used by the author (including deduction and induction), the presence of logical fallacies (if any), and the appropriateness and sufficiency of
     the evidence provided.

C.   Consider these questions:

     ▪ Which sentences support the author's thesis?

     ▪ Which sentences introduce a new premise or a turn in the argument?

     ▪ Which sentences contain evidence that supports the thesis? What
        kind of evidence?

     ▪ Are there any flaws in the reasoning?

     ▪ How would you sum up the thesis in your own words?

     ▪ Are you convinced?

from THE END OF SEX: HOW HOOKUP CULTURE IS LEAVING A GENERATION UNHAPPY, SEXUALLY UNFULFILLED, AND CONFUSED ABOUT INTIMACY

Donna Freitas

*Having received a doctorate in religion and having taught at two
universities, Donna Freitas is now an author, journalist, and
broadcaster. She has published novels for adults and young adults, as
well as nonfiction books dealing with topics such as sex and spirituality.*

Topic: *Is excessive drinking the major cause of the "hookup" culture
at some of our colleges?*

There are many studies about alcohol on college campuses. These   [1]
studies generally look at overall consumption, frequency of consumption, the size of the drinking population at different universities, and
the effects of alcohol on student decision-making and sexual activity.
In a 2008 study published in the journal *Adolescence*, approximately
25 percent of college students reported that they had recently engaged in binge drinking. Other studies have reported even higher
numbers of binge drinkers on campus, with figures of up to 40 percent.
According to the *Adolescence* study, about another 30 percent of the
students reported frequent social drinking, and 12 percent reported
occasional social drinking. The percentages were higher for women
than for men in each category. All of this means that more than half
of the campus population drinks regularly. These trends were very evident in my study as well. Talk of hookup culture almost inevitably led
to talk of alcohol and getting drunk.[1]

During my one-on-one interviews with students, it quickly be-   2
came clear that there was nothing subtle about the amount of alcohol consumed on campus every weekend. The relationships between
drinking and the party scene, and between alcohol and hookup culture, was impossible to miss. There was a pervasive perception among
students not only that everyone was drinking, but that everyone
was drinking *hard*, that is, drinking in order to get wasted, and that
the getting-wasted part had its purpose, too: to ease a person into the
mood necessary for a hookup. Perhaps not surprisingly, most of the
students with whom I spoke said they did not drink in this manner —
much as in the *Adolescence* study. Students would readily admit that
they were *around* alcohol regularly, and that they drank some, but they
tended to see excessive alcohol consumption as something others did,
rather than as something they did themselves — at least not as something they did very often.

Common answers to survey questions about the nature of college   3
social life often cited alcohol. "The number one activity probably on
most campuses is drinking," said one first-year man at a Catholic school.
A sophomore woman, also on a Catholic campus, said, "At night … a
good majority of this campus goes out and drinks." When pressed to
say more about why people drank so much, this same young woman
attributed it to the challenges of the higher education experience
today. "I think part of it is being in college, it's such a stressful time,
there's so much going on, there's so many expectations required," she
explained. "And, [drinking is] a chance to relax from all that and hang
out with friends and to be able to let loose. I think for some people it's
an escape — to get away from things that are really bothering them.
But I think a lot of it is just that people are really stressed."

One young man, also a first-year student at a Catholic college,   4
had only one word for me when I asked what people usually did on
the weekends at his school: "Drink." Yet he went on to say that,
although he did participate a little, he felt that he was different in
his drinking habits from everybody else on campus. "I do [drink]
sometimes, but I am very moderate with it. Where[as] a lot of
people came here and as soon as they had that freedom, they ran
with it." When asked why alcohol was so appealing to people
on his campus, he, too, distanced himself from the sort of drinking he believed everyone else was doing. "Alcohol can be a catalyst for conversation," he said. "Like something mind-altering
can spark some kind of imagination. But some people abuse it
completely, and feel compelled to do it every night of the week.

I don't really admire that in anyone. It's upsetting to see a lot of kids falling into it."

This student's comment about alcohol as a "catalyst for conversation" was really a veiled statement about how students hook up. Most of the students I interviewed stated this more plainly, such as a sophomore woman from a Catholic college, who said; "I think that alcohol is the catalyst of finally making [something into] an intimate relationship. [Alcohol] just makes it easier. You would never walk up to someone and just start making out with them if you weren't intoxicated. It makes your inhibitions go." A male student who was a junior at a secular university cited alcohol as *the* determining factor in hookup culture. Without alcohol, he said, hookup culture wouldn't even exist.

5

This student also said that first-year students, in particular, were fixated on expectations to hook up and used alcohol to get themselves into the right mindset. "Alcohol flows much easier here than it did at home in high school," he explained. "So when people are drunk their inhibitions are let go — that's just common knowledge — and people feel freer to use alcohol as an excuse or as the real reason why they're feeling less inhibited to be promiscuous." These types of comments seem to be corroborated by the evidence. According to a 2007 study published in the journal *Addictive Behaviors*, 32 percent of students reported having unprotected sex after drinking. Overall, the study showed that a whopping 55 percent of the sexual encounters on campus with someone who was not a steady partner involved alcohol.[2]

6

Alcohol is key to the perpetuation of hookup culture on campus. It plays a huge part in the poor decisions students often make — and later regret. At evangelical colleges, which are dry, and where only a tiny sliver of the population breaks the rules by drinking and partying, hookup culture — at least as students at Catholic, private-secular, and public institutions know it — simply does not exist.[3] Although it would be difficult to establish a definitive causal relationship between drinking culture and hookup culture, the correlation, at least, seems fairly obvious.

7

But is *everyone* on campus really getting wasted and hooking up? In my interviews and online survey, the "me vs. everyone else" motif was quite prominent. Students talked about alcohol as if it were an all-powerful, extremely pervasive factor on campus affecting everyone's behavior — everyone *else's* behavior, at least. They did not often believe it was an important factor in their own behavior.

8

One of the online survey questions asked how often it had been the case that when a student had engaged in sexual activity, he

9

or she had also been drinking alcohol or using a drug (see Table 2.1). Nearly a quarter of the students answering this question responded that they had "never" drunk alcohol or used drugs during sexual activity. Also, more than a quarter answered they had "rarely" drunk or used drugs during sexual activity. Together these respondents represented more than 50 percent of the students who took the online survey. This still left approximately 48 percent of the students. These students admitted in the survey that they had been drinking or using a drug at least some of the time when they had been engaging in sexual activity. Forty-eight percent is a significant number, certainly, but it is a far cry from "everybody." Thus, if we assume that the students who took the survey were accurately reporting their own use of alcohol and drugs during sexual activity, we can see that there is a fairly significant discrepancy between perceptions of the correlation between alcohol use and sexual activity and the reality.

One likely interpretation of these results is that students simply lie   10
to their peers about all sorts of things — whether they are still a virgin, how many times they've hooked up (men up their numbers, women do the opposite), and exactly how drunk they were the night before

TABLE 2.1: Survey Data
Sexual Activity and Use of Alcohol or Drugs

How often is it the case when you have engaged in sexual activity that you have also been drinking alcohol or using a drug?	Response Percent	Response Count (776 students)
Never	24.5%	190
Rarely	27.3%	212
More often had not been drinking or using a drug	20.6%	160
Equal times had been drinking or using a drug as not	11.9%	92
More often had been drinking or using a drug than not	9.4%	73
Frequently	4.8%	37
All the time	1.5%	12

when they engaged in x, y, and z. Alcohol has always been the great excuse for all sorts of behavior, but never before have students been so dependent on it to explain away their sexual encounters, both to others and to themselves. The incentive to either be, or at least appear to be, drunk on Thursday, Friday, and Saturday nights is high. Saying that you were drunk when you did something — even if you were not — will often get you a pass from peers. The shock of what someone did the night before — how far they went, who they were with, where they did whatever it was they did — can be lessened or even waved away if a person can say they were trashed at the time. Admitting to sobriety makes a person more fully responsible for his or her behavior.[4]

The student I interviewed who cited alcohol as the determining   11
factor in hookup culture, like many other students, felt that alcohol was a key ingredient of the hookup because it allowed people to excuse themselves from responsibility for whatever sexual intimacy occurred. The first time this young man had had sex was during a hookup. "Alcohol went into the decision," he said about this experience. "I guess [my partner and I] just started hooking up and started having unprotected sex and then I just stopped and said [to myself], 'Wait, what am I doing? This is stupid!' But then I kind of blocked it out of my memory for a while."

I heard many similar stories. It's disconcerting to listen to so many   12
students talk about how they relinquished their agency for sexual decision-making because of alcohol. This young man's stammering phrases of "I guess" and "I just," and the way he reported blocking out what had happened — his claim to confusion, in other words — were revealing. They showed that he was trying to justify his behavior and absolve himself of responsibility because he was drunk. The way he described this sexual encounter made it sound as if he had suddenly woken up and was surprised to find himself in bed with a woman, as if the alcohol had acted of its own accord and without his consent. This kind of talk begs consideration of the nature of sexual consent itself within hookup culture. Is there indeed a relationship between drinking and the hookup that diminishes a person's sexual agency? And, if so, what does "consent" mean here? How does one give consent to have sex if so many people use alcohol to relinquish responsibility for whatever "happens"?

In general, my survey data and the narratives of the students show   13
that although students appear to revel in hookup culture when in public, in private they admit that much of the sexual activity in hookups is unwanted, at worst, and ambivalent, at best.

When alcohol is the self-medicating medium of choice, the   14
conversation about sexual assault becomes very complicated. The
41 percent of students in my survey who reported being profoundly
upset about hooking up said the encounters made them feel, among
other things, used, miserable, disgusted, and duped. Most disturbing
of all were those who likened their hookups to "abuse." Within hookup
culture, it is too simplistic to have conversations about date rape and
"no means no," since this culture is one that by definition *excludes dating*, almost prohibiting it, while promoting using copious amounts of
alcohol. Taken together, it has students not only *not* saying no, but
barely saying anything at all, including yes.

Researchers have begun to investigate the relationship between   15
alcohol consumption, sexual assault, and hookup culture on campus.
An article in the *Journal of Interpersonal Violence* found that, with
respect to alcohol consumption generally, 41 percent of student
participants drank one to two times per week, and 28 percent
drank more than twice per week. Fifty-six percent of these students
said that when they drank, their intention was to get drunk. These
statistics are perhaps not surprising, given the way American culture
glorifies drinking on college campuses. Yet, according to these researchers, the prevalence of hooking up drastically increased when
alcohol was involved, as did the prevalence of unsafe sex and
sexual assault. 'The study showed that 62 percent of unwanted sex
occurred because the student's "judgment was impaired due to
drugs and alcohol."[5]

In a follow-up study in the same journal, researchers claimed that   16
approximately 26 percent of college students in their first and second
years of college had had sex with someone they had just met when
they were under the influence of alcohol; 40.4 percent had had sex with
someone they knew, but with whom they were not in a relationship,
while under the influence of alcohol. The accompanying statistics on
sexual assault on campus in this study were startling. Approximately
44 percent of the women participating in the study reported at least
one unwanted sexual encounter while in college, and 90 percent of
this unwanted sex took place during a hookup. Of all the reported incidents of unwanted sex, 76.2 percent involved alcohol, which played a
significant role in blurring the lines of consent. The researchers found
that often, the victim was too drunk to properly give consent. Often,
the victim did not really remember what had happened after waking
up the next day.[6]

1. Donna E. Howard, Melinda A. Griffin, and Bradley O. Boekeloo, "Prevalence and Psychosocial Correlates of Alcohol-Related Sexual Assault Among University Students," *Adolescence* 43 (2008).

2. Jennifer L. Brown and Peter A. Vanable, "Alcohol Use, Partner Type, and Risky Sexual Behavior Among College Students: Findings from an Event-Level Study." *Addictive Behaviors* 32, no. 12 (2007): 2940–2952. See also William F. Flack Jr., Marcia L. Caron, Sarah J. Leinen, Katherine G. Breitenbach, Ann M. Barber, Elaine N. Brown, et al., "'The Red Zone': Temporal Risk for Unwanted Sex Among College Students," *Journal of Interpersonal Violence* 23, no. 9 (2008).

3. Donna Freitas, *Sex and the Soul: Juggling Sexuality, Spirituality, Romance and Religion on America's College Campuses (New York: Oxford University Press, 2008), 75–92, 113–125.*

4. For more discussion of this tendency, see also Brown et al., "Alcohol Use, Partner Type."

5. William F. Flack Jr., Kimberly Daubman, and Marcia Caron, "Risk Factors and Consequences of Unwanted Sex Among University Students: Hooking Up, Alcohol, and Stress Response," *Journal of Interpersonal Violence* 22, no. 2 (2007): 139–157.

6. Flack et al., "'The Red Zone.'"

EYE FOR AN EYE: THE CASE FOR REVENGE
Thane Rosenbaum

Now a senior fellow at New York University, Thane Rosenbaum is a frequent speaker at universities and cultural centers and on other media. His books include fiction and two works of nonfiction critical of our legal system. This article appeared in the Chronicle of Higher Education.

Topic: *Is the fulfillment of revenge the most important component of justice?*

A surefire way to establish one's moral superiority—certainly in our society and in most Western nations—is to renounce any interest in revenge. No matter the damage done, the outrageousness of the conduct, or the magnitude of the loss, most people will reflexively wave off any suggestion that vengeance is what they desire. Indeed, they will indignantly deny having a vengeful streak, as if nothing could be so shameful as the simple wish to settle a score. Take your pick of maxims: "Vengeance is beneath me"; "I'm not out for revenge, I just want to make sure this doesn't happen to someone else"; "All I care about is justice, not revenge."

[Yet] A call for justice is always a cry for revenge. By placing their faith   2
in the law, those who justifiably wish to see wrongdoers punished are
not disavowing vengeance. If anything, they are seeking to be avenged
by the law. No matter what they say, victims aren't choosing justice over
vengeance; they are merely capitulating to a cultural taboo, knowing that
the protocol in polite society is to repudiate revenge. But make no mistake:
When it comes to the visceral experience of being a victim, revenge and
justice are one and the same.

And everyone should feel similarly. After all, there is no justice unless   3
victims feel avenged, when they believe that a wrong has been righted
and honor restored. And revenge is never just if it is disproportionately
delivered — if the retaliation exceeds what is justly deserved, measure for
measure. Indeed, vengeance is not irrational (the common knock on revenge) — it's healthy and entirely human. Insisting that justice will suffice
when revenge is what victims really want is both intellectually dishonest
and factually untrue. Besides, in modern societies where vigilantism is disal-
lowed, we all on some level reasonably believe that it is only by leveraging
the law — and having the legal system serve as our proxy — that vengeance
can be actually achieved....

What's so shameful about the emotional clarity and moral imperative   4
of getting even? Why all the hypocrisy surrounding revenge?

Before the Internet, those with a fondness for porn were left with little   5
choice but to sneak into adult theaters in the seedy section of town wearing
oversized raincoats and wide-brimmed hats. To be caught in the compromised position of standing in the ticket line while another PTA parent just
happened to drive by was difficult to explain away. Society has long ban-
ished the perverted from the ranks of respectable company....

Revenge shares a similar public shame (though it is probably more ac-   6
ceptable to confess to having a kinky taste for porn than to acknowledge
harboring feelings of revenge). The vengeful are deemed out of control,
emotionally unhinged, perpetually angry, and unable to turn the cheek and
move on with their lives. Yet the revenge film — think *Gladiator, Braveheart,
True Grit, Death Wish* — remains immensely popular, with decades of box-
office appeal. If revenge is so shameful, then why don't audiences charge
out of theaters in protest? Why, instead, do they settle into their seats with
their blood rushing and their minds driven mad by the possibility that a fic-
tional wrongdoer will escape punishment before the closing credits?

We watch revenge films without embarrassment because on some   7
primal level we know that just deserts are required in the moral universe,
that those who commit crimes must be punished according to their blame-
worthiness, and that wrongs must ultimately be righted. It's not our lust for

violence that explains why we applaud payback, but our absolute need to live in a world that promotes fairness, law and order, and social peace. We're all better off when wrongdoers are punished.

Without the debt canceling, equalizing, restorative dimensions of revenge, faith in humankind is lost and the world makes less sense. That's precisely what people mean when they lament that there is "no justice in the world"—a wrongdoer has gotten away with murder, and all who depend, morally and emotionally, on the sum-certainty of vengeance are left helpless, dumbfounded, and enraged. The revenge we are so often denied in our private lives is experienced vicariously—courtesy of the movies.

So if justice and revenge are fundamentally the same, why can't we be more honest about the role that revenge plays in our lives? It's finally time to humanize justice by restoring the face of vengeance. Doing so is not an invitation to lawlessness but a mandate that the law must act with the same moral entitlement, and the same spirit of human fulfillment, as the righteous avenger.

Vengeance is as old as man himself. It is an instinct at the very core of our emotions; indeed, it's a byproduct of our evolutionary history. Human survival depended greatly on convincing neighboring clans, tribes, and states that no attack or moral injury would go unanswered. Payback was nonnegotiable and self-regulating. Reclaiming one's honor was not undertaken out of haphazard rage. To avenge was to achieve justice, and to do what was just necessitated the taking of revenge.

The philosopher Robert C. Solomon has pointed out that "vengeance is the original meaning of justice. The word 'justice' in the Old Testament and in Homer virtually always refers to revenge.... Not that the law and the respect for the law are unimportant, of course, but one should not glibly identify these with justice and dismiss the passion for vengeance as something quite different and wholly illegitimate."

For much of human history, the resolution of disputes was a private matter. States were not yet in the business of maintaining legal systems or, for that matter, punishing wrongdoers for crimes committed against another. Law and order was enforced at the most local of levels. Governments became involved—essentially taking a monopoly on vengeance—only during the Enlightenment, when the social contract obligated citizens to surrender to, and faithfully accept, the rule of law. To hold up their end of the bargain, states collected taxes to erect courthouses and police stations, and filled them with personnel responsible for keeping the peace. Governments assumed the role of surrogate avenger, minus the emotional involvement that a true avenger would naturally possess.

But regardless of who becomes the designated revenge-taker—   13
either the state, with its impersonal security apparatus, or the avenger, who
is discharging his personal duty—human beings can no more suppress
their revenge impulse than can they curb their instincts for sex and hunger
for food. Getting even is a biological necessity. We need our revenge,
notwithstanding how feverishly religions and governments have worked
to eradicate it from the human experience. Vengeance can be curtailed, but
it can never be truly undone, nor should it. Vengeance keeps returning …
well … with a vengeance.

The *lex talionis*, the law of the talion, which provides for the right of   14
retaliation, has its origins in the Old Testament and in Hammurabi's Code,
and sets forth the basic formulation of reciprocity in response to moral
injury—measure for measure. "An eye for an eye," misunderstood as a
mantra for the bloodthirsty, has attained a thuggish reputation. But it has
an altogether different meaning. If anything, "an eye for an eye" is a check
on excess. It demands exactness and has no tolerance for recklessness. The
wrongdoer who causes someone to lose an eye will have to forfeit one of
his own—no more, no less. And not out of pure hate, but in accordance
with what is due.

The talion establishes a boundary for human loss. A debt is created,   15
and the avenger is entitled to take the measure of his or her loss as payback. The wrongdoer is entitled to no discount, and the avenger is held to a
standard that allows for no excess.

Society should always reject the wrongdoer who takes an eye and not   16
the avenger who is duty-bound to even the score. Those who, like Gandhi,
say "An eye for an eye makes the whole world blind" ignore their own moral
blindness. Telling victims to accept their loss without recourse is not a sign
of virtue—it's proof of cowardice. Turning the cheek may have religious
significance to practicing Christians, but it is an awkward facial maneuver
not readily practiced in the moral universe where the repayment of all debts
is mandated.

There is a paradox in our distaste for "an eye for an eye." Most peo-   17
ple abhor having to accept discounts in their professional or private lives.
Businesses insist that invoices be paid in full; landlords evict tenants who
are delinquent in paying rent; retailers gnash their teeth at having to mark
down an item that should have sold at full price; those who emerge from
bankruptcy are often socially exiled for paying pennies on the dollar to satisfy their debts; marriages fall apart when one spouse simply won't carry
an equal load. The Beatles seemed to understand the principle when they
wrote "the love you take is equal to the love you make."

We all want reciprocity, and we want the ledgers we keep with business associates and intimate partners to be balanced. Indeed, we expect it. Those who stand on principle and demand fair payment — insisting on precision and always inflexible about price — are thought to be righteous. And yet, when it comes to the most crushing of debts, the losses that are simply too much to bear, the injuries that are truly a matter of life and death — the murder or rape of a loved one, large-scale human suffering, an assault on dignity so great that honor is not easily recaptured — our math skills suddenly fail us, and we become reluctant to support equivalent punishments. A new calculus is created, one that doesn't add up. 18

So we tolerate a legal system where over 95 percent of all cases are resolved with a negotiated plea — bargained down from what the wrongdoer rightfully deserved. That means that convicted criminals are rarely asked to truly repay their debt to society. Even worse, this math-phobic system tragically discounts the debt owed to the victim, who is grossly shortchanged. 19

In Rhode Island, in 1983, Michael Woodmansee was sentenced to 40 years in prison for gruesomely murdering a 5-year-old boy, Jason Foreman. (Woodmansee allegedly ate the boy's flesh and shellacked his bones.) Rhode Island permits the early release of prison inmates for good behavior and for working prison jobs during their incarceration. In 2011, Woodmansee was scheduled to be released, having served only 28 years of his negotiated plea. From the moment of sentencing, with the trial aborted for a plea bargain, Woodmansee had already shortchanged the state of Rhode Island and the boy's father, John Foreman, of what was owed. Now it was measurably worse. On hearing that his son's murderer was soon to be a free man, Foreman said, "If this man is released anywhere in my vicinity, or if I can find him after the fact, I do intend to kill this man." 20

Many criticized Foreman: How could he so openly and unapologetically admit that he was planning to take justice into his own hands? (Woodmansee was voluntarily committed to a mental institution, and so his life was spared.) But who could blame Foreman for feeling that traditional justice had failed him, and that personal vengeance was now absolutely necessary? 21

Plea bargains, with their bargain-basement rationales, epitomize the degree to which our legal system has too little respect for victims and even less regard for the moral imperative that justice must be done. What is paramount under the talionic principle seems to be optional under our laws. A justice system that recognized the duty it owed to victims would not rely so heavily on this method of resolution, which casually distorts the truth and trivializes the remedy. 22

By definition, plea bargains are breaches of the social contract, because 23
they enable states to leave unfulfilled their obligation to punish on behalf
of their citizens. These are the very same citizens who, through the force of
law, have been deprived of their ancient right to personally enact revenge.
The justice system can't have it both ways: outlawing personal vengeance
while at the same time devaluing legal punishment. The public places its
faith in the state, but it is unworthy of that faith unless it can fully accept its
role as proxy—the revenge denied to victims must be undertaken by the
government, because states have assumed the task of punishment to be
theirs alone.

Part II

WRITING ABOUT SOURCES

Presenting Your Sources to Your Reader

In Chapter 1, you were the reader; now, you are the writer. How do you tell your reader about the sources that you have read? How do you present the ideas of each source fairly and accurately?

- Janet is a social worker presenting a complex case to a committee deciding whether a patient is ready to leave an institution. Janet will have to take the files and notes of many years and marshal the evidence into a comprehensive summary with enough detail to be convincing but not repetitive. Chapter 2 shows you how to present a source through summary: the technique of conveying information and ideas briefly, yet completely.

- Parker is a director of human resources at a department store presenting a report about an incident that occurred between a sales assistant and a customer that may result in the worker being fired. Parker will have to find out what was said, consulting witnesses, and then quote the exact words that were exchanged, making it clear who said what, in order to provide a fair and accurate basis for judgment. Chapter 3 describes the rules to follow when you apply quotation: recording the precise language used by a source as well as that person's name.

- Greg is a junior executive in a manufacturing firm that is considering buying out another company, and he has been asked to speak to a range of stockholders and assess their reactions. Greg will have to take his notes of each conversation and present each person's views in a way that conveys the individuality of those opinions. Chapter 4 gives you practice in paraphrase: the method of expressing the ideas of others accurately and succinctly in your own words.

In the academic world, summary, quotation, and paraphrase are the building blocks of writing from sources. They enable you to demonstrate your understanding of the source while integrating these ideas into your own work. They also help you avoid the dishonest "borrowings," called plagiarism, that occur when the reader cannot tell who wrote what and, therefore, gives you credit for work that you did not do. Whether you summarize, quote, or paraphrase, you must always *acknowledge*, or *document*, your source by including that person's name.

▪2▪
Summarizing Sources

When you annotate a text, when you ask yourself questions about its contents, you are helping yourself to understand what you are reading. When you write a summary, you are *recording* your understanding for your own information. When you include the summary in an essay of your own, you are *reporting* your understanding to your reader. In fact, you have already been using summary in your marginal notes when you express an author's idea in a phrase or sentence.

Summarizing a source usually means *condensing ideas or information.* You are not expected to include every repetition and detail. Rather, you extract only those points that seem important—the main ideas, which in the original text may have been interwoven with less important material. A summary of several pages can sometimes be as brief as one sentence.

When writing a brief summary, you should add nothing new to the material in the source, nor should you change the emphasis or provide any new interpretation or evaluation. For the sake of clarity and coherence, you may rearrange the order of the ideas; however, as summarizer, you should strive to remain in the background.

The writer of a research essay depends on summary as a means of referring to source materials. When you discuss another piece of writing, you generally have to summarize the contents briefly so that your reader understands the material that you intend to analyze. Summary also enables you to present and explain the ideas of several sources all dealing with the same subject.

> ### Reasons for Summarizing
>
> 1. To record your understanding of a text that you've read for your own notes
> 2. To report your own account of what you've read to your readers
> 3. To express that account clearly but succinctly, emphasizing the main ideas without introducing your own ideas
> 4. To present the ideas of a group of sources so that each receives fair representation and all have a place in the structure of your essay

Summarizing a Paragraph

Before you can begin to summarize a short text—a paragraph, for example— you must read the passage carefully and understand the significance of each idea and how it is linked to the other ideas. Sometimes, the paragraph will contain a series of examples that can be summarized inductively.

The following paragraph can be summarized adequately by one of its own sentences. Which one?

> It is often remarked that science has increasingly removed man from a position at the center of the universe. Once upon a time the earth was thought to be the center and the gods were thought to be in close touch with the daily actions of humans. It was not stupid to imagine the earth was at the center, because, one might think, if the earth were moving around the sun, and if you threw a ball vertically upward, it would seem the ball should come down a few feet away from you. Nevertheless, slowly, over many centuries, through the work of Copernicus, Galileo, and many others, we have mostly come to believe that we live on a typical planet orbiting a typical star in a typical galaxy, and indeed that no place in the universe is special.
>
> GORDON KANE, from "Are We the Center of the Universe?"

summarizing sentence?

summarizing sentence?

The first sentence is a broader generalization and a more comprehensive summary than the last sentence. Even when you find a strong sentence that suggests the main idea of the paragraph, you often need to tinker with that sentence, expanding its meaning by giving the language a more general focus. Here is a paragraph in which no one sentence is broad enough to sum up the main idea, but which contains a scattering of useful phrases:

> In a discussion [with] a class of teachers, I once said that I liked some of the kids in my class much more than others and that, without saying which ones I liked best, I had told them so. After all, this is something that children know,

whatever we tell them; it is futile to lie about it. Naturally, these teachers were horrified. "What a terrible thing to say!" one said. "I love all the children in my class exactly the same." Nonsense; a teacher who says this is lying, to herself or to others, and probably doesn't like any of the children very much. Not that there is anything wrong with that; plenty of adults don't like children, and there is no reason why they should. But the trouble is that they feel they should, which makes them feel guilty, which makes them feel resentful, which in turn makes them try to work off their guilt with indulgence and their resentment with subtle cruelties — cruelties of a kind that can be seen in many classrooms. Above all, it makes them put on the phony, syrupy, sickening voice and manner, and the fake smiles and forced, bright laughter that children see so much of in school, and rightly resent and hate.

JOHN HOLT, from How Children Fail

Here, you might begin by combining key phrases: "a teacher who says" that she "love[s] all the children" "is lying, to herself or to others," and makes herself and the children "feel resentful." However, this kind of summarizing sentence resembles a patchwork, with the words and phrasing pulled straight out of the original. Even if you acknowledged the borrowings, by using quotation marks, as above, you would still be left with a weak sentence that is neither yours nor the author's. It is far better to construct an entirely new sentence of your own, such as this one:

> In John Holt's view, although it is only natural for teachers to prefer some students to others, many teachers cannot accept their failure to like all equally well and express their inadequacy and dissatisfaction in ways that are harmful to the children.

Finally, some paragraphs give you no starting point at all for the summary and force you to write an entirely new generalization. How would you summarize this paragraph?

> When we pick up our newspaper at breakfast, we expect — we even demand — that it bring us momentous events since the night before. We turn on the car radio as we drive to work and expect "news" to have occurred since the morning newspaper went to press. Returning in the evening, we expect our house not only to shelter us, to keep us warm in winter and cool in summer, but to relax us, to dignify us, to encompass us with soft music and interesting hobbies, to be a playground, a theater, and a bar. We expect our two-week vacation to be romantic, exotic, cheap, and effortless. We expect a faraway atmosphere if we go to a nearby place; and we expect everything to be relaxing, sanitary, and Americanized if we go to a faraway place. We expect new heroes every season, a literary masterpiece every month, a dramatic spectacular every

week, a rare sensation every night. We expect everybody to feel free to disagree, yet we expect everybody to be loyal, not to rock the boat or to take the
Fifth Amendment. We expect everybody to believe deeply in his religion, yet
not to think less of others for not believing. We expect our nation to be strong
and great and vast and varied and prepared for every challenge; yet we expect
our "national purpose" to be clear and simple, something to give direction to
the lives of nearly two hundred million people and yet that can be bought
in a paperback at the corner drugstore for a dollar.

DANIEL BOORSTIN, from *The Americans: The National Experience*

What holds this paragraph together? Boorstin's set of examples begins by
taking us through the passage of time—a day, the seasons of the year (with
holidays)—and expands from events to entertainment to civil liberties. The
word *expect* ties them together. Are we expecting everyone to be exactly like
us? Do we exist simply to consume? Are we insisting on perfection? We expect
more than we can possibly get, Boorstin tells us, more through his barbed tone
than through any explicit statement. A summary will convey the futility of those
expectations:

Daniel Boorstin points out that Americans expect to have an entertaining,
safe, comfortable, and ethical life in a rich and complex country guided by
clear-sighted political leadership; but Boorstin's tone makes it clear that
such expectations are unrealistic and can never be fulfilled.

Notice that this summarizing sentence includes Boorstin's name—twice.
Mentioning the author's name emphasizes that what you are summarizing is
not your own work. By making it clear who is responsible for what, you are
avoiding any possibility of *plagiarizing*—borrowing from your source without
acknowledgment.

Summarizing a Brief Passage

1. Find a summarizing sentence within the passage (and, if you are
   using it in your own essay, put it in quotation marks); *or*
2. Combine elements within the passage into a new summarizing
   sentence; *or*
3. Write your own summarizing sentence.
4. Cite the author's name somewhere in the summary, and use quotation marks around any borrowed phrases.

EXERCISE 7: Summarizing a Paragraph

As your instructor indicates, summarize one or more of the following paragraphs by doing *one* of three things:

A. Underline a sentence that will serve as a comprehensive summary; *or*

B. Combine existing phrases; then rewrite the sentence, based on these phrases, to create a comprehensive summary; *or*

C. Invent a new generalization to provide a comprehensive summary.

Be prepared to explain your summary in class discussion.

1. Many parents hire nannies rather than sending their children to day care precisely because they want their children to develop personal, emotional relationships with the people who care for them. But can the emotional labor of care really be bought? The worker may carry out the physical work of care, entering into a sort of intimacy with the children, but her caring engenders no mutual obligations, no entry into a community, and no real human relationship — just money. A worker may care for a child over many years, spending many more hours with that child than the child's natural mother does, but should the employer decide to terminate the relationship, the worker will have no further right to see the child. As far as the employer is concerned, money expresses the full extent of her obligation to the worker. To the worker, this view is deeply problematic; indeed, it denies the worker's humanity and the very depth of her feelings. Juliette, a nanny from Côte d'Ivoire working in Parma, recalled, "I cared for a baby for his first year.… The child loves you as a mother, but the mother was jealous and I was sent away. I was so depressed then, seriously depressed. All I wanted was to go back and see him.… I will never care for a baby again. It hurts too much."

BRIDGET ANDERSON, from "Just Another Job?
The Commodification of Domestic Labor," *Global Woman*

2. With the rise of sites like Facebook, MySpace, LinkedIn, and others, features like discussion pages or walls and user profiles have become ubiquitous. But there's a good reason for this: In many cases, the simple ability to communicate and coordinate with others is enough to get people to act together for a common goal, whatever that goal might be. While social networking sites like Facebook mostly started out simply as places for people to write about their favorite books or movies, chat with their friends, or post photos of last night's party (the common goal, in other words, being to form social bonds and seem "cool" to one's classmates), in recent years these goals have gotten a bit more lofty, as social and political movements of all stripes — be it

for protests against the policies of the Burmese junta (which garnered more than three hundred thousand supporters on Facebook in a matter of two weeks) or grassroots environmental campaigns — have migrated there. The simple ability to communicate with like-minded others, form bonds over mutual interests, and form coordinated plans is enough to draw motivated people looking to participate in a cause, and get them to cooperate effectively.

YOCHAI BENKLER, from *The Penguin and The Leviathan*

3. The university is a place that is truly saturated with copies and copying. In large lecture courses, the students come to class dressed up in chaotic but well-defined subcultural fashions, which they can read almost instantaneously on each other (and on me). They move through a maze of corporate branding, which controls everything from drinking water to the bathroom walls. They are encouraged to learn through the act of repeating information, quoting, appending citations, in the traditional academic way; but with access to the Internet, to computers that can copy, replicate, and multiply text at extraordinary speed, they are also exhorted not to imitate too much, not to plagiarize, and to always acknowledge sources. They are ordered not to copy — but they are equally aware that they will be punished if they do not imitate the teacher enough!

MARCUS BOON, from *In Praise of Copying*

4. Most troubling for the future of saving are the credit habits of college students. A 2008 survey by Sallie Mae concluded that many students "use credit cards to live beyond their means." Eighty-four percent of undergraduates had credit cards — half of them possessing *four or more*. One-fifth of them carried balances of $3,000 to $7,000. Only 17 percent paid their bill in full each month. Over the past two decades the industry has bombarded undergraduates with solicitations, assisted by colleges that permitted on-campus vendors often in exchange for kickbacks.[84] Students were an easy mark. Prior to 2010, they could sign up for credit cards without parental permission upon turning eighteen. Where once American schools ran savings programs to encourage thrift, credit card companies now cultivate an entire generation addicted to consumer debt.

SHELDON M. GARON, from *Beyond Our Means:
Why America Spends While the World Saves*

84. Sallie Mae, *How Undergraduate Students Use Credit Cards*, 2009, http://www.salliemae.com/NR/rdonlyres/0BD600F1-9377-46EA-AB1F-6061FC763246/10744/SLMCreditCardUsageStudy41309FINAL2.pdf, accessed May 17, 2010.

5. Research portrays Americans as increasingly insecure, isolated, and lonely.[5] We work more hours than ever before, often at several jobs. Even high school and college students, during seasons of life when time should be most abundant, say that they don't date but "hook up" because "who has the time?" We have moved away, often far away, from the communities of our birth. We struggle to raise children without the support of extended families. Many have left behind the religious and civic associations that once bound us together.[6] To those who have lost a sense of physical connection, connectivity suggests that you make your own page, your own place. When you are there, you are by definition where you belong, among officially friended friends. To those who feel they have no time, connectivity, like robotics, tempts by proposing substitutions through which you can have companionship with convenience. A robot will always be there, amusing and compliant. On the Net, you can always find someone. "I never want to be far from my BlackBerry," a colleague told me. "That is where my games are. That is where my sites are. Without it, I'm too anxious."

SHERRY TURKLE, from *Alone Together: Why We Expect More from Technology and Less from Each Other*

5. Hugh Gusterson and Catherine Besteman, eds., *The Insecure American: How We Got Here and What We Should Do About It* (Los Angeles: University of California Press, 2009).

6. See, for example, Robert D. Putnam, *Bowling Alone: The Collapse and Revival of American Community* (New York: Simon and Schuster, 2001); Gusterson and Besteman, eds., *The Insecure American*; Theda Skocpol, *Diminished Democracy: From Membership to Management in American Civic Life* (Norman: University of Oklahoma Press, 2003).

6. Are we saving enough? The standard economic view is that at any given time a person has well-defined preferences that stipulate whether he or she will choose to save some portion of a monthly paycheck or spend it all. In other words, people know exactly what they want and what they do not want. In that sense, the savings of any given household is a direct outcome of its members' personal preferences. Economists see these preferences as the sacrosanct realm of the individual. If someone is in debt up to the eyeballs, it is because that person prefers to discount future consumption very heavily relative to current consumption. One may believe that, for whatever reason, it is much better to buy the new car and new clothes now than to worry about the future, if it ever shows up. Many economists believe, then, that savings is a matter of individual choice, and questions about "too much" or "too little" have a moral punch that is not relevant to the decision making

of rational people. Who are we to question what this or that person wants out of life?

RONALD T. WILCOX, from *Whatever Happened to Thrift?*
Why Americans Don't Save and What to Do About It

Summarizing a Text or an Article

When you want to summarize an excerpt from a book or a short article in a few sentences, how do you judge which points are important and which are not? Some texts, especially newspaper and periodical articles, have rambling structures; you may not even have fully developed paragraphs in which to identify topic sentences. Are there any standard procedures to help you decide which points to include in your summary?

Summarizing an Article

1. Read the entire article more than once and note key points.
2. Ask yourself why the article was written and published.
3. Look for repetitions of and variations on the same idea.

Read the excerpt from *How Children Succeed: Grit, Curiosity, and the Hidden Power of Character* by Paul Tough, an author who has written extensively about education. Some of the main points are indicated in the margins. Would you add any? How would you turn these notes into a summary?

Background: This text quotes Jeff Nelson, who cofounded OneGoal, a training organization that encourages underachieving high school students to aspire to earn a college degree. There is also a reference to the "marshmallow experiment," in which small children could opt to receive one treat (a marshmallow) if they wanted it immediately, or two treats (two marshmallows) if they were willing to wait for their reward. The second group was shown to benefit in later life from their ability to defer gratification.

from HOW CHILDREN SUCCEED
Paul Tough

Recently, two labor economists at the University of California, Philip   1
Babcock and Mindy Marks, analyzed surveys of time use by college students

from the 1920s through the present. They found that in 1961, the average full-time college student spent twenty-four hours a week studying outside of the classroom. By 1981, that had fallen to twenty hours a week, and in 2003, it was down to fourteen hours a week, not much more than half of what it had been forty years earlier. This phenomenon transcended boundaries: "Study time fell for students from all demographic subgroups," Babcock and Marks wrote, "for students who worked and those who did not, within every major, and at four-year colleges of every type, degree structure, and level of selectivity." And where did all those extra hours go? To socializing and recreation, mostly. A separate study of 6,300 undergraduates at the University of California found that students today spend fewer than thirteen hours a week studying, while they spend twelve hours hanging out with friends, fourteen hours consuming entertainment and pursuing various hobbies, eleven hours using "computers for fun," and six hours exercising.

over 42 years, work time almost halved

affects all students

free time spent having a good time

To many observers, these statistics are cause for alarm. But Jeff Nelson sees this situation as an opportunity for his students. He recalled for me his own freshman year at the University of Michigan, when he did what a lot of other upper-middle-class kids do at the beginning of their college careers: he didn't work very hard. For some affluent students, freshman year is about drinking heavily; for others, it's about pledging a fraternity or trying to write for the student newspaper. That time is certainly not always wasted, but it generally doesn't contribute much to a student's academic outcomes. And so Nelson sees freshman year as a "magical timeframe" for OneGoal students "where they can radically close the achievement gap." As Nelson explained his theory in one of our early conversations, "Freshman year is this unique moment in time. Kids who have not had to persevere as much walk into college and they coast, for the most part. Or they're partying too hard. And in that moment, if our kids are working diligently and building relationships with professors and studying and using all of the skills that we've trained them to use, they can close the gap. We've seen it time and time again, that all of a sudden a kid who might have been three or four grade levels behind in high school has caught up in a really significant way to his peers by the beginning of sophomore year."

2

"But" = turn warning or opportunity?

wasted time has no academic purpose

Nelson: freshman year is easy for some, not so easy for students unprepared for academic work

catch up by concentrating on developing academic skills

Her first fall at Western Illinois, Kewauna took introductory courses — English 100, Math 100, Sociology 100. None of them was easy for her, but the course she found most challenging was Biology 170, Introduction to Health Careers. The professor was a popular lecturer, so the class was pretty full, and most of the students were upperclassmen. On the first day of class, Kewauna did what Michele Stefl had recommended: she politely introduced herself to the professor before class, and then she sat in the front row, which until Kewauna sat down was occupied entirely by white girls. The other

3

Kewauna = extended example

dealt with difficult course content by putting herself forward

African American students all tended to sit at the back, which disappointed Kewauna. ("That's what they *expect* you to do," she said when we talked by phone that fall. "Back in the civil rights movement, if they told you you had to sit in the back, you wouldn't do it.")

asked for help from the faculty

Her biology professor used a lot of scientific terms in his lectures that Kewauna wasn't familiar with. So she came up with a strategy: every time he used a word she didn't understand, she wrote it down and put a red star next to it. At the end of the class, she waited until all the other students who wanted to talk to the professor had taken their turns, and then she went through each red-starred word with him, one by one, asking him to explain them.

4

asked for help from fellow students and tutor

Kewauna spent a lot of time interacting with all her professors, in fact. She was a regular at office hours, and she e-mailed them whenever she wasn't clear on assignments. She also tried to make one or two acquaintances among the students in each of her classes, so that if she needed help with homework and couldn't reach the professor, she'd have someone to ask. Through her freshman-support program, she found a writing tutor — she had always had "grammar issues," she told me, as well as trouble with spelling and punctuation — and she made a practice of going over with her tutor every paper she wrote before handing it in. Finally, in December, she felt she had internalized enough about comma splices and dependent clauses, and she handed in her final English paper without going over it

5

was successful

challenging environment

little money

with the writing tutor. She got an A.

Still, it was a difficult semester for Kewauna, She was always short of money and had to economize everywhere she could. At one point, she ran out of money on her meal card and just didn't eat for two days. She was studying all the time, it felt like. Every paper was a challenge, and at the end of the semester, she stayed up practically all night, three nights in a row, studying for finals. But her hard work was reflected in her final grades that semester: two B pluses, one A, and, in biology, an A plus. When I spoke to her a few days before Christmas, she sounded a bit depleted, but proud too. "No matter how overwhelming it is, no matter how exhausting it is, I'm not going to give up," she said. "I'm never the type to give up. Even when I played hide-and-go-seek when I was little, I would be outside till eight o'clock, until I found everyone. I don't give up on nothing, no matter how hard."

6

little free time

perseverance

Kewauna's grades actually improved in her second semester, and at the end of her freshman year, her cumulative GPA stood at 3.8. There were still three years to go, lots of time for things to go wrong, for

7

setbacks and mistakes and crises. But Kewauna seemed certain of where she was heading and why — almost unnervingly so. What was most remarkable to me about Kewauna was that she was able to marshal her prodigious noncognitive capacity — call it grit, conscientiousness, resilience, or the ability to delay gratification — all for a distant prize that was, for her, almost entirely theoretical. She didn't actually *know* any business ladies with briefcases downtown; she didn't even know any college graduates except her teachers. It was as if Kewauna were taking part in an extended, high-stakes version of Walter Mischel's marshmallow experiment, except in this case, the choice on offer was that she could have one marshmallow now or she could work really hard for four years, constantly scrimping and saving, staying up all night, struggling, sacrificing — and then get, not two marshmallows, but some kind of elegant French pastry she'd only vaguely heard of, like a Napoleon. And Kewauna, miraculously, opted for the Napoleon, even though she'd never tasted one before and didn't know anyone who had. She just had faith that it was going to be delicious.

ability to focus on goal

K's strengths are not intellectual

goal = remote outside K's experience

ability to sacrifice to achieve reward

Not all of Kewauna's fellow OneGoal students are going to take to the deal with the same conviction. And it won't be clear for another couple of years whether the leadership skills Kewauna and her classmates were taught are powerful enough to get them through four years of college. But so far, OneGoal's overall persistence numbers are quite good. Of the 129 students, including Kewauna, who started OneGoal as juniors at ten Chicago high schools in the fall of 2009, ninety-four were enrolled in four-year colleges as of May 2012. Another fourteen were enrolled in two-year colleges, for an overall college-persistence total of 84 percent. Which left only twenty-one students who had veered off the track to a college degree: twelve who left OneGoal before the end of high school, two who joined the military after high school, two who graduated from high school but didn't enroll in college, and five who enrolled in college but dropped out in their freshman year. The numbers are less stellar but still impressive for the pilot-program cohort, students for whom OneGoal was a weekly afterschool class. Three years out of high school, 66 percent of the students who enrolled in the program as high-school juniors are still enrolled in college. Those numbers grow more significant when you recall that OneGoal teachers are deliberately selecting struggling students who seem especially unlikely to go to college.

8

the "deal" won't work for everyone

84% success rate measured by staying in college

students selected are below average academically

Jeff Nelson would be the first to admit that what he has created is far from a perfect solution for the widespread dysfunction of the country's

9
need for educated labor force

ideal = raise academic level of pre-college students so OneGoal won't be needed

human-capital pipeline. Ideally, we should have in place an education and social-support system that produces teenagers from the South Side who *aren't* regularly two or three or four years behind grade level. For now, though, OneGoal and the theories that underlie it seem like a most valuable intervention, a program that, for about fourteen hundred dollars a year per student, regularly turns underperforming, undermotivated, low-income teenagers into successful college students.

1. Read the entire article more than once and note key points.

One of the first things you'll notice is that the passage is built on a contrast between well-prepared freshmen who can afford to waste their time and poorly prepared freshmen who will flounder and fail unless they're willing to work to their utmost capacity. That contrast is illustrated by setting off Kewauna's story against the background of her more carefree classmates. But there's also a second, implicit contrast between Kewauna and her peers—other underachieving students, including those in the OneGoal program—who may not "take to the deal with the same conviction" as Kewauna has and who may therefore be less successful. What is "the deal"? Students receive the know-how to compete for good grades in return for pledging to invest all their free time and energy in implementing that know-how.

2. Ask yourself why this passage was included in Paul Tough's book.

What point did the author want to make? One easy—but wrong—answer is that Tough wants to present Kewauna's dramatic situation. You should try not to confuse the facts of her story with the underlying reasons for telling that story. Here is a one-sentence summary that concentrates too heavily on Kewauna:

> Despite poor preparation for college, Kewauna, with the help of the OneGoal program, was successful in her freshman year.

This summary is certainly true, but is it enough? The writer is ignoring all the information that Tough provides about how and why Kewauna manages to succeed under extremely difficult circumstances. The summary is all fact, no interpretation.

Here's another summary that focuses on Tough's original point of contrast:

> Studies have shown that many students waste their time in college, but Kewauna's experience demonstrates that hard work will get results.

Again, the summary is off the mark because it doesn't ask why Tough is making this contrast. In fact, it may be a mistake to devote half the summary to the time-wasting habits of the average freshman since only the first 20% of this excerpt is concerned with their experience. Not only is Tough much less interested in those average freshmen, but the excerpt in its entirety suggests that comparing the two groups—the time-wasters and the Kewaunas—is like comparing apples and oranges since their goals, their skills, and their ability to harness their skills to achieve their goals are so very different.

3. Look for repetitions of and variations on the same theme.

Many of the marginal comments refer to the ways in which the Kewaunas on any campus can benefit from "the deal" and catch up with their classmates by developing academic skills. Tough singles out Kewauna's perseverance and her ability to focus on goals and engage in behaviors that are alien to her past experience. What's notable here is that these strengths are not intellectual, but psychological. Self-belief drives Kewauna's transformation.

This interpretation—which you may notice comes entirely from the marginal notes—can form the basis of a satisfactory summary:

> Students who are underprepared for college work can succeed provided that they have the self-belief and perseverance that will help them adjust to a new intellectual and social environment.

Note the importance of "provided that": Tough briefly acknowledges that the deal won't work for everyone, which is an important enough point to include in the summary, if you can tuck it in.

There is one more point that may be worth including: toward the end, Tough alludes to a larger context for Kewauna's story. He is concerned about the "widespread dysfunction of the country's human-capital pipeline." In other words, there is a political interest in enabling America's Kewaunas to succeed and thus ensuring a highly skilled pool of labor for the economy. That point can be included in a longer, slightly different summary:

> To ensure that the United States has a well-educated labor force and that poorly prepared students have the opportunity to earn college degrees, support programs like OneGoal must be more widely established to help such students harness the force of their character and their self-belief and be motivated to succeed.

EXERCISE 8: Summarizing an Article

A. Carefully read "Is a Picture Worth a Thousand Notes?" by Jessica Higgins, twice.

B. Determine the article's purpose and make marginal notes of the points that the author emphasizes.

C. Then write a comprehensive summary in two or three sentences.

IS A PICTURE WORTH A THOUSAND NOTES?

Jessica Higgins

Jessica Higgins teaches English composition and literature at Broward College and has published short stories in Bartleby Snopes, *an online literary magazine. This article first appeared in the* Chronicle of Higher Education.

Background: Most newspapers and many popular periodicals present their articles in very short paragraphs, often no more than one or two sentences each. As that practice differs from the characteristic structure of academic writing, and as the brevity of the paragraphs can make it difficult to follow the way ideas are linked, the number of paragraphs in this article — and comparable articles throughout the book — has been reduced with no alteration to the text.

In a class this past December, after I wrote some directions on the board for students about their final examination, one young woman quickly snapped a picture of the board using her smartphone. It wasn't the first time a student had taken a picture instead of taking notes, nor was she the only student in that class who was using this photographic note-taking method. But perhaps because she was sitting in the front row, or perhaps because her phone flashed, she drew my attention. 1

When I looked in her direction, she sheepishly apologized: "Sorry. Was it wrong to take a picture?" I assured her that she needn't apologize and that I didn't see it as wrong. But I did ask why she had taken a picture instead of writing down notes. "I'm just curious," I explained. 2

For several years now I've observed this new trend in note taking, and in recent months I've noticed an increase in its frequency. Some students try covertly to take pictures of the board or, curiously, the PowerPoint presentations. I say "curiously" because I post my PowerPoint presentations online. 3

The students sit, scrunched in their desks, and attempt, silently and stealthily, to snap pictures throughout the class — as if their phones came with an invisibility-granting cloaking device. Others are bolder and, like the young woman described above, sit in the front and snap away with flashes 4 on. "I can't read my own handwriting," the young woman explained. "It's best if I take a picture of your writing so I can understand the notes."

That remark sparked a classwide conversation about taking a picture versus taking notes. For those in the photo-snapping camp, motives extended beyond their inability to comprehend their own penmanship. Some took pictures of notes because they knew their phone was a safe place to store material. They might lose paper, they reasoned, but they wouldn't lose their phone. Some took photos because they wanted to capture exactly the manner in which I had noted information on the board. Others told me that during class they liked to be able to listen to the discussion without the distraction of writing notes.

Students have been using laptops and tablets in the classroom for years to circumvent some of the tedium of taking notes by hand. Students have also brought small voice recorders to class in order to record the lecture. The logic of convenience that students use to defend those devices has been transferred to the smartphone: With a portable computer in their pocket, why wouldn't they make good use of its applications?

Yet the use of cameras as note takers, expedient as it may be, does raise significant questions for the classroom. What of the privacy of other students? Does clandestine photographic note taking violate intellectual-property laws? What of institutional and professorial policies on cellphone use? Those matters are important, but a different question has piqued my interest: Is a picture an effective replacement for the process of note taking?

Instructors encourage students to take notes because the act of doing so is more than merely recording necessary information — it helps pave the way for understanding. Encouraging students to take notes may be an old-fashioned instructional method, but just because a method has a long history doesn't mean it's obsolete. Writing things down engages a student's brain in auditory, visual, and kinesthetic learning — a view supported by longstanding research. The act of writing down information enables a person to begin committing it to memory, and to process and synthesize it, establishing the building blocks of learning new concepts.

Taking a picture does indeed record the information, but it omits some of the necessary mental engagement that taking notes employs. So can the two be equally effective? The answer to that question is difficult to gauge, and short of hooking up students to electrodes and monitoring their brain waves as they take pictures or write notes, I'm not sure how to measure the neurological efficacy of either method. For now, I allow students to take notes however they see fit — handwritten, typed, voice-recorded, or photographed — because I figure that some notes, no matter the method of documentation, are better than none.

Summarizing a Complex Essay

Sometimes, you need to summarize a reading containing a number of complex and abstract ideas, a reading that may be disorganized and therefore difficult to understand and condense. The best way to prepare for such a summary is to *make marginal notes* and then *write a list* with each key point expressed in a sentence.

Here is an essay by Bertrand Russell, a distinguished British mathematician and philosopher of the early twentieth century. The essay is annotated with marginal notes and followed by a preliminary list of key ideas, a statement of Russell's thesis, and the final summary.

Russell's essay is difficult, so be sure to read it slowly, and more than once. If you get confused at any point, try referring to the list of notes that follows (see p. 93); but be sure to *go back to the essay* after you have identified and understood each numbered point.

First Stage: Marginal Notes

THE SOCIAL RESPONSIBILITY OF SCIENTISTS
Bertrand Russell

Bertrand Russell was a British philosopher, logician, and social critic whose interests ranged from mathematics to education. Winner of the Nobel Prize for literature in 1950, Russell was regarded as a controversial figure, in part because of his activities as an anti-war protester.

responsibility
for how
discoveries
are used?

some scientists:
no

scientists as
public-spirited
citizens

some scientists
work in the
public interest;
others work
for the
government

Science, ever since it first existed, has had important effects in matters that lie outside the purview of pure science. Men of science have differed as to their responsibility for such effects. Some have said that the function of the scientist in society is to supply knowledge, and that he need not concern himself with the use to which this knowledge is put. I do not think that this view is tenable, especially in our age. The scientist is also a citizen; and citizens who have any special skill have a public duty to see, as far as they can, that their skill is utilized in accordance with the public interest. Historically, the functions of the scientist in public life have generally been recognized. The Royal Society was founded by Charles II as an antidote to "fanaticism" which had plunged England into a long period of civil strife. The scientists of that time did not hesitate to speak out on public issues, such as religious toleration and the folly of prosecutions for witchcraft. But although science has, in various ways at various times, favored what may be called a humanitarian outlook, it has from the first had an intimate and sinister connection with war. Archimedes sold his skill to the Tyrant of Syracuse for use against the Romans; Leonardo secured a salary from

1
2

3

4

the Duke of Milan for his skill in the art of fortification; and Galileo got employment under the Grand Duke of Tuscany because he could calculate the trajectories of projectiles. In the French Revolution the scientists who were not guillotined were set to making new explosives, but Lavoisier was not spared, because he was only discovering hydrogen which, in those days, was not a weapon of war. There have been some honorable exceptions to the subservience of scientists to warmongers. During the Crimean War the British government consulted Faraday as to the feasibility of attack by poisonous gases. Faraday replied that it was entirely feasible, but that it was inhuman and he would have nothing to do with it.

influence of the media

Modern democracy and modern methods of publicity have made the problem of affecting public opinion quite different from what it used to be. The knowledge that the public possesses on any important issue is derived from vast and powerful organizations: the press, radio, and, above all, television. The 5

governments lack information

knowledge that governments possess is more limited. They are too busy to search out the facts for themselves, and consequently they know only what their underlings think good for them unless there is such a powerful movement in a different sense that politicians cannot ignore it. Facts which ought 6 to guide the decisions of statesmen—for instance, as to the possible lethal qualities of fallout—do not acquire their due importance if they remain buried in scientific journals. They acquire their due importance only when they become known to so many voters that they affect the course of the elections. In general, there is an opposition to widespread publicity for such facts. This

special interests suppress information

opposition springs from various sources, some sinister, some comparatively 7 respectable. At the bottom of the moral scale there is the financial interest of the various industries connected with armaments. Then there are various effects of a somewhat thoughtless patriotism, which believes in secrecy and in

public is squeamish

what is called "toughness." But perhaps more important than either of these is the unpleasantness of the facts, which makes the general public turn aside to 8 pleasanter topics such as divorces and murders. The consequence is that what ought to be known widely throughout the general public will not be known unless great efforts are made by disinterested persons to see that the information reaches the minds and hearts of vast numbers of people. I do not think this work can be successfully accomplished except by the help of men of sci-

scientists have a public duty to speak

ence. They, alone, can speak with the authority that is necessary to combat the misleading statements of those scientists who have permitted themselves to 9 become merchants of death. If disinterested scientists do not speak out, the others will succeed in conveying a distorted impression, not only to the public but also to the politicians.

It must be admitted that there are obstacles to individual action in our age which did not exist at earlier times. Galileo could make his own telescope.

scientific research depends on funding

But once when I was talking with a very famous astronomer he explained   10
that the telescope upon which his work depended owed its existence to
the benefaction of enormously rich men, and, if he had not stood well with
them, his astronomical discoveries would have been impossible. More frequently, a scientist only acquires access to enormously expensive equipment
if he stands well with the government of his country. He knows that if he
adopts a rebellious attitude he and his family are likely to perish along with
the rest of civilized mankind. It is a tragic dilemma, and I do not think that
one should censure a man whatever his decision; but I do think—and I
think men of science should realize—that unless something rather drastic is
done under the leadership or through the inspiration of some part of the scientific world, the human race, like the Gadarene swine, will rush down a steep
place to destruction in blind ignorance of the fate that scientific skill has prepared for it.

It is impossible in the modern world for a man of science to say with any
honesty, "My business is to provide knowledge, and what use is made of the
knowledge is not my responsibility." The knowledge that a man of science provides may fall into the hands of men or institutions devoted to utterly unworthy
objects. I do not suggest that a man of science, or even a large body of men of
science, can altogether prevent this, but they can diminish the magnitude of
the evil.

support more benign research

There is another direction in which men of science can attempt to pro-   11
vide leadership. They can suggest and urge in many ways the value of those
branches of science of which the important and practical uses are beneficial
and not harmful. Consider what might be done if the money at present spent
on armaments were spent on increasing and distributing the food supply of
the world and diminishing the population pressure. In a few decades, poverty
and malnutrition, which now afflict more than half the population of the globe,
could be ended. But at present almost all the governments of great states consider that it is better to spend money on killing foreigners than on keeping their
own subjects alive. Possibilities of a hopeful sort in whatever field can best be
worked out and stated authoritatively by men of science; and, since they can do
this work better than others, it is part of their duty to do it.

As the world becomes more technically unified, life in an ivory tower becomes increasingly impossible. Not only so; the man who stands out against
the powerful organizations which control most of human activity is apt to find
himself no longer in the ivory tower, with a wide outlook over a sunny landscape, but in the dark and subterranean dungeon upon which the ivory tower
was erected. To risk such a habitation demands courage. It will not be necessary
to inhabit the dungeon if there are many who are willing to risk it, for everybody knows that the modern world depends upon scientists, and, if they are

speaking out
together lessens
the risk

insistent, they must be listened to. We have it in our power to make a good   12
world; and, therefore, with whatever labor and risk, we must make it.

Second Stage: List of Notes

1. Should scientists try to influence the way their discoveries are used?

2. One point of view: the scientist's role is to make the discovery; what happens afterward is not his concern.

3. Russell's point of view: scientists are like any other knowledgeable and public-spirited people; they must make sure that the products of their knowledge work for, not against, society.

4. In the past, some scientists have made public their views on controversial issues like freedom of religion; others have been servants of the war machine.

5. The power to inform and influence the public is now controlled by the news media.

6. Government officials are too busy to be well informed; subordinates feed them only enough information to get them re-elected.

7. It is in the interests of various groups, ranging from weapons makers to patriots, to limit the amount of scientific information that the public receives.

8. The public is reluctant to listen to distasteful news.

9. Since the public deserves to hear the truth, scientists, who are respected for their knowledge and who belong to no party or faction, ought to do more to provide the public with information about the potentially lethal consequences of their discoveries. By doing so, they will correct the distortions of those scientists who have allied themselves with warmongers.

10. It is very difficult for scientists to speak out since they depend on government and business interests to finance their work.

11. While scientists cannot entirely stop others from using some of their discoveries for antisocial purposes, they can support other, more constructive kinds of research.

12. Speaking out is worth the risk of incurring the displeasure of powerful people; since the work of scientists is so vital, the risk isn't too great, especially if they act together.

Third Stage: Establish a Thesis

Russell's thesis: Contrary to the self-interested arguments of many scientists and other groups, scientists have a social responsibility to make sure that their work is used for, not against, the benefit of humanity.

Fourth Stage: Summary

two views of the scientists' responsibility = framework

obstacles to scientific freedom of speech

the need to act despite obstacles = thesis

(1) Some scientists, as well as other groups, consider that they need not influence the way in which their discoveries are used. (2) However, Bertrand Russell, in "The Social Responsibility of Scientists," believes that scientists have a responsibility to make sure that their work is used for, not against, the benefit of humanity. (3) In modern times, he argues, it has been especially difficult for concerned scientists to speak out (a) because many powerful groups prefer to limit and distort what the public is told, (b) because government officials are too busy to be thoroughly informed, (c) because scientists depend on the financial support of business and government, and (d) because the public itself is reluctant to hear distasteful news. (4) Nevertheless, Russell maintains that scientists have the knowledge and the prestige to command public attention, and their work is too vital for their voices to be suppressed. (5) If they act together, they can warn us if their work is likely to be used for an antisocial purpose and, at least, they can propose less destructive alternatives.

This summary of Russell's essay is not a simple compilation of phrases taken from the text, nor a collection of topic sentences, one from each paragraph. Rather, it is a clear, coherent, and unified summary of Russell's ideas, expressed in the student's own voice and words.

A *framework* is immediately established in the first two sentences of the summary, which contrast the two alternative views of the scientist's responsibility. The third sentence, which describes the four obstacles to scientific freedom of speech, illustrates the *rearrangement of ideas* that is characteristic of summary. While reviewing the list of notes, the summarizer has noticed that points 6, 7, 8, and 10 each refer to a reason why scientific truth may be suppressed; she has therefore brought them together and lined them up in a parallel construction based on the repeated word *because*. Finally, the last two sentences contain a *restatement of Russell's thesis* and point out that the obstacles to action are not as formidable as they seem.

Notice that the Russell summary excludes points 1, 4, and 5 on the list of notes: point 1 is included in the presentation of points 2 and 3; point 4 is an example, one that is not essential to an understanding of the essay; and point 5 is not directly related to Russell's argument. In summarizing Russell's essay, you should not include side issues, such as the dangers of making scientific secrets public, for that would be arguing with Russell. Such ideas should be reserved for a full-length essay in which you develop an argument of your own.

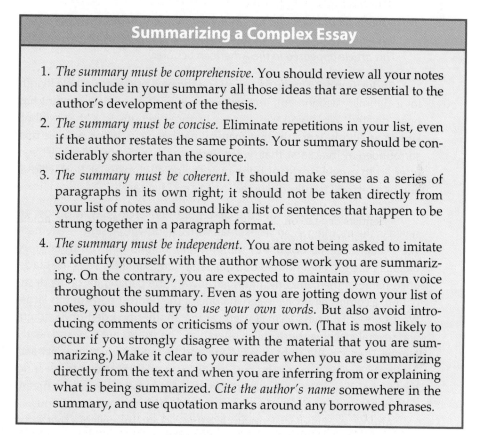

Summarizing a Complex Essay

1. *The summary must be comprehensive.* You should review all your notes and include in your summary all those ideas that are essential to the author's development of the thesis.

2. *The summary must be concise.* Eliminate repetitions in your list, even if the author restates the same points. Your summary should be considerably shorter than the source.

3. *The summary must be coherent.* It should make sense as a series of paragraphs in its own right; it should not be taken directly from your list of notes and sound like a list of sentences that happen to be strung together in a paragraph format.

4. *The summary must be independent.* You are not being asked to imitate or identify yourself with the author whose work you are summarizing. On the contrary, you are expected to maintain your own voice throughout the summary. Even as you are jotting down your list of notes, you should try to *use your own words.* But also avoid introducing comments or criticisms of your own. (That is most likely to occur if you strongly disagree with the material that you are summarizing.) Make it clear to your reader when you are summarizing directly from the text and when you are inferring from or explaining what is being summarized. *Cite the author's name* somewhere in the summary, and use quotation marks around any borrowed phrases.

ASSIGNMENT 1: Summarizing an Essay

Summarize one of the following two essays. Before you begin your summary (on your second reading):

A. Underline and annotate (in the margins) key ideas and arguments.

B. Make a preliminary list of points to potentially include in your summary.

C. Identify the thesis.

D. Rearrange your list of points into coherent paragraphs; the ideas should be linked as one sentence leads to the next.

Use your own words as much as possible.

MAKING SPARKS FLY: HOW OCCUPATIONAL EDUCATION CAN LEAD TO A LOVE OF LEARNING FOR ITS OWN SAKE

Mike Rose

A professor at UCLA and the author/editor of ten books, Mike Rose has won numerous awards for his research in public education. This article appeared in the American Scholar.

Background: To make this essay and the next one a reasonable length for a summary assignment, approximately 20% of its original content has been deleted. When you see a series of three periods (…), that symbol, known as ellipsis, indicates that material has been cut. When you see text surrounded by [brackets], that symbol indicates that a few words have been inserted to provide a clear bridge over the deleted material. Both ellipsis and brackets will be fully discussed in the next chapter.

As I exit the freeway into the center of the overcast city, it is close to seven in the morning. A homeless man with a handwritten sign — "Vietnam vet" — stands at the bottom of the off-ramp. Behind him is a three-story building, the top floor burned out; big, fat-lettered graffiti covers the blackened name of the company. I turn left toward the parking lot of my destination, a community college serving one of the poorest parts of this large, West Coast city. I pass a small used-car lot, another boarded-up building, and several machine shops still in operation. The streets are gray and nearly empty. Then, on the right, the college and heightened activity. Cars and buses are pulling over to the curb to drop people off; students, wearing backpacks, weave their bicycles in and out of traffic; the light turns green, and a crowd that just got off a commuter train streams onto the campus.

After years of neglect, students like these — and the colleges that serve them — are the focus of national attention. Though many states are slashing education budgets, federal and private philanthropic initiatives are helping people who are economically, and often educationally, disadvantaged pursue further education and job training. I play a tiny role in this effort as part of a research team that is trying to get a better handle on what enables or impedes educational success for this group. What makes it possible for these students to walk onto this campus an hour after sunrise, heading toward a nursing, or electrical construction, or English class? What jobs — if they have them — are flexible enough to allow time for school? Or are these people going from here to work or coming in after the night shift? What child-care arrangements do they have? How about transportation? Though many of the college's students are local, a number come from fairly far away by bus or train to attend its well-respected occupational programs. One young woman I interviewed gets up at 3:30 in the morning to begin the trek to her 7:00 a.m. class. Hardships of that order are obviously threats to achievement. But I'm just as interested — more so, really — in what it is that pulls these students forward, the desire that gets them through the door. I understand it just a little better every time I visit a place like this.

Come along with me for the first day of one of the college's programs for people who have low academic skills (many of them didn't finish high school) but who want to prepare for a skilled trade. Because of confidentiality agreements I've signed in order to do my research, I'm deliberately keeping the college anonymous, and I've changed students' names. Otherwise, I'm giving you the day-to-day events as I saw them.

The director of the program is standing at a lectern at the front of a large classroom; before her are 25 or so students sitting quietly in plastic chairs at eight long tables. The director has a serious demeanor, but her voice is inviting. Behind her hang an expansive white board and a screen for PowerPoint or video. I lean back and look around the windowless room: the walls are bare, institutional cream, clean and spare. The students are black and Latino, a few more women than men. Most appear to be in their early 20s to early 30s, with one man, who looks like he's had a hard time of it, in his mid-40s. "Welcome to college," the director says. "I congratulate you." She then asks each of them to talk a little about what motivates them and why they're here.

The economic motive looms large. One guy laughs. "I don't want to work a crappy job all my life," he says. A woman in the back says she wants to get her high school diploma "to get some money to take care of myself." But people give a lot of other reasons for being here, too: to "learn more," to be a "role model for my kids," to get "a career to support my daughter," to "have a better life." The director turns to the older man. "I'm illiterate," he says in a halting voice, "and I want to learn to read and write."

The semester before, when students wrote out their reasons for attending the program, their range of responses was even wider. Again, the economic motive was central, but there were also these comments, some written in neat cursive, some in scratchy uneven print: "learning new things I never thought about before"; "I want my kids too know that I can write and read"; "Hope Fully with this program I could turn my life around"; "to develope better social skills and better speech"; "I want to be somebody in this world"; "I like to do test and essay like it is part of my life."

Combined, these testimonies offer a rich vision of the goals of education. What is curious, though, is that nearly every speech and policy document and op-ed piece on educational initiatives aimed at poor people is focused wholly on schooling's economic benefits. Speaking in September 2009 at a community college in Troy, New York, President Obama said "the power of these institutions [is] to prepare students for 21st century jobs." Given the complex nature of the economy in our time — not only the recession but the changing nature and distribution of work — one hopes the president's statement is accurate. The people in this program would certainly want it to be true. But they are also here for so much more. They want to do something good for themselves and their families. They want to be better able to help their kids with school. They want to have another go at education and change what it means to them. They want to learn new things and to gain a sense — and the certification — of competence. They want to redefine who they are. A lot is riding on this attempt to reenter school; no wonder, as I sit in this classroom, the hope and desire are almost palpable.

At the table right in front of me, a slight young woman with *Love* woven on the back of her black sweatshirt is leaning in toward the director as she talks. Whenever the director gives out a piece of information — about textbooks, about the tutoring center — she takes notes. I know from talking to so many other students over the years the sense of excitement they feel at a time like this, a sense of life opening up, but also the foreignness of it all, the uncertainty.

8

The director announces that it's time for a quick tour of the campus, and off we go to the bookstore, the administration building, the office for students with disabilities. The students walk in groups of two or three, talking, looking at this new campus landscape. A few walk alone. The young woman in the black sweatshirt stays close to the director. Toward the end of the tour, we pause before the child-care center. The director asks, "Who has kids?" A number of people say they do, raising their hands. The young woman slips her pen into the pocket of her Love sweatshirt and brings her hand slowly to her shoulder.

9

What my team is finding so far about the possible barriers to success for students like her supports the research that's already been done. Students tend to drop out of school for reasons other than academics. Poor basic skills, especially significant problems with reading, make college very difficult. And students do flunk out. But the main reasons people quit have to do with their circumstances beyond the campus: child care, finances, housing, and family disruption, ranging from injury or serious illness to divorce to immigration problems. As I was writing this, I got a phone call from a student I've come to know — a young man doing well in one of the occupational programs — asking me if I had any leads on where he might go for housing or shelter. He was suddenly homeless and on the verge of dropping out of college. He wasn't alone. Three of his classmates were

10

living in shelters near the campus. A fourth had been sleeping for several weeks behind the dumpster by the library.

No wonder that, along with the hope and sense of possibility they express, these students also voice, sometimes within the same sentence, the worry that this rug too will be pulled out from under them. I remember an older woman in an adult literacy program talking about failure in terms of falling: "Not falling down on my legs or knees, but falling down within me." Most of these students do not have a history of success, especially in school, and they want this time to be different, but if one thing goes wrong — an accident, a job lost — there's little reserve to draw on.   11

Many of the occupational programs at the college have been in operation since the mid-20th century, if not earlier. One such program, welding, which sits farther into the heart of the campus, has provided generations of students with a powerful trade, enabling them to make a decent living. It's one of the programs where I have been spending a lot of my time.   12

The welding lab is a huge room, rows of work benches down the middle and sheltered stalls along the walls. Welding equipment — gas tanks, the consoles for different electric welding processes, cutting machines, vises and grips — is spread throughout the room; rows of pipes and conduits and vents are crisscrossed along the walls and overhead. Walk in the lab during class, and you'll think you've entered Vulcan's workshop. Thirty or more students are practicing their techniques. Sparks fly up from the work stations, and from inside the stalls fiercely bright light pulses and dies. You'll need a mask to get close to the students. Everything is loud: the discordant symphony of welding's pops and crackles; the continuous hammering as the novice welders knock slag off their welds or peen a weld to improve its ductility. Voices rise above the din: the instructor tells one guy, and three others watching, to "look at your angle, man, look at your angle" and "don't push the electrode, glide it." Even with the vents, the strong acrid smell of electrical heat fills the air. This is where knowledge and skill are forged.   13

Over two years, students will develop physical adroitness with welding's tools and attune their senses to welding's demands. They will become proficient in the use of various gas and electric welding processes, each having advantages for different metals, structures, and conditions. They will learn about metallurgy and electricity. They will learn the vocabulary of welding and its many symbols and will develop a level of literacy and numeracy that enables them to read the welding code, pass certification exams, and function on the job. They will learn problem solving, troubleshooting, decision making — thinking in a careful and systematic way about what they're doing and why.   14

Not all vocational programs provide such solid preparation for a career, but, before the recession, most of the welding program's students were able to find jobs. What strikes me about good occupational programs, though, are the other things they make possible, the things that people rarely talk about. These programs provide a meaningful context for learning and a home base, a small community with a common goal. For many participants, school has not offered this kind of significance, and the results can extend beyond economic benefits, the kind typically associated with a more liberal course of study, the kind of education that first group of students I mentioned said they entered the college's basic-skills program to achieve.   15

Elias, Cynthia, and Bobby are pursuing both a certificate in welding and an associate of science degree. I've observed them in class, read their writing, and had a number of conversations with them, some focused on their education, and some just casual chitchat walking from one part of the campus to another. Not everyone in the program is as engaged by school as these three, but what is happening to them happens frequently enough to catch your attention.   16

Elias is in his first semester. In his mid-20s, medium height and build, clean-cut, he readily talks trash with the other men, but just as easily becomes well-spoken and reflective. I first noticed him in the basic-math class the welding instructor conducts before taking his students into the shop. The students work on the mathematics of converting fractions and calculating area, but also on solving word problems that involve welding. Elias was an eager participant, watching intently as his instructor laid out a problem, volunteering answers — some right, some wrong — then taking the instructor's feedback and looking down at the page, calculating again.   17

Elias's mathematical knowledge upon entering the program was at about the level of adding and subtracting simple fractions. The stuff he's doing now feels new to him, since he "checked out" of high school early on and eventually dropped out. During his late teens and early 20s he "ran the streets and was into drugs." But, and here his eyes widen as if waking up, one day he had this realization that he was going nowhere and wanted to turn his life around. He works as an entry-level car mechanic but, since he's single with no kids, wants to adjust his schedule to accommodate more schooling. "This is the first time," he says, "school means anything to me."   18

When she ran for an office in student government, Cynthia, one of the few women in the program, printed a flyer showing her in full welding garb — leather apron, gloves, mask flipped up to reveal her round face, almond eyes, and hint of a smile. *Vote 4 updating curriculum and equipment and for improving campus communication.* Her welding classmates   19 distributed the flyers for her. She'd never done anything like this before, she told me. She'd never run for office in high school and had avoided any kind of public speaking. But as she was beginning her second year, her welding instructor—for reasons not entirely clear—pushed and prodded her to go on this political journey. His instincts were true. During the campaign, I was observing a class in another department when Cynthia visited to give her two-minute stump speech. She said she was running to fight for more resources and to get a student voice into a current conflict between the academic and trade departments. Standing still in front of the room, her hands folded in front of her, she lacked the polish of some of the other candidates, but she was articulate and quietly passionate, the fluency that comes from authentic belief. She wanted to make a difference.

Bobby is about five foot eight, barrel chested, buzz cut, looks to be in his mid-to-late 40s. He's completed the welding certification but is still in school pursuing his academic degree and assisting in the welding program. You'll meet more than a few people like Bobby on this campus, in trouble with the law since he was 13: pills, meth, multiple incarcerations. About seven years ago during one of his times in jail, it came to him: "What am I doing? What's my life going to be?" He found religion and began the journey to various halfway houses and occupational centers. Then he found the welding program. Bobby has a jittery energy about him—his arms flap out from the sides of his body when he walks—but when he shakes your hand, it's with a full grip, and he looks you straight in the eye and holds the gaze. I remember thinking of those corneal scans in futuristic movies; he's taking your full measure in a blink. Bobby asked me to read one of his English compositions; it was on leadership, using his elected position in the campus chapter of the American Welding Society as the main example. He insisted I give him my opinion and any suggestions as to how to make it better. I've also talked to him about an art history course he's taking, a general education requirement. He liked it, found it interesting. We talked about a field trip he had taken to a museum. He was amazed that he could identify different styles and periods of art. Bobby's got what musicians call "big ears"; he's wide open, curious about everything. "Not a day goes by," he said to me when we were talking about the art course, "where you don't learn something—otherwise, something's wrong with you."

Regardless of whether Elias has ever seen the kinds of math problems he's now doing—and given his chaotic school record, it's hard to know if he has—he is engaged with them as if for the first time. Mathematics now means something to him. It is not only central to what he wants to do for a living, it has also become part of his attempt to redefine who he is. Cynthia,

20

21

by running for office, is hurling herself into a political and rhetorical world that is new to her, an act of courage and experimentation. She is finding her way into institutional life and the public sphere, and in so doing she is acquiring an on-the-ground civic education. Bobby is in full cognitive throttle. After so many years of kicking around, chasing dope, bouncing in and out of jail, he's found solidity at the college, a grounding that frees him up in a way that he never knew on the streets. Yes, he's eager to finish up here and transfer to a four-year school, but he's taking it all in along the way — essays, museums.

Fostering this kind of learning and growth is in a society's best interest. What is remarkable is how rarely we see it depicted in our media, how absent it is in both highbrow and popular culture. Even more remarkable is how rarely our thinking and talking about education makes room for this vocationally oriented explosion of mind. As I noted earlier, it certainly isn't reflected in current education policy and politics. My worry is that if we don't see this kind of development, and if it's not present in our political discourse, then we won't create the conditions to foster and advance it.   22

Why are the experiences of the participants in that basic-skills program at the community college or those of Elias, Cynthia, and Bobby not present in the public sphere?   23

One reason, as I've said, is an education policy that for several decades has been so directed toward the economic benefits of education. Of the other goals of education that have formed the American tradition from Jefferson to John Dewey — intellectual, civic, social, and moral development — only the civic gets an occasional nod these days. The economic rationale is a reasonable political pitch, commonsensical and pragmatic, but students' lives and aspirations get reduced in the process.   24

A further piece of the puzzle has to do with social class. Few policymakers have spent much time at colleges that serve a mostly working-class population. And the journalists who write the stories we do get about such students tend to focus on their hardships and determination (which are worthy of depiction) or on their failures. What we rarely get, and maybe some journalists do not see, are the many positive *educational* dimensions of these students' time in school.   25

Another element connected to social class and deeply rooted in American educational history is the sharp distinction made between academic and vocational study, a distinction institutionalized in the early-20th-century high school. The vocational curriculum prepared students for the world of work, usually blue-collar, service, or basic-technology work, while the academic curriculum emphasized the arts and sciences and the cultivation of mental life. From the beginning, Dewey predicted   26 the problems that this divide would create, and over the past three decades, school reformers have been trying to undo them: the artificial compartmentalizing of knowledge, the suppressing of the rich cognitive content of work, and the limiting of intellectual development of students in a vocational course of study. But Dewey's wisdom and reformers' efforts notwithstanding, the designation "academic" still calls up intelligence, smarts, big ideas, while the tag "vocational" conjures quite the opposite....

Elias, Cynthia, and Bobby have the ability to pursue a liberal studies curriculum, and I suspect they'd find much there to engage them. But in their present circumstances, they couldn't follow such a course exclusively. It is precisely its grounding in work and its pathway to decent employment that makes their educational journey possible. Their vocational commitment doesn't negate the liberal impulse but gives rise to it.   27

When Cynthia was delivering her stump speech in that class I observed, she spoke about the political discord on campus between the academic and vocational faculty and pledged to try to do something about it. "I'm in welding," she said, "but I'm pursuing an associate's degree, too. These don't have to be in conflict. I want to unite that gap." Cynthia was talking about conflict over turf and resources, but that conflict arises from a troubling history of philosophical claims about knowledge and intellectual virtue. Speaking from her experience, she was onto something that eluded her elders. Her life and the lives of the other students we've met demonstrate that habits of mind, reflection and thoughtfulness, exploration and experimentation can be sparked both in classrooms and in the workshop, reading a book and learning a trade. We ourselves have to disrupt our biases and binaries and be more creative in fusing book and workshop for those who go to school to fashion a better life.   28

IS FACEBOOK MAKING US LONELY?

Stephen Marche

Stephen Marche, a novelist, has written on cultural topics for Esquire, *the* New York Times, *and* Atlantic, *where this article appeared. His most recent book is* How Shakespeare Changed Everything.

Yvette Vickers, a former *Playboy* playmate and B-movie star, best known for her role in *Attack of the 50 Foot Woman*, would have been 83 last August, but nobody knows exactly how old she was when she died. According to the Los Angeles coroner's report, she lay dead for the better part of a year before a neighbor and fellow actress, a woman named Susan Savage, noticed cobwebs and yellowing letters in her mailbox, reached through a   1 broken window to unlock the door, and pushed her way through the piles of junk mail and mounds of clothing that barricaded the house. Upstairs, she found Vickers's body, mummified, near a heater that was still running. Her computer was on too, its glow permeating the empty space.

The *Los Angeles Times* posted a story headlined "Mummified Body of Former Playboy Playmate Yvette Vickers Found in Her Benedict Canyon Home," which quickly went viral. Within two weeks, by Technorati's count, Vickers's lonesome death was already the subject of 16,057 Facebook posts and 881 tweets. She had long been a horror-movie icon, a symbol of Hollywood's capacity to exploit our most basic fears in the silliest ways; now she was an icon of a new and different kind of horror: our growing fear of loneliness. Certainly she received much more attention in death than she did in the final years of her life. With no children, no religious group, and no immediate social circle of any kind, she had begun, as an elderly woman, to look elsewhere for companionship. Savage later told *Los Angeles* magazine that she had searched Vickers's phone bills for clues about the life that led to such an end. In the months before her grotesque death, Vickers had made calls not to friends or family but to distant fans who had found her through fan conventions and Internet sites.

Vickers's web of connections had grown broader but shallower, as has happened for many of us. We are living in an isolation that would have been unimaginable to our ancestors, and yet we have never been more accessible. Over the past three decades, technology has delivered to us a world in which we need not be out of contact for a fraction of a moment. In 2010, at a cost of $300 million, 800 miles of fiber-optic cable was laid between the Chicago Mercantile Exchange and the New York Stock Exchange to shave three milliseconds off trading times. Yet within this world of instant and absolute communication, unbounded by limits of time or space, we suffer from unprecedented alienation. We have never been more detached from one another, or lonelier. In a world consumed by ever more novel modes of socializing, we have less and less actual society. We live in an accelerating contradiction: the more connected we become, the lonelier we are. We were promised a global village; instead, we inhabit the drab cul-de-sacs and endless freeways of a vast suburb of information.

At the forefront of all this unexpectedly lonely interactivity is Facebook, with 845 million users and $3.7 billion in revenue last year. The company hopes to raise $5 billion in an initial public offering later this spring, which will make it by far the largest Internet IPO in history. Some recent estimates put the company's potential value at $100 billion, which would make it larger than the global coffee industry—one addiction preparing to surpass the other. Facebook's scale and reach are hard to comprehend: last summer, Facebook became, by some counts, the first Web site to receive 1 trillion page views in a month. In the last three months of 2011, users generated an average of 2.7 billion "likes" and comments every day. On whatever scale you care to judge Facebook—as a company, as a culture, as a country—it is vast beyond imagination....

When you... set up your Friends circle, the program specifies that you   5
should include only "your real friends, the ones you feel comfortable shar-ing private details with." That one little phrase, *Your real friends*—so quaint, so charmingly mothering—perfectly encapsulates the anxieties that social media have produced: the fears that Facebook is interfering with our real friendships, distancing us from each other, making us lonelier; and that so-cial networking might be spreading the very isolation it seemed designed to conquer.

Facebook arrived in the middle of a dramatic increase in the quantity   6
and intensity of human loneliness, a rise that initially made the site's prom-ise of greater connection seem deeply attractive. Americans are more soli-tary than ever before. In 1950, less than 10 percent of American households contained only one person. By 2010, nearly 27 percent of households had just one person. Solitary living does not guarantee a life of unhappiness, of course. In his recent book about the trend toward living alone, Eric Klinenberg, a sociologist at NYU, writes: "Reams of published research show that it's the quality, not the quantity of social interaction, that best predicts loneliness." True. But before we begin the fantasies of happily ec-centric singledom, of divorcees dropping by their knitting circles after work for glasses of Drew Barrymore pinot grigio, or recent college graduates with perfectly articulated, Steampunk-themed, 300-square-foot apartments or-ganizing croquet matches with their book clubs, we should recognize that it is not just isolation that is rising sharply. It's loneliness, too. And loneliness makes us miserable.

We know intuitively that loneliness and being alone are not the same   7
thing. Solitude can be lovely. Crowded parties can be agony. We also know, thanks to a growing body of research on the topic, that loneliness is not a matter of external conditions; it is a psychological state. A 2005 analysis of data from a longitudinal study of Dutch twins showed that the tendency toward loneliness has roughly the same genetic component as other psychological problems such as neuroticism or anxiety.

Still, loneliness is slippery, a difficult state to define or diagnose. The   8
best tool yet developed for measuring the condition is the UCLA Loneliness Scale, a series of 20 questions that all begin with this formulation: "How often do you feel...?" As in: "How often do you feel that you are 'in tune' with

the people around you?" And: "How often do you feel that you lack companionship?" Measuring the condition in these terms, various studies have shown loneliness rising drastically over a very short period of recent history. A 2010 AARP survey found that 35 percent of adults older than 45 were chronically lonely, as opposed to 20 percent of a similar group a decade earlier. According to a major study, roughly 20 percent of Americans — about 60 million people — are unhappy with their lives because of loneliness. Across the Western world, physicians and nurses have begun to speak openly of an epidemic of loneliness.

The new studies on loneliness are beginning to yield some surprising preliminary findings about its mechanisms. Almost every factor that one might assume affects loneliness does so only some of the time, and only under certain circumstances. People who are married are less lonely than single people, one journal article suggests, but only if their spouses are confidants. If one's spouse is not a confidant, marriage may not decrease loneliness. A belief in God might help, or it might not, as a 1990 German study comparing levels of religious feeling and levels of loneliness discovered. Active believers who saw God as abstract and helpful rather than as a wrathful, immediate presence were less lonely. "The mere belief in God," the researchers concluded, "was relatively independent of loneliness."   9

But it is clear than social interaction matters. Loneliness and being alone are not the same thing, but both are on the rise. We meet fewer people. We gather less. And when we gather, our bonds are less meaningful and less easy. The decrease in confidants — that is, in quality social connections — has been dramatic over the past 25 years. In one survey, the mean size of networks of personal confidants decreased from 2.94 people in 1985 to 2.08 in 2004. Similarly, in 1985, only 10 percent of Americans said they had no one with whom to discuss important matters, and 15 percent said they had only one such good friend. By 2004, 25 percent had nobody to talk to, and 20 percent had only one confidant.   10

In the face of this social disintegration, we have essentially hired an army of replacement confidants, an entire class of professional carers. As Ronald Dworkin pointed out in a 2010 paper for the Hoover Institution, in the late '40s, the United States was home to 2,500 clinical psychologists, 30,000 social workers, and fewer than 500 marriage and family therapists. As of 2010, the country had 77,000 clinical psychologists, 192,000 clinical social workers, 400,000 nonclinical social workers, 50,000 marriage and family therapists, 105,000 mental-health counselors, 220,000 substance-abuse counselors, 17,000 nurse psychotherapists, and 30,000 life coaches. The majority of patients in therapy do not warrant a psychiatric diagnosis.   11

This raft of psychic servants is helping us through what used to be called regular problems. We have outsourced the work of everyday caring.

We need professional carers more and more, because the threat of societal breakdown, once principally a matter of nostalgic lament, has morphed into an issue of public health. Being lonely is extremely bad for your health. If you're lonely, you're more likely to be put in a geriatric home at an earlier age than a similar person who isn't lonely. You're less likely to exercise. You're more likely to be obese. You're less likely to survive a serious operation and more likely to have hormonal imbalances. You are at greater risk of inflammation. Your memory may be worse. You are more likely to be depressed, to sleep badly, and to suffer dementia and general cognitive decline. Loneliness may not have killed Yvette Vickers, but it has been linked to a greater possibility of having the kind of heart condition that did kill her.   12

And yet, despite its deleterious effect on health, loneliness is one of the first things ordinary Americans spend their money achieving. With money, you flee the cramped city to a house in the suburbs or, if you can afford it, a McMansion in the exurbs, inevitably spending more time in your car. Loneliness is at the American core, a by-product of a long-standing national appetite for independence: The Pilgrims who left Europe willingly abandoned the bonds and strictures of a society that could not accept their right to be different. They did not seek out loneliness, but they accepted it as the price of their autonomy. The cowboys who set off to explore a seemingly endless frontier likewise traded away personal ties in favor of pride and self-respect. The ultimate American icon is the astronaut: Who is more heroic, or more alone? The price of self-determination and self-reliance has often been loneliness. But Americans have always been willing to pay that price....   13

In his 2000 book *Bowling Alone*, Robert D. Putnam attributed the dramatic post-war decline of social capital — the strength and value of interpersonal networks — to numerous interconnected trends in American life: suburban sprawl, television's dominance over culture, the self-absorption of the Baby Boomers, the disintegration of the traditional family. The trends he observed continued through the prosperity of the aughts, and have only become more pronounced with time: the rate of union membership declined in 2011, again; screen time rose; the Masons and the Elks continued their slide into irrelevance. We are lonely because we want to be lonely. We have made ourselves lonely....   14

Which brings us to a ... fundamental question: Does the Internet make people lonely, or are lonely people more attracted to the Internet?   15

The question has intensified in the Facebook era. A recent study out of Australia (where close to half the population is active on Facebook),   16 titled "Who Uses Facebook?," found a complex and sometimes confounding relationship between loneliness and social networking. Facebook users had slightly lower levels of "social intelligence"—the sense of not feeling bonded with friends—but "significantly higher levels of family loneliness"—the sense of not feeling bonded with family. It may be that Facebook encourages more contact with people from outside of our household, at the expense of our family relationships—or it may be that people who have unhappy family relationships in the first place seek companionship through other means, including Facebook. The researchers also found that lonely people are inclined to spend more time on Facebook: "One of the most noteworthy findings," they wrote, "was the tendency for neurotic and lonely individuals to spend greater amounts of time on Facebook per day than non-lonely individuals." And they found that neurotics are more likely to prefer to use the wall, while extroverts tend to use chat features in addition to the wall.

Moira Burke, until recently a graduate student at the Human-Computer Institute at Carnegie Mellon, used to run a longitudinal study of 1,200 Facebook users. That study, which is ongoing, is one of the first to step outside the realm of self-selected college students and examine the effects of Facebook on a broader population, over time. She concludes that the effect of Facebook depends on what you bring to it. Just as your mother said: you get out only what you put in. If you use Facebook to communicate directly with other individuals—by using the "like" button, commenting on friends' posts, and so on—it can increase your social capital. Personalized messages, or what Burke calls "composed communication," are more satisfying than "one-click communication"—the lazy click of a like. "People who received composed communication became less lonely, while people who received one-click communication experienced no change in loneliness," Burke tells me. So, you should inform your friend in writing how charming her son looks with Harry Potter cake smeared all over his face, and how interesting her sepia-toned photograph of that tree-framed bit of skyline is, and how cool it is that she's at whatever concert she happens to be at. That's what we all want to hear. Even better than sending a private Facebook message is the semi-public conversation, the kind of back-and-forth in which you half ignore the other people who may be listening in. "People whose friends write to them semi-publicly on Facebook experience decreases in loneliness," Burke says.

On the other hand, non-personalized use of Facebook—scanning your friends' status updates and updating the world on your own activities via your wall, or what Burke calls "passive consumption" and "broadcasting"—correlates to feelings of disconnectedness. It's a lonely business, wandering

17

18

the labyrinths of our friends' and pseudo-friends' projected identities, trying to figure out what part of ourselves we ought to project, who will listen, and what they will hear. According to Burke, passive consumption of Facebook also correlates to a marginal increase in depression. "If two women each talk to their friends the same amount of time, but one of them spends more time reading about friends on Facebook as well, the one reading tends to grow slightly more depressed," Burke says. Her conclusion suggests that my sometimes unhappy reactions to Facebook may be more universal than I had realized. When I scroll through page after page of my friends' descriptions of how accidentally eloquent their kids are, and how their husbands are endearingly bumbling, and how they're all about to eat a home-cooked meal prepared with fresh local organic produce bought at the farmers' market and then go for a jog and maybe check in at the office because they're so busy getting ready to hop on a plane for a week of luxury dogsledding in Lapland, I do grow slightly more miserable. A lot of other people doing the same thing feel a little bit worse, too.

Still, Burke's research does not support the assertion that Facebook   19 creates loneliness. The people who experience loneliness on Facebook are lonely away from Facebook, too, she points out; on Facebook, as everywhere else, correlation is not causation. The popular kids are popular, and the lonely skulkers skulk alone....

John Cacioppo, the director of the Center for Cognitive and Social   20 Neuroscience at the University of Chicago, is the world's leading expert on loneliness. In his landmark book, *Loneliness*, released in 2008, he revealed just how profoundly the epidemic of loneliness is affecting the basic functions of human physiology. He found higher levels of epinephrine, the stress hormone, in the morning urine of lonely people. Loneliness burrows deep: "When we drew blood from our older adults and analyzed their white cells," he writes, "we found that loneliness somehow penetrated the deepest recesses of the cell to alter the way genes were being expressed." Loneliness affects not only the brain, then, but the basic process of DNA transcription. When you are lonely, your whole body is lonely.

To Cacioppo, Internet communication allows only ersatz intimacy.   21 "Forming connections with pets or online friends or even God is a noble attempt by an obligatorily gregarious creature to satisfy a compelling need," he writes. "But surrogates can never make up completely for the absence of the real thing." The "real thing" being actual people, in the flesh. When I speak to Cacioppo, he is refreshingly clear on what he sees as Facebook's effect on society. Yes, he allows, some research has suggested that the greater the number of Facebook friends a person has, the less lonely she is. But he argues that the impression this creates can be misleading. "For the most part," he says, "people are bringing their old friends, and feelings of loneliness or connectedness, to Facebook." The idea that a Web site could deliver a more friendly, interconnected world is bogus. The depth of one's social network outside Facebook is what determines the depth of one's social network within Facebook, not the other way around. Using social media doesn't create new social networks; it just transfers established networks from one platform to another. For the most part, Facebook doesn't destroy friendships — but it doesn't create them, either.

In one experiment, Cacioppo looked for a connection between the loneliness of subjects and the relative frequency of their interactions via Facebook, chat rooms, online games, dating sites, and face-to-face contact. The results were unequivocal. "The greater the proportion of face-to-face interactions, the less lonely you are," he says. "The greater the proportion of online interactions, the lonelier you are." Surely, I suggest to Cacioppo, this means that Facebook and the like inevitably make people lonelier. He disagrees. Facebook is merely a tool, he says, and like any tool, its effectiveness will depend on its user. "If you use Facebook to increase face-to-face contact," he says, "it increases social capital." So if social media let you organize a game of football among your friends, that's healthy. If you turn to social media instead of playing football, however, that's unhealthy.... 22

"Facebook can be terrific, if we use it properly," Cacioppo continues. "It's like a car. You can drive it to pick up your friends. Or you can drive alone." But hasn't the car increased loneliness? If cars created the suburbs, surely they also created isolation. "That's because of how we use cars," Cacioppo replies. "How we use these technologies can lead to more integration, rather than more isolation." 23

Loneliness is certainly not something that Facebook or Twitter or any of the lesser forms of social media is doing to us. We are doing it to ourselves. Casting technology as some vague, impersonal spirit of history forcing our actions is a weak excuse. We make decisions about how we use our machines, not the other way around. Every time I shop at my local grocery store, I am faced with a choice. I can buy my groceries from a human being or from a machine. I always, without exception, choose the machine. It's faster and more efficient, I tell myself, but the truth is that I prefer not having to wait with the other customers who are lined up alongside the conveyor belt: the hipster mom who disapproves of my high-carbon-footprint pineapple; the lady who tenses to the point of tears while she waits to see if the gods of the credit-card machine will accept or decline; the old man whose clumsy feebleness requires a patience that I don't possess. Much better to bypass the whole circus and just ring up the groceries myself. 24

Our omnipresent new technologies lure us toward increasingly super-   25
ficial connections at exactly the same moment that they make avoiding
the mess of human interaction easy. The beauty of Facebook, the source of
its power, is that it enables us to be social while sparing us the embarrassing reality of society — the accidental revelations we make at parties, the
awkward pauses, the farting and the spilled drinks and the general gau-
cherie of face-to-face contact. Instead, we have the lovely smoothness of a
seemingly social machine. Everything's so simple: status updates, pictures,
your wall.

But the price of this smooth sociability is a constant compulsion to as-   26
sert one's own happiness, one's own fulfillment. Not only must we contend
with the social bounty of others; we must foster the appearance of our own
social bounty. Being happy all the time, pretending to be happy, actually attempting to be happy — it's exhausting. Last year a team of researchers led
by Iris Mauss at the University of Denver published a study looking into "the
paradoxical effects of valuing happiness." Most goals in life show a direct
correlation between valuation and achievement. Studies have found, for
example, that students who value good grades tend to have higher grades
than those who don't value them. Happiness is an exception. The study
came to a disturbing conclusion:

> Valuing happiness is not necessarily linked to greater happiness. In
> fact, under certain conditions, the opposite is true. Under conditions
> of low (but not high) life stress, the more people valued happiness,
> the lower were their hedonic balance, psychological well-being, and
> life satisfaction, and the higher their depression symptoms.

The more you try to be happy, the less happy you are....   27

Self-presentation on Facebook is continuous, intensely mediated, and   28
possessed of a phony nonchalance that eliminates even the potential for
spontaneity. ("Look how casually I threw up these three photos from the
party at which I took 300 photos!") Curating the exhibition of the self has
become a 24/7 occupation. Perhaps not surprisingly, then, the Australian
study "Who Uses Facebook?" found a significant correlation between
Facebook use and narcissism: "Facebook users have higher levels of total
narcissism, exhibitionism, and leadership than Facebook nonusers," the
study's authors wrote. "In fact, it could be argued that Facebook specifically
gratifies the narcissistic individual's need to engage in self-promoting and
superficial behavior."

Rising narcissism isn't so much a trend as the trend behind all other   29
trends. In preparation for the 2013 edition of its diagnostic manual, the
psychiatric profession is currently struggling to update its definition of narcissistic personality disorder. Still, generally speaking, practitioners agree

that narcissism manifests in patterns of fantastic grandiosity, craving for attention, and lack of empathy. In a 2008 survey, 35,000 American respondents were asked if they had ever had certain symptoms of narcissistic personality disorder. Among people older than 65, 3 percent reported symptoms. Among people in their 20s, the proportion was nearly 10 percent. Across all age groups, one in 16 Americans has experienced some symptoms of NPD. And loneliness and narcissism are intimately connected: a longitudinal study of Swedish women demonstrated a strong link between levels of narcissism in youth and levels of loneliness in old age. The connection is fundamental. Narcissism is the flip side of loneliness, and either condition is a fighting retreat from the messy reality of other people.

A considerable part of Facebook's appeal stems from its miraculous   30
fusion of distance with intimacy, or the illusion of distance with the illusion of intimacy. Our online communities become engines of self-image, and self-image becomes the engine of community. The real danger with Facebook is not that it allows us to isolate ourselves, but that by mixing our appetite for isolation with our vanity, it threatens to alter the very nature of solitude. The new isolation is not of the kind that Americans once idealized, the lonesomeness of the proudly nonconformist, independent-minded, solitary stoic, or that of the astronaut who blasts into new worlds. Facebook's isolation is a grind. What's truly staggering about Facebook usage is not its volume — 750 million photographs uploaded over a single weekend — but the constancy of the performance it demands. More than half its users — and one of every 13 people on Earth is a Facebook user — log on every day. Among 18-to-34-year-olds, nearly half check Facebook minutes after waking up, and 28 percent do so before getting out of bed. The relentlessness is what is so new, so potentially transformative. Facebook never takes a break. We never take a break. Human beings have always created elaborate acts of self-presentation. But not all the time, not every morning, before we even pour a cup of coffee. Yvette Vickers's computer was on when she died.

Nostalgia for the good old days of disconnection would not just be   31
pointless, it would be hypocritical and ungrateful. But the very magic of the new machines, the efficiency and elegance with which they serve us, obscures what isn't being served: everything that matters. What Facebook has revealed about human nature — and this is not a minor revelation — is that a connection is not the same thing as a bond, and that instant and total connection is no salvation, no ticket to a happier, better world or a more liberated version of humanity. Solitude used to be good for self-reflection and self-reinvention. But now we are left thinking about who we are all the time, without ever really thinking about who we are. Facebook denies us a pleasure whose profundity we had underestimated: the chance to forget about ourselves for a while, the chance to disconnect.

·3·

Quoting Sources

I hate quotations. Tell me what you know.

Ralph Waldo Emerson (1849)

By necessity, by proclivity, and by delight, we all quote.

Ralph Waldo Emerson (1876)

Like Emerson in 1849, most writers hope to rely entirely on what they know and to express their knowledge in their own words. But, as Emerson realized later, our ideas are rarely original. Someone has usually gone part of the way before, so why not build on that person's discoveries—and, perhaps, use their actual words?

In academic writing, presenting the words of another writer through quotation is the most basic way to support your own ideas. Quotation enables you to give credit to your sources for both borrowed ideas and borrowed words.

1. *Appropriate quotation* tells your reader that you know when to quote and when not to quote; you never allow your sources' words to dominate your writing.

2. *Correct quotation* tells your reader that you respect your sources, that you know how to distinguish between your own work and theirs, and that you will not *plagiarize*—make unacknowledged use of another writer's words and ideas.

Reasons to Use Quotation
1. To support a point
2. To preserve vivid or technical language
3. To comment on the quotation
4. To distance yourself from the quotation

Reasons for Quoting

1. Quoting for Support

You will most often refer to another writer's work as evidence to support one of your own points. To ensure that the evidence retains its full meaning and impact, you may retain the author's original language, instead of putting the sentences in your own words. Very often, quoted material appears in an essay as an *appeal to authority*; the source being quoted is important enough or familiar enough with the subject (as in an eyewitness account) to make the original words worth quoting. For example, the only quotation in a *New York Times* article describing political and economic chaos in Bolivia presents the opinion of a government official:

> Even the Government acknowledges its shaky position. "The polity is unstable, capricious and chaotic," Adolfo Linares Arraya, Minister of Planning and Co-ordination, said. "The predominance of crisis situations has made the future unforeseeable."

The minister's words in themselves seem vague and glib, and therefore not especially quotable. But his position as representative of the government makes the minister's exact words necessary evidence for the reporter's presentation of the Bolivian crisis.

2. Quoting Vivid or Technical Language

The wording of the source material may be so apt or concise that the point will be lost if you express it in your own words. You will want to quote a sentence that is very compact or that relies on a striking image to make its point. For example, here is a paragraph from a review of a book about Vietnamese history:

> Not many nations have had such a history of scrapping: against Mongols and Chinese seeking to dominate them from the north, and to the

south against weaker and more innocent peoples who stood in the way of the Vietnamese march to the rich Mekong Delta and the underpopulated land of Cambodia. Mr. Hodgkin [the author] quotes from a poem by a medieval Vietnamese hero: "By its tradition of defending the country / the army is so powerful it can swallow the evening star."

The quotation adds authentic evidence to the reviewer's discussion and provides a memorable image for the reader.

It is also important to keep the precise terminology of a *technical or legal document*. Changing one word of the text can significantly change its meaning. Here is a sentence from the final paragraph of a Supreme Court decision upholding the civil rights of three tenth-graders who had been suspended by school officials for "spiking" the punch at a meeting of an extracurricular club:

> We hold that a school board member is not immune from liability for damages if he knew or reasonably should have known that the action he took within his sphere of official responsibility would violate the constitutional rights of the student affected, or if he took the action with the malicious intention to cause a deprivation of constitutional rights or other injury to the student.

Virtually every word of the sentence has potential impact on the way this decision will be interpreted in subsequent legal suits. Note, for example, the distinction between "knew" and "reasonably should have known" and the way in which "intention" is qualified by "malicious."

3. Quoting Another Writer to Comment on the Quotation

In your essay, you may want to analyze or comment on the language used by another writer. Your readers should have that writer's exact words in front of them if they are to get the full benefit of your commentary; *you have to quote it in order to talk about it.* Thus, when a writer reviewing Philip Norman's biography of the Beatles wants to criticize the biographer's style, he must supply a sample quotation so that his readers can make up their own minds.

> Worst of all is the overwritten prologue, about John Lennon's death and its impact in Liverpool: "The ruined imperial city, its abandoned river, its tormented suburban plain, knew an anguish greater than the recession and unemployment which have laid Merseyside waste under bombardments more deadly than Hitler's blitz." A moment's thought should have made Norman and his publishers realize that this sort of thing, dashed off in the heat of the moment, would quickly come to seem very embarrassing indeed.

4. Quoting to Gain Distance

Authors generally use quotation to distinguish between themselves and other authors they are citing. Sometimes, however, you want to distance yourself from *your own* choice of language. For example, you may use quotation marks to indicate that a word or phrase is not in common or standard use. A phrase may be *obsolete*, no longer in current usage:

> Many "flower children" gathered at the rock festivals of the late 1960s.

Or a phrase may be *slang*, not yet having been absorbed into standard English:

> According to some students, the actor Aziz Ansari is "mad" funny.

In effect, you want to use the phrase and at the same time "cover" yourself by signaling your awareness that the phrase is not quite right: you are distancing yourself from your own vocabulary. On the whole, it is better to take full responsibility for your choice of words and to avoid using slang or obsolete vocabulary, with or without quotation marks.

You can achieve a different kind of distance when you use quotation marks to suggest *irony*:

> The actor was joined by his "constant companion."

The quoted phrase is a familiar *euphemism*, a bland expression substituted for a more blunt term. Again, by placing it in quotation marks, the author is both calling attention to and distancing him- or herself from the euphemism.

Quotation marks also serve as a means of *disassociation* for journalists who wish to avoid taking sides on an issue or making editorial comments.

> A fire that roared through a 120-year-old hotel and took at least 11 lives was the work of a "sick arsonist," the county coroner said today. Robert Jennings, the Wayne County coroner, said that he had told county officials that the building was a "fire trap."

The author of this article did not want the responsibility of attributing the fire to a "sick arsonist" or labeling the building a "fire trap"—at any rate, not until the findings of an investigation or a trial make the terminology unquestionably true. Thus, he is careful not only to use quotation marks around certain phrases but also to acknowledge the precise source of the statement.

Using Quotations

> ## How to Quote
>
> 1. *Insert quotation marks* to indicate that you are borrowing certain words, as well as certain ideas, that appear in your writing.
> 2. *Insert a citation* containing the source's name to give credit for both ideas and words to the author.
>
> | **Citation** | **Quotation** |
> |---|---|
> | Theodore Roosevelt said, | "Speak softly and carry a big stick; you will go far." |

Direct Quotation: Separating Quotations from Your Own Writing

The simplest way to quote is to combine the acknowledgment of the author—known as the *citation* (written by you)—with the words you are quoting (exactly as they were said or written by your source). This method of quotation joins together two separate statements, with punctuation—comma or colon—bridging the gap, and a capital letter beginning the quoted sentence.

St. Paul declared, "It is better to marry than to burn."

In his first epistle to the Corinthians, St. Paul commented on lust: "It is better to marry than to burn."

In both these forms of direct quotation, the quoted words are not fully integrated into the grammatical structure of your sentence:

- The *quotation marks* separate the citation and the quotation.
- The *comma* or *colon* separates the citation and the quotation.
- The *capital letter* at the beginning of the quotation separates the citation and the quotation.

These separating devices make it clear that two voices appear in the sentence: yours and your source's. In general, you should choose this kind of direct quotation when you want to differentiate between yourself and the quoted words, perhaps because you disagree with them.

The *colon* is used less frequently than the comma. It usually follows a group of words that can stand alone as a complete sentence. As such, the colon separates a complete idea of your own from a complementary or supporting idea taken from your source.

Direct Quotation: Integrating Quotations into Your Sentences

In an alternative kind of direct quotation, *only the quotation marks indicate that you are using someone else's words.*

> St. Paul declared that "it is better to marry than to burn."

> Alvin Toffler defined future shock as "the shattering stress and disori-entation that we induce in individuals by subjecting them to too much change in too short a time."

There is no other signal for the reader that separates citation from quotation—no comma or colon, no capital letter. The first word of the quoted material, in this second type of direct quotation, is *not* capitalized, even if it was capitalized in the source.

Source

Beware of all enterprises that require new clothes.

HENRY DAVID THOREAU

Quotation

Thoreau warned his readers to "beware of all enterprises that require new clothes."

The effect is very smooth, and the reader's attention is not distracted from the flow of words.

The Two Kinds of Direct Quotation

Separated	Integrated
■ Comma or colon and quotation marks separate citation and quotation.	■ No punctuation but quotation marks separates citation and quotation.
■ The first letter of the quotation is capitalized.	■ The first letter of the quotation is not capitalized.
■ You are distinguishing between your ideas and those of your source.	■ You are integrating your ideas with those of your source.

Indirect Quotation

You may be tempted to use indirect quotation, in which you report, rather than quote what the source has written. But you would be wise to insert quotation marks whenever you use a source's exact words, whether written or oral.

Direct Quotation

Robert Ingersoll condemned those who deny others their civil liberties: "I am the inferior of any man whose rights I trample underfoot."

Indirect Quotation

Robert Ingersoll proclaimed that he was the inferior of any man whose rights he trampled underfoot.

The indirect quotation does not indicate whose language appears in this sentence. In fact, the lack of quotation marks strongly indicates that the words aren't Ingersoll's—yet they are! Changing "I" to "he" and the present to the past tense has made no real difference: the basic phrasing of the sentence remains Ingersoll's. *To imply, as this indirect quotation could, that the wording is yours, not Ingersoll's, would be plagiarism.*

For this reason, writers use indirect quotation with great care. If one of the two forms of direct quotation does not seem appropriate, you should invent your own wording—called *paraphrase*—to express the source's original statement.

The Historical Present Tense

Certain ideas and statements remain true long after their creators have died. By convention, writers often refer to these statements in the present tense. Conventions are agreements, written or unwritten, that a certain practice should be generally used.

Shakespeare *states*, "This above all: to thine own self be true."

When you are devoting part of your own essay to an exploration of another writer's ideas, you may prefer to present those ideas using a common ground of time through the present tense, called the *historical present*. The historical present is almost always used when you refer to important documents that remain in force long after they were created. Obvious examples include the Constitution, the Declaration of Independence, the laws of Congress, Supreme Court decisions, the charter of your state government, and the bylaws governing your college or university.

The Constitution *guarantees* that women—and, indeed, all citizens—
shall have the vote in elections; Amendment XIX *states* that the right to
vote "shall not be denied or abridged by the United States or by any State
on account of sex."

Punctuating Direct Quotations: Opening the Quotation

You have already learned about punctuating the beginning of the quotation:

1. In a separated direct quotation, the citation is followed by a comma or a colon.
2. In an integrated direct quotation, the citation is followed by no punctuation at all.

Some writers tend to forget this second point and include an unnecessary
comma:

Incorrect Quotation

Ernest Hemingway believed that, "what is moral is what you feel good
after and what is immoral is what you feel bad after."

Remember that an integrated quotation should have no barriers between
citation and quotation:

Correct Quotation

Ernest Hemingway believed that "what is moral is what you feel good
after and what is immoral is what you feel bad after."

In the integrated direct quotation, remember that the first letter of the quotation
is not capitalized.

Punctuating Direct Quotations: Closing the Quotation

There is no easy way to remember the proper sequence of punctuation for closing a quotation. The procedure was determined long ago by conventional and
arbitrary agreement, originally for the convenience of printers. Although other
countries abide by different conventions, in the United States the following
rules apply—and *there are no exceptions.*

1. All periods and commas are placed inside the terminal quotation marks.

It does not matter whether the period belongs to your sentence or to the quoted
sentence: it goes *inside* the marks. This is the most important rule and the

one most often ignored. Don't resort to ambiguous devices such as placing the marks directly over the period.

> P. T. Barnum is reputed to have said that "there's a sucker born every minute."
> ↑

> P. T. Barnum is reputed to have said that "there's a sucker born every minute," and Barnum's circuses undertook to entertain each and every one.
> ↑

Notice that, in the second example, the comma at the end of the quotation belongs to the framework sentence, not to the quotation itself; nevertheless, it goes *inside* the marks.

2. Semicolons, colons, and dashes are generally placed outside the terminal quotation marks.

Semicolons, colons, and dashes should be regarded as the punctuation for *your* sentence, and not for the quotation.

> George Santayana wrote that "those who cannot remember the past are condemned to repeat it"; today, we are in danger of forgetting the lessons of history.   ↑

3. Question marks and exclamation points are sometimes placed inside the quotation marks and sometimes placed outside.

- ▪ If the quotation is itself a question or an exclamation, the mark or point goes *inside* the quotation marks.

> In 1864, General Sherman signaled the arrival of his reinforcements: "Hold the fort! I am coming!"
> ↑

The exclamation is General Sherman's; the exclamation point goes inside the quotation.

- ▪ If your own sentence is a question or an exclamation, the mark or point goes *outside* a quotation placed at the very end of your sentence.

> Can anyone today agree with Dumas that "woman inspires us to great things and prevents us from achieving them"?
> ↑

Dumas was *not* asking a question; the question mark goes at the very end of the sentence, after the quotation marks.

> Sigmund Freud's writings occasionally reveal a remarkable lack of insight: "The great question that has never been answered, and which I have not yet been able to answer despite my thirty years of research into the feminine soul, is: What does a woman want?"
> ↑

Freud himself asked this famous question; the question mark goes inside the quotation.

> Freud was demonstrating remarkably little insight when he wrote,
> "What does a woman want?" citing his "thirty years of research
> into the feminine soul"!   ↑
>   ↑

The exclamation is the writer's, not Freud's; the exclamation point goes outside the quotation marks.

■ It is possible to construct a sentence that ends logically in two question marks (or exclamation points): one for the quotation and one for your own sentence. In such cases, you need include only one—and, by convention, it should be placed *inside* the quotation marks:

> What did Freud mean when he asked, "What does a woman want?"
>   ↑

These rules about punctuation apply only to the quotation of complete sentences or long phrases. Whether it is a quotation or an obsolete, slang, or ironic reference, *a single word or a brief phrase should be fully integrated into your sentence, without being preceded or followed by commas.*

> Winston Churchill's reference to "blood, sweat and tears" rallied the
> English to prepare for war.

Interrupting Quotations

Sometimes you want to break up a long quotation or to vary the way you quote your sources by interrupting a quotation and placing the citation in the middle.

> "I do not mind lying," wrote Samuel Butler, "but I hate inaccuracy."
> ↑   ↑   ↑   ↑

Butler's statement is divided into two separate parts, and therefore you need to use *four* quotation marks: two introductory and two terminal. The citation is joined to the quotation by a comma on either side. There are two danger points:

■ If you forget to use the marks at the beginning of the second half of the quotation, you are failing to distinguish your words from Butler's.

■ You must also put the first comma *inside* the terminal quotation marks (because commas *always* go inside the terminal quotation marks) and put the comma that concludes the citation *before* the quotation marks (because it is *your* comma, not Butler's).

Quoting Inside a Quotation

Sometimes a statement that you want to quote already contains a quotation. In that case, you must use two sets of quotation marks, double and single, to help your reader to distinguish between the two separate sources:

- *Single quotation marks* are used for the words already quoted by your source (and this is the *only* time when it is appropriate to use single quotation marks).

- *Double quotation marks* are used around the entire quotation.

> Goethe at times expressed a notable lack of self-confidence: "'Know thyself?' If I knew myself, I'd run away."

> At the beginning of World War I, Winston Churchill observed that "the maxim of the British people is 'Business as usual.'"

Presenting an Extended or Block Quotation

Occasionally, you may have reason to present an extended quotation, a single extract from the same source that runs *more than four printed or typewritten lines*. For extended quotations, you must, by conventional rule, set off the quoted passage by *indenting the entire quotation on the left*:

- Introduce an extended quotation with a colon.

- Start each line of the quotation one inch (or one-half inch) from the left-hand margin; stop each line at your normal right-hand margin.

- Some instructors prefer single-spacing within extended quotations; some prefer double-spacing. If possible, consult your instructor about the style appropriate for your course or discipline. If you are given no guidelines, use double-spacing.

- Omit quotation marks at the beginning and end of the quoted passage; the indented margin (and the introductory citation) will tell your readers that you are quoting.

Here is an example of an extended quotation:

> Although he worked "hard as hell" all winter, Fitzgerald had difficulty finishing *The Great Gatsby*. On April 10, 1924, he wrote to Maxwell Perkins, his editor at Scribner's:
>
> > While I have every hope & plan of finishing my novel in June... even [if] it takes me 10 times that long I cannot let it go unless it has the very best I'm capable of in it or even as I feel sometimes better than

I'm capable of. It is only in the last four months that I've realized how much I've—well, almost *deteriorated*....What I'm trying to say is just that...at last, or at least for the first time in years, I'm doing the best I can.

EXERCISE 9: Quoting Correctly

A. Correct the errors in the following sentences:

1. Dealing with backstabbers, Eminem commented there was one thing I learned." "They're only powerful when you got your back turned".

2. Do you agree with Jerry Seinfeld that: "A bookstore is one of the only pieces of evidence we have that people are still thinking?"

3. H. L. Mencken cynically remarked that, "Nobody ever went broke underestimating the intelligence of the American public.

4. Oscar Wilde believed that, "after a good dinner', one can forgive anybody", even one's own relations".

5. The American historian Barbara Tuchman wrote about the ineptitude of generals, arguing that: "The power to command frequently causes failure to think".

6. Obesity is on the rise around the world, says Ann Becker. The Harvard anthropologist reports that the "Sudden increase in eating disorders among teenage girls in Fiji may be linked to "Western ideals of beauty" and to the arrival of television in the 1990s.

7. Donald Trump offered this advice—"there's the old story about the boxer after a fight who said: 'that wasn't so tough." What was really tough was my father hitting me on the head with a hammer."

8. Before the Revolutionary War, Patrick Henry made a passionate speech, "is life so dear or peace so sweet, as to be purchased at the price of chains and slavery"? "Forbid it, Almighty God"! I know not what course others may take, but as for me, give me liberty or give me death."!

B. Use quotations from the following group as directed:

- Choose one quotation and write a sentence that introduces a direct quotation with separation.

- Choose a second quotation and write a sentence that introduces a direct quotation with integration.

- Choose a third quotation and write a sentence that interrupts a quotation with a citation in the middle.

1. I don't know anything about music. In my line you don't have to. (Elvis Presley)

2. All wish to possess knowledge, but few, comparatively speaking, are willing to pay the price. (Juvenal, Roman poet who lived around 100 AD)

3. I wake up every morning at nine and grab for the morning paper. Then I look at the obituary page. If my name isn't on it, I get up. (Benjamin Franklin)

4. Making predictions is difficult, particularly about the future. (Samuel Goldwyn, Hollywood producer)

5. Stage fright is always waiting outside the door. You either battle or walk away. (Laurence Olivier, British stage and film actor)

6. Money, it turned out, was exactly like sex, you thought of nothing else if you didn't have it and thought of other things if you did. (James Baldwin, American novelist)

7. Those things over there are my husbands. (Kingsley Amis, challenged to produce a sentence whose meaning depended on an apostrophe)

8. Man, it has been said, is a dining animal. Creatures of the inferior races eat and drink; man only dines. (Isabella Beeton, author of *Mrs. Beeton's Book of Household Management*, 1861)

Quoting Accurately

Quoting is not a collaboration in which you try to improve on your source's words. Don't make minor changes or carelessly leave words out, but faithfully transcribe the exact words, the exact spelling, and the exact punctuation that you find in the original.

Source

Those who corrupt the public mind are just as evil as those who steal from the public purse.

ADLAI STEVENSON

Inexact Quotation

Adlai Stevenson believed that "those who act against the public interest are just as evil as those who steal from the public purse."

Exact Quotation

Adlai Stevenson believed that "those who corrupt the public mind are just as evil as those who steal from the public purse."

Even if you notice an error (or what seems to be an error), you still must copy the original wording. For example, old-fashioned spelling should be retained, as well as regional or national dialect and archaic spelling conventions:

> One of Heywood's *Proverbes* tells us that "a new brome swepeth clean."

> In one of his humorous stories, Colonel Davy Crockett predicted the reactions to his own death: "It war a great loss to the country and the world, and to ole Kaintuck in particklar. Thar were never known such a member of Congress as Crockett, and never will be agin. The painters and bears will miss him, for he never missed them."

If the material that you are quoting contains errors of syntax, punctuation, or spelling, you can use a conventional way to point out such errors and inform the reader that the mistake was made not by you, but by the source. The Latin word *sic* (meaning "thus") is placed in square brackets and inserted immediately after the error. The [sic] signals that the quotation was "thus" and that you, the writer, were aware of the error, which was not the result of your own carelessness in transcribing the quotation.

In the following example, [sic] calls attention to an error in subject-verb agreement:

> Richard Farson points out that "increased understanding and concern has [sic] not been coupled with increased rights."

You may also want to use [sic] to indicate that the source used archaic spelling:

> In describing Elizabeth Billington, an early nineteenth-century singer, W. Clark Russell observed that "her voice was powerful, and resembled the tone of a clarionet [sic]."

It would be tedious, however, to use [sic] to indicate each misspelling in the Davy Crockett quotation; in your essay about Crockett, you could, instead, explain his use of dialect as you discuss his life and writing.

Tailoring Quotations to Fit Your Writing

There are several ways to change quotations to fit the quoted material naturally into your own sentences. Like [sic], these devices are conventions, established by generally accepted agreement: *you cannot improvise; you must follow these rules.* Usually, the conventional rules require you to inform your reader that a change is being made. In other words, they make clear the distinction between your wording and the author's.

Using Ellipses to Delete Words

It is permissible to delete words from a quotation, provided that you indicate to the reader that something has been omitted. Your condensed version is as accurate as the original; it is just shorter. But you must remember to insert the conventional symbol for deletion, *three spaced dots*, called an *ellipsis*. Once made aware by the three dots that your version omits part of the original, any reader who wants to see the omitted portion can consult the original source.

Source

Since the rise of the first neolithic cultures, man has hanged, tortured, burned, and impaled his fellow men. He has done so while devoutly professing religions whose founders enjoined the very opposite upon their followers. It is as though we carried with us, from some dark tree in a vanished forest, an insatiable thirst for cruelty.

LOREN EISELEY

Quotation with Ellipsis

Loren Eiseley tells us that "since the rise of the first neolithic cultures, man has hanged, tortured, burned, and impaled his fellow men. . . . It is as though we carried with us, from some dark tree in a vanished forest, an insatiable thirst for cruelty."

Notice that:

- The three dots are spaced equally, with one space between each dot and the next, and before the first and after the last.
- The dots *must* be three—not two or five.
- The first period is retained, to provide terminal punctuation for the first part of the quotation.

If you wish to delete the end of a quotation, and the ellipsis coincides with the end of your sentence, you must use the three dots, plus a fourth to signify the sentence's end.

Quotation with Terminal Ellipsis

Loren Eiseley provides a harrowing picture of man's darker nature: "Since the rise of the first neolithic cultures, man has hanged, tortured, burned, and impaled his fellow men. He has done so while devoutly professing religions whose founders enjoined the very opposite. . . ."

Here, you'll note:

- There are four dots, three to indicate a deletion and a fourth to indicate the period at the end of the sentence.

- The first dot is placed immediately after the last letter.
- The sentence ends with quotation marks, as usual, with the marks placed *after* the dots, not before.

Three dots can also link two separate quotations from the same paragraph in your source; the ellipsis will indicate the deletion of one or more sentences. You may do this only if the two sentences that you are quoting are fairly near each other in the original. When you use an ellipsis to bridge one or more sentences, use only *one* set of quotation marks. Your full quotation, with an ellipsis in the middle, is still continuous—a single quotation—even though there is a gap.

Source

In one sense there is no death. The life of a soul on earth lasts beyond his departure. You will always feel that life touching yours, that voice speaking to you, that spirit looking out of other eyes, talking to you in the familiar things he touched, worked with, loved as familiar friends. He lives on in your life and in the lives of all others that knew him.

ANGELO PATRI

Quotation with Ellipsis

Patri states that "in one sense there is no death. The life of a soul on earth lasts beyond his departure....He lives on in your life and in the lives of all others that knew him."

The source's meaning must always be exactly preserved, despite the deletion represented by the ellipsis.

Source

As long as there are sovereign nations possessing great power, war is inevitable.

ALBERT EINSTEIN

Inexact Quotation

Einstein believes that "as long as there are sovereign nations...war is inevitable."

It would not be accurate to suggest that Einstein believed in the inevitability of war merely because sovereign nations exist. To extract only a portion of this statement with an ellipsis is to oversimplify and thus to distort the evidence.

An ellipsis can be used to make a quotation fit more smoothly into your own sentence. But ellipses should *not* be used to condense long, tedious quotations or to replace summary and paraphrase. If you want to quote only a brief extract from a lengthy passage, then simply quote that portion and ignore the surrounding material.

Using Brackets to Insert Words

Brackets have an opposite function: an ellipsis signifies deletion; *brackets signify addition or alteration.* Brackets are not the same as parentheses. Parentheses would be confusing for this purpose, for the quotation might itself include a parenthetical statement, and the reader could not be sure whether the parentheses contained the author's insertion or yours. Instead, brackets, a relatively unusual form of punctuation, are used as a conventional way of informing the reader that material has been inserted. (You have already seen how to use brackets with [sic], which enables you to comment on the material that you are quoting.) You simply insert the information *inside* the quotation, placing it in square brackets:

- Brackets are used to clarify vague language. You may, for example, choose to quote only the last portion of a passage, omitting an important antecedent:

  Source

  It is the nature of desire not to be satisfied, and most men live only for the gratification of it.

  Aristotle

  Quotation with Brackets

  Aristotle notes that "most men live only for the gratification of [desire]."

- Brackets are also used to complete a thought that depends on an earlier sentence—an antecedent—which you have left out of the quotation.

  Source

  A well-trained sensible family doctor is one of the most valuable assets in a community....Few men live lives of more devoted self-sacrifice.

  Sir William Osler

  Quotation with Brackets

  The great surgeon Sir William Osler had enormous respect for his less famous colleagues: "Few men live lives of more devoted self-sacrifice [than good family doctors]."

In this, as in the first example, the quotation marks are placed *after* the brackets, even though the quoted material ends after the word "self-sacrifice." The explanatory material inside the brackets is considered part of the quotation, even though it is not in the source's own words.

Reasons to Use Brackets
■ To explain a vague word
■ To replace a confusing phrase
■ To suggest an antecedent
■ To correct an error in a quotation
■ To adjust a quotation to fit your own writing

You may put your own explanatory comments in brackets if they are brief. You might, for example, want to include an important date or name as essential background information. But whatever is inside the brackets should fit smoothly into the quotation and should not distract the reader. For example, do not use brackets to argue with the author you are quoting. The following running dialogue with the entertainer Sophie Tucker is poorly conveyed through the use of brackets.

Confusing Use of Brackets

Sophie Tucker suggests that up to the age of eighteen "a girl needs good parents. [This is true for men, too.] From eighteen to thirty-five, she needs good looks. [Good looks aren't that essential anymore.] From thirty-five to fifty-five, she needs a good personality. [I disagree because personality is important at any age.] From fifty-five on, she needs good cash."

EXERCISE 10: Using Ellipses and Brackets in Quotations

A. Choose one of the following quotations. By using ellipses, incorporate a portion of the quotation into a sentence of your own; remember to acknowledge the author's name.

B. Choose a second quotation. Incorporate a portion of the quotation into another sentence of your own; insert your own words in brackets to clarify one or more of the quoted words.

1. A lifetime of happiness! No man alive could bear it; it would be hell on earth. (George Bernard Shaw)

2. I have never taken any exercise, except sleeping and resting, and I never intend to take any. Exercise is loathsome. And it cannot be any benefit when you are tired, and I am always tired. (Mark Twain)

3. Money has never made man happy, nor will it. There is nothing in its nature to produce happiness. The more of it one has the more one wants. (Benjamin Franklin)

4. An engaged woman is always more agreeable than a disengaged. She is satisfied with herself. Her cares are over, and she feels that she may exert all her powers of pleasing without suspicion. (Jane Austen)

5. The Internet is like alcohol in some sense. It accentuates what you would do anyway. If you want to be a loner, you can be more alone. If you want to connect, it makes it easier to connect. (Esther Dyson)

6. Serious sport has nothing to do with fair play. It is bound up with hatred, jealousy, boastfulness, disregard of all rules, and sadistic pleasure in witnessing violence. In other words, it is war minus the shooting. (George Orwell)

Giving Credit to the Source

Citing the Author's Name

The first time that you refer to a source, use the author's full name—without Mr. or Miss, Mrs., or Ms.

First Reference

John Stuart Mill writes, "The opinion which it is attempted to suppress by authority may possibly be true."

After that, should you need to cite the author again, use the *last name only*. Conventional usage discourages casual and distracting references such as "John thinks," "JSM thinks," or "Mr. Mill thinks."

Second Reference

Mill continues to point out that "all silencing of discussion is an assumption of infallibility."

When you cite the author's name:

- At first reference, you may (and usually should) include the *title* of the work from which the quotation is taken:

    In *On Liberty*, John Stuart Mill writes...

- Avoid referring to the author twice in the same citation, once by name and once by pronoun.

    In John Stuart Mill's *On Liberty*, he writes...

- If there is a long break between references to the same author, or if the names of several other authors intervene, you may wish to repeat the full name and remind your reader of the earlier citation.

In addition to his warnings about the dangers of majority rule, which were cited earlier in the discussion of public opinion, John Stuart Mill also expresses concern about "the functions of police; how far liberty may legitimately be invaded for the prevention of crime, or of accident."

- Finally, unless you genuinely do not know it, use the author's name!

Choosing the Introductory Verb

The introductory verb in the citation can tell your reader something about your reasons for presenting the quotation and its context in the work that you are quoting. Will you choose "J. S. Mill says," or "J. S. Mill writes," or "J. S. Mill thinks," or "J. S. Mill feels"? Those are the most common introductory verbs—so common that they have become boring! As the senses are not directly involved in writing, avoid "feels" entirely. And, unless you are quoting someone's spoken words, substitute a more accurate verb for "says."

Here are some introductory verbs:

argues	adds	concludes
establishes	explains	agrees
emphasizes	believes	insists
finds	continues	maintains
points out	declares	disagrees
notes	observes	states
suggests	proposes	compares

Of course, once you stop using the all-purpose "says" or "writes," you have to remember that verbs are not interchangeable and that you should choose the verb that best suits your purpose.

The citation should suggest the relationship between your own ideas (in your previous sentence) and the statement that you are about to quote.

Examine the quotation before writing the citation to define the way in which the author makes a point:

- Is it being asserted forcefully?
  Use "argues" or "declares" or "insists."
- Is the statement being offered only as a possibility?
  Use "suggests" or "proposes" or "finds."
- Does the statement immediately follow a previous reference?
  Use "continues" or "adds."

For clarity, the introductory verb may be expanded:

Mill is aware that...
Mill stresses the opposite view.

Mill provides one answer to the question.
Mill makes the same point as Bentham.
Mill erroneously assumes...

But make sure that the antecedent for the "view" or the "question" or the "point" can be found in the previous sentences of your essay.

Note that all the examples of introductory verbs are given in the *present tense*, which is the conventional way of introducing most quotations.

Varying Your Sentence Patterns

Even if you choose a different verb for each quotation, the combination of the author's name, introductory verb, and quotation can become repetitious and tiresome. One way to vary the citations is occasionally to place the name of the source in a less prominent position, tucked into the quotation instead of calling attention to it at the beginning.

1. As was discussed on page 122, you can interrupt the quotation by placing the citation in the middle.

"I made my mistakes," acknowledged Richard Nixon, "but in all my years of public service, I have never profited from public service. I have earned every cent."

2. You can phrase the citation as a subordinate clause or phrase, thus avoiding the monotonous "X says that..." pattern.

In Henry Kissinger's opinion, "Power is 'the great aphrodisiac.'"

As John F. Kennedy declares, "Mankind must put an end to war or war will put an end to mankind."

3. You should avoid placing the citation after the quotation.

The author's name at the end may weaken the statement, especially if the citation is pretentiously or awkwardly phrased:

Awkward Citation

"I am the inferior of any man whose rights I trample underfoot," as quoted from the writings of Robert Ingersoll.

Clear Citation

A champion of civil liberties, Robert Ingersoll insisted, "I am the inferior of any man whose rights I trample underfoot."

Two Rules Should Govern Your Choice of Citation
1. Don't be too fancy.
2. Be both precise and varied in your phrasing.

Deciding What to Quote

Use quotation sparingly! If quoting seems to be your primary purpose in writing, your reader will assume that you have nothing of your own to say. Quote only when you have a clear reason for doing so:

- when you are intending to analyze or explain a quotation,
- when you are sure that its wording is essential to the author's meaning,
- or when you simply cannot rephrase it in your own words.

Citing Primary Sources

You will probably want to quote authorities in the field, especially primary sources: original works—often by historical figures—that other authors have commented on or authentic voices from a previous era. A secondary source is a writer commenting on events or works in which he or she has had no direct involvement. (For an explanation of primary and secondary sources, see pp. 358–359.) Here, for example, Lewis Lapham, the editor of *Harper's*, is writing about America as a nation of immigrants, citing primary sources: first an American president and then a notable explorer:

name of
the source

context for the
quotation

name in the
middle of the
quotation

source's name

> We are a nation of parvenus, all bound to the hopes of tomorrow, or next week, or next year. John Quincy Adams put it plainly in a letter to a German correspondent in the 1820s who had written on behalf of several prospective émigrés to ask about the requirements for their success in the New World. "They must cast off the European skin, never to resume it," Adams said. "They must look forward to their posterity rather than backwards to their ancestors."
>
> We were always a mixed and piebald company, even on the seventeenth century colonial seaboard, and we accepted our racial or cultural differences as the odds that we were obliged to overcome or correct. When John Charles Frémont (a.k.a. The Pathfinder) first descended into California from the East in

context

1843, he remarked on the polyglot character of the expedition accompanying him south into the San Joaquin Valley:

block quotation/
no quotation
marks

ellipsis

> Our cavalcade made a strange and grotesque appearance, and it was impossible to avoid reflecting upon our position and composition in this remote solitude…still forced on south by a desert on one hand and a mountain range on the other; guided by a civilized Indian, attended by two wild ones from the Sierra; a Chinook from the Columbia; and our own mixture of American, French, German—all armed; four or five languages heard at once; above a hundred horses and mules, half-wild; American, Spanish and Indian dresses and equipments intermingled—such was our composition.

John Quincy Adams's statement is tightly phrased, with the first half of each sentence balancing the second; Lapham would have found it difficult to express it half as well in his own words. Frémont's description has the authenticity of experience that is hard to capture using secondhand words.

Citing Primary Sources: "Petrified"

In this excerpt from "Petrified," John Lahr, a drama critic and biographer of theatrical figures, writing here for the *New Yorker,* is examining the mental and physical disintegration that performers can feel when they suffer stagefright. Before each quotation, Lahr provides a context and then lets the words of, first, a famous actor and, then, a distinguished musician suggest the horror of the experience.

quoting to
emphasize the
word

hard to use other
words

interrupted
quotation/image
of an enemy
waging war

rejection of the
performing life

In a sense, the term "stagefright" is a misnomer—fright being a shock for which one is unprepared. For professional performers, the unmooring terror hits as they prepare to do the very thing they're trained to do. According to one British medical study, actors' stress levels on opening night are equivalent "to that of a car-accident victim." When Sir Laurence Olivier was in his sixties, he considered retiring from the stage because of stagefright. It "is always waiting outside the door," he wrote in *Confessions of an Actor.* "You either battle or walk away." The Canadian piano virtuoso Glenn Gould, who suffered from disabling stagefright, did walk away, abandoning the public platform for the privacy of the recording studio. "To me the ideal artist-to-audience relationship is one to zero," he said.

Citing Primary Sources: A Consumer's Republic

Historical figures and celebrities aren't the only primary sources who merit quotation. In this extract from *A Consumer's Republic,* Lizabeth Cohen, who teaches American Studies at Harvard University, describes the rise of the shopping center or, as she puts it, the "feminization of public space." Many of Cohen's primary sources are ordinary people from the 1950s and 1960s. Notice that

Cohen tends to use this standard pattern: source's name – description of context – colon – quotation. Unlike Lapham's and Lahr's magazine articles, this is an academic work, based on extensive research, and so the sources are documented with notes. The need for documentation is explained in greater detail at the end of this chapter and in Chapter 10.

This was a new phrase in 1958.

When "the whole family [was] shopping together," as marketer Pierre Martineau put it in 1958, men played a greater role in household purchasing. Survey after survey documented husbands' increasing presence alongside their wives at shopping centers, which made evenings and weekends by far the busiest time there, creating peaks and valleys in shopping that had not affected downtown stores nearly as much. In many suburban centers more than half the volume was done at night. At Bergen Mall the peak traffic count was at 8 p.m., and shopping was very heavy on Saturdays as well. A May Company executive described how this imbalance created special problems in branch-store

quotation — succinct, but is the quotation needed?

operation: "The biggest day in the suburban store will be ten times the poorest day, instead of five as it usually is downtown." The manager of the Tots 'n Teens toy store in Shoppers World in Framingham, Massachusetts, tried to explain to less experienced mall sellers how the new-style suburban shopping actually worked: "It's a curious thing about a shopping center. Most of our daytime

authentic voice

shoppers are women who are just looking around. It's hard to sell them during the day but if they're at all interested, they'll be back at night — with their husbands. That's when we do the real business."[51]

Shopping centers responded to suburban couples' growing tendency to shop together with stores and programming specifically designed to further encourage families to turn shopping chores into leisure time spent at the mall.

Quote sounds like a board chair! Is it needed?

William M. Batten, board chair of JCPenney, for example, recalled "the broadening of our lines of merchandise and our services to encompass a fuller spectrum of family activity" as the company began building stores in shopping centers rather than on Main Street in the late 1950s and 1960s. Only then did Penney's start selling appliances, hardware, and sporting goods, and offering portrait studios, restaurants, auto service, and Singer sewing instruction. *Business Week* reported that department stores were scurrying to respond as well: Federated Department Stores started a new Fedway chain to attract the whole family and

striking phrase — integrated quotation

in its F. & R. Lazarus store in Columbus was "making a real effort to take the curse of femininity off the big store" by selling more male-oriented merchandise.[52]

51. Martineau, "Customers' Shopping Center Habits Change Retailing," p. 16; Feinberg, *What Makes Shopping Centers Tick*, p. 97; Oaks, *Managing Suburban Branches of Department Stores*, p. 72; Irving Roberts, "Toy Selling Techniques in a Shopping Center," *Playthings*, July 1953, p. 112; also see "Lenox Toy & Hobby Selects Good Location in Atlanta Shopping Center — 1,200 Sales a Week," *Playthings*, May 1961, p. 99.

Figure 3-1 Large, open, well-lighted departments with year-round air conditioning permit Bambergers to handle large crowds easily.

RWDSU Local 1-S. Courtesy of Robert F. Wagner Labor Archives, New York University, from its Department Store Workers, Local 1-S Collection

RWDSU Local 1-S. Courtesy of Robert F. Wagner Labor Archives, New York University, from its Department Store Workers, Local 1-S Collection

Figure 3-2 Do-it-yourself delivery is popular with suburban customers — and so is the "togetherness" of family shopping.

These photographs from Macy's annual report to shareholders the year its Garden State Plaza opened conveyed the prevalence of women shoppers but also hinted at the growing importance of the "'togetherness' of family shopping," referred to in the bottom caption. Reproduced from R.H. Macy & Co., Inc., *1957 Annual Report.*

52. JCPenney, "An American Legacy, A 90th Anniversary History," brochure (1992), pp. 22, 25, JCPenney Archives, Plano, TX; Mary Elizabeth Curry, *Creating an American Institution: The Merchandising Genius of J.C. Penney* (New York: Garland, 1993), pp. 311–13; William M. Batten, *The Penney Idea: Foundation for the Continuing Growth of the J.C. Penney Company* (New York: Newcomen Society in North America, 1967), p. 17. The opening of the JCPenney store in Garden State Plaza in 1958 is featured in a film, *The Past Is a Prologue* (1961), which is one of several fascinating movies made by the company that has been collected on a video, *Penney Premieres*, available through the JCPenney Archives. Also see *Penney News* 24 (November–December 1958): 1, 7 on the new Paramus store; JCPenney Archives.

Selecting Quotations

1. *Never quote something just because it sounds impressive.* The style of the quotation—the level of difficulty, the choice of vocabulary, and the degree of abstraction—should be compatible with your own style.

2. *Never quote something that you find difficult to understand.* When the time comes to decide whether to quote, rapidly read the quotation and observe your own reactions. If you become distracted or confused, your reader will be, too.

3. *Quote primary sources—if they are clear and understandable.* A person who witnessed the Chicago Fire has a better claim to have his original account presented verbatim than does a historian, writing a century later.

EXERCISE 11: Why Quote?

A. Read this excerpt from *The End of Men: And the Rise of Women,* by Hanna Rosin, twice.

B. Make marginal notes.

C. Be prepared to comment on Rosin's use of quotation.

from THE END OF MEN: AND THE RISE OF WOMEN
Hanna Rosin

A journalist specializing in religion and politics, Hanna Rosin is a writer and editor at Atlantic *and at* Slate. The End of Men *is her second book.*

Background: Rosin is exploring the causes and consequences of the rapid decline in the percentage of American households with married couples.

The sociologist Kathryn Edin spent five years talking with mothers in the inner suburbs of Philadelphia. Many of these neighborhoods, she found, had turned into matriarchies, with women making all the decisions and dictating what the men should and should not do. "I think something feminists have missed," Edin told me, "is how much power women have" when they're not bound by marriage. The women, she explained, "make every important decision" — whether to have a baby, how to raise it, where to live. "It's definitely 'my way or the highway,'" she said. "Thirty years ago, cultural norms were such that the fathers might have said, 'Great, catch me if you can.' Now they are desperate to father, but they are pessimistic about whether they can meet her expectations. So they have the babies at nineteen or twenty, but they

1

just don't have the jobs to support them." The women don't want them as husbands, and they have no steady income to provide. So what do they have?

"Nothing," Edin says. "They have nothing. The men were just annihilated in the recession of the nineties, and things never got better. Now it's just awful." 2

The situation today is not, as Edin likes to say, a "feminist nirvana." After 3 staying steady for a while, the portion of American children born to unmarried parents jumped to 40 percent in the past decade. A child born to an unmarried mother, once a stigma, is now the "new normal," *The New York Times* reported in a 2012 front page story, as more than half of births to American women under thirty occurred outside marriage. Many of these single mothers are struggling financially; the most successful are working and going to school and hustling to feed the children, and then falling asleep in the elevator of the community college. Still, they are in charge. "The family changes over the past four decades have been bad for men and bad for kids, but it's not clear they are bad for women," says sociologist Brad Wilcox.

Over the years, researchers have proposed different theories to explain 4 the erosion of marriage in the lower classes: the rise of welfare, the disappearance of work for men, or in the eyes of conservative critics such as Charles Murray, plain old moral decay. But Edin thinks the most compelling theory is that marriage has disappeared because women are now more economically independent and thus able to set the terms for marriage — and usually they set them too high for the men around them to reach. "I want that white-picket-fence dream," one woman told Edin, and the men she knew just didn't measure up, so she had become her own one-woman mother/father/nurturer/provider. Or as Edin's cowriter, the sociologist Maria Kefalas, puts it, "everyone watches *Oprah*" — or whatever the current *Oprah* equivalent is. "Everyone wants a big wedding, a soul mate, a best friend." But among the men they know, they can't find one.

Some small proof for this theory that women don't marry because they're 5 on top can be found in a recent study of Florida Lottery winners, called "Lucky in Life, Unlucky in Love?: The Effect of Random Income Shocks on Marriage and Divorce," published in the *Journal of Human Resources* in 2011. Researchers discovered that women who recently won the lottery were significantly less likely to marry, whereas for men it made no difference. Women who had won relatively large prizes ($25,000–$50,000) in the Florida Lottery were 41 to 48 percent less likely to marry than women who won less than $1,000, suggesting that money does in fact affect women's decisions.

It's far from definitive, but the results do confirm a certain picture. The 6 whole country's future could look much as the present does for many lower-class African-Americans: The mothers pull themselves up, but the men don't follow. First-generation college-educated white women may join their black counterparts in a new kind of middle class, where marriage is increasingly rare.

These changes are not merely spreading around the fringes; they are fundamentally altering the core of American middle-class life, as Wilcox and his colleagues chronicle in a groundbreaking report called "When Marriage Disappears: The Retreat from Marriage in Middle America." Wilcox's work concentrates on what he calls the "moderately educated middle," meaning the 58 percent of Americans who do not have a college degree but are not high-school dropouts, either, and might have some higher education. This is the class that used to strive upward and model itself on the upper classes. Now, in this vast swath of Middle America, "marriage, that iconic middle-class institution, is foundering," writes Wilcox, and at an "astonishingly fast pace."

By nearly every important social measure, Middle America is starting to look like high-school-dropout America. By the late 1990s, 37 percent of moderately educated women were divorcing or separating within ten years of their first marriage, almost the same rate as among women who didn't finish high school and more than three times that of college graduates. Middle America also caught up in rates of infidelity and number of sexual partners. By the late 2000s, nonmarital childbirths accounted for 44 percent of children born to moderately educated mothers and 6 percent of children born to highly educated mothers. Teenagers in Middle America are now less likely to say they would be embarrassed if they got pregnant, and less likely to have a strong desire to attend college.

The middle class still aspires to a happy soul-mate marriage, but increasingly their life experience is not matching up. From the 1970s to the 2000s, the percent of spouses who reported they were "very happy" in their marriages dropped among moderately educated Americans from 68 to 57 percent. Marriage, writes Wilcox, "is in danger of becoming a luxury good attainable only to those with the material and cultural means to grab hold of it." As Kefalas puts it, "Stable marriage has become a class privilege in America, just like good school and access to health care and healthy foods."

Page 92. The sociologist Kathryn Edin: Kathryn Edin and Maria Kefalas, *Promises I Can Keep: Why Poor Women Put Motherhood Before Marriage* (Berkeley and Los Angeles: University of California Press, 2005).

Page 93. After staying steady for a while: The National Center for Health Statistics reports that 41 percent of children are now born to unmarried parents. In 2002, that figure was 34 percent, according to Stephanie J. Ventura, "Changing Patterns of Nonmarital Childbearing in the United States," NCHS Data Brief No. 18, May 2009. http://www.cdc.gov/nchs/data/databriefs/db18.pdf.

Page 93. Now the "new normal": Jason DeParle and Sabrina Tavernise, "Unwed Mothers Now a Majority Before Age of 30," *The New York Times,* February 17, 2012.

Page 94. Chronicle in a groundbreaking report: Wilcox, ed., "When Marriage Disappears."

EXERCISE 12: What to Quote

A.   As your instructor indicates, read either the excerpt from *Women from the Ankle Down: The Story of Shoes and How They Define Us*, by Rachelle Bergstein, or the excerpt from *The Steal: A Cultural History of Shoplifting*, by Rachel Shteir. Read the excerpt twice.

B.   Decide which phrases or sentences, if any, would be worth quoting in a research essay. If this were an essay assignment, your choice would depend on your essay topic and proposed thesis.

from WOMEN FROM THE ANKLE DOWN: THE STORY OF SHOES AND HOW THEY DEFINE US
Rachelle Bergstein

Rachelle Bergstein has written fiction and non-fiction for numerous websites. Women from the Ankle Down *is her first book.*

Today, the average woman often owns upward of ten, twenty, fifty pairs of shoes, some of which have very little practical use and languish in the back of the closet until just the right occasion arises. This is thanks, in part, not only to factories but also to industrial leaders like DuPont, which introduced low-cost artificial materials into the market in the early 1960s. On the heels of the cookie-cutter 1950s, youthful consumers were willing to experiment with style, and they tested out new, outrageous designs like the *cuissarde* — a sexy thigh-high boot — with aplomb. Then, in the 1980s, another important development: sneaker companies, eager to promote their technologically innovative product, courted sports stars to appear as spokesmodels, and the age of the celebrity endorsement was born. Finally, progress came full circle when, during the late 1980s and early 1990s, the reign of the fairy-tale cobbler with his handmade, bespoke shoes returned. These glamorous, high-quality shoes could be purchased for a considerable price, and expressions of status — always subtly enmeshed with the worlds of footwear and fashion — became as conspicuous as the ruby red soles of a pair of Christian Louboutins.

These days, when women pick out their shoes, they find themselves, consciously or not, negotiating between the choices that have already been made for them by the fashion elite — the group of powerful designers, editors, and stylists who determine which shoes to show on the runways, and then to feature on the pages of popular magazines — and the prerogatives of personal style. As most women understand, lacing up a pair of Doc Martens or Converse Chuck Taylors sends a different message than shuffling through a restaurant in Crocs or strutting down the sidewalk in a pair of Jimmy Choos. It's up to each individual to decide who she wants to be in any given moment, and what information

Image copyright © The Metropolitan Museum of Art/Art Resource, NY

Figure 3-3 This evening boot (1957) by French designer Roger Vivier for Christian Dior features blue silk satin, blue cotton lace, glass beads, sequins, and leather.

she'd like her footwear to convey. Shoes have evolved to take on unique personalities and to communicate with the world in precise nonverbal language. If you ask a woman why she loves shoes she'll tell you that they're beautiful, that they make her feel good, that they have the ability to transform an outfit from simple jeans and a T-shirt into something showstopping and spectacular. These are just a handful of reasons why, at the height of this recent recession, footwear sales continued to rise while overall retail profits plummeted.

from THE STEAL: A CULTURAL HISTORY OF SHOPLIFTING
Rachel Shteir

Head of dramaturgy at DePaul University, Rachel Shteir has published three books, including the award-winning Striptease.

What's new about shoplifting today is that it has become a cultural phenomenon — a silent epidemic, driven by pretty much everything, in our era. Some scholars connect it to traditional families' disintegration, the American love of shopping, the downshifting of the middle class, global capitalism, immigration, the replacement of independent stores with big chains, and the lessening of faith's hold on conduct. Shoplifting gets tangled up in American cycles of spending and saving, and boom and bust, and enacts the tension between the rage to consume conspicuously and the intention to live thriftily. The most recent suspects include the Great Recession, the increasing economic divide between rich and poor, and an ineffectual response to

1

the shamelessness of white-collar fraudsters: the shoplifter as the poor man's Bernard Madoff.

Yet many shoplifters see themselves as escape artists, stealing out of inscrutable cravings and unexamined desires. Having lost their old solaces, people shoplift as an anodyne against grief or to avenge themselves against uncontrollable forces or as an act of social aggression, to hurl themselves away from their identities as almost-have-nots. Whatever form shoplifting takes, it is as difficult to stamp out as oil spills or alcoholism.

2

Integrating Quotations into Your Paragraphs

Now that you know how to present the words of others accurately and with an appropriate citation to the author, you must learn to incorporate quotations smoothly into your paragraphs, supporting—not preempting—your own ideas.

Using Quotations in Your Writing

1. **Quotations generally belong in the body of the paragraph, not at the beginning as a replacement for the topic sentence.**

   The topic sentence should establish—in your own words—what you are about to explain or prove. *The quotation should appear later in the paragraph, as supporting evidence.*

2. **Let the quotation make its point; your job is to explain or interpret its meaning, not to translate it word for word.**

   Once you have presented a quotation, you need not provide an exact repetition of the same idea in your own words, making the same point twice. Instead, follow up a quotation with an *explanation* of its relevance to your paragraph or an *interpretation* of its meaning. Make sure that your commentary does more than echo the quotation.

In the following student example, the quotation used in the fifth sentence adds interest to the paragraph because of the shift in tone and the shift to a sharper, narrower focus.

topic sentence

explanation of
topic sentence

example

Some parents insist on allowing their children to learn through experience. Once a child has actually performed a dangerous action and realized
its consequences, he will always remember the circumstances and the
possible ill effects. Yvonne Realle illustrates the adage that experience is
the best teacher by describing a boy who was slapped just as he reached
for a hot iron. The child, not realizing that he might have been burned,

quotation
interpreting the
example

elaboration of the
topic sentence

had no idea why he had been slapped. An observer noted that "if he had learned by experience, if he'd suffered some discomfort in the process, then he'd know enough to avoid the iron next time." In the view of parents like Yvonne Realle, letting a child experiment with his environment will result in a stronger lesson than slapping or scolding the child for trying to explore his surroundings.

Instead of looking at another completed paragraph that includes a quotation, let's reverse the process by starting with a simple quotation and seeing how it is used in the development of a paragraph. In an article on shopping written for the *Guardian*, a British newspaper, Jess Cartner-Morley is presenting the following thesis:

> Men tend to view shopping as a chore, a necessary way of obtaining things they need; for women, it is a leisure activity and a reward.

Cartner-Morley intends to include a quotation by Charles Revson, a major figure in the cosmetics industry:

> "In the factory we make cosmetics; in the store we sell hope."

The connection between the thesis and the quotation can be found in the words "reward" and "hope." So Cartner-Morley establishes a topic sentence—as well as a follow-up, explanatory sentence—that makes the connection in general terms:

> Certainly, it is clear that in a consumer society, shopping has come to stand for much more than just buying things. It is your ticket to an idealized self.

Shopping as "reward" has led to shopping as a "ticket to an idealized self," and that, in turn, leads to Revson's compact and catchy sentence—well worth quoting—about cosmetics as a symbol of "hope."

To introduce the quotation, Cartner-Morley uses an explanatory citation identifying Revson:

> Charles Revson, who founded Revlon in 1932, figured this out long ago, saying, "In the factory we make cosmetics; in the store we sell hope."

And then Cartner-Morley completes the paragraph by building on "long ago" in the citation and contrasting 1932 with 2004:

> But it is in recent years that the culture of shopping has become increasingly about image rather than substance.

Now she is ready to move on and discuss the way the idealized image of self is developed and marketed. The paragraph is only four sentences long—short and easy to follow—but it makes its point clearly by working toward the quotation and then away from it. The quotation strongly supports Cartner-Morley's thesis but can do so only because it is embedded in a strong paragraph.

Read through the complete paragraph and see how well it hangs together:

> Certainly, it is clear that in a consumer society, shopping has come to stand for much more than just buying things. It is your ticket to an idealized self. Charles Revson, who founded Revlon in 1932, figured this out long ago, saying, "In the factory we make cosmetics; in the store we sell hope." But it is in recent years that the culture of shopping has become increasingly about image rather than substance.

Academic writers may deal with more complex topics, but they use precisely the same techniques for incorporating quotations—the evidence of authoritative sources—into their paragraphs. Here is a paragraph from Dick Teresi's *Lost Discoveries: The Ancient Roots of Modern Science—From the Babylonians to the Maya*. Teresi is a science writer who bridges academic and popular audiences. Here, he is beginning a chapter on the origins of the science of geology:

topic sentence

example

closer focus

> Prehistoric peoples must have had intimate knowledge of the qualities of the stones they depended on in order to live. Neanderthal humans in the Middle Pleistocene crafted stone tools of a specific form known as Mousterian.[1] They used two methods: by chipping at the stone core to create the tool, and by using the chips themselves as the tools.[2] Geologist Gordon Childe says that

support: authority (quotation)

> "both procedures demand both great dexterity and considerable familiarity with the properties of the stone utilized. Just bashing two stones together is not likely to yield a useable flake or core tool. To produce either the blow must be struck with precisely the right force and at the correct angle on a flat sur-

shift in focus to the present

> face."[3] Modern geology students who have attempted to make their own tools in this fashion can vouch for the difficulty involved. One student told me she

support: brief anecdote

> spent a full morning trying to make a stone cutting tool from two pieces of flint she found on the beach.

1. Kenneth F. Weaver, "The Search for Our Ancestors," *National Geographic* 168 (Nov. 1985): 616.

2. Gordon Childe, "The Prehistory of Science: Archaeological Documents," in Guy S. Metraux and François Crouzet (eds.), *The Evolution of Science: Readings from the History of Mankind* (New York: New American Library, Mentor Books, 1963), pp. 39, 40.

3. Ibid.

Notice that Teresi's paragraph contains *three footnotes* to document the sources of his information as well as the quotation. Cartner-Morley is writing for a newspaper and is not expected to do more than identify sources by name and, if appropriate, provide some background. Complete information about when and how to document sources can be found in Chapter 10.

EXERCISE 13: Integrating Quotations into a Paragraph

A. The following paragraph is taken from a student's essay, "The Compulsive Gambler." The second excerpt comes from *The Psychology of Gambling*, by Edmund Bergler.

Choose one appropriate supporting quotation from the Bergler excerpt, decide where to place it in the student paragraph, and insert the quotation correctly and smoothly into the paragraph. Remember to lead into the quotation by citing the source. Be prepared to explain your choice of quotation and your choice of placement.

Student Paragraph

One obvious reason for gambling is to make money. Because some gamblers are lucky when they play, they never want to stop. Even when quite a lot of money has been lost, they go on, assuming that they can get rich through gambling. Once a fortune is made, they will feel really powerful, free of all dependency and responsibilities. Instead, in most cases, gambling becomes a daily routine. There is no freedom, no escape.

Source

Every gambler gives the impression of a man who has signed a contract with Fate, stipulating that persistence must be rewarded. With that imaginary contract in his pocket, he is beyond the reach of all logical objection and argument. The result of this pathologic optimism is that the true gambler never stops when he is winning, for he is convinced that he must win more and more. Inevitably, he loses. He does not consider his winnings the result of chance; to him they are a down payment on that contract he has with Fate which guarantees that he will be a permanent winner. This inability to stop while fortune is still smiling is one of the strongest arguments against the earnest assumption, common to all gamblers, that one can get rich through gambling.

B. The following paragraph is taken from a student's essay, "Why the Public Loves Celebrities." The second excerpt comes from *Fame Attack: The Inflation of Celebrity and Its Consequences*, by Chris Rojek.

Choose one appropriate supporting quotation from the Rojek excerpt, decide where to place it in the student paragraph, and insert the quotation correctly and smoothly into the paragraph. Remember to lead into the quotation by citing the source. Be prepared to explain your choice of quotation and your choice of placement.

Student Paragraph

In the 21st century, celebrities are seen as larger than life. We don't want to idolize people who are just like us. We want them to have all the material advantages that we yearn for and may never possess. Their lives, and often their personalities, are filled with excess. They seem to do as they please. In the eyes of the public, celebrities represent godlike beings.

Source

Celebrities like Britney Spears, Jay-Z, Beyoncé, Paris Hilton, Jodie Marsh, Simon Cowell and Kanye West, are often portrayed in the media and perceived by the public as divas and prima donnas. Although they may engage in impromptu asides and occasionally cast themselves as regular guys, the locus of their fame resides in being more glamorous, wealthier, having more glitzy appeal, business opportunities and being free of normal social conventions.

These are the celebrities who present a public image of living a frontier existence in which emotional and psychological pressures are greater than for the ordinary person. As a result, the normal rules of everyday life do not apply. Theirs is the world of private airplanes, helipads, chauffeur-driven stretch limos, maids, personal chefs, bodyguards, tantrums, enormous performance fees and heedless consumption. The PR-Media hubs that work for them want the public to know it. For celebrity icons the nucleus of fame is a public image of exoticism. They are the rare and colorful birds of the jungle. They fly higher than other celebrities and the rest of us. So their demand for public attention knows no limits. They are stellar.

Avoiding Plagiarism

Quoting without quotation marks is one kind of *plagiarism*. Even if you cite the source's name somewhere on your page, a word-for-word quotation without quotation marks would still be considered plagiarism.

Plagiarism is the unacknowledged use of another writer's words or ideas. The only way to acknowledge that you are using someone else's actual words is through citation and quotation marks.

Chapter 10 discusses plagiarism in detail. At this point, you should understand that:

- If you plagiarize, you will never learn to write.
- Literate people consider plagiarism to be equivalent to theft.
- Plagiarists eventually get caught!

It is easy for an experienced reader to detect plagiarism. Every writer, professional or amateur, has *a characteristic style or voice* that readers quickly learn to recognize. The writer's voice becomes so familiar that the reader notices when the style changes and a new, unfamiliar voice appears. When there are frequent acknowledged quotations, the reader simply adjusts to a series of new voices. But when there are unacknowledged quotations, *the absence of quotation marks* and *the change of voices* usually suggest to an experienced reader that the work is poorly integrated and probably plagiarized.

Instructors are well aware of style and are trained to recognize inconsistencies and awkward transitions. A revealing clue is the patched-together, mosaic effect. The next exercise will improve your own perception of shifting voices and encourage you to rely on your own characteristic style as the dominant voice in everything that you write.

EXERCISE 14: Identifying Plagiarism

The following paragraphs contain several plagiarized sentences.

A.   Examine the *language* and *tone* of each sentence, as well as the *continuity* of the entire paragraph.

B.   Then underline the plagiarized sentences.

1.   The Beatles' music in the early years was just plain melodic. It had a nice beat to it. The Beatles were simple lads, writing simple songs simply to play to screaming fans on one-night stands. There was no deep, inner meaning to the lyrics. Their songs included many words like I, and me, and you. As the years went by, the Beatles' music became more poetic. *Sergeant Pepper* is a stupefying collage of music, words, background noises, cryptic utterances, orchestral effects, hallucinogenic bells, farmyard sounds, dream sequences, social observations, and apocalyptic vision, all masterfully blended together on a four-track tape machine over nine agonizing and expensive months. Their music was beginning to be more philosophical, with a deep, inner, more secret meaning. After it was known that they took drugs, references to drugs were seen in many songs. The "help" in Ringo's "A Little Help from My Friends" was said to have meant pot. The songs

were poetic, mystical; they emerged from a self-contained world of bizarre carnival colors; they spoke in a language and a musical idiom all their own.

2. Before the Civil War, minstrelsy spread quickly across America. Americans all over the country enjoyed minstrelsy because it reflected something of their own point of view. For instance, Negro plantation hands, played usually by white actors in blackface, were portrayed as devil-may-care outcasts and minstrelmen played them with an air of comic triumph, irreverent wisdom, and an underlying note of rebellion, which had a special appeal to citizens of a young country. Minstrelsy was ironically the beginning of black involvement in the American theater. The American people learned to identify with certain aspects of the black people. The Negro became a sympathetic symbol for a pioneer people who required resilience as a prime trait.

·4·

Paraphrasing Sources

Some passages are worth quoting for the sake of their precise or elegant style or their distinguished author. But many sources that you will use in your college essays are written in more ordinary language or by more ordinary writers. Rather than quoting bland material, you should provide your readers with a clear paraphrase.

> *Paraphrase is the point-by-point recapitulation of another person's ideas, expressed in your own words.*

When you paraphrase, you retain everything about the original writing but the words.

Reasons for Using Paraphrase

Paraphrasing helps your readers to gain a detailed understanding of your sources and, indirectly, to accept your thesis as valid. There are two major reasons for using paraphrase in your essays.

1. Use paraphrase to present information or evidence whenever there is no special reason for using a direct quotation.

Many sources don't have sufficient authority or a distinctive enough style to justify your quoting their words. The following illustration, from a *New York Times* article, paraphrases a report written by an anonymous group of "municipal auditors" that was not considered worth quoting. Note the initial reference to the source of the information ("a report issued yesterday") and the follow-up reminders ("they said"; "the auditors said").

> A city warehouse in Middle Village, Queens, stocked with such things as snow shovels, light bulbs, sponges, waxed paper, laundry soap and tinned herring, has been found to be vastly overstocked with some items and lacking in others. Municipal auditors, *in a report issued yesterday*, said that security was fine and that the warehouse was quicker in delivering goods to city agencies than it was when the auditors made their last check.... But in one corner of the warehouse, *they said*, nearly 59,000 paper binders, the 8½-by-11 size, are gathering dust, enough to meet the city's needs for nearly seven years. Nearby, there is a 10½-year supply of cotton coveralls.
>
> Both the overstock and shortages cost the city money, *the auditors said*. They estimated that by reducing warehouse inventories, the city could save $1.4 million, plus $112,000 in interest....

2. Use paraphrase to give your readers an accurate and comprehensive account of ideas taken from a source — ideas that you intend to explain, interpret, or disagree with in your essay.

The first illustration comes from a *Times* article about the data and photographs provided by *Voyager 2* as it explored the farthest reaches of the solar system. In summarizing a press conference, the article paraphrases various scientists' descriptions of what *Voyager* had achieved during its journey near Triton, one of the moons of the planet Neptune. Note the limited use of carefully selected quotations within the paraphrase.

> Out of the fissures [on Triton], roughly analogous to faults in the Earth's crust, flowed mushy ice. There was no eruption in the sense of the usual terrestrial volcanism or the geyser-like activity discovered on Io, one of Jupiter's moons. It was more of an extrusion through cracks in the surface ice.
>
> Although scientists classify such a process as volcanism, Dr. Miner said it could better be described as a "slow-flow volcanic activity." A somewhat comparable process, he said, seemed to have shaped some of the surface features of Ariel, one of the moons of Uranus.
>
> Dr. Soderblom said Triton's surface appeared to be geologically young or "millions to hundreds of millions of years old." The absence of many impact craters was the main evidence for the relatively recent resurfacing of the terrain with new ice.

The next example shows how paraphrase can be used more briefly, to present another writer's point of view as the basis for discussion. Again, the writer of this description of a conference on nuclear deterrence has reserved quotation to express the precise point of potential dispute:

> Scientists engaged in research on the effects of nuclear war may be "wasting their time" studying a phenomenon that is far less dangerous than the natural explosions that have periodically produced widespread extinctions of plant and animal life in the past, a University of Chicago scientist said last week. Joseph V. Smith, a professor of geophysical sciences, told a conference on nuclear deterrence here that such natural catastrophes as exploding volcanoes, violent earthquakes, and collisions with comets or asteroids could produce more immediate and destructive explosions than any nuclear war.

Using Paraphrase as Preparation for Reading and Writing Essays

Paraphrase is sometimes undertaken as an end in itself to improve your understanding of a complex passage. When you grasp an essay at first reading, when its ideas are clearly stated in familiar terms, then you can be satisfied with annotating it or writing a brief summary. But when you find an essay hard to understand, writing down each sentence in your own words forces you to stop and make sense of what you have read, helping you work out ideas that may at first seem beyond your comprehension.

When you take notes for an essay based on one or more sources, you should mostly paraphrase. Quote only when recording phrases or sentences that clearly merit quotation. All quotable phrases and sentences should be transcribed accurately in your notes, with quotation marks separating the paraphrase from the quotation.

Writing a Paraphrase

In a good paraphrase, the sentences and the vocabulary do not duplicate those of the original. *You cannot merely substitute synonyms for key words and leave the sentences otherwise unchanged; that is plagiarism in spirit, if not in fact.* Word-for-word substitution won't demonstrate that you have understood the ideas.

The level of abstraction within your paraphrase should resemble that of the original: it should be neither more general nor more specific. If you do not understand a sentence, do not try to guess or cover it up with a vague phrase that slides over the idea. Instead:

- Look up difficult words.
- Think of what they mean and how they are used together.

- Consider how the sentences are formed and how they fit into the context of the entire paragraph.
- Then, to test your understanding, write down your version of the original.

Remember that a good paraphrase makes sense by itself; it is coherent and readable, without requiring reference to the original essay.

Guidelines for a Successful Paraphrase

- A paraphrase must be accurate.
- A paraphrase must be complete.
- A paraphrase must be written in your own voice.
- A paraphrase must make sense by itself.

Writing a Paraphrase: *The Prince*

Here, side by side with the original, is a free paraphrase of an excerpt from Niccolo Machiavelli's *The Prince*. This passage exemplifies the kind of text—very famous, very difficult—that really benefits from a comprehensive paraphrase. *The Prince* was written in 1513. This version of the original text (on the left), as translated from the Italian by Tim Parks, was published in 2009.

Source: Machiavelli

So, a leader doesn't have to possess all the virtuous qualities I've mentioned, but it's absolutely imperative that he seem to possess them. I'll go so far as to say this: if he had those qualities and observed them all the time, he'd be putting himself at risk. It's seeming to be virtuous that helps; as, for example, seeming to be compassionate, loyal, humane, honest and religious. And you can even be those things, so long as you're always mentally prepared to change as soon as your interests are threatened. What you have to understand is that a ruler, especially a ruler new to power,

Paraphrase

It is more important for a ruler to give the impression of goodness than to be good. In fact, real goodness can be a liability, but the pretense is always very effective. It is all very well to be virtuous, but it is vital to be able to shift in the other direction whenever circumstances require it.

After all, rulers, especially recently elevated ones, have a duty to perform which may absolutely require them to act against the dictates of faith and compassion and kindness.

One must act as circumstances require and, while it's good to be

can't always behave in ways that would make people think a man good, because to stay in power he's frequently obliged to act against loyalty, against charity, against humanity and against religion. What matters is that he has the sort of character that can change tack as luck and circumstances demand, and, as I've already said, stick to the good if he can but know how to be bad when the occasion demands.

So a ruler must be extremely careful not to say anything that doesn't appear to be inspired by the five virtues listed above; he must seem and sound wholly compassionate, wholly loyal, wholly humane, wholly honest and wholly religious.... Everyone sees what you seem to be, few have experience of who you really are, and those few won't have the courage to stand up to majority opinion underwritten by the authority of state. When they're weighing up what someone has achieved — and this is particularly true with rulers, who can't be held to account — people look at the end result. So if a leader does what it takes to win power and keep it, his methods will always be reckoned honorable and widely praised. The crowd is won over by appearances and final results. And the world is all crowd: the dissenting few find no space so long as the majority have any grounds at all for their opinions.

virtuous if you can, it's better to be bad if you must.

In public, however, the ruler should appear to be entirely virtuous, and if his pretense is successful with the majority of people, then those who do see through the act will be outnumbered and impotent, especially since the ruler has the authority of government on his side.

In the case of rulers, even more than for most men, the end justifies the means. If the ruler is able to assume power and administer it successfully, his actions will always be judged proper and satisfactory; for the common people will accept the pretense of virtue and the reality of success, and the astute will find no one is listening to their warnings.

Paraphrase and Summary

To clarify the difference between paraphrase and summary, here is a paragraph that *summarizes* the excerpt from *The Prince*.

According to Machiavelli, perpetuating power is a more important goal for a ruler than achieving personal goodness or integrity. Although he should act virtuously if he can, and always appear to do so, it is more important for him to adapt quickly to changing circumstances. The masses will be so swayed by his pretended virtue and by his success that any opposition will be ineffective. The wise ruler's maxim is that the end justifies the means.

Summary Versus Paraphrase

Here, again, are the guidelines for writing a brief summary, applying them to *The Prince*:

1. *A summary is comprehensive.* Like the paraphrase, the summary of *The Prince* says more than "the end justifies the means." While that is probably the most important idea in the passage, it does not by itself convey Machiavelli's full meaning. For one thing, it contains no reference at all to princes and how they should rule—and that, after all, is Machiavelli's subject.

2. *A summary is concise.* The summary should say exactly as much as you need—and no more. The summary of *The Prince* is considerably shorter than the paraphrase.

3. *A summary is coherent.* The summary links together the passage's most important points in a unified paragraph that makes sense on its own. The ideas need not be presented in the same sequence as that of the original passage, as they are in the paraphrase.

4. *A summary is independent.* What is most striking about the summary, compared with the paraphrase, is the writer's attitude toward the original text. While the paraphraser has to follow closely the sequence of Machiavelli's ideas and point of view, the summarizer does not. Characteristically, Machiavelli's name is cited in the summary, calling attention to the fact that it presents another person's ideas.

You might use either summary or paraphrase to refer to this passage in an essay. Which you would choose to use depends on your topic, on the way you are developing your essay, and on the extent to which you wish to discuss Machiavelli:

- In an essay citing Machiavelli as only one among many political theorists, you might use the four-sentence summary; then you might briefly comment on Machiavelli's ideas before going on to summarize (and perhaps compare them with) another writer's theories.

In an essay about a contemporary politician, you might analyze the way in which your subject does or does not carry out Machiavelli's strategies; then you probably would want to familiarize your readers with *The Prince* in some detail through paraphrase. You might include the full paraphrase, interspersed, perhaps, with an analysis of your present-day "prince."

Comparing Paraphrase and Summary

Paraphrase

- Reports your understanding to your reader
- Records a relatively short passage
- Records every point in the passage
- Records these points in their original order
- Includes no interpretation

Summary

- Reports your understanding to your reader
- Records a passage of any length
- Selects and condenses, recording only the main ideas
- Changes the order of ideas when necessary
- Explains and (if the writer wishes) interprets

Writing an Accurate Paraphrase: "Divorce and the Family in America"

The basic purpose of paraphrase is to present a source's ideas as they appear in the original text. When paraphrase fails to convey the substance of the source, there are four possible explanations:

1. *Misreading*: The writer genuinely misunderstood the text.
2. *Projecting*: The writer projected his or her own ideas into the text.
3. *Guessing*: The writer had a spark of understanding and constructed a paraphrase from that spark, but ignored too much of the original text.
4. *Summarizing*: The writer presents only a few of the main ideas, omitting necessary material.

Read this excerpt from Christopher Lasch's "Divorce and the Family in America," which analyzes the changing role of the child in family life. Then examine each of the three paraphrases that follow, deciding whether it conveys

Lasch's principal ideas and, if not, why it has gone astray. Compare your reactions with the analysis that follows each paraphrase.

Source: Christopher Lasch

The family by its very nature is a means of raising children, but this fact should not blind us to the important change that occurred when child-rearing ceased to be simply one of many activities and became the central concern — one is tempted to say the central obsession — of family life. This development had to wait for the recognition of the child as a distinctive kind of person, more impressionable and hence more vulnerable than adults, to be treated in a special manner befitting his peculiar requirements. Again, we take these things for granted and find it hard to imagine anything else. Earlier, children had been clothed, fed, spoken to, and educated as little adults; more specifically, as servants, the difference between childhood and servitude having been remarkably obscure throughout much of Western history....It was only in the seventeenth century in certain classes that childhood came to be seen as a special category of experience. When that happened, people recognized the enormous formative influence of family life, and the family became above all an agency for building character, for consciously and deliberately forming the child from birth to adulthood.

from "Divorce and the Family in America," *Atlantic*

Paraphrase A: Guessing and Projecting

The average family wants to raise children with a good education and to encourage, for example, the ability to read and write well. They must be taught to practice and learn on their own. Children can be treated well without being pampered. They must be treated as adults as they get older and experience more of life. A parent must build character and the feeling of independence in a child. No longer should children be treated as kids or servants, for that can cause conflict in a family relationship.

This paraphrase has very little in common with the original excerpt. True, it is about child rearing, but the writer chooses to give advice to parents, rather than present the contrast between early and modern attitudes toward children, as Lasch does. Since the only clear connection between Lasch's text and this paragraph is the reference to servants, the writer was probably confused by the passage, and (instead of slowing down the process and paraphrasing it sentence by sentence) guessed — mistakenly — at its meaning. There is also some projection of the writer's ideas about family life. Notice how assertive the tone is; the writer seems to be admonishing parents rather than presenting Lasch's detached analysis.

Paraphrase B: Guessing and Projecting

When two people get married, they usually produce a child. They get married because they want a family. Raising a family is now different from the way it used to be. The child is looked upon as a human being, with feelings and thoughts of his own. Centuries ago, children were treated like robots, little more than hired help. Now, children are seen as people who need a strong, dependable family background to grow into persons of good character. Parents are needed to get children ready to be the adults of tomorrow.

Although it comes closer to conveying the sense of Lasch's paragraph, this paraphrase also includes guessing (beginning) and projecting (end). The middle sentences do present Lasch's basic point, but the beginning and the end move so far away from the main ideas that the paraphrase as a whole does not bear much resemblance to the original text. It also includes an exaggeration: are servants "robots"?

Paraphrase C: Incomplete Paraphrase

Though the family has always been an important institution, its child-rearing function has only in recent centuries become its most important activity. This change has resulted from the relatively new idea that children have a special, unique personality. In the past, there was little difference seen between childhood and adulthood. But today people realize the importance of family life, especially the family unit as a means of molding the personalities of children from childhood to adulthood.

While this paraphrase is certainly the most accurate of the three, it is too brief to be a complete paraphrase. In fact, the writer seems to be summarizing, not paraphrasing. Lasch's main idea is there, but the following points are missing:

- There is a tremendous difference between pre-seventeenth-century and twenty-first-century perceptions of childhood.
- Before the seventeenth century, it was difficult to distinguish between the status and treatment of children and that of servants.
- Child rearing has now become of overriding ("obsessive") importance to the family.
- Children are different from adults in that they are less hardened and less experienced.

The author of Paraphrase C has done a thorough job of the beginning and the end of Lasch's passage, and evidently left the middle to take care of itself. But a paraphrase cannot be considered a reliable "translation" of the original text unless all the supporting ideas are given appropriate emphasis. The second omission is the most serious criticism.

Paraphrase D: Comprehensive Paraphrase

Though the family has always been the institution responsible for bringing up children, only in recent times has its child-raising function become the family's overriding purpose and its reason for being. This striking shift to the child-centered family has resulted from the gradual realization that children have a special, unique personality, easy to influence and easy to hurt, and that they must be treated accordingly. Special treatment for children is the norm in our time; but hundreds of years ago, people saw little or no difference between childhood and adulthood, and, in fact, the child's role in the family resembled that of a servant. It was not until the seventeenth century that people began to regard childhood as a distinctive stage of growth. That recognition led them to understand what a powerful influence the family environment must have on the child and to define "family" as the chief instrument for molding the child's personality and moral attitudes.

EXERCISE 15: Identifying a Good Paraphrase

A. Read the excerpt from *Crying* by Tom Lutz, twice. Look up any unfamiliar vocabulary. Then read the three paraphrases that follow.

B. Examine each paraphrase and decide whether it conforms to the guidelines for paraphrasing.

C. Ask yourself whether the paraphrase contains any point that is not in the original excerpt and whether the key points of the original are *all* clearly presented in the paraphrase. Does the writer understand the text?

[Today], to be called a "sensitive male" is in many contexts a compliment. Crying by men can now be interpreted as strength rather than weakness. Crying by women can be seen as instability, rather than the moral responsiveness it implied a century ago. In the late 1960s, the idea that women were more "emotional" and men more "rational" came under explicit attack as sexist ideology, as some argued that identifying women with emotionalism was necessarily demeaning and debilitating in a culture that prized rationality. But at the same time, an opposite argument was afloat—the idea that women's emotionalism constitutes a kind of moral superiority: cold rationality promulgated war and oppression, while an emotional approach to life encouraged empathy and harmony. The "patriarchal tradition" had seen emotion as a kind of degraded thinking, a kind of polluted cognition, and some feminists turned this argument on its head, claiming instead that emotion was the full human response, of which rational thought was only a part. To insist on rationality, according to this way of thinking, was to limit oneself to a fraction of one's equipment for understanding oneself and others.

In this context, two complimentary [sic] arguments about crying gained currency. Women had been socialized into crying instead of expressing anger, and men, socialized into a fear of tears, tended to express anger when they should be crying. Women needed to stop crying and get angry, and men needed to stop being angry and start crying. That these two arguments might be at loggerheads did not seem to bother anyone. Never before had there been such a clamor for change in people's basic emotional makeup. The biological and social sciences were called on to establish both the nature of gender difference and its cultural contingency, and thus the malleability of those differences.

TOM LUTZ, from *Crying*

Paraphrase 1

It's in women's nature to cry and in men's nature to hold back their tears. Women have always been emotional creatures in a world of reason. But that concept is no longer popular. Some feminists have argued that emotionalism is better than reason and that women have wrongly been regarded as inferior to men. But this claim disregards the value of the rational mind. Society needs someone to take charge in times of war and other crises.

Some say that the world might be better off if women were more angry and men cried more. But this argument doesn't make sense, nor does trying to change the basic differences between the sexes. Even science doesn't fully understand how the differences between the sexes came about, and whether it is possible or desirable to change the balance.

Paraphrase 2

Throughout history, men and women have had separate roles and have dealt with their feelings differently. Men were stoic, women were emotional, and women were seen as the lesser sex, indulging their feelings rather than engaging in rational thought. With the rise of feminism, there has been more emphasis on the importance of empathy and pressure to reverse the traditional roles, to make women tougher and men more sensitive.

Whether these role reversals would be more beneficial to society isn't clear. Nor is it clear whether it's even possible to make men more like women and women more like men.

Paraphrase 3

These days, it's acceptable for men to cry; far from compromising their masculinity, their ability to shed tears can be regarded as an asset.

In contrast, rather than demonstrating their capacity for empathy, as it used to, crying in women seems now less desirable, suggesting an erratic tendency to give way to their moods. For several decades, the traditional labels—men are stoic and cerebral, women are full of feeling—have begun to lose their currency because they seem so sexist. On the one hand, since our society has historically been controlled by men and has given the highest value to rational behavior, women's supposed tendency to act on their feelings, using only a modified form of logic, has turned them into second-class citizens. But, now, women's capacity for empathic understanding has begun to be valued as more completely human and as healthier for society than men's rationalism.

Complex social attitudes towards crying at the beginning of the 21st century have stemmed from these changing values and changing beliefs about the two sexes. In the past, it was in society's interest to encourage women to channel their more violent emotions into tears. And, similarly, the "manly" man was taught to suppress his tears and express his rage. Now, there has been pressure to reverse these tendencies, even though they would still end up diametrically opposed to each other. Society has been using science to question what it is to be a man or a woman, as well as to explore the usefulness of the original stereotypes and the potential for them to change.

Paraphrasing a Difficult Text

Since translating another writer's words into your own can be difficult, a paraphrase is often written in two stages.

1. In your first version, you work out a *word-for-word* paraphrase, staying close to the sentence structure of the original, as if you are writing a translation.
2. In your second version, you work from your word-for-word paraphrase, reconstructing and rephrasing the sentences to make them more natural and more characteristic of your own writing style.

Writing a paraphrase that is faithful to the original text is impossible if you are uncertain of the meaning of any of the words. To paraphrase a difficult passage:

- Use a dictionary, especially if the passage contains unfamiliar or archaic language.
- Write down a few possible synonyms for each difficult word, making sure that you understand the connotations of each synonym.
- Choose the substitute that best fits the context of the text.

Too often, the writer of a paraphrase forgets that there *is* a choice and quickly substitutes the first synonym in the dictionary. Even when appropriate synonyms have been carefully chosen, the first version of a paraphrase can look peculiar and sound dreadful. While the old sentence structure has been retained, the key words have been yanked out and new ones plugged in.

Writing a Paraphrase: "Of Marriage and Single Life"

To illustrate the pitfalls of this process, here is a short excerpt from Francis Bacon's essay "Of Marriage and Single Life," written around 1600. Some of the phrasing and word combinations are archaic and may sound unnatural, but nothing in the passage is too difficult for modern understanding *if* the sentences are read slowly and carefully.

> He that hath wife and children hath given hostages to fortune; for they are impediments to great enterprises, either of virtue or mischief. Certainly, the best works and of greatest merit for the public have proceeded from the unmarried or childless men: which both in affection and means have endowed the public.

Here is the passage's main idea: *unmarried men, without the burden of a family, can afford to contribute to the public good.* But by now you must realize that such a brief summary is not the same as a paraphrase, for it does not fully present Bacon's reasoning.

Paraphrase A: Poor Word Choice

He who has a wife and children has *bestowed prisoners to riches*; for they are *defects* in huge *business organizations* either for *morality* or *damage.*

Paraphrase B: Better Word Choice

He who has a wife and children has *given* a *pledge* to *destiny*; for they are *hindrances* to large *endeavor*, either for *good* or for *ill.*

Neither sentence is easy to understand; but the second has potential, while the first makes no sense. Yet, in *both* cases, the underlined words are synonyms for the original vocabulary. In Paraphrase A the words do not fit Bacon's context; in Paraphrase B they do.

For example, it is misleading to choose "business organizations" as a synonym for "enterprises," since the passage doesn't actually concern business but refers to any sort of undertaking requiring freedom from responsibility. "Impediment" can mean either "defect" (as in speech impediment) or "hindrance" (as in impediment to learning); but—again, given the context—it is the second meaning that Bacon has in mind.

A phrase like *hostages to fortune* offers special difficulty, since it is a powerful image expressing a highly abstract idea. No paraphraser can improve on the original wording or even find an equivalent phrase. What is Bacon trying to express? A bargain made with life—the renunciation of future independence in exchange for a family. Wife and children become a kind of pledge ("hostages") to ensure one's future social conformity. The aptness and singularity of Bacon's original phrase are measured by the difficulty of paraphrasing three words in less than two sentences!

Correct though the synonyms may be, the passage from Bacon cannot be left as it is in Paraphrase B, for no reader could readily understand this stilted, artificial sentence. It is necessary to rephrase the paraphrase, ensuring that the meaning of the words is retained, but making the sentence sound more natural. The first attempt at "freeing up" the paraphrase stays as close as possible to the literal version, leaving everything in the same sequence but using a more modern idiom:

Paraphrase C: Unclear

Married men with children are hindered from embarking on any important undertaking, good or bad. Indeed, unmarried and childless men are the ones who have done the most for society and have dedicated their love and their money to the public good.

The second sentence (which is simpler to paraphrase than the first) has been inverted here, but the paraphrase is still a point-by-point recapitulation of Bacon. Paraphrase C is acceptable, but can be improved, both to clarify Bacon's meaning and to introduce a more personal voice. What exactly *are* these unmarried men dedicating to the public good? "Affection and means." And what is the modern equivalent of means? money? effort? time? energy?

Paraphrase D: Improved

A man with a family has obligations that prevent him from devoting himself to any activity that pleases him. On the other hand, a single man or a man without children has a greater opportunity to be a philanthropist. That's why most great contributions of energy and resources to the good of society are made by single men.

The writer of Paraphrase D has not supplied a synonym for "affection," which may be too weak a motivation for the philanthropist as he is described here.

Paraphrase E: Successful

The responsibility of a wife and children discourages a man from taking risks with his money, time, and energy. The greatest social benefactors have been men who have adopted the public as their family.

The second sentence here is the only one of the five versions that approaches Bacon's economy of style. "Adopted the public" is not quite the same as "endowed the public" with one's "affection and means"; but nevertheless, this paraphrase is successful because it speaks for itself. It has a life and an importance of its own, independent of Bacon's original passage, yet it makes the same point that Bacon does.

Guidelines for Paraphrasing a Difficult Passage

1. Look up in a dictionary the meanings of all the words of which you are uncertain. Pay special attention to the difficult words, considering the context of the whole passage.
2. Write a paraphrase by substituting appropriate synonyms within the original sentence structure.
3. Revise your first paraphrase, keeping roughly to the same length and number of sentences as the original but using your own sentence style and phrasing throughout. You may prefer to put the original passage aside at this point and work entirely from your own version.
4. Read your final paraphrase aloud to make sure that it makes sense.

EXERCISE 16: Paraphrasing a Difficult Text

Paraphrase one of the following paragraphs, using the guidelines in the box above. (Your instructor may assign a specific paragraph for the entire class to paraphrase; you may be asked to work in a group with your classmates.)

1. We all know that there are gradations of intimacy and that there is a friendship deeper than a Facebook friend. The lucky ones among us have people with whom we are genuinely close: those who will help us in an emergency, whom we could call at midnight with a problem, with whom we feel mutual obligations, who provide us with social identity and place, and without whom our lives would be tangibly compromised. Facebook and the like promote intimacy lite. Lite intimacies in social media create a background din of disclosure, confession, closeness, and familiarity. It isn't inherently fake or objectionable.… But there's a danger that the lite intimacies of the sentimental culture might deplete the resources of our true intimacies. If the intimate building blocks that once belonged mostly to a domestic partner

or family—the sharing of a million little details about our moods, and what we ate for breakfast, and our daily rituals and secret gripes—now belong to everyone on Facebook in the world of lite intimacy, then how much deeper do we need to go to find the everyday material out of which to recognize, solidify, and build that deeper intimacy? Do we have to scream emotions louder to be heard over the cacophony of the lite intimacy? A mild hypothesis for the new social life of our age: the easier it is to be close but not intimate in public, the easier it is to be close but not intimate in private.

PAMELA HAAG, from "Death by Treacle,"
The American Scholar

2. Conversation with strangers invariably brings awkward moments and slight but annoying interpersonal risks. Moving through the metropolis, we are overwhelmed by the number of strangers passing close to us. Sociologist Robin Dunbar has suggested that we are really only comfortable with 150 (or so) human contacts, but in the modern metropolis we encounter five times that number while leaving our office buildings to visit the local roach coach. At home we are husbands and wives, moms and dads. At the office we are colleagues, experts, working stiffs, bosses, or lackeys. But in between these geographically separate roles, there is little to provide the interpersonal context on which the modern personality depends. With nothing to shape ourselves against, introversion is the most familiar and prudent course to safeguard psychic energy. We wrap invisible technological shells around us like hamster balls and become "i-Pods" as we move from site to site in our native urban landscape. The sense of dissatisfaction we sometimes experience in our urban environment is often inexplicable since we don't really have a clear picture of the kind of life we were designed for or why we are missing it. Meanwhile, technological distractions have become our most accessible means of providing interpersonal security as we hurry through the public spaces where we are least defined and most vulnerable.

GILES SLADE, from *The Big Disconnect:*
The Story of Technology and Loneliness

3. It is somewhat ironic to note that grading *systems* evolved in part because of [problems in evaluating performance]. In situations where reward and recognition often depended more on who you knew than on what you knew, and lineage was more important than ability, the cause of justice seemed to demand a method whereby the individual could demonstrate specific abilities on the basis of objective criteria. This led to the establishment of specific standards and public criteria as ways of reducing

prejudicial treatment and, in cases where appropriate standards could not be specified in advance, to the normal curve system of establishing levels on the basis of group performance. The imperfect achievement of the goals of such systems in no way negates the importance of the underlying purposes.

WAYNE MOELLENBERG, from "To Grade or Not to Grade — Is That the Question?"

4. Our country has embarked on an unparalleled experiment, inspired by ideals of self-command and cultivated humanity. Unlike all other nations, we ask a higher education to contribute a general preparation for citizenship, not just a specialized preparation for a career. To a greater degree than all other nations, we have tried to extend the benefits of this education to all citizens whatever their class, race, sex, ethnicity, or religion. We hope to draw citizens toward one another by complex mutual understanding and individual self-scrutiny, building a democratic culture that is truly deliberative and reflective, rather than simply the collision of unexamined preferences. And we hope in this way to justify and perpetuate our nation's claim to be a valuable member of a world community of nations that must increasingly learn how to understand, respect, and communicate, if our common human problems are to be constructively addressed.

MARTHA C. NUSSBAUM, from *Cultivating Humanity: A Classical Defense of Reform in Liberal Education*

5. In humorously attributing the design to "Mr. Per[i]wig" and identifying "Miss Heel" as the printmaker, the accompanying text cites two of the elements used to form this figure. To modern eyes the design looks surreal, but it is actually a fashionable, erotic variant of a seventeenth-century print type. Known as Nobody prints, these featured figures composed only of legs and heads, with nothing in between, and the resulting verbal-visual pun was aimed critically at a specified target. Here, the elegant female "no-body" is composed of a huge, elaborately dressed wig sitting atop a bare derriere, with her lower extremities clad in white silk stockings, red garters, and high-heeled pumps. Like other fashion satires that mocked the latest trends, this print took aim at the enormous hairdos and wigs that women favored in Britain and France in the decades before the French Revolution. The title and the partial nudity frankly acknowledge the sexual appeal of the fashion while simultaneously suggesting that those who followed it lacked sense, since the figure not only has no body but also is literally brainless.

CONSTANCE MCPHEE AND NADINE ORENSTEIN, from *Infinite Jest: Caricatures and Satire from Leornado to Levine*

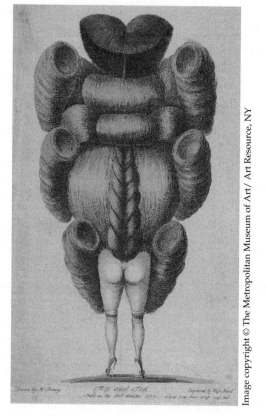

Figure 4-1 Anonymous, "Top and Tail," 1777

Using Paraphrase with Quotation and Summary

The paraphrased ideas of other writers should never dominate your essay, but should always be subordinate to *your* ideas.

> *Most academic writers rely on a combination of quotation, paraphrase, and summary to present their sources and to support their theses.*

To illustrate the way in which these three techniques of presentation can be successfully combined, here is an extract from an article by Conor Cruise O'Brien that depends on a careful mixture of paraphrase, summary, and quotation. In "Violence—And Two Schools of Thought," O'Brien gives an account of a medical conference concerned with the origins of violence. Specifically, he undertakes to present and (at the end) comment on the ideas of two speakers at the conference.

from VIOLENCE — AND TWO SCHOOLS OF THOUGHT
Conor Cruise O'Brien

summary

The opening speakers were fairly representative of the main schools of thought which almost always declare themselves when violence is discussed. The first school sees a propensity to aggression as biological but capable of being socially conditioned into patterns of acceptable behavior. The second sees it as essentially created by social conditions and therefore capable of being removed by benign social change.

quotation

The first speaker held that violence was "a bio-social phenomenon." He rejected the notion that human beings were blank paper "on which the environment can write whatever it likes." He described how a puppy could be conditioned to choose a dog food it did not like and to reject one it did like. This

paraphrase

was the creation of conscience in the puppy. It was done by mild punishment. If human beings were acting more aggressively and anti-socially, despite the advent of better social conditions and better housing, this might be because permissiveness, in school and home, had checked the process of social conditioning, and therefore of conscience-building. He favored the reinstatement of conscience-building, through the use of mild punishment and token re-

quotation

wards. "We cannot eliminate violence," he said, "but we can do a great deal to reduce it."

summary

The second speaker thought that violence was the result of stress; in almost all the examples he cited it was stress from overcrowding. The

paraphrase/ quotation

behavior of apes and monkeys in zoos was "totally different" from the way they behaved in "the completely relaxed conditions in the wild." In crowded zoos the most aggressive males became leaders and a general reign of terror

paraphrase/ quotation

set in; in the relaxed wild, on the other hand, the least aggressive males ruled benevolently. Space was all: "If we could eliminate population pressures, violence would vanish."

summary

The student [reacting to the argument of the two speakers] preferred the second speaker. He [the second speaker] spoke with ebullient confidence, fast but clear, and at one point ran across the vast platform, in a lively imitation of the behavior of a charging ape. Also, his message was simple and hopeful. Speaker one, in contrast, looked sad, and his message sounded faintly sinister.

author's comment

Such impressions, rather than the weight of argument, determine the reception of papers read in such circumstances.

summary/ paraphrase

Nonetheless, a student queried speaker two's "relaxed wild." He seemed to recall a case in which a troop of chimpanzees had completely wiped out another troop. The speaker was glad the student had raised that question because it proved the point. You see, where that had occurred, there had been an

1

2

3

4

5

quotation

*author's
comment*

overcrowding in the jungle, just as happens in zoos, and this was a response to overcrowding. Conditions in the wild, it seems, are not always "completely relaxed." And when they attain that attributed condition — through the absence of overcrowding — this surely has to be due to the "natural controls," including the predators, whose attentions can hardly be all that relaxing, or, indeed, all that demonstrative of the validity of the proposition that violence is not a part of nature. Speaker two did not allude to predators. Nonetheless, they are still around, on two legs as well as on four.

Although we do not have the texts of the original papers given at the conference to compare with O'Brien's description, this article seems to present a clear account of a complex discussion. In the first paragraph, O'Brien uses brief summaries to help us distinguish between the two speakers; next, he provides us with two separate, noncommittal descriptions of the two main points of view.

The balance among quotation, paraphrase, and summary works very effectively. O'Brien quotes for two reasons: *aptness of expression* and *the desire to distance himself from the statement*. For example, he chooses to quote the *vivid image* of the blank paper "on which the environment can write whatever it likes." And he also selects points for quotation that he regards as *open to dispute* — "totally different"; "completely relaxed"; "violence would vanish." Such strong statements are often quoted so that writers won't be accused of either toning down or exaggerating the meaning in their paraphrases.

In the last two paragraphs, it is not always easy to determine where O'Brien's paraphrase of the speakers' ideas ends and his own opinions begin. In Paragraph 4, his description of the student's reactions to the two speakers appears objective. At the end of the paragraph, however, we learn that O'Brien is scornful of the criteria that the student is using to evaluate these ideas. But at first we cannot be sure whether O'Brien is describing the *student's observation* or giving *his own account* of the speaker's platform maneuvers. It would be clearer to us if the sentence began: "According to the responding student, the second speaker spoke with ebullient confidence...." Similarly, the last sentence of Paragraph 4 is undoubtedly O'Brien's opinion, yet there is nothing to indicate the transition from the student to O'Brien as the source of commentary.

This confusion of point of view is especially deceptive in Paragraph 5 as O'Brien moves from his paraphrased and neutral account of the dialogue between student and speaker to his own opinion that certain predators influence behavior in civilization as well as in the wild. It takes two readings to notice the point — can you find it? — at which O'Brien has stopped paraphrasing and begins to speak in his own voice. Such confusions could have been clarified by inserting citations — the name of the source or appropriate pronoun — in the appropriate places.

Reasons to Use Quotation

- You can find no words to convey the economy and aptness of phrasing of the original text.
- A paraphrase might alter the statement's meaning.
- A paraphrase would not clearly distinguish between your views and the author's.

EXERCISE 17: Distinguishing among Quotation, Paraphrase, Summary, and Commentary

A.   Read "Maybe Money Does Buy Happiness After All," by David Leonhardt, twice.

B.   In the margin, indicate where the author uses quotation (Q), paraphrase (P), summary (S), and commentary (C). As necessary, distinguish between summary of the source and summary of the topic or context.

C.   In class discussion, be prepared to evaluate the use of quotation, paraphrase, and summary, and to indicate those places in the article where, in your opinion, one of the techniques is inappropriately or unnecessarily used, where the transition from one technique to the other is not clearly identified, or where the source is not clearly cited.

MAYBE MONEY DOES BUY HAPPINESS AFTER ALL

David Leonhardt

For over a decade, David Leonhardt's columns about economics have appeared in the New York Times, *where this article was first published. Leonhardt has also written for* Business Week *and the* Washington Post.

In the aftermath of World War II, the Japanese economy went through one of the greatest booms the world has ever known. From 1950 to 1970, the economy's output per person grew more than sevenfold. Japan, in just a few decades, remade itself from a war-torn country into one of the richest nations on earth. Yet, strangely, Japanese citizens didn't seem to become any more satisfied with their lives. According to one poll, the percentage of people who gave the most positive possible answer about their life satisfaction actually fell from the late 1950s to the early '70s. They were richer but apparently no happier.   1

This contrast became the most famous example of a theory known as the Easterlin paradox. In 1974, Richard Easterlin, then an economist at the   2

University of Pennsylvania, published a study in which he argued that economic growth didn't necessarily lead to more satisfaction. People in poor countries, not surprisingly, did become happier once they could afford basic necessities. But beyond that, further gains simply seemed to reset the bar. To put it in today's terms, owning an iPod doesn't make you happier, because you then want an iPod Touch. Relative income — how much you make compared with others around you — mattered far more than absolute income, Mr. Easterlin wrote.

The paradox quickly became a social science classic, cited in academic journals and the popular media. It tapped into a near-spiritual human instinct to believe that money can't buy happiness. As a 2006 headline in the *Financial Times* said, "The Hippies Were Right All Along About Happiness."

But now the Easterlin paradox is under attack. Last week, at the Brookings Institution in Washington, two young economists — from the University of Pennsylvania, as it happens — presented a rebuttal of the paradox. Their paper has quickly captured the attention of top economists around the world. It has also led to a spirited response from Mr. Easterlin. In the paper, Betsey Stevenson and Justin Wolfers argued that money indeed tends to bring happiness, even if it doesn't guarantee it. They point out that in the 34 years since Mr. Easterlin published his paper, an explosion of public opinion surveys has allowed for a better look at the question. "The central message," Ms. Stevenson said, "is that income does matter."

Gallup polls done around the world clearly [show] that life satisfaction is highest in the richest countries. The residents of these countries seem to understand that they have it pretty good, whether or not they own an iPod Touch. If anything, Ms. Stevenson and Mr. Wolfers say, absolute income seems to matter more than relative income. In the United States, about 90 percent of people in households making at least $250,000 a year called themselves "very happy" in a recent Gallup poll. In households with income below $30,000, only 42 percent of people gave that answer. But the international polling data suggests that the under-$30,000 crowd might not be happier if they lived in a poorer country.

Even the Japanese anomaly isn't quite what it first seems to be. Ms. Stevenson and Mr. Wolfers dug into those old government surveys and discovered that the question had changed over the years. In the late 1950s and early '60s, the most positive answer the pollsters offered was, "Although I am not innumerably satisfied, I am generally satisfied with life now." (Can you imagine an American poll offering that option?) But in 1964, the most positive answer became simply, "Completely satisfied." It is no wonder, then, that the percentage of people giving this answer fell. When you look only at the years in which the question remained the same, the share of people calling themselves "satisfied" or "completely satisfied" did rise.

To put the new research into context, I called Daniel Kahneman, a Princeton psychologist who shared the 2002 Nobel Prize in economics. He has spent his

3

4

5

6

7

career skewering economists for their belief that money is everything and has himself written about the "aspiration treadmill" at the heart of the Easterlin paradox. Yet Mr. Kahneman said he found the Stevenson-Wolfers paper to be "quite compelling." He added, "There is just a vast amount of accumulating evidence that the Easterlin paradox may not exist."

I then called Mr. Easterlin, who's now at the University of Southern California and who had received a copy of the paper from Ms. Stevenson and Mr. Wolfers. He agreed that people in richer countries are more satisfied. But he's skeptical that their wealth is causing that satisfaction. The results could instead reflect cultural differences in how people respond to poll questions, he said. He would be more persuaded, he continued, if satisfaction had clearly risen in individual countries as they grew richer. In some, it has. But in others — notably the United States and China — it has not. "Everybody wants to show the Easterlin paradox doesn't hold up," he told me. "And I'm perfectly willing to believe it doesn't hold up. But I'd like to see an informed analysis that shows that." He said he liked Ms. Stevenson and Mr. Wolfers personally, but he thought they had put out "a very rough draft without sufficient evidence."   8

They, in turn, acknowledge that the data on individual countries over time is messy. But they note that satisfaction has risen in 8 of 10 European countries for which there is polling back to 1970. It has also risen in Japan. And a big reason it may not have risen in the United States is that the hourly pay of most workers has not grown much recently. "The time-series evidence is fragile," Mr. Wolfers said. "But it's more consistent with our story than his."   9

So where does all this leave us? Economic growth, by itself, certainly isn't enough to guarantee people's well-being — which is Mr. Easterlin's great contribution to economics. In this country, for instance, some big health care problems, like poor basic treatment of heart disease, don't stem from a lack of sufficient resources. Recent research has also found that some of the things that make people happiest — short commutes, time spent with friends — have little to do with higher incomes.   10

But it would be a mistake to take this argument too far. The fact remains that economic growth doesn't just make countries richer in superficially materialistic ways. Economic growth can also pay for investments in scientific research that lead to longer, healthier lives. It can allow trips to see relatives not seen in years or places never visited. When you're richer, you can decide to work less — and spend more time with your friends.   11

Affluence is a pretty good deal. Judging from [those poll results] the people of the world seem to agree. At a time when the American economy seems to have fallen into recession and most families' incomes have been stagnant for almost a decade, it's good to be reminded of why we should care.   12

Giving Credit to Your Paraphrased Sources

In academic writing the clear acknowledgment of the source is not merely a matter of courtesy or clarity; it is an assurance of the writer's honesty.

When you paraphrase another person's ideas, you must cite the author's name, as you do when you quote, or else risk being charged with plagiarism. Borrowing ideas is just as much theft as borrowing words.

You omit the quotation marks when you paraphrase, but you must not omit the citation. The name of the source should be smoothly integrated into your sentence, following the guidelines used for citation of quotations. The source's name need not appear at the beginning of the sentence, but it should signal the beginning of the paraphrase:

Not everyone enjoys working, but most people would agree with Jones's belief that work is an essential experience of life.

The writer of the essay is responsible for the declaration that "not everyone enjoys working" and that most people would agree with Jones's views; but the belief that "work is an essential experience of life" is attributed to Jones. Here, the citation is well and unobtrusively placed; there are no quotation marks, so presumably Jones used a different wording.

Citing Sources

- When you *quote*, there can never be any doubt about where the borrowed material begins and where it ends: the quotation marks provide a clear indication of the boundaries.
- When you *paraphrase*, although the citation of the author's name may signal the *beginning* of the source material, your reader may not be sure exactly where the paraphrase *ends*. There is no easy method of indicating the end of paraphrased material. (As you will see in Chapter 10, the author's name or a page number in parentheses works well if you are using MLA documentation.) You can signal the end of a paraphrase simply by starting a new paragraph. However, you may want to incorporate more than one person's ideas into a single paragraph. *When you present several points of view in succession, be careful to acknowledge the change of source by citing names.*

Writing a Paragraph That Incorporates Paraphrase and Quotation: *Jarhead*

Now, let's look at the writing process in reverse again. Instead of observing the finished product and analyzing how a writer has used several sources, you'll see exactly how one source can be used to support one paragraph of an essay.

The topic of the essay is *soldiers and the code of war*. The student writer is working with the following thesis: *Given the nature of modern warfare, soldiers find it difficult to think of themselves as heroes.* One relevant source is *Jarhead*, a memoir about Anthony Swofford's training as a Marine and his experiences during the first Gulf War. Here is an excerpt.

from JARHEAD

Anthony Swofford

As we drive in the tactical convoy toward the airfield, we occasionally pass a POW internment area, nothing more than a few-hundred-foot circle of concertina wire, and in the center a mass of surrendered men, constrained with plastic thumb cuffs. Marines walk the perimeter with M16s. We drive close enough to the wire so that I see the faces of the POWs, and the men look at us and smile. Occasionally an embarrassing scene of thanks unfolds as a detainee is processed, the detainee kneeling in front of his once enemy and now jailor, weeping and hugging the Marine's legs. I suspect the performances are equal parts genuine and dramatic, men genuinely happy at the prospect of not dying and smart enough to please their fierce and potentially deadly jailors with an act of supplication.

It's easier to surrender than to accept surrender. The men who surrender do so with blind faith in the good hearts and justice of the men and the system they surrender to. They are faithful and faith is somewhat easy. Those who accept the surrendering men must follow the rules of justice. This requires not faith, but labor and discipline.

I feel more compassion for the dead Iraqi soldiers I witnessed yesterday than I do for these men, alive and waving the propaganda pamphlets with vigor and a smile as they await processing. These live men were my enemy just before surrendering, while the dead men are quite simply dead. Moments before surrendering, these incarcerated men might have tried to kill me, so until very recently they were capable of receiving my bullets. The dead men have been incapable of killing me for days or weeks or at least hours and so I would not have shot them. When I'd considered my enemy in the past, I'd been able to imagine them as men similar to me, similarly caught in a trap of their own making, but now that I see these men breathing and within arm's reach, witness them smiling and supplicating and wanting to be my friend, *my friend*, even as I am on my way to kill their fellow soldiers, I no longer care for the men or their safety or the cessation of combat. The enemy are caught in an unfortunate catch-22, in that I care for them as men and fellow unfortunates as long as they are not within riflesight or they're busy being dead, but as soon as I see them living, I wish to turn upon them my years of training and suffering, and I want to perform some of the despicable acts I've learned over the prior few years, such as trigger-killing them from one thousand yards distant, or gouging their hearts with my sharp bayonet.

How do you write a paragraph that conveys Swofford's testimony about a soldier's life and links it to the proposed thesis of the essay? Here are four versions of a possible paragraph:

First Version: Plagiarized

acceptable summary

Soldiers are so caught up in the tension of battle and the fear of being killed that they can't suddenly feel compassion for the enemy when they are defeated and become prisoners. A soldier may feel more comfortable with a dead man than with a live prisoner of war. You can't kill the enemy one day and be expected to regard them as nice people the next day.

no mention of Swofford = plagiarism

This is a reasonable summary of the Swofford passage. Unfortunately, there is no mention of the source. The reader has no idea that Swofford's experience is being described, and the writer is moving very close to plagiarism.

Second Version: Plagiarized

no topic sentence

underlining indicates plagiarism

In *Jarhead*, Anthony Swofford tells us about the time he came to a prisoner of war camp during the Gulf War and sees <u>an embarrassing scene of thanks</u> as prisoners weep and clutch their captors' legs. Swofford concludes that the prisoners have an easier time than their jailors since <u>it's easier to surrender than to accept surrender.</u> He can't understand how they can want to be his friend when he's performed so many <u>despicable acts</u> and has killed so many of their fellow soldiers.

This version cites Swofford as the source but plagiarizes his words. The writer is not paraphrasing, but, rather, stringing together bits of Swofford's phrases. The paragraph also lacks a topic sentence that explains why Swofford is being cited.

Third Version: Acceptable

good presentation of Swofford; supports topic sentence

It's easy for soldiers fighting a brutal war to lose their sense of humanity. Anthony Swofford's *Jarhead* tells us about an incident that happened to him when he was a Marine fighting in the first Gulf War. He sees a group of prisoners trying to placate their captors, and that makes him examine

a quotation would make the experience more immediate

his own resentment at the fact that they are alive and happily trying to stay alive. Swofford can't bring himself to see them as human beings. After all, later that day he might have to kill men just like them in the enemy's army.

This is a good presentation of the source because it provides just enough material from Swofford to support the point of the topic sentence. But the writer could and should have used quotation to give some immediacy to Swofford's experience.

Fourth Version: Successful

topic sentence

good mixture of quotation and paraphrase

full documen-tation: author's name, work's title, page number

Soldiers are trained to kill routinely, and to do that efficiently they can't let themselves think of the enemy as people like themselves. In *Jarhead*, Anthony Swofford describes his disgust at an "embarrassing scene of thanks" at a prisoner of war camp during the first Gulf War. Feeling ambivalent, he wants to think of the enemy "as men similar to me," but finds it hard to endure the sight of the prisoners carrying on the business of life by trying to please their captors. The enemy dead don't cause as much moral conflict for him as the living enemy. Swofford's conclusion is that "it's easier to surrender than to accept surrender" (227). It takes a lot of effort and self-control for a soldier to kill one day and be expected to take care of the enemy the next day. Swofford's experience helps me to understand what happened in Abu Ghraib jail.

The writer makes a point in the topic sentence and then convincingly uses paraphrase and quotation to support that point. The citation to Swofford is clear, and the quoted material is appropriate. Equally important, the writer doesn't just recount Swofford's experience but makes comments that link the source to the writer's own purposes in writing the essay. Finally, notice that the writer *documents* the source not only by citing the author's name and the work but also by inserting after the second quotation the page number where the paraphrased and quoted material can be found. You'll learn about the formal documentation of sources in Chapter 10.

EXERCISE 18: Paraphrasing without Plagiarism

A. Read each paragraph twice. Then read the three brief paraphrases taken from student essays.

B. As you read the paraphrases, consider whether the structure of the phrases and sentences seems to be the student's work or the original author's and whether the choice of words seems *for the most part* to be the student's or the author's. At what point does the balance tip and the fair use of common language turn into plagiarism?

C.   Determine whether each paraphrase:

■ accurately conveys the author's meaning

■ distorts his or her meaning

■ plagiarizes his or her words in order to express the original meaning

Set 1

> To prepare…lamb in either the Neapolitan or Roman style is simple, but first the cook must deal with the question of squeamishness, for guests tend to react to baby lamb as if it were the family poodle. Surely it is not an act of kindness to kill an innocent lamb, but neither is it kind to kill the innocent pigs and cattle that supply the B.L.T.s and Big Macs that we thoughtlessly devour by the billion. Human beings are omnivores who in their various cultures — or under extreme conditions in any culture — will kill and eat almost anything, including one another.
>
> JASON EPSTEIN, from "The Science of the Lambs,"
> The *New York Times* magazine, 17 March 2002: 66.

Note that an acceptable paraphrase can reasonably include some language from the source: words that are basic or common or words that are essential to the meaning. For example, conveying Jason Epstein's meaning would be difficult without using the word "lamb." But what about "innocent lamb"?

Paraphrase 1

Jason Epstein observes that serving lamb at dinner can be difficult if the guests have scruples about eating meat. It's one thing to react with horror at slaughtering and eating a family pet or a wooly lamb, but Epstein wonders whether we have the same scruples about slaughtering the less attractive and endearing but no less innocent steers and pigs consumed daily in hamburgers and B.L.T.s. All human beings are capable of killing and eating other living creatures if their needs require it (66).

Paraphrase 2

According to Jason Epstein, squeamish guests can be a problem when they react to a dish of baby lamb as if they were being asked to eat the family poodle. Although killing an innocent lamb isn't an act of kindness, it's just as bad to kill the innocent cattle and pigs that we eat in B.L.T.s and Big Macs. We have to accept the fact that human beings are omnivores who will eat whatever their cultures require, including (under extreme conditions) each other (66).

Paraphrase 3

Jason Epstein thinks that guests who refuse to eat lamb create problems for the cook, but they simply don't want to be responsible for the death of an innocent animal. In Epstein's view, whether it's a baby lamb or a cow or a pig, slaughtering living creatures to provide food for our lunches and dinners is cruel and inhumane. It's unfortunate that our cultures encourage us to eat whatever we want to and that usually means living animals, even each other (66).

Set 2

Freudian readings of cannibal tales argue that such stories present the world from the child's point of view — hence the importance of oral satisfaction, pleasure and survival (eating or being eaten). In traditional psychoanalytic terms, stories of cannibalism are usually interpreted as a disfigured form of parental aggression or a projection of the child's own all-consuming greed.

MIKITA BROTTMAN, from "Celluloid Cannibals That Feed Our Darkest Fears," *Chronicle of Higher Education*, 2 March 2001: B15.

Deciding which of the source's words can be reasonably used becomes more difficult when you are writing about a discipline that has its own unique terms of reference. Brottman is using the language of psychology. Conveying the meaning of "oral satisfaction" or "projection" is a challenge, but you should try as much as possible to use your own words.

Paraphrase 1

Mikita Brottman notes that many cannibal tales are written from the child's point of view and emphasize oral satisfaction, pleasure, and the need to survive. From a Freudian point of view, such stories are interpreted as a distorted form of parental aggression or a projection of the child's greed (B15).

Paraphrase 2

According to Freudian theory, stories about cannibals tend to be told from a child's perspective and therefore emphasize the comforting reassurance that children receive from the act of eating combined with relief that they themselves are not serving as someone's meal. Underlying these stories of cannibalism is the child's fear that his parents will harm him or that he will harm himself and others by excessive eating (Brottman, B15).

Paraphrase 3

Brottman tells us that Freudians look at stories about cannibals as a child would. Children are happy when they eat and are fearful when they think someone might eat them. They worry that their parents will hurt them or that they will eat too much (B15).

Set 3

Binge drinking in college used to be associated primarily with males, but a 1997 study of 116 four-year colleges, conducted by researchers at Harvard University, found that 39 percent of women and 49 percent of men had binged in the two previous weeks....Now, several studies reported this year indicate a further increase in the percentage of college women drinking.

DEVON JERSILD, from "Alcohol in the Vulnerable Lives of College Women," *Chronicle of Higher Education*, 31 May 2002: B10.

When you are dealing with facts or statistics, you may have little choice but to use your source's wording. There may be few options for inventing your own phrasing. Still, the sentences in your paraphrase should follow your own structure, not your source's.

Paraphrase 1

A survey in 1997 showed that the number of women college students who engage in excessive drinking (39%) was almost as high as that of male students (49%), who are more traditionally associated with binge drinking. Recent surveys confirm this trend toward an excessive use of alcohol among college women (Jersild, B10).

Paraphrase 2

Although binge drinking in college used to be associated primarily with males, a 1997 Harvard study found that 39 percent of women and 49 percent of men had binged in the two previous weeks. More recent studies indicate that this trend is continuing.

Paraphrase 3

Jersild cites a Harvard study showing that more men than women engage in binge drinking (B10).

EXERCISE 19: Writing a Paragraph That Incorporates Paraphrase and Quotation

A. Read the following excerpt from *The Better Angels of Our Nature: Why Violence Has Declined*, by Steven Pinker, twice.

B. Assume that you're working on an essay about "Improvements in the Treatment of Animals for Research" or "Is Progress in Medical Research

Worth the Pain Suffered by Laboratory Animals?" (Or make up a comparable topic of your own.) Write a paragraph that supports one of these topics, and use Pinker as your source.

C. Remember to include appropriate and accurate citations of the author's name and, if your instructor requests it, provide the page number in parentheses. (This excerpt appeared on pages 454–456 of Pinker's book. Slashes indicate the page breaks.)

From THE BETTER ANGELS OF OUR
NATURE: WHY VIOLENCE HAS DECLINED
Steven Pinker

Holder of a prestigious professorship at Harvard, Steven Pinker is an experimental psychologist. His books include How the Mind Works, The Stuff of Thought, *and, most recently,* The Better Angels of Our Nature.

Let me tell you about the worst thing I have ever done. In 1975, as a twenty-year-old sophomore, I got a summer job as a research assistant in an animal behavior lab. One evening the professor gave me an assignment. Among the rats in the lab was a runt that could not participate in the ongoing studies. / So, he wanted to use it to try out a new experiment. The first step was to train the rat in what was called a temporal avoidance conditioning procedure. The floor of a Skinner box was hooked up to a shock generator, and a timer that would shock the animal every six seconds unless it pressed a lever, which would give it a ten-second reprieve. Rats catch on quickly and press the lever every eight or nine seconds, postponing the shock indefinitely. All I had to do was throw the rat in the box, start the timers, and go home for the night. When I arrived back at the lab early the next morning, I would find a fully conditioned rat.

But that was not what looked back at me when I opened the box in the morning. The rat had a grotesque crook in its spine and was shivering uncontrollably. Within a few seconds, it jumped with a start. It was nowhere near the lever. I realized that the rat had not learned to press the lever and had spent the night being shocked every six seconds. When I reached in to rescue it, I found it cold to the touch. I rushed it to the veterinarian two floors down, but it was too late, and the rat died an hour later. I had tortured an animal to death.

As the experiment was being explained to me, I had already sensed it was wrong. Even if the procedure had gone perfectly, the rat would have spent twelve hours in constant anxiety, and I had enough experience to know that laboratory procedures don't always go perfectly. My professor was a radical behaviorist, for whom the question "What is it like to be a rat?" was simply incoherent. But I was not, and there was no doubt in my mind that a rat could feel pain. The professor wanted me in his lab; I knew that if I refused, nothing bad would happen. But I carried out the procedure anyway, reassured by the ethically spurious but psychologically reassuring principle that it was standard practice....

The reason I bring up this blot on my conscience is to show what *was* standard practice in the treatment of animals at the time. To motivate the animals to work for food, we starved them to 80 percent of their free-feeding weight, which in a small animal means a state of gnawing hunger. In the lab next door, pigeons were shocked through beaded keychains that were fastened around the base of their wings; I saw that the chains had worn right through their skin, exposing the muscle below. In another lab, rats were shocked through safety pins that pierced the skin of their chests. In one experiment on endorphins, animals were given unavoidable shocks described in the paper as "extremely intense, just subtetanizing" — that is, just short of the point where the animal's muscles would seize up in a state of tetanus. The callousness extended outside the testing chambers. One researcher was known to show his anger by picking up the nearest unused rat and throwing it against a wall. Another shared a cold joke with me: a photograph, printed in a scientific journal, of a rat that had learned to avoid shocks by lying on its furry back while pressing the food lever with its forepaw. The caption: "Breakfast in bed."

4

I'm relieved to say that just five years later, indifference to the welfare of / animals among scientists had become unthinkable, indeed illegal. Beginning in the 1980s, any use of an animal for research or teaching had to be approved by an Institutional Animal Care and Use Committee (IACUC), and any scientist will confirm that these committees are not rubber stamps. The size of cages, the amount and quality of food and veterinary care, and the opportunities for exercise and social contact are strictly regulated. Researchers and their assistants must take a training course on the ethics of animal experimentation, attend a series of panel discussions, and pass an exam. Any experiment that would subject an animal to discomfort or distress is placed in a category governed by special regulations and must be justified by its likelihood of providing "a greater benefit to science and human welfare."

5

Any scientist will also confirm that attitudes among scientists themselves have changed. Recent surveys have shown that animal researchers, virtually without exception, believe that laboratory animals feel pain.[240] Today a scientist who was indifferent to the welfare of laboratory animals would be treated by his or her peers with contempt.

The change in the treatment of laboratory animals is part of yet another rights revolution: the growing conviction that animals should not be subjected to unjustifiable pain, injury, and death. The revolution in animal rights

6

is a uniquely emblematic instance of the decline of violence, and it is fitting that I end my survey of historical declines by recounting it. That is because the change has been driven purely by the ethical principle that one ought not to inflict suffering on a sentient being. Unlike the other Rights Revolutions, movement for animal rights was not advanced by the affected parties themselves: the rats and pigeons were hardly in a position to press their case. Nor has it been a by-product of commerce, reciprocity, or any other positive-sum negotiation; the animals have nothing to offer us in exchange for our treating them more humanely. And unlike the revolution in children's rights, it does not hold out the promise of an improvement in the makeup of its beneficiaries later in life. The recognition of animal interests was taken forward by human advocates on their behalf, who were moved by empathy, reason, and the inspiration of the other Rights Revolutions. Progress has been uneven, and the animals themselves, if they could be asked, would not allow us to congratulate ourselves too heartily just yet. But the trends are real, and they are touching every aspect of our relationship with our fellow animals.

240. Scientists believe animals feel pain: Herzog, 2010, p. 209.

Presenting Sources: A Summary of Preliminary Writing Skills

1. **Annotation: underlining the text and inserting marginal comments on the page.**

    The notes explain points that are unclear, define difficult words, emphasize key ideas, point out connections to previous or subsequent paragraphs, or suggest the reader's own reactions to what is being discussed.

2. **Paraphrasing: recapitulating, point by point, using your own words.**

    A paraphrase is a faithful and complete rendition of the original, following much the same order of ideas. Although full-length paraphrase is practical only with relatively brief passages, it is the most reliable way to explain and present a text. Paraphrasing a sentence or two, together with a citation of the author's name, is the best method of presenting another person's ideas within your own essay.

3. **Quotation: including another person's exact words within your own writing.**

    Although quotation requires the least amount of invention, it is the most technical of all these skills, demanding an understanding of conventional and complex punctuation. In your notes and in your essays, quotation should be a last resort. If the phrasing is unique, if the presentation is subtle, if the point at issue is easily misunderstood or hotly debated, quotation may be appropriate. When in doubt, paraphrase.

4. **Summary: condensing the text into a relatively brief presentation of the main ideas.**

Unlike annotation, a summary should make sense as an independent, coherent piece of writing. Unlike paraphrase, a summary includes only main ideas. However, the summary should be complete in the sense that it provides a fair representation of the work and its parts.

Part III

WRITING ABOUT SOURCES IN AN ESSAY

The End Product of Research Is a Complete Document Drawn from Your Sources and Yourself

So far, you have been working with sources on a small scale, presenting sources through summary, quotation, and paraphrase. But on the job, whether you are an academic or another kind of professional, you'll be expected to complete your assignments, report on your projects, or present your research by preparing a document that offers a thesis to be proved, and cites evidence that convincingly proves that thesis. Naturally, the evidence in large part will come from your sources, but your own good judgment matters just as much, for you must explain and interpret what you have learned. In this way, *writing from sources becomes a partnership between you and your sources.*

This process is as essential in the business world as it is at the university. At the beginning of Part II, three professionals were assigned projects requiring the presentation of sources. Janet, the social worker, determining whether a patient is ready to leave institutional care, will have to provide a balanced summary, including quotation and paraphrase, and then submit her own recommendation to the committee. Similarly, Parker, the human resources manager, must reconstruct a play-by-play account of the incident in the department store, relying heavily on quotation and paraphrase, so that all the parties involved will accept this version of events and understand who, if anyone, was at fault. Greg, the junior executive providing feedback from stockholders about a merger, needs to convince his superiors that his portrayal of the various reactions — through paraphrase, summary, and quotation — reflects the reality and variety of their opinions, that he has listened to his sources and understands their views.

Before you can prepare complex documents like these, you need to practice on a smaller scale. First, a *single source* serves as a stimulus for you to develop your own ideas in a full-length essay that blends both voices, yours and your source's. Chapter 5 contains two strategies for writing an essay based on a single source.

- You can use your source as the basis for the development of your own ideas by writing as essay on a similar or related topic, citing the source when and as necessary.

- You can explain the difference between your source and yourself by writing about the two, one at a time, and, in the process, develop an argument that supports or refutes your source's thesis.

While you were learning to summarize, quote, and paraphrase, your only purpose was to present the source fairly and completely. You kept your own views out of the exercise or assignment. Now, it is you who must find a thesis—decide what it is that you want to say about the topic—and work out the structure and direction of your essay.

Most of the time, in college or in the workplace, writing from sources includes more than one source. Blending together a variety of sources is usually called *synthesis*. When you are synthesizing sources, the *wrong strategy* is to present each source, one at a time, without considering what they have in common and without offering any perspective of your own. Instead, you have to search for a *broad generalization that will link your sources together*, that will convey the ways in which they share the same views and yet differ from each other. These generalizations will help you to find the starting point for your essay's thesis and organization, while the ideas of your sources will serve as the evidence that supports your conclusions. When you and your classmates are assigned the same set of readings to write about, your teacher hopes to receive, not an identical group of essays, but rather a range of individual interpretations with a common starting point in common sources.

Chapter 6 shows you how to work with multiple sources by applying techniques of synthesis:

- Analyzing each source in a search for common themes;
- Establishing common denominators or categories that cut across the separate sources and provide the structure for your essay;
- Evaluating each source's relative importance as you decide which ones to emphasize; and,
- As you write your essay, citing references from several different sources in support of each single point.

The easiest way to learn how to synthesize is to start with material taken from oral interviews and surveys. After the process becomes familiar, you move on to analyzing a group of written sources, using the readings as the basis for a multiple-source essay.

·5·
Writing the Single-Source Essay

When you write from a source, you must understand the writer's ideas as thoroughly as you understand your own. The first step is to read carefully through the source essay, using the skills for comprehension that you learned about in previous chapters: *annotation*, *paraphrase*, and *summary*. Once you can explain to your reader what the source is all about, you can start to write your own essay.

Strategy One: Developing an Essay Based on a Source

This strategy gives you the freedom to develop your own ideas and present your own point of view in an essay that is only loosely linked to a source. Reading an assigned essay helps you to generate ideas and topics and provides you with information to cite in your own essay; but the thesis, scope, and organization of your essay are entirely your own.

1. Looking for a Topic

As always, you begin by studying the assigned essay carefully, establishing its thesis, structure, and main ideas. As you read, start brainstorming: listing ideas of your own that interest you and might be worth developing. Your essay need not cover exactly the same material as the source essay. What you want is a *spin-off* from the original reading, not a summary.

Here is one student's preliminary list of topics for an essay based on Blanche Blank's "A Question of Degree." (Blank's essay can be found on pp. 12–16.) Notice that, initially, this student's ideas are mostly personal and mostly expressed as questions:

- "selling college": how do colleges recruit students? how did I choose this college? has my college experience met my expectations?

- "practical curriculum": what are my courses preparing me for? what is the connection between my courses and my future career? why am I here?

- "college compulsory at adolescence": what were my parental expectations? teachers' expectations? did I have any choice?

- "employment discrimination based on college degrees": what kinds of jobs now require a B.A.? was it always like that? what other kinds of training are possible—for clerks? for government workers? for teacher's aides?

- "financing college": how much is tuition? are we getting what we pay for? is education something to be purchased, like a winter coat?

- "dignity of work": job experience/work environment

- "joylessness in university life": describe students' attitudes—is the experience mechanical? is the environment bureaucratic?

- "hierarchical levels": what do the different college degrees mean? should they take as long as they do? should a B.A. take four years?

2. Exploring Strategies

If you read a source a few times without thinking of a topic or if you can't see how your ideas can be developed into an essay, test some standard strategies, applying them to the source essay in ways that might not have occurred to the original author. Here, for example, are some strategies that generate topics for an essay based on "A Question of Degree."

Process

You might examine in detail one of the processes that Blank describes only generally:

- You could write about your own experience to explain the ways in which teenagers are encouraged to believe that a college degree is essential, discussing high school counseling and college catalogs and analyzing the unrealistic expectations that young students are encouraged to have.

- If you have sufficient knowledge or experience, you might describe the unjust manipulation of hiring procedures that favor college graduates or the process by which a college's liberal arts curriculum gradually becomes "practical."

Illustration

If you focused on a single discouraged employee, showing in what ways ambition for increased status and salary have been frustrated, or a single disillusioned college graduate, showing how career prospects have failed to measure up to training and expectations, your strategy would be an illustration proving one of Blank's themes.

Definition

Definition often emerges from a discussion of the background of an issue:

- What should the work experience be like?
- What is the function of a university?
- What is a good education?

By attempting to define one of the components of Blank's theme in terms of the ideal, you are helping your reader to understand her arguments and evaluate her conclusions more rationally.

Cause and Effect

- You can examine one or more of the reasons why a college degree has become a necessary credential for employment. You can also suggest a wider context for discussing Blank's views by describing the kind of society that encourages this set of values. In either case, you will be accounting for, but not necessarily justifying, the nation's obsession with degrees.
- You can predict the consequences, good or bad, that might result if Blank's suggested legislation were passed.
- You might explore some hypothetical possibilities and focus on the circumstances and causes of a situation different from the one that Blank describes. What if everyone in the United States earned a college degree? What if education after the eighth grade were abolished? By taking this approach, you are radically changing the circumstances that Blank depicts but still sharing her concerns and exploring the principles discussed in her essay.

Problem and Solution

If Cause and Effect asks "why," then Problem and Solution explains "how." Blank raises several problems that, in her view, have harmful social consequences. What are some solutions? What changes are possible? How can we bring about such changes?

- How can we change students' expectations of education and make them both more realistic and more idealistic?
- How can we change the workplace so that no one feels demeaned?

Note that exploring such solutions means that you are basically in agreement with Blank's thesis.

Comparison

You can alter the reader's perspective by moving the theme of Blank's essay to another time or place:

- Did our present obsession with education exist a hundred years ago? Is it a problem outside the United States at this moment? Will it probably continue throughout the twenty-first century?
- Focusing on contemporary America, how do trends in education and employment compare with trends in other areas of life—housing, finance, recreation, child rearing, or communications?

With all these potential comparisons, you begin with a description of Blank's issue and contrast it with another set of circumstances, past or present, real or hypothetical.

Before choosing any of these speculative strategies and topics, you must consider the limits of the assignment:

- What is practical in a brief essay?
- Will the topic require further research?
- When fully developed, will the topic retain some connection to the source essay?

For example, there may be some value in comparing the current emphasis on higher education with monastic education in the Middle Ages. Can you write such an essay? How much research will it require? Will a discussion of monastic education help your reader to understand Blank's ideas? Or will you immediately move away from your starting point—your source essay—and find no opportunity to return to it? Do you have a serious objective, or are you simply making the comparison "because it's there"?

3. Taking Notes

Consider how you might develop an essay based on one of the topics suggested in the previous section. Notice that the chosen topic is expressed as a question.

Topic: What is the function of a university today?

- After thinking about the topic, start your list of notes *before* you reread the essay, to make sure that you are not overly influenced by the author's point of view and to enable you to include some ideas of your own in your notes.
- Next, review the essay and add any relevant ideas to your list, *remembering to indicate when an idea originated with the source and not with you.*

Here is a complete list of notes for an essay defining the *function of a university for our time.* The paragraph references to Blanche Blank, indicate which points were made by Blank and where in her essay they can be found. (Note that several entries contain no reference to Blank's essay.)

WHAT THE UNIVERSITY SHOULD DO

1. increase students' understanding of the world around them
   e.g., to become more observant and aware of natural phenomena (weather, for example) and social systems (like family relationships)

2. help students live more fulfilling lives
   to enable them to test their powers and know more and become more versatile; to speak with authority on topics that they didn't understand before

3. help students live more productive lives
   to increase their working credentials and qualify for more interesting and well-paying jobs (B. B., Paragraphs 3–9)

4. serve society by creating better informed, more rational citizens
   not only through college courses (like political science) but through the increased ability to observe and analyze and argue (B. B., Paragraphs 3, 14)

5. contribute to research that will help to solve scientific and social problems (not a teaching function) (B. B., Paragraphs 3, 14)

6. serve as a center for debate to explore the issues of the day
   people should regard the university as a source of unbiased information and counsel; notable people should come to lecture (B. B., Paragraphs 3, 14)

7. serve as a gathering place for great teachers
   students should be able to regard their teachers as worth emulating

8. allow students to examine opportunities for personal change
   and growth
   > this includes vocational goals, e.g., career changes (B. B., Paragraph 4)

WHAT THE UNIVERSITY SHOULD NOT DO

9. it should not divide the haves from the have-nots
   > college should not be considered essential; it should be possible to
   > be successful without a college degree (B. B., Paragraphs 8, 10)

10. it should not use marketing techniques to appeal to the greatest
    number
    > what the university teaches should be determined primarily by the
    > faculty and to a lesser extent by the students; standards of achieve-
    > ment should not be determined by students who haven't learned
    > anything yet

11. it should not ignore the needs of its students and its community by
    clinging to outdated courses and programs

12. it should not cooperate with business and government to the extent
    that it loses its autonomy (B. B., Paragraphs 6, 9)

13. it should not be an employment agency and vocational center to the
    exclusion of its more important functions (B. B., Paragraphs 6, 9, 16)

4. Writing a Thesis

These notes, divided into what a university should and should not do, already
suggest a *definition strategy*, with its emphasis on differentiation. To develop a
thesis, look for themes that are emphasized throughout the list:

- The university should help its students to gain knowledge and develop
  intellectually.
- The university should help its students to become better human beings
  and citizens.
- The university does not help its students if it serves primarily as a
  screening mechanism for employers.
- The university does not help its students if it tries to sell itself as a
  destination to every potential student.

Like the list of notes, the thesis drawn from those notes is based on *contrast*. The four key points above—two positive, two negative—are presented in reverse order (negative, then positive) in a thesis statement about what the university should not be and what it should be.

> *Thesis: As Blanche Blank points out, a university education is not a commodity to be marketed and sold; a university should be a resource center for those who want the opportunity to develop their intellectual powers and lead more productive, useful, and fulfilling lives.*

Because Blanche Blank is the starting point in the development of this essay and will be referred to in many of the paragraphs, her name is cited in the thesis. Notice that not every entry in the notes was incorporated into the thesis. Many of the secondary points are likely to creep into the essay anyway!

Moving from source to thesis, through lists of notes, is a process of *narrowing the topic*, an important stage in writing an essay. You'll see this process happen again in the next chapter when you synthesize multiple sources.

5. Structuring Your Essay

Having made all the preliminary decisions, you are ready to plan the structure of your essay:

- Mark those portions of your source that you will need to support your thesis.
- Check whether your notes accurately paraphrase the source.
- Double-check to make sure that you are giving the source credit for all paraphrased ideas.
- If appropriate, include some examples from your own experience.

Organize your notes by arranging them in a logical sequence, which is usually called an *outline*. Some outlines use numbers and letters; some don't. But *all outlines represent the relationship of ideas by their arrangement on the page*: major points at the margin, supporting points and evidence underneath and slightly to the right:

- Divide your notes into groups or categories, each of which will be developed as a separate paragraph or sequence of related paragraphs.
- Decide the order of your categories (or paragraphs).

▪ Incorporate in your outline some of the points from Blanche Blank's essay that you intend to include. Cite the paragraph number of the relevant material with your outline entry. If the source paragraph contains several references that you expect to place in different parts of your outline, use a sentence number or a set of symbols or a brief quotation for differentiation.

Here is one section of the completed outline for an essay on "Defining a University in the Twenty-First Century." This section incorporates notes 3, 13, 9, and 8 from the list on pages 193–194

I. The university should help students to live more productive lives, to increase their working credentials, and to qualify for more interesting and well-paying jobs. (Paragraph 6—last sentence)

   A. But it should not be an employment agency and vocational center to the exclusion of its more important functions. (Paragraph 9—"servicing agents"; Paragraph 12—"joylessness in our university life"; Paragraph 16)

   B. It should not divide the haves from the have-nots; success without a college degree should be possible. (Paragraph 2—"two kinds of work"; Paragraph 17)

II. The university should allow students to examine the opportunities for personal growth and change; this includes vocational goals, e.g., career changes. (Paragraph 4—"an optional and continuing experience later in life")

Although you may need to be flexible once you start writing, you should assume that every entry in your outline will become a paragraph and that you will write your essay following the sequence of your outline, paragraph by paragraph.

6. Writing the Essay

When you write from sources, you strive for an appropriate balance between your own ideas and those of your source. *But it is your voice that should dominate the essay.* You, after all, are writing it; you are responsible for its contents and its effect on the reader. For this reason, all the important "positions" in the structure of your essay should be filled by you. The topic sentences of the paragraphs, as well as the essay's introduction and conclusion, should be written in your own words and should stress your views, not those of your author. On the other hand, your reader should not be allowed to lose sight of the source essay; it should be treated as a form of *evidence* and referred to whenever it is relevant, but always as a context in which to develop your own strategy and assert your own thesis.

Here is the completed paragraph based on Points I and IA in the outline:

topic sentence

explanation: personal experience

source: summary

examples

source: paraphrase and quotation

quotation

To achieve certain goals, all of us have agreed to take four years out of our lives, at great expense, for higher education. What I learn here will, I hope, give me the communication skills, the range of knowledge, and the discipline to succeed in a career as a journalist. But, as Blanche Blank points out, a college education may not be the best way to prepare for every kind of job. Is it necessary to spend four years at this college to become a supermarket manager? a computer programmer? a clerk in the Social Security office? If colleges become no more than high-level job training or employment centers, or, in Blank's words, "servicing agents" to screen workers for business, then they lose their original purpose as centers of a higher form of learning. Blank is rightly concerned that, if a college degree becomes a mandatory credential, I and my contemporaries will regard ourselves "as prisoners of economic necessity," alienated from the rich possibilities of education by the "joylessness in our university life."

7. Revising the Essay

Your work isn't finished until you have reviewed your essay carefully to ensure that the organization is logical, the paragraphs are coherent, and the sentences are complete. To gain some distance and objectivity, most people put their work aside for a while before starting to revise it. Problems usually arise in three areas.

Overall Structure

If you followed your outline or your revised list of notes, your paragraphs should follow each other fairly well. But extraneous ideas—some of them good ones—tend to creep in as you write, and sometimes you need to make adjustments to accommodate them. As you look carefully at the sequence of paragraphs, make sure that they lead into each other. Your object is to make it easy for your reader to understand when and how you move from one point to the next. Are *parallel points* presented in a series or are they scattered throughout the essay? Sometimes, two paragraphs need to be *reversed*, or two paragraphs belong together and need to be *merged*. In addition, your reader should be guided through the sequence of paragraphs by the "traffic signals" provided by *transitional phrases*, such as "in addition" or "nevertheless" or "in fact." The transitions need not be elaborate: words like "also," "so," and "too" help the reader to follow the connections between your sentences and between your ideas.

Paragraph Development

The paragraphs should be of roughly comparable length, each containing a *topic sentence* (preferably but not necessarily placed at the beginning), *explanatory sentences, details or examples* provided by your source or yourself, and (possibly) *quotations from your source*. It's important to have this mix of general material and detail to keep your essay from being too abstract or too specific. Make sure that every sentence contributes to the point of the paragraph. Look for sentences that have nothing to say, or sentences that repeat the same point. If, after such deletions, a paragraph seems overly brief or stark, consider what illustrations or details might be added to support and add interest to the topic. Check back to the source to see if there are still some points worth paraphrasing or quoting.

Sentence Style

Your writing should meet a basic acceptable standard:

- Is the *sentence style* monotonous, with the same pattern repeated again and again? Look for repetitions, and consider ways to vary the style, such as starting some sentences with a phrase or subordinate clause.

- Are you using the same *vocabulary* again and again? Are too many of your sentences built around "is" or "are"? Search for stronger verbs, and vary your choice of words, perhaps consulting a thesaurus. But think twice about using words that are totally new to you, or you'll risk sounding awkward.

- Are you adhering to *basic grammar and punctuation*? Are the sentences complete? Eliminate fragments or run-ons. Check for apostrophes, for subject-verb agreement, for quotation marks. Don't let careless errors detract from your hard work in preparing and writing this essay. And use a spellchecker!

Guidelines for Writing a Single-Source Essay

1. Identify the source essay's thesis; analyze its underlying themes and its strategy; and construct a rough list of its main ideas.

2. After brainstorming, decide on two or three possible essay topics related to your work in Step 1, and narrow down one of them. (Be prepared to submit your topics for your teacher's approval and, in conference, to choose the most suitable one.)

3. Write down a list of notes about your own ideas on the topic; distinguish between your points and points that are derived from the source.

4. Write a thesis of your own that fairly represents the key ideas on your list. Mention the source in your thesis if appropriate.

5. If you have not done so already, choose a strategy that will best carry out your thesis; it need not be the same strategy as the source essay's.

6. Mark (by brackets or underlining) those paragraphs or sentences in the source that will help to develop your topic.

7. Draw up an outline for your essay. Revise your outline: combine repetitious points; bring together similar and related points. Decide on the best sequence for your paragraphs.

8. Decide which parts of the reading should be cited as evidence; place paragraph or page references to the source in the appropriate sections of your outline. Then decide which sentences of the reading to quote and which to paraphrase.

9. Write the rough draft, making sure that, whenever possible, the topic sentence of each paragraph expresses your views, introduces the material that you intend to present in that paragraph, and is written in your voice. Later in the paragraph, incorporate references to the source, and link your paragraphs together with transitions. Do not be concerned about a bibliography for this single-source essay. Cite the author's full name and the exact title of the work early in your essay. (See pp. 131–133 for a review of citations.)

10. Write an introduction that contains a clear statement of your thesis, as well as a reference to the source essay and its role in the development of your ideas. The introduction tells your reader why you've chosen this topic and this thesis, why it is interesting to you. Draft a conclusion that recapitulates the main ideas of your essay, including the thesis.

11. Review your first draft to note problems with organization, transitions, or language. Proofread your first draft very carefully to correct errors of grammar, style, reference, and spelling.

12. Prepare the final draft. Even if you use a spellchecker, proofread again.

ASSIGNMENT 2: Writing an Essay Based on a Single Source

A. As your instructor indicates, read "Faux Friendship," "Manual Labor, All Night Long," or "A Million First Dates," twice. Look up unfamiliar words in your dictionary. One of these three essays will serve as the starting point for an essay of your own. Assume that the essay you are planning will be approximately three pages long, or 600–900 words.

B. Using Steps 1 and 2 in the guidelines on page 199, think of *three* possible topics for an essay of that length, and submit the most promising (or, if your instructor suggests it, all three) for approval.

C. Plan your essay by working from notes to an outline. Be prepared to submit your thesis and outline of paragraphs (with indications of relevant references to the source) to your teacher for approval.

D. Write a rough draft after deciding which parts of the source essay should be cited as evidence, distributing references to the source among appropriate sections of your outline, and determining which parts of the source should be quoted and which should be paraphrased.

E. Write a final draft of your essay, and then proofread the draft before submitting the final version to your instructor.

FAUX FRIENDSHIP

William Deresiewicz

The author of three books, including the recent Excellent Sheep, *William Deresiewicz writes for the* Nation, *the* New Republic, *and the* American Scholar. *He has been nominated for two national awards for criticism. This article appeared in the* Chronicle of Higher Education.

We live at a time when friendship has become both all and nothing at all. Already the characteristically modern relationship, it has in recent decades become the universal one: the form of connection in terms of which all others are understood, against which they are all measured, into which they have all dissolved. Romantic partners refer to each other as boyfriend and girlfriend. Spouses boast that they are each other's best friends. Parents urge their young children and beg their teenage ones to think of them as friends. Adult siblings, released from competition for parental resources that in traditional society made them anything but friends (think of Jacob and Esau), now treat one another in exactly those terms. Teachers, clergymen, and even bosses seek to mitigate and legitimate their authority by asking those they oversee to regard them as friends. We're all on a first-name basis, and when we vote for president, we ask ourselves whom we'd rather have a beer with. As the anthropologist Robert Brain has put it, we're friends with everyone now.

Yet what, in our brave new mediated world, is friendship becoming? The   2
Facebook phenomenon, so sudden and forceful a distortion of social space,
needs little elaboration. Having been relegated to our screens, are our friendships now anything more than a form of distraction? When they've shrunk to
the size of a wall post, do they retain any content? If we have 768 "friends," in
what sense do we have any? Facebook isn't the whole of contemporary friendship, but it sure looks a lot like its future. Yet Facebook—and MySpace, and
Twitter, and whatever we're stampeding for next—are just the latest stages of
a long attenuation. They've accelerated the fragmentation of consciousness,
but they didn't initiate it. They have reified the idea of universal friendship, but
they didn't invent it. In retrospect, it seems inevitable that once we decided to
become friends with everyone, we would forget how to be friends with anyone.
We may pride ourselves today on our aptitude for friendship—friends, after
all, are the only people we have left—but it's not clear that we still even know
what it means....

Now we can see why friendship has become the characteristically modern   3
relationship. Modernity believes in equality, and friendships, unlike traditional
relationships, are egalitarian. Modernity believes in individualism. Friendships
serve no public purpose and exist independent of all other bonds. Modernity
believes in choice. Friendships, unlike blood ties, are elective; indeed, the rise
of friendship coincided with the shift away from arranged marriage. Modernity believes in self-expression. Friends, because we choose them, give us back
an image of ourselves. Modernity believes in freedom. Even modern marriage
entails contractual obligations, but friendship involves no fixed commitments.
The modern temper runs toward unrestricted fluidity and flexibility, the endless play of possibility, and so is perfectly suited to the informal, improvisational
nature of friendship. We can be friends with whomever we want, however we
want, for as long as we want.

Social changes play into the question as well. As industrialization uprooted   4
people from extended families and traditional communities and packed them
into urban centers, friendship emerged to salve the anonymity and rootlessness
of modern life. The process is virtually instinctive now: You graduate from college, move to New York or L.A., and assemble the gang that takes you through
your 20s. Only it's not just your 20s anymore. The transformations of family life
over the last few decades have made friendship more important still. Between
the rise of divorce and the growth of single parenthood, adults in contemporary households often no longer have spouses, let alone a traditional extended
family, to turn to for support. Children, let loose by the weakening of parental
authority and supervision, spin out of orbit at ever-earlier ages. Both look to
friends to replace the older structures. Friends may be "the family we choose,"
as the modern proverb has it, but for many of us there is no choice but to make

our friends our family, since our other families — the ones we come from or the ones we try to start — have fallen apart. When all the marriages are over, friends are the people we come back to. And even those who grow up in a stable family and end up creating another one pass more and more time between the two. We have yet to find a satisfactory name for that period of life, now typically a decade but often a great deal longer, between the end of adolescence and the making of definitive life choices. But the one thing we know is that friendship is absolutely central to it.

Inevitably, the classical ideal [of friendship] has faded. The image of the   5
one true friend, a soul mate rare to find but dearly beloved, has completely disappeared from our culture....That glib neologism "bff," which plays at a life-long avowal, bespeaks an ironic awareness of the mobility of our connections: Best friends forever may not be on speaking terms by this time next month. We save our fiercest energies for sex. Indeed, between the rise of Freudianism and the contemporaneous emergence of homosexuality to social visibility, we've taught ourselves to shun expressions of intense affection between friends — male friends in particular, though even Oprah was forced to defend her rela-tionship with her closest friend — and have rewritten historical friendships, like Achilles' with Patroclus, as sexual. For all the talk of "bromance" lately (or "man dates"), the term is yet another device to manage the sexual anxiety kicked up by straight-male friendships — whether in the friends themselves or in the peo-ple around them — and the typical bromance plot instructs the callow bonds of youth to give way to mature heterosexual relationships. At best, intense friendships are something we're expected to grow out of.

As for the moral content of classical friendship, its commitment to virtue   6
and mutual improvement, that, too, has been lost. We have ceased to believe that a friend's highest purpose is to summon us to the good by offering moral advice and correction. We practice, instead, the nonjudgmental friendship of unconditional acceptance and support — "therapeutic" friendship, in Robert N. Bellah's scornful term. We seem to be terribly fragile now. A friend fulfills her duty, we suppose, by taking our side — validating our feelings, supporting our decisions, helping us to feel good about ourselves. We tell white lies, make excuses when a friend does something wrong, do what we can to keep the boat steady. We're busy people; we want our friendships fun and friction-free....

With modernity's elevation of youth to supreme status as the most vital   7
and authentic period of life, friendship became the object of intense emotion in two contradictory but often simultaneous directions. We have sought to prolong youth indefinitely by holding fast to our youthful friendships, and we have mourned the loss of youth through an unremitting nostalgia for those friendships. One of the most striking things about the way the 20th century understood friendship was the tendency to view it through the

filter of memory, as if it could be recognized only after its loss, and as if that loss were inevitable.

The culture of group friendship reached its apogee in the 1960s. Two   8
of the counterculture's most salient and ideologically charged social forms were the commune — a community of friends in self-imagined retreat from a heartlessly corporatized society — and the rock'n'roll "band" (not "group" or "combo"), its name evoking Shakespeare's "band of brothers" and Robin Hood's band of Merry Men, its great exemplar the Beatles. Communes, bands, and other 60s friendship groups (including Woodstock, the apotheosis of both the commune and the rock concert) were celebrated as joyous, creative places of eternal youth — havens from the adult world. To go through life within one was the era's utopian dream; it is no wonder the Beatles' break-up was received as a generational tragedy. It is also no wonder that 60s group friendship began to generate its own nostalgia as the baby boom [generation] began to hit its 30s. *The Big Chill*, in 1983, depicted boomers attempting to recapture the magic of a late-60s friendship circle. ("In a cold world," the movie's tagline reads, "you need your friends to keep you warm.") *Thirtysomething*, taking a step further, certified group friendship as the new adult norm. Most of the characters in those productions, though, were married. It was only in the 1990s that a new generation, remaining single well past 30, found its own images of group friendship in *Seinfeld*, *Sex and the City*, and, of course, *Friends*. By that point, however, the notion of friendship as a redoubt of moral resistance, a shelter from normative pressures and incubator of social ideals, had disappeared. Your friends didn't shield you from the mainstream, they were the mainstream.

And so we return to Facebook. With the social-networking sites of the new   9
century — Friendster and MySpace were launched in 2003, Facebook in 2004 — the friendship circle has expanded to engulf the whole of the social world, and in so doing, destroyed both its own nature and that of the individual friendship itself. Facebook's very premise — and promise — is that it makes our friendship circles visible. There they are, my friends, all in the same place. Except, of course, they're not in the same place, or, rather, they're not my friends. They're simulacra of my friends, little dehydrated packets of images and information, no more my friends than a set of baseball cards is the New York Mets.

I remember realizing a few years ago that most of the members of what   10
I thought of as my "circle" didn't actually know one another. One I'd met in graduate school, another at a job, one in Boston, another in Brooklyn, one lived in Minneapolis now, another in Israel, so that I was ultimately able to enumerate some 14 people, none of whom had ever met any of the others. To imagine that they added up to a circle, an embracing and encircling structure, was a belief, I realized, that violated the laws of feeling as well as geometry. They were a set of points, and I was wandering somewhere among them. Facebook seduces us,

however, into exactly that illusion, inviting us to believe that by assembling a list, we have conjured a group. Visual juxtaposition creates the mirage of emotional proximity. "It's like they're all having a conversation," a woman I know once said about her Facebook page, full of posts and comments from friends and friends of friends. "Except they're not."

Friendship is devolving, in other words, from a relationship to a feeling — 11 from something people share to something each of us hugs privately to ourselves in the loneliness of our electronic caves, rearranging the tokens of connection like a lonely child playing with dolls. The same path was long ago trodden by community. As the traditional face-to-face community disappeared, we held on to what we had lost — the closeness, the rootedness — by clinging to the word, no matter how much we had to water down its meaning. Now we speak of the Jewish "community" and the medical "community" and the "community" of readers, even though none of them actually is one. What we have, instead of community, is, if we're lucky, a "sense" of community — the feeling without the structure; a private emotion, not a collective experience. And now friendship, which arose to its present importance as a replacement for community, is going the same way. We have "friends," just as we belong to "communities." Scanning my Facebook page gives me, precisely, a "sense" of connection. Not an actual connection, just a sense.

What purpose do all those wall posts and status updates serve? On the 12 first beautiful weekend of spring this year, a friend posted this update from Central Park: "[So-and-so] is in the Park with the rest of the City." The first question that comes to mind is, if you're enjoying a beautiful day in the park, why don't you give your iPhone a rest? But the more important one is, why did you need to tell us that? We have always shared our little private observations and moments of feeling — it's part of what friendship's about, part of the way we remain present in one another's lives — but things are different now. Until a few years ago, you could share your thoughts with only one friend at a time (on the phone, say), or maybe with a small group, later, in person. And when you did, you were talking to specific people, and you tailored what you said, and how you said it, to who they were — their interests, their personalities, most of all, your degree of mutual intimacy. "Reach out and touch someone" meant someone in particular, someone you were actually thinking about. It meant having a conversation. Now we're just broadcasting our stream of consciousness, live from Central Park, to all 500 of our friends at once, hoping that someone, anyone, will confirm our existence by answering back. We haven't just stopped talking to our friends as individuals, at such moments, we have stopped thinking of them as individuals. We have turned them into an indiscriminate mass, a kind of audience or faceless public. We address ourselves not to a circle, but to a cloud....

Sex [and the City] and *Friends* went off the air just five years ago, and already we live in a different world. Friendship (like activism) has been smoothly integrated into our new electronic lifestyles. We're too busy to spare our friends more time than it takes to send a text. We're too busy, sending texts. And what happens when we do find the time to get together? I asked a woman I know whether her teenage daughters and their friends still have the kind of intense friendships that kids once did. Yes, she said, but they go about them differently. They still stay up talking in their rooms, but they're also online with three other friends, and texting with another three. Video chatting is more intimate, in theory, than speaking on the phone, but not if you're doing it with four people at once. And teenagers are just an early version of the rest of us. A study found that one American in four reported having no close confidants, up from one in 10 in 1985. The figures date from 2004, and there's little doubt that Facebook and texting and all the rest of it have already exacerbated the situation. The more people we know, the lonelier we get.   13

The new group friendship, already vitiated itself, is cannibalizing our individual friendships as the boundaries between the two blur. The most disturbing thing about Facebook is the extent to which people are willing—are eager—to conduct their private lives in public. "Hola cutie-pie! i'm in town on wednesday. lunch?" "Julie, I'm so glad we're back in touch. xoxox." "Sorry for not calling, am going through a tough time right now." Have these people forgotten how to use e-mail, or do they actually prefer to stage the emotional equivalent of a public grope? I can understand "[So-and-so] is in the Park with the rest of the City," but I am incapable of comprehending this kind of exhibitionism. Perhaps I need to surrender the idea that the value of friendship lies precisely in the space of privacy it creates: not the secrets that two people exchange so much as the unique and inviolate world they build up between them, the spider web of shared discovery they spin out, slowly and carefully, together. There's something faintly obscene about performing that intimacy in front of everyone you know, as if its real purpose were to show what a deep person you are. Are we really so hungry for validation? So desperate to prove we have friends?   14

But surely Facebook has its benefits. Long-lost friends can reconnect, far-flung ones can stay in touch. I wonder, though. Having recently moved across the country, I thought that Facebook would help me feel connected to the friends I'd left behind. But now I find the opposite is true. Reading about the mundane details of their lives, a steady stream of trivia and ephemera, leaves me feeling both empty and unpleasantly full, as if I had just binged on junk food, and precisely because it reminds me of the real sustenance, the real knowledge, we exchange by e-mail or phone or face-to-face. And the whole theatrical quality of the business, the sense that my friends are doing their   15 best to impersonate themselves, only makes it worse. The person I read about, I cannot help feeling, is not quite the person I know.

As for getting back in touch with old friends — yes, when they're people you really love, it's a miracle. But most of the time, they're not. They're someone you knew for a summer in camp, or a midlevel friend from high school. They don't matter to you as individuals anymore, certainly not the individuals they are now, they matter because they made up the texture of your experience at a certain moment in your life, in conjunction with all the other people you knew. Tear them out of that texture — read about their brats, look at pictures of their vacation — and they mean nothing. Tear out enough of them and you ruin the texture itself, replace a matrix of feeling and memory, the deep subsoil of experience, with a spurious sense of familiarity. Your 18-year-old self knows them. Your 40-year-old self should not know them....

Finally, the new social-networking Web sites have falsified our understanding of intimacy itself, and with it, our understanding of ourselves. The absurd idea, bruited about in the media, that a MySpace profile or "25 Random Things About Me" can tell us more about someone than even a good friend might be aware of is based on desiccated notions about what knowing another person means: First, that intimacy is confessional — an idea both peculiarly American and peculiarly young, perhaps because both types of people tend to travel among strangers, and so believe in the instant disgorging of the self as the quickest route to familiarity. Second, that identity is reducible to information: the name of your cat, your favorite Beatle, the stupid thing you did in seventh grade. Third, that it is reducible, in particular, to the kind of information that social-networking Web sites are most interested in eliciting, consumer preferences. Forget that we're all conducting market research on ourselves. Far worse is that Facebook amplifies our longstanding tendency to see ourselves ("I'm a Skin Bracer man!") in just those terms. We wear T-shirts that proclaim our brand loyalty, pique ourselves on owning a Mac, and now put up lists of our favorite songs. "15 movies in 15 minutes. Rule: Don't take too long to think about it."

So information replaces experience, as it has throughout our culture. But when I think about my friends, what makes them who they are, and why I love them, it is not the names of their siblings that come to mind, or their fear of spiders. It is their qualities of character. This one's emotional generosity, that one's moral seriousness, the dark humor of a third. Yet even those are just descriptions, and no more specify the individuals uniquely than to say that one has red hair, another is tall. To understand what they really look like, you would have to see a picture. And to understand who they really are, you would have to hear about the things they've done. Character, revealed through action: the two eternal elements of narrative. In order to know people, you have to listen to their stories.

16

17

18

But that is precisely what the Facebook page does not leave room for, or   19
500 friends, time for. Literally does not leave room for. E-mail, with its rapid-
fire etiquette and scrolling format, already trimmed the letter down to a certain
acceptable maximum, perhaps a thousand words. Now, with Facebook, the box
is shrinking even more, leaving perhaps a third of that length as the conventional limit for a message, far less for a comment. (And we all know the deal on
Twitter.) The 10-page missive has gone the way of the buggy whip, soon to be
followed, it seems, by the three-hour conversation. Each evolved as a space for
telling stories, an act that cannot usefully be accomplished in much less. Posting information is like pornography, a slick, impersonal exhibition. Exchang-
ing stories is like making love: probing, questing, questioning, caressing. It is
mutual. It is intimate. It takes patience, devotion, sensitivity, subtlety, skill — and
it teaches them all, too....

We have given our hearts to machines, and now we are turning into   20
machines. The face of friendship in the new century.

MANUAL LABOR, ALL NIGHT LONG:
THE REALITY OF PAYING FOR COLLEGE
Alana Semuels

Alana Semuels has been a journalist at the Los Angeles Times
and the Boston Globe, *frequently writing about issues related to
economic inequality. She is presently a staff writer at* Atlantic,
where this article was published.

Most college students are busy. But Alexis McLin's schedule is even more   1
jam-packed than the average student's. One day last week, for instance, she
attended a lab from 3 p.m. to 6:45, went to dinner with her mother, and then
at midnight went in to work at UPS, where she sorts packages from midnight
to 4:30 a.m. McLin, 21, is training to be a teacher, and so after she got off work
and had some breakfast, she drove to an elementary school at 7:40 a.m and
observed classes for four hours. That afternoon she attended a parent-teacher
conference, capping off more than 24 hours straight of work and school with
no sleep.

It wasn't an unusual day for McLin, who is attending the University of   2
Louisville for free through a program that pays her tuition if she works the
overnight shift at UPS and keeps her grades above a C. The program, called
Metropolitan College, has been held up as a model of a public-private partnership, helping students pay for school while filling holes in the workforce.

Indeed, McLin, a chipper redhead whom I interviewed at the UPS facility at   3
two in the morning last week, told me this was the only way she could attend

college, as her family can't afford the tuition. But even her family is incredulous at the hours she keeps. She works five nights a week at UPS from midnight until 4:30 a.m., and still finds time to go to classes, participate in color guard, and fulfill student-teaching responsibilities. "It was really hard in the beginning, but I got used to it," the junior told me. "I've become more responsible and more organized with my time."

Tour the UPS facility between midnight and 4 a.m. Monday through Friday and you'll see many students like McLin sorting mail envelopes, dragging heavy containers full of packages to and from airplanes, and unloading carts of mail onto conveyor belts, 155 miles of which chug around the facility. Of the 6,000 people working there on any given night shift, about 2,000 of them are in the Metropolitan College program, which gives in-state tuition to the night-shift workers to attend either the University of Louisville or Jefferson Community and Technical College during the day. (Metropolitan College isn't a university itself, just the name of the program.)

The program was created in the late 1990s after UPS had trouble with turnover: In a booming economy, at the wages it was paying, the company couldn't keep workers on the night shift for more than a month or two. It was also having labor problems: In 1997, the Teamsters held a 15-day strike at UPS demanding more part-time jobs and higher wages at the company. (Student workers now make $10 an hour, but when the program started, they made $8.50.)

When UPS threatened to locate an expansion of its busy air hub elsewhere, state and city leaders held an emergency meeting to come up with an idea for retaining workers. Their proposal: City government would pay half of students' tuition; UPS the other half. Together, the full-tuition benefit would be enough to keep night-shift workers on the rolls. Since then, turnover on the night shift has dropped from 70 percent to 20 percent annually, and 14,000 students have worked at UPS while attending school. "It's a win-win because it has stabilized our workforce considerably, and the Commonwealth gets a much better-educated workforce," Mike Mangeot, a UPS spokesman, told me as we drove around the busy airport—the largest automated package-handling facility in the world—at three in the morning.

It's not just tuition: Students also receive benefits such as health insurance, and are paid bonuses for finishing college and the semester. They also get counseling to help them juggle their responsibilities, and many students end up working their way up the corporate ladder at UPS after they graduate. (They're also paid for the hours they work.)

But as I walked through the long rows of students pushing envelopes to conveyor belts and into the open air where teenagers pulled cargo off jet planes, I wondered if the system really is win-win. I was having trouble staying awake and alert as we got closer and closer to dawn, and I couldn't imagine being able to focus on homework or college lectures later on in the day. The UPS/Metropolitan College model helps students pay for college, and for that it should be lauded. But can college students really work the night shift five nights a week and stay alert enough at school to understand what is happening in their classes? In the richest country in the world, shouldn't there be a less hellish way to finance a college diploma?

* * *

For the first 200 or so years after Harvard, the first college in America, was founded in 1636, students either studied the classics or technical topics such as science or agriculture. But in the mid-1800s, leaders of schools including Harvard and Yale, concerned that wealthy families were starting to see college as useless, began to embrace a curriculum that both prepared students for the working world and gave them a broad education in a number of topics. In 1869, Charles W. Eliot, who was soon appointed president of Harvard, laid out his vision for what he called "a practical education" in a piece in *Atlantic*. "The fact is, that the whole tone and spirit of a good college ought to be different in kind from that of a good polytechnic or scientific school," he wrote. "In the college, the desire for the broadest culture, for the best formation and information of the mind, the enthusiastic study of subjects for the love of them without any ulterior objects, the love of learning and research for their own sake, should be the dominant ideas," he wrote. Eliot spent much of the next 40 years making Harvard into a place where students could get a "practical education," which combined exploration and abstract learning with the acquisition of useful skills.

9

At the time, a college education was only accessible to the most elite: In 1940, only 6 percent of males had completed four years of college, according to the National Center for Educational Statistics; fewer than half of Americans had finished eighth grade.

10

But college attainment rates began to grow steadily after World War II, when the G.I. Bill sent millions of returning soldiers to college and helped promote a more democratic notion of who could get a college degree. (It is important to note, however, that the effects of the G.I. Bill did not fall equally to all Americans, and many black veterans, particularly in the South, did not benefit at all.) College completion rates rose from 6 percent of males to 12 percent by 1962. Women and minorities began to attend college in greater numbers, too. These trends accelerated in the later part of the 20th century and early 21st: College enrollment climbed from 25 percent of 18-to-24-year-olds in 1967 to 41 percent in 2012.

11

But as more students began attending college, the new institutions that   12
sprang up to educate students didn't have the endowments of the older
schools. And as colleges began to compete against one another to attract
students and faculty, they started spending more money on things like
sports teams, new buildings, and personnel. Tuition and fees have gone up
1,120 percent since 1978 alone, according to Bloomberg.

Today, affordability is the factor most challenging students' ability to go   13
to college. And as students struggle with how to pay for school, many are finding they don't have as much time for — let alone want to spend their limited
money on — "learning and research for their own sake." Fearing the specter of
loans hanging over them forever, many students try to finish college as quickly
as possible, live at home, and work one or two jobs during school to save money.
Their main concerns aren't whether they have time to take all of the fascinating and varied classes in the course catalog, but instead how they can get all
their credit hours in without going so deep into debt that they'll never escape.
Though they've been told that a college education is what they need to succeed in America, the stress of paying for that education challenges their ability to
benefit from it.

In 2011, about 71 percent of undergraduates worked while enrolled in   14
college, according to a recent Census report. And they're working more hours,
rather than fewer, according to the National Center for Education Statistics. The
share of those working fewer than 20 hours per week has declined, to about
15 percent in 2007, while the percentage of those working between 20 and
34 hours increased to 21 percent. Working a small number of hours — say, less
than 15 — can be beneficial to a student, especially if that job is on campus, said
Laura Perna, a professor at Penn's Graduate School of Education who is also the
executive director of the Alliance for Higher Education and Democracy. A job on
campus provides another way for the student to be integrated into the campus,
and it is usually flexible so that a student can take whatever classes he or she
wants, or work less during exam periods.

But working more than 15 or so hours can be detrimental to a student's   15
academic performance, she said. "It's often very difficult for students, with the
stress of trying to manage multiple responsibilities," she said. "The fact that
there's only so many hours in a day — when you're allocating a certain number
of hours to paid employment, the energy you have to be engaged with your
academic requirements declines." Working all night can be challenging for
students, especially those who have early morning classes or exams. A study
published last year in the *Journal of Nature and Science of Sleep* found that sleep
deprivation and daytime sleepiness in college students can result in lower
grade point averages, increased risk of academic failure, and impaired mood.

Subjects who were tested after 35 hours of sleep deprivation, for example, saw scores drop two letter grades when compared to non-sleep-deprived subjects. Students who slept for nine hours a night or more had much higher GPAs than those who slept for fewer than six hours a night.

It's not just the physical strain of sleep deprivation that affects students. When students are so overworked, Perna said, they aren't able to spend as much time paying attention to learning, and to enjoying the learning experience. Indeed, none of the students I saw at the UPS center were likely spending many late nights cramming for exams with friends, or talking about literature with people they'd just met, or taking extra time on a science experiment, just because they found it interesting. Instead, many of the students have to plan every minute of their day to squeeze in work, sleep, classes, and homework. "When you're trying to simultaneously hold down a job and stay enrolled and make satisfactory academic progress, there can be an absence of attention to the enjoyment of the learning experience," Perna said.

Still, some students don't mind trading that "enjoyment of the learning experience" for an absence of loans. Tori Ziegler started out college attending the University of Kentucky and living in the dorms. By the end of her first semester, though, Ziegler began to worry about the size of the loans she was taking out, and how she was going to pay them back. She transferred to the University of Louisville and Metropolitan College and started working as a sorter on the night shift at UPS. "I wasn't going to be able to finish school if I didn't find some way to get it paid for," she told me.

16

17

Photo by Alana Semuels. Courtesy *The Atlantic.*
Reprinted by permission.

Figure 5-1 Sorters at UPS

Photo by Alana Semuels. Courtesy *The Atlantic*. Reprinted by permission.

Figure 5-2 Workers unload mail off a plane at UPS WorldPort.

Sorting is tough work—in some jobs, you stand between lines of quick-moving conveyor belts as mail chugs down a chute; when the parcels reach you, you move them into compartments on the conveyor belt as quickly as you can. In other jobs, you take the mail that's fallen into a bag destined for, say, Lincoln, Nebraska, zip up those bags and load them onto a container bound for an airplane. In the summer, the sorting area, located atop the floors and floors of automated machinery at UPS, can get incredibly hot, students told me. "It's manual labor, definitely," Ziegler said. "At first, it was a big adjustment, I was sore and tired. But I knew it was the only way I was going to get to go to school."

When in school, Ziegler said, her planner was her best friend—she'd write down everything she had to do during the week and plan every minute. Some days, if she got behind on homework, she'd try and finish it when she got off work, around six in the morning, and then sleep for a couple hours before doing it all again. She had to show up at work, but she also had to do well at school: If students get below a "C" they have to repay UPS the tuition for that class. But Ziegler said she was motivated to make the UPS program work. "Both of my parents were pretty adamant—do this, so you can do better than we did," she told me (neither of her parents graduated from college). "I knew that I had to do it, but there were times I thought I would never make it."

Ziegler worked the night shift for the rest of college, and finished in December with a degree in sociology. Soon after, a job at UPS in the HR department opened up, and she now works for the HR department from 9 p.m. to 5 a.m., five days a week. She doesn't regret missing the "college experience,"

18

19

20

she told me; she preferred living at home to living in the dorms, and liked socializing with the people she met at UPS more than with those at school.

But Ziegler's school experience was vastly different than the liberal-arts education that Charles Eliot envisioned in his *Atlantic* article and that has been held up as a model of American education for more than a century. Indeed, Eliot wrote that in order to get a good education, students shouldn't work manual labor while enrolled. Referring to the Rensselaer Polytechnic Institute, which at the time had students perform manual labor, Eliot wrote that "the experiment of making manual labor a part of the regular curriculum has been tried, and has failed." Young children may be able to work in factories for half a day and then learn to read and write, Eliot argued, but for advanced instruction, students need more time for intellectual pursuits. "To be sure, a young man cannot read and write 14 hours a day; but when he cannot be studying books he can be catching butterflies, hunting for flowers and stones, experimenting in a chemical laboratory, practicing mechanical drawing, sharpening his wits in converse with bright associates, or learning manners in ladies [sic] society," he wrote. "Any of these occupations is much better for him than digging potatoes, sawing wood, laying brick, or setting type."

21

* * *

While I was in Kentucky, I also visited Berea College, set in a bucolic small town in the eastern part of the state. Berea, founded in 1855 as the first co-ed, non-segregated school in the South, is a "work college": It provides its students free tuition, and, in exchange, they must work on campus for 10 to 15 hours a week. Berea is one of just seven "work colleges" in the United States. Many, like Berea, provide free or reduced tuition in exchange for work. All try to incorporate that work experience into a student's academic life, so that students don't have to sacrifice their education to earn money.

22

Located on the edge of Appalachia, Berea serves many low-income students who would have had to take out large loans to attend college at all (99 percent of first-year students are eligible for Pell Grants). The jobs assigned to students vary from serving food in the dining halls to working in the public-relations office of the school, and are limited to 10 to 15 hours a week. I talked to Brittany Kenyon and Lisa Rivera, a freshman and a sophomore coming out of one of Berea's picturesque brick dorms on a recent weeknight: Kenyon works cleaning the dorms; Rivera works for dining services. Both said they'd chosen Berea in part because they wouldn't have to take out loans. But they're getting a good education, too. Work never gets in the way of school, they told me. "They schedule you around your classes here," Kenyon told me. "The classes come first, if you have an hour here, and hour there, that's when you work."

23

The freedom of not having to pay for school has allowed some students   24
to use their time to invest back in the community. One student I talked to,
Ethan Hamblin, was able to work for a foundation that encouraged grassroots
philanthropy in Appalachia. He is still employed there today, although he
already graduated.

The work-college model is lauded by both students and education advo-   25
cates, but it's not practical for most universities. Berea, for instance, runs off a
hefty $1 billion endowment. But there are schools that are trying to use the
work-college model to make tuition more affordable. Paul Quinn College, a private liberal-arts institution in Texas that serves minorities, recently announced
that it was launching what it's calling a "New Urban College Model" that will integrate work into students' college experience as a way to reduce tuition costs.

The school launched the program because many of its students were   26
struggling with how to pay for school, Michael Sorrell, the college's president,
told me. Beginning this fall, students will spend some time working for the
school for their first two years, and then will work for companies outside of the
university for their second two years. Students will not work more than 20 hours
a week, he told me. With Pell Grants and the work credit, students should only
have to pay a few thousand dollars a semester, he said, down from the $23,850
in tuition the school had been charging. Sorrel says he wants his students to still
be able to get a liberal-arts education. But helping them organize their work
experience through college will allow them to do that, while still paying for college, he said. "If your students are already working and you don't help them,
then they're going to get whatever jobs they can, and those jobs aren't always
compatible with their classes," he said.

I hadn't mentioned UPS when we talked, but Sorrell brought up the prob-   27
lem of students taking night-shift work without my prompting. Before starting
this program, he said, many of the students at Paul Quinn found jobs at a
FedEx facility nearby, working the midnight shift. They often struggled to stay
up for the night shift and achieve academically. "If you get off work at 3, 4 a.m.,
you're not going to your 8 a.m. class," he said. "And if you go to the 8 a.m. class,
you're not really there."

"It should never have been defined as either/or," he said. "I don't think   28
students are well-served not being given an opportunity to focus on learning."
Where we've gone wrong, Sorrell, said, is making students feel like they have to
chose between a liberal-arts education and an affordable education that also
prepares them for the real world. He's hoping that Paul Quinn's program will
allow them to do both.

* * *

It's easy to pick on Metropolitan College and the bargain Louisville struck with   29
UPS. After all, UPS wasn't paying people enough to stay in part-time jobs, so
it got Louisville to pitch in a subsidy to make those jobs attractive to low-
income people who wanted to go to college. But it also could be argued
that the more options students have in paying for college, the better. Just
11 percent of low-income students who are first in their family to attend
college will have a degree six years after enrolling because of the many
challenges, financial and academic, that they face. And while it might have
once been possible for students to work their way through college on grit
alone, tuition has risen so much faster than the minimum wage that a student
would now have to work 991 hours to pay for one year of public university
tuition, one study found.

Until we find a way to make college more affordable, it can't hurt to give   30
students more ways to pay for college. As long as they know they have options.
Students should be aware that they can take out loans and not work during
school, Perna told me, or that they can get a job and work and study throughout. They should know that there are Pell Grants available and state loans,
in some cases. They should know there are programs such as Metropolitan
College, but also that they don't have to do them to go to school.

I wondered how much choice students enrolled in Metropolitan College   31
felt they had: The city would pay half of their college tuition if they pledged to
work for UPS, but otherwise, they were on their own. A friend who grew up in
Louisville joked to me that students there have two choices to get a free ride
to college: work the night shift at UPS or "get shot at," by joining the military.
But then I talked to Ilya Lyalin, who is now 26, and worked for UPS during a few
years of college. He wouldn't have been able to attend school without Metropolitan College: His parents, Russian immigrants, told him after his first year of
low grades at Jefferson Community and Technical College, that they weren't
going to pay for school anymore, and that he should drop out and get a job.
"I basically had an option of either leaving school or going to UPS and working
there and staying in school," he told me.

He thought seriously about dropping out, but a few friends were doing   32
Metropolitan College, so he applied and started working as a loader, taking
packages off a conveyor belt and stacking them in containers. When Lyalin
started working in the summer, it was horrible, he said. He stayed up all night
in the heat to load packages while supervisors harangued him to move faster.
Once school started again, it was even worse. His friends would be hanging out,
and he'd have to leave and go to work. It got worse when he transferred to
the University of Louisville, which had much more of a traditional college atmosphere. "I hated it. I was the type of college student that would just be out on

weeknights, hanging out with friends, and I felt like that's it, my life is over," he said. "Everybody says college is supposed to be amazing. I was like, this is great, but I'm going to get out of here and realize I didn't make any friends — or get to do anything."

But he had signed the contract with UPS that said they would pay for his semester, and if he dropped the job, he'd have to repay the company. So he stuck with it. And things started getting less miserable. He got a lucky break when he got transferred to a different department that sorted irregular packages, where the work tended to be slower and he sometimes even had some time to study. He even continued to do a second job, working at a kiosk at a mall, to earn more money.   33

Lyalin had to quit the UPS job after he decided to study engineering. The classes and homework required to study calculus and physics required Lyalin's full brain power, and he found it was all but impossible to have the capacity to do the course work on no sleep. He did it for one semester, and it was hell. He'd work until 5 a.m. and then sleep until calculus class at 9 a.m., and be up for the rest of the day studying and working. The worst was every Tuesday when there would be a calculus test at 8 a.m. His GPA began to tumble. "It was two hours of sleep every night for the whole semester," he said. "It was the hardest thing I've ever had to do." When he stopped working for UPS, his life changed. He joined a fraternity, started interning with an engineering company, finished his bachelor's, and then got his master's in engineering.   34

But what fascinates me about Lyalin is that he looks back fondly on his time at UPS, and sometimes kicks himself for dropping it. Yes, he drank energy drinks to stay up, and yes, his teeth rotted from those energy drinks, and yes, he sometimes had to drink NyQuil to make himself sleep at six in the morning, and yes, his coursework suffered, but he got two years of college, for free, saved up a lot of money and became more disciplined about sleep and homework. Yes, coming from a low-income family changed his college experience, he said, but money changes everything. If money weren't an object, he would have studied politics instead of engineering, for instance. And he'd tried to reduce the role money played in his college experience: He'd applied to scholarships and grants before college, and had even been a finalist for one, but didn't receive a penny in financial aid.   35

Now, Lyalin has $30,000 in loans to pay off from the rest of his schooling. He has a job in Louisville, and is glad he went to college. But when he looks back, he's thankful he had UPS, miserable as it was at the time. When all is said and done, he prefers the night shift to the loans that now hover over him, and will, he says, for many years. "The loans are much worse than working there," he told me. "I just feel like I'm caged in." Friends who don't have loans are buying houses, adopting dogs, traveling the world. Even though he has a good   36 job and managed to get through college and graduate school, with much of his tuition covered, Lyalin is still paying the price for being poor.

A MILLION FIRST DATES: HOW ONLINE DATING IS THREATENING MONOGAMY
Dan Slater

A journalist for many periodicals, including the New York Times *and the* Washington Post, *Dan Slater is the author of* Love in the Time of Algorithms. *This article appeared in* Atlantic.

After going to college on the East Coast and spending a few years bouncing around, Jacob moved back to his native Oregon, settling in Portland. Almost immediately, he was surprised by the difficulty he had meeting women. Having lived in New York and the Boston area, he was accustomed to ready-made social scenes. In Portland, by contrast, most of his friends were in long-term relationships with people they'd met in college, and were contemplating marriage.

Jacob was single for two years and then, at 26, began dating a slightly older woman who soon moved in with him. She seemed independent and low-maintenance, important traits for Jacob. Past girlfriends had complained about his lifestyle, which emphasized watching sports and going to concerts and bars. He'd been called lazy, aimless, and irresponsible with money.

Before long, his new relationship fell into that familiar pattern. "I've never been able to make a girl feel like she was the most important thing in my life," he says. "It's always 'I wish I was as important as the basketball game or the concert.'" An only child, Jacob tended to make plans by negotiation: if his girlfriend would watch the game with him, he'd go hiking with her. He was passive in their arguments, hoping to avoid confrontation. Whatever the flaws in their relationship, he told himself, being with her was better than being single in Portland again. After five years, she left.

Now in his early 30s, Jacob felt he had no idea how to make a relationship work. Was compatibility something that could be learned? Would permanence simply happen, or would he have to choose it? Around this time, he signed up for two online dating sites: Match.com, a paid site, because he'd seen the TV ads; and Plenty of Fish, a free site he'd heard about around town. "It was fairly incredible," Jacob remembers. "I'm an average-looking guy. All of a sudden I was going out with one or two very pretty, ambitious women a week. At first I just thought it was some kind of weird lucky streak."

After six weeks, Jacob met a 22-year-old named Rachel, whose youth and good looks he says reinvigorated him. His friends were jealous. Was this The One? They dated for a few months, and then she moved in. (Both names have been changed for anonymity.)

Rachel didn't mind Jacob's sports addiction, and enjoyed going to   6
concerts with him. But there were other issues. She was from a blue-collar military background; he came from doctors. She placed a high value on things he didn't think much about: a solid credit score, a 40-hour workweek. Jacob also felt pressure from his parents, who were getting anxious to see him paired off for good. Although a younger girlfriend bought him some time, biologically speaking, it also alienated him from his friends, who could understand the physical attraction but couldn't really relate to Rachel.

In the past, Jacob had always been the kind of guy who didn't break up   7
well. His relationships tended to drag on. His desire to be with someone, to not have to go looking again, had always trumped whatever doubts he'd had about the person he was with. But something was different this time. "I feel like I underwent a fairly radical change thanks to online dating," Jacob says. "I went from being someone who thought of finding someone as this monumental challenge, to being much more relaxed and confident about it. Rachel was young and beautiful, and I'd found her after signing up on a couple dating sites and dating just a few people." Having met Rachel so easily online, he felt confident that, if he became single again, he could always meet someone else.

After two years, when Rachel informed Jacob that she was moving out, he   8
logged on to Match.com the same day. His old profile was still up. Messages had even come in from people who couldn't tell he was no longer active. The site had improved in the two years he'd been away. It was sleeker, faster, more efficient. And the population of online daters in Portland seemed to have tripled. He'd never imagined that so many single people were out there.

"I'm about 95 percent certain," he says, "that if I'd met Rachel offline, and   9
if I'd never done online dating, I would've married her. At that point in my life, I would've overlooked everything else and done whatever it took to make things work. Did online dating change my perception of permanence? No doubt. When I sensed the breakup coming, I was okay with it. It didn't seem like there was going to be much of a mourning period, where you stare at your wall thinking you're destined to be alone and all that. I was eager to see what else was out there."

The positive aspects of online dating are clear: the Internet makes it easier   10
for single people to meet other single people with whom they might be compatible, raising the bar for what they consider a good relationship. But what if online dating makes it *too* easy to meet someone new? What if it raises the bar for a good relationship *too* high? What if the prospect of finding an ever-more-compatible mate with the click of a mouse means a future of relationship instability, in which we keep chasing the elusive rabbit around the dating track?

Of course, no one knows exactly how many partnerships are undermined   11
by the allure of the Internet dating pool. But most of the online-dating-company executives I interviewed… agreed with what research appears to

suggest: the rise of online dating will mean an overall decrease in commitment. "The future will see better relationships but more divorce," predicts Dan Winchester, the founder of a free dating site based in the U.K. "The older you get as a man, the more experienced you get. You know what to do with women, how to treat them and talk to them. Add to that the effect of online dating." He continued, "I often wonder whether matching you up with great people is getting so efficient, and the process so enjoyable, that marriage will become obsolete."

"Historically," says Greg Blatt, the CEO of Match.com's parent company, "relationships have been billed as 'hard' because, historically, commitment has been the goal. You could say online dating is simply changing people's ideas about whether commitment itself is a life value." Mate scarcity also plays an important role in people's relationship decisions. "Look, if I lived in Iowa, I'd be married with four children by now," says Blatt, a 40-something bachelor in Manhattan. "That's just how it is."   12

Another online-dating exec hypothesized an inverse correlation between commitment and the efficiency of technology. "I think divorce rates will increase as life in general becomes more real-time," says Niccolò Formai, the head of social-media marketing at Badoo, a meeting-and-dating app with about 25 million active users worldwide. "Think about the evolution of other kinds of content on the Web — stock quotes, news. The goal has always been to make it faster. The same thing will happen with meeting. It's exhilarating to connect with new people, not to mention beneficial for reasons having nothing to do with romance. You network for a job. You find a flatmate. Over time you'll expect that constant flow. People always said that the need for stability would keep commitment alive. But that thinking was based on a world in which you didn't meet that many people."   13

"Societal values always lose out," says Noel Biderman, the founder of Ashley Madison, which calls itself "the world's leading married dating service for discreet encounters" — that is, cheating. "Premarital sex used to be taboo," explains Biderman. "So women would become miserable in marriages, because they wouldn't know any better. But today, more people have had failed relationships, recovered, moved on, and found happiness. They realize that that happiness, in many ways, depends on having had the failures. As we become more secure and confident in our ability to find someone else, usually someone better, monogamy and the old thinking about commitment will be challenged very harshly."   14

Even at eHarmony — one of the most conservative sites, where marriage and commitment seem to be the only acceptable goals of dating — Gian Gonzaga, the site's relationship psychologist, acknowledges that commitment is at odds with technology. "You could say online dating allows people to get into   15 relationships, learn things, and ultimately make a better selection," says Gonzaga. "But you could also easily see a world in which online dating leads to people leaving relationships the moment they're not working—an overall weakening of commitment."

Indeed, the profit models of many online-dating sites are at cross-purposes   16
with clients who are trying to develop long-term commitments. A permanently paired-off dater, after all, means a lost revenue stream. Explaining the mentality of a typical dating-site executive, Justin Parfitt, a dating entrepreneur based in San Francisco, puts the matter bluntly: "They're thinking, *Let's keep this idiot coming back to the site as often as we can*." For instance, long after their accounts become inactive on Match.com and some other sites, lapsed users receive notifications informing them that wonderful people are browsing their profiles and are eager to chat. "Most of our users are return customers," says Match.com's Blatt.

In 2011, Mark Brooks, a consultant to online-dating companies, published   17
the results of an industry survey titled "How Has Internet Dating Changed Society?" The survey responses, from 39 executives, produced the following conclusions:

- "Internet dating has made people more disposable."
- "Internet dating may be partly responsible for a rise in the divorce rates."
- "Low quality, unhappy and unsatisfying marriages are being destroyed as people drift to Internet dating sites."
- "The market is hugely more efficient....People expect to—and this will be increasingly the case over time—access people anywhere, anytime, based on complex search requests....Such a feeling of access affects our pursuit of love;...the whole world (versus, say, the city we live in) will, increasingly, feel like the market for our partner(s). Our pickiness will probably increase."
- "Above all, Internet dating has helped people of all ages realize that there's no need to settle for a mediocre relationship."

Alex Mehr, a co-founder of the dating site Zoosk, is the only executive   18
I interviewed who disagrees with the prevailing view. "Online dating does nothing more than remove a barrier to meeting," says Mehr. "Online dating doesn't change my taste, or how I behave on a first date, or whether I'm going to be a good partner. It only changes the process of discovery. As for whether you're the type of person who wants to commit to a long-term monogamous relationship or the type of person who wants to play the field, online dating has nothing to do with that. That's a personality thing."

Surely personality will play a role in the way anyone behaves in the realm   19
of online dating, particularly when it comes to commitment and promiscuity. (Gender, too, may play a role. Researchers are divided on the question

of whether men pursue more "short-term mates" than women do.) At the same time, however, the reality that having too many options makes us less content with whatever option we choose is a well-documented phenomenon. In his 2004 book, *The Paradox of Choice*, the psychologist Barry Schwartz indicts a society that "sanctifies freedom of choice so profoundly that the benefits of infinite options seem self-evident." On the contrary, he argues, "a large array of options may diminish the attractiveness of what people *actually* choose, the reason being that thinking about the attractions of some of the unchosen options detracts from the pleasure derived from the chosen one."

Psychologists who study relationships say that three ingredients generally determine the strength of commitment: overall satisfaction with the relationship; the investment one has put into it (time and effort, shared experiences and emotions, etc.); and the quality of perceived alternatives. Two of the three—satisfaction and quality of alternatives—could be directly affected by the larger mating pool that the Internet offers.   20

At the selection stage, researchers have seen that as the range of options grows larger, mate-seekers are liable to become "cognitively overwhelmed," and deal with the overload by adopting lazy comparison strategies and examining fewer cues. As a result, they are more likely to make careless decisions than they would be if they had fewer options, and this potentially leads to less compatible matches. Moreover, the mere fact of having chosen someone from such a large set of options can lead to doubts about whether the choice was the "right" one. No studies in the romantic sphere have looked at precisely how the range of choices affects overall satisfaction. But research elsewhere has found that people are less satisfied when choosing from a larger group: in one study, for example, subjects who selected a chocolate from an array of six options believed it tasted better than those who selected the same chocolate from an array of 30.   21

On that other determinant of commitment, the quality of perceived alternatives, the Internet's potential effect is clearer still. Online dating is, at its core, a litany of alternatives. And evidence shows that the perception that one has appealing alternatives to a current romantic partner is a strong predictor of low commitment to that partner.   22

"You can say three things," says Eli Finkel, a professor of social psychology at Northwestern University who studies how online dating affects relationships. "First, the best marriages are probably unaffected. Happy couples won't be hanging out on dating sites. Second, people who are in marriages that are either bad or average might be at increased risk of divorce, because of increased access to new partners. Third, it's unknown whether that's good or bad for society. On one hand, it's good if fewer people feel like they're stuck in relationships. On the other, evidence is pretty solid that having a stable romantic partner means all kinds of health and wellness benefits." And that's even   23 before one takes into account the ancillary effects of such a decrease in commitment — on children, for example, or even society more broadly.

Gilbert Feibleman, a divorce attorney and member of the American Academy of Matrimonial Lawyers, argues that the phenomenon extends beyond dating sites to the Internet more generally. "I've seen a dramatic increase in cases where something on the computer triggered the breakup," he says. "People are more likely to leave relationships, because they're emboldened by the knowledge that it's no longer as hard as it was to meet new people. But whether it's dating sites, social media, e-mail — it's all related to the fact that the Internet has made it possible for people to communicate and connect, anywhere in the world, in ways that have never before been seen." 24

Since Rachel left him, Jacob has met lots of women online. Some like going to basketball games and concerts with him. Others enjoy barhopping. Jacob's favorite football team is the Green Bay Packers, and when I last spoke to him, he told me he'd had success using Packers fandom as a search criterion on OkCupid, another (free) dating site he's been trying out. 25

Many of Jacob's relationships become physical very early. At one point he's seeing a paralegal and a lawyer who work at the same law firm, a naturopath, a pharmacist, and a chef. He slept with three of them on the first or second date. His relationships with the other two are headed toward physical intimacy. He likes the pharmacist most. She's a girlfriend prospect. The problem is that she wants to take things slow on the physical side. He worries that, with so many alternatives available, he won't be willing to wait. 26

One night the paralegal confides in him: her prior relationships haven't gone well, but Jacob gives her hope; all she needs in a relationship is honesty. And he thinks, *Oh my God*. He wants to be a nice guy, but he knows that sooner or later he's going to start coming across as a serious ass. While out with one woman, he has to silence text messages coming in from others. He needs to start paring down the number of women he's seeing. 27

People seeking commitment — particularly women — have developed strategies to detect deception and guard against it. A woman might withhold sex so she can assess a man's intentions. Theoretically, her withholding sends a message: *I'm not just going to sleep with any guy that comes along*. Theoretically, his willingness to wait sends a message back: *I'm interested in more than sex*. 28

But the pace of technology is upending these rules and assumptions. Relationships that begin online, Jacob finds, move quickly. He chalks this up to a few things. First, familiarity is established during the messaging process, which also often involves a phone call. By the time two people meet face-to-face, they already have a level of intimacy. Second, if the woman is on a dating site, there's a good chance she's eager to connect. But for Jacob, the most crucial difference between online dating and meeting people in the "real" world is the sense of urgency. Occasionally, he has an acquaintance in common with a woman he 29 meets online, but by and large she comes from a different social pool. "It's not like we're just going to run into each other again," he says. "So you can't afford to be too casual. It's either 'Let's explore this' or 'See you later.'"

Social scientists say that all sexual strategies carry costs, whether risk to reputation (promiscuity) or foreclosed alternatives (commitment). As online dating becomes increasingly pervasive, the old costs of a short-term mating strategy will give way to new ones. Jacob, for instance, notices he's seeing his friends less often. Their wives get tired of befriending his latest girlfriend only to see her go when he moves on to someone else. Also, Jacob has noticed that, over time, he feels less excitement before each new date. "Is that about getting older," he muses, "or about dating online?" How much of the enchantment associated with romantic love has to do with scarcity (*this person is exclusively for me*), and how will that enchantment hold up in a marketplace of abundance (*this person could be exclusively for me, but so could the other two people I'm meeting this week*)?   30

Using OkCupid's Locals app, Jacob can now advertise his location and desired activity and meet women on the fly. Out alone for a beer one night, he responds to the broadcast of a woman who's at the bar across the street, looking for a karaoke partner. He joins her. They spend the evening together, and never speak again.   31

"Each relationship is its own little education," Jacob says. "You learn more about what works and what doesn't, what you really need and what you can go without. That feels like a useful process. I'm not jumping into something with the wrong person, or committing to something too early, as I've done in the past." But he does wonder: When does it end? At what point does this learning curve become an excuse for not putting in the effort to make a relationship last? "Maybe I have the confidence now to go after the person I really want," he says. "But I'm worried that I'm making it so I can't fall in love."   32

Strategy Two: Arguing against Your Source

The simplest way to argue against someone else's ideas is to establish *complete separation between the source and yourself*. The structure of your essay breaks into two parts, with the source's views presented first, and your own reactions given equal (or greater) space immediately afterward. Instead of treating the reading as evidence in support of your point of view and blending it with your own ideas, you write an essay that first *analyzes* and then *refutes* your source's basic themes.

Look, for example, at Roger Sipher's "So That Nobody Has to Go to School If They Don't Want To." The late Roger Sipher, a professor emeritus in the history department at the State University of New York at Cortland, had a special interest in educational standards.

SO THAT NOBODY HAS TO GO TO SCHOOL
IF THEY DON'T WANT TO
Roger Sipher

A decline in standardized test scores is but the most recent indicator that American education is in trouble. 1

One reason for the crisis is that present mandatory-attendance laws force many to attend school who have no wish to be there. Such children have little desire to learn and are so antagonistic to school that neither they nor more highly motivated students receive the quality education that is the birthright of every American. 2

The solution to this problem is simple: Abolish compulsory-attendance laws and allow only those who are committed to getting an education to attend. 3

This will not end public education. Contrary to conventional belief, legislators enacted compulsory-attendance laws to legalize what already existed. William Landes and Lewis Solomon, economists, found little evidence that mandatory-attendance laws increased the number of children in school. They found, too, that school systems have never effectively enforced such laws, usually because of the expense involved. 4

There is no contradiction between the assertion that compulsory attendance has had little effect on the number of children attending school and the argument that repeal would be a positive step toward improving education. Most parents want a high school education for their children. Unfortunately, compulsory attendance hampers the ability of public school officials to enforce legitimate educational and disciplinary policies and thereby make the education a good one. 5

Private schools have no such problem. They can fail or dismiss students, knowing such students can attend public school. Without compulsory attendance, public schools would be freer to oust students whose academic or personal behavior undermines the educational mission of the institution. 6

Has not the noble experiment of a formal education for everyone failed? While we pay homage to the homily, "You can lead a horse to water but you can't make him drink," we have pretended it is not true in education. 7

Ask high school teachers if recalcitrant students learn anything of value. Ask teachers if these students do any homework. Quite the contrary, these students know they will be passed from grade to grade until they are old enough to quit or until, as is more likely, they receive a high school diploma. At the point when students could legally quit, most choose to remain since they know they are likely to be allowed to graduate whether they do acceptable work or not. 8

Abolition of archaic attendance laws would produce enormous dividends.   9

First, it would alert everyone that school is a serious place where one goes   10
to learn. Schools are neither day-care centers nor indoor street corners. Young
people who resist learning should stay away; indeed, an end to compulsory
schooling would require them to stay away.

Second, students opposed to learning would not be able to pollute the   11
educational atmosphere for those who want to learn. Teachers could stop
policing recalcitrant students and start educating.

Third, grades would show what they are supposed to: how well a student is   12
learning. Parents could again read report cards and know if their children were
making progress.

Fourth, public esteem for schools would increase. People would stop   13
regarding them as way stations for adolescents and start thinking of them as
institutions for educating America's youth.

Fifth, elementary schools would change because students would find out   14
early that they had better learn something or risk flunking out later. Elementary
teachers would no longer have to pass their failures on to junior high and high
school.

Sixth, the cost of enforcing compulsory education would be eliminated.   15
Despite enforcement efforts, nearly 15 percent of the school-age children in our
largest cities are almost permanently absent from school.

Communities could use these savings to support institutions to deal   16
with young people not in school. If, in the long run, these institutions
prove more costly, at least we would not confuse their mission with that of
schools.

Schools should be for education. At present, they are only tangentially so.   17
They have attempted to serve an all-encompassing social function, trying to be
all things to all people. In the process they have failed miserably at what they
were originally formed to accomplish.

1. Presenting Your Source's Point of View

Sipher opposes compulsory attendance laws. You, on the other hand, can see
advantages in imposing a very strict rule for attendance. In order to challenge
Sipher convincingly, you begin by *acknowledging his ideas and presenting them to
your readers*. State them as fairly as you can, without pausing to argue with him
or to offer your own point of view about mandatory attendance.

At first it may seem easiest to follow Sipher's sequence of ideas (especially
since his points are so clearly numbered). But Sipher is more likely to dominate
the argument if you follow the structure of his essay, presenting and answering

each of his points one by one; for you will be arguing on *his* terms, according to *his* conception of the issue rather than yours. Instead:

- Make sure that your reader understands what Sipher is actually saying,
- See if you can find any common ground between your points of view, and
- Begin your rebuttal.

A. Briefly summarize the issue and the reasons why the author wrote the essay.

You do this by writing a brief summary, as explained in Chapter 2. Here is a summary of Sipher's article:

> Roger Sipher argues that the presence in the classroom of unwilling students who are indifferent to learning can explain why public school students as a whole are learning less and less. Sipher therefore recommends that public schools discontinue the policy of mandatory attendance. Instead, students would be allowed to drop out if they wished, and faculty would be able to expel students whose behavior made it difficult for serious students to do their work. Once unwilling students were no longer forced to attend, schools would once again be able to maintain high standards of achievement; they could devote money and energy to education, rather than custodial care.

You can make such a summary longer and more detailed by paraphrasing some of the author's arguments and, if you wish, quoting once or twice; such a summary is likely to require several paragraphs.

B. Analyze and present some of the basic principles that underlie the author's position on this issue.

In debating the issue with the author, you will need to do more than just contradict his main ideas: Sipher says mandatory attendance is bad, and you say it is good; Sipher says difficult students don't learn anything, and you say all students learn something useful; and so on. This point-by-point rebuttal shows that you disagree, but it provides no *common context* so that readers can decide who is right and who is wrong. You have no starting point for your counterarguments.

Instead, ask yourself why the author has taken this position, one that you find so easy to reject:

- What are the foundations of his arguments?
- What larger principles do they suggest?
- What policies is he objecting to? Why?
- What values is he determined to defend?

You are now analyzing Sipher's specific responses to the practical problem of attendance in order to *identify his premises* and *infer some broad generalizations* about his philosophy of education.

Although Sipher does not include such generalizations in this article, his views on attendance appear to derive from a *conflict of two principles*:

- the belief that education is a right that may not be denied to children under any circumstances, and

- the belief that education is a privilege to be earned.

Sipher advocates the second position. So, after your initial summary of the article, you should analyze that position in a separate paragraph.

> Sipher's argument implies that there is no such thing as the right to
> an education. A successful education can only depend on the student's will-
> ing presence and active participation. Passive or rebellious students cannot
> be educated and should not be forced to stay in school. Sipher is telling us
> that, although everyone has the right to an opportunity for education, its
> acquisition is actually the privilege of those who choose to work for it.

Through this analysis of Sipher's position, you have established a common context—*eligibility for education*—within which you and he disagree. There is little room for compromise here; it is hard to reconcile the belief that education should be a privilege with the concept of education as an entitlement. Provided with a clear understanding of the differences between you, your reader can choose between your opposing views. At the same time, it's clear that this point and no other is the essential point for debate; thus, you will be fighting on ground that *you* have chosen.

Your analysis also establishes that Sipher's argument is largely *deductive*: a series of premises that derive their power from an appeal to parents' fears that their children (who faithfully attend) will have their education compromised by the unwilling students (who don't). His *supporting evidence* consists of one allusion to the testimony of two economists and one statistic. Both pieces of evidence confirm the subsidiary idea that attendance laws haven't succeeded in improving attendance. His third source of support—the adage about leading a horse to water—deals more directly with the problem of students reluctant to learn; but can it be regarded as serious evidence?

2. Presenting Your Point of View

C. *Present your reasons for disagreeing with your source.*

Once you have established your opponent's position, you may then develop your own counterarguments by writing down your reactions and pinpointing the exact reasons for your disagreement. (All the student examples analyzed in this section are taken from such preliminary responses; they are *not* excerpts from finished essays.) Your reasons for disagreeing with Sipher might fit into one of three categories:

- You believe that his basic principle is not valid (Student B).
- You decide that his principle, although valid, cannot be strictly applied to the practical situation under discussion (Student C).
- You accept Sipher's principle, but you are aware of other, stronger influences that diminish its importance (Student E).

Whichever line of argument you follow, it is impossible to present your case successfully if you wholly ignore Sipher's basic principle, as Student A does:

Student A

make them attend   Sipher's isn't a constructive solution. Without strict attendance laws, many students wouldn't come to school at all.

Nonattendance is exactly what Sipher wants: he argues that indifferent students should be permitted to stay away, that their absence would benefit everyone. Student A makes no effort to refute Sipher's point; he is, in effect, saying to his source, "You're wrong!" without explaining why.

Student B, however, tries to establish a basis for disagreement:

Student B

education is too
important to give
students a choice

If mandatory attendance were to be abolished, how would children acquire the skills to survive in an educated society such as ours?

According to Student B, the practical uses of education have become so important that a student's very survival may one day depend on having been well educated. Implied here is the principle, in opposition to Sipher's, that receiving an education cannot be a matter of choice or a privilege to be earned. What children learn in school is so important to their future lives that they should be forced to attend classes, even against their will, for their own good.

But this response is still superficial. Student B is confusing the desired object—*getting an education*—with one of the means of achieving that object—*being present in the classroom*. Attendance, the means, has become an end in itself. Since students who attend but do not participate will not learn, mandatory attendance cannot by itself create an educated population.

On the other hand, although attendance may not be the *only* prerequisite for getting an education, the student's physical presence in the classroom is certainly important. In that case, should the decision about attendance, a decision likely to affect much of their future lives, be placed in the hands of those too young to understand the consequences?

Student C

students are not mature enough to be given a choice

The absence of attendance laws would be too tempting for students and might create a generation of semi-illiterates. Consider the marginal student who, despite general indifference and occasional bad behavior, shows some promise and capacity for learning. Without a policy of mandatory attendance, he might choose the easy way out instead of trying to develop his abilities. As a society, we owe these students, at whatever cost, a chance at a good and sound education.

Notice that Student C specifies a "chance" at education. Here is a basic point of accommodation between Student C's views and Sipher's. *Both agree in principle that society can provide the opportunity, but not the certainty, of being educated.* The distinction here lies in the way in which the principle is applied. With his argument based on a sweeping generalization, Sipher makes no allowances or exceptions: there are limits to the opportunities that society is obliged to provide. Student C, however, believes that society must act in the best interests of those too young to make such decisions; for their sake, the principle of education as a privilege should be less rigorously applied. Students should be exposed to the conditions for (if not the fact of) education, whether they like it or not, until they become adults, capable of choice.

Student D goes even further, suggesting that not only is society obliged to provide the student with educational opportunities, but schools are responsible for making the experience as attractive as possible.

Student D

if schools were less boring, students would attend

Maybe the reason for a decrease in attendance and an unwillingness to learn is not that students do not want an education, but that the whole system of discipline and learning is ineffective. If schools concentrated on making classes more appealing, the result would be better attendance, and students would learn more.

In Student D's analysis, passive students are like consumers who need to be encouraged to take advantage of an excellent product that is not selling well. To encourage good attendance, the schools ought to consider using more attractive marketing methods. Implicit in this view is *a transferral of blame from the student to the school.* Other arguments of this sort might blame the parents, rather than the schools, for not teaching their children to understand that it is in their own best interests to get an education.

Finally, Student E accepts the validity of Sipher's view of education but finds that the whole issue has become subordinate to a more important problem.

Student E

our security requires that students stay in school

We already have a problem with youths roaming the street, getting into serious trouble. Just multiply the current number of unruly kids by five or ten, and you will come up with the number of potential delinquents that will be hanging around the streets if we do away with the attendance laws that keep them in school. Sipher may be right when he argues that the quality of education would improve if unwilling students were permitted to drop out, but he would be wise to remember that those remaining inside school will have to deal with those on the outside sooner or later.

In this perspective, *security becomes more important than education*. Student E implicitly accepts and gives some social value to the image (rejected by Sipher) of school as a prison, with students sentenced to mandatory confinement.

Student E also ignores Sipher's tentative suggestion (in paragraph 16) that society provide these unwilling students with their own "institutions," which he describes only in terms of their potential costs. What would the curriculum be? Would these institutions be "special schools" or junior prisons? And when these students "graduate," how will they take their place in society?

3. Structuring Your Essay

A reasonably full response, like those of Students C and E, can provide the material for a series of paragraphs that argue against Sipher's position. Here, for example, is Student E's statement analyzed into *the basic topics for a four-paragraph rebuttal* within the essay. (The topics are on the left.)

Student E

danger from drop-outs if Sipher's plan is adopted (III)

custodial function of school (II)

concession that Sipher is right about education (I)

interests of law and order out-weigh interests of education (IV)

We already have a problem with youths roaming the street, getting into serious trouble. Just multiply the current number of unruly kids by five or ten, and you will come up with the number of potential delinquents that will be hanging around the streets if we do away with the attendance laws that keep them in school. Sipher may be right when he argues that the quality of education would improve if unwilling students were permitted to drop out, but he would be wise to remember that those remaining inside school will have to deal with those on the outside sooner or later.

Here are Student E's four topics, with the sequence reordered, in outline format. The student's basic agreement with Sipher has become the starting point.

I.   Sipher is right about education.
  A. It is possible that the quality of education would improve if unwilling students were allowed to drop out.
II. School, however, has taken on a custodial function.
  A. It is attendance laws that keep students in school.
III. If Sipher's plan is adopted, dropouts might be a problem.
  A. Youths are already roaming the streets, getting into trouble.
  B. An increase in the number of unruly kids hanging out in the streets means even greater possibility of disorder.
IV. The interests of law and order outweigh the interests of education.
  A. Educators will not be able to ignore the problems that will develop outside the schools if students are permitted to drop out at will.

Student E can now write a brief essay, with a summary and analysis of Sipher's argument, followed by four full-length paragraphs explaining each point. If a longer essay is assigned, Student E should go to the library to find supporting evidence—statistics and authoritative testimony—to develop these paragraphs. A starting point might be issues that Sipher omits: how do these non-attenders fare later on when they look for work? What methods have been successful in persuading such students to stay in school?

Guidelines for Writing a One-Source Argument

■ Present your source's point of view.

  1. Briefly summarize the issue and the reasons that prompted the author to write the essay.

  2. Analyze and present some of the basic principles that underlie the author's position on this issue.

■ Present your point of view.

  3. Present your reasons for disagreeing with (or, if you prefer, supporting) your source.

ASSIGNMENT 3: Writing an Argument Based on a Single Source

A. Read "What Our Education System Needs Is More F's," "What If Marriage Is Bad for Us?," and the excerpt from *What's So Great about America*. As the starting point for an essay, select one source with which you disagree. (Or, with your instructor's permission, bring in an essay that you are certain you disagree with, and have your instructor approve your choice.)

B.   Write a two-part summary of the essay, the first part describing the author's position and explicitly stated arguments, the second analyzing the principles underlying that position.

C.   Then write your own rebuttal of the author's point of view.

The length of your essay will depend on the number and complexity of the ideas that you find in the source and the number of counterarguments that you can assemble. The minimum acceptable length for the entire assignment is two printed pages (approximately 500–600 words).

WHAT OUR EDUCATION SYSTEM NEEDS IS MORE F'S
Carl Singleton

Carl Singleton, a faculty member at Fort Hays State University, is the editor of Vietnam Studies. *This article appeared in the* Chronicle of Higher Education.

I suggest that instituting merit raises, getting back to basics, marrying the university to industry, and…other recommendations will not achieve measurable success [in restoring quality to American education] until something even more basic is returned to practice. The immediate need for our educational system from prekindergarten through post-Ph.D. is not more money or better teaching but simply a widespread giving of F's.

Before hastily dismissing the idea as banal and simplistic, think for a moment about the implications of a massive dispensing of failing grades. It would dramatically, emphatically, and immediately force into the open every major issue related to the inadequacies of American education.

Let me make it clear that I recommend giving those F's — by the dozens, hundreds, thousands, even millions — only to students who haven't learned the required material. The basic problem of our educational system is the common practice of giving credit where none has been earned, a practice that has resulted in the sundry faults delineated by all the reports and studies over recent years. Illiteracy among high-school graduates is growing because those students have been passed rather than flunked; we have low-quality teaching because of low-quality teachers who never should have been certified in the first place; college students have to take basic reading, writing, and mathematics courses because they never learned those skills in classrooms from which they never should have been granted egress.

School systems have contributed to massive ignorance by issuing unearned passing grades over a period of some 20 years. At first there was a tolerance of students who did not fully measure up (giving D's to students who should have received firm F's); then our grading system continued to deteriorate (D's became C's, and B became the average grade); finally we arrived at total accommodation (come to class and get your C's, laugh at my jokes and take home B's).

Higher salaries, more stringent certification procedures, getting back to basics will have little or no effect on the problem of quality education unless and until we insist, as a profession, on giving F's whenever students fail to master the material.

5

Sending students home with final grades of F would force most parents to deal with the realities of their children's failure while it is happening and when it is yet possible to do something about it (less time on TV, and more time on homework, perhaps?). As long as it is the practice of teachers to pass students who should not be passed, the responsibility will not go home to the parents, where, I hope, it belongs. (I am tempted to make an analogy to then Gov. Lester Maddox's statement some years ago about prison conditions in Georgia — "We'll get a better grade of prisons when we get a better grade of prisoners" — but I shall refrain.)

6

Giving an F where it is deserved would force concerned parents to get themselves away from the TV set, too, and take an active part in their children's education. I realize, of course, that some parents would not help; some cannot help. However, Johnny does not deserve to pass just because Daddy doesn't care or is ignorant. Johnny should pass only when and if he knows the required material.

7

Giving an F whenever and wherever it is the only appropriate grade would force principals, school boards, and voters to come to terms with cost as a factor in improving our educational system. As the numbers of students at various levels were increased by those not being passed, more money would have to be spent to accommodate them. We could not be accommodating them in the old sense of passing them on, but by keeping them at one level until they did in time, one way or another, learn the material.

8

Insisting on respecting the line between passing and failing would also require us to demand as much of ourselves as of our students. As every teacher knows, a failed student can be the product of a failed teacher.

9

Teaching methods, classroom presentations, and testing procedures would have to be of a very high standard — we could not, after all, conscionably give F's if we have to go home at night thinking it might somehow be our own fault.

10

The results of giving an F where it is deserved would be immediately evident. There would be no illiterate college graduates next spring — none. The same would be true of high-school graduates, and consequently next year's college freshmen — all of them — would be able to read.

11

I don't claim that giving F's will solve all of the problems, but I do argue that unless and until we start failing those students who should be failed, other

12

suggested solutions will make little progress toward improving education. Students in our schools and colleges should be permitted to pass only after they have fully met established standards; borderline cases should be retained.

The single most important requirement for solving the problems of education in America today is the big fat F, written decisively in red ink millions of times in schools and colleges across the country.

13

WHAT IF MARRIAGE IS BAD FOR US?
Laurie Essig and Lynn Owens

Both authors teach sociology at Middlebury College. Laurie Essig has published two books, writes frequently for the Chronicle of Higher Education, *where this article appeared, and writes a blog called "Love, Inc" for* Psychology Today. *Lynn Owens is the author of one book.*

...The belief that marriage is good for us also explains why gay and lesbian activists have been fighting so hard for same-sex marriage. According to Freedom to Marry, the national organization behind much of the gay-marriage movement, marriage is "the most powerful expression we have for the affirmation of love and commitment, a source of social recognition...that hold(s) two people together through life's ups and downs." Marriage is also the source of more than a thousand federal rights and responsibilities, not to mention cheaper gym memberships, social approval, and all those gifts that arrive on your wedding day.

2

Where there are policy disputes, you can expect social scientists to weigh in with their supposedly objective data. One noteworthy example is Mark Regnerus's recent op-ed essay in the *Washington Post,* urging young people to get married. Regnerus argues that "today, as ever, marriage wisely entered into remains good for the economy and the community, good for one's personal well-being, good for wealth creation, and, yes, good for the environment, too."

3

Marriage promises to save the poor, empower gays and lesbians, and socialize the young. In support of those promises, the romantics wax about love and happiness, the pragmatics tout rights and security, and the experts crunch the numbers. But as critical sociologists, we find ourselves agreeing most strongly with Marx—Groucho—who quipped, "Marriage is a wonderful institution, but who wants to live in an institution?"

Institutions serve two purposes, practical and ideological. We will do well to keep both in mind in evaluating the benefits that marriage supposedly offers.

4

Marriage makes you rich. Advocates claim that marriage increases wealth. That makes sense; if the key to a successful marriage is hard work, you

5

should at least get paid for it. It's true that married people are wealthier than unmarried people, but it's not marriage that makes you rich. Marriage is not randomly distributed across the population. People who get married (and stay married) tend to be wealthier and whiter than people who do not. For instance, 95 percent of white women will marry at some point in their lifetime, while only 43 percent of black women will.

To say marriage creates wealth is to confuse correlation with causation. If there is more wealth in Manhattan than in Brooklyn, that does not mean that moving to Manhattan will make you wealthier. In fact, moving—and marrying—may make you poorer, given the high start-up costs. A move requires first and last months' rent, a moving van, and lots of bubble wrap. A marriage often demands a wedding, and with the average cost of weddings at $30,000, getting married is going to cost you.   6

Nor will moving into marriage necessarily increase your earnings or earning potential. If you're poor and have little education, saying "I do" won't get you off welfare or make minimum wage any less a dead end. If you already have means, marriage might help. Be careful, though, because even when marriage does produce wealth, divorce often destroys it. If you are getting married for the economic benefits, better make sure it's forever.   7

Marriage is traditional. As Frank Sinatra once crooned: "Love and marriage / go together like a horse and carriage....It's an institute you can't disparage / Ask the local gentry and they will say it's elementary." But there is nothing elementary about the form of marriage as we practice it today. Despite the claims of sociologists, politicians, and marriage advocates on all sides, marriage has changed over time and exists differently in different cultures.   8

Marriage as we imagine it today developed during the late 1800s, when it became "for love" and "companionate." Until that point, one married for material and social reasons, not romance. Women required marriage for survival; men did not. That left men free to behave as they wished: Prostitutes and buggery were part of many a married man's sexual repertoire. But then the Victorians (with their sexual prudishness) and first-wave feminists (with their sense that what's good for the goose is good for the gander) insisted that antiprostitution and antisodomy laws be enacted, and that married men confine their sexual impulses to the conjugal bed. The result was enforced lifelong sexual monogamy for both parties, at least in theory.   9

That might have seemed reasonable in 1900, when the average marriage lasted about 11 years, a consequence of high death rates. But these days, when a marriage can drag on for half a century, it can be a lot of work. Laura Kipnis calls marriage a "domestic gulag," a forced-labor camp where the inmates have to spend all their time outside of work working on their marriage.   10

And if the dyadic couple locked in lifelong monogamy was a radical new form, so was the family structure it spawned. The nuclear family is primarily   11 a mutant product of the nuclear age. Before World War II, most Americans lived among extended family. The definition of family was not the couple and their offspring, but brothers, sisters, aunts, uncles, and grandparents as well. With the creation of suburbs for the middle classes, large numbers of white Americans began participating in the radical family formation of two married parents plus children in a detached house separated from extended family.

Although the nuclear family is idealized as "natural" and "normal" by our   12
culture (*Leave It to Beaver*) and our government ("family values"), it has always been both a shockingly new way of living and a minority lifestyle. Even at its height, in the early 1970s, only about 40 percent of American families lived that way. Today that number is about 23 percent, including stepfamilies. The nuclear family is not only revolutionary; it is a revolution that has failed for most of us.

Marriage makes you healthy. According to the Centers for Disease   13
Control and Prevention, married people have better health than those who are not married. A closer look at the data, however, reveals that married and never-married Americans are similar; it's the divorced who seem to suffer. The lesson might be to never divorce, but an even more obvious lesson to be drawn from the research might be to never marry.

Naomi Gerstel and Natalia Sarkisian's research shows that married couples   14
are more isolated than their single counterparts. That is not a function just of their having children. Even empty-nesters and couples without children tend to have weak friendship networks. Marriage results in fewer rather than more social ties because it promises complete fulfillment through the claims of romance. We are instructed by movies, pop songs, state policy, and sociology to get married because "love is all you need." But actually we humans need more. We need both a sense of connection to larger networks—to community, to place—and a sense of purpose that is beyond our primary sexual relationships.

For those reasons, marriage has been self-destructing as a social form.   15
The marriage rate in the United States is at an all-time low. In 1960 about two-thirds of adult Americans were married. Today only slightly more than half of Americans live in wedded bliss. Actually, even the bliss is declining, with fewer married Americans describing their unions as "very happy."

Maybe it's the decline in happiness that has caused an increasing num-   16
ber of Americans to say "I don't," despite Hollywood's presenting us with happy ending after happy ending and a government bent on distributing civil rights on the basis of marital status. Apparently no amount of propaganda or coercion can force humans to participate in a family form so out of sync with what we actually need.

With all that marriage supporters promise—wealth, health, stability,   17
happiness, sustainability—our country finds itself confronted with a paradox: Those who would appear to gain the most from marriage are the same ones

who prove most resistant to its charms. Study after study has found that it is the poor in the United States who are least likely to wed. The people who get married are the same ones who already benefit most from all our social institutions: the "haves." They benefit even more when they convince everyone that the benefits are evenly distributed.

Too often we are presented with the false choice between a lifelong, loving marriage and a lonely, unmarried life. But those are far from the only options. We should consider the way people actually live: serial monogamy, polyamory, even polygamy.   18

Instead of "blaming the victims" for failing to adopt the formative lifestyles of the white and middle class, we should consider that those avoiding marriage might know exactly what they are doing. Marriage is not necessarily good for all of us, and it might even be bad for most of us. When there is broad, seemingly unanimous support for an institution, and when the institution is propped up by such disparate ideas as love, civil rights, and wealth creation, we should wonder why so many different players seem to agree so strongly. Perhaps it's because they are supporting not just marriage but also the status quo.   19

We can dress up marriage in as many beautiful white wedding gowns as we like, but the fundamental fact remains: Marriage is a structure of rights and privileges for those who least need them and a culture of prestige for those who already have the highest levels of racial, economic, and educational capital.   20

So when you hear activists and advocates — gay, Christian, and otherwise — pushing to increase not only marriage rights but also marriage rates, remember these grouchy words of Marx: "Politics is the art of looking for trouble, finding it everywhere, diagnosing it incorrectly, and applying the wrong remedies." Marriage is trouble. Americans haven't failed at marriage. Marriage has failed us.   21

from WHAT'S SO GREAT ABOUT AMERICA
Dinesh D'Souza

Born in India, Dinesh D'Souza, a writer, filmmaker, and political commentator, is the author of 16 books and numerous articles. His work is known for its strongly conservative and Christian point of view.

Background: *What's So Great about America* was published in 2002. You may want to consider whether there have been changes in American life since 2002 that would make D'Souza's argument less convincing.

The [immigrant] who sees America for the first time typically experiences emotions that alternate between wonder and delight. Here is a country where   1 *everything works*: the roads are clean and paper smooth, the highway signs are clear and accurate, the public toilets function properly, when you pick up the telephone you get a dial tone, you can even buy things from the store and then take them back. For the Third World visitor, the American supermarket is a thing to behold: endless aisles of every imaginable product, fifty different types of cereal, multiple flavors of ice cream. The place is full of countless unappreciated inventions: quilted toilet paper, fabric softener, cordless telephones, disposable diapers, roll-on luggage, deodorant. Most countries even today do not have these benefits: deodorant, for example, is unavailable in much of the Third World and unused in much of Europe.

"What the immigrant cannot help noticing is that America is a country where the poor live comparatively well." This fact was dramatized in the 1980s, when CBS television broadcast an anti-Reagan documentary, "People Like Us," which was intended to show the miseries of the poor during an American recession. The Soviet Union also broadcast the documentary, with a view to embarrassing the Reagan administration. But by the testimony of former Soviet leaders, it had the opposite effect. Ordinary people across the Soviet Union saw that the poorest Americans have television sets and microwave ovens and cars. They arrived at the same perception of America that I witnessed in a friend of mine from Bombay who has been unsuccessfully trying to move to the United States for nearly a decade. Finally I asked him, "Why are you so eager to come to America?" He replied, "Because I really want to live in a country where the poor people are fat."

"The point is that the United States is a country where the ordinary guy has a good life. This is what distinguishes America from so many other countries." Everywhere in the world, the rich person lives well. Indeed, a good case can be made that if you are rich, you live better in countries other than America. The reason is that you enjoy the pleasures of aristocracy. This is the pleasure of being treated as a superior person. Its gratification derives from subservience: in India, for example, the wealthy enjoy the satisfaction of seeing innumerable servants and toadies grovel before them and attend to their every need.

In the United States the social ethic is egalitarian, and this is unaffected by the inequalities of wealth in the country. Tocqueville noticed this egalitarianism a century and a half ago, but it is, if anything, more prevalent today. For all his riches, Bill Gates could not approach a homeless person and say, "Here's a $100 bill. I'll give it to you if you kiss my feet." Most likely the homeless guy would tell Gates to go to hell! The American view is that the rich guy may have more money, but he isn't in any fundamental sense better than you are. The American janitor or waiter sees himself as performing a service, but he doesn't see himself as inferior to those he serves. And neither do the customers see him that way: they are generally happy to show him respect and appreciation on

2

3

4

a plane of equality. America is the only country in the world where we call the waiter "Sir," as if he were a knight.

The moral triumph of America is that it has extended the benefits of comfort and affluence, traditionally enjoyed by very few, to a large segment of society. Very few people in America have to wonder where their next meal is coming from. Even sick people who don't have proper insurance can receive medical care at hospital emergency rooms. The poorest American girls are not humiliated by having to wear torn clothes. Every child is given an education, and most have the chance to go on to college. The common man can expect to live long enough and have free time to play with his grandchildren.

Ordinary Americans enjoy not only security and dignity, but also comforts that other societies reserve for the elite. We now live in a country where the construction workers regularly pay $4 for a nonfat latte, where maids drive very nice cars, where plumbers take their families on vacation to Europe. As Irving Kristol once observed, there is virtually no restaurant in America to which a CEO can go to lunch with the absolute assurance that he will not find his secretary also dining there. Given the standard of living of the ordinary American, it is no wonder that socialist or revolutionary schemes have never found a wide constituency in the United States. As sociologist Werner Sombart observed, all socialist utopias in America have come to grief on roast beef and apple pie.

Thus it is entirely understandable that people would associate the idea of America with a better life. For them, money is not an end in itself; money is the means to a longer, healthier, and fuller life. Money allows them to purchase a level of security, dignity, and comfort that they could not have hoped to enjoy in their native countries. Money also frees up time for family life, community involvement, and spiritual pursuits: thus it produces not just material, but also moral, gains. All of this is true.

▪6▪
Synthesizing Sources for the Multiple-Source Essay

Until now, most of your writing assignments have been based on information derived from a *single* source. Now, as you begin to organize a wider range of materials, you will try to present the ideas of your sources in all their variety while at the same time maintaining your own perspective. How can you describe each author's ideas without taking up too much space for each one? How can you fit all your sources smoothly into your essay without allowing one to dominate?

Many of the oral sources used in the first part of this chapter have their equivalents in professional writing. Lawyers, doctors, engineers, social workers, and other professionals often work from notes taken in interviews and surveys to prepare case notes, case studies, legal testimony, reports, and market research.

Analyzing Multiple Sources

When you write from sources, your object is to present a thesis statement of your own that is based on your examination of a variety of views. Some of these views may conflict with your own and with each other. Because of this diversity, organizing multiple sources can be more difficult than working with even the most complex single essay.

Generalizing from Examples

In academic writing, a common theme often connects apparently dissimilar ideas or facts found in a group of sources. The writer looks for that common theme and presents it to the reader as a *generalization*.

240

To demonstrate this process, assume that you have been asked to consider and react to seven different but related situations.

A.   In a sentence or two, write down your *probable reaction* if you found yourself in each of the following situations.* Write quickly; this exercise calls for immediate, instinctive responses.

1. You are walking behind someone. You see him take out a cigarette pack, pull out the last cigarette, put the cigarette in his mouth, crumple the package, and nonchalantly toss it over his shoulder onto the sidewalk. What would you do?

2. You are sitting on a train and you notice a person (same age, sex, and type as yourself) lighting up a cigarette, despite the no smoking sign. No one in authority is around. What would you do?

3. You are pushing a shopping cart in a supermarket and you hear the thunderous crash of cans. As you round the corner, you see a two-year-old child being beaten, quite severely, by his mother, apparently for pulling out the bottom can of the pile. What would you do?

4. You see a teenager that you recognize shoplifting at the local discount store. You're concerned that she'll get into serious trouble if the store detective catches her. What would you do?

5. You're driving on a two-lane road behind another car. You notice that one of its wheels is wobbling more and more. It looks as if the lugs are coming off one by one. There's no way to pass, because cars are coming from the other direction in a steady stream. What would you do?

6. You've been waiting in line (at a supermarket or gas station) for longer than you expected and you're irritated at the delay. Suddenly, you notice that someone very much like yourself has sneaked in ahead of you in the line. There are a couple of people before you. What would you do?

7. You've raised your son not to play with guns. Your rich uncle comes for a long-awaited visit and he brings your son a .22 rifle with lots of ammunition. What would you do?

B.   Read over your responses to the seven situations and try to form two general statements (in one or two sentences each), one about *the circumstances in which you would take action* and a second about *the circumstances in which you would choose to do nothing.* Do not simply list the incidents, one after the other, divided into two groups.

To form your first generalization, you examine the group of situations in which you *do* choose to take action and determine what they have in common. It is also important to examine the "leftovers," and to understand why these incidents did not warrant your interference. One effective approach is to look

*Adapted from "Strategy 24" in Sidney B. Simon et al., *Values Clarification* (New York: Hart, 1972).

at each situation in terms of either its *causes* or its *consequences*. For example, in each case there is *someone to blame*, someone who is responsible for creating the problem—except for number 5, where fate (or poor auto maintenance) threatens to cause an accident.

As for consequences, in some of the situations (littering, for example), there is *little potential danger*, either to you or to the public. Do these circumstances discourage action? In others, however, the possible victim is oneself or a member of one's family. Does self-interest alone drive one to act? Do adults tend to intervene in defense of children—even someone else's child—since they cannot stand up for themselves? Or, instead of calculating the consequences of not intervening, perhaps you should imagine *the possible consequences of interference.* In which situations can you expect to receive abuse for failing to mind your own business? Would this prevent you from intervening?

Read through the seven examples again:

- Each item is intended to illustrate a specific and very different situation. Although it does not include every possible example, the list as a whole constitutes *a set of public occasions for interfering with a stranger's conduct.*

- Since you probably would not choose to act in every situation, you cannot use the entire list as the basis for your generalization. Rather, you must establish *a boundary line*, differentiating between those occasions when you would intervene and those times when you would decide not to act. The exact boundary between intervention and nonintervention will probably differ from person to person, as will the exact composition of the list of occasions justifying intervention. Thus, there is no one correct generalization.

This process of analysis results in a set of guidelines for justifiably minding other people's business.

Forming a Generalization from Examples

You can clarify your ideas and opinions about an abstract issue by:

1. inventing a set of illustrations

   [*seven opportunities for potential intervention*]

2. marking off a subgroup according to your own standards

   [*intervention desirable only in situations 3 (the child beaten in the supermarket), 5 (the wobbly wheel), and 7 (the gift of a gun)*]

3. forming a generalization that describes the common characteristics of the subgroup

   [*intervention only to protect someone from physical harm*]

Finding Common Meanings

Differentiating among examples and forming generalizations becomes more difficult when your evidence comes from several different sources, not just a prepared list. Working with multiple sources usually begins with the *analysis of ideas.*

> *Analysis is first breaking down a mass of information into individual pieces and then examining the pieces to see how they relate to each other.*

As you underline and annotate your sources, you look for similarities and distinctions in meaning, as well as the basic principles underlying what you read. Only when you have taken apart the evidence of each source to see how it works can you begin to find new ways of putting everything back together again in your own essay.

To illustrate this kind of analysis, assume that you have asked five people what the word **foreign** means. You want to provide a reasonably complete definition of the word by exploring all the different meanings (or connotations—the ideas that a word suggests beyond its literal meaning) that the five sources provide. If each one of the five people gives you a completely different answer, then you will not have much choice in the organization of your definition. In that case, you would probably present each separate definition of *foreign* in a separate paragraph, citing a different person as the source for each one. But responses from multiple sources almost always overlap, as these do. Notice the *common meanings* in this condensed list of the five sources' responses:

John Brown: "Foreign" means unfamiliar and exotic.

Lynne Williams: "Foreign" means strange and unusual.

Vijay Patel: "Foreign" means strange and alien (as in "foreign body").

Maria Garcia: "Foreign" means exciting and exotic.

Bob Friedman: "Foreign" means difficult and incomprehensible (as in "foreign language").

The paragraphs of your definition of "foreign" will be organized around common meanings, not the names of the five sources. That is why the one-source-per-paragraph method should hardly ever be used (except on those rare occasions when all the sources completely disagree).

> *When you organize ideas taken from multiple sources, never devote one paragraph to each page of your notes, simply because all the ideas on that page happen to have come from the same source.*

If you did so, each paragraph would have a topic sentence that might read, "Then I asked John Brown for his definition," as if John Brown were the topic for discussion, instead of his views on "foreign." And if John Brown and Maria Garcia each get a separate paragraph, there will be some repetition because both think that one of the meanings of "foreign" is "exotic." "Exotic" should be the topic of one of your paragraphs, not the person (or people) who suggested that meaning.

Analyzing Shades of Meaning

Here is a set of notes, summarizing the ideas of four different people about the meaning of the word **individualist**. How would you analyze these notes?

> *Richard Becker*: an "individualist" is a person who is unique and does not "fall into the common mode of doing things"; would not follow a pattern set by society. "A youngster who is not involved in the drug scene just because his friends are." A good word; it would be insulting only if it referred to a troublemaker.

> *Simon Jackson*: doing things on your own, by yourself. "She's such an individualist that she insisted on answering the question in her own way." Sometimes the word is good, but mostly it has a bad connotation: someone who rebels against society or authority.

> *Lois Asher*: one who doesn't "follow the flock." The word refers to someone who is very independent. "I respect Jane because she is an individualist and her own person." Usually very complimentary.

> *Vera Lewis*: an extremely independent person. "An individualist is a person who does not want to contribute to society." Bad meaning: usually antisocial. She first heard the word in psych class, describing the characteristics of the individualist and "how he reacts to society."

At first glance, all four sources seem to say much the same thing: the individualist is different and *independent*.

Having identified the basis for a definition, you need to establish the *context* in which the four sources are defining this word: all the responses define the individualist *in terms of other people*—either the "group," or the "flock," or "society." Oddly enough, it is not easy to describe the individualist as an individual, even though it is that person's isolation that each source is emphasizing. One has to be independent of something outside oneself—the group.

So, you have now established the context for your definition: whatever is unique about the individualist is defined by the gap between that person and everyone else. Now you must *differentiate between the views of your sources*: Obviously Lois Asher thinks that to be an individualist is a good thing; Vera

Lewis believes that individualism is bad; and the other two suggest that both connotations are possible. But simply describing the opinions of the four sources—positive or negative—stops short of defining the word according to those reactions. On what values do these sources base their judgments?

- Richard Becker and Lois Asher, two people who suggest a favorable meaning, describe the group from which the individual is set apart in similar and somewhat disapproving terms: "common"; "pattern set by society"; "follow the flock." Becker and Asher both seem to suggest *a degree of social conformity or sameness that the individualist is right to reject*, as Becker's youngster rejects his friends' drugs.

- But Vera Lewis, who thinks that the word's connotation is bad, sees the individualist in a more benign society, with which the individual ought to identify himself and to which he ought to contribute. To be antisocial is to be an undesirable person—from the point of view of Lewis and society.

- Simon Jackson (who is ambivalent about the word) uses the phrases "by yourself" and "on your own," which suggest the isolation and the lack of support, as well as the admirable independence, of the individualist. In Jackson's view, the individualist's self-assertion becomes threatening to all of us in society ("antisocial") only when the person begins to rebel against authority.

Probably for Jackson, and certainly for Vera Lewis, the ultimate authority should rest with society as a whole, not with the individualist. Even Richard Becker, who admires independence, draws the line at allowing the individualist complete autonomy: when reliance on one's own authority leads to "troublemaking," the term becomes an insult.

EXERCISE 20: Analyzing Shades of Meaning in Multiple Sources

A. Analyze the following set of notes for a definition of the word *inquisitive*.

B. Find the underlying terms or concepts that can lead to a common context for defining *inquisitive*.

C. Write *two generalizations* that might serve as *topic sentences* for a two-paragraph definition. (Do not use "favorable" and "unfavorable" as your two topics.)

Gino Carella: curious; won't settle for the obvious; always wants to know more; can be dangerous; "the Spanish Inquisition tortured people."

Ferdi Lopez: asks a lot of questions; wants to know your life story; okay within limits, but can seem like snooping; "they may not respect your privacy."

Marie Melmotte: nosy; pries into your affairs; intrusive; doesn't know when to stop asking questions; "newspaper reporters are inquisitive, always trying to get personal details to make a good story."

Lucy Snowe: searching for answers; probing; want to find out; better to be inquisitive than indifferent; "scientists and explorers are inquisitive about the world around them, and their discoveries benefit everyone."

Maggie Tulliver: not satisfied with easy answers; persistent; often have no sense of the limits of appropriate behavior; "they want to know more because it makes them feel powerful."

Synthesizing Multiple Sources: The Lottery

Once you have analyzed your sources and discovered their common themes and their contexts, their similarities and differences, you then reassemble these parts into a more coherent whole. This process is called *synthesis*. Although at first you may regard analysis and synthesis as contradictory operations, they are actually overlapping stages of a single, larger process.

Analysis and Synthesis

To illustrate the way in which analysis and synthesis work together, let us examine a set of answers to the questions: "Would you buy a **lottery** ticket? Why?" First, read through these summaries of all seven responses.

Mary Smith: She thinks that lottery tickets were made for people to enjoy and win. It's fun to try your luck. She looks forward to buying her ticket, because she feels that, for a few dollars, you have a chance to win a lot more. It's also fun scratching off the numbers to see what you've won. Some people don't buy tickets because they think the lottery is a big rip-off; but "a few dollars can't buy that much today, so why not spend it and have a good time?"

John Jones: He would buy a lottery ticket for three reasons. The first reason is that he would love to win. The odds are like a challenge, and he likes to take a chance. The second reason is just for fun. When he has two matching tickets, he really feels happy, especially when he thinks that dollars can be multiplied into hundreds or thousands. "It's like Russian roulette." The third reason is that part of the money from the lottery goes toward his education. The only problem, he says, is that they are always sold out!

Michael Green: He has never bought a lottery ticket in his life because he doesn't want to lose money. He wants to be sure of winning. Also, he says that he isn't patient enough. The buyer of a lottery ticket has to be very patient to wait for his chance to win. He thinks that people who buy tickets all the time must enjoy "living dangerously."

Anne White: Buying a lottery ticket gives her a sense of excitement. She regards herself as a gambler. "When you win ten dollars or twenty dollars you get a thrill of victory, and when you see that you haven't, you feel the agony of defeat." She thinks that people who don't buy tickets must be very cautious and non-competitive, since the lottery brings "a sense of competition with you against millions of other people." She also knows that the money she spends on tickets goes toward education.

Margaret Brown: She feels that people who buy tickets are wasting their money. The dollars spent on the lottery could be in the bank, getting interest. Those people who buy tickets should expect to have thrown out their money, and should take their losses philosophically, instead of jumping up and down and screaming about their disappointment. Finally, even if she could afford the risk, the laws of her religion forbid her to participate in "any sort of game that is a form of gambling."

William Black: He would buy a lottery ticket, because he thinks it can be fun, but he wouldn't buy too many, because he thinks it's easy for people to get carried away and obsessed by the lottery. He enjoys the anticipation of wanting to win and maybe winning. "I think that you should participate, but in proportion to your budget; after all, one day you might just be a winner."

Elizabeth Watson: She wouldn't buy a lottery ticket because she considers them a rip-off. The odds are too much against you, 240,000 to 1. Also, it is much too expensive, "and I don't have the money to be throwing away on such foolishness." She thinks that people who indulge themselves with lottery tickets become gamblers, and she's against all kinds of gambling. Such people have no sense or self-control. Finally, "I'm a sore loser, so buying lottery tickets just isn't for me."

Making a Chart of Common Ideas

Since you are working with seven sources with varying opinions, you need a way to record the process of analysis. One effective way is to make a *chart of commonly held views*. To do so, follow these two steps, which should be carried out *simultaneously*:

1. Read each statement carefully, and identify each separate reason that is being cited for and against playing the lottery by writing a number above or next to the relevant comment. When a similar comment is made by another person, use *the same number* to provide a key to the final list of common reasons. In this step, you are analyzing your

sources. Here is what the first two sets of notes might look like once the topic numbers have been inserted:

Mary Smith: She thinks that lottery tickets were made for people to enjoy and win ①. It's fun to try your luck ②. She looks forward to buying her ticket, because she feels that, for a few dollars, you have a chance to win a lot more ② ①. It's also fun scratching off the numbers to see what you've won. Some people don't buy tickets because they think the lottery is a big rip-off ③; but "a few dollars can't buy that much today, so why not spend it and have a good time?" ①

John Jones: He would buy a lottery ticket for three reasons. The first reason is that he would love to win. The odds are like a challenge ②, and he likes to take a chance ①. The second reason is just for fun. When he has two matching tickets, he really feels happy, especially when he thinks that dollars can be multiplied into hundreds or thousands ②. "It's like Russian roulette." The third reason is that part of the money from the lottery goes toward his education ④. The only problem, he says, is that they are always sold out!

2. At the same time as you number each of your reasons within the statements, also write a list or *chart of reasons* on a separate sheet of paper. Each reason should be assigned *the same number* you wrote next to it in the original statement. Don't make a new entry when the same reason is repeated by a second source. Next to each entry on your chart, put the names of the people who have mentioned that reason. You are now beginning to *synthesize* your sources. (This process is also known as *cross-referencing*.)

Here's what your completed list of reasons might look like:

Reason		Sources
1.	People play the lottery because it's fun.	Smith; Jones
2.	People play the lottery because they like the excitement of taking a chance and winning.	Smith; Jones; Green; White; Black
3.	People don't play the lottery because they think it's a rip-off.	Smith; Watson

4. People play the lottery because they are contributing to education.   Jones; White

5. People don't play the lottery because they have better things to do with their money.   Green; Brown; Watson

6. People play the lottery because they like to gamble.   White; Brown; Watson

7. People who play the lottery and those who refuse to play worry about the emotional reactions of the players.   Green; White; Brown; Black; Watson

The process of synthesis starts as soon as you start to make your list. The list of common reasons represents the reworking of seven separate sources into a single new pattern that can serve as the basis for an essay.

Distinguishing between Reasons

One of the biggest problems in synthesis is deciding, in cases of overlapping, whether you actually have one reason or two. Since overlapping reasons were deliberately not combined, the preceding list may be unnecessarily long:

- *Reasons 1 and 2*: The difference between the experiences of *having fun* and *feeling the thrill of excitement* is a difference in sensation that most people would understand. You might ask yourself, "Would someone play the lottery just for fun without the anticipation of winning? Or would someone experience a thrill of excitement without any sense of fun at all?" If one sensation can exist without the other, you have sufficient reason for putting both items on your chart. Later on, the similarities, not the differences, might make you want to combine the two; but, at the beginning, it is important to note down exactly what ideas and information are available to you.

- *Reasons 2 and 6*: The distinction between the *thrill of excitement* (2) and the *pleasure of gambling* (6) is more difficult to perceive. The former is, perhaps, more innocent than the latter and does not carry with it any of the obsessive overtones of gambling.

- *Reasons 3 and 5*: Resenting the lottery because it is a *rip-off* (3) and resenting the lottery because the players are *wasting their money* (5) appear at first glance to be similar reactions. However, references to the rip-off tend to emphasize the "injured victim" whose money is being whisked away by a public agency. In other words, Reason 3 emphasizes *self-protection from robbery*; Reason 5 emphasizes *the personal virtue of thrift*.

▪ *Reason 7*: This is not really a reason at all. Some comments in the notes do not fit into a tidy list of reasons for playing, yet they provide a valuable insight into human motivation and behavior as expressed in lottery playing. An exploration of the emotions that characterize the player and the nonplayer (always allowing for the lottery preference of the source) might be an interesting way to conclude an essay.

Deciding on a Sequence of Topics

The topics in your chart appear in the same random order as your notes. Once the chart is completed, you should decide on *a more logical sequence of topics* by re-ordering the entries in the list. You can make an indirect impact on your reader by choosing a logical sequence that supports the pattern that you discovered in analyzing your sources.

Here are two possible ways to arrange the "lottery" reasons. Which sequence do you prefer? Why?

1. fun	1. fun
2. excitement	2. rip-off
3. gambling	3. excitement and gambling
4. education	4. misuse of money
5. rip-off	5. education
6. misuse of money	6. personality of the gambler
7. personality of the gambler	

The right-hand sequence *contrasts the advantages and disadvantages* of playing the lottery. Moving back and forth between paired reasons calls attention to the relation between opposites and, through constant contrast, makes the material interesting for the reader. The left-hand sequence places all the advantages and disadvantages in two groups, providing an opportunity to *explore positive and negative reactions to the lottery separately* without interruption, therefore encouraging more complex development. Both sequences are acceptable.

EXERCISE 21: Identifying Common Ideas

This exercise is based on a set of interview notes, answering the question "Would you give money to a beggar?"

A.   Read through the notes.

1. Identify distinct and different reasons by placing numbers next to the relevant sentences.

2. As you number each new reason, add an entry to the chart. (The first reason is already filled in.)

B.   Arrange the numbered reasons in a logical sequence. If it makes sense to you, combine those reasons that belong together. Be prepared to explain the logic behind your sequence of points. If you can find two possible sequences, include both, explaining the advantages of each.

Reason   *Sources*

1.   I can afford to give to beggars.

2.

3.

4.

5.

6.

7.

8.

9.

10.

Would You Give Money to a Beggar?

Jonathan Cohen: When asked for money on the street, I often apply a maxim of a friend of mine. He takes the question, "Have you got any spare change?" literally: if he has any loose change, he hands it over, without regard for his impression of what the money's for, since he doesn't think ulterior motives are any of his business. Since I can always afford the kind of contribution that's usually asked for—fifty cents or a dollar—or am at least less likely to miss it than the person asking me for it, I usually take the request as the only qualification of "need." I'm more likely to give out money if I don't have to go into my billfold for it, however, and would rather give out transit tokens or food, if I have them. But I want to be sympathetic; I often think, "There but for the grace of God go I."

Jennifer Sharone: I hate to think about what people who beg have to undergo; it makes me feel so fortunate to be well dressed and to have good food to eat and a home and a job. Begging seems kind of horrifying to me—that in this country there are people actually relying on the moods of strangers just to stay alive. I give to people who seem to have fallen on hard times, who aren't too brazen, who seem embarrassed to be asking me for money. I guess I do identify with them a lot.

Michael Aldrich: If a person meets my eye and asks plainly and forthrightly (and isn't falling-down drunk), I try to empty my pocket, or at least come up with a quarter or two. If the person has an unusually witty spiel—even if it's outlandish—I give more freely. I don't mind giving small change; it's quick and easy. I try not to think about whether or not the person really "needs" the money—how could you ever know? On some level, I think that if someone's begging, they need the money. Period. There's an old guy who stands on my corner—he's been there for years. I always give him money, if I have the change. If I don't have it, he says a smile will do. I would hate to think of him going without a meal for a long time or having to sleep out in the rain. He reminds me of my father and my uncle.

Marianne Lauro: I used to give people money, but frankly, I'm too embarrassed by the whole process. It seems to me that folks who really couldn't be all that grateful for somebody's pocket change still make an effort to appear grateful, and then I'm supposed to get to feel magnanimous when I really feel ridiculous telling them they're welcome to a couple of coins that don't even amount to carfare. So the whole transaction seems vaguely humiliating for everyone concerned. Really, the city or the state or the federal government should be doing something about this—not expecting ordinary people, going home from work, or whatever, to support people who have mental or physical impairments or addictions, especially when you're never sure what their money will be used for. But maybe I'm just rationalizing now—maybe the most "humane" thing about these kinds of transactions is the mutual embarrassment.

Donald Garder: I try, when possible, to respond to the person approaching me, by looking at them, perhaps even making eye contact, which frequently lends some dignity to the moment. But then I don't always reach into my pocket. I often give to people with visible physical handicaps, but rarely to someone who's "young and able-bodied." Sometimes I feel guilty, but I'm never sure if the person is for real or not—I've known people who swindled people out of money by pretending to be homeless, so I have a nagging doubt about whether or not a beggar is legitimate.

Darrin Johnson: I never give on the subway—I hate the feeling of entrapment, of being held hostage. The "O.K., so I have you until the next stop so I'm going to wear you down with guilt until I get the money out of you." I really resent that. I flatly refuse to give under those circumstances because it just pisses me off. I might give to somebody just sitting on the street, with a sign and a cup or something—someone who isn't making a big scene, who leaves it up to me whether I give or not. But I hate feeling coerced.

Jenny Nagel: I never give to people on the streets anymore—there are places where people who are really in need can go if they're really starving or need drug treatment or something. Someone once told me, after I'd given money to some derelict looking guy, that he'd probably buy rubbing alcohol or boot polish and melt it down for the alcohol content—that my money was just helping him kill himself. After that I never gave to anyone on the street. I'd rather make a contribution to a social agency.

Paul O'Rourke: I used to give money or if asked I'd give a cigarette. But one day a beggar let loose with a stream of obscenities after I gave him some money. A lot of these people are really messed up—the government should be looking after them, doing more to help them; if they keep getting money from people off the street, they'll just keep on begging. So now I volunteer once a month at a food pantry, and give to charitable organizations, rather than hand out money on the street.

Organizing Multiple Sources: Student Promotion

Playing the lottery is not a subject that lends itself to lengthy or abstract discussion; therefore, charting reasons for and against playing the lottery is not a great challenge. The article that follows defines an educational and social problem without taking sides or suggesting any solutions. The reporter's sources simply cite aspects of the problem and express baffled concern.

Twenty students were asked to read the article and to offer their opinions; these are presented following the article. As you read the article and the student opinions, assume that you plan to address the issue and synthesize the opinions in an essay of your own.

from RULE TYING PUPIL PROMOTION
TO READING SKILL STIRS WORRY
Gene I. Maeroff

A strict new promotion policy requires the public schools to hold back seventh-grade pupils until they pass the reading test. The difficulty will be compounded this year by a requirement that new seventh graders also pass a mathematics test. 1

"I am frightened that we may end up losing some of these kids, creating a whole new group of dropouts who leave school at junior high," said Herbert Rahinsky, principal of Intermediate School 293, on the edge of the Carroll Gardens section of Brooklyn. 2

Students like Larry, who is 16 years old and in the seventh grade at I.S. 293, are repeating the grade because they scored too low on the reading tests last June to be promoted. If Larry does not do well enough on the test this spring, he will remain in the seventh grade in the fall. 3

An analysis by the Board of Education has shown that about 1,000 of the 8,871 students repeating the seventh grade are already 16 years of age or older. At least one 18-year-old is repeating the seventh grade.   4

Normally, a seventh grader is 12 years old.   5

When the promotion policy, which threatened to hold back students with low reading scores in the fourth and seventh grades, was implemented in 1980, it was hailed by many observers as a welcome effort to tighten standards.   6

But as the program has continued, certain students have failed to show adequate progress. These youngsters are in jeopardy of becoming "double holdovers" in the seventh grade. Some were also held back at least once in elementary school. . . .   7

Authorities theorize that these youngsters form a hard core of poor readers for whom improvement is slow and difficult. Such students often were not held back in prior years because it was easier to move them along than to help them.   8

Educators now wonder whether repeated failure will simply lessen the likelihood of students persisting in school long enough to get a regular diploma.   9

Student Opinions

Diane Basi: If these students are pushed through the system and receive a diploma, not being able to read beyond a seventh-grade level, we will be doing them and society a grave injustice. What good will it do to have a diploma if you cannot read or write? In the end, the students will be hurt more if they are just promoted through the system.

Jason Berg: A student should not be repeatedly held back on the basis of one test. A student's overall performance should be taken into consideration, such as classwork, participation, and attitude. If a student is not up to par for some reason on the day of the test, all the work and effort that was put into school during the year goes down the drain.

Rafael Del Rey: This strict rule has unfortunate consequences. The students who are being forced out don't comprehend what is being taught to them. Exasperated and feeling like social outcasts and inferior beings, it is no wonder that many drop out without skills or goals. Low reading scores mean that students have been neglected by the school system. Educators should be interested in more than just test scores.

Anita Felice: It is extremely embarrassing to be a 16-year-old in a class of 12-year-olds. Such poor students should be promoted to a special program with other students who have the same problems. In time, there should be some improvement in their reading scores. Being held back will only cause frustration and eventually cause them to drop out. Test scores should be a lot less important than they are now.

Joe Gordon: By enforcing a rigid standard, the schools are actually promoting an increased dropout rate and, by doing so, are harming the student and society. What about the teachers? Sometimes students fail a teacher, and for that reason fail the class.

Margaret Jenkins: After two tries, a student should be able to pass a test. It's to the child's advantage to learn and keep learning while moving upward in school. Holding them back is for their own good.

Rachel Limburg: It isn't fair to those students who can do the work just to push these students along. It also isn't fair to the kids who can't pass the test because eventually they are going to have to earn a living. We should look for new ways to help them find their talents and prepare them to face the future.

Barbara Martin: It's a hard question, but I think you have to look at the cost in terms of money, as well as frustration and embarrassment. I'm sorry for kids who are left back, but it's only going to be a problem for everyone later when they can't get a job. Work today is increasingly technical, and everyone needs basic skills. This policy is tough love, and it's necessary.

Len McGee: This policy isn't good enough because it doesn't deal with the individual student; it deals with seventh-graders as a whole. The individual's problems and motivation are not taken into consideration. Sometimes exam pressure defeats intelligence. If left back, the student is trapped in a revolving door and is likely to lose interest in school.

Tina Pearson: It's a mistake to pass students solely on the basis of the reading score. It may show they have learned to read well. But it doesn't mean they learned well in their other classes. Perhaps they worked especially hard on reading and English but just coasted along in their other subjects.

Julius Pena: Automatic promotion is a guarantee that the weak student will face future problems. Making the student repeat is for his own good. Imagine how frustrating it would be for someone who can't fill out a job application. Of course, you shouldn't just throw the student back into the class, but give as much encouragement as possible.

Mark Pullman: We must have certain standards in our educational system. This is a challenge for these students, and repeating the course may encourage them to try harder, making them smarter and better prepared to face life's challenges.

Anthony Raviggio: Strict standards are best for the student. In the long run, individuals who really want the college degree will be glad to remember the ordeal they went through in junior high. It's better to make them keep trying and succeed than to let them think it's okay to fail.

Vivian Ray: If a child has been held back in elementary school and held back again in junior high, it should become quite apparent to teachers and parents that the child has a problem. Being slow to learn is not sufficient reason to hold back a child. The child should be promoted and put in a slower class with more students like himself.

Bernice Roberts: I think there's too much concern for the feelings of the "poor" student and too little concern for the needs of society. Eighteen-year-olds who can't read are likely candidates for welfare. I don't want to have the responsibility of carrying some illiterate kid who couldn't be bothered to learn when he was in school.

Althea Simms: The tough standards are good for these students because they will be motivated to become more serious about doing well. There are kids who don't care whether or not they study for their exams since they know they're going to be promoted to the next grade anyway. Knowing that you may be held back is a strong motivator to study harder.

Patricia Sokolov: Not all students are intellectually gifted, nor is the progress of the nation solely dependent on the effort of intellectuals. Laborers and blue-collar workers have been credited throughout our history for their great contribution to the wealth and progress of our country. Educators should be more concerned with nurturing students' individual potential and less concerned with passing tests.

Matthew Warren: What's the point of promoting a student who won't be able to keep up in his new classes, much less perform his job properly when he's out in the working world? Standards should be enforced regardless of age. What's age? It's just a number.

Michael Willoughby: Educators should recognize that some students don't have the capacity, for whatever social, genetic, or psychological reasons, to fulfill the educators' traditional expectations. An alternative effort must be made, emphasizing vocational skills and also basic reading and math, that will permit students to progress at their own pace.

Betty Yando: I am concerned about the large number of dropouts and their dismal prospects. Why should a student, despite obvious learning disabilities, be forced to continue in an exasperating educational process in which he is making little or no progress? The standards by which we determine whether an individual will make a good worker and a good citizen are too high.

Organizing Multiple Sources

1. **Summarize the facts of the issue.**
   Write a brief, objective summary of the issue under discussion (in this case, the problem described in the article). Your summary of this article should convey both the *situation* and the *two key ideas* that are stressed. Try structuring your paragraph to contrast the conflicting opinions.

2. **Establish your own point of view.**
   End your summary with a statement of your own reaction to suggest a possible direction for your essay. This step is more important than it might at first seem. Once you begin to analyze a mass of contradictory opinion, you may find yourself being completely convinced by first one source and then another, or you may try so hard to stay neutral that you end up with no point of view of your own at all. You need to find a vantage point for yourself from which to judge the credibility of the statements that you read. Of course, you can (and probably will) adjust your point of view as you become more familiar with all the arguments and evidence that your sources raise. Do not regard your initial statement of opinion as a thesis to be proven, but rather as a *hypothesis—an idea to be tested, modified, or even abandoned.*

3. **Synthesize your evidence.**
   Label your set of opinions and *establish categories*. The 20 statements following the article are all personal reactions to withholding promotion because of poor performance and the issue of maintaining standards versus individual needs. For each statement, follow these steps:

   A. *Read each statement carefully and think about its exact meaning.* First, get a rough idea of what each statement says—do a mental paraphrase, if you like. You will naturally notice which "side" the author of each statement is on. There is a tendency to want to stop there, as if the "yes" or "no" is all that one needs to know. But your object is not only to find out which side of an issue each person prefers, but also to understand why that side was chosen.

   B. *Try to pick out the chief reason put forth by each person, or, even better, the principle that lies behind each argument.* Sum up the reasoning of each person in a word or phrase.

   C. When you have labeled the statements, *review your summarizing phrases to see if there is an abstract idea, used to describe several statements, that might serve as a category title.* (Some change in the wording may be necessary.) Once two or three categories become obvious, consider their relationship to each other. Are they parallel? Are they contrasting? Then attempt to see how the smaller categories fit into the pattern that is beginning to form.

How the Three Steps Work

Following is one student's exploration of the article on promotion and the 20 student opinions.

1. **Summarizing.** Here the student identifies the article to which he and his sources are responding, summarizing the issue and the nature of the conflict.

> In the *New York Times*, Gene I. Maeroff reported that seventh-grade students, who formerly would pass into the eighth grade despite failing their reading tests, are now required to repeat the year until they can pass the test. Some repeaters in the seventh grade are now older than 16. The school system adopted this new rule in order to maintain standards for promotion. But the students most affected apparently don't have the skills to meet those standards. Some educators, questioning the change in policy, are concerned that such students may not stay "in school long enough to get a regular diploma."

2. **Hypothesizing** (stating your own point of view). Here the student expresses an opinion that suggests the possible direction for an essay. At this point, the student has not studied the group of opinions that accompanies the article.

> School authorities have a dilemma. On the one hand, it's in society's interest to produce graduates who have mastered basic skills. Students who pass the reading test will benefit from the rest of their education and then qualify for and hold down good jobs. But, in many cases, the inability to pass the test does not mean that the students didn't try to the best of their capabilities. Holding them back again and again won't ensure that they pass. Later on, when no one wants to hire them, society will have to support them through welfare programs. Perhaps a new vocational track could be developed with less rigorous testing to accommodate children who can't learn well.

3. **Synthesizing** (labeling your set of opinions and establishing categories). In this step, the student moves away from the article to examine the opinions of others who have read the article, determining first *the position of each respondent and then the reasoning behind the position*. Here, the statements of the 20 respondents are repeated, with a summarizing label following each statement.

Student Opinions

Diane Basi: If these students are pushed through the system and receive a diploma, not being able to read beyond a seventh-grade level, we will be doing them and society a grave injustice. What good will it do to have a diploma if you cannot read or write? In the end, the students will be hurt more if they are just promoted through the system.

Basi: literacy necessary for employment; otherwise, individual and society both suffer

Jason Berg: A student should not be repeatedly held back on the basis of one test. A student's overall performance should be taken into consideration, such as classwork, participation, and attitude. If a student is not up to par for some reason on the day of the test, all the work and effort that was put into school during the year goes down the drain.

Berg: test scores less important than individual potential

Rafael Del Rey: This strict rule has unfortunate consequences. The students who are being forced out don't comprehend what is being taught to them. Exasperated and feeling like social outcasts and inferior beings, it is no wonder that many drop out without skills or goals. Low reading scores mean that students have been neglected by the school system. Educators should be interested in more than just test scores.

Del Rey: test scores less important than individual self-esteem

Anita Felice: It is extremely embarrassing to be a 16-year-old in a class of 12-year-olds. Such poor students should be promoted to a special program with other students who have the same problems. In time, there should be some improvement in their reading scores. Being held back will only cause frustration and eventually cause them to drop out. Test scores should be a lot less important than they are now.

Felice: test scores less important than individual self-esteem

Joe Gordon: By enforcing a rigid standard, the schools are actually promoting an increased dropout rate and, by doing so, are harming the student and society. What about the teachers? Sometimes students fail a teacher, and for that reason fail the class.

Gordon: society suffers if high standards lead to dropping out

Margaret Jenkins: After two tries, a student should be able to pass a test. It's to the child's advantage to learn and keep learning while moving upward in school. Holding them back is for their own good.

Jenkins: enforcing tough sttandards builds character

Rachel Limburg: It isn't fair to those students who can do the work just to push these students along. It also isn't fair to the kids who can't pass the test because eventually they are going to have to earn a living. We should look for new ways to help them find their talents and prepare them to face the future.

Limburg: fairness requires that both good and bad students get an education

Barbara Martin: It's a hard question, but I think you have to look at the cost in terms of money, as well as frustration and embarrassment. I'm sorry for kids who are left back, but it's only going to be a problem for everyone later when they can't get a job. Work today is increasingly technical, and everyone needs basic skills. This policy is tough love, and it's necessary.

Martin: literacy necessary for employment; otherwise, individual and society both suffer

Len McGee: This policy isn't good enough because it doesn't deal with the individual student; it deals with seventh-graders as a whole. The individual's problems and motivation are not taken into consideration. Sometimes exam pressure defeats intelligence. If left back, the student is trapped in a revolving door and is likely to lose interest in school.

McGee: society suffers if high standards lead to dropping out

Tina Pearson: It's a mistake to pass students solely on the basis of the reading score. It may show they have learned to read well. But it doesn't mean they learned well in their other classes. Perhaps they worked especially hard on reading and English but just coasted along in their other subjects.

Pearson: promotion should be based on a variety of skills

Julius Pena: Automatic promotion is a guarantee that the weak student will face future problems. Making the student repeat is for his own good. Imagine how frustrating it would be for someone who can't fill out a job application. Of course, you shouldn't just throw the student back into the class, but give as much encouragement as possible.

Pena: enforcing standards builds character; but offer more help

Mark Pullman: We must have certain standards in our educational system. This is a challenge for these students, and repeating the course may encourage them to try harder, making them smarter and better prepared to face life's challenges.

Pullman: enforcing tough standards builds character

Anthony Raviggio: Strict standards are best for the student. In the long run, individuals who really want the college degree will be glad to remember the ordeal they went through in junior high. It's better to make them keep trying and succeed than to let them think it's okay to fail.

Raviggio: enforcing tough standards builds character

Vivian Ray: If a child has been held back in elementary school and held back again in junior high, it should become quite apparent to teachers and parents that the child has a problem. Being slow to learn is not sufficient reason to hold back a child. The child should be promoted and put in a slower class with more students like himself.

Ray: provide alternate track

Bernice Roberts: I think there's too much concern for the feelings of the "poor" student and too little concern for the needs of society. Eighteen-year-olds who can't read are likely candidates for welfare. I don't want to have the responsibility of carrying some illiterate kid who couldn't be bothered to learn when he was in school.

Roberts: the problem is lack of effort, not lack of ability; it's not society's problem

Althea Simms: The tough standards are good for these students because they will be motivated to become more serious about doing well. There are kids who don't care whether or not they study for their exams since they know they're going to be promoted to the next grade anyway. Knowing that you may be held back is a strong motivator to study harder.

Simms: the problem is lack of effort, not lack of ability

Patricia Sokolov: Not all students are intellectually gifted, nor is the progress of the nation solely dependent on the effort of intellectuals. Laborers and blue-collar workers have been credited throughout our history for their great contribution to the wealth and progress of our country. Educators should be more concerned with nurturing students' individual potential and less concerned with passing tests.

Sokolov: test scores less important than individual potential

Matthew Warren: What's the point of promoting a student who won't be able to keep up in his new classes, much less perform his job properly when he's out in the working world? Standards should be enforced regardless of age. What's age? It's just a number.

Warren: literacy necessary for employment

Michael Willoughby: Educators should recognize that some students don't have the capacity, for whatever social, genetic, or psychological reasons, to fulfill the educators' traditional expectations. An alternative effort must be made, emphasizing vocational skills and also basic reading and math, that will permit students to progress at their own pace.

Willoughby: provide alternate track

Betty Yando: I am concerned about the large number of dropouts and their dismal prospects. Why should a student, despite obvious learning disabilities, be forced to continue in an exasperating educational process in which he is making little or no progress? The standards by which we determine whether an individual will make a good worker and a good citizen are too high.

Yando: individual suffers if high standards lead to dropping out

From this list, the student can establish eight categories that cover the range of topics. Here is the list of categories:

Categorizing the Sources' Opinions

Category	Source	Notes
Literacy is necessary for employment	Warren	
	Basi Martin	Otherwise, individual and society both suffer.
The problem is lack of effort, not lack of ability	Simms	
	Roberts	If students can't meet standards, it's not society's fault.
Society suffers if high standards lead to dropping out	Gordon McGee Yando	
Enforcing tough standards builds character	Jenkins Pullman Raviggio	
	Pena	Society should also offer more help to the individual student.
Test scores are less important than individual potential	Sokolov	
	Berg Pearson	Promotion should be based on a variety of skills.
Test scores are less important than individual self-esteem	Del Rey Felice	
Society owes an education to bad students as well as good ones	Limburg	
Society should offer an alternative track for failing students	Ray Willoughby	

Evaluating Sources

Although you are obliged to give each of your sources serious and objective consideration and a fair presentation, synthesis also requires a certain amount of *selection*. Certainly, no one's statement should be immediately dismissed as trivial or crazy. *But do not assume that all opinions are equally convincing and deserve equal representation in your essay.* You owe it to your reader to evaluate the evidence, partly through what you choose to emphasize and partly through your explicit comments about flawed and unconvincing statements.

The weight of a group of similar opinions can add authority to an idea. If most of your sources hold a similar view, you will probably give that idea proportionate prominence in your essay. However, majority rule should not govern the structure of your essay. Your own perspective determines the thesis of your essay, and you must analyze the range of arguments provided by your sources and decide which have the greatest validity. You may find an idea highly persuasive even though only one or two sources have supported it. In the end, your original hypothesis, either confirmed or altered in the light of your increased understanding, becomes the *thesis* of your essay:

- Sift through all the statements and decide which ones seem *thoughtful and well-balanced*, supported by convincing reasons and examples, and which seem to be thoughtless assertions that rely on stereotypes or unsupported references. Your evaluation of the sources may differ from someone else's, but you must assert your own point of view.

- Review the hypothesis that you formulated before you began to analyze the sources. *Decide whether that hypothesis is still valid* and will become your thesis, or whether, as a result of your full exploration of the subject, you wish to change it or abandon it for another.

Writing a Thesis

For the essay on "student promotion," here are some questions that you would have to answer before writing your thesis:

- If students fail tests, is it necessarily their fault? To what extent should they be penalized?

- What is the purpose of using test scores as the primary criterion for promotion? Does enforcing such a barrier benefit society?

- What are the human consequences of making students repeat grades indefinitely?

■ Is there a better way of assessing progress than a single exam? Is there any other way of making sure that high standards are maintained?

The answers to these questions are likely to determine your thesis and shape the basic structure of your essay, supported by selected comments from the twenty students. Your thesis might focus on the plight of the teenager repeating a grade for the third time:

It is pointless to humiliate adolescents by making those who fail a reading test repeat the grade indefinitely. Rather than destroy their self-esteem, the educational system should provide them with a track towards graduation that is within their abilities.

Or your thesis might assert that a high school diploma should signify a high standard and the purpose of the test is to determine who meets that standard:

No one benefits if students are allowed to graduate from high school without learning basic skills. Automatic promotion will lower standards of achievement, and the next generation of workers will lack the necessary skills to succeed.

Writing a Synthesis Essay

Organizing Ideas and Material: Spend some time planning your sequence of ideas and considering possible *strategies*. Do your topic and materials lend themselves to a cause-and-effect structure, or definition, or problem and solution, or comparison, or argument? In writing about the issue of school promotion, you might want to use an overall *problem-solution* strategy, at the same time *arguing* for your preferred solution.

Developing Topic Sentences: Before starting to write each paragraph, review the relevant group of your sources' statements. By now, you should be fully aware of the reasoning underlying each point of view and the pattern connecting them all. But because your reader does not know as much as you do, you need to explain your main ideas in enough detail to make all the complex points clear. Remember that your reader has neither made a list nor even read the original sources. It is therefore important to include *some explanation in your own voice*, in addition to naming sources.

Presenting Sources as Evidence: If possible, you should use all three methods of reference: *summary, paraphrase,* and *quotation.* (See the paragraph in Exercise 22 as an appropriate model.) As a rule, paraphrase is far more effective than quotation. Remember that the first sentence presenting any new idea (whether the topic sentence of a new paragraph or a shift of thought within a paragraph) should be written *entirely in your own voice,* as a generalization, without any reference to your sources.

To summarize, the paragraphs of your essay should include the following elements:

- *Topic sentence*: Introduce the theme of the paragraph, and state the idea that is a common element tying this group of opinions together.

- *Explanation*: Support or explain the topic sentence. Later in the paragraph, if you are dealing with a complex group of statements, you may need a connecting sentence or two, showing your reader how one reason is connected to the next. For example, an explanation might be needed in the middle of the "enforcing tough standards builds character" paragraph as the writer moves from the need for "tough love" to the obligation of society to offer more help.

- *Paraphrase or summary*: Present specific ideas from your sources in your own words. In these cases, you must of course *acknowledge your sources* by citing names in your sentence.

- *Quotation*: Quote from your sources only when the content or phrasing of the original statement justifies word-for-word inclusion. In some groups of statements, there may be several possible candidates for quotation; in others, there may be only one; often you may find no source worth quoting. For example, read the statements made by Sokolov, Berg, and Pearson once again. Could you reasonably quote any of them? Although Berg and Pearson both take strong positions well worth presenting, there is no reason to quote them and every reason to use paraphrase. You might want to quote Sokolov's first sentence, which is apt and well-balanced.

As you present the opinions of your sources in the body of your essay, *you should remain neutral*, exploring the problem and analyzing each point of view without bias. In the final paragraphs of your essay, you present your own conclusions, in your own voice, arguing for maintaining society's standards or nurturing the individual student, or recommending ways to accommodate both sides.

Citing Sources in a Synthesis Essay

- *Cite the source's full name*, whether you are quoting, paraphrasing, or summarizing.
- *Try not to begin every sentence with a name*, nor should you introduce every paraphrase or quotation with "says."
- *Each sentence should do more than name a person*; don't include sentences without content: "Mary Smith agrees with this point."
- If possible, *support your general points with references from several different sources*, so that you will have more than one person's opinion or authority to cite.
- When you have several relevant comments to include within a single paragraph, *consider carefully which one should be placed first—and why.*
- You need not name every person who has mentioned a point (especially if you have several almost identical statements); however, *you may find it useful to sum up two people's views at the same time*, citing two sources for a single paraphrased statement:

  Mary Smith and John Jones agree that playing the lottery can be very enjoyable. She finds a particular pleasure in scratching off the numbers to see if she has won.

- *Cite only one source for a quotation*, unless both have used exactly the same wording. In the example above, the citation would not make sense if you quoted "very enjoyable."
- If an idea under discussion is frequently mentioned in your sources, *convey the relative weight of support* by citing "five people" or "several commentators." Then, after summarizing the common response, cite one or two specific opinions, with names. But try not to *begin* a paragraph with "several people"; remember that, whenever possible, the topic sentence should be a generalization of your own, without reference to the supporting evidence.
- *Discuss opposing views within a single paragraph as long as the two points of view have something in common.* Radically different ideas should, of course, be explained separately. Use transitions like "similarly" or "in contrast" to indicate the relationship between opinions.

EXERCISE 22: Analyzing a Paragraph Based on Synthesis of Sources

A. Read the following paragraph, twice.

B. Decide which sentences (or parts of sentences) belong to each of these categories: topic sentence, explanation, summary, paraphrase, quotation.

C. Insert the appropriate label in the left margin, and bracket the sentence or phrase illustrating the term.

D. Be prepared to explain the components of the paragraph in class discussion.

Reading test scores may not always be a valid basis for deciding whether students should be promoted or made to repeat the seventh grade. According to Jason Berg, Tina Pearson, and Patricia Sokolov, proficiency in reading is just one factor among many that should count toward promotion. Pearson points out that students with high scores in reading don't necessarily excel in other subjects. In her view, it is unfair to base the decision on just one area of learning. Berg finds it equally unfair that one test should be valued more highly than a year's achievements. But the issue here is not limited to academic competence. Both Berg and Sokolov attach more importance to a student's character and potential than to intellectual attainments. Berg's definition of "overall performance" includes general contributions to the class that demonstrate a positive attitude. For Berg, the context is the classroom; for Sokolov, it is the nation. In her view, intellect alone won't make the nation thrive: "Laborers and blue-collar workers have been credited throughout our history for their great contribution to the wealth and progress of our country." Our primary concern should be to educate good citizens rather than good readers.

Citing Sources for Synthesis

When you yourself have interviewed people as part of a survey, you realize that it's important to indicate who they are and what they represent. To illustrate a particularly deft use of citation in synthesizing a group of interviews, here is an excerpt from *Moral Freedom* by Alan Wolfe, a sociologist who has published several books exploring American national identity. Based on interviews with ordinary Americans, *Moral Freedom* attempts to define an era in which moral certainties are eroding. In this section, Wolfe is recording opinions about *the disappearance of loyalty in everyday life*.

As you read, notice that both paragraphs begin with a sentence or two in which Wolfe sums up and comments on what his interviewees have told him. Then he introduces Quincy Simmons, Kellie Moss, and Laverne Eaton, one at a time, each with a *brief biographical description* that moves seamlessly—within the same sentence—into a paraphrase or quotation expressing their views. (In this excerpt, the citations have been italicized.) The *transitions*—where Wolfe moves from person to person or from paraphrase to commentary—are extremely clear. You're never in doubt about whose voice you're hearing. This is an excellent model for the presentation of oral evidence.

from MORAL FREEDOM:
TILL CIRCUMSTANCES DO US PART
Alan Wolfe

topic sentence

citation of source

quotation

summary

quotation

transition and
new topic sentence

explanation

link to 1st source

introduction
of 2nd source

quotation

transition
to 3rd source

quotation

summary

quotation

No other institution in American life provokes such bittersweet reflections of loyalty lost as the business corporation. *Quincy Simmons*, who is now 47 years old, came to America from one of the Caribbean islands and eventually settled in the Hartford area. A small businessman who makes his living painting and remodeling, *Mr. Simmons remembers* that "in the old days you got a job and for both the company and the employee it would be different." *He is struck* by these differences between then and now. Then, "you go back home and at the same time the company will see that you get reasonable pay or whatever for the work you do. But now it goes back to greed, everybody's thinking about the money."

Mr. Simmons's views are surely influenced by the wave of downsizings that took place in his city. Known as the home of the American insurance industry, Hartford was hit hard by managed care, a rationalization of health care costs that, for a time, cut into the profits of such large insurers in the area as Aetna or the Hartford. Given the traumatic effects of economic consolidation on the region, *Mr. Simmons's lament* was repeated by so many of his neighbors, and in words so close to his, as to constitute a kind of folk truth. Since the big companies started merging, as *Kellie Moss, a retired bank clerk*, puts it, "there's no heart. It takes the heart and soul out of a company. They make more money — and it all comes down to money — but they don't take care of it. Everything is merging, merging, merging. Push this one out, buy this one out, get him out." *Laverne Eaton, a 55-year-old grandmother*, could see the changes in her own life. She worked for the same company for 32 years before retiring. "They cared about us; we cared about them; we would work ourselves silly because it was important to the company, and the company always showed in kind that they cared about us," *she recalls*. Her son now works for the same firm, and his experiences are entirely different. For him, "there's no loyalty and people don't care about doing the job that they're hired to do."

ASSIGNMENT 4: Writing an Essay Synthesizing Multiple Sources

A. Read "Helping First-Year Students Help Themselves," by Christine B. Whelan, twice.

B. Write a summary of the point at issue, and then present your own opinion of this issue.

C. Use the statements that follow as a basis for a synthesis essay. These statements were written in response to the questions: *Are today's college students immature compared with previous generations and, if so, why? If there is a problem, who should be responsible for solving it?* Analyze each statement, label each kind of reason, and organize all the categories in a chart.

D. Write an essay that presents the full range of opinion, paraphrasing and, where relevant, quoting from representative sources.

To provide a more well-rounded variety of views, your instructor may ask your class to submit brief responses to Whelan's article.

HELPING FIRST-YEAR STUDENTS HELP THEMSELVES
Christine B. Whelan

A sociologist who is presently a senior fellow at the University of Wisconsin (Madison), Christine B. Whelan has written articles for leading newspapers and has published three books concerned with self-improvement in the areas of marriage and college life. This article appeared in the Chronicle of Higher Education.

First-year college students have always arrived on campus full of anxieties: Will I be able to keep up academically? Will I get along with my roommates? Will it be fun? Recently, however, an increasing number feel unable to cope with the emotional demands of college life, and transitional worries have morphed into longer-term fears: Why isn't life falling into place for me? 1

According to a yearly national survey of more than 200,000 first-year students conducted by researchers at the University of California at Los Angeles, college freshmen are increasingly "overwhelmed," rating their emotional health at the lowest levels in the 25 years the question has been asked. Such is the latest problem dropped at the offices of higher-education administrators and professors nationwide: Young adults raised with a single-minded focus on gaining admission to college now need help translating that focus into ways to thrive on campus and beyond. 2

As a college professor specializing in the social psychology of behavioral change, I began noticing the trend several years ago, when many of my students — first at the University of Iowa, then at the University of Pittsburgh — came to me complaining that they felt baited-and-switched. Trained to excel at specific tests and often bolstered by oversupportive parents, they didn't understand why the job offers weren't forthcoming, why their relationships weren't working, why everything seemed so much harder than they'd expected. I call this cohort "Generation WTF" because of that crass, often-heard exclamation of frustration. 3

Much has been written about why so many students are in such a predicament. Perhaps it was a generation of helicopter parents. Maybe it was a 4 cultural shift toward, and acceptance of, the idea of "emerging adulthood," which extends youth well beyond the teenage years. Other research points to growing narcissism and declining empathy among college students — in essence condemning a generation's poor moral character. Certainly the bad economy is exacerbating stress levels for both young adults and their parents.

But to pin all students' stress on loans and a challenging job market misses   5
the larger point: Many young adults weren't taught the basic life skills and coping mechanisms for challenging times. While a rising economic tide may have allowed such students to succeed without strong personal-management strategies, college administrators and professors now must do more than describe the water in which many of our students are drowning. Life rafts of behavioral change, awareness of self-presentation, and social graces are necessary to get students from that stressed-out "what the #%$&?" feeling to one of control — over both their day-to-day behavior and their future choices.

The consequences for students who lack those skills have become increasingly clear both on campus and after graduation. At Pitt, where I teach, and at   6
other institutions, student-life administrators have noticed a marked decrease in resiliency, particularly among first-year students. That leads to an increase in everything from roommate disagreements to emotional imbalance and crisis. After graduation, employers complain that a lack of coping mechanisms makes for less proficient workers: According to a 2006 report by the Conference Board, a business-research group, three-quarters of surveyed employers said incoming new graduates were deficient in "soft" skills like communication and decision making.

Parents and high-school educators certainly have a role to play, but college administrators and professors cannot abdicate their role as an influential   7
socialization force to guide young adults toward better self-management.

After working closely with Generation WTF, I know that it comprises   8
well-meaning young people who genuinely want to improve. Such students are eager to make personal improvements when given the tools to do so and the leeway to customize advice to suit their individual needs. Gallup polling shows that previous generations didn't turn to self-improvement until their 40s. But Generation WTF is the product of a therapeutic culture adept at talking about emotional health at a younger age, ready to embrace ideas of self-help with ease.

I have harnessed this comfort with inward assessment in an introductory   9
sociology course I teach, yielding major improvement in students' well-being. For many students it is the first time that anyone has asked them to explain why they want to achieve a particular goal, and what specific steps they are taking to get there. Dennis, a first-year student in one of my sociology classes, wrote in a paper: "Motivation for me used to be found in others, never in myself. I always needed to be yelled at or pushed to do something." After completing a simple worksheet on goal-setting — and embracing the opportunity to set

and execute any goal he wanted — he decided to make his part-time job a more meaningful experience: "When I set a goal to create a team at work, to get everyone involved and share their opinions, I sort of became a leader. And that sparked more motivation to try to do a good job."

The way to combat the decline in emotional health among first-year 10 students is to offer them opportunities to build such self-efficacy from the start. For example, giving them worksheets to track how they spend their time and money is an empowering exercise. Much academic stress can be eliminated when students see exactly how much time they waste online and watching TV, or how much money they could save by buying fewer snacks on the run.

Teaching interpersonal skills of self-presentation is also essential, as it 11 makes students' interactions with roommates, professors, and professional colleagues flow more smoothly. By following suggestions popularized by Dale Carnegie during the Great Depression — to think in terms of the interests of others, smile, and express honest and sincere appreciation — my Generation WTF students report being happily stunned by more-successful interviews, better relationships with family members, and more-meaningful interactions with friends.

Yes, times are tough, and that's part of the stress felt by first-year students. 12 But that must not encourage parents to swoop in and fix their offspring's problems, or educators to lament the decline in moral character of today's young people. I tell students that the goal of my course is to help them rebrand that WTF of frustration into one of empowerment for a wise, tenacious, and fearless future.

While much of my advice seems revolutionary to them, adults from 13 previous generations know that I'm simply teaching a return to core values of self-control, honesty, thrift, and perseverance — the basic skills that will allow those in "emerging adulthood" to get on with life.

Comments:

Bob Bernstein: The skills that Whelan describes may be desirable for getting ahead in life, but I'm not sure that college is the right place to learn them. We are here to get an education. If you feel too frustrated or inadequate to take advantage of the opportunity, then maybe you don't belong in college.

Tom Chang: It's hard to accept that students who are old enough to vote and marry and support themselves should be the kind of basket cases that Whelan writes about. If Whelan is right, maybe they should focus on their academic work, and their instructors should focus on teaching their courses. I don't see college as a self-help center.

Andrea Cilic: Young people certainly don't all mature at the same time, and I question Whelan's conclusion that a whole generation is suffering from this lack of focus and lack of confidence. In my experience at college, some do, and some don't. For the ones who aren't sure of themselves and how to behave, it's useful to have support services on campus. But I don't think we should all be lumped together as socially inept the way Whelan makes it sound.

Mark Grego: I think a lot of my contemporaries are a bit soft, as Whelan describes them, and don't really know how to take care of themselves and get ahead in life without mommy and daddy behind them. My parents have told me about how tough it was for them to get a good start, and they made sure I knew how to work hard and take advantage of opportunities, particularly the opportunity to go to college. I feel sorry for my classmates who seem a bit lost, but I'm not sure it's the college's responsibility to solve their problems.

Elizabeth Grunwald: I don't see how you can separate the academic part of college from the personal growth part of college. It's not just about learning course content; it's how we deal with the experience of being in college, meeting the instructor's standards for a good grade, getting along with other students, making the right choices, not just about what courses we take, but how we spend our time and even who we spend it with. Those skills are integral to college, and will be useful all through life. Students who don't have them should be helped to acquire them.

Miguel Gutierrez: If students lack the ability to focus today, it's because there are so many distractions that our teachers and our parents never had. It's normal now to spend a lot of time on social media and simply checking up on what's happening. The student who doesn't do that will probably stand out as being different or odd. I don't know how you change that. Getting tough with students and restricting their access to electronic equipment just won't work.

Declan Mangan: Whelan mentions "helicopter parents." Does she mean they function as a sort of rescue service when their kids get into trouble? I can see that some kids my age would feel abandoned, especially if they go away to college, without the constant reminders of what's the right thing to do and the right choice to make and the sense that there's someone behind you who cares about you. In that sense, the school does need to step in and take the place of a parent. But what's the alternative? Should parents withdraw their support as soon as their children become teenagers? Helicopter parents are better than absent parents.

Ruth Martinez: The only thing I can think of to avoid the problem Whelan describes is to include "maturity" and "good focus" and "self-confidence" as requirements for acceptance to college. Maybe colleges shouldn't just look at academic and extra-curricular achievement, but also at the whole person. Isn't that what interviews are for?

Margaret Matthews: What's the point of graduating a class of students at the end of four years who don't have the skills to get on in the world? I don't care whose fault it is. If you restrict the curriculum to academic subjects, you are letting down your students. Colleges do have a responsibility to encourage students to grow into responsible adults. "Responsible" means being able to take care of themselves and to be thoughtful about other people, to make good choices in life.

Jenny McKenzie: Many colleges do not attempt to bring their freshmen up to speed by offering courses in areas like good study habits, time management, decision-making. I imagine that students who take those courses will benefit and will be more likely to graduate, and on time, with a good GPA. It's really a matter of practicality. If colleges want a good record of student success, then they have to help the students to make it happen.

Martin O'Sullivan: I don't think the problem is primarily the fault of parents. A lot of it comes from opening the doors of the colleges to practically anyone who wants to enroll. If admission was restricted to students who were well prepared for academic work, many of these issues wouldn't arise. Students would have the confidence and the interest to get involved in their courses because they want to be educated. I don't think everyone in college really wants to be there, but it's a requirement now for getting the right kind of job.

Raj Patel: We no longer live in an era when a college education belonged to the elite. Why should students be deprived of the opportunity to learn just because their homes and their schools didn't teach that kind of knowledge? If they are exposed to academic work and also given enough support to make them believe that they can master this material, that they're good enough, then some of them, at least, will benefit from the experience and lead a different kind of life from the one that their parents had. Colleges need to encourage that kind of student.

Larry Prentice: One crucial factor is financial support. The students that Whelan describes may be lost, and frustrated, and unable to settle down because they are not sure whether they can afford to be where they are. Many students come from families that cannot help them with the costs of their college education. Many students, even those with scholarships and other financial aid, find it hard to acquire the things that other students take so lightly. Wondering whether you are going to be able to buy the books for your course would make it very difficult to settle down to learning what's being taught.

Beth Selig: I had a roommate who hardly talked to me and who never seemed to be able to pry herself from her iPad. She certainly lacked interpersonal skills (although she may have been great in her tweets). I'm not sure any amount of extra help and support groups would have made any difference. I think colleges have to come to terms with the fact that their students are lost in technology and that taking English and math courses certainly can't compete.

Georgia Shaw: It's hard to be motivated when your motivations have always been provided for you. My parents, and the parents of all my friends, were always very sure about what was best for me. They weren't cruel or nasty about it; they just had certain expectations and made sure that we lived up to them. It's true that there's a kind of vacuum now that I'm away from home, but I think that the guidance that I had throughout my childhood has equipped me well enough to make the transition to being on my own. I and my contemporaries may flounder for a while, but we will get somewhere in the end.

Francesca Silva: You can't behave as if you know how to get along in the world until you've been out in the world. I and my friends have mostly had to have jobs since we were in our early teens. We know how to present ourselves, to look reliable, to attend to business, to please our bosses. We know the value of a paycheck. There's very little a college can do to bring that kind of knowledge in its students. They will acquire it little by little.

LaToya Simms: No one in my family has ever even started college, much less received a diploma. My family has mostly done blue-collar work or work in the lower levels of the health profession. Sure, they are clean and neat and hard-working, but they have never learned the kind of presentation skills and "social graces" that Whelan mentions. I don't think I or my family should be stigmatized for lacking those skills. And I don't see what they have to do with gaining a college education.

Victor Szabo: If the problem can be fixed by bringing students back to reality, then learning to use timesheets and budgeting money and even smiling at people when you don't really feel like it would all be very helpful. One way to do this would be to encourage a mentoring system, in which third-and fourth-year students would simply communicate what they had learned about getting along in college. I think that students would accept these lessons much more easily from their near-contemporaries.

Tony Torres: In my school, everything was geared to passing tests with a high grade. Nothing else mattered because test scores would get you into a good college and would also make the school look good against comparable schools. The content of what you were learning wasn't really important. So we were trained to perform, and to regurgitate facts, but we weren't taught what to do with that knowledge, much less how to behave in work or social situations. It's not surprising that, once they got to college, my classmates more or less fell apart. They were unable to handle a life that wasn't programmed for them.

Sophie Trevino: I worked hard to get to college and am very grateful to be here. I am really appalled by some of my classmates who act as if they're entitled to succeed, that they'll get their grades and their diploma just by showing up in class — sometimes. I don't think that colleges should waste their resources on helping students to become more responsible people. Students who are lazy, even arrogant, should be held up to the highest standards, and if they cannot meet those standards, it's their problem. Either they'll motivate themselves into a diploma or they won't.

When to Synthesize and When to Compare

Synthesis is a method; it is not an end in itself. Some works do not lend themselves to synthesis, which tends to *emphasize similarities* at the expense of interesting differences between sources.

The academic writer needs to distinguish between material that is appropriate for synthesis and material whose individuality should be recognized and preserved. One example of the latter is *fiction;* another is *autobiography.* Assume that three writers are reminiscing about their first jobs: one was a clerk in a drugstore, the second a telephone operator, and the third plowed his father's fields. In their recollections, the reader can find several similar themes: accepting increased responsibility; sticking to the job; learning appropriate behavior; living up to the boss's or customers' or father's expectations. But, just as important, the three autobiographical accounts *differ* sharply in their context and circumstances, in their point of view and style. You cannot lump them together in the same way that you might categorize statements about the lottery or opinions about begging, for they cannot be reduced to a single common experience. The three are not *interchangeable;* rather, they are *comparable.*

Comparison and synthesis both involve analyzing the ideas of several sources and searching for a single vantage point from which to view them. However, there is an important difference. *The writer of a synthesis constructs a new work out of the materials of the old; the writer of a comparison tries to leave the sources intact throughout the organizational process, so that each retains its individuality.* For comparison, you must have two or more works of similar length and complexity that deal with the same subject and that merit individual examination.

When you are assigned an essay topic, and when you assemble several sources, you are not likely to want to *compare* the information that you have recorded in your notes; rather, you will *synthesize* the material into a complete presentation of the topic. One of your sources may be an encyclopedia, another a massive survey of the entire subject, a third may devote several chapters to a scrutiny of that one small topic. In fact, these three sources are really not comparable, nor is your primary purpose to distinguish between them or to understand how they approach the subject differently. You are only interested in the results that you can achieve by using and building on this information.

Synthesizing Sources in Academic Essays

So far, the sources that you have worked with in this chapter have been transcripts of informal statements of opinion. But unless you're including interviews or a survey as part of your research, when you write an essay for your college courses, you'll be using mostly *written* sources: *published documents in print or electronic form*. Written sources vary enormously, not only in their length and their targeted audience, but also in their treatment of the topic and in their reliability.

In a way, your relationship with your sources changes as they grow in number. When you worked with a single source, you were essentially engaging in a conversation with one person.

> *When you work with multiple sources, you're like the* **moderator of a roundtable discussion** *in which you choose who speaks and which points each speaker is allowed to make.*

In the excerpt from Alan Wolfe's *Moral Freedom* on page 268, he is managing the "discussion" quite easily because he has interviewed the sources, asking the questions and setting the agenda. None of his sources is going beyond the limits he has set. The role of the moderator becomes more challenging when you are working with written sources or other kinds, like films, that all have agendas of their own and aren't even aware of your questions.

Using Documentation When Synthesizing Sources: *The Naked Crowd*

To illustrate this process, let's look at an excerpt from Jeffrey Rosen's *The Naked Crowd*. Rosen teaches law at George Washington University and frequently writes about the legal aspects of issues like privacy. In *The Naked Crowd*, he is concerned with Americans' lack of security—on many levels—since 9/11. In this excerpt, he is developing some theories about the way in which we express our fears through stigmatizing others. The comments in the margin help you to track the way in which Rosen embeds his sources into the structure of his argument, both as evidence for what he wants to say and as a spur toward the development of new ideas.

Because this is an academic work (although published for a general audience), Rosen is using formal documentation: endnotes. You can find out about Rosen's sources by checking the endnotes at the back of his book (or, in this case, at the end of the excerpt). As you read, notice that, while some sources get cited only by endnote, others get cited by endnote and also by name within the text:

- When he's dealing with *facts or statistics*, Rosen has to acknowledge where he found the information, but there's no need to cite the person who produced the document. So, he provides an endnote but no citation in the text.

- When he's dealing with *ideas*, he is back to conducting that roundtable discussion, and each participant has to be acknowledged as a *source* (in the endnote) and as a *person* (in the citation within the text). This distinction is important to the smooth and effective presentation of research.

- *Anything that isn't endnoted or accompanied by a source's name in the text can be attributed to Rosen and Rosen alone.*

As you read through the passage, try to pinpoint the places where Rosen stops using a source and advances the analysis or argument himself. Also, see if you can find the one place where he includes an unacknowledged source.

Finally, since many of your instructors will expect you to use MLA style, rather than notes, you should start to become familiar with the way MLA documentation appears on the page. At the end of the excerpt, Rosen's fifth paragraph is repeated, this time with MLA parenthetical citations incorporated into the text. Also see Chapter 12.

from THE NAKED CROWD

Jeffrey Rosen

One of the most salient features of stigma is fear. But today, we fear different attributes than our twentieth-century predecessors did. Instead of fearing unfamiliar races, nations, or religions, people in a more individualistic and egalitarian world are hesitant to make moral judgments about others but we have no hesitation about showing an obsessive concern about the visible signs of our own marketability, such as personal hygiene, physical fitness, health, and sexual attractiveness. We increasingly focus, therefore, on medical risks rather than moral risks. As Alan Wolfe has argued, "When nonjudgmental people make judgments, they often defer to the scientific and medical authorities whom they cite in avoiding making judgments in other situations."[7] Wolfe explores the ways that we medicalize our moral judgments—cloaking our opposition to smoking in the purported health risks of secondhand smoke rather than in our disapproval of the smoker's lack of self-control, for example—and the ways

names Wolfe 3 times: quotation and summary

1

that we try to explain away our moral disapproval of self-destructive behavior by chalking it up to addiction rather than choice. In contrast to the moralistic Victorian era, Wolfe suggests, America has "entered a new era in which virtue and vice are redefined in terms of public health and addiction." Smoking and obesity are attacked as symbols of a failure of discipline that used to be associated with a failure of moral character.[8] And conditions or diseases that are feared to be contagious may lead the tainted individuals or places to be stigmatized with a ruthlessness that the ancient Greeks would have recognized.

Stearns cited in endnote: summary

Today, individuals and objects can become stigmatized not merely because they are infected with a contagious disease, but because they are symbolically contaminated in a way that others fear might be contagious. Paul Rozin of the University of Pennsylvania has studied the ways that fear of contagion can lead individuals to avoid even the briefest contact with an object that poses no actual health risk. Rozin gives the following example: You are about to drink a glass of juice, when a friend drops a cockroach in it. You refuse to drink it, on the grounds that cockroaches are dirty and might carry disease. The friend pours a new glass of juice and drops a dead sterilized cockroach into it, ensuring that there is no longer a safety issue. You refuse to drink again, confessing that the drink has been spoiled because it has been "cockroached" by brief contact with a disgusting object: What motivates you to spurn the juice is not a rational fear of disease, but a visceral reaction that is best described as being grossed out. The health risk turns out to be a masquerade for a psychological aversion that is harder to justify in rational terms.

names Rozin 3 times: paraphrase and brief quotation

The response to the cockroach, Rozin argues, illustrates what he calls "the law of contagion."[9] Because we respond more emotionally to negative than positive images, even the briefest physical contact with an object that is perceived to be contaminated can lead a person or an object to be perceived as contaminated as well. Once an object or a person has been spoiled or stigmatized, it may be very hard to remove the stigma: The cockroached juice remains objectionable even if the cockroach has been sterilized. And if there are psychological or moral fears lurking behind a medicalized fear, no amount of reassurance about physical risks will remove the stigma: This is why there is widespread reluctance to touch people with AIDS. The result may be the permanent shunning of individuals who are not, in fact, contagious but who engage our deep and ineradicable fears of contagion, which are rooted in a disgust that we dare not publicly express.

After 9/11, the most dramatic illustration of the principle of contagion was America's response to fears of anthrax. Four letters containing anthrax were mailed to congressional and media leaders in October 2001, leading to 23 cases of anthrax infections and five deaths by the end of November. But the disruption that resulted was wildly disproportionate to the actual risk: The Hart

government Web site cited: summary of event

2

3

4

Senate Office Building was closed for months and decontaminated at a cost of $22 million. After traces of anthrax were found in its mailroom, the U.S. Supreme Court evacuated its courtroom for the first time since the building opened in 1935, and held a special session down the street at the U.S. Court of Appeals for the D.C. Circuit. When traces of spores were found at almost two dozen off-site mail facilities that served federal buildings throughout Washington, including the White House, the CIA, and the State Department and the Justice Department, mail to all federal government offices was shipped to Ohio to be decontaminated, delaying its delivery for months. The postmaster general told Congress that the total cost of the anthrax attacks could exceed $5 billion.[10]

After the anthrax attacks, many citizens reported increased levels of fear. During the month of October, the FBI investigated 2,500 reports of suspected anthrax attacks, many of which turned out to involve harmless substances such as talcum powder. There was a surge in purchases of gas masks and Cipro, the anthrax antibiotic. Three out of ten people surveyed in a Gallup Poll at the end of October said they had thought about buying a gas mask or Cipro, and more than half said they were considering handling their mail more cautiously.[11] In another poll, half said they had some concern about contracting anthrax, although the other half had little or no concern.[12] More than a third of Americans reported washing their hands after opening Christmas cards.[13] Whether this behavior should be interpreted as a limited panic by an irrational minority or as "reluctance to panic"[14] by the calmer majority is open to debate; but it demonstrates a level of concern vastly disproportionate to the actual threat of infection.

More striking than the fluctuating polls were the rituals that the government adopted in order to expunge the stigma of a mail system that had been tainted in just the way that Rozin's experiments with cockroaches suggest. Once the postal service had been marked in the public mind as a bearer of contamination, even the most remote possibility of contact with a letter that had passed through one of the facilities where a few anthrax spores had been detected became a source of public fear and disgust. Soon after the attacks, on the advice of the Centers for Disease Control and Prevention, universities and other private employers advised their employees to wash their hands after handling mail and to wear latex gloves when opening envelopes. Months after the attacks, the post office adopted elaborate procedures for the permanent irradiation, in off-site facilities, of letters addressed to federal offices, resulting in substantial delays. And a post office report issued in March 2002 promised to implement a "multi-layered, multi-year Emergency Preparedness Plan" to protect customers and employees from exposure to biohazardous material and safeguard the mail system from future attacks. The plan includes the deployment of technology to identify and track all retail mail in the United States; to scan each letter for possible contamination; to sanitize mail addressed to targeted groups; and

(margin annotations)

news article cited: summary

news articles cited: summaries

Glass & Schoch-Spana cited in endnote but not named: brief quotation

names Rozin: reminder/ no endnote

government report cited: summary

5

6

to expand the use of "e-beam and X-ray irradiation" of contaminated mail. It aspires in the next few years to develop an "intelligent mail system" that would allow "capturing and retaining data to enable tracking and tracing of mail items, data mining to allow forensic investigation, and positive product tracking to eliminate anonymous mail." Within four years of its implementation, the program is estimated to cost up to $2.4 billion a year.[15]

Recall that these extraordinary rituals, which have permanently changed the way mail is delivered in America, were triggered by an attack that claimed only five lives. But the rituals were designed not to purify the mail but to eliminate the stigma that has attached itself to the American postal system. Like the early Christians who understood stigmata as bodily signs of holy grace, and thus transformed the symbols of Christ's ultimate sacrifice into symbols of divine favor, we are attempting to purge the stigma of anthrax by reenacting a ritual of reassurance. In this sense, the scanning of envelopes for anthrax is similar to the rituals that require us to remove our shoes at the airport or to use plastic knives in the sky. Like a religious rite, its purpose is psychological rather than empirical. Just as people take Communion to remind themselves that Jesus died on the Cross and sacrificed Himself for their sins, so people remove their shoes to give themselves the illusion of being protected from future shoe bombers. Like believers taking the leap of faith, they are more concerned about ritualized expressions of safety than about safety itself.

Our response to the anthrax attacks after 9/11 is only one example of the tendency of crowds to think in terms of emotional images rather than reasoned arguments, which helps to explain why different groups respond differently to unfamiliar risks. In a Gallup Poll taken soon after September 11, 69 percent of the women surveyed said they were "very worried" that their families might be victimized by terrorist attacks. Only 46 percent of the men were similarly concerned. Paul Slovic's work suggests that in thinking about a range of risks—from the hazards of nuclear waste to the possibility of being victimized by crime and violence—men tend to judge the risks as smaller and less threatening than women.[16] Better educated, richer people perceive themselves to be less at risk than their poorer counterparts. People of color tend to be more fearful of risk than white people. And white men consistently perceive risks to be lower than everyone else, including white women and men and women of color.

When Slovic examined the data more closely, however, he found that not all white men are less fearful than everyone else. The "white male effect," he discovered, seemed to be caused by about 30 percent of the white men surveyed, who judged risks to be extremely low. The rest of the white men didn't perceive risks very differently from all the other groups.[17] What distinguished the 30 percent of less fearful white men from everyone else? They shared certain characteristics that had more to do with their worldview than with

names Slovic twice: paraphrase

7

8

9

their sex. The calmer white men tended to be less egalitarian than everyone else: A majority agreed with the proposition that America has gone too far in pursuing equal rights. They tended to display more trust in authorities, agreeing that government and industry could be relied on to manage technological risks. By wide margins, they felt very much in control of risks to their own health, and they agreed that if a risk was small, society could impose it on other individuals without their consent. They believed that individuals should be able to take care of themselves. In short, they were more politically conservative, more hierarchical, more trusting of authority, and less egalitarian than most of their fellow Americans.

One reason that relatively conservative white men seem to be less concerned about risk than their fellow citizens is that people are most fearful of risks they perceive as beyond their ability to control. Many Americans preferred to drive rather than to fly in the months following September 11, even though their risks of being killed in a car crash were greater than their risks of being killed in another terrorist attack. At the wheel of a car, people have an illusion of control that they can't achieve as passengers on a plane, and, therefore, they tend to underestimate the risk of driving and overestimate the risk of flying. It isn't easy to imagine yourself in situations you haven't personally experienced, which means that people have a hard time making decisions about unfamiliar and remote risks. This is why people fear most being a victim of those crimes that they are, in fact, least likely to experience. Women worry most about violent crime, even though they have the lowest risk of being victims, while young men worry the least, even though they have the highest risk. Because of their physical differences, men have a greater illusion of control over their ability to respond to violent crime than women do. In areas where women feel more in control than men, however, they are more likely to engage in risky behavior. When it comes to social risks — such as asking strangers for directions — women turn out to be more intrepid than men. Because men are more reluctant than women to risk the humiliation of appearing foolish before strangers, they perceive the ordeal to be more socially risky.

10

In the case of terrorism after 9/11, in fact, men and women appear to be equally at risk. But the best explanation for why men perceive the risk of future terrorist attacks to be lower than women do is that men tend to be angrier than women about the 9/11 attacks, while women tend to be more fearful. In a study of 1,000 Americans conducted a few weeks after 9/11, a group of scholars at Carnegie Mellon University found that women believed they had a greater chance of being hurt in a future terrorist attack than men did. Eighty-one percent of the difference between men's and women's perception of risk could be explained by the fact that women reported lower degrees of anger about the attacks, and higher degrees of fear.[18] Fear is more likely to arise in people who

11

study cited: summary

feel uncertain and unable to control future events, while anger is more likely to arise in people who are more confident of their ability to control their environment. Because angrier people have a greater sense of personal control than fearful ones, they tend to be less pessimistic about the possibility of future attacks.

source?

Despite these gender differences, both men and women dramatically overestimated the risks of a future attack after 9/11: The respondents saw a 20 percent chance that they would be personally hurt in a terrorist attack within the next year, and a nearly 50 percent chance that the average American would be hurt. Thankfully, these predictions proved to be wrong, and there was no attack comparable to those on the World Trade Center in the twelve months following 9/11. But the predictions seemed alarmist even when they were made: They could have come true only if an attack of similar magnitude occurred nearly every day for the following year. This shows how liable people are to exaggerate the risk of terrorism because of their tendency to evaluate probabilities in emotional rather than empirical terms. . . .

12

names Le Bon: no endnote

names Tversky & Kahneman: quotation and summary

The tendency of crowds to make judgments about risks based on visual images rather than on reasoned arguments results in another mental shortcut that leads us to overestimate the probability of especially dramatic risks. People fixate on the hazards that catch their attention, which means those that are easiest to imagine and recall. As Gustave Le Bon recognized in *The Crowd*, a single memorable image will crowd out less visually dramatic risks in the public mind and will lead people wrongly to imagine that they are more likely to be victims of terrorism than of mundane risks, like heart disease. The Nobel Prize winners Amos Tversky and Daniel Kahneman have called this the "availability heuristic,"[20] which they define as the tendency to assume that an event is likely to recur if examples of it are easy to remember. . . . For the same reason, people overestimate the frequency of deaths from dramatic disasters such as tornadoes, floods, fire, and homicide, and underestimate the frequency of deaths from diabetes, stomach cancer, stroke, and asthma.[21]

13

Viscusi cited in endnote but not named: summary

Sunstein named: brief quotation

When presented with two estimations of risk—one high and the other low—people tend to believe the high risk estimation regardless of whether it comes from government or industry.[22] This bias toward the worst-case scenario is another example of the fact that crowds, when their emotions are intensely engaged, tend to focus on the vividness of a particularly unpleasant risk rather than on its likelihood. This phenomenon, which Cass Sunstein calls "probability neglect,"[23] can lead to behavioral changes that strike experts as irrational, such as buying gas masks and Cipro and canceling flights while continuing to drive and eat Big Macs. The print and electronic media play an important role in contributing to this behavior, but it is a role that can't be separated from the demands of the public itself. Most journalists can tell stories of editors who

14

Tocqueville named: paraphrase and quotation

have pressured them to describe worst-case scenarios, in order to scare the audience into thinking that the story in question is somehow relevant to their lives. As Tocqueville noted in his discussion of why American writers are bombastic, citizens in democratic societies spend most of their time contemplating themselves, and can be tempted to stop gazing at their navels only when they are confronted with the largest and most gripping of subjects. Writers, therefore, have an incentive to attract the attention of the crowd by exaggerating the significance of every topic: If they report that things aren't as bad as they might be, the public won't pay attention. Because of this unfortunate dynamic, Tocqueville reported, "the author and the public corrupt one another at the same time."[24]

Best named 3 times: quotation and paraphrase

When reporting on essentially random risks, there is especially great pressure on reporters to exaggerate the scope and probability of the danger, in order to make more people feel that they, too, could be victims. Joel Best of Southern Illinois University has examined the "moral panics" about dramatic new crimes that seized the public attention in the 1980s and 1990s, such as freeway violence in 1987, wilding in 1989, stalking around 1990, children and guns in 1991, and so forth. In each of these cases, Best writes, the television media seized on two or three incidents of a dramatic crime, such as freeway shooting, and then claimed that it was part of a broader trend. By taking the worst and most infrequent examples of criminal violence and melodramatically claiming they were typical, TV created the impression that everyone was at risk, thereby increasing its audience. Although the idea of random violence appeals to our democratic sensibilities — if violence is random, then everyone is equally at risk — Best points out that "most violence is not patternless, is not pointless, nor is it increasing in the uncontrolled manner we imagine."[25] After purported trends failed to pan out in most of the cases described above, the media spotlight moved on in search of new and even more melodramatic threats.

15

7. Alan Wolfe, *Moral Freedom: The Search for Virtue in a World of Choice* (New York: W.W. Norton, 2001), p. 88.

8. Peter N. Stearns, *Battleground of Desire: The Struggle for Self-Control in Modern America* (New York: NYU Press, 1999), p. 325.

9. Paul Rozin, "Technological Stigma: Some Perspectives from the Study of Contagion," in *Risk, Media and Stigma*, pp. 31–35.

10. See <http://www.usps.com/news/2001/press/mailsecurity/allfaq.htm>.

11. Richard Benedetto, "Poll Finds Anthrax Fear But No Panic," *USA Today*, October 23, 2001, p. A4.

12. J. Mozingo, "Poll: Floridians Not Panicked," *The Miami Herald*, October 25, 2001, p. 3B.

13. Tom Pelton, "36% of Americans Wash Up after Handling Mail," *The Baltimore Sun*, December 18, 2001, p. 8A.

14. See, generally, Thomas A. Glass and Monica Schoch-Spana, "Bioterrorism and the People: How to Vaccinate a City against Panic," in *Confronting Biological Weapons*, CID 34, January 15, 2002, p. 222.

15. See, generally, *U.S. Postal Service Emergency Preparedness Plan for Protecting Postal Employees and Postal Customers from Exposure to Biohazardous Material and for Ensuring Mail Security against Bioterror Attacks*, March 6, 2002, available at <http://www.usps.com/news/2002/epp/welcome.htm>.

16. Paul Slovic, "Trust, Emotion, Sex, Politics and Science: Surveying the Risk-Assessment Battlefield," in Paul Slovic, *The Perception of Risk* (Sterling, Va.: Earthscan, 2000), p. 396.

17. Ibid., pp. 398–99.

18. Jennifer S. Lerner, Roxana M. Gonzalez, Deborah A. Small, and Baruch Fischoff, "Effects of Fear and Anger on Perceived Risks of Terrorism: A National Field Experiment," *Psychological Science* (2002).

20. See Amos Tversky and Daniel Kahneman, "Availability: A Heuristic for Judging Frequency and Probability," 5 *Cognitive Psychology* 207 (1973).

21. Ibid., p. 107.

22. W. Kip Viscusi, "Alarmist Decisions with Divergent Risk Information," 107 *Ec. Journal* 1657 (1997).

23. Cass Sunstein, "Probability Neglect: Emotions, Worst Cases, and Law," 112 *Yale L.J.* 61 (2002).

24. Alexis de Tocqueville, *Democracy in America*, eds. Harvey C. Mansfield and Delba Winthrop, vol. 2, part 1, ch. 18 (Chicago: University of Chicago Press, 2000), p. 464.

25. Joel Best, *Random Violence: How We Talk about New Crimes and New Victims* (Berkeley: University of California Press, 1999), p. 10.

The Naked Crowd, Paragraph 5
with MLA Documentation

After the anthrax attacks, many citizens reported increased levels of fear. During the month of October, the FBI investigated 2,500 reports of suspected anthrax attacks, many of which turned out to involve harmless substances such as talcum powder. There was a surge in purchases of gas masks and Cipro, the anthrax antibiotic. Three out of ten people surveyed in a Gallup Poll at the end of October said that they had thought about buying a gas mask or Cipro, and more than half said they were considering handling their mail more cautiously (Benedetto). In another poll, half said they had some concern about contracting anthrax, although the other half had little or no concern (Mozingo). More than a third of Americans reported washing their hands after opening Christmas cards

(Pelton). Whether this behavior should be interpreted as a limited panic by an irrational minority or as "reluctance to panic" (Glass and Schoch-Spana 222) by the calmer majority is open to debate; but it demonstrates a level of concern vastly disproportionate to the actual threat of infection.

Note: The bibliography would provide further information about these references.

EXERCISE 23: Integrating Three Academic Sources

According to some social commentators, many people use the Internet, especially social media, as a means of self-advertisement.

A. Read the following three excerpts and identify the common themes.

B. Write two or three paragraphs, based on these sources, exploring the extent to which using the Web may be encouraging us to re-brand or re-package our personalities.

C. For the purposes of this exercise, you may limit your documentation to citing the names of the three sources; no formal documentation is needed.

Note: Do not discuss one source per paragraph.

**from THE CULT OF THE AMATEUR:
HOW TODAY'S INTERNET
IS KILLING OUR CULTURE**
Andrew Keen

Andrew Keen was the founder of Audiocafe.com, an Internet music company. He has expressed his views on media and participatory technology through articles in journals such as the Weekly Standard *and* Newsweek, *as well as in his columns for the* London Telegraph, *and through appearances on PBS, NPR, and other television news programs.*

The *New York Times* reports that 50 percent of all bloggers blog for the sole purpose of reporting and sharing experiences about their personal lives. The tagline for YouTube is "Broadcast Yourself." And broadcast ourselves we do, with all the shameless self-admiration of the mythical Narcissus. As traditional mainstream media is replaced by a personalized one, the Internet has become a mirror to ourselves. Rather than using it to seek news, information, or culture, we use it to actually BE the news, the information, the culture.

This infinite desire for personal attention is driving the hottest part of the new Internet economy—social-networking sites like MySpace, Facebook, and Bebo. As shrines for the cult of self-broadcasting, these sites have become tabula rasas of our individual desires and identities. They claim to be all about "social networking" with others, but in reality they exist so that we can advertise ourselves: everything from our favorite books and movies, to photos from our summer vacations, to "testimonials" praising our more winsome qualities or re-capping our latest drunken exploits. It's hardly surprising that the increasingly tasteless nature of such self-advertisements has led to an infestation of anony-mous sexual predators and pedophiles.

from THE APP GENERATION: HOW TODAY'S YOUTH NAVIGATE IDENTITY, INTIMACY, AND IMAGINATION
Howard Gardner and Katie Davis

A developmental psychologist, the author of numerous books on learning theory, and the winner of MacArthur and Guggenheim grants, Howard Gardner worked with Katie Davis at the Project Zero research group at Harvard. Now on the faculty of the University of Washington, Katie Davis is especially interested in the effects of digital media on adolescents.

Facebook and other social network sites emphasize self-presentation by organizing their sites around users' individual profiles. The standard elements of a profile on Facebook—friend list, profile picture, inventories of personal tastes and activities—are used to package the self for public consumption. Presen-tation and performance are also central on YouTube, where users become the stars of their own video channels. A few of them—including Justin Bieber, a teen heartthrob whom many adolescent girls would like to "marry"—have earned widespread celebrity for their homemade videos, offering others the misleading promise that anyone with a camera and Internet access can achieve similar renown. The discourse of fame surrounding new media technologies like YouTube parallels the growing emphasis on individualistic values that researchers have observed in tween-focused TV shows.[15] Indeed, they point out that many of these shows engage youth across a variety of media platforms, encouraging their participation by holding out the promise that they, too, can become stars like their favorite TV personalities. Perhaps one needs to add to Erikson's ensemble of possible outcomes of the fifth life crisis a new category: "implausible identity."   1

The educators of low-income youth were particularly concerned about the impact of reality TV on their students. One educator observed that young   2 people increasingly find their role models on MTV rather than in their family or their neighborhood. These television personalities embody a glamorous, self-centered lifestyle that demands little effort or concern for matters beyond their personal and immediate satisfaction. Several participants pointed to such cultural influences to explain one educator's observation: "Many of our students, even though they aspire to other things, if they could, they would rather be someone in the entertainment industry, or a sports figure." This view is supported by published research indicating that many teens would rather be the personal assistant to a celebrity than to be themselves a prominent executive, author, or researcher.[16] The desire for a celebrity connection is particularly widespread among unpopular kids and kids with low self-esteem.

3   Apps also prove instructive in contemplating the rise of the packaged self. Individualism and self-focus are evident in the vast marketplace of apps, which gives youth endless opportunity to personalize their digital experience according to their (at least seemingly) distinct combination of interests, habits, and social connections. Just as no two snowflakes are alike, the same could be said (or claimed) of the array of apps on a person's cell phone. Indeed, the app icon itself is worthy of note. One could argue that the icon serves less to signify the purpose of an app and more to represent a particular brand and the lifestyle, values, and general cachet associated with it. In other words, part of an app's appeal lies in its external representation rather than its internal functionality.

4   Packaging oneself for others involves an element of performance. An app that gained considerable popularity among teens in 2012 illustrates this performative aspect of identity in a digital age. Snapchat lets users take pictures and short videos with their phone (or other mobile device), add text or drawings, and send them to a fellow Snapchat user for a specified length of time (up to ten seconds) before poof! they vanish magically. After considerable cajoling in 2012, Molly convinced Katie to download Snapchat. Something that stood out immediately for Katie was the stagecraft involved in each Snapchat message that Molly sent to her. A typical message might include a "selfie" of Molly making a funny face, overlaid with a wry comment about a thought she just had. Katie concluded that Snapchat exchanges are not so much a conversation between two people, as with standard text messages, but rather a series of mini-performances for an audience of one.

15. Uhls and Greenfield, "Rise of Fame."

16. Jake Halpern, *Fame Junkies: The Hidden Truths behind America's Favorite Addiction* (Boston: Houghton Mifflin, 2007).

from VIRTUALLY YOU: THE DANGEROUS POWERS OF E-PERSONALITY
Elias Aboujaoude

The author/editor of three books, Elias Aboujaoude is a psychiatrist on the faculty at the Stanford School of Medicine; his research centers on obsessive compulsive behavior.

The result of all [our] online interactions is the unwitting creation of an e-identity, a virtual whole that is greater than its parts and that, despite not being real, is full of life and vitality. Unfettered by old rules of behaving, social exchange, etiquette, or even netiquette, this virtual personality is more assertive, less restrained, a little bit on the dark side, and decidedly sexier. Its advantages cannot be underestimated: This "e-personality" can act as a liberating force for the real-life individual, allowing the person to transcend debilitating shyness, let go of stultifying inhibitions, and forge connections and friendships that would be impossible otherwise. In many cases, the virtual version nicely complements the actual person and acts as an extension of his real-life persona. Seen under the best possible light, it is bolder, stronger, and more efficient than the real-life original. It is what makes voicing an unpopular point of view and organizing against an injustice easier to do over instant messaging and on social networking sites. It spurs action and confers bravery and takes cyber-disobedience from Facebook to Freedom Square in Tehran, in the form of hundreds of thousands of wired and suddenly emboldened freedom lovers, carrying out what was dubbed Iran's "Twitter Revolution" in the summer of 2009. (On the eve of renewed student protests later in the year, one of the first measures taken by the Iranian government was to choke off Internet access.)

It is also what makes breaking up with a significant other easier over e-mail and allows us to put an end, less messily or so we think, to an unsatisfying relationship that has gone on too long, without the awkwardness of a conversation that we know we should have but which we keep delaying. Seen from this perspective, this is our action-oriented side at its most efficient best, moving past mountains of inertia, cutting through layers of real-life red tape, social etiquette, and business protocol, to expeditiously and relatively painlessly consummate all manner of transactions in cyberspace. Given these advantages, having a virtual persona can be like acquiring the proverbial third hand: It empowers the person sitting at the computer desk and can even serve as an incentive to become more assertive, effective, and efficient offline as well.

For my friend Laurie and many others, however, the flip side of enhanced productivity, expediency, and courage can be confusion, pain, and disorientation in the real world. That is so because the online self is also dangerous and irresponsible, running roughshod over our caution and self-control. It can encourage us to pursue unrealistic or unhealthy goals; it can make us feel smarter and more knowledgeable than is warranted; and it can encourage us to behave more selfishly and recklessly. By promising both immediate fantasy fulfillment and anonymity, the Internet makes it difficult to resist going to eBay and buying that unneeded leather jacket or waltzing into a "social network" and pretending to be thinner, more popular, and more successful than we really are. It allows us to reinvent the portions of ourselves we are unhappy with, and it offers the freedom to engage in behaviors that our more responsible selves might put a stop to in the harsh light of day. As the Internet presents itself as a godsend and the answer to old yearnings and needs, it is creating unfamiliar and dangerous challenges — ones that strike at the core of who we are or who we want to be. Indeed, if logging on begins as an attempt to fulfill our human need for self-expression and connectedness, it often gives voice to some less mature and antisocial impulses, aspects of ourselves that have historically been kept in check by culture, expectation, religion, and what one might call the social contract. The consequences of allowing these psychological forces to go unchecked can be far-reaching.

One needs to look beyond the unquestionable universe of new opportuni- 4
ties that the virtual world represents — a revolution equal in scope and potential to the Industrial Revolution — to see the dramatic transformations taking place in the most basic ways we behave, communicate, and identify ourselves in the world. When we log on to the Internet, or lose ourselves in a texting exchange, we become, to varying degrees, different individuals. Unconsciously, we take on a new personality that in some cases bears little resemblance to the one familiar to us from our offline lives. It takes but a moment of self-reflection to realize that our typed words often do not sound like us, our online purchases are less thought out than those at the local mall, our cyberspace hookups are less responsible, and our online personal profiles, well, stretch credulity. It takes but a little self-scrutiny to be hit by the realization that we really should know better than to text and drive. Yet in that "state," we feel free, invincible and immune, like "nothing can touch me now." Why should we want to log off?

The person we become can be a conscious creation of our wild imagi- 5
nations, as on the Web site Second Life, where over sixteen million virtual "residents" — cyberspace avatars built from scratch — live in a parallel world of work, play, and romance. Or it can be a deliberate repackaging of our most attractive or attention-grabbing traits, as on social networking sites like MySpace, which has over 100 million active accounts, or Facebook, with over 500 million users. Whether on Second Life, MySpace, or Facebook, subscribers consciously and intentionally reinvent their biographies in part or in whole, presenting to the large virtual audience a new version of themselves, one that may in some cases bear little resemblance to the "real me." More often than not,

however, this new self emerges unintentionally and unconsciously, through e-mail, blogging, texting, message boards, e-tail, sexual pursuits, and innumerable other interactions in cyberspace. Assessing the breadth and nature of a person's online activities, then holding them up against the real-life person we think we know, we can appreciate how foreign and removed virtual personality can be.

ASSIGNMENT 5: Synthesizing Academic Sources

A. Read excerpts from Christina Hoff Sommers' *The War Against Boys*, Peg Tyre's *The Trouble with Boys*, Michael Kimmel's *Guyland*, and Hanna Rosin's *The End of Men*, twice.

B. Use these sources to write an essay on the following topic: *Boys tend to be less successful than girls—academically and socially—in their school years. Is this a problem and if so, what should be done about it?* As you analyze your sources and explore their themes and their differences, develop a thesis that responds to the topic. Follow the guidelines for writing a synthesis essay (p. 264–266), and cite the sources appropriately within your paragraphs. If your instructor asks you to use formal documentation, consult Chapter 10 as well as the forms in Chapter 12. The essay should be three pages long.

from THE WAR AGAINST BOYS: HOW MISGUIDED FEMINISM IS HARMING OUR YOUNG MEN
Christina Hoff Sommers

Known for her conservative views, Christina Hoff Sommers is the author/co-author/editor of seven books, including a textbook on ethics. She has gained public attention for her exploration of the defects of the feminist movement.

The girl-crisis advocates have succeeded in projecting an image of males as predators and females as hapless victims. They have convinced school administrators, leaders of teachers' unions, and officials in the U.S. Department of Education to support them and fund them. They have been able to implement their curricula and policies in many of the nation's classrooms. They could hardly have done these things if they were not addressing genuine problems that school officials are trying to solve.

Sex differences in violence are very real: physically, males *are* more aggressive than females.[47] Cross-cultural studies confirm the obvious: boys are universally more bellicose. In a classic 1973 study of the research on male-female differences, Eleanor Maccoby and Carol Jacklin conclude that, compared to girls, boys engage in more mock fighting and more aggressive fantasies. They insult and hit one another and retaliate more quickly when attacked: "The sex difference [in aggression] is found as early as social play [begins] — at 2 or 2½."[48] The equity specialists look at these insulting, hitting, chasing, competitive creatures and see them as proto-criminals.

It is precisely in drawing this conclusion that they go badly wrong, for they fail to distinguish between healthy and aberrant masculinity. Criminologists distinguish between "hypermasculinity" (or "protest masculinity"), on the one hand, and the normal masculinity of healthy young males, on the other. Hypermasculine young men do, indeed, express their maleness through antisocial behavior — mostly against other males, but also through violent aggression toward and exploitation of women. Healthy young men express their manhood in competitive endeavors that are often physical. As they mature, they take on responsibility, strive for excellence, achieve, and "win." They assert their masculinity in ways that require physical and intellectual skills and self-discipline. In American society, healthy, normal young men (which is to say, the overwhelming majority) don't batter, rape, or terrorize women; they respect them and treat them as friends.   3

Unfortunately, many educators have become persuaded that there is truth in the relentlessly repeated proposition that masculinity per se is the cause of violence. Beginning with the factual premise that most violence is perpetrated by men, they move hastily (and fallaciously) to the proposition that maleness is the leading cause of violence. By this logic, every little boy is a potential harasser and batterer.   4

Of course, when boys are violent or otherwise antisocially injurious to others, they must be disciplined, both for their own betterment and for the sake of society. But most boys' physicality and masculinity are not expressed in antisocial ways.   5

It is very rare these days to hear anyone praising masculinity. The dissident feminist writer Camille Paglia is a refreshing exception. Her observations are effective antidotes to the surfeit of disparagements. For Paglia, male aggressiveness and competitiveness are animating principles of creativity: "Masculinity is aggressive, unstable, combustible. It is also the most creative cultural force in history."[49] Speaking of the "fashionable disdain for 'patriarchal society' to which nothing good is ever attributed," she writes, "but it is patriarchal society that has freed me as a woman. It is capitalism that has given me the leisure to sit at this desk writing this book. Let us stop being small-minded about men and freely acknowledge what treasures their obsessiveness has poured into culture."[50] Men, writes Paglia, "created the world we live in and the luxuries we enjoy"[51]: "When I cross the George Washington Bridge or any of America's great bridges, I think — men have done this. Construction is a sublime male poetry."[52]   6

47. In talking about sex differences, it is important to bear in mind that the characterizations do not apply to all girls, not even all "normal" boys or girls. Although there are any number of gentle and shy boys who shrink from violence, it is said that boys are more aggressive than girls because on the whole they are. And although there are many girls who are less nurturing than the average boy, it is said that girls are more nurturing than boys because, on average, they are.

48. Eleanor Emmons Maccoby and Carol Nagy Jacklin, *The Psychology of Sex Differences*, vol. 1 (Palo Alto, Calif.: Stanford University Press, 1974), p. 352.

49. Camille Paglia, *Sex, Art, and American Culture* (New York: Vintage, 1992), p. 53.

50. Camille Paglia, *Sexual Personae: Art and Decadence from Nefertiti to Emily Dickinson* (New Haven, Conn.: Yale University Press, 1990), p. 37.

51. Paglia, *Sex, Art, and American Culture*, p. 24.

52. Paglia, *Sexual Personae*, p. 37.

from THE TROUBLE WITH BOYS: A SURPRISING REPORT CARD ON OUR SONS, THEIR PROBLEMS AT SCHOOL, AND WHAT PARENTS AND EDUCATORS MUST DO

Peg Tyre

A journalist specializing in education, Peg Tyre has written for national periodicals and published two books. The foundation where she is director of strategy encourages and supports the aspirations of students who could not otherwise afford to go to college.

We know that children who hear and speak plenty of words tend to learn to read more readily. We also know that in the home most little boys speak fewer words and get read to slightly less than girls. It would stand to reason, then, that kindergarten — which is designed to be a language-rich environment — would enable the boys to catch up. Kindergarten, however, seems to make things worse. In the fall term of kindergarten, girls outperform boys by 0.9 points in reading. By the spring semester, the difference has nearly doubled to 1.7 points.

Early in elementary school, classes divide — sometimes formally, sometimes informally — into good readers and not-so-good readers. Too often, the gap between them widens every year in what reading researchers call the "Matthew effect," after a New Testament parable about the rich getting richer and the poor getting poorer. In first grade, a child in the not-so-good reading group reads an average of 16 words in a week, and a skilled reader reads an average of 1,933 words. As any primary school teacher will tell you, the more kids read, the better they read. The inverse is also true. By the end of fifth grade, boys who are poor readers are at a disadvantage from which they will never recover. By middle school, a poor reader reads 100,000 words a year, an average reader 1 million words, and a voracious reader 10 million words.

Around fourth and fifth grade, another factor comes into play as well. Good readers take a leap forward as they move from learning to read to reading to learn. The curriculum demands it. It's no longer enough to be able to "sound out" words. Children have to comprehend sentences and paragraphs from history and science books and make inferences from those texts. Kids who don't make that jump fall into what experts have dubbed the "fourth-grade slump." They are stuck trying to figure out how to decode the word *everglades*, for instance, while other kids are learning about the kinds of animals that live in those Florida swamps. It's an important cognitive leap.   3

By every measure, the fourth-grade slump hits boys harder than it hits girls. This is reflected in boys' engagement in school and in reading. In 2006, Scholastic, a publisher of materials for children, commissioned one of the nation's top polling firms, Yankelovitch, to do a study of the attitudes of nine-year-old boys and girls toward reading. Children were asked if they like to read. More girls than boys were reading enthusiasts (49 percent of boys, 57 percent of girls). More boys than girls said that they didn't like it (10 percent of boys answered "not at all," 6 percent of girls). Those little boys become what Thomas Newkirk, professor of English at the University of New Hampshire and author of the seminal book *Misreading Masculinity: Boys, Literacy and Popular Culture*, calls "reluctant readers." "Boys don't like reading," he says, "so they don't read." It's a disastrous decision. When they turn off reading so young, says Newkirk, "they can't build up enough stamina to read in a sustained way."   4

The fourth-grade slump draws those boys inexorably toward the "eighth-grade cliff." Because girls read so much better than boys, struggling boy readers, perhaps defensively looking for reasons why they're not succeeding, begin to express the opinion that reading is "feminine." Then they go out of their way to avoid things that they classify as "girlie" activities. It's a silly, self-defeating pattern, but boys find plenty of support for this attitude in their families and their culture. Mom is the person who usually reads them a bedtime story. Mom is the person who makes up the grocery list or follows the recipe. Mom is the person who is most likely to buy books, read magazines, and take books out of the library. She's the person they're most likely to barge in on reading a novel.   5

What do boys conclude about the world of reading? Men don't read. So boys begin to check out, and the consequences are almost inevitable.   6

142. *In the fall term of kindergarten.* "Trends in Education Equity of Girls and Women, 2004," National Center for Education Statistics, U.S. Dept. of Education, http://nces.ed.gov/pubs2005/2005016.pdf

142. *The "Matthew effect"* See Matthew 25:29: "For to everyone who has will more be given and he will have abundance. But from one who has not, even what he has will be taken away." See Keith Stanovich, "Matthew Effect in Reading: Some Consequences of Individual Differences in the Acquisition of Literacy," *Reading Research Quarterly* 21, no. 4 (1986): 360–407.

Note: The number that precedes each note refers to the page number on which the information being documented appears in the original text.

from GUYLAND: THE PERILOUS WORLD WHERE BOYS BECOME MEN
Michael Kimmel

A sociologist at SUNY Stony Brook, Michael Kimmel has published twenty books in men's studies, his field of specialization. He is the editor of the academic journal Men and Masculinities.

The evidence is overwhelming that boys of all ages are having trouble in school. They are underachieving academically, acting out behaviorally, and disengaging psychologically. Many are failing to develop those honorable traits we often associate with masculinity — responsibility, thoughtfulness, discipline. Boys drop out of school, are diagnosed as emotionally disturbed and commit suicide four times more often as girls; they get into fights twice as often. Boys are six times more likely to be diagnosed with Attention Deficit and Hyperactivity Disorder (ADHD). They score consistently below girls on tests of reading and verbal skill, and have lower class rank and fewer honors than girls.

Yet while everyone agrees that boys are in trouble, we don't necessarily agree on the source of the crisis, and thus we strongly disagree about its remedies. To hear some tell it, the source of boys' problems is, in a word, girls, who have eclipsed boys in school achievement and honors, college admissions, and attendance. This is not the fault of the girls themselves, others argue, but the fault of "misguided" feminists who, in their zeal to help girls get ahead, have so transformed elementary and secondary education as to make it a hostile environment for boys.

Boys seem to have "lost out" to girl power, and now "the wrong sex may be getting all the attention in school." Pop psychologist Michael Gurian claims schools "feminize" boys, forcing active, healthy, and naturally rambunctious boys to conform to a regime of obedience, giving them the message, he says, that "boyhood is defective." Another pundit writes that "school is a terrible place for boys. In school they are trapped by 'The Matriarchy' and are dominated by women who cannot accept boys as they are. The women teachers mainly wish to control and to suppress boys."

By far the most sustained fusillade against feminism as the cause of boys' woes comes from Christina Hoff Sommers, formerly a philosophy professor and now a resident anti-feminist pundit at the American Enterprise Institute. In her 2000 book, *The War Against Boys*, Sommers claims that schools are an "inhospitable" environment for boys, where their natural propensities for rough and tumble play, competition, aggression, and rambunctious violence are cast as social problems in the making. Efforts to transform boys, to constrain or curtail them, threaten time-tested and beneficial elements of masculinity and run counter to nature's plan. These differences, she argues, are "natural, healthy, and, by implication, best left alone." The last four words of her book are "boys will be boys" — to my mind, the four most depressing words in educational policy discussions today. They imply such abject resignation: Boys are such wild, predatory, aggressive animals that there is simply no point in trying to control them.

The idea that feminist reforms have led to the decline of boyhood is both educationally unsound and politically untenable. It creates a false opposition between girls and boys, assuming that the educational reforms undertaken to enhance girls' educational opportunities have actually hindered boys' educational development. But these reforms — new initiatives, classroom reconfigurations, teacher training, increased attentiveness to students' processes and individual learning styles — actually enable larger numbers of *students* to get a better education, boys as well as girls. Further, "gender stereotypes, particularly those related to education," hurt both girls and boys, and so challenging those stereotypes and expressing less tolerance for school violence and bullying, and increased attention to violence at home, actually enables both girls *and* boys to feel safer at school.

What's more, the numbers themselves may be deceiving. First, more *people* — both male and female — are enrolling in college than ever before. Female rates are going up faster than male rates, but both are increasing. Second, while it's true that more women than men are enrolling in college, that discrepancy has more to do with race than gender. Among middle- and upper-income white students there is virtually no gender gap at all in college enrollments, which suggests that boys' suffering — at least the suffering of the boys these pundits are talking about — isn't as widespread a disaster as they predict. According to Jacqueline King at the American Council on Education, half of all middle- and upper-income white high-school graduates going to college this year are male. What accounts for the gender gap are the statistics regarding working class, black, and Latino college students: In all three groups, women are far more likely than men to go to college.

And although girls are catching up to boys in science and math, and far outdistancing them in English and languages, the cause is neither the disappearance of some putative math gene nor the machinations of some feminist

4

5

6

7

science cabal. It has to do with the ways in which boys and girls experience masculinity and femininity. Again, it's about *gender*—about the Guy Code,—and that means the only way that parents and teachers are going to be able to meet this new wrinkle in our educational institutions is by paying attention to gender.

Let's take the science and math side of the equation first. Much of the work of developmental psychologists suggests that when girls hit adolescence these once-assertive, confident, and proud young girls "lose their voice," as psychologist Carol Gilligan so memorably put it. At a slightly earlier age, as William Pollack and others have found, when the Boy Code kicks in, boys seem to become *more* confident, even beyond their abilities. You might even say that boys *find* their voices, but it is the inauthentic voice of bravado, of constant posturing, of foolish risk-taking, and gratuitous violence. The Boy Code teaches them that they are supposed to be in power, and thus they begin to act like it.

That is to say: At adolescence, *girls suppress ambition, boys inflate it*. Girls are more likely to undervalue their abilities, especially in the more traditionally "masculine" educational arenas such as math and science. As a result, only the most able and most secure girls take such courses. The few girls whose abilities and self-esteem are sufficient to enable them to "trespass" into a male domain skew female data upward. By contrast, too many boys who overvalue their abilities remain in difficult math and science courses longer than they should; they pull the boys' mean scores down....

A parallel process is at work in English and foreign languages, where girls' test scores far outpace boys. But this is hardly the result of "reverse discrimination"; rather, it is because the boys bump up against the Guy Code. While boys tend to regard any sort of academic success as feminizing—notice how they pick on the nerds or the geeks—English is seen as especially "feminine." Boys who study literature are seen as "effeminate, enfeebled bookworms." Ethnographic research has consistently found that boys profess disinterest in English because of what it might say about their (inauthentic) masculine pose. "Most guys who like English are faggots," commented one boy. The traditional liberal arts curriculum is seen as feminizing. Unlike math and science, where there is little room for opinion and conjecture, the language arts and social sciences are about human experience, and so studying them requires that you discuss human experience—something that leaves many guys feeling uncomfortable.

Boys tend to hate English and foreign languages for the same reasons that girls love them. There are no hard and fast rules, but rather one expresses one's opinion about the topic and everyone's opinion is equally valued. "The answer can be a variety of things, you're never really wrong," observed one boy. "It's not like math and science where there is one set answer to everything." Another boy noted:

> I find English hard. It's because there are no set rules for reading texts.… English isn't like math where you have rules on how to do things and where there are right and wrong answers. In English you have to write down how you feel and that's what I don't like.

Compare this to the comments of girls in the same study: 12

> I feel motivated to study English because…you have freedom in English—unlike subjects such as math and science—and your view isn't necessarily wrong. There is no definite right or wrong answer and you have the freedom to say what you feel is right without it being rejected as a wrong answer.

Interestingly, girls assume they'll be wrong—they like subjects where   13
their answers are "not necessarily wrong," while boys assume they'll be right, so they like subjects where there is no gray area. Girls like English because it's harder to be wrong; guys hate it because it's harder to be right. In that sense, it is not the school experience that "feminizes" boys, but rather the ideology of traditional masculinity that keeps boys from wanting to succeed.

The pressure on boys and young guys to conform, first to the Boy Code and   14
then to the Guy Code, is intense and unforgiving. Might that constant pressure actually be what lies behind the problems boys are having in school? And the fear of failure—of being seen as a geek or a sissy, of becoming a target, or of the shame that attends being a passive bystander—is not only what lies behind guys' poor performance academically, but also what lies behind so much of the behavior that baffles the adults in their lives, and leaves so many young guys with knots in their stomachs every time they eat in the cafeteria, go to the bathroom, stand by their locker, walk out onto the playground, change their clothes in the locker room, or even walk from one class to the next. For so many boys, only by shutting down completely, becoming stoic, expressionless robots, can they navigate those public spaces. Is it any wonder that boys are having trouble in school?

71. *The "War Against Boys"?* Some of this section is based on "'What About the Boys?' What the Current Debates Tell Us—And Don't Tell Us—About Boys in School" in *Michigan Feminist Studies*, 14, 1999, pp. 1–28.

71. *Diagnosed with Attention Deficit and Hyperactivity Disorder (ADHD).* See for example Brad Knickerbocker, "Young and Male in America: It's Hard Being a Boy" in *Christian Science Monitor*, April 29, 1999.

71. *Lower class rank and fewer honors than girls.* Knickerbocker, "Young and Male." URL for this article is
http://www.csmonitor.com/durable/1999/04/29/fpls3-csm.shtml

71. *He says, that "boyhood is defective."* Article in *New York Times* and Elium book are cited in Susan Faludi, *Stiffed* (New York: William Morrow, 1998), p. 46; Gurian is cited in G. Pascal Zachary, "Boys Used to Be Boys, But Do Some Now See Boyhood as a Malady" in *Wall Street Journal*, May 2, 1997.

71. *"Mainly wish to control and to suppress boys."* Cited in Debbie Epstein, Janette Elwood, Valerie Hey, and Janet Maw, "Schoolboy Frictions: Feminism and 'Failing' Boys" in *Failing Boys* (Buckingham: Open University Press, 1998), p. 7.

72. *"Healthy, and, by implication, best left alone."* Christina Hoff Sommers, *The War Against Boys* (New York: Simon and Schuster, 2000), p. 75.

74 *Liberal arts curriculum is seen as feminizing.* Tamar Lewin, "American Colleges Begin to Ask, Where Have all the Men Gone?" in *New York Times*, December 6, 1998, p. A26. See also Michele Cohen, "A Habit of Healthy Idleness: Boys' Underachievement in Historical Perspective" in *Failing Boys*, edited by Debbie Epstein, Janette Elwood, Valerie Hey, and Janet Maw (Buckingham: Open University Press, 1998), p. 28.

75. *How you feel and that's what I don't like.* Wayne Martino, "Gendered Learning Practices: Exploring the Costs of Hegemonic Masculinity for Girls and Boys in Schools" in *Gender Equity*: *A Framework for Australian Schools* (Canberra: 1997), p. 133.

75. *Without it being rejected as a wrong answer.* Wayne Martino, "Gendered Learning Practices," p. 134. See also Wayne Martino and Bob Meyenn, *What About the Boys?: Issues of Masculinity in Schools* (Buckingham: Open University Press, 2001).

75. *That boys are having trouble in school?* Susan McGee Bailey and Patricia B. Campbell, "The Gender Wars in Education" in *WCW Research Report*, 1999/2000.

from THE END OF MEN: AND THE RISE OF WOMEN
Hanna Rosin

A journalist specializing in religion and politics, Hanna Rosin is a writer and editor at Atlantic *and at* Slate. The End of Men *is her second book.*

Background: You may want to view an eight-minute *TED Talk* given by Hanna Rosin in 2010 on "New Data on the Rise of Women."

The Nation's Report Card (officially the National Assessment of Educational Progress [NAEP]) is a series of tests that's been given every few years since the late 1960s by the Department of Education, as a kind of check-in on the progress of students in different grades. In the latest assessment, girls scored much higher than boys in reading, but girls have always scored higher in reading. The only significant change over the last decade or so is a dip in twelfth-grade boys' scores. The dip is most acute for boys from poor and minority families but is not exclusive to them. At the end of high school, nearly one in four white sons of college-educated parents scored "below basic" on the reading section of the NAEP, compared to 7 percent of girls. In math, scores of both boys and girls have been steadily improving, but in the last few years girls have been closing the gap.

In any given year the differences are not alarming, and in some years boys in certain grades even do better than girls. But cumulatively the numbers paint a picture of an education system that plays to girls' strengths, and a new generation of girls who are confident and ready to rise to those expectations. Schools have in effect become microcosms of the larger economy. Richard Whitmire, author of *Why Boys Fail*, summarizes the trend this way: "The world has gotten more verbal; boys haven't." In the late 1990s, educators acted on the correct assumption that all jobs now require more sophisticated writing. Cops now need advanced degrees and practice in communication skills; factory workers are expected to be able to fill out elaborate orders. Society expects most workers to have college-level literacy, even if their day-to-day jobs do not really require that.

Schools responded accordingly and began pushing verbal skills earlier in the curriculum. Now a typical pre-kindergartner learns what a first-grader used to learn. The verbal curriculum heats up long before boys are mature enough to handle it. As a result, they start to think of themselves early on as failures in school. Their discouragement builds and, many years down the road, schools face what Whitmire calls the ninth-grade bulge. That year often produces much larger classes than subsequent years, because classes are full of boys waiting it out until they are old enough to drop out altogether. Girls meanwhile amp up their ambition as they progress through school. They are more likely than boys to take college-preparatory classes, including geometry, algebra II, chemistry, biology, and foreign languages, although boys are more likely to take physics. A University of Michigan study found that 67 percent of female high school seniors say they plan to graduate from a four-year college, compared with 55 percent of male students.

Beyond straight verbal skills, boys tend to get tripped up by what researchers call "noncognitive skills," meaning the ability to focus, organize yourself, and stay out of trouble. Boys of every race and background have a much higher incidence of school disciplinary and behavior problems and suspensions, and they spend far fewer hours doing homework. They are much more likely to be in special ed programs or diagnosed with a disability or some form of autism. Teachers consistently rate girls as being less disruptive and putting in more effort than boys in high school. And these days the temptations that can siphon

2

3

4

off effort are much greater. Boys and girls both fritter away time on technology, but studies show that boys tend to do it in much longer blocks, spending hours after school playing video games. In fact, a consensus is forming that the qualities most predictive of academic success are the ones that have always made up the good girl stereotype: self-discipline and the ability to delay gratification. In other words, the ability to spend two hours doing your homework before you take out the PlayStation.

Page 161. In the latest assessment: "The Nation's Report Card: Reading 2011," NCES 2012-457, National Center for Education Statistics. http://nces.ed.gov/pubsearch/pubsinfo.asp?pubid=2012457.

Page 161. Nearly one in four white sons: Richard Whitmire, *Why Boys Fail: Saving Our Sons from an Educational System That's Leaving Them Behind* (AMACOM, 2010), p. 25.

Page 161. In math, scores of both boys and girls: National Assessment of Educational Progress 1990, 1992, 1996, 2000, 2003, 2005, 2007, 2009 and 2011 Mathematics Assessments, National Center for Education Statistics.

Page 162. "The world has gotten more verbal": Whitmire, *Why Boys Fail*, p. 28.

Page 162. Ninth-grade bulge: Whitmire, *Why Boys Fail*, p. 21.

Page 162. They are more likely than boys: See tables 157 and 159 in "Digest of Education Statistics: 2010," National Center for Education Statistics. http://nces.ed.gov/programs/digest/d10/.

Page 162. University of Michigan study: Jerald G. Bachman, Lloyd D. Johnston, and Patrick M. O'Malley, "Monitoring the Future: Questionnaire Responses from the Nation's High School Seniors, 2010," University of Michigan Institute for Social Research, 2011.

Part IV

WRITING FROM RESEARCH

Research Can Bridge the Academic and Business Worlds

There is a point at which professional writing and academic writing begin to diverge. Legal writing, technical writing, business writing, writing in the health and welfare professions—all provide few opportunities to engage in research as the basis for preparing documents. Still, the director of a mental health unit might tell Janet, the social worker, that the district is considering adding music therapy to their range of services and ask her to draw on her college experience in the arts and psychology to prepare a report about the success rate and costs of such programs in other states. Parker could be assigned to use his background in economics to explore the range of pension plans available to retail workers across the country as his department store reviews possibilities for expanding its benefits program. And Greg's manufacturing company is ready to decide on a location for a new factory, but is concerned about the dangers of natural disasters like flooding or fire, so Greg reviews his old geography texts and goes off to find out about meteorological conditions at the proposed site. All of these reports will involve research—at the library, online, and in interviews. Janet, Parker, and Greg will find it helpful to have had some training and practice in evaluating sources, synthesizing the material to form a recommendation (very much like a thesis), and writing it up in a coherent, persuasive document. Those skills, and more, are what Part IV will emphasize.

But the more immediate purpose for which this book, and particularly Part IV, prepares you is the writing of essays for your college courses. Most long essays and term papers are based on research. You'll be expected to formulate your opinion or respond to a topic, and then to validate and support your response by searching for and citing authorities. Unlike the multiple-source essays in Chapter 6, a research essay assignment rarely comes with pre-packaged sources. As soon as you start your research, you will find yourself dealing with a multitude of sources from which you will have to make your own selection of readings.

- In the electronic databases and computer catalogs, you'll have to judge quickly which books and periodicals are worth locating.

- At the shelves and on the computer screen, you'll have to skim a variety of books, articles, and Web sites rapidly to choose the ones that may be worth reading at length.

- At the library table and on the computer screen, you'll have to decide which information is worth writing up as part of your notes, which pages need to be downloaded, duplicated, or printed out, and which sources can be ignored.

In Chapters 7, 8, and 9, you will be given explicit guidelines for locating, evaluating, and taking notes from sources.

So far, the process seems like the one that Janet, Parker, and Greg would be using to prepare a comprehensive report with a convincing recommendation. It's in Chapter 10 that the two worlds—business and academic—really diverge. For the academic researcher, the *process* is just as important as the conclusion. And the crucial component of the process is *accountability*. In your college writing, you will, in substantial part, be judged on whether you have made it clear which source is responsible for which idea and on which page of the source that information can be found. Of course, you will also be expected to establish your own thesis and structure, and your paragraphs will have to be written in your own voice, with the sources serving as evidence for your own views. In Chapter 10, you will be shown that, in addition to turning in a coherent essay, you must also account for your sources using a system that includes the familiar skills of summary, quotation, paraphrase, and the citation of authors. This system is called *documentation*.

What should your essay look like when it's completed? For reference, in Chapter 11, you can examine two essays that demonstrate how to write a persuasive, analytical research essay, each one using a common method of documentation.

▪7▪
Beginning Research

Chapter 7 shows you many ways to develop a topic for a research essay as you search for information in the library and on the Internet. You can use databases and search engines to identify and locate a range of books, periodical articles, and Web sites that are appropriate for academic research. At the same time, you'll learn to organize these sources into a formal bibliography.

Topic Narrowing

When you start your research, sometimes you will know exactly what you want to write about, and sometimes you won't. Your instructor may assign a precise topic. Or you may start with a broad subject and then narrow the focus yourself. Or you may develop an idea that you wrote about in your single- or multiple-source essay.

Ask yourself these practical questions as you think about your topic and before you begin collecting material for your essay:

- How much time do I have?
- How long an essay am I being asked to write?
- How complex a project am I ready to undertake?

Narrowing Your Topic

1. Whether your instructor assigns a broad topic for your research paper or you are permitted to choose your own topic, do some preliminary searching for sources to get background information.

2. As you see what's available, begin to break down the broad topic into its components. Try thinking about a specific point in time or the influence of a particular event or person if your topic is *historical* or *biographical*. Try applying the standard strategies for planning an essay (see p. 199 in Chapter 5) if you're going to write about a *contemporary* subject. Try formulating the reasons for and against if you're going to write an *argument*.

3. Once you have some sense of the range of available material, consider the *scope* of your essay. If the scope is too broad, you run the risk of presenting a superficial overview. If the scope is too narrow, you may run out of material.

4. As you read, consider *your own perspective* and what interests you about the person, event, or issue. If you really want to know more about the topic, your research will progress more quickly and you're more likely to get your essay in on time.

5. Formulate a few *questions* to help you structure your reading and research. As you read, you should stay within that framework, concentrating on materials that add to your understanding of the topic, skimming lightly over those that don't.

6. As answers to these questions emerge, think about a potential *thesis* for your essay—a hypothesis that you would like to prove.

Topic Narrowing: Biographical and Historical Subjects

Biographical and historical topics have an immediate advantage: they can be defined and limited by space and time. Events and lives have clear beginnings, middles, and ends, as well as many identifiable intermediate stages. You probably won't want to undertake the full span of a biography or a complete historical event, but you could select a specific point in time as the focus for your essay.

Writing about People

Assume, for example, that by choice or assignment your broad subject is *Franklin Delano Roosevelt* (FDR), who was president of the United States for twelve years—an unparalleled term of office—from 1933 until 1945. You begin by reading *a brief overview of FDR's life*. An encyclopedia article of several pages might be a starting point. This should give you enough basic information to decide which events in FDR's life might interest you enough to sustain you through the long process of research. You might also read encyclopedia articles about the major events and issues that formed the background to FDR's career: the Great Depression, the New Deal, the changing role of the president.

Choosing a Point in Time: Now, instead of tracing *all* the events in which he participated during his 63 years, you might decide to describe FDR at the point when his political career was apparently ruined by polio. Your focus would be *the man in 1921*, and your essay might develop a thesis drawing on any or all of the following topics—his personality, his style of life, his physical handicap, his experiences, his idea of government—at *that* point in time. Everything that happened to FDR after 1921 would be relatively unimportant to your chosen perspective. Another student might choose a different point in time and describe *the new president in 1933* against the background of the Depression. Yet another might focus on an intermediate point in FDR's presidency and construct a profile of the *seasoned president* in 1940, at the brink of America's entry into World War II, when he decided to run for an unprecedented third term in office.

Finding a Focus: The topic might be made even more specific by focusing on *a single event and its causes*. For example, the atomic bomb was developed during FDR's presidency and was used in Japan shortly after his death:

- What was FDR's attitude toward atomic research?
- Did he advocate using the bomb?
- Did he anticipate its consequences?
- How has 70 years changed our view of the atomic bomb and FDR's role in its development?

Or you might want to study Roosevelt in the context of his political party:

- How did he influence the Democratic Party?
- How did the party's policies influence his personal and political decisions?
- What role did Roosevelt play in the establishment of the United States as a "welfare state"?
- How has the Democratic Party changed since his time?

This kind of profile attempts to describe a historical figure, explore his or her motives and experiences, and, possibly, apply them to an understanding of current issues. In effect, your overriding impression of character or intention becomes the basis for the thesis, the controlling idea of your essay.

Writing about Events

You can also view a *historical event* from a similar specific vantage point. Your broad topic might be the Civil War, which lasted four years, or the Berlin Olympics of 1936, which lasted a few weeks, or the Los Angeles riots of 1991, which lasted a few days. Rather than cover a long span of time, you might focus on an intermediate point or stage, which can serve to illuminate and characterize the entire event.

The *Battle of Gettysburg*, for example, is a broad topic often chosen by those interested in the even broader topic of the Civil War. Since the three-day battle, with its complex maneuvers, can hardly be described in a brief narrative, you would want to narrow the focus even more. You might describe the battlefield and the disposition of the troops, as a journalist would, at a single moment in the course of the battle. In this case, your thesis might demonstrate that the disposition of the troops at this point was typical (or atypical) of tactics used throughout the battle, or that this moment did (or did not) foreshadow the battle's conclusion.

Finding a Focus: In writing about history, you also have to consider your own point of view. If, for example, you set out to recount an episode from the Civil War, you first need to *establish your perspective*: Are you describing the Union's point of view? the Confederacy's? the point of view of the politicians of either side? the generals? the civilians? industrialists? hospital workers? slaves in the South? black freedmen in the North?

The "day in the life" approach can also be applied to *social and technological changes that had no specific date*:

- When and under what circumstances were primitive guns first used in battle?
- What was the reaction when the first automobile drove down a village street? When television was first introduced into American homes?
- What was it like to shop for food in Paris in 1810?
- In Chicago in 1870?
- In any large American city in 1945?

Instead of attempting to write a complete history of the circus from Rome to Ringling, try portraying *the particular experience of a single person*:

- What was it like to be an equestrian performer in Astley's Circus in London in 1805?
- A chariot racer in Pompeii's Circus Maximus in 61 BC?

Setting a tentative target date helps you to focus your research, giving you a practical way to judge the relevance and the usefulness of each of your sources.

Establishing a Thesis and a Strategy

As you narrow your topic and begin your reading, watch for your emerging thesis—a *clear impression of the person or event* that you wish your reader to receive. Whether you are writing about a sequence of events, like a battle or a flood, or a single event or issue in the life of a well-known person, you will still need both a *thesis* and a *strategy* to shape the direction of your essay. A common strategy for biographical and historical topics is the *cause-and-effect sequence*—reasons why a certain decision was made or an event turned out one way and not another:

- Why did the United States develop the atomic bomb before Germany did?
- Why did President Truman decide to use the atomic bomb against Japan as the war was ending?

Your thesis should contain your own view of the person or event that you're writing about:

- "FDR had no choice but to support the development of the atomic bomb."
- "The development of the supermarket resulted in major changes to American family life."
- "The imposition of term limits for the presidency after FDR's fourth term in office was [or was not] good for the United States [or for democracy in the United States or for political parties in the United States or for politicians in the United States]."

Finally, do not allow your historical or biographical portrait to become an exercise in creative writing. Your evidence must be derived from and supported by well-documented sources, not just your imagination. The "Napoleon might have said" or "Stalin must have thought" in some biographies and historical novels is often a theory or an educated guess. If the theory is firmly rooted in research, the author should provide documentation and a bibliography to substantiate it.

Topic Narrowing: Contemporary Subjects

If you chose to write about the circus in 61 BC or 1805, you would find a limited assortment of books describing traditional kinds of circus activity. More recently, however, reviews and features are printed—and preserved for the researcher—every time Ringling Brothers opens in a new city. Your research for an essay about the circus today might be endless and the results unmanageable unless, quite early, you focus your approach.

Finding a Focus: The usual way is to analyze a topic's component parts and select *a single aspect* as the tentative focus of your essay:

- Do you want to write about circus acts? Do you want to focus on animal acts or, possibly, the animal-rights movement's opposition to the use of animals for circus entertainment? Or the dangers of trapeze and high-wire acts?

- How has the circus adapted to contemporary culture? What does the trend to small, one-ring circuses or the advent of the "new age" Cirque de Soleil tell us about people's taste today? Why are circuses still so popular in an age of instant electronic entertainment?

- How does the circus function as an economic organization? What are the logistics of circus management — transport, for example — or marketing? How has modern entertainment (e.g., TV, the Internet) altered the business of circuses?

One practical way to begin narrowing a topic is to do a *computer search.* Descriptors and keywords can suggest possibilities for the direction of your essay.

Yet another way to narrow your perspective is to apply different strategies to possible topics. Suppose that *food* is your broad topic. Your approach might be *descriptive,* analyzing *causes and effects:* you could discuss recommendations about what we ought to eat and the way in which our nutritional needs are best satisfied. Or you could deal with the production and distribution of food — or, more likely, a specific kind of food — and use *process description* as your approach. Or you could analyze a different set of *causes:* Why don't we eat what we ought to? Why do so many people have to diet, and why aren't diets effective? Or you could plan a *problem-solution* essay: What would be the best way to educate the public about proper nutrition?

Within the narrower focus of *food additives*, there are numerous ways to develop the topic:

- To what degree are additives dangerous?
- What was the original purpose of the Food and Drug Act of 1906?
- What policies does the Food and Drug Administration carry out today?
- Would individual rights be threatened if additives like artificial sweeteners were banned?
- Can the dangers of food additives be compared with the dangers of alcohol?

On the other hand, your starting point could be *a concrete object*, rather than an abstract idea: you might decide to write about the Big Mac. You could describe its contents and nutritional value, or recount its origins and first appearance on the food scene, or compare it to best-selling foods of past eras, or evaluate its relative popularity in different parts of the world. All of these topics require research.

If you have a few approaches in mind before you begin intensive reading, you can distinguish between sources that are potentially useful and sources that probably will be irrelevant. Your initial impression of the topic will develop into a *hypothesis*, a theory that may or may not be true, depending on what you find in your research. What you *cannot* do at this stage is formulate a definite thesis. Your thesis will probably answer the question that you asked at the beginning of your research. Although, from the first, you may have your own theories about the answer, you cannot be sure that your research will confirm your hypotheses. Your thesis should remain tentative until your reading has given your essay content and direction. *Remember, though, you have to ask the question first in order to look for the answers.*

Topic Narrowing: Issues for Argument

Most people want to argue about an issue that has significance for them. If no issue immediately occurs to you, try *brainstorming*—jotting down possible ideas in a list. Recall conversations, news broadcasts, class discussions that have made you feel interested, even argumentative. Keep reviewing the list, looking for one that satisfies the following criteria:

- *Your topic should allow you to be objective.* Your reader expects you to present a well-balanced account of both sides of the argument. Too much emotional involvement with a highly charged issue can be a handicap. If, for example, someone close to you was killed in an incident involving a handgun, you are likely to lose your objectivity in an essay on gun control.

- *Your topic should have appropriate depth.* Don't choose an issue that is too trivial: "Disney World is better than Disneyland." Similarly, don't choose an issue that is too broad or too abstract: "Technology has been the bane of the modern world" or "A life without God is not worth living." Your topic should lend itself to a clear, manageable path of research. Using the keywords "god" and "life" in a database search will produce a seemingly unending list of books and articles. Where will you begin?

- *Your topic should have appropriate scope.* Consider the terms of your instructor's assignment. Some topics can be explored in ten pages; others require more lengthy development. Some require extensive research; others can be written using only a few selected sources. Stay within the assigned guidelines.

- *Your topic should have two sides.* Some topics are nonissues: it would be hard to get anyone to disagree about them. "Everyone should have the experience of work" or "Good health is important" are topics that aren't worth arguing. (Notice that they are also far too abstract.) Whatever the issue, the opposition must have a credible case.

- *Your topic can be historical.* There are many issues rooted in the past that are still arguable. Should President Truman have authorized dropping the atomic bomb on Japan? Were there better alternatives to ending slavery than the Civil War? Should Timothy McVeigh have been executed, or the Rosenbergs, or Sacco and Vanzetti?

- *Your topic should be practical.* It may be tempting to argue that tuition should be free for all college students, but, in the process, you would have to recommend an alternative way to pay for the cost of education—something that state and federal governments have yet to figure out.

- *Your topic should have sufficient evidence available to support it.* You may not know for sure whether you can adequately defend your argument until you have done some research. A local issue—should a new airport be built near our town?—might not have attracted a substantial enough body of evidence.

- *Your topic should be within your range of understanding.* Don't plan an essay on "the consequences of global warming" unless you are prepared to present scientific evidence, much of which is written in highly technical language. Evidence for topics in the social sciences can be equally difficult to comprehend, for many depend on surveys that are hard for a nonprofessional to evaluate. Research on literacy and teaching methods, for example, often includes data (such as reading scores on standardized tests) that require training in statistics.

Many of these criteria also apply to choosing a historical narrative or a contemporary subject. What's important in writing any essay—especially one involving a commitment to research—is that the topic interest you. If you are bored while writing your essay, your reader will probably be just as bored while reading it.

EXERCISE 24: Narrowing a Topic

Here are ten different ways of approaching the broad topic of *poverty in America.*

A. Decide which questions would make good starting points for an eight-to-ten-page research essay. Consider the practicality and the clarity of each question, the probable availability of research materials, and the likelihood of being able to answer the question in approximately nine pages.

B. Try rewriting two of the questions that seem too broad, narrowing the focus.

1. How should the nation deal with poverty in its communities?

2. What problems does your city or town encounter in its efforts to make sure that its citizens live above the poverty level?

3. What are the primary causes of poverty today?

4. Whose responsibility is it to help the poor?

5. What effects does a life of poverty have on a family?

6. What can be done to protect children and the aged, groups that make up the largest proportion of the poor?

7. Does everyone have the right to freedom from fear of poverty?

8. Which programs for alleviating poverty have been particularly successful, and why?

9. Should all those receiving welfare funds be required to work?

10. What nations have effectively solved the problem of poverty, and how?

C. Make up several questions that would help you to develop the broad topic of *restricting immigration to America* for an eight-to-ten-page research essay.

EXERCISE 25: Proposing a Topic

The following topic proposals were submitted by students who had been given a week to choose and narrow their topics for an eight-to-ten-page research essay.

A. Consider the scope and focus of each proposal, and decide which ones suggest *practical* topics for an essay of this length.

B. If the proposal is too broad, be prepared to offer suggestions for narrowing the focus.

Student A

Much of the interest in World War II has been focused on the battlefield, but the war years were also a trying period for the public at home. I intend to write about civilian morale during the war, emphasizing press campaigns to increase the war effort. I will also include a description of the way people coped with brownouts, shortages, and rationing, with a section on the victory garden.

Student B

I intend to deal with the role of women in feudal life, especially the legal rights of medieval women. I would also like to discuss the theory of chivalry and its effects on women, as well as the influence of medieval literature on society. My specific focus will be the ideal image of the medieval lady.

Student C

I have chosen the Lindbergh kidnapping case as the subject of my essay. I intend to concentrate on the kidnapping itself, rather than going into details about the lives of the Lindberghs. What interests me is the planning of the crime, including the way in which the house was designed and how the kidnapping was carried out. I also hope to include an account of the investigation and courtroom scenes. Depending on what I find, I may argue that Hauptmann was wrongly convicted.

Student D

I would like to explore methods of travel one hundred and fifty years ago, and compare the difficulties of traveling then with the conveniences of traveling now. I intend to stress the economic and social background of the average traveler. My focus will be the Grand Tour that young men used to take.

Student E

I'd like to explore quality in television programs. Specifically, I'd like to argue that popular and critically acclaimed TV shows of today are just as good as comparable programs ten and twenty years ago and that there really hasn't been a decline in popular taste. It may be necessary to restrict my topic to one kind of television show—situation comedies, for example, or coverage of sports events.

Student F

I would like to do research on several aspects of adolescent peer groups, trying to determine whether the overall effects of peer groups on adolescents are beneficial or destructive. I intend to include the following topics: the need for peer acceptance, conformity, personal and social adjustment, and peer competition. I'm not sure that I can form a conclusive argument, since most of the information available on this subject is purely descriptive, but I'll try to present an informed opinion.

Locating Sources

Research takes place in three overlapping stages:

- Identifying and locating possible sources;
- Quickly reviewing each source and noting its potential usefulness—or lack of usefulness—to your topic (and possibly downloading or copying extracts from the useful ones);
- Recording or saving basic facts about each potentially useful source for possible inclusion in a bibliography.

It's rare that you'll be able to locate all your sources first, read through them, choose those that are worth including in your essay, and then record all your basic information. Research isn't that tidy. At a later stage of your work, you may come across a useful database and find new materials that must be reviewed, recorded, and included in your essay.

The three most common kinds of sources are *books*, *periodicals* (including magazines, newspapers, and scholarly journals), and *Web sites*. Most books and periodicals are published in print form; you can hold them in your hands (or read periodical articles from back issues by inserting microfilm or microfiche into reading machines). Web sites and a few periodicals are located in cyberspace on the Internet and appear only on your computer screen. Depending on your topic, other sources for research might include recorded interviews and lectures, videos and films, radio broadcasts, filmed productions of plays, and recorded music.

Are Libraries Obsolete?

Every library is different; no library is typical. So, describing the system used by your university library is best left to the librarians, who will almost certainly provide tours of the facility. Given the wonders of modern technology, you may question whether you need to visit the library at all.

It's true that you can do a good deal of research on your computer without ever entering the library. You can obtain information about potential sources for your topic; you can download Web material for later use; you can find the complete texts of many periodical articles and even books—all on your computer screen. But you'll still need to use the library:

- To obtain most scholarly books
- To read periodical articles that aren't available on the Internet
- To look for older articles in print indexes
- To use microfilm and microfiche machines
- To obtain and use CD-ROMs
- To get assistance from reference librarians

The last reason is probably the most important one. Librarians provide essential support for your research. They'll show you how the library is organized; how to navigate the stacks of books, online catalogs, and databases; and how to target and refine a computerized search. Much of this information will be available on the home page of your library's Web site; but it's hard to improve on having your questions answered by a real person in real time.

Computer Searches

Searching for sources is best done online through *electronic databases*. Since databases generally list books or periodical articles, but not both, you'll have to engage in at least two separate searches to find a full range of materials. And searching for Web sites requires using a *search engine*, which is nothing more than another kind of database.

Databases and search engines have to manage huge amounts of constantly changing information. To avoid overflowing lists and unmanageable systems, each new work is scanned and then listed only under those *subject headings* (often called *keywords* or *descriptors*) that are relevant to its content. This key organizing principle is called *cross-referencing*: a method of obtaining a standardized, comprehensive list of subject headings that can be used to index information. One example of such a list, used by many libraries as an index for books, is the *Library of Congress Subject Headings,* or LCSH.

Searching for Lawrence of Arabia

Let's assume that you've decided to write about *Lawrence of Arabia*. T. E. Lawrence was a key figure in the Middle East campaigns of World War I, a British scholar fascinated by the desert, whose guerrilla tactics against the Turks succeeded partly because he chose to live like and with the Bedouin tribes who fought with him. You've enjoyed the 1962 award-winning movie about Lawrence, but you'd like to find out whether it accurately represents his experience. Here are some issues and questions about Lawrence's life that might intrigue you:

- Acclaimed as a hero after the war, Lawrence chose to enlist in the Royal Air Force at its lowest rank, under an assumed name. Why?

- He died at the age of 46 in a mysterious motorcycle crash. Was this an accident?

- He contributed to the development of a new kind of military tactic. Why was his kind of guerrilla warfare so effective? Is it still in use today?

- He hoped to gain political independence for the Bedouin tribes. What prevented him?

What Is Boolean Searching?

Boolean searching is the standard way to search a database. Named after George Boole, a nineteenth-century mathematician, this method focuses your topic to get the best possible results. If you are too broad in your wording, you'll get an interminable list of sources, which will be unmanageable; if you're too specific in your wording, you'll get a very short list, which can bring your research to a dead halt.

To carry out a Boolean (or advanced) search, you refine your topic by *combining words*, using *phrases* to express complex subjects, and inserting "operators" — AND, OR, NOT — between keywords. (Sometimes, the operators are symbols, such as +, rather than words.) In effect, you must ask yourself what you do and what you don't want to know about your topic. Let's apply these guidelines to a database search for information about Lawrence of Arabia.

"Lawrence of Arabia" — in quotation marks — is your subject expressed as a phrase: the search will include only those sources in which the entire phrase is found and not those in which both "Lawrence" and "Arabia" appear only separately.

"Lawrence of Arabia" AND "guerrilla warfare" limits the search to those sources that contain *both* phrases. A book about Lawrence that omits guerrilla warfare won't appear in the results list, and vice versa.

"Lawrence of Arabia" OR "T. E. Lawrence" expands the search by expressing the topic two ways and potentially multiplying the number of sources found.

"Lawrence of Arabia" NOT "motion picture" limits the search by excluding sources that focus on the film rather than the man.

Starting with an Encyclopedia: One place to begin your search about Lawrence of Arabia is an *encyclopedia*, which will provide you with a brief overview of his life and so help you to narrow down your topic. There are several general encyclopedias listed in the Google directory (under "reference"), some of which are free to use. Exercise caution if you use *Wikipedia*, the free online encyclopedia "that anyone can edit," since the articles are written and edited by readers and the information is not always authoritative. The best choice — *Encyclopedia Britannica Online* (*EBO*) — is pay-to-view only. So, access it through your library's online link.

If you consult *EBO*, you'll be prompted to type in a question or keyword. So, you type "Lawrence of Arabia." Remember: the quotation marks identify your keyword as a single *phrase*, so your results will be restricted to information about the Lawrence you're looking for. Without quotation marks, Lawrence of Arabia will be interpreted as a request for information about anyone or anything named Lawrence and any material about Arabia.

In its response, *EBO* offers you a choice: an article about T. E. Lawrence or an article about *Lawrence of Arabia* (motion picture). At this stage, you'll probably want to click on and read both; you may want to compare the movie version with Lawrence's actual experiences. In fact, clicking on the entry for T. E. Lawrence provides you with links to other articles, such as "Guerrilla Leader," "Advisor on Arab Affairs," and "Postwar Activities," as well as icons for "Additional Reading" and "Related Articles." Choosing and reading any of these articles can help you decide what aspect of Lawrence's life you want to write about.

Carrying out research is all about choices:

- You start to narrow down your topic by considering just what it is that you want to find and then expressing it briefly in a word or phrase.

- You type a request into a database, and you receive a list of topics or sources to choose from.

- You read an article about your subject, and at the end you find a list of additional articles to choose from headed "Bibliography" or "Further Reading."

- You look at a Web site, and throughout the text you see *hyperlinks* that will lead you to related Web pages.

Finding sources is not difficult; the real challenge is deciding which ones to read first.

Using Computer Searches to Locate Books

Databases that contain books are usually place-specific. In other words, each library produces a computerized database that lists all the books housed in its building or group of buildings. The library in the next town will have a different database for its holdings. Your own college library almost certainly has such a database listing all the books on its shelves, organized and search-able by author, by title, and by subject. You can also search comparable data-bases for other libraries in the area or major libraries across the globe. If you want to examine a full range of the books in existence on Lawrence of Arabia, you can look up that topic in the database of the Library of Congress or the New York Public Library, both of which are available online. If you locate a book that seems important for your research and your own library does not have it, your librarian can probably arrange for an *interlibrary loan* from a library that does.

Searching a Database

Let's search the Library of Congress Online Catalog (LCOC) for books about Lawrence of Arabia. The URL for the most recent version is catalog.loc.gov/ index-htm. If you want to narrow down your topic, don't use the "Quick Search," but immediately click on "Advanced Search."

- You type in *Lawrence of Arabia*; click the drop-down menu to the right; and highlight and click "as a phrase." No quotation marks are necessary.
- You *don't* click the "Keyword Anywhere" entry on the right, making sure that you can view the full range of available sources.
- You want to obtain information about the man, Lawrence of Arabia, rather than the film *Lawrence of Arabia*, so you rule out prints of the movie and recordings of its sound track by clicking "NOT" twice, and typing in *motion picture* and *sound recording*.
- You click "Search."

Choosing Books to Review

Your search for Lawrence of Arabia produces 120 items; however, many of them are irrelevant to your immediate purpose. The first 15, for example, do not have authors listed. They refer to various types of media, including television documentaries about Lawrence and images of him, including one of his funeral procession. You may want to examine and choose some pictures or films of Lawrence to accompany your essay, but not at this early stage.

The 105 other entries—all of which refer to books—contain a good many duplicates. Repetition is a recurring problem in computerized searches. The same book can appear as a reprint (with the same contents, but a new cover, probably paperback) or in a new edition (with revisions or new material). For example, your search list contains four entries for *Great Contemporaries* by Winston Churchill (which includes a chapter about Lawrence); each entry refers to a different edition of the same book.

Other entries are inappropriate for a variety of reasons. Some are fiction (*Scorpion's Bite, Murder of Lawrence of Arabia*, or *Marconi's Dream*, which includes a short story titled "Dancing with Lawrence of Arabia"). Others focus on *very narrow* aspects of Lawrence's career and character: you don't want to begin your research by reading *Military Mavericks: Extraordinary Men of Battle* or *Great Bastards of History: The True and Riveting Accounts of the Most Famous Illegitimate Children Who Went on to Achieve Greatness*.

Most of the biographies of Lawrence in the LCOC search list were written 30 or more years ago. At some point, you may want to inspect one or two biographies by authors who actually knew Lawrence (although personal knowledge sometimes creates issues of bias—see pp. 354–355 in Chapter 8). For now, it makes sense to look at some *recent* biographies since those authors probably have had access to the widest range of material about Lawrence. Most databases will sort the titles for you in reverse order of publication, most recent first. Figure 7-1 shows seven of the most likely titles.

This short list contains four biographies of Lawrence, one collection of his letters, one very recent study of Lawrence and the Middle East, and an "encyclopedia" devoted entirely to his life. What will you look at first?

- Tabachnick's encyclopedia—248 pages—might prove very useful later on when you want to find specific information about a particular event or person connected to Lawrence as it consists of a comprehensive series of alphabetized entries.

- Lawrence's "Selected Letters" will certainly provide you with supporting material in his own words—once you're at the stage when you know what points you need to support.

- Hulsman's discussion of Lawrence and the Middle East will be extremely helpful—but only if that turns out to be the focus of your essay.

- MacLean's biography is written for a juvenile audience—something that this (and other databases) don't tell you, but which becomes apparent when you try to locate the book and find it in the children's library.

So, three entries on your short list are worth following up on immediately: Brown, James, and Wilson.

Examining the Full Record: After you click on an item on a search list, you can find maximum information about the work by selecting the icon, usually

[33]	Brown, Malcolm, 1930-	Lawrence of Arabia : the life, the legend / Malcolm Brown.	2005
[56]	Hulsman, John C., 1967-	To begin the world over again : Lawrence of Arabia and the invention of the Middle East / John Hulsman.	2009
[60]	James, Lawrence, 1943-	Golden warrior : the life and legend of Lawrence of Arabia / Lawrence James.	2008
[74]	Lawrence, T. E. (Thomas Edward), 1888-1935.	Lawrence of Arabia : the selected letters / edited by Malcolm Brown.	2007
[84]	MacLean, Alistair, 1922-1987.	Lawrence of Arabia / Alistair MacLean.	2006
[109]	Tabachnick, Stephen Ely.	Lawrence of Arabia : an encyclopedia / Stephen E. Tabachnick.	2004
[122]	Wilson, Jeremy.	Lawrence of Arabia : the authorized biography of T. E. Lawrence / Jeremy Wilson.	1990

Figure 7-1 Selected recent biographies of Lawrence from the LCOC

at the top of the screen, labeled "Full Record" or "Full View." As figures 7-2 to 7-4 demonstrate, each screen includes important information such as:

- The length of the book,
- Whether it has an index (so you can look up topics quickly),
- Whether it has notes and a bibliography (so you can locate additional sources), and
- The scope of the book, with a list of "subjects" as a clue to the specific contents.

Assuming that all three were available in your library, which book would you examine first—Brown, James, or Wilson?

- *Brown's biography* (Figure 7-2) has the advantage of being a brief overview, but the "record" suggests that he's most interested in Lawrence's role in the Middle Eastern campaign, and that might limit your research at this stage. Brown's documentation is also extremely slender.

- *James's biography* (Figure 7-3) seems midway between the two: long enough to provide sufficient information, yet not as exhaustive— and exhausting—as Wilson's. But, like Brown, James focuses on Lawrence's role in the war and may not offer the necessary overview of Lawrence's life.

- *Wilson's "authorized" biography* (Figure 7-4) is going to be an important resource, no matter what topic you eventually choose. This is clearly the standard work in the field, with extensive documentation that will enable you to locate other helpful sources. Choosing the "abridged" version makes sense since 406 pages will be quite enough for a preliminary overview.

Following Cross-Referenced Hyperlinks: Cross-referencing in an electronic database provides you with one more set of choices. If you click on any

Type of Material: Book (Print, Microform, Electronic, etc.)
Personal Name: Brown, Malcolm, 1930-
Main Title: Lawrence of Arabia : the life, the legend / Malcolm Brown.
Published/Created: New York : Thames & Hudson, 2005.
Related Names: Imperial War Museum (Great Britain)   *— probable emphasis on military strategy*
Description: 208 p. : ill. (some col.), col. maps ; 27 cm.   *— relatively brief book*
ISBN: 9780500512388
0500512388
Notes: "Published in association with the Imperial War Museum"--T.p. verso.
Includes bibliographical references (p. 205) and index.   *— one page of notes*
Subjects: Lawrence, T. E. (Thomas Edward), 1888-1935.
Lawrence, T. E. (Thomas Edward), 1888-1935 --Pictorial works.
Soldiers --Great Britain --Biography.
Middle East specialists --Biography.   *— emphasis on World War I*
World War, 1914-1918 --Campaigns --Arab countries.

Figure 7-2 Abridged LCOC for Brown, from the full record

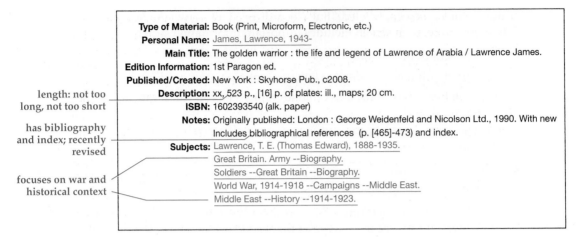

length: not too long, not too short

has bibliography and index; recently revised

focuses on war and historical context

Type of Material: Book (Print, Microform, Electronic, etc.)
Personal Name: James, Lawrence, 1943-
Main Title: The golden warrior : the life and legend of Lawrence of Arabia / Lawrence James.
Edition Information: 1st Paragon ed.
Published/Created: New York : Skyhorse Pub., c2008.
Description: xx, 523 p., [16] p. of plates: ill., maps; 20 cm.
ISBN: 1602393540 (alk. paper)
Notes: Originally published: London : George Weidenfeld and Nicolson Ltd., 1990. With new
Includes bibliographical references (p. [465]-473) and index.
Subjects: Lawrence, T. E. (Thomas Edward), 1888-1935.
Great Britain. Army --Biography.
Soldiers --Great Britain --Biography.
World War, 1914-1918 --Campaigns --Middle East.
Middle East --History --1914-1923.

Figure 7-3 Abridged LCOC for James, from the full record

"authorized": Lawrence's estate allowed Wilson access to private records

very long; many pictures

focus on military career as well as complete life

Type of Material: Book (Print, Microform, Electronic, etc.)
Personal Name: Wilson, Jeremy.
Main Title: Lawrence of Arabia : the authorized biography of T. E. Lawrence / Jeremy Wilson.
Published/Created: New York : Atheneum, 1990, c1989.
Description: xi, 1188 p. : ill., maps : 25 cm. ————— 32 pages of plates
ISBN: 0689119348
Notes: Includes bibliographical references and index.
Subjects: Lawrence, T. E. (Thomas Edward), 1888-1935.
Great Britain. Army --Biography.
Soldiers --Great Britain --Biography.
World War, 1914-1918 --Campaigns --Middle East.
Middle East --History --20th century.

Figure 7-4 Abridged LCOC for Wilson, from the full record

of the underlined subjects listed in the "Full Record" of a work—*Lawrence, T. E. (Thomas Edward), 1888–1935*, for example—the next screen will display numerous subtopics related to Lawrence, ranging from his death and burial to his psychology. If, for example, you click on "Military Leadership," you're referred to Oliver Butler's *The Guerrilla Strategies of Lawrence and Mao*, which compares the military exploits of Lawrence with those of Mao Zedong, the Chinese Communist leader. And the screen for the Butler book also contains another hyperlinked subject list, including guerrilla warfare, that would allow you to continue your search for this topic.

Using WorldCat

WorldCat is an enormously popular database that builds on already existing libraries (including the Library of Congress) to provide researchers with a vast number of books, articles, and various types of media from which to search. Unlike the LCOC, WorldCat's advanced search doesn't allow you to exclude aspects of the keyword by using "NOT," so an initial search for Lawrence of Arabia—all formats—resulted in 2,805 entries. A "books only" search produced a list of 806 items. A new search, this time using *T. E. Lawrence* as the keyword, resulted in over 14,000 books, listed in order of *relevance*. Unfortunately, the standard used to determine "relevance" is rather dubious. The first 50 entries, most of them written by Lawrence himself, are all "relevant," but, after that, other authors named Lawrence begin to creep in, and the list becomes useless.

One reason for the very long list is that it includes some unpublished doctoral dissertations. *Originality and Inspiration: The Roots of T. E. Lawrence's Military Success* may (or may not) be just what you need to develop an essay on Lawrence's guerrilla tactics. But keep in mind that the dissertation is unpublished and has therefore not been subject to full peer review, so there's no way of knowing whether finding and reading it is actually worth your time. Searching in cyberspace usually means that a computer algorithm or formula, rather than experienced judgment, decides what comes first. When using a catch-all database like WorldCat, be prepared to reject a good many entries before you come across something that seems worth examining.

Searching for Books

1. Get an overview of your subject by reading an encyclopedia article.

2. Carry out an advanced search using your own library's database or the Library of Congress Online Catalog.

3. Take advantage of the search limits available in an advanced search: expand or narrow the scope of your keywords; consider whether you want the results listed by relevance or date.

4. As you read through the list of search results, put a check next to books that are likely to provide general knowledge about your subject and might be useful now, and other books containing more specific information that you may want to come back to when you've narrowed your topic. Use the "print," "save," or "e-mail" capability to create and keep one short list of books to examine now and a second list of books to keep in reserve.

5. Examine the "Full Record" of the books on your short list, and, considering each one's length, scope, and documentation, decide which one(s) to look at first.

6. As necessary, find more sources by using the hyperlinks available on the "Full Record" subject lines and by consulting the bibliographies in some of the books that you find in the library.

Searching Bibliographies: Don't neglect a traditional, non-computerized way of identifying sources: look in the bibliographies of standard works on the subject, like Wilson's. The books on Lawrence will probably be shelved together in your library stacks, and you'll want to examine the *table of contents, index,* and *bibliography* of several before deciding which ones merit your time.

Using Computer Searches to Locate Periodical Articles

Finding appropriate periodical articles is a more massive task than looking for books. Each issue of a periodical contains a dozen or so articles; each year, thousands of periodicals appear in English alone; many of the best ones have been publishing for decades, a few for centuries. *No single database can catalog all the newspaper, magazine, and journal articles on a specific topic.*

Moreover, as you've seen, electronic searches tend to generate lists that are inflated with repetitious and irrelevant items. Given the vast amount of material available and the idiosyncrasies of most search mechanisms, you need to carefully control the terms of your initial search request. The more opportunity the database gives you to define the direction and limits of your search, the more likely it will be that the result—the search list—will be clean, relevant, and useful to your project.

Searching Databases

Periodical databases don't all provide the same sort of information:

- Some databases provide only bibliographical listings of articles (sometimes called *citations*) and leave you to find the article in bound volumes on your library shelves, in another electronic database, on microfilm, or on the Web.
- Other databases provide *abstracts* of the articles that they list. An abstract is a brief summary—a few sentences—that helps you to decide whether you want to locate and read the entire article.
- Some databases include *extracts*—samples from the article.
- A few databases will produce the *full text*, sometimes for a fee.
- And other databases provide all of the above—sometimes only an abstract, sometimes the full article.

Like databases for books, electronic databases for periodicals allow you to choose between a *basic* search and an *advanced* search. Depending on the database, the advanced search might allow you to:

- Limit the range of sources by discipline (only history? or the social sciences? or all available journals?),
- Refine your search with Boolean connectives (NOT motion picture),

- Request only popular periodicals (magazines and newspapers) or only academic journals,
- Exclude certain types of articles (book reviews?),
- Specify a time span for your search (2000–the present?) and/or
- Restrict your search to articles that have been peer reviewed.

That last option can be significant: *peer review* means that a journal requires each of its articles to be read and approved by authorities in the field before it's accepted for publication. Peer review is, in effect, a guarantee of reasonable quality.

You may need to search in more than one database, starting with the periodical database in your campus library, which should list all the articles in all the newspapers, magazines, and journals that the library owns or can access electronically. Your library will also have a long list of the other periodical databases available to you online. For example, Columbia University lists over 300 online databases for the social sciences, ranging from *Abstracts in Social Gerontology* to *Medieval Travel Writing*. More general in their scope, the *Social Sciences Index* and the *Humanities Index* are often good starting points for topics within those broad disciplinary areas. Some databases, such as the *Reader's Guide*, focus on general-interest periodicals—magazines, newspapers—rather than scholarly journals.

Searching for Scholarly Journals

The number of journals searchable in academic databases varies from over 500 (*Project MUSE*), to 2,000 (*JSTOR* and *ScienceDirect*), to 13,000 (*Ingenta*). But the size of the database doesn't change the essential fact of electronic searching: the list resulting from your search will almost certainly contain numerous articles that have no substantial connection to your topic. Lawrence of Arabia may be mentioned once—in comparison with someone else or as a type of hero—or an article about British foreign policy or Middle Eastern democracy will include his name in a historical summary. And, once again, many entries are likely to be book reviews, which are rarely useful to the beginning researcher. That's why it's important to read the abstract before you waste time finding an article.

Don't forget to *narrow down your search specifications*, or you will have an unmanageable number of articles to look at. A ProQuest Research Library search for "Lawrence of Arabia," limited to the last 20 years, resulted in 2,482 listings. ProQuest enables you to further restrict your search to "only scholarly journals" (or "audio and video" if that's your interest). And you can also request only articles that have been "peer-reviewed." With those specifications, a new "Lawrence of Arabia" search reduced the list to 379 articles.

Unfortunately, sorted by "relevance," nine out of the first ten items on the list were book reviews, which are not very useful for your purposes. So, you need to try once again, this time using a NOT operator to screen out book reviews. Even with all those restrictions, the resulting list of 75 isn't a great deal of use: most of the articles either mention Lawrence only peripherally or are concerned with very minor aspects of his life (for example, postage stamps issued with his picture). Only one item in the first 20 listings is really worth looking at: "Lawrence of Arabia: Image and Reality," focusing on the reasons for his enduring reputation. Still, these results are not as discouraging as they seem. If you can find three or four scholarly articles among the 75 that can become sources for your research essay, your bibliography will become better balanced with a mix of books, articles, and Web sites.

Two Tips for Database Searching

1. Never assume that the first few listings are the most important, even if they're the most recent or "relevant," and so ignore the rest of the list. The machine doing the ordering is not necessarily logical.

2. No single database is likely to contain all the material you'll need. It always pays to look a little further.

Using Computer Searches to Locate Web Sites

Web sites can be created by anyone who wants to set one up: government agencies, schools, businesses, nonprofit organizations, and individuals. Because they are ideal for distributing up-to-date information to a worldwide audience, many Web sites are maintained by corporations for advertising purposes. Other sites enable people with an interest or hobby to display their knowledge in a public setting—often, a blog. These are reasons you need to make doubly sure that information for research obtained through the Web is accurate and objective. As you'll learn in Chapter 8, not all Web sites are reliable or worth citing in your essay. Before you take notes or print out content, get some sense of the author's credentials and the material's reliability.

The distinctive qualities of the Web—the speed with which it can be updated and searched, and the huge amount of information it contains—are both its strength and its weakness. Web sites change and disappear without any notice, and the information that you thought you had on Monday may be unavailable by Friday. The Web contains lots of material about today's issues, but rarely goes back more than a few years. It is huge, but indiscriminate. You can search for anything, but often find nothing useful for your purpose. Unless you're very focused in your search requirements, you're likely to receive a list of sites that seem randomly chosen and ranked. As Danny O'Brien wrote in "The Fine Art of Googling," search engines "may know the contents of all Web pages, but they know the meaning of none." Good research does not start and end with point and click.

Using Search Engines

Most people routinely use search engines to access the millions of sites available on the Web. Unfortunately, practically all search engines can produce a hodgepodge of results, mostly irrelevant to the topic you're searching for. One built-in disadvantage of search engines is that the descriptions come directly from the sites' owners and may or may not be accurate summaries of the contents. *There's little or no peer review on the Web.*

So, to achieve a reasonable results list, your search has to be *well-targeted.* Even an "advanced" search for "Lawrence of Arabia" on Google won't limit the terms of the search sufficiently to exclude sites that are inappropriate or irrelevant to your topic. Such a search in 2014 produced 125,000 hits, most of them about the film or its music. If that happens, an *alternative descriptor* should be tried. A search for "T. E. Lawrence"—his actual name—has more promising results, partly because the specifications allow you to require that "T. E. Lawrence" appear in the title of the Web page, which eliminates the large number of sites that mention his name only once.

If you look at the first 100 items on this list, you'll find a varied mixture of sites, a few worth pursuing, some possible, many useless for your purpose. The process is time-consuming, because the good and bad are jumbled together, and you have to exercise some judgment about what you decide to click on and follow up. The best prospects are by no means in the first 20 or even the first 50 items on the list. Book reviews, book sellers, astrological horoscopes, and notices of events like exhibitions about Lawrence are sandwiched in between short overviews of his life (from respectable sources like Public Broadcasting System and Clio), but these overviews are almost identical and lack depth and detail. You can find a great many *pictures of Lawrence*—through a Tumblr site (#28) curated by a high school social studies teacher; an attractive collection of "pins" of Lawrence in different poses (#84); and a BBC documentary from YouTube (#19). One *video* that appears more than once in the list contains an interview with Scott Anderson, a former war correspondent, who has written a book about Lawrence. Anderson may be a goldmine of important insights, but the interviewer wants to focus on the comparison between the hero of the movie and Lawrence himself, and the interview does not go anywhere interesting. Another typical Web offering is a *Web chat* with a few "historians"—you would have to check their credentials to use this material, and they're not offering their full names—about the way Lawrence is regarded in Arabia today. An interesting topic, but these are short "sound bites" on the page, with lots of irrelevant digression.

What, then, is worth following up in the first 50 hits of a "T. E. Lawrence" Google search? A site called Al-Bab (#94)—intended to "introduce non-Arabs to the Arab world and their culture"—contains a number of possible *links to other books and other Web pages.* #91 on the list is a scholarly page about "T. E. Lawrence and the Arab Cause at the Paris Peace Conference," which might be very useful if you want to write about the political consequences of Lawrence's activities in the Middle East. And #81 contains *a short essay by Lawrence himself* about the pleasure of riding a motorcycle and his love for his "Brough Superior" machine, which, if quoted in the right place, might add a human touch to your essay. But the most promising site is actually #3, which is maintained by Jeremy Wilson, who wrote the authorized biography of Lawrence. This page contains a good deal of impeccably sourced and documented information, as well as links to other sites of interest. On the other hand, much of this material was unobtainable in 2014 as the site was being rebuilt—a peril of Web research—and, in fact, there seems to be little here that can't be learned from exploring Wilson's book—a form of one-stop shopping.

Another option would be to use *Google Scholar,* which presents itself as an academic search engine with results drawn from articles in scholarly journals. However, the search results for "T. E. Lawrence" contain the usual quota of irrelevant and bizarre entries, many of which are clearly on the list because some other Lawrence's name was cited once in an article about feeding cows or motorcycle helmets. Like its parent Google, Google Scholar provides few sites that you would be likely to cite in a mainstream college essay. *An easy search is not necessarily a successful search.* You'll learn more about evaluating Web sites in the next chapter.

Using Other Sources from the Internet

A source is only as good as the reputation of its author. If you want to use material from Facebook, a chat room, a blog, a Tweet, an e-mail, or any other Web medium, *be very sure that you know who the writer is and whether that person has a provable claim to be an authority on the subject of your essay.* When in doubt, don't use it.

E-mail is a bit of a special case. It's possible for you to approach an authority, sending your own e-mail, and ask for assistance in exploring a research topic. If you know the e-mail address of an expert in that field, you can send a courteous message, asking questions or requesting specific information. Keep in mind, though, that academic and professional authorities have little time to answer unsolicited e-mails and, as the number of e-mail inquiries has increased, many are less willing to participate in students' research. Soliciting a response by e-mail is most likely to succeed if your topic focuses on a local or regional event or issue and you approach someone involved in the project. *Remember that any information obtained through e-mail that is subsequently used in an essay must have its source cited.* See Chapter 12 for appropriate documentation.

Managing Web Searches

- Refine your search by choosing an "advanced" or "guided" search page and using exact phrases and other "operators" to limit the results. The more precise your search instructions, the greater the number of meaningful responses.

- If your search yields a list of a thousand sites, look at the first 50. If there's nothing worthwhile, refine your search, or try another search engine or database.

- Don't settle for the first sites you find that seem remotely connected to your topic. Keep on searching until the information is solid.

- Avoid commercial sites selling products. They rarely contain material appropriate for academic research.

- Watch out for dead links—Web sites that were indexed months or even years ago and are no longer being maintained by their owners.

- Don't just add interesting possibilities to your "Favorites" or "Bookmarks" for later reading. The material will pile up. If you read (or, at least, skim) as you go along, you'll learn enough about your topic to give some direction to your search.

- Don't be tempted to open every link you come to and pursue stray pieces of information just because they're there. Before you click on a link, consider whether this information is likely to be useful to your present project. Surfing isn't research.

- Maintain concrete and reasonable expectations for your search. Decide what you want to get out of each session on the Internet, and concentrate on that goal. Search with a purpose.

Using Computer Searches to Locate Images and Other Media

You can often increase the effectiveness of your research essay by including pictures, charts and graphics, audio, or video. A historical topic—biography or event—easily benefits from a presentation that includes images, footage, or recordings of people or places. But you can also use media to support the analysis of a contemporary issue. Chapter 9 will explore some ways to integrate such media into your essay.

At a point in your research when your thesis has already begun to take shape, you may want to look at a few databases to see what kinds of media are available and whether they will suit your purpose. As you've just seen, almost any search for "Lawrence of Arabia" yields a large number of photographs, most of which are stills or posters from the motion picture. Several

The last known photograph of Lawrence.
Clouds Hill 1935

[Home] [More]

Brough Superior Motorcycles

© National Trust Images

Figure 7-5 Lawrence of Arabia

images are worth including in an essay, including the last photograph of Lawrence taken before his death, showing him astride his Brough motorcycle (Figure 7-5). In fact, the picture comes from the Web site for Brough Superior Motorcycles, which contains some useful material about Lawrence as both hero and motorcyclist.

A number of Web sites feature databases of photos and videos appropriate for academic work. Most require registration and, possibly, a fee. In addition to YouTube, here are a few useful sites to try:

- **www.memory.loc.gov**
  This free Library of Congress site contains images and sound recordings to illustrate a range of topics related to American history and culture.

- **http://tvnews.vanderbilt.edu/?SID=20130827391906738**
  This site features clips from TV news.

- **www.globalimageworks.com**
  This site contains footage and stock shots in the areas of entertainment, news, and nature.

- **www.gettyimages.com**
  This is a huge collection of images, photos, videos, and music (including archival material from the BBC).

- **www.apimages.com**
  This site calls itself "the world's largest collection of historical and contemporary photos."

- **www.producerslibrary.com**
  This is a library of stock photos and footage from old films.

Interviewing and Field Research

As well as books, articles, films, videos, Web sites, and other materials, personal interviews and field research can be worthwhile resources for your research essay. A well-conducted interview with an expert in the field or your own observations of an event or an environment can be a source of valuable information.

Interviewing

You will want to interview experts or authorities who are both knowledgeable and appropriate sources of information about your specific topic. The faculty on your campus may offer expert knowledge and may also serve as sources of referrals to other authorities in the field at nearby colleges and universities. To further your research project on Lawrence of Arabia, you might identify a faculty member with an interest in Lawrence and his era in the department of:

- Political Science (the Arab Revolt),
- History (World War I and Lawrence's military campaign),
- Psychology (Lawrence's complex motivation), or
- Literature (*Seven Pillars of Wisdom* — Lawrence's major published work).

Or, if your focus were on Lawrence as a strategist or guerrilla leader, you might appropriately consult a source with military (or diplomatic) experience. Faculty in the film department might provide access to someone in the movie industry with direct knowledge of the making of David Lean's *Lawrence of Arabia*.

Planning an Interview

Write, e-mail, or phone in advance to arrange an appointment once you have focused your topic and identified candidates for interviews. Allow enough time to make initial contact and then to wait a week or two, if necessary, until the person has enough time to speak with you at length. When you call or write to those whom you hope to interview, politely identify yourself; then briefly describe your topic and the special focus of your essay. Ask for an interview of 20 to 30 minutes at a later time convenient for the subject. If appropriate, mention the name of the person who suggested this source, or refer to the publication in which you saw the subject's name. Your objective is to convey your own serious interest in the topic and in your subject's knowledge of the topic. If someone is reluctant to be interviewed, you should retreat gracefully. At the same time, don't hesitate to ask for a referral to someone else who might be in a better position to provide helpful information.

Preparing for an Interview

Because your interview, whether in person or on the phone, will probably be brief, you need to plan in advance what you intend to say and ask so that you can use the time effectively. Review your research notes and make a focused list of questions in writing beforehand, tailoring them to your specific paper topic and to your source's area of knowledge. It can be helpful to prepare a questionnaire, leaving space between the questions for you to take notes, which can be used, with variations, for a whole series of personal interviews.

Recording Information during an Interview

If you plan to use a recorder, make sure you ask your subject's permission in advance; test the equipment beforehand (especially if it's borrowed for the occasion); and know how to operate it smoothly. When the interview is about to begin, check again to see if your subject has any objection to your recording the conversation. Then, to avoid making your subject self-conscious, put the recorder in an unobtrusive place.

Even if you plan to record the interview, come prepared to take careful notes; bring notebook and pens, as well as your list of questions or questionnaire. If your subject presents a point so well that you know you'll want to quote it, write it down rapidly but carefully, and—then and there—read it back to make sure that you have transcribed the statement correctly.

Conducting the Interview

Briefly remind your subject of the essay topic and your reason for requesting the interview. Then get right down to your "script": ask each question clearly, without hurrying, be alert to recognize when the question has been fully answered (there is usually a pause), and move briskly on to the next question. Otherwise, let your subject talk freely, with minimum interruption.

Sometimes, a particular question will capture your subject's interest, and you will get a more detailed answer than you expected. Be aware of the time limit for the interview; but if you see a promising line of questioning that you didn't anticipate, and your subject seems relaxed and willing to prolong the conversation, take advantage of the opportunity and ask follow-up questions. What if your subject digresses far away from the topic of your essay? At the first opportunity, ask whether there is a time constraint. If there is, politely indicate that you have three or four more questions to ask and you hope that there will be enough time to include them.

At the end, your subject should, ideally, offer to speak with you again, if necessary, to fill any gaps. To maintain that good impression, be sure to send a brief note of thanks to your subject no longer than a day or two after the interview. Later on, you may want to send a copy of the completed essay.

Using Interview Sources in Your Essay

Since the purpose of the interview is to gather information (and to provide yourself with a few apt quotations), you need to have clear notes to work from as you organize your essay. If you used a recorder, you should transcribe the interview as soon as you can; if you took notes, you should go over them carefully, clarify confusing words, and then type a definitive version. Transcribe the interview accurately, without embroidering or revising what your subject actually said. Keep the original notes and tapes; your instructor may want to review them along with your essay. Remember to document in your essay each use of material taken from your interview, whether it is ideas or words, with a parenthetical reference. See Chapter 12 for the appropriate form.

Field Research

Like interviewing, field research is a way of supplementing the material you take from texts and triggering new ideas about your topic. When you engage in field research, you are gathering information directly, acting as an observer, investigator, and evaluator within the context of an academic or professional discipline:

- If you are asked by your anthropology instructor to describe and analyze a family celebration as an ethnographer would, your observations of Thanksgiving dinner at home would be regarded as field research.

- When the nursing program sends students to a nearby hospital for their clinical practice and asks for a weekly report on their work with patients, these students are doing field research.

- Students, participating in a cooperative education program involving professional internships, prepare reports on their work experiences based on field research.

Whatever the course, your instructor will show you how to connect your field research activities to the theories, procedures, and format characteristic of that discipline.

Field research usually involves the observation of a group of people in order to form a hypothesis about their behavior, test that hypothesis, and determine its significance. You might, for example, be asked to observe your fellow students in the library or at a football game to form conclusions about their patterns of behavior. Such a field research project would fall into three stages: gathering information, analyzing that information, and writing the essay.

Gathering the Information

Field research entails a specified number of observations, usually determined in advance, that can range from a few sessions to an entire semester (or, in the case of anthropologists or sociologists, a year or more). As a new researcher, you would probably be expected to perform a limited number of separate observations, according to a predetermined schedule. At each session, you would take notes, in response to a list of questions or guidelines that you've prepared in advance. These questions set up a framework for your observations and, possibly, a potential structure for your essay.

If, for example, your project involved observation of students using the new lounge, you might be trying to find out:

- How many students are spending time in the lounge?
- Who are they and how long do they stay there?
- What kinds of activities do they engage in?

While you're carrying out your observation of the lounge, you are simply trying to record your subjects' activities accurately, to provide notes for future interpretation. You're not as yet trying to write a narrative or understand the significance of what you're seeing. If, as is quite likely, someone speaks to you during your observation periods, take advantage of the opportunity to do a little formal interviewing and possibly gain a useful quotation for your essay.

After a couple of sessions, you may feel that you have a general idea of the range of students' behavior at the site, so you can begin to look specifically for repeated instances of certain activities: studying together or individually, eating, relaxing. But you will need to keep an open mind about what you observe as your subjects' behavior may not conform to your planned questions and your tentative hypothesis.

Analyzing Your Information

After a few sessions of observation, you start to review your notes to try to understand what you have seen and figure out what you have learned. Your object is to establish categories and generalizations that describe your subjects' pattern of behavior. To support these general categories, you pull out of your notes specific references to behavior that match the category, noting the date and time of each instance. You may want to chart your observations to represent at a glance such variables as these: How many students studied or socialized? Which activities were associated with males or with females? If your sessions took place during different times of the day, the hour would be another variable to record on your chart.

As you identify categories, you need to ask yourself some questions to help you characterize each one and define the differences among some of your subjects' behaviors. For example: Are these differences determined by gender or by preferred methods of learning, like solitary or group study? As you think through the possible conclusions to be drawn from your observations, record them in your notebook, for these preliminary analyses will later become part of your essay.

Writing an Essay Based on Field Research

An essay based on field research generally follows a format appropriate to the particular discipline in the social sciences. Your instructor will provide detailed guidelines and, perhaps, refer you to an article in a professional journal to use as a model. For the essay analyzing student behavior, you might present your findings according to the following outline:

Purpose: In the first section, you state the problem—the purpose of your field research—clearly indicating the question(s) you set out to investigate.

Method: Here, you explain your choice of site, the times and number of your observation sessions, and the general procedure for observation that you followed, including any exceptions to or deviations from your plan.

Observations: Next, you record the information you gathered from your observations, not as a list of random facts, but as categories or groupings that make the facts coherent to the reader. In many disciplines, this kind of information can be presented through charts, graphs, or tables.

Analysis: The heart of your essay, here is where you explain to your readers the significance of your observations. If, for example, you decided that certain activities were gender related, you would describe the basis for that distinction. Or you could discuss your conclusion that students use the lounge primarily as a meeting place to socialize. Or you might make the connection between studying as the most prevalent student activity and the scheduling of midterms during the time of your observations.

Conclusions: At the end of your essay, you remind your readers—and the instructor who is evaluating your work—that your purpose throughout has been to answer the questions and clarify the problems posed in the first paragraph. Would your research encourage your college to open more lounges like this one, or to change the decor or hours, or would your research justify its closure on the grounds of insufficient or inappropriate use?

ASSIGNMENT 6: Writing an Essay Based on Interviews or Field Research

A. Interviewing

1. Choose a topic from the following list; or think of a question that might stimulate a wide range of responses, and submit the question for your teacher's approval. Try to avoid political issues and very controversial subjects that may make it difficult for you to guide the interview and prevent you from getting a full range of opinion. You want a topic in which everyone you interview can take an interest, without becoming intensely partisan.

Suggestions for Topics

- Is "traditional" dating still desirable today?
- Is there a right age to get married?
- What are the ingredients for a lasting marriage?
- Should children be given the same first names as their parents?
- Is it better to keep a friend by not speaking your mind or risk losing a friend by honesty?
- Should community service become a compulsory part of the high school curriculum?
- Should English be made the official language of the United States?
- Are laws banning the use of phones in cars an infringement of individual rights?
- Is graffiti vandalism?
- Should animals be used in laboratory research?
- Should colleges ban drinking alcohol on campus and in fraternity houses?
- How should ethics be taught in schools?
- How should the commandment "honor thy parents" be put into practice today?
- What, if anything, is wrong with the nuclear family?
- Are students forced to specialize too soon in their college experience?
- Should schools stay in session all year round?
- Should citizens have to pay a fine for not voting?
- Should movies have a rating system?
- Should children's TV or computer time be rationed?
- Should parents be held legally or financially responsible for damage done by their children?

▨ At what age is it acceptable for children to work (outside the family)?

▨ Should high school students be tested for drug use?

▨ Should hosts who serve alcohol be held responsible if their guests are involved later in auto accidents?

▨ Should students have to maintain passing grades in order to participate in school athletics?

▨ How should society deal with homeless people?

▨ When should parents cease to be financially responsible for their children?

2. Once your topic is decided (and, if necessary, approved), interview at least six people, or as many as you need to get a variety of reactions for your survey. (Some of your sources should be students in your class.) If you wish, use the following format for conducting each interview:

> Name: (first and last: check the spelling!)
>
> Do you think . . . . ?
>
> Why do you think so? What are some of your reasons? (later)
> Are there any other reasons?
>
> Why do you think people who take the opposite view would do so?
>
> Do any examples come to your mind to illustrate your point?
>
> Quotation:

3. Take careful and complete notes of the comments that you receive. (*You will be expected to hand in all your notes, in their original form, with your completed essay.*) Keep a separate sheet for each person. If one of your sources says something worth quoting, write down the exact words; read them back to make sure that what you have quoted is what the speaker meant to say; then put quotation marks around the direct quotation. Otherwise, use summary or paraphrase.

4. List the ideas from your notes and arrange the points in a sequence of your choice.

5. Write a summary of your notes that presents the full range of opinion, paraphrasing and (occasionally) quoting from representative sources. After analyzing the arguments of your sources, conclude with one or two paragraphs explaining which point of view, in your opinion, has the most validity, and why.

B. Field Research

1. Select a topic appropriate for engaging in field research on your campus, in your dormitory, or in your workplace. For example, you might want to learn about how students occupy their time during large lecture courses; by auditing two or three lecture classes over a period

of time and taking notes about students' behavior, you could test the theory that professors should provide printed lecture notes or that mobile phones should be banned in the classroom.

2. Present your topic to your instructor for approval and, after carrying out your research, organize your notes and prepare your essay according to the instructions on page 335.

Saving and Recording Information for Your Bibliography

Before the computer and the copying machine were invented, a researcher in the library had to make immediate and firm choices: deciding which material was worth including in an essay, taking notes from the material, and then returning books and journals to the shelves. Later on, those notes would become the basis for the essay. But the twenty-first century does provide some convenient backup alternatives. As well as taking notes, it makes sense to *copy or download key pages from books and articles* so that, as you write, you can check your version of the material against the actual text. Having that text at hand discourages inadvertent plagiarism since you will be in no doubt about which ideas and language are the source's and which are yours. Copies also make it possible to write comments in the margin and circle or highlight key points.

Once you have located and briefly examined a book or periodical article or a Web site and decided that it is probably worth including in your essay, you should not only copy or save selected pages, but also write a few preliminary notes to yourself about the *source's probable usefulness*. Jot down your opinion of the work's scope and contents, strong or weak points, and relevance to your topic, as well as any impressions about the author's reliability as a source. Often, you can make these tentative judgments by examining the "Full Record" or the table of contents, and leafing or scrolling through the pages.

Notes are also useful for your bibliography and essential if you're asked to submit an annotated bibliography. *A bibliography is a complete list of all the works that you use in preparing your essay.* What's included in a bibliography can differ at various stages of your work:

- A *preliminary* or *working* bibliography, sometimes called "Works Consulted," consists of all the sources that you find worth recording and saving as you do your research. You may or may not cite them in your essay.

- A *final* bibliography (usually called "Works Cited" or "References") consists of the sources that you have actually used in writing your essay.

- An *annotated* bibliography includes a sentence or two after each item, describing the work's scope and specific focus and suggesting its relevance and usefulness to the development of your topic. An example of an annotated bibliography is provided on pages 342–343.

Copying and Recording Print Material

Copying Text: Do place the book or journal carefully in the copier to *avoid cutting off material* at the top, bottom, or sides of the page; days or weeks later, if you want to quote, it may be difficult to reconstruct missing language. Equally important, make sure that the *page numbers* show on the copies, since those numbers are crucial in the citation of your sources. Also, keep in mind that you may not always remember how that extract fit into the author's sequence of ideas. Write down a brief *explanation of context* at the top of the first copied page: the focus of the chapter, the author's previous point.

Copying the Bibliography: As you develop your preliminary bibliography, it can be helpful to copy some or all of the sources listed in the bibliography of a key text.

Copying the Copyright Page: To record basic publication information about a book legibly and accurately, copy the title page and the copyright page (the back of the title page) at the same time that you copy extracts. For a periodical article, copy the cover of the magazine or journal and the table of contents. Of course, if you used a database to identify books and periodical articles, most of the information that you need will be included in the results list. (That's one reason why it's useful to download or print the results pages of your database searches.) But even if you have those lists saved on your computer, the information that you'll need will be scattered over a number of downloaded files. At some point, you'll have to put it all together in a single file.

Recording Your Working Bibliography: Start the computer file or notebook list for your working bibliography early in the research process, and every time you find a source you're likely (but not necessarily certain) to use, add it to the list. Transcribe the information from the databases that you've downloaded and the stack of title pages that you've copied. Or, if you use a word processing program or a bibliographic software program that automatically prepares a bibliography in any of the standard formats, enter the data about each new source into the fields of the database. It's important to be accurate and consistent in recording each entry. Check the spelling of the author's name. Don't abbreviate unless you're sure you'll remember the significance of each symbol.

The majority of college research essays use MLA (Modern Language Association) style for documentation. To prepare a final bibliography in MLA style (or, indeed, in most other styles), you should include the following facts in your preliminary list:

For Print Books

- the full name of the author(s)
- the exact title, italicized
- the name of the editor(s) (for an anthology) or the name of the translator (for a work first written in a foreign language)

- the name of the publisher
- the original date of publication and the date of the new edition or reprint, if the book has been reissued
- the inclusive page numbers and any other information for a specific chapter or other section (such as the author and title of an introduction or of a selection within an anthology)
- the full name of the series (if it is one volume in a series)
- the volume number, if the book is part of a multivolume work
- the call number, so that you will not need to return to the catalog if you decide to locate the book again

For Print Articles

- the full name of the author(s)
- the title of the article, in quotation marks
- the exact title of the periodical, italicized
- the volume and issue numbers (if any) and the date and season of the issue
- the inclusive page numbers of the article

Copying and Recording Web Material and Other Media

Downloading or saving material from the Web is the equivalent of copying print texts. Since the content of a Web site can change from day to day—or the site itself can disappear—it's a good idea to *download and/or save to a file* if you have any inclination at all to use the source. Once you're sure a document is a solid source worth rereading, click "Save As" on the File menu, choosing a name that will be easily recognizable and (if you want to save space on your hard drive and you need the text only) selecting a "text only" option rather than saving the complete document, graphics and all. If the document is large, you may want to highlight extracts and then copy and paste them to a file in your word processing program. Early on in your research, *create a new folder* named for your paper topic and, after that, save all Web material to that folder, so it won't be scattered all over your hard drive. Printing out a Web document is also helpful. Web graphics can be distracting; computer screens are hard on the eyes. Having a print copy also makes it easier to put comments in the margins and highlight important points.

Keep a record of URLs—the Web addresses—so that if you want to go back to a page you can do so easily. (Be careful with the spelling of Web addresses.) Don't assume that you'll remember a URL. If you've downloaded Web material, saving it under a convenient name, you may have to search hard to reconstruct its address. It's safest to have a single file that records all your sources, with complete bibliographic information. And save it! And back it up by copying it to an external drive!

Compile your working bibliography by adding information about Web sources to the file where you're storing data about print sources. Many Web documents were previously or simultaneously published in print; in those cases, include both the print and the electronic data. (If you read the material on the Web, you must cite the Internet source in your bibliography.) Journal articles often have DOIs, or digital object identifiers—unique numbers assigned to electronic content. Be sure to include the DOI if your source has one. On many sites, the kind of bibliographic information shown in print sources is not provided or is difficult to find. Look for and record any of the following items that you can identify:

For Web Material

- the name of the author(s) of the article or other document and/or of the person(s) or sponsor(s) who created the site
- the title of the article or other document, in quotation marks
- the title of the book or periodical or of the site, italicized, or a description, such as *Home page*
- any volume number, issue number, or other identifying number
- any print publication information, including the date
- the date of publication on the Web, or of the most recent update (usually at the bottom of the "page")
- the range or total number of pages, paragraphs, or other sections, if they are numbered on the site
- the name of the database, italicized (if applicable)
- the URL or DOI (digital object identifier, if any)
- the date of access, if no publication date is listed

Obviously, this information can vary depending on the kind of document you're intending to use. An individual's home page, for example, would require nothing more than the author's name, the indication that it is a home page, the publication date, and the URL. But serious research is much more likely to depend on Web sites with academic or professional (or even commercial) sponsorship, and it's necessary to indicate all those details in the bibliography. Examples of bibliographical entries for citing Web sources can be found in Chapter 12.

Presenting an Annotated Bibliography

Here's what some of the information you've recorded about Lawrence of Arabia looks like when you've turned it into an *annotated bibliography* (following MLA style). The references to "Sources Consulted" in the title means that not every source will necessarily be cited in your essay. Some only provided background information or leads to other sources.

The Myth of Lawrence of Arabia in the Movies:
An Annotated List of Sources Consulted

television: interview

Anderson, Scott. Interview by Steve Hindy, *Local 10*. WP2G, 21 July 2014. Not much depth to the interview, but Anderson does compare his new book with the portrayal of Lawrence in the film.

book

Butler, Oliver J. *The Guerrilla Strategies of Lawrence and Mao: An Examination.* Butler, 1974. Useful background for understanding the success of Lawrence's campaigns against the Turks and evaluating the movie's accuracy, particularly the bombing of the train.

Web: article

Evans, C. T., and Andrew Clubb. "T. E. Lawrence and the Arab Cause at the Paris Peace Conference." *The Paris Peace Conference*, 27 Mar. 2014, Charles T. Evans, www.ctevans.net/Versailles/Diplomats/Lawrence/Lawrence.html. A scholarly take on Lawrence's legacy in the Middle East as it was shaped in Versailles at the peace conference.

book

Hodson, Joel C. *Lawrence of Arabia and American Culture: The Making of a Transatlantic Legend.* Greenwood, 1995. This book focuses on the impact the Lawrence myth had on American culture. The last part is particularly useful in analyzing the movie's presentation of Lawrence, especially his alleged homosexuality.

book

James, Lawrence. *The Golden Warrior: The Life and Legend of Lawrence of Arabia.* Skyhorse, 2008. Useful biography emphasizing Lawrence's strategy in the Middle East. Maps are helpful.

article

Kauffmann, Stanley. "On Films: The Return of El Aurans. *Lawrence of Arabia* Reissued, Restored to Its Original Length." *The New Republic*, 20 Feb. 1989, pp. 26–28. One of the most eminent film critics reassesses the significance of the film.

photo

Last Known Photograph of Lawrence: Clouds Hill, 1935. Dropbears, 2009, www.dropbears.com/b/brough_superior/players.htm. Photograph. A photo of Lawrence on his Brough Superior motorcycle.

film

Lawrence of Arabia. Directed by David Lean, Horizon Pictures, 1962. The one and only.

website

Lawrence of Arabia—The Life, the Legend. Imperial War Museum London, www.iwm.org.uk/upload/package/54/Lawrence/index.htm. Accessed 5 Sept. 2014. This site is related to and sponsored by a *book*

special exhibition about Lawrence at the Imperial War Museum in 2005–2006.

Web: article

Lawrence, T. E. *The Letters of T. E. Lawrence of Arabia.* 1938. Edited by David Garnett, Spring, 1964. This is a comprehensive collection of Lawrence's correspondence, which provides an especially detailed and moving picture of his later years in the RAF.

---. "The Road." *The Vintagent,* 30 Sept. 2007, thevintagent.blogspot .com/2007/09/te-lawrence-road-taken-from-mint.html. A charming description by Lawrence of the pleasures of riding his Brough motorcycle.

book

---. *The Seven Pillars of Wisdom.* Pike, 1926. Lawrence's own interpretation of what happened in the campaign against the Turks is written in a flowery and sometimes opaque style. Nevertheless, it's essential reading.

Web: video

T. E. Lawrence and Arabia. BBC, 1986, YouTube, 14 Dec. 2012, www .youtube.com/watch?v=B9UfvVDN_nc. Contains newsreel footage from the period and interviews with Lawrence's contemporaries, including his brother.

Web: article

Walters, Irene. "The Lawrence Trail." *Contemporary Review,* vol. 272, no. 1587 Jan. 1998, pp. 205–210. *Free Library,* www.thefreelibrary.com /The+Lawrence+Trail.-a020615180. This is little more than a personal narrative following Lawrence's path through the desert in the 1917 campaign. Useful only for local color.

Web: blog

Whitaker, Brian. "T. E. L." *Al-Bab,* 28 July 2009, www.al-bab.com. Attempts to present Lawrence from a contemporary Arabian perspective.

book

Wilson, Jeremy. *Lawrence of Arabia: The Authorised Biography of T. E. Lawrence.* Heinemann, 1989. Although not the most recent, this is the most comprehensive of the biographies of Lawrence and covers every aspect of his life. The bibliography could be more helpful.

website

---. *T. E. Lawrence Studies.* Castle Hill Press, 2012, www.telstudies.org /index.shtml. This is a superb, searchable Web site containing information about Lawrence, maps and chronology, bibliography, and a link to the journal.

journal article

Wilson, Michael. "Lawrence of Arabia: Elements and Facets of the Theme." *Cineaste,* vol. 21, no. 4, 1995, pp. 30–32. This article, though brief, provides interesting insights into how the screenwriter thought he was representing Lawrence's life.

Web: article

Wyatt-Brown, B. "Lawrence of Arabia: Image and Reality." *Journal of the Historical Society,* vol. 9, no. 4, Dec. 2009, pp. 515–548. *Wiley Online Library,* doi:10.1111/j.1540-5923.2009.00286.x. Very useful article. Worth a second reading.

How Much Research Is Enough?

Research is open-ended. You can't know in advance how many sources will provide adequate support for your topic. Your instructor may require that you consult at least five authorities, or ten, or fifteen; but that is probably intended to make sure that everyone in your class does a roughly equal amount of research. Quantity is not the crucial issue. There's little point in compiling the required number of source materials if the works on your list are minor, or trivial, or peripheral to the topic. Your bibliography could contain hundreds of sources—whole sections of a database or whole pages of an index—but would that be the basis for a well-documented essay?

You should try to achieve a good mix of sources in your bibliography, a balance of books, periodical articles, and Web material. Generally, the print sources—books and periodicals—should dominate the bibliography. Keep in mind that a book accessed from the Web remains a book for purposes of balance.

At various stages of your research, you may think that you have located enough sources. When that happens, try asking yourself these questions:

- Do my sources include a few of the "standard" books on my topic by well-known authorities? The most recent books? Contemporary accounts (if the topic is historical)?

- Have I checked databases and indexes to find the most authoritative periodical articles, whether in print or on the Web? Have I included the best ones among my sources?

- Does Web material supplement my research, rather than dominate it?

- Have I discussed any questions about my research with my instructor or with a librarian?

- Have I taken notes of my own ideas and thoughts about the topic?

- Without consulting sources, can I talk about the subject convincingly and fluently? Have I succeeded in doing this with a friend?

- Is a point of view or thesis emerging from my research?

- Have I gathered a critical mass of information, copied excerpts, and downloaded material so that my essay has the prospect of substantial support?

- Do I feel ready to start writing my essay?

EXERCISE 26: Compiling a Working Bibliography

Here are three topics for a research essay dealing with the broad topic of *advertising*, followed by a bibliography of 17 articles, arranged in order of their publication dates. Each item in the bibliography is followed by a brief description of its contents.

A. Examine the bibliography carefully and choose a set of sources for possible inclusion in a preliminary bibliography, for *each* of the three essay topics. Depending on the topic, which articles should you read? You are not expected to locate and read these articles; use the notes to help you make your decisions.

B. List the numbers of the articles that you select underneath each topic. You will notice that some of the articles can be used for more than one topic.

Topics

i) Feminists have argued that the image of women created by the advertising industry remains a false and objectionable one. Is that claim valid?

ii) How do advertising agencies go about manipulating the reactions of consumers?

iii) To what extent does advertising serve the public? harm the public?

1. Vranica, Suzanne. "Sirius Ad Is Best Bet for Most Sexist." *The Wall Street Journal,* 1 Apr. 2004, p. B6. This article is about the award given each year for advertising's most sexist commercial or advertisement and describes the various tasteless finalists. Although some advertising people think that higher standards of decency will eventually be imposed, others say that "edgy" ads appeal to young consumers.

2. Klempner, Geoffrey. "Ethics and Advertising." *Cardiff Centre for Ethics, Law and Society,* June 2004, www.ccels.cardiff.ac.uk/pubs/klempnerpaper.html. In a philosophical article (with references to Plato and Wittgenstein), this "professional metaphysician" attempts to "deconstruct the dream world of advertising" and the ways in which advertisers seduce us, and concludes that advertising is only as moral as the consumers it serves.

3. Drumwright, Minette E., and Patrick E. Murphy. "How Advertising Practitioners View Ethics: Moral Muteness, Moral Myopia, and Moral Imagination." *Journal of Advertising,* vol. 33, no. 2, Summer 2004, pp. 7–24, doi: 10.1080/00913367.2004.10639158. This article describes a study that

concluded that a large proportion of advertising professionals have a blind spot — "moral myopia" — about ethical issues when they arise. They believe that, if the consumers will accept it, then an advertising practice has to be morally acceptable and there's no need for concern.

4. Vagnoni, Anthony. "Ads Are from Mars, Women Are from Venus." *Print: America's Graphic Design Magazine*, vol. 59, no. 2, March 2005, pp. 52–56, connection.ebscohost.com/c/articles/16360212/ads-are-from-mars-women-are-from-venus. An advertising executive believes that ads targeted at women tend to be tasteless and even offensive, and, in return, women are ignoring most ads. The article contrasts strategies presently used to attract male and female consumers but does not attempt to solve the problem.

5. Singer, Emily. "They Know What You Want." *New Scientist*, 31 July 2004, pp. 36. Singer describes "neuromarketing," a new kind of technology that scans consumers' brains while they are shopping and comparing products. Advertisers hope to learn more about the origins of brand preference and brand loyalty so that they can better predict customer behavior.

6. Johnson, Scott. "Lies and Entertainment." *Adweek*, 27 Feb. 2006, www.adweek.com/news/advertising/lies-and-entertainment-84207. The rise of the Internet means that it's easier for lies to pass as truth. Knowing this, consumers are skeptical about advertising claims. They choose the products that they buy not because they believe the content of the ads on Web sites, but because they are entertained by the ads. This article provides tips for making ads amusing and likeable.

7. Mlotkiewicz, David. "Attracting Sales to Your Business." *Franchising World*, April 2006, www.franchise.org/attracting-sales-to-your-business. No business is going to do well without a marketing plan and effective sales techniques. The object is to make the customer trust the brand so much that there's no choice when it's time to buy. If a franchise is going to thrive, it must create brand loyalty.

8. Zimmerman, Amanda, and John Dahlberg. "The Sexual Objectification of Women in Advertising: A Contemporary Cultural Perspective." *Journal of Advertising Research*, vol. 48, no. 1, 2008, pp. 71–79. Since the 1960s, feminists have made great efforts to stop advertisers from using women in suggestive poses to sell products. This article explores the way the present generation of young women is reacting to ads that use sexual content as a selling device. It concludes that most are not offended by these portrayals.

9. Dittmar, Helga, Emma Halliwell, and Emma Stirling. "Understanding the Impact of Thin Media Models on Women's Body-Focused Affect: The Roles of Thin-Ideal Internalization and Weight-Related Self-Discrepancy Activation in Experimental Exposure Effects." *Journal of Social and Clinical Psychology*, vol. 28, no. 1, 2009, pp. 43–72, guilfordjournals.com/doi/abs/10.1521/jscp.2009.28.1.43. In a study of responses to ads with thin models, women, influenced by their own poor body image, tended to internalize the idea that it's best to be thin, and the result is that they felt even worse about themselves.

10. Durkin, K., and K. Rae. "Women and Chocolate Advertising: Exposure to Thin Models Exacerbates Ambivalence." *European Psychiatry*, vol. 24, no. 1, Supplement 1, 2009, p. S743, dx.doi.org/10.1016/S0924-9338(09)70976-9. This study showed women a variety of media images, with thin and fat models, and analyzed the extent to which these women felt more guilt (after seeing thin models) and less guilt (after seeing overweight models) about eating chocolate.

11. Feiereisen, Stephanie, Amanda L. Broderick, and Susan P. Douglas. "The Effect and Moderation of Gender Identity Congruity: Utilizing 'Real Women' Advertising Images." *Psychology and Marketing*, vol. 26, no. 9, September 2009, pp. 813–843, onlinelibrary.wiley.com/doi/10.1002/mar.20301/abstract. Women have positive responses to ads that make a direct appeal to their gender. Other influences include national culture.

12. Yu, Jay (Hyunjae), and Brenda J. Cude. "Possible Disparities in Consumers' Perceptions Toward Personalized Advertising Caused by Cultural Differences: U.S. and Korea." *Journal of International Consumer Marketing*, vol. 21, no. 4, August 2009, pp. 251–69, www.tandfonline.com/doi/abs/10.1080/08961530802282166#.Vz80COQuzdk. How do consumers react to personalized advertising, using a person's actual name in unsolicited e-mails, letters, and phone calls? This study, focusing on reactions in Korea and the U.S., indicated that consumers generally respond negatively, but more negatively in America than in Korea.

13. Bratu, Sofia. "The Phenomenon of Image Manipulation in Advertising." *Economics, Management, and Financial Markets*, vol. 5, no. 2, June 2010, pp. 333–8, http://connection.ebscohost.com/c/articles/52730274/phenomenon-image-manipulation-advertising. This article seems to be written in jargon: "Amos et al. hold that repeated pairings of a brand and celebrity strengthen the associative link consumers establish

between brand and celebrity. Bermeitinger et al. say that positive values indicate more consumption of the primed product than the nonprime product."

14. Sutton, Denise. *Globalizing Ideal Beauty: How Female Copywriters of the J. Walter Thompson Advertising Agency Redefined Beauty for the Twentieth Century.* Palgrave Macmillan, 2009. Decades ago, at the Thompson agency, female copywriters created unusual and even erotic ads to sell beauty products to women.

15. Sukumar, Snigda. "Impact of Female Sexual Objectification in Advertising for Women." *Advances in Management,* vol. 4, no. 12, 2011, www .managein.net/bk_issue/abst_4_12.htm. This article is about the consequences of the sexual objectification of women in advertising and other media, focusing on issues like depression and low self-esteem.

16. Wilson, Pam. "Advertising in the Public Interest?" *Media Literacies for the 21st Century,* 21 Feb. 2011, http://medialiteracies21st.blogspot.com/2011 /02/advertising-in-public-interest.html. Public service announcements are an important kind of advertising. It's vital to produce attractive public service ads that will rouse the audience's interest.

17. Kilbourne, Jean. "Killing Us Softly 3: Advertising's Images of Women." Media Education Foundation, 2000, www.mediaed.org/cgi-bin/commerce .cgi?preadd=action&key=206. An analysis of numerous print and media ads demonstrating prevailing gender stereotypes about women's appearance and behavior.

EXERCISE 27: Finding and Selecting Sources

Each of the historical figures on the following list has been the subject of a motion picture. (The dates and, where necessary, titles of the films are in parentheses.) Choose one figure and then compile a preliminary bibliography for an essay that sets out to determine *to what extent the film is authentic.* (Since this is a *preliminary* bibliography and you're not being asked to write the essay, you need not have seen the film in order to start the research process.)

Using databases and search engines, search for sources that are clearly linked to your topic. Print out a list of the first 20 or 30 items from each search, eliminate those that are obviously commercial or trivial, and choose those that might appropriately be included in a preliminary bibliography. You do not have to examine the books, articles, or Web sites in order to make your selection; base your choices on the descriptions, summaries, or abstracts provided by the database or search engine. If you don't find sufficient material in your first search, keep trying.

Your preliminary bibliography should contain at least 12 items, with a balance of one-third books, one-third print periodical articles, and one-third Web material. Hand in the results lists from your searches with the appropriate choices marked. If your instructor requests it, also prepare a formal bibliography using MLA format.

Abraham Lincoln (2012)
Alexander the Great
    (*Alexander* 2004)
Alfred Hitchcock (*Hitchcock* 2012;
    The Girl 2012)
Alfred Kinsey (*Kinsey* 2004)
Benito Juárez (*Juarez* 1939)
Charlie Chaplin (*Chaplin* 1992)
Charles Gordon (*Khartoum* 1966)
Charles Lindbergh (*Spirit of
    St. Louis* 1957)
Che Guevara (*Che* 2008)
Cleopatra (1963)
Cole Porter (*Night and Day* 1946;
    De-Lovely 2004)
Dian Fossey (*Gorillas in the Mist*
    1988)
El Cid (1961)
Erwin Rommel (*The Desert Fox*
    1951)
Eva Perón (*Evita* 1996)
Gandhi (1982)
George III (*The Madness of King
    George* 1994)
George VI (*The King's Speech* 2010)
George Patton (*Patton* 1970)
Hans Christian Andersen (1952)
Harvey Milk (*Milk* 2008)
Helen Keller (*The Miracle Worker*
    1962)

Howard Hughes (*The Aviator*
    2004)
Jackie Robinson (*42* 2013)
James Brown (*Get On Up* 2014)
Jim Morrison (*The Doors* 1991)
John Dillinger (*Public Enemies* 2009)
John F. Kennedy (*JFK* 1991)
Johnny Cash (*Walk the Line* 2005)
Kurt Cobain (*Last Days* 2005)
Larry Flynt (*The People vs. Larry
    Flynt* 1996)
Lenny Bruce (*Lenny* 1974)
Loretta Lynn (*Coal Miner's
    Daughter* 1980)
Louis Kahn (*My Architect* 2003)
Marie Curie (*Madame Curie* 1943)
Marilyn Monroe (*My Week with
    Marilyn* 2011)
Mark Zuckerberg (*The Social
    Network* 2010)
Michael Collins (1996)
Mike Tyson (*Tyson* 2008)
Mikhail Kutuzov (*War and Peace*
    1956)
Mozart (*Amadeus* 1984)
Muhammad Ali (*Ali* 2001)
Oscar Wilde (1997)
Philippe Petit (*Man on Wire* 2008)
Queen Elizabeth I (*Elizabeth* 1998,
    2006)

Queen Elizabeth II (*The Queen* 2007)
Queen Victoria (*Mrs. Brown* 1997)
Ray Charles (*Ray* 2004)
Richard Nixon (*Nixon* 1995; *Frost/Nixon* 2008)
Thomas Jefferson (*Jefferson in Paris* 1995)
Tina Turner (*What's Love Got to Do with It* 1993)
Truman Capote (*Capote* 2005; *Infamous* 2006)

Tsar Nicholas II (*Nicholas and Alexandra* 1971)
Ty Cobb (*Cobb* 1994)
Vincent Van Gogh (*Lust for Life* 1956)
William Gilbert or Arthur Sullivan (*Topsy-Turvy* 1999)
William Randolph Hearst (*Citizen Kane* 1941)
Wyatt Earp (*My Darling Clementine* 1946)

ASSIGNMENT 7A: Preparing a Proposal for a Research Essay

A. Choose a broad topic that you will research and develop into an extended essay of ten or more pages.

■ If you have a *person or an event* in mind, but do not have enough knowledge to decide on a focus or target date, do some preliminary reading first. Start with an encyclopedia article or an entry in a biographical dictionary; then use the online databases and search engines, as well as any bibliographies that you find along the way.

■ If you select a *contemporary subject or issue for argument*, search for books, journal and newspaper articles, and Web sites to help you formulate a few questions that might be explored in your essay.

B. Compile a preliminary bibliography, based on your search results. At this point, you need not have examined all the sources, taken notes, or planned the organization of your essay. Your purpose is to assess the *amount* and, as much as possible, the *quality* of the material that is available. Whether or not your instructor asks you to hand in your preliminary bibliography, make sure that the publication information that you record is accurate and legible. Indicate which sources your library has available and which may be difficult to obtain.

C. After you have read enough sources to decide what interests you, submit a topic proposal to your instructor, describing the probable scope and focus of your essay. (If you are interested in more than one topic, suggest a few possibilities.) Be prepared to change the specifics of your proposal as you learn more about the number and availability of your sources. Assignment 7B, dealing with writing the research essay, can be found at the end of Chapter 9, p. 439.

▪8▪
Evaluating Sources

It's hard to write about most subjects from your own knowledge and experience. As a rule, you have to rely on the evidence of others, usually in written form, published in print or on the Web. If that evidence is questionable, then your work loses its credibility. For this reason, it's essential that—before you start writing or even reading at length—you evaluate each potential source to determine whether it's solid enough to support your essay.

Evaluating sources doesn't have to take a great deal of time. You have to read enough of each text to make some judgments about its *substance* and its *tone*. You have to understand what kind of work it is—whether it's *believable*, whether it's *appropriate* for the essay that you're writing. You need to be sure it's *relevant* to your topic. And since a good source should be *authoritative*, you must explore the author's claims and give them serious consideration.

Evaluating Print Sources

Let's assume that you've begun research for an essay on *animal rights*. You've often wondered about the motivations of vegetarians. As a meat eater yourself, you're curious about the arguments used by animal rights advocates to discourage the slaughter of living creatures for the table. You are also aware of an ongoing controversy about the use of animals in medical experiments.

Your college library holds many of the books and periodicals that have turned up in your database searches. How do you determine which ones to read seriously? How do you weigh one source of evidence against another and decide whose ideas should be emphasized in your essay? Since all the books and articles have been chosen for publication, each one has presumably undergone some form of selection and review. Would it have been published if its author's authority was questionable? Why is it necessary to inquire further?

Credentials

At the most basic level, you want to find out whether the author of a book or article about animal rights can be trusted to know what he or she is writing about. Here's where the person's education and professional experience become relevant. Is the writer an academic? If so, what's the field of specialization?

- A *psychologist* might provide insights into the personal beliefs motivating vegetarians, but would probably be less concerned with the ideology of the animal rights movement.
- A *philosopher* will present theoretical arguments about the ethics of killing other creatures, but the analysis may be too abstract to provide you with concrete examples for developing your thesis.
- An *economist* might seem to be an unlikely source to support this topic, but the movement toward vegetarianism has had serious consequences for the agricultural economy as well as the retail world of the supermarket.
- A *home economist* might turn up on a database search for "animal rights" AND vegetarianism, but the authors of cookbooks and guides to good nutrition are unlikely to possess academic qualifications.

Do these concerns matter? What kind of an essay are you writing, anyway? One that stresses the theoretical arguments behind the animal rights movement? The psychological motivation? The economic consequences? The practical applications in the kitchen? Your research is now helping you to narrow down your topic.

An author's background is important. Here's how you can find out about it quickly and easily:

- Check a book's *preface* (including acknowledgments), which will often contain biographical information.
- Read the *blurb* on the jacket cover—often laudatory—which should include some basic facts among the hype.
- Look for *thumbnail biographies* at the beginning or end of periodical articles, or grouped together somewhere in the issue. Be aware that such brief biographies (often written by the authors themselves) can be vague or even misleading. "A freelance writer who frequently writes about this topic" can describe a recognized authority or an inexperienced amateur.
- Do a *Web search* using the author's name. See what other books and articles the author has published.

- Consult one of the many *biographical dictionaries and encyclopedias* available on the Web.

- Check the *Book Review Index* on the Web. If the book is a recent one, there will probably be many reviews available.

- Routinely check the level and extent of the *documentation* that the author provides. Footnotes or parenthetical notes and a comprehensive bibliography usually indicate a scholarly commitment to the subject.

Credentials: Peter Singer: Peter Singer is the author of *Animal Liberation: A New Ethics for Our Treatment of Animals.* After a database search turns up this title, you find the book on the library shelves, note that it was published in 1975 (but revised in 1990), and wonder whether it's worth delving into a book that's more than 40 years old. So you search for Singer's name in the *Britannica Online* encyclopedia and find the following:

Singer, Peter (Albert David) born July 6, 1946, Melbourne, Austl.
Australian ethical and political philosopher, best known for his work in bioethics and his role as one of the intellectual founders of the modern animal rights movement.

Singer's Jewish parents emigrated to Australia from Vienna in 1938 to escape Nazi persecution following the Anschluss. Three of Singer's grandparents were subsequently killed in the Holocaust. Growing up in Melbourne, Singer attended Scotch College and the University of Melbourne, where he earned a B.A. in philosophy and history (1967) and an M.A. in philosophy (1969). In 1969 he entered the University of Oxford, receiving a B.Phil. degree in 1971 and serving as Radcliffe Lecturer in Philosophy at University College from 1971 to 1973. At Oxford his association with a vegetarian student group and his reflection on the morality of his own meat eating led him to adopt vegetarianism. While at Oxford and during a visiting professorship at New York University in 1973–74, he wrote what would become his best-known and most influential work, *Animal Liberation: A New Ethics for Our Treatment of Animals* (1975). Returning to Australia, he lectured at La Trobe University (1975–76) and was appointed professor of philosophy at Monash University (1977); he became director of Monash's Centre for Human Bioethics in 1983 and codirector of its Institute for Ethics and Public Policy in 1992. In 1999 he was appointed Ira W. DeCamp Professor of Bioethics in the University Center for Human Values at Princeton University.

The article notes that Singer views ethical issues from a utilitarian point of view and so advocates actions that result in the greatest good for the greatest number of people. He has written, cowritten, or edited 46 books, the most recent in 2013, some in areas of pure philosophy, but most dealing with matters of ethical choice. He was chosen as the author of *Encyclopedia Britannica*'s article on ethics.

What do you learn from this information? Singer holds impeccable academic credentials and has had a long academic career at estimable universities. As a philosopher, he is likely to root his work on animal rights in abstract arguments. As an ethicist, he is likely to provide plenty of concrete examples to illustrate his arguments.

So far, *Animal Liberation* seems like an excellent choice for your preliminary bibliography and, quite probably, your final bibliography. Is there anything more that you need to know about Singer and his work?

Impartiality

Sometimes you have to consider whether an author has any personal interest in a subject, especially if it's a contentious one like animal rights. In the simplest terms, a declared vegetarian is likely to argue against using animals for food and may present those arguments in a way that's less than impartial. There's nothing intrinsically wrong with having one's own point of view. Few people succeed in being totally detached or objective, whether about their beliefs or their areas of professional expertise. But there's a big difference between an acknowledged *personal interest* and an *underlying prejudice*.

The issue here is *bias*: the special interest or personal preference that might affect an author's opinion or treatment of a subject. The existence of bias needn't prevent you from using and citing a source. It's simply one factor that can affect your understanding of an author's ideas. A *dogmatic* writer may want to convert you at all costs. A *narrow-minded* writer will ignore or downplay opposing points of view. You may conclude that either is too biased to be credible. But a third author, who also cares passionately about a subject, may argue the issue strongly and yet remain credible. Such writers are usually aware of and acknowledge their bias—and seek to *persuade* or *convince* rather than bludgeon their readers into submission. If you think that an author has a special interest in the subject, either disregard the bias as harmless, or adjust your judgment to allow for its influence, or—if the bias is clearly prejudice in disguise—reject the source as not worth your time.

Impartiality: Peter Singer: Looking further at the *Britannica* profile, you notice that Peter Singer's books tend to have strong titles, urging action: *Animal Liberation, In Defence of Animals, Ethics into Action, Democracy and Disobedience*. Clearly, he's not an ivory tower philosopher, and so, curious to learn more about his activities, you do a Web search. You don't even have to click on any of the items on the results lists to learn that Singer has been called the world's "most controversial ethicist" and that a petition was started to protest his appointment to a named chair at Princeton. There are references to his "infanticide excesses" and "utilitarian horrors" as well as comparisons with Hitler's Nazism. On the other hand, other Web sites support his views and praise his reasoned defense of his ethical beliefs.

Since these searches have taken only a few minutes, you try one more, and find an article in *Contemporary Authors* that provides an analysis of reactions by reviewers to many of Singer's works. Focusing on those that deal with *Animal Liberation*, you find praise for his documentation and for his "quite unhysterical and engaging" style. He is also referred to as a propagandist, and he is apparently a successful one, since *Animal Liberation* is described by one reviewer as "one of the most thoughtful and persuasive books that I have read in a long time."

What can you conclude now? That the present controversy over Singer may or may not concern his 1975 work, which is the one that's most relevant to your research. That he has his detractors and his supporters, which is understandable given his contentious subject. That you should judge for yourself by reading *Animal Liberation*, while being alert for the possibility of a biased presentation.

Style and Tone

Writers aim their work at particular audiences and adjust the content and style accordingly. A children's book about kindness to animals would be an unsuitable candidate for inclusion in a research paper; both style and content would be too simplified to be taken seriously. At the other extreme, technical papers in the sciences and social sciences are often written in a dense style, with a vocabulary incomprehensible to someone outside the discipline; essentially, one academic is writing for an audience of peers. You would probably want to avoid reading—and citing—a journal article that focuses on the methodology for a survey of animal rights activists or analyzes the chemical basis of nutrients needed in a vegetarian diet.

Nonfiction books are often categorized as:

Popular: intended to attract the widest possible audience and, therefore, be accessible to people with a wide range of educational backgrounds. A popular treatment of a serious subject is likely to emphasize colorful detail and stories rather than abstract, complex ideas.

General interest: intended for an audience that is interested in a subject but has no special grounding in it. General interest books provide a thorough introduction, with some level of complexity, but without a lot of technical description.

Academic: intended for a limited audience in the field. An academic book is usually published by a university press and contains a level of scholarship and depth of analysis that might well be beyond the comprehension of the general public.

As a rule, you would do well to include some general-interest books and some purely academic books—at the more accessible end of the academic spectrum—in your preliminary bibliography.

To determine whether a book is appropriate and potentially useful for your research, look at the *table of contents*, the *introduction*, and a *sample* from a middle chapter that will give you a sense of style and tone. Also check the *index* to see how often your topic appears. Does the book have a *bibliography*? Notes or other documentation to make it academically credible?

Periodicals also serve a wide range of readers. Most have a marketing "niche," appealing to a specific audience with well-defined interests and reading habits. Since readership varies so greatly, articles on the same subject in two different periodicals are likely to differ widely in their content, point of view, and presentation. A newsmagazine like *Time* or *Newsweek* might provide factual information on an animal rights demonstration; the article would be short and lively, filled with concrete illustrations and quotations. It would not have the same purpose, nor cite the same kinds of evidence, nor use the same vocabulary as a longer article on the animal rights movement in a general-interest periodical like *Psychology Today*. And that, in turn, would have little in common with an essay in a scholarly journal on the moral basis of the contractarian argument supporting the rights of animals. Researchers must allow for this wide variation in style and tone when they select and use their sources.

Articles in social science journals tend to follow a conventional structure and use professional terminology that can sometimes seem like jargon. At the beginning of such articles, you're likely to find a *"review of the literature"*: a summary of the contributions that other sociologists or psychologists have made to an understanding of the topic. Here's a typical paragraph taken from "Social Work and Speciesism," an article by David B. Wolf in the journal *Social Work*:

> There are many connections between our treatment of animals and environmental integrity; these touch on issues such as hunger, poverty, and war. Toffler (1975) suggested that the most practical hope for resolving the world's food crisis is a restriction of beef eating that will save billions of tons of grain. Ehrlich and Ehrlich (1972) reported that production of a pound of meat requires 40 to 100 times as much water as the production of a pound of wheat. Altschul (1964) noted that in terms of calorie units per acre, a diet of grains, vegetables, and beans will support 20 times as many people as a diet of meat....

In effect, Wolf is summarizing the evidence of his sources in the topic sentence and then citing them, one by one. This pattern of presentation should not be imitated in an essay written for a basic writing course, *nor is it usually a good idea to include such a "review of the literature" within your essay*. You would be quoting or paraphrasing Wolf, who is paraphrasing Toffler or Altschul. Better to eliminate the middleman (Wolf) and go directly to the source (Altschul or Toffler).

You can often decide to dismiss or pursue an article just by considering the title of the periodical. In a ProQuest search for journal articles on "animal rights," the results list included periodicals ranging from *Chemical and Engineering News* to *Poultry World* to *Transport Topics* to *Vegetarian Times*. It's highly unlikely that articles in any of those four periodicals would be suitable for a research essay on "animal rights." What about *Gender and Society*? If you're especially interested in gender issues and wonder whether activism on behalf of animals may be gender-specific, that might be an excellent article to review for your preliminary bibliography. *Animal Law*? That depends on the technical level of the article. You'd have to see it to decide whether the issues are presented in accessible language or in professional "legalese." *Audubon*? Here, again, the issue is audience. Is the article intended to appeal to a limited group of nature lovers, or is its content intended for a broader audience?

> *The style and tone of a book or article should be appropriate for your level of research.*

If you find a source too erudite, then you'll have difficulty understanding it and presenting it to your readers. If you find that a source is written in a superficial, frivolous, or overly emotional style, then it's not serious or authoritative enough to include in your essay.

Style and Tone: Peter Singer: In the case of Singer's *Animal Liberation*, you've already found out from the *Contemporary Authors* summary that his style is regarded as accessible; according to one reviewer, it was "intended for the mass market." Something can also be learned about the style and tone of a book just by considering the *publisher*. Most of Singer's books come from Oxford University Press or Cambridge University Press, but *Animal Liberation* was published by Random House, a "general interest" company eager to sell books to the general public. Finally, you open the book to a chapter that particularly interests you and glance at a few sentences:

> Becoming a vegetarian is not merely a symbolic gesture. Nor is it an attempt to isolate oneself from the ugly realities of the world, to keep oneself pure and so without responsibility for the cruelty and carnage all around. Becoming a vegetarian is the most practical and effective step one can take toward ending both the killing of nonhuman animals and the infliction of suffering upon them.

The language is clear; the sentences compelling. You hope that Singer will at some point present the arguments of the nonvegetarian and realize that, if he does not, it will be your job to find the appropriate sources and do so.

Currency

One further indication of a work's usefulness for your purpose is its *date*. Only in the last few years has animal rights emerged as an issue of international importance. As a rule, in the sciences and social sciences, the most recent sources usually replace earlier ones. Unless you're interested in writing a historical review of attitudes toward animals, your research would probably focus on works published over the last 10 or 20 years. An article about vegetarianism as practiced in the 1930s would probably be of little value to you. On the other hand, Singer's 1975 *Animal Liberation* is now regarded as a seminal work—a key influence on later writers about animal rights—and would therefore not lose currency.

For research on historical and biographical topics, you need to know the difference between *primary* and *secondary* sources.

> *A primary source is a work that is itself the subject of your essay or (if you are writing a historical research essay) a work written during the period that you are writing about that gives you direct or primary knowledge of that period.*

"Primary source" is frequently used to describe an original document—such as the Constitution—or memoirs and diaries of historical interest, or a work of literature that, over the years, has been the subject of much written commentary. Your interview or survey notes are primary sources.

> *A secondary source can be any commentary written both after and about the primary source.*

A history textbook is usually a secondary source. So are most biographies. While you generally study a primary source for its own sake, the secondary source is important—often, it only exists—because of its primary source:

- If you are asked to write an essay about *Huckleberry Finn*, and your instructor tells you not to use any secondary sources, you are to read only Mark Twain's novel and not consult any commentaries.
- T. E. Lawrence's *Seven Pillars of Wisdom* is a secondary source if you are interested in guerrilla warfare, but a primary source if you are studying Lawrence.
- If you read archival issues of the *New York Times* to acquire information about Lawrence's desert campaign in World War I, you are using the newspaper as a primary source since it was written during the period you are studying. But when you look up a *Times* movie review of *Lawrence of Arabia*, then you are locating a secondary source in order to learn more about your primary subject.

Currency is not always essential for research about historical and biographical subjects, which usually includes primary sources. Even out-of-date secondary sources can be occasionally useful. Lowell Thomas's 1924 biography of T. E. Lawrence is still of moderate interest in part because Thomas was present during the desert campaigns and could provide firsthand (although not necessarily unbiased) information. Nevertheless, because research is always unearthing new facts about people's lives, Thomas's work has long been superseded by new biographies providing a broader range of information. *For a biographical or historical essay, you should consult some primary sources, one or two secondary sources written at the time of the event or during the subject's lifetime, and the most recent and reliable secondary sources.* It is the sources in the middle—written a few years after your target date, without the perspective of distance—that often lack authenticity or objectivity.

Evaluating the authors of books and articles shouldn't dominate your research process. If you're building a preliminary bibliography of 10–15 sources and you're writing an essay in which you anticipate that no single source will be emphasized, don't waste time looking up every author. On the other hand, if you're likely to be working with only a few key sources, invest some time in finding out about these authors and their qualifications.

Evaluating Web Sources

Checking the credibility of *print sources*—books and periodical articles—can strengthen your research. It is useful to do so, but not always essential. Evaluating the reliability of *Web sources* can be crucial to the quality of your essay. It should become a routine part of your research practice.

You need to evaluate Web sources for two reasons:

- *An overabundance of information.* The profusion of material on the Web far exceeds the number of available print articles and books. What do you do when the keyword "animal rights" in a Yahoo! search produces 681,000 Web sites? First, you refine your search; next, you evaluate what's left and decide which sites are worth examining.

- *An absence of editorial or peer review.* When a book or article is submitted for print publication, editors or specialist reviewers judge its quality, accuracy, and timeliness, based on their knowledge of comparable material. If the work is published, the reader can assume that it meets reasonably high standards. There is no comparable process for reviewing most material appearing on the Web. No one at Google or Yahoo! or Chrome is responsible for making choices or maintaining standards. Each of the 681,000 Web sites on animal rights is presented as equal to the rest. Even search engines that claim to rank responses do not actually do so in a meaningful way. "Relevance" is not the same as quality. The basis for ranking—if any—tends to be commercial, not intellectual.

Here are a few ways to avoid the quagmire of endless results lists:

1. Start your search with *academic* databases that include Web material. When a college library or academic organization compiles or endorses a database, the contents are likely to have some claim to reliability. That is by no means true of databases that are compiled randomly or those that accept payment from sites in return for inclusion at the top of search engine lists.

2. If, initially, you don't know which databases are academic or if your access is limited to general search engines, that's all the more reason to narrow down your topic with an *advanced Boolean search*. (See p. 317.)

3. Scan the search engine's results list looking for Web sites sponsored by *academic institutions* or *government agencies*, and access them first.

4. One or two reliable, comprehensive sites can lead you, via *hyperlinks*, to the best material about your subject on the Web. For example, one of the links in the 681,000-hit Yahoo! search on animal rights led to a Google Directory that, in turn, listed four sites, all sponsored by government or academic institutes, that serve as clearinghouses for Web sites about animal rights. One, from the University of British Columbia, provides 32 links to relevant and credible sites, some of which are appropriate for a college-level essay.

Since the Web is still a new medium, with very few rules or standard procedures, evaluating Web sites can be a hit-or-miss process. But the categories are the same as those for evaluating works in print: credentials, impartiality, style and tone, and currency.

Credentials

With print sources, the material's credibility greatly depends on the author's *qualifications*. With Web sources, credibility is linked to the knowledgeability and seriousness of the *individual* or the disinterested commitment of the *organization* that originated and maintains the site. If the name of an individual appears on the site as owner, then you must try to assess that person's background and credentials and determine his or her likely credibility in your area of research:

- Does the site contain a link to the owner's home page?
- Is there a section of the site specifically about the owner (often called "About Me")?

- What else has the owner published?
- Does he appear in other writers' bibliographies?
- Has she any professional experience in a discipline appropriate to this subject?

Often, you'll find no single person taking responsibility for the site. Instead, there will be a *sponsoring organization*, which will probably include an "About Us" section, describing the group's collective purpose or "mission." If there's no "About" link, then it may be possible to do a Web search for more information about the sponsor:

- Is the organization commercial or nonprofit? (The ".com" and ".org" in the URL used to distinguish between the two, but that's no longer the rule.)
- What's the reason for creating a site about this topic?
- Is there a political or cultural agenda?
- If the sponsor is commercial, what's the motive for expending resources on this Web site?

Another element to look for is *documentation*. Appropriate documentation tells you that the author or sponsor understands the basic requirements for presenting academic scholarship; seeing bibliographical references or endnotes gives you some assurance that the information contained in the site comes from reliable sources. Documentation found in Web pages may consist of hyperlinks to other Web sources; you will want to click on some of these, to evaluate the quality of the linked sources and perhaps add them to your bibliography.

Impartiality

People and organizations usually create Web sites not to provide a fair, well-balanced account of an issue, but to sell something: a product, a cause, a point of view, a lifestyle. Bias isn't to be avoided on the Web; it's considered a legitimate basis for self-presentation. So you do have to scrutinize and evaluate what you find.

As you begin to read a Web page, consider the *nature of the content*. Is it purely personal opinion? Is it self-serving? Is it advocacy? Commercial? Ideological? Academic? Does the owner apparently have an ax to grind? Does the site present fact or opinion? Or does it present opinion as fact? Are you the target of propaganda for a cause or advertising for a product? Can you tell the difference between the site of a pet food company with a feature on animal welfare, that of an advocacy group organizing a rally against cruelty to animals, and that of a university veterinary department publishing a report on the use of animals in experiments?

Whatever the degree of bias, worthwhile Web material should provide reasonable support for its assertions. As you begin to read, consider the following:

- Does the site have a discernible thesis or point, or was it put on the Web purely to indulge the owner's desire for self-revelation?
- Is there a clear context established for the material?
- Does the author make an initial statement of intention, purpose, and scope? Is that statement coherent? Does it make sense?

Many sites are the spatial equivalent of a soundbite. Their authors don't engage in complex analysis and argument:

- Is there supporting evidence?
- Is there a logical sequence of ideas or just a series of claims?
- Is there a convincing level of fact and detail?
- Does the author anticipate and deal with potential objections to opinions?
- Is the evidence mostly anecdotal, depending on stories ("It happened to me")?
- Are examples and anecdotes relevant to the topic?

You needn't automatically exclude poorly supported or one-sided Web material (or print sources) from your bibliography. Instead, make yourself aware of the flaws in your sources and, if you choose to include them in your essay, compensate for their deficiencies by adding stronger or complementary sources so that your essay will become better balanced and better supported.

Style and Tone

In a freewheeling medium like the Web, there are few rules about style or tone. Many sites, particularly home pages developed by individual owners or blogs that serve as personal journals, will be presented informally, as if the writer were delivering a monologue or holding a one-sided conversation. This lack of balance or purpose should raise some doubts as soon as you click on and start reading the site:

- Is the material *clearly focused* and *coherent*?
- Is the *tone* dispassionate? Conversational? Hysterical?
- Is the *language* inflammatory? Frivolous? Is it full of superlatives?
- Is the *argument* presented in neutral language, or are there innuendoes about those holding opposing views?
- Does the writer follow the basic rules of *grammar*?

- Can the material be *summarized* or *paraphrased*? Be particularly wary with blogs, as the uncredentialed blogger is likely to post self-indulgent, opinionated entries.

As with print material, it is helpful to consider the intended *audience*. Web sites frequently target niche audiences. What sort of user does a specific Web page hope to attract?

- Is the site intended for the general public? Then the content may be worth your consideration.

- Is it aimed at juveniles? If so, the approach and style are probably too simplistic to be useful for an academic essay.

- Does the author assume that the reader shares a common religious background or political assumptions? A reader unfamiliar with these beliefs or causes may find the contents hard to understand or accept.

- Is the sponsor a local group that's appealing to a grassroots audience? The site's purpose and level of detail may be so narrow that it is likely to interest only those who live in that area.

The *appearance of the site* itself can help you to evaluate the content:

- Is there any logic to its construction? Is it well designed? Easy to use? Or is it sprawling and hard to follow?

- Does it have a plan or method of organization? If it's a large site, are there links—on the home page and elsewhere—that enable you to go directly to pages that interest you?

- Are additions and updates integrated into existing material, or left dangling at the end?

- Are there graphics? Do they help your understanding of the site, or do they distract you?

Currency

In print sources, currency is estimated in *decades*; in Web sources, it's often a matter of *months or even days*. If you don't download or print material quickly, you may not have access to that information when you actually need it. The site may have disappeared from the Web.

Other sites will linger on even when they have lost their currency. The owners are no longer taking responsibility for regular maintenance and updating. If the subject of your essay is a current issue and you need to find and use up-to-the-minute sources, you should be very careful to *check the date at the end of each Web site*. And, whatever the subject, you should note the date of the site's last update to include a complete reference to the site in your bibliography.

Evaluating Sources

	Books	Periodicals	Web sites/E-mails
Credentials	■ Appropriate specialization for your topic ■ Appropriate and sufficient educational background ■ Includes credible documentation	■ Appropriate specialization for your topic ■ Appropriate and sufficient educational background ■ Includes credible documentation, appropriate for its length	■ Appropriate specialization for your topic ■ Indication of relevant experience and recognition by others in the field ■ Evidence of some acceptable documentation
Impartiality	■ Absence of dogmatic or biased tone ■ Willingness to consider other points of view	■ Absence of dogmatic or biased tone ■ Willingness to consider other points of view	■ Serious intention ■ Bias kept within reasonable limits ■ Opinion distinguished from fact ■ Hidden agendas at a minimum ■ Evidence of reasoned argument
Style and Tone	■ Written for a general-interest or academic audience ■ If academic, written in an accessible style	■ Periodical intended for a reasonably broad audience ■ Style and tone consistent with other periodicals (and books) in your bibliography ■ Language accessible to someone outside that field of specialization	■ Coherent, calm, even-handed, open-minded, purposeful
Currency	■ If appropriate to your topic, bibliography should include primary and secondary sources ■ Bibliography should contain the most recent research about your topic	■ Unless your topic requires you to include primary sources, recent articles should dominate your periodicals list	■ Available for a reasonable length of time (Web site) ■ Maintained and updated (Web site)

Evaluating Web Sources about Animal Rights

To demonstrate some of these evaluative criteria, let's look at a few of the hundreds of Web sites found in a Google search using the keywords "animal rights." As usual, the results list includes several *commercial* sites selling products totally unrelated to the subject of the search. Most of the others are sponsored by *organizations or individuals actively advocating the cause of equal rights for animals* and urging the public to join in protesting various instances of "speciesism." Such sites are typically crammed with news stories about animal exploitation; links to like-minded organizations; offers for products and services (often supporting vegetarianism); and invitations to participate in online discussions, attend rallies and events, and register for membership—often requiring fees or contributions—in the common cause. The range of links on one site includes "The Joy of Adopting an Older Animal," "Featured Shelter of the Month," "Ways to Help Animals without Leaving Your Computer," "Dogs in Heaven," and "Tiny Tim—a Kitten's Story."

Sites Sponsored by Organizations

The home page of **www.all-creatures.org** is typical. Crowded with lists and choices, the site is busy and difficult to navigate. The links and options are all intended to educate the reader about the plight of animals and encourage participation in their defense. On the home page, pictures of animals compete for space with lists of "action alerts" and campaigns, an "Animal Exploitation Photo Journal," and a blog by the Joyful Curmudgeon. Various news items have been selected to inspire, inform, and touch the hearts of site visitors.

Similarly, **www.animalrightsstand.com** (Figure 8-1) welcomes you and invites you to action through "Critter Trivia," in which we learn that Sir Isaac Newton, discoverer of gravity, also invented the cat door, and "Animal Humor," which features a joke about a dancing canine. These sites seem aimed at an intellectually unsophisticated audience who, the sponsors hope, will be moved to action by the pathos and force of these human-interest stories. Although some of the links are useful, *most of the information on the majority of these sites is not appropriate for research* into the issues surrounding animal rights.

As a medium of communication, the Web serves as an international pulpit for anyone with a cause. Yet the strength of sites like **www.all-creatures.org** and **www.animalrightsstand.com** lies in their ability to project a strong sense of community, often reinforced by an emphasis on *local interests.* You're invited to join campaigns and be kept informed about the activities wherever you live. A typical local site will provide details of fund-raising bake sales and vegan potluck suppers. Sites like these, while admirable as grassroots operations, are little more than a distraction for researchers looking for more broadly based information.

Figure 8-1 Animal Rights Stand Web site

Animal rights is a provocative topic that lends itself to a hard sell and offers no amnesty to opposing views. For example, **www.animalrightsstand. com** sells a T-shirt with a slogan that offers two options: "Be kind to animals" or "Burn in hell."

Very few sites dealing with this topic take a more neutral stance. What varies is *the tone in which the propaganda is presented*. Consider, for example, the content and presentation of the Americans for Medical Progress (AMP) Web site (Figure 8-2). The "About AMP" page contains a small picture of an appealing white mouse on the masthead. Prominently featured on the "About" page is a straightforward statement about the organization and its purpose: to "protect society's investment in research by nurturing public understanding of and support for the humane, necessary, and valuable use of animals in medicine...to foster a balanced public debate on the animal research issue, ensuring that among the voices heard are those whose lives have been touched by research... [to distribute] timely and relevant news, information and analysis about animal rights extremism...." There are links to press releases and studies describing the breakthroughs that have resulted from animal research, as well as to government documents such as the "Public Health Service Policy on Human Care and Use of Animals." Consistent with its mission to inform both researchers and the general public, the site's content has a temperate and accommodating tone.

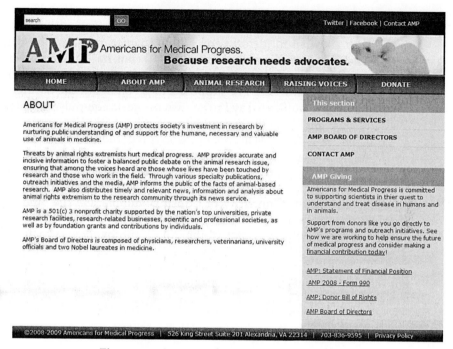

Figure 8-2 Americans for Medical Progress Web site

Nevertheless, AMP doesn't rely entirely on an appeal to reason and social conscience. It has a cause to advocate, and it does so by motivating its audience to support that cause financially—by seeking donations—and emotionally—by inviting everyone to "let the world hear your story." Among the "resources" provided is a group of posters featuring endearing children and contented animals.

Although the AMP site includes a section on how to become an active advocate for animal research, it avoids the abstract question of whether violent actions are appropriate in defense of animal rights. (Some pro animal-rights sites express fewer doubts.) If you intend to make this issue the focus of your research, you might gain some helpful material by clicking on the links provided on the AMP site—as long as you remain aware of the *underlying bias* and make an effort to balance your presentation.

It's reassuring that, according to the "About AMP" page, AMP is a registered charity and the sponsoring organization provides an address and phone number at the bottom of the home page (many sites do not). The site's *credibility* is enhanced by a listing of the Board of Directors that includes some Nobel laureates; but there are also several representatives of the pharmaceutical industry, which stands to benefit a great deal from continuing to use animals in developing new drugs. On balance, this is a site that merits some cautious exploration.

Sites Owned by Individuals

Some Web sites fail to identify any author, owner, or sponsor; others do so unconvincingly. Brian Carnell, at **brian.carnell.com**, has a mission to expose the flaws in the animal rights movement. He is sparing in his biographical description: "I think this is where I'm supposed to go on about the boring details of who I am etc. Just suffice to say I'm an extreme geek, compulsive writer, insomniac and general pain-in-the-ass-know-it-all."

In contrast, Chris MacDonald, who prepared a list of links for the W. Maurice Young Center for Applied Ethics, offers a two-page biography (plus picture) that includes his academic qualifications, professional experience, research, and Web sites. It's significant that the Center for Applied Ethics is affiliated with the University of British Columbia. On the other hand, the WWW Virtual Library, which provides a long list of links on animal welfare, is described as "the oldest catalog of the Web...run by a loose confederation of volunteers" who develop Web sites in their particular areas of expertise. The description includes an offer to anyone who's interested to prepare a site for the Virtual Library—no credentials requested or apparently required. It's this casual approach to competency that makes research on the Web so risky.

Balancing Your Sources

It takes time and patience to evaluate Web sources. You have to inspect each site to make sure it's reliable before considering it for your preliminary bibliography. Is it authoritative? Is it at an appropriate level? Will it make a contribution to your essay? And however carefully you select Web sources, your research can't stop there.

If you want your essay to be successful and receive a commensurate grade, don't get all or even most of your sources from the Internet.

Many important authors still publish their work only in traditional print forms. If you don't include these sources in your research, your essay will lack balance and completeness.

How will your instructor realize that your research is exclusively from the Web? In "How the Web Destroys the Quality of Students' Research Papers," Professor David Rothenberg says that "it's easy to spot a research paper that is based primarily on information collected from the Web," partly because no books are included in the bibliography. Most disturbing to Professor Rothenberg is the mindlessness of the Web research process:

> You toss a query to the machine, wait a few minutes, and suddenly a lot of possible sources of information appear on your screen. Instead of books that you have to check out of the library, read carefully, understand, synthesize and then tactfully excerpt, these sources are quips, blips, pictures, and short

summaries that may be downloaded magically to the dorm-room computer screen. Fabulous! How simple! The only problem is that a paper consisting of summaries of summaries is bound to be fragmented and superficial, and to demonstrate more of a random montage than an ability to sustain an argument through 10 to 15 double-spaced pages.

There are no shortcuts to thorough research. Use the Internet as you would use any tool available to you, but try to resist its facile charms.

Integrating Sources

So far, we've been looking at ways to evaluate sources one by one, making sure that each is worth including in your research. But sources won't appear in your essay one at a time. They must work well together. They must be *compatible*.

Authors write for different audiences. Their work varies in tone, in style, in level of detail. As we've seen, the sources that you find on the Web or in the library may have nothing at all in common but their subject. Before you can decide which ones belong together in your essay, you need to be able to describe them. As you glance through a book, or an article, or Web material, ask yourself:

- Does the *content* seem primarily theoretical or practical?
- How often does the author offer *concrete evidence* to support conclusions? What kind of evidence? Facts? Examples? Anecdotes? Documentation?
- Does the author's *thesis* depend on a series of broad propositions, logically linked together?
- What is the *scope* of the work? Does it include many aspects of your broad subject, or does it focus on one?
- How abstract or technical is the *language*? Do you have difficulty understanding the sentences or following the argument?

In the end, the sources that you include in your essay should be at roughly the same *level of difficulty*. This does not mean that they should be identical: the same range of ideas, the same length, the same style and depth of evidence. But it does mean you should be able to move from one to the other easily as you write about them; you should be able to integrate them into your own approach to the subject.

Analyzing Three Sources: Animal Rights

Here are descriptions of and excerpts from three different sources—all books—dealing with the subject of animal rights:

1. This book is an extended consideration of the arguments for and against strict enforcement of animal rights that relies heavily on philosophical

abstractions to make its points; the author supports the use of animals in medical experiments.

> A number of authors [have] contributed to an image of humans as the great despoilers, the beings who are always out of place and can do nothing right in the natural world. Some paint an idyllic and completely unrealistic picture of pristine, peaceful nature, beyond our blundering rapacious hands. Others exclaim despairingly that the world would be a better place without humans.... What these ideas have in common is a nostalgia for simpler times and a veiled lament for a lost Edenic paradise. In fact, guilt and the need for repentance through self-punishment pervade much contemporary writing on the environment and our relationship to animals. The fable of the Fall of Man has now acquired a secular guise, and a group of righteous pop environmental philosophers and animal liberationists are the new self-appointed apostles of redemption.
>
> MICHAEL ALLEN FOX, from *The Case for Animal Experimentation: An Evolutionary and Ethical Perspective*

Fox's language is abstract. He hardly touches on the issues of animal exploitation but rather wants to understand this growing impulse to identify with the more natural environment represented by animals.

2. The second book explains the history of the animal rights movement, taking a neutral stance. The authors rely on concrete evidence to demonstrate that animal rights campaigners are often the products of their culture.

> The meat and food industry has inadvertently contributed to the anthropomorphic intuitions that drive animal protection demands. At least since Charlie the Tuna, food commercials have thoroughly personified their own products. In one commercial, two anthropomorphic cows shoot at a Lea and Perrins bottle, "the steak sauce only a cow could hate." The only speaking parts in an ad for Roy Rogers' chicken club sandwich belong to two fast-talking goldfish. Talking chickens, fish, and other animals seem clever, but they also remind sensitive viewers of the origins of their food.
>
> JAMES M. JASPER and DOROTHY NELKIN, from *The Animal Rights Crusade: The Growth of a Moral Protest*

Jasper and Nelkin are more concerned with practical cause and effect: advertising strategies portraying animals as if they were human have encouraged people to identify with the animal rights movement. It's easy to follow the examples of Charlie the Tuna and the Roy Rogers goldfish.

3. The third book is a sociological study of animal rights activists and their motivations. The text relies heavily on interview transcripts.

A quietly spoken public servant, Rhett decided some years ago to take the step to animal rights activism. He claims it was the inconsistency in our treatment of animals that was the catalyst for his activism and the cause of some tension in his personal relationships:

> But I can tell you that when I was a child, I was presented with an inconsistency which always stuck in my mind. And that was that my father would never eat fowl, and at Christmas time he would always have a chop or something like that. And the reason was that when he was a child, his father brought home some chickens. The kids had made pets of them, and then they were served up for Christmas dinner. He was so upset that he refused to participate in the killing of chooks [young birds]....This was when I was quite young, and I could see that he was being inconsistent, but I'm grateful for the inconsistency because if I hadn't had that example of someone who was sensitive, I mean, who knows? It might have taken me ten more years or something. I don't know.
>
> LYLE MUNRO, from *Compassionate Beasts: The Quest for Animal Rights*

Rhett's personal experiences are of a very different order. He doesn't have a thesis to prove; he doesn't provide you with a topic sentence that shows you where this excerpt might be placed in your essay. It's up to you to interpret his musings and determine how—or whether—they fit in with the other sources.

Integrating Three Sources: Animal Rights

Can these three sources be integrated into the same essay? They aren't equivalent; in many ways, they aren't even similar. But each is relevant and interesting in its own way.

What you *don't* want to do is to plunk down excerpts from these three sources side by side, in adjoining sentences. Remember that your sources are your evidence. So, how you use these three sources depends on the kind of essay you intend to write. They serve to illustrate *your* ideas, your understanding of the issues involved in the animal-rights movement.

■ *Is your thesis abstract?* If you intend to emphasize the political and philosophical premises underlying this issue—do animals have the same rights that humans do?—then you'll focus your attention on Fox's book, summarizing his arguments and, in the process, figuring out what you really believe. In this way, you determine your research priorities—and your thesis. As you develop that thesis, you'll go on to read other books like Fox's and find many of the same ideas with new arguments and new conclusions. You'll notice that authors writing on this abstract level tend to be familiar with each other's theories and argue with each other on paper. The same names will appear again and again. Your essay will become one more voice in an ongoing dialogue.

- *Is your thesis more practical?* You might be more interested in the relatively rapid emergence of this movement. Why has animal rights become such a hot issue? Is it our affluence that enables us to express concern about the plight of animals? Is it our increasing urbanization? Or is it the absence of other compelling causes? This thesis would be more "popular" in its approach to the subject and would not emphasize theoretical, abstract sources. That doesn't diminish its value: a popularization is a simplification of a difficult subject. In a sense, a college research essay has to be "popular" since it serves as evidence of a student's understanding of the subject, not as a contribution to scholarly knowledge. Your thesis would be supported by *secondary sources* such as Jasper and Nelkin or by *primary sources* like the evidence of activists such as Rhett.

- *Are your sources and approach appropriate to the level of your course?* In an introductory course, you are expected only to grasp the fundamental concepts that are basic to the discipline, so your instructor will probably not want you to go out of your depth in hunting scholarly sources for your essay. In an advanced course, you are preparing to do your own research, so you need to demonstrate your understanding of the work of others as well as the methods that are commonly used in that field. In an advanced course, the popular approach can be regarded as superficial.

- *Are your sources appropriate to your level of understanding?* You should include in your bibliography only sources that you yourself understand. If you come across a difficult source that seems too important to leave out, do consult your instructor, or a librarian, or the staff of the writing center on your campus. But never cite sources whose writing makes no sense to you, no matter how eminent and qualified these authorities may be.

- *Are your sources appropriate to the assigned length of your essay?* If you're writing fewer than ten pages, you would be wise to limit your sources to those that blend well together because they are of the same order of difficulty. The writers don't have to agree with each other, but their scope and approach should be roughly equivalent. A longer essay of ten pages or more enables you to position different kinds of sources in different parts of the essay, each where it will have the most convincing effect.

There is actually a *common theme* that runs through the three excerpts from books on animal rights. Fox writes about our generalized feelings of guilt for having plundered our natural heritage; Jasper and Nelkin imply that our anthropomorphic identification with cartoon animals has made us into guilty vegetarians; and Munro's Rhett describes his father's ambivalence about eating chicken, which brings him close to guilt by association. All three excerpts support the following paragraph, which analyzes one of the more complex motivations underlying the animal rights movement. (Note that the sources are documented using MLA style; this process of documentation will be explained in Chapter 10.)

topic sentence	Animal-rights activists pursue their cause with great passion and intensity, as if the fate of the Earth depended on the success of their mission.
explanatory sentence	They seem to be trying to compensate for or even undo all the harm that man has done to the natural environment and particularly to its living creatures. In Michael Allen Fox's view, their yearning to return to the
1st source: summary and quotation	Garden of Eden is linked to a sense of guilt and a compulsion to atone for our culture's crimes against nature. He refers, somewhat contemptuously, to a "nostalgia for simpler times" that seems unrealistic and
student's comment	sentimental (20). Fox seems to be saying that we wallow too easily in a kind of Disneyland view of animals. James M. Jasper and Dorothy Nelkin
2nd source: summary	support that view when they describe the anthropomorphic world of commercials in which Charlie the Tuna and the Roy Rogers goldfish become our friends (149). It's also easy to read that kind of sentimentality
transition	into the personal experience of Rhett, an animal-rights activist, whose father never got over the guilt of eating the chickens that had been his
3rd source: summary	pets (Munro 95).

You will have noticed that this paragraph is essentially *negative* about the animal-rights movement, reflecting Fox's bias. (Indeed, the paragraph relies heavily on Fox's ideas, which makes sense since he offers more of them than the other authors do.) Depending on your chosen thesis, you could build on the implication that animal rights is little more than sentimental claptrap; or you could argue against Fox's point, pointing out that Rhett and his father are displaying an admirable sensitivity to the needs of living creatures. Where you take these ideas is up to you; it's your essay.

> ## Choosing Sources
>
> As you choose sources for your essay, consider the following:
> - the scope of the source and the extent to which it deals with your topic;
> - the depth of detail, the amount and kind of evidence presented, the documentation of sources, and the level of analysis and theory;
> - the degree to which you understand and feel comfortable with the author's language and style; and
> - the way in which possible sources could be used together in your essay.

EXERCISE 28: Evaluating Internet Sources

The first eight sources have been excerpted from the first few pages of Web sites found in an advanced Google search using the keywords "Battle of Wounded Knee" NOT "1973." (The search was focused on the 1890 battle, rather than the demonstration that took place at the same site in 1973.) The last two sources are short videos, from YouTube, on the same topic. The purpose of the search was to compile a *preliminary bibliography* for an essay examining the extent to which the U.S. government carried out an aggressive policy of extermination against Native Americans in the nineteenth century. The Web material in this exercise was not chosen at random but represents some of the typical sites found in the search. The excerpts have not been edited.

A. Read through the eight excerpts and view the two videos.

B. Making allowances for repetition, examine the way in which each source presents information about the Battle of Wounded Knee, paying special attention to tone and style. Consider the probable audience for which each site was intended.

C. Then decide which sources you would read through to the end, which video you would view a second time, and which ones, if any, you would be likely to include in a preliminary bibliography for a 10- to 12-page essay assigned in an introductory-level course.

1. Tensions had been running high on Pine Ridge Reservation in South Dakota for months because of the growing popularity of a new Indian spiritual movement known as the Ghost Dance. Many of the Sioux at Pine Ridge had only recently been confined to reservations after long years of resistance, and they were deeply disheartened by the poor living conditions and deadening tedium of reservation life. The Ghost Dance movement taught

that the Indians were defeated and confined to reservations because they had angered the gods by abandoning their traditional ways. If they practiced the Ghost Dance ritual and rejected white ways, many Sioux believed the gods would create the world anew, destroy the unbelievers, and bring back murdered Indians and the giant herds of bison.

By late 1890, Pine Ridge Indian agent James McLaughlin was alarmed by the movement's increasing influence and its prediction that all non-believers — presumably including whites — would be wiped out. McLaughlin telegraphed a warning to Washington, D.C. that: "Indians are dancing in the snow and are wild and crazy. We need protection now." While waiting for the cavalry to arrive, McLaughlin attempted to arrest Sitting Bull, the famous Sioux chief, who he mistakenly believed was a Ghost Dance supporter. U.S. authorities killed Sitting Bull during the arrest, increasing the tensions at Pine Ridge rather than defusing them.

On December 29, the 7th Cavalry under Colonel James Forsyth surrounded a band of Ghost Dancers under the Sioux Chief Big Foot near Wounded Knee Creek and demanded they surrender their weapons. Big Foot and his followers had no intention of attacking anyone, but they were distrustful of the army and feared they would be attacked if they relinquished their guns. Nonetheless, the Sioux agreed to surrender and began turning over their guns. As that was happening, a scuffle broke out between an Indian and a soldier, and a shot was fired. Though no one is certain which side fired it, the ensuing melee was quick and brutal. Without arms and outnumbered, the Sioux were reduced to hand-to-hand fighting with knives, and they were cut down in a withering rain of bullets, many coming from the army's rapid-fire repeating Hotchkiss guns. By the time the soldiers withdrew, 146 Indians were dead (including 44 women and 18 children) and 51 wounded. The 7th Cavalry had 25 dead and 39 wounded.

Although sometimes referred to as a battle, the conflict at Wounded Knee is best seen as a tragic and avoidable massacre. Surrounded by heavily armed troops, it is highly unlikely that Big Foot's band would have deliberately sought a confrontation.

2. The events at Wounded Knee (South Dakota) on December 29, 1890, cannot be understood unless the previous 400 years of European occupation of the *New World* are taken into consideration. As Dee Brown has pointed out in *Bury My Heart at Wounded Knee* (pp. 1–2):

> 'So tractable, so peaceable, are these people,' Columbus wrote to the King and Queen of Spain [referring to the Tainos on the island of San Salvador, so was named by Columbus], 'that I swear to your Majesties there is not in the world a better nation. They love their neighbors as

themselves, and their discourse is ever sweet and gentle, and accompanied with a smile; and though it is true that they are naked, yet their manners are decorous and praiseworthy.'

All this, of course, was taken as a sign of weakness, if not heathenism, and Columbus being a righteous European was convinced the people should be 'made to work, sow and do all that is necessary and to *adopt our ways*.' Over the next four centuries (1492–1890) several million Europeans and their descendants undertook to enforce their ways upon the people of the New World.

Many accounts (from both sides: US Army and Lakota) of this shameful episode exist, and many of those can be found on the Internet. The following is a brief, edited description (from *The Great Chiefs* volume of Time-Life's *The Old West* series) of events. Links to further resources and descriptions follow.

3. <u>Wounded Knee, A Wound That Won't Heal</u> Did the Army Attempt to Cover-up the Massacre of Prisoners of War?

Historical reference material from:
The Official Bulletin National Indian War Veterans U.S.A. <u>Section One</u>, <u>Section Two</u>, <u>Section Three</u> and <u>Section Four</u>.
<u>The Medals of Wounded Knee</u>
<u>Medals</u> of dis-Honor
…<u>more Medals of dis-Honor</u>
<u>Medals of</u> dis-Honor Campaign

An email campaign has been initiated so as to force the U.S. Government to rescind the <u>twenty medals of dis-Honor</u> awarded participants in the Massacre at Wounded Knee. Your help is solicited…an input form is provided for your convenience

<u>Lieutenant Bascom</u> Gets His Due

<u>Rescindment Petition Comments</u>

<u>Senator McCain Responds to the Rescindment Petition</u>

<u>My Response to McCain</u>

<u>Wokiksuye Canpe Opi…a site dedicated to rescindment of the "medals of dis-Honor."</u>

4. Eyewitness to a Massacre
Philip Wells was a mixed-blood Sioux who served as an interpreter for the Army. He later recounted what he saw that Monday morning:

'I was interpreting for General Forsyth (*Forsyth was actually a colonel*) just before the battle of Wounded Knee, December 29, 1890. The captured

Indians had been ordered to give up their arms, but Big Foot replied that his people had no arms. Forsyth said to me, 'Tell Big Foot he says the Indians have no arms, yet yesterday they were well armed when they surrendered. He is deceiving me. Tell him he need have no fear in giving up his arms, as I wish to treat him kindly.' Big Foot replied, 'They have no guns, except such as you have found.' Forsyth declared, 'You are lying to me in return for my kindness.'

5. The round up of the Lakota was in response to the growing fear and igno- rance on the part of the US Govt. The white people did not know about the culture, beliefs, or lives of the Lakota and saw them as a threat to the society they were trying to preserve: the white society. The Lakota were seen as outsiders; the "other" in a world where a person's looks and background determined who belonged here. Through much of American history, where a person was born also determined if they belonged. Ironically, the Native Americans were here on this land first, but were treated as though they were visitors. Their assumption was that because they look different or act different, they are not the same; they are not Americans. The white people refused to recognize the Lakota's right to the land and did everything in their power to remove them. This ignorance led to violence in an obvious act of proving power and control.

Col. James W. Forsyth ordered the Sioux people to be disarmed. A shot was fired and the fighting ensued. The federal troops fired on the Lakota with rifles and powerful, rapid-shooting Hotchkiss guns. Sioux casualties totaled 153 dead and 44 wounded, half of whom were unarmed women and children. Survivors were pursued and butchered by US troops. Cavalry losses totaled 25 dead and 39 wounded. Charges were brought against Col. Forsyth for his part in the bloodshed, but a court of inquiry exonerated him.

At the time, and continually after, people regarded the confrontation as a massacre. This terrible blow to the Lakota people proved to break down their strength in fighting back. To subsequent generations of Indians, it "symbolized the injustices and degradations inflicted on them by the US government" (Robert Utley). It later served as an inspiration for the 1973 occupation at Wounded Knee.

We must never forget this moment in US history of the horrific destruc- tion of human life and liberty. For many, the picture of US history is filled with tales of brave rebels, fighting for a belief in equality, such as the ideals which started and founded the nation. However, not many recognize the hypocritical actions of the nation which went against this idea of equality. This is just another example where the question of "Who belongs?" and "Who has a right to 'American' liberties?" is tested. The Lakota were never allowed a place in the nation, forced to give up their land and suffered immensely in loss of lives and rights. The Wounded Knee massacre serves as a reminder to a time when those people seen as "foreigners" were exterminated and refused their rights as Americans.

6. No one knows what caused the disturbance, no one claims the first shot, the Wounded Knee Massacre began fiercely with the Hotchkiss guns raining fragmentation shells into the village at a combined rate of 200 or more rounds a minute. The 500 well armed Cavalry Troopers were well positioned using crossing fire to methodically carry out what is known as the Wounded Knee Massacre.

   Almost immediately most of the Sioux Indian men were killed. A few Sioux Indians mustered enough strength barehanded to kill 29 soldiers and wound 39 more. The bravery of these people was to no avail for as long as an Indian moved, the guns kept firing. Unarmed Sioux Indian Women and children were Mercilessly Massacred. A few ran as far as three miles only to be chased by the long knives of the Cavalry and put to death.

   Of the original 350 Indians one estimate stated that only 50 survived. Almost all historical statistics report over 200 Indians being killed on that day but government figures only reported the Indian dead as 64 men, 44 women and girls, and 18 babies. All of the bodies were buried in one communal grave.

   If the Battle of the Little Big Horn had been the beginning of the end, Wounded Knee was the finale for the Sioux Indians. This was the last major engagement in American history between the Plains Indians and the U. S. Army. Gone was the Indian dream, pride and spirit.

7. Annotation: President Benjamin Harrison offered these comments about the Wounded Knee massacre.

   Document: That these Indians had some complaints, especially in the matter of the reduction of the appropriation for rations and in the delays attending the enactment of laws to enable the Department to perform the engagements entered into with them, is probably true; but the Sioux tribes are naturally warlike and turbulent, and their warriors were excited by their medicine men and chiefs, who preached the coming of an Indian messiah who was to give them power to destroy their enemies. In view of the alarm that prevailed among the white settlers near the reservation and of the fatal consequences that would have resulted from an Indian incursion, I placed at the disposal of General Miles...all such forces as were thought by him to be required. He is entitled to the credit of having given thorough protection to the settlers and of bringing the hostiles into subjection with the least possible loss of life.

8. "Sometimes dreams are wiser than waking," says Black Elk, Oglala Sioux Indian who took part in the Ghost Dance Religion during the late nineteenth century. The Wounded Knee epidemic took place in December 29, 1890

between the U.S. government and the Sioux Indians in South Dakota. Primarily, the outbreak occurred at Wounded Knee in part result of the growing support of the Ghost Dance Religion. Army leaders feared the religion would lead to an Indian uprising and called for troops to be sent to keep things under control. Thus, the hostilities that drug out between the U.S. government and the Sioux Indians in South Dakota are an important historical event that unfolded in U.S. western history. When reviewing the Wounded Knee battle, it is of utmost importance for various teachers who want to gain more knowledge of this epidemic that took place to fully understand insights about when, where, what, and why this battle occurred in 1890 in South Dakota. Furthermore, the Sioux Ghost Dance Religion played a crucial role in "triggering" the hostilities and events that lead up to the Wounded Knee battle.

First, before going into depth about the history of Wounded Knee Creek battle, it is important to understand the need for history. Why do we study and need to know history? Well, David E. Kyvig and Myron A. Marty believe history is an essential part of human development: We all need to know who we are, how we have become what we are, and how to cope with a variety of situations in order to conduct our own lives successfully. We also need to know what to expect from people and institutions around us. Organizations and communities require the same self understanding in order to function satisfactorily. For individuals and groups alike, experience produces a self-image and a basis for deciding how to behave, manage problems, and plan ahead. We remember sometimes accurately, sometimes not-what occurred, the causes of certain responses or changes, and learn reactions to different circumstances. These memories, positive and negative, help determine our actions.

9. Massacre at Wounded Knee 1890. YouTube, 18 June 2006. http://www.youtube.com/watch?v=dc7fZonjD1M

10. The Massacre at Wounded Knee 1890. YouTube, 2 Aug. 2008. www.youtube.com/watch?v=r8KRklpDWrE

EXERCISE 29: Choosing Internet Sources

The following list of sixteen Web sites has been compiled from searches using the keywords "TV Violence."

A. Assume that you are preparing a preliminary bibliography for an essay examining *the links between violence on television and violent crimes in American schools*.

B. Review the list of Web sites and choose those that you would definitely want to explore. Be prepared to give your reasons for including or excluding each site.

Your instructor may ask you to click on some or all of the sites before you do your ranking. If some sites are no longer being maintained, you may be asked to do a new search on the same topic, choosing and submitting brief descriptions of several sites (preferably noncommercial), with their URLs, and indicating those that, in your opinion, seem relevant and reliable.

1. APA HelpCenter: Warning Signs of TV Violence
   www.apahelpcenter.org
   The American Psychological Association provides basic information to the nation's youth about warning signs of violent behavior, including violence in schools.

2. Children and Television Violence
   www.abelard.org/tv/tv.php
   Abelard's front page. Violence on television affects children negatively, according to psychological research. Brief summaries of sources, but no documentation.

3. National Television Violence Study
   www.media-and-violence-research-brief-2013-3.pdf
   The National Television Violence Study 1996–97 contains recommendations of a large scientific study of television violence. Sponsored by the University of California at Santa Barbara.

4. TV and Film Violence
   www.cybercollege.com/violence.htm
   A brief report on the CyberCollege Internet Web site outlining the relationship between exposure to TV violence and acts of aggressiveness later in life. CyberCollege offers "free educational services." Last updated 2013.

5. Research: Violence in Children's TV
   i-parents.illinois.edu/research/wilson.html
   Dr. Barbara Wilson has written a short article about which elements of the plots for children's programs are likely to encourage violence. The types of programs are categorized. Sources are cited.

6. Children and Television Violence
   www.allsands.com/kids/childtelevision_twd_gn.htm
   An essay on television violence and children. Eight sources cited. No author or date. Allsands's articles are written by "professional journalists and experts."

7. The Effects of Media Violence
   www.youtube.com/watch?v=q1pSPw9uVwA
   This 7-minute film is excerpted from a longer PBS program on TV violence broadcast after the shootings at Newtown. It consists of an interview with an academic expert on TV violence and a novelist. Broadcast 22 Dec. 2012.

8. Telecommunications Act of 1996

   www.fcc.gov/telecom.html
   Full text of the Telecommunications Law is available via FTP. Source:
   Pub Docs US Congress.

9. Violent Media Is Good for Kids

   www.motherjones.com/politics/2000/06/violent-media-good-kids-0
   Comic book author Gerard Jones argues that violence in videogames
   and other media give [sic] children a tool to master their rage.

10. Children and TV Violence/American Academy of Child & Adolescent
    Psychiatry

    www.aacap.org/cs/root/facts_for_families/children_and_tv_violence
    Describes some simple methods parents can use to shield their
    children from TV violence. Last updated in 2011.

11. TV Bloodbath/Violence on Prime Time Broadcast TV

    **www.parentstv.org/PTC/publications/reports/stateindustryviolence/
    main.asp**
    Uses statistics from 2003 and earlier to show that TV violence is
    becoming more graphic. Examples from *Buffy the Vampire Slayer* and
    The X-Files. Sponsored by Parents Television Council, whose mission is
    to "Clean Up TV Now."

12. Pulling the Plug on TV Violence

    **https://www.healthychildren.org/English/family-life/Media/Pages/
    Pulling-the-Plug-on-TV-Violence.aspx**
    Aimed at parents, this site contains a list of ways to prevent children
    from being influenced by violence on TV. The sponsor is the American
    Academy of Pediatrics. Updated in 2013.

13. How Violence in the Media Effects Children

    https://www.youtube.com/watch?v=bEfSlqr5STg
    A short YouTube film (5.45 minutes) discusses the dangers of TV
    violence and features a history of media violence. Uploaded 9 Dec. 2012.

14. Surprise! TV Violence Isn't Portrayed Accurately

    **http://psychcentral.com/blog/archives/2009/05/20/surprise-tv-
    violence-isn't-portrayed-accurately**
    A short 2009 blog by John Grohol, PsyD, commenting on the Mayo
    Clinic's research.

15. How TV Violence Can Affect Your Child

    **http://www.pureintimacy.org/h/how-tv-violence-can-affect-your-
    child/**
    Writing for a Christian organization, Focus on the Family, Shana
    Schutte suggests that "when your child watches too much TV, with too
    much violence, you might get more than you bargained for."

16. Television Violence and Aggression: A Retrospective Study
    swacj.org/swjcj/archives/5.1/4%20Slotsve.pdf
    Published in the *Southwest Journal of Criminal Justice* by four academics
    at universities in Texas, this paper contains analysis of evidence from
    statistical surveys, as well as a long list of resources.

EXERCISE 30: Evaluating Sources

Each of the following extracts comes from a book, article, or Web site about
cyberbullying or trolling.

A. Carefully examine the distinctive way in which each passage presents its
    information, noting especially:

    - the author's apparent purpose
    - the amount and kind of evidence that is cited, and how it is
      documented
    - the expectations of the audience's knowledge and understanding
    - the relative emphasis on generalizations and abstract thinking
    - the characteristic tone and vocabulary
    - the date of publication

B. Decide how—or whether—you would use these sources together in a
    single research essay exploring this question: *What do cyberbullying and
    trolling reveal about American culture in the early 21st century?*

C. Prepare some tentative responses to this question as the basis for a possible
    thesis. Then decide which sources you would be likely to use in writing your
    essay. Be prepared to justify your choices.

Note that these are brief *extracts* from books, articles, and Web sites: many
of them may begin or end abruptly since space does not permit providing their
full context.

1. cyberbullying

The use of electronic communication to bully a person, typically by sending
messages of an intimidating or threatening nature: 1

    children may be reluctant to admit to being the victims of cyberbullying

troll

INFORMAL Make a deliberately offensive or provocative online posting   2
with the aim of upsetting someone or eliciting an angry response from
them:

    [NO OBJECT] *if people are obviously trolling then I'll delete your posts and
do my best to ban you*

[WITH OBJECT]: *you folks taking this opportunity to troll me, you really need to reassess your values in your life*

Oxford Dictionaries. Oxford University Press (2014). 15 Sept. 2014.
www.oxforddictionaries.com

2. Unlike with traditional bullying, the identity of the cyberbully is often un-known (close to half of the victims did not know the identity of the perpetra-tor, in one study). This leads to higher levels of anxiety among victims , who don't know who their enemy is and who they should protect themselves against. Instead of their vigilance centering on a specific bully, possibly with a limited number of accomplices, cyberbullying victims are diffus-ingly, confusingly vigilant, unable to know who the aggressor is and where the next blow will come from. Avoiding the playground or the school bus — as problematic as those options are — and staying closer to home does not make them feel safer: Victims are now available to be attacked twenty-four hours a day, seven days a week, and there is no time when a threat or a taunt cannot be launched in their direction in the form of an e-mail or a text message. To make matters worse, complaining to parents, once a source of reassurance and support for some victims, can, from the child's perspective, backfire: Kids live in deadly fear of their cell phones being taken away or their Internet access being curtailed by a concerned parent.

The lack of access to each other's emotions during a cyberbullying episode compounds the pain. "When people tease or bully face-to-face," Kowalski writes, "they use off-record markers (winks, smiles, etc.) to indicate the intent behind their behavior" and to assess its impact. Such nonverbal cues — with the possible exception of emoticons, which I will talk about later — are largely lacking during the virtual attack. The result is that the perpetrators are more out of touch with the pain they are inflicting because it is invisible to them, and the victims cannot know if the perpetrators are truly bullying them or "just kidding." Naturally, the victims' instinct of self-preservation makes them assume the worst about the attack and the attacker and convinces them that someone is really out to get them. A host of negative consequences can then ensue from bad grades to social withdrawal, depression, and a general suspiciousness and mistrustfulness of the world.

In part because of anonymity, "more individuals are potential cyber bullies than potential schoolyard bullies." However, it is not just the num-ber of perpetrators that has increased but also "the magnitude of threats, taunts, and so on, that they are willing to deliver." The increased number of attackers, and the more vitriolic nature of the attacks, show how very naturally and almost automatically the dark side of children emerges online, and the real dangers attendant on that.

ELIAS ABOUJAOUDE, from *Virtually You:*
The Dangerous Powers of the E-Personality (2011)

3. Solitude in cyberspace is all right in small doses, but studies of e-mail usage indicate that exclusive use of e-mail as a social interface impairs chronic users' abilities to read nonverbal social cues and leaves the extensive social neural networks of their brains underdeveloped.[6] Moreover, as Gary Small observes, "Digital Immigrants note worsening of depression symptoms from too much exposure to technology. Previous studies have shown that social isolation clearly increases the risk for depression and worsens its symptoms. Despite the availability of social networks, email, and instant messaging, these electronic communication modes lack the emotional warmth of direct human contact and worsen a person's feelings of isolation."[7]

1

Among cyber natives, low self-esteem, depression, and isolation contribute to the testiness responsible for flaming, cyberbullying, and generalized lack of empathy and interpersonal skill. Early in my online career, when strangers made intense attacks against my personality rather than the substance of my blogs, older bloggers told me it was possible to gauge how much time an attacker spent online by the violence of the attack. Such people cannot gauge the real psychological impact of their attacks on others. They have lost the gift of empathy in much the same way that chronically lonely people do, simply because the neural pathways of social connection have not been used enough. They are socially clumsy, awkward, and very poor "mind-readers," who need considerable reentry time to readjust to community life. I believe this disconnection is endemic to cyber life and further disconnects us from one another.

2

My colleagues at *HuffingtonPost.com* also told me that cyberbullies are loners with low self-esteem. The bully's satisfaction in tearing you down lies in making you feel worse about yourself than they do about themselves. Now there is evidence to support this intuition.[8] But the violence of their attacks (what I call the "chained-dog effect") result from the lack of empathy in a disassociated, textual medium. Cyberbullies have no satisfyingly visible impact on *others*, so they generally choose the most offensive response like a chained dog barking as you pass by on the street: "I'd tear you apart if I could get to you," they seem to say. In all the years I wrote for *HuffPo*, the shrill vituperation of bloggers trying to intimidate never became an insignificant part of the job. These days, whenever the curt, megalomaniacal voice of the isolated cyber native rings out across the web, I find an excuse to discontinue communication politely but as firmly as possible.

3

Cyber-crazies are damned souls that float through the ether of cyberspace. You must learn to identify and avoid them. Like addicts, only they can decide to help themselves.

Note: This book is documented with endnotes.

GILES SLADE, from The Big Disconnect (2012)

4. The Internet is hardly the medium with the highest density of anonymous or offensive communications. A high school's bathroom stalls may be the winner in that category. But Facebook, or a similar Internet site visited and easily discovered by the same high school's students, may well be the canvas of choice for the contemporary offensive graffitist. It is useful then to compare these, and then other media, in order to think about the legal environment in which juvenile—as well as mature but false—communications take place.

 Environments, or media, can be compared from the perspective of the law or from that of the communicator. For one who wishes to communicate nasty remarks about a classmate, employer, or competitor, considerations of social standing, legal consequences, audience size, interactivity, and effort are all likely to play roles. A juvenile posting will have real bite—whether on an Internet site, on handbills left around a building, or on the bathroom wall—if something more than a simple slur is produced. Details can generate a defamation claim, unless author and publisher can remain unknown, and they also make possible the communication of socially useful, if painful, information. "Amy X is a slut"[1] is quintessentially juvenile, especially as a signal of interest, and no fun for Amy X or her true friends to read. Still, it is not clear that anyone suffers grave harm, not just because of the familiar aphorism about sticks and stones but also because of the irony that the more commonplace such taunts are, the less seriously anyone will take them. One response to the slut slur is for one's friends to shout out a thousand claims of that status attached to all sorts of people in order to diminish further the value of the first communication. The alternative and not unknown reaction is for an informed or well-intentioned passerby to attempt to expunge the offensive message so that it is not further communicated. Such short messages are typical of bathroom wall postings, and do not even attempt to convey much information. In contrast, "Y stole $150 from me" or "Z loved a dog behind Bartlett Hall," are slight rewordings of observed markings, and I hesitate to be so crude as to refer to them in print except that they are unusual. The details make these claims slightly more memorable and even credible, though not for the usual reason that details facilitate falsification. The claim that Y is a thief, if true, is a good example of an anonymous insult that might provide socially useful information—either because it deters other thieves, who fear shaming, or because it warns others to be wary of Y. The same cannot easily be said for the other comment. I hesitate to label these as unusual examples of *effective* juvenile communications because we do not know the authors' aims or knowledge. Each author ran the small risk of attracting vandalism or defamation charges, or perhaps even revenge by an informed target. Revenge may well be the most serious risk; it is ironic that the target will have more success in identifying the culprit if the original claim is detailed and true, or at least based on some real events. I return to accuracy and social utility below, but for now let us assume that the communications are exaggerations or outright falsehoods and, at best, a juvenile reaction to something about Y or Z that the writer finds distasteful.

When the offensive graffitist uses the bathroom wall he runs up against   3
the medium's constraints; the Internet now provides a superior medium for one who wishes to spread juvenile or malicious speech. One can scratch or spray paint a wall for a variety of reasons, but the audience for that speech is limited, and the greater the offense with respect to both content and audience, the more quickly the communication will be erased. Moreover, the juvenilist who works on the bathroom wall with paint or knife must work quickly to avoid detection and prosecution. Thus, a longer and often more credible message is hard to cast. In obvious contrast, the juvenilist on the Internet is empowered by the ability to communicate in leisurely fashion and to do so from afar. The old-fashioned graffitist risks disciplinary action in a school or workplace, and police attention elsewhere, because in a real environment the graffitist has committed a crime — namely vandalism — even as he is open to a claim of defamation. On the Internet there is no vandalism and, with respect to defamation, the risk of detection and social sanction is close to zero so long as the author chooses a site where anonymity is secure.

Note: This book is documented with endnotes.

SAUL LEVMORE, from "The Internet's Anonymity Problem,"
in *The Offensive Internet*, eds. Saul Levmore and
Martha C. Nussbaum (2010)

5. Cyberbullies differ from face-to-face bullies in that cyberbullies can remain   1
"virtually" anonymous by impersonating others or by hijacking another's account. Cyberbullies are not known by their victims almost half the time and cyberbullying often occurs off school grounds (Greene, 2006). The sharing or stealing of youths' private passwords occurs with relative frequency. For example, a 2001 Pew Internet research study found that 22% of teens between the ages of 12 and 17 had shared a password

with a friend or with someone they knew (Schrock & Boyd, 2011). Another study found that 13% of 4th–6th graders and 15% of 7th–9th graders experienced someone using their password without their permission (McQuade & Sampat, 2008). The ability to hide behind fake screen names or to steal someone else's screen name allows perpetrators to say things to each other that they would never say face-to-face "[and] may lead some perpetrators to remain unconvinced that they are actually harming their target [or that] they are doing anything wrong" (Kowalski & Limber, 2007, p. S28). As one kid stated "on Facebook, you can be as mean as you want" (Hoffman, 2010). Unlike face-to-face bullying that is limited to the immediate victim or bystanders, cyberbullies can spread their abuse across their entire electronic contact list in a matter of seconds, which may also serve to heighten victims' perceptions of vulnerability (Kowalski & Limber, 2007; Ollove, 2010). Perhaps most disturbing is that these harmful comments can be delivered at any time of the day or night by youth who cannot see the pain they are inflicting on their victims (Hinduja & Patchin, 2007; Underwood, Rish-Scott, & Springer, 2011).

One of the most challenging and distinct features of cyberbullying, compared with face-to-face bullying, is the degree to which parents and adults may not understand the nature or impact of cyberbullying. For example, many parents hold inaccurate beliefs about the risks their children face when they communicate online, parents underestimate the amount of information their children post online, and parents are often unaware of how online sites are used (DeHue, Bolman, & Vollink, 2008; Holladay, 2010; Rosen, Cheever, & Carrier, 2008). Many parents do not routinely supervise or monitor their teenager's electronic communications and also underestimate, to a significant degree, their child's involvement in making fun of a peer online (Holladay, 2010). Many parents also lag behind their children and teens in their understanding of and use of technology, which make cyberbullying incidents "very difficult for adults to detect or track" (Center for Mental Health in Schools at UCLA, 2011, p. 1).

An entirely new set of hostile behaviors is unique to cyberenvironments. These behaviors are identified and described in Table 3.1. Among these four bullying behaviors unique to cyberenvironments, it appears that *outing and trickery* and *picture or video clip bullying* are most common. For example, 20% of survey respondents reported someone sharing private information without their permission, and another 16% of respondents reported someone posting embarrassing pictures or video of them without their permission (Cass & Anderson, 2011). However, it is important to note that sexting (or *picture or video clip bullying*) appears to be much less common among minor children than previously thought. A recent study found that 10% of children between the ages of 10 and 17 have used a cell phone to send or receive sexually suggestive images and that only 1 in 100 has sent "images considered graphic enough to violate child pornography laws" (i.e., images that included full or partial nudity) (O'Connor, 2011).

Other forms of cyberbullying include the spreading of false rumors   4
and the posting of "mean" messages on Internet pages or by text message (Cass & Anderson, 2011). Girls commonly target each other with labels such as "slut," "whore," and "bitch" while boys attack other boys a great deal for being "gay" or questioning their sexual orientation (Holladay, 2010; Wolak, Finkelhor, Mitchell, & Ybarra, 2008).

Several additional findings illustrate the uniqueness of cyberbullying   5
compared with other forms of bullying. For example, there is some evidence that certain youths may be more likely to engage in cyberbullying or to be victimized by cyberbullying compared with other forms of bullying. Specifically, one study found that 64% of youth who reported being harassed online did not report being bullied in person (Ybarra, Dlener-West, & Leaf, 2007). This may be due to the fact that socially anxious teens may find the Internet and related technologies as a means to communicate without fear or anxiety as well as a way to exact revenge on perpetrators of face-to-face bullying. While having more friends is a protective factor for face-to-face bullying, having more friends is not a protective factor against cyberbullying (Wang, Iannotti, & Nansel, 2009). Teens may also be more reluctant to report instances of electronic bullying since a report of electronic bullying may result in a restriction in cell phone or Internet use (Kowalski & Limber, 2007).

DAVID R. DUPPER, from *School Bullying* (2013)

6. One question we get asked a lot is whether technology has created whole   1
new groups of people who bully and are bullied. Think about it: If someone feels tempted to be cruel to someone else, but is afraid of getting caught, chickening out, or being beaten up, he might turn to the Internet, especially if that person is super comfortable using social media and other online tools. On the surface, it seems like there are *plenty* of reasons someone might bully others online but not in real life.

While this way of thinking seems logical, it doesn't appear to be what   2
is actually going on. Most often, those who bully in person also bully online. And those who don't bully in person at school or elsewhere aren't very likely to bully others online, either. Similarly, those who are bullied offline (at school or elsewhere) are more likely to also be bullied online. In fact, one of our surveys found that teens who bullied others in person were more than twice as likely both to be bullied and to bully others online. We also learned that kids who had been bullied in person were almost three times as likely to be cyberbullied.

So bullying in person and bullying online involve many of the same people, and in general they're more similar than they are different. However, they *do* differ in a few important ways: 3

- One big difference is that **targets of cyberbullying don't always know who is bullying them.** A person who's bullying from behind a computer or cell phone can mask her identity using screen names or anonymous email addresses. However, we've found in our research that many teens who are cyberbullied know (or think they know) exactly who is targeting them. And it's almost always one of their peers, such as a former friend, a former boyfriend or girlfriend, or the new romantic partner of the former boyfriend or girlfriend. And often, if a person being bullied looks closely at what is being said, he will see clues about who is behind it. (Check out **Chapter 3** for more about how someone who is cyberbullying can be identified.)   4

- Second, **cyberbullying has the potential to go viral** in a way that physical or in-person bullying generally doesn't. A large number of people (at school, in the neighborhood, in the city, and even around the world) can be involved in a cyberbullying incident, or they can at least find out about it with a few taps on a screen or clicks of a mouse. This can make bullying even more painful because it feels like absolutely everyone knows about it. When we were bullied in middle school, only the bully and his buddies were usually there at the time. Afterward, a few classmates might have heard about it — but that was about it. In the case of cyberbullying, though, it's possible for a much larger audience to see or know what happened. This can definitely make cyberbullying much harder to deal with. However, it also means that there are more opportunities for someone to step up and stop the bullying or to stand with the target. That bystander-turned-upstander could be you! (We talk more about what you can do in **Chapter 4.**)   5

- Third, it is often easier to be cruel online because **cyberbullying can be done from just about anywhere.** That means that the person doing the bullying doesn't always see the effect of his or her words on others. Some people might not even realize or understand the true extent of the pain they are inflicting.   6

- Fourth, **cyberbullying sometimes goes on for a long time** because many adults don't have the time or technological know-how to keep track of everything that's happening online. This doesn't necessarily mean that they don't care. It's just that they sometimes don't get it, or don't know what to do. Again, this is where you can step in — with the help of what you'll learn from this book.   7

My best friend and I weren't friends anymore. She was well liked in school, so she ended up turning everyone against me. The bullying first started with girls threatening to jump me and saying that I'd had sex with   8 *every guy on the basketball team. I felt betrayed and miserable. Then one day I got on Facebook and there were so many guys asking to be my friend and sending sexual messages to me. I also had girls tagging me in rude pics and comments, and there was a page up that listed all the guys/girls I'd had sex with — but none of it was true. I started not caring about myself and how I dressed or looked. My grades started to drop. I didn't eat lunch because everyone I used to sit with was against me.*

—Gabi, 17, Georgia

JUSTIN W. PATCHIN AND SAMEER HINDUJA from *Words Wound* (2014)

7. The computer and other information and communication technologies   1
(ICTs, e.g. androids, iPhones, iPads, etc.) have created a global, interactive communication and social networking community which transcend personal, geographical, sociopolitical, and socioeconomic boundaries. In 2005, there were more than one billion internet users and two billion mobile phone users worldwide (Privetera & Campbell, 2009). The use of these technologies by children, adolescents, and adults for communication has both positive and negative outcomes. One of the negative consequences of online communities whose existence relies on these technologies is cyberbullying. Concerns about the abuse and misuse of ITCs as well as the harmful effects on victims of some online activity have been discussed in the literature and researched within child/adolescent populations for more than a decade (Bruno, 2004; Cowie & Colliety, 2010; Wolak, Finkelhor, Mitchell, & Ybarra, 2010). Over the past 15 years, we have witnessed a trend, in which those who bully and those who are bullied in cyberspace through the misuse of ICTs, has become a global phenomenon occurring in countries throughout Asia, Europe, the Middle and Far East, North and South America, Africa and Australia. Moreover, cyberbullying affects a much broader age demographic than conventional/traditional bullying and what was reported earlier in the literature on cyberbullying. It is now occurring among older adolescents, college students, and older adults in the workplace (Aricak et al., 2008; Bhat, 2008; Liau Khoo & Ang, 2005; Muir, 2005; Pellegrini & Long, 2002; Slonje & Smith, 2008; Smith & Williams, 2004; Walrave & Heirman, 2011).

Cyberbullying has been defined as the intentional and repeated harm   2
inflicted through the use of computers, cell phones, or other electronic devices (Kowalski & Limber, 2007; Patchin, Burgess-Proctor, & Hinduja, 2009; Burgess-Proctor, Patchin, & Hinduja, 2010). It has been compared to traditional bullying by some research which has found similarities in terms of the characteristics outlined in the American Psychological Association document (2004). By definition, it is a form of aggression; however, not all aggressive acts use technology. For example, research has shown that cyberbullies also bully in conventional ways (Smith et al., 2008; Williams & Guerra, 2007).

Thus, theories on the psychological processes and consequences of traditional bullying might be applied to the study of cyberbullying.

JUNE F. CHISHOLM AND STOREY K. DAY, from
"Current Trends in Cyberbullying," *Journal of Social Distress and the Homeless*, 22 (1), 2013. 9 Sept. 2014
http://www.maneyonline.com/doi/ref/10.1179/1053078913Z.0000000007

8. **Abstract**

While online, some people self-disclose or act out more frequently or   1
intensely than they would in person. This article explores six factors that interact with each other in creating this online disinhibition effect: dissociative anonymity, invisibility, asynchronicity, solipsistic introjection, dissociative imagination, and minimization of authority. Personality variable also will influence the extent of this disinhibition. Rather than thinking of disinhibition as the revealing of an underlying "true self," we can conceptualize it as a shift to a constellation within self-structure, involving clusters of affect and cognition that differ from the in-person constellation.

JOHN SULER, from "The Online Disinhibition Effect,"
CyberPsychology & Behavior 7.3 (June 2004). 12 Sept. 2014
http://online.liebertpub.com/doi/abs/10.1089/1094931041291295

9. *Note: Violentacrez, the moderator at Reddit.com, is regarded as "the biggest troll on the Web."*

It is important to note that trolling is not a one-size-fits-all behavioral   1
category. I've worked with certain trolls who take great pleasure in taunting the friends and family of murdered teenagers. I've worked with other trolls who are disgusted by this sort of behavior and instead restrict their focus to trolling other trolls. Some trolls are very intelligent, and have extremely interesting things to say about trolling, while others have no real opinion about anything they do, other than the fact that it makes them laugh. Just as there are many different kinds of trolls, there are many different ways to troll. Some trolling is relatively innocuous, for example trolling that re-directs targets to absurd images or videos. Some trolling meets the legal criteria for harassment, and can persist for weeks or even months.

In addition to acknowledging the wide variety of trolling behaviors, it is   2
just as important to note that simply saying nasty things online does not make someone a subcultural troll, nor does engaging in "good faith" (for lack of a better term) racism or sexism or homophobia. Not necessarily, any-way. Trolling in the subcultural sense may be afoot in these instances, but maybe not, immediately complicating the impulse to declare every aggres-sive or otherwise unsavory online behavior an act of trolling—an impulse regularly exercised by those in the mainstream media.

How, then, is it possible to know when someone is in fact trolling (as opposed to being genuinely racist, sexist, or otherwise ignorant)? In most cases, self-identifying trolls will slip in a subtle reference to trolling — a kind of subcultural calling card. This calling card isn't intended for the target, in fact is rarely perceptible to the target, but rather is geared towards other trolls. Not only does the reference claim victory for the initiating troll, it also tends to incite further trolling behaviors. This is how most raids get started — a troll essentially calls for backup, and other trolls, who are attuned to these sorts of signals, come running.

> WHITNEY PHILLIPS, from "What an Academic Who Wrote Her Dissertation on Trolls Thinks of Violentacrez," *Atlantic* (15 Oct. 2012) 8 Sept. 2014. http://www.theatlantic.com/technology/archive/ 2012/10/what-an-academic-who-wrote-her-dissertation- on-trolls-thinks-of-violentacrez/263631

10. Brandon Turley didn't have friends in sixth grade. He would often eat alone at lunch, having recently switched to his school without knowing anyone. While browsing MySpace one day, he saw that someone from school had posted a bulletin — a message visible to multiple people — declaring that Turley was a "fag." Students he had never even spoken with wrote on it, too, saying they agreed.

Feeling confused and upset, Turley wrote in the comments, too, asking why his classmates would say that. The response was even worse: He was told on MySpace that a group of 12 kids wanted to beat him up, that he should stop going to school and die. On his walk from his locker to the school office to report what was happening, students yelled things like "fag" and "fatty." "It was just crazy, and such a shock to my self-esteem that people didn't like me without even knowing me," said Turley, now 18 and a senior in high school in Oregon. "I didn't understand how that could be."

As many as 25% of teenagers have experienced cyberbullying at some point, said Justin W. Patchin, who studies the phenomenon at the University of Wisconsin-Eau Claire. He and colleagues have conducted formal surveys of 15,000 middle and high school students throughout the United States, and found that about 10% of teens have been victims of cyberbullying in the last 30 days.

Online bullying has a lot in common with bullying in school: Both behaviors include harassment, humiliation, teasing and aggression, Patchin said. Cyberbullying presents unique challenges in the sense that the perpetrator

Figure 8-3 Brandon Turley, 18, who experienced cyberbullying in middle school, designed the WeStopHate.org Web site.

can attempt to be anonymous, and attacks can happen at any time of day or night.

There's still more bullying that happens at school than online, however, Patchin said. And among young people, it's rare that an online bully will be a total stranger.

"In our research, about 85% of the time, the target knows who the bully is, and it's usually somebody from their social circle," Patchin said.

Patchin's research has also found that, while cyberbullying is in some sense easier to perpetrate, the kids who bully online also tend to bully at school. "Technology isn't necessarily creating a whole new class of bullies," he said.

ELIZABETH LANDAU, from "When Bullying Goes High-Tech,"
CNN.com (15 Apr. 2013). 17 Sept. 2014.
www.cnn.com/2013/02/27/health/cyberbullying-online-bully-victims

11. With technology and the Internet ruling today's society, why is cyberbullying still a taboo topic?

Think about it. When do you hear about it? It's not an issue that's dis-   2
cussed that often and when it is, it's very focused on middle school and
high school-aged students. Additionally, it only becomes a relevant topic
in the media when someone has physically harmed themselves because
they have been a victim of cyberbullying. But let's get one thing straight —
cyberbullying is serious in ANY context and is NOT age sensitive.

In fact, I would argue that cyberbullying is just as prominent if not more   3
prominent in college-aged students. College culture and social media
makes it easy for cyberbullies to thrive. With college confession pages and
apps that allow anonymous posting, cyberbullying is gaining momentum
without people even realizing it because it's being glorified. In certain contexts it's used as entertainment, but I know from personal experience that
cyberbullying is nothing to make light of.

Prior to my freshman year of college, I wasn't cyberbullied at all and   4
thought I never would be. Luckily, bullying in general was never a huge
problem for me. However, that all changed overnight and turned into
about 2 years of relentless online harassment.

I was cyberbullied for my first 2 years of college by someone I had never   5
met before. Let me repeat — I did not know this person at all, in any way.
But that doesn't prevent cyberbullies from attacking their victims. When
cyberbulliers are behind the screen, they don't care what they say or who
it's about. They feel invincible because no one can immediately stop them.
Their victims become somewhat powerless and start to feel hopeless as
they try to decide how to deal with it.

As a cyberbullying victim, I can tell you that this is one of the most frus-   6
trating parts of the situation. I was on top of the world, excelling in my
academics and in my athletics, but no matter how much confidence you
might have, you feel conflicted about what to do and how you feel about
yourself. In my situation, part of me knew that nothing my cyberbully and
her friends said was true. Nothing they said could phase me. I wouldn't let
them get to me. I would be the bigger person. I could ignore it.

However, when being cyberbullied becomes part of your everyday life,   7
you start to feel discouraged to the point where you can't ignore the situation. The other part of me was bothered by what they said. I cried multiple
times. I couldn't just let it go. I questioned my value as a person. I didn't
know what the next attack would be. Sometimes I wanted to lash back at
them. I was straight up *angry*.

Like many other cyberbullying victims, throughout my experience   8
I struggled to not become consumed by the situation. This is particularly hard to do when you're cyberbullied on social media platforms like

Facebook and Twitter—things that most people check frequently on a daily basis. Cyberbullying is also hard to ignore when the attacks are so personal. The comments my cyberbully and her friends made about me were all based on the things in my life that were important to me, things that I love. They criticized by body, my athletics, my major, where I went to school, etc. All the things I am proud of were being degraded, which started to make me feel unaccomplished and unsuccessful in my college career.

These cyber attacks would happen multiple times a week—so often   9
that they became a daily expectation. Not only was I finding out about the attacks on my own, but I had multiple other people telling me about them as well. So many people started to find out that I was being cyberbullied. The situation was starting to go beyond just me.

My cyberbully and her friends went as far as to write mean comments on   10
photos of me on my friend's profile, causing my friends to become involved as they tried to defend me. I felt surrounded and trapped in the midst of it, never knowing what would happen next or when they'd stop. So bad that I thought about it in the morning and thought about it at night—the situation was clouding my mind in a way that nothing ever had before.

Now, I know what some people might be thinking—just set your   11
accounts to private and/or block them, right? Yes, I understand why this solution seems simple and trust me, I went back and forth with it. But in my experience I felt like I shouldn't have to do that. My cyberbully was already trying to have so much power over me—why should I, as a victim, have to alter my social media accounts and how I interact on them?

Still, I knew I had to do something because I was reaching a breaking   12
point. I decided that I was either going to overcome the issue or I was going to let it consume me. I consulted my family and friends for advice and support—resolving the issue became a group effort. My family and friends reminded me of every challenge I had faced before. They reassured me that I am strong, I am successful, I am worth something, and nothing anyone says about me can undermine my character or my accomplishments. I had to channel all my energy and focus it into all the good things I had in my life and when the days were tough, I had a team of encouraging and loving people on my side. They are the ones that know the real me and more importantly, I know the real me—ultimately, that's all that matters.

It was a process to get back to feeling normal, but one of the most im-   13
portant things I learned was the power of kindness. The saying "kill them with kindness" has never applied to my life more than when I was cyberbullied. I tried to treat others how I wanted to be treated and in the end,

this helped stop my cyberbully and her friends. There was even a day that I unexpectedly came face-to-face with my cyberbully at the mall, and even though she tried to avoid me, I approached her confidently and politely said hi and asked how she was doing. Lead by being a positive role model — it's more powerful than hurtful words ever will be.

HAILEY ELLIS, from "A Victim's Story: My Experience With College Cyberbullying," *The Lala* (1 June 2015). 17 Dec. 2014. http://thelala.com/experience-cyberbullying-college/

·9·

Writing the Research Essay

In Chapter 9, you take the evidence and information that you have found in your sources and transform them into an essay. Now, you truly begin to make the sources your own—by taking notes; by developing a thesis; by deciding which information is relevant and important to that thesis; by organizing the material into a sequence of paragraphs in support of the thesis; and, finally, by expressing your ideas and presenting your evidence to the reader, as far as possible in your own words.

Saving Information

By now, you should have accumulated a quantity of notes that serve as the raw materials for your essay. Here, the term "notes" refers to any of *the products of your research*: your own summaries and paraphrases, quotations, photocopies of book pages and articles, printouts and downloaded copies of Web material, class lecture notes, stories and pictures clipped from newspapers and magazines, transcripts of interviews, and jottings of your own ideas about the topic.

Research also requires you to *take notes*: you read through a text, sometimes quickly and sometimes slowly, deciding as you go which information you might want to use in your essay and recording it as summary, paraphrase, and quotation. Before the days of computers, notes were usually handwritten on index cards or lined pads, ready to be organized into a sequence that would become the outline of an essay. Many students still prefer this slow but thorough way of absorbing ideas and information. Indeed, according to "Fare Thee Well, My Pen," in the *New York Times*, a recent study shows that pen-and-ink note-takers "have a tendency to retain more information than those who used keyboards."

But technology does offer an easy alternative. Text from a book goes through a copy machine and becomes a photocopied page; the words of the text remain the same. Online articles or Web sites get downloaded and appear in a file on your computer screen; the words of the text remain the same. Certainly, having a copy of the original text can be useful: for example, you may want to quote a small portion in your essay. But, at some point, most of the text will have to be rewritten in your own words, in your own voice. Otherwise, you will not be writing an essay; you will be compiling an anthology of quotations.

Downloading presents a particular temptation. The information is available right there, on your screen, and by clicking a few keys you can transfer it directly into the file you've created for your research essay. You can keep on cutting and pasting from other Web sites and database articles, and type in or scan some extracts from photocopies; you'll end up with something that contains sentences and paragraphs and meets the minimum number of assigned pages. It may look like an essay—but will it read like an essay or an electronic scrapbook?

The cut-and-paste method of writing an essay involves no writing. Your instructor will easily observe that the writing component of the assignment hasn't been fulfilled and will grade the "essay" accordingly.

Learning to write essays means learning to speak for yourself. Learning to write research essays means using the skills of summary and paraphrase to present your sources. And you can't delay doing that until you're at the point of writing the essay. What's the solution? Take notes!

Taking Notes

If it's your preference or if your access to a computer is limited, by all means use the traditional, reliable method of taking *handwritten notes on index cards or a pad of paper.* But if you opt for convenience, establish *a new computer file* at the onset of your research. This file will not be the one used for the writing of your essay; it will be exclusively for notes. As you start working with each new source, open that file, put the bibliographical information about that source clearly at the start of a new section, and *type in your version of the material* that you may want to use. Don't copy-type (except for the occasional quotation). Use your own words.

When you've finished writing notes on all your sources, you'll have one long file ready to be printed out and reorganized, or simply reorganized on the screen, ready to transfer into your essay file. The difference is that, this way, you will be cutting and pasting *your own work.*

Here are some guidelines for note taking:

1. *Wait to take notes.* Don't start taking notes until you have compiled most of your preliminary bibliography. Choosing materials to copy and to download will help you gradually to understand the possibilities of your subject and decide on a potential thesis. But if you start taking notes from the first few texts that you find, you may be wasting time

pursuing an idea that will turn out to be impractical or that the evidence ultimately won't support.

2. *Use photocopies and printouts.* Unless it's prohibitively expensive, try to take notes from photocopies of books and articles, rather than the texts themselves; that way, you'll always have the copies handy to refer to if there's a confusion in your notes. (The copies will also be useful if your instructor asks you to submit some of your sources.) Print out down-loaded material and work from the printed copy. It's hard to take good notes if you don't have the text in front of you as you write.

3. *Use paraphrase and summary.* As you learned in Chapter 4, quotation should be the exception, not the rule. Copying the author's language word-for-word will make it more difficult for you to shift to your own writing style later on. You want to avoid producing an anthology of cannibalized quotations. The effort of paraphrasing and summarizing also helps you to understand each new idea. In your notes, always try to explain the author's exact meaning.

4. *Cite evidence.* Include evidence to support the broader ideas that you're writing about. If your topic is corruption in the Olympic games, don't simply allude to issues like the use of performance-enhancing drugs or the influence of network television in the scheduling of events. Cite facts to illustrate your point. You won't remember the range of evidence as you're writing the essay unless you include examples in your notes.

5. *Separate yourself from your source.* Differentiate your own ideas from those that you are paraphrasing. When you take notes, you're working slowly and concentrating on what you're reading. It's at that time that you're most likely to develop your own comments and ideas, spinning them off from the text. Be careful to indicate in your notes what's yours and what's the source's. Later on, you'll need to know which material to document. Using square brackets [like these] around your own ideas is a good way of making this distinction or use the tracking program on your word processor.

6. *Record page numbers.* Keep a running record of page references. You'll need to cite the exact page number for each reference, not an approxi-mate guess. It isn't enough to write "pp. 285–91" after a few paragraphs of notes. Three weeks or three hours later, how will you remember on which page you found the point that you're about to cite in your essay? If you're quoting or paraphrasing a source in some detail, make a slash and insert a new page number to indicate exactly where you turned the page. Put quotation marks around all quotations *immediately*.

7. *Record bibliographical data.* Always include complete bibliographical in-formation for each source. If you don't have a clear record of details like place of publication, volume number, or URL, you won't be able to hand in a complete bibliography. Either start a new file just for bibliography or include that information at the beginning of each section of your notes. Refer back to the lists of necessary information at the end of Chapter 7.

Taking Good Notes

1. Don't start taking notes until you have compiled most of your preliminary bibliography.
2. Try to take notes from photocopies of books and articles and printouts of sources, rather than the texts themselves.
3. Use paraphrase and summary, rather than quotation.
4. Include evidence to support the broader ideas that you're writing about.
5. Differentiate your own ideas from those that you are paraphrasing.
6. Keep a running record of page references.
7. Always include complete bibliographical information for each source.

Taking Notes by Source: Organizationally, you can take notes by source or by topic. Taking notes by source is the more obvious way. You start your computer file (or your cards or pad) with the first source, presenting information in the order of its appearance in the book or article. Then you go on to the second source, the third, and so on. Figure 9-1 shows notes for an essay, organized by source, describing *the 1871 fire that devastated Chicago*. The source (described in detail earlier in the file) is the *New York Times* for October 15, 1871:

- Each item in the list is assigned a number; this will be useful later on, when you are organizing your notes to write your essay.

- The source has also been assigned an identifying letter; if you have two sources with the same name (for example, the *Times* for two different dates), you'll be able to distinguish between them.

Taking Notes by Topic: The disadvantage of taking notes by source is that your notes remain raw material, with no organizational pattern imposed on them. Taking notes by topic is a more sophisticated system:

1. Decide on the basic events or issues that your essay will cover.
2. Assign each of those topics a separate section of your notes file.
3. Place each new piece of information under the relevant topic.

For example, early in the note-taking process, one student decided that she would definitely write about the *aftermath of the Chicago fire*; one section of her notes would be devoted to efforts to contain and put out the blaze. After that, every time she came across a new point about *firefighting*—no matter what the source—she scrolled through (or searched) her notes file,

NY Times, 10/15/71, p. 1   Source J

1. city normal again
2. still martial rule; Gen. Sheridan in charge
3. citizens working at night to watch for new outbreak of fire
4. newspapers moved to other locations
5. estimate 1,000 dead
6. earlier reports of looting and loss of life not exaggerated
7. waterworks won't open until next day
8. two-thirds of the city still using candlelight
9. suffering mostly among "humbler classes"
10. businessmen are "buoyant"
11. bread is 8 cents
12. saloons are closed at 9:00 p.m. for one week

Figure 9-1 Notes grouped by source

looking for the topic name and then adding that new information. Similar sections were established to deal with *food supplies* and *looting*. Figure 9-2 shows a sample of her notes.

Organizing notes by topic makes it much easier to organize your essay. In fact, because your information is already categorized, you can often skip a whole stage in the process and begin to write your essay from your notes without much additional synthesis. But taking notes by topic does require you to make a list, either written or mental, of possible categories or note topics while

Firefighting

All engines and hose carts in city come (NYT 10/8, p. 5)
Water station on fire, with no water to put out small fires
    (Hall, p. 228)
All engines out there; fire too big to stop (NYT 10/8, p. 5)
Fire department "demoralized"; bad fire previous night; men
were drinking afterward; fire marshal "habitually drunk"
    (NYT 10/23, p. 2)

Figure 9-2 Notes grouped by topic

you're still doing your research. And you may not be completely sure about your thesis and structure that early in the process. When you take notes by topic, it's also vital to make sure that *each* point is followed by its source and the relevant page number.

EXERCISE 31: Taking Notes on Three Topics

Assume that you are doing historical research and that you have come across the following source in the library. After doing a preliminary evaluation of the passage, take a set of notes for an essay entitled "Class Differences in Early Chinese History," a second set of notes for an essay entitled "The Historical Role of Chinese Women as Ornaments," and a third set of notes for an essay entitled "The Illusion of Beauty: How Women Have Sacrificed Themselves for Fashion."

from THE HONOR CODE: HOW MORAL REVOLUTIONS HAPPEN
Kwame Anthony Appiah

Presently a professor at New York University, Kwame Anthony Appiah is the author of more than fifteen non-fiction books as well as numerous essays, primarily in areas of political theory and intellectual history. He has also written detective fiction.

Background: In *The Honor Code,* Chinese foot-binding is one of several extended examples of brutal or inhumane practices that only came to an end when challenged and overcome by a national sense of honor or shame.

The Beginnings of the Golden Lotus

The precise origins of footbinding are shrouded in controversy. There are traditions that associate its beginnings with the poet-king Li Yu, last of the Southern Tang rulers, who held out against Song rule until 975. (If this is right, then footbinding began nearly fifteen hundred years after the death of Confucius.) Howard Levy, author of one of the first modern histories of footbinding, records a reference in the work of a twelfth-century commentator to a text, now lost, which described Li Yu's "favored palace concubine," a woman known as "Lovely Maiden," "who was a slender-waisted beauty and a gifted dancer. He had a six-foot high lotus constructed for her out of gold....Lovely Maiden was ordered to bind her feet with white silk cloth to make the tips look like the points of a moon sickle. She then danced in the centre of the lotus, whirling about like a rising cloud."[12] Whatever the merits of the story as history, the bound foot of a Chinese woman came to be known as a golden lotus or lily.

1

Footbinding began as a sign of elevated status in an extremely hierarchical   2
society. By the late thirteenth century, Levy writes, "families which claimed
aristocratic lineage came to feel compelled to bind the feet of their girls … as a
visible sign of upper-class distinction." The distinction was possible because
women of the upper classes — aristocrats at the court or gentry in the provinces —
did not need to work in the fields, as peasant women did, or take long walks
to the market. In fact, their bound feet kept them from straying far from home,
thus guaranteeing, as a fourteenth-century treatise put it (in an argument that
was to be repeated many times over the centuries), their chastity.[13]

The golden lotus is connected from its beginnings with female honor.   3
And, since honor was one of the essential prerequisites for respectable
marriage — which was an arrangement between families, not the choice of
individuals — Chinese women who expected to marry men of any social status
needed to have their feet bound. Men came to long for small-footed women;
and this painful practice was made bearable to women — as they endured it
themselves, and as they witnessed the pain of daughters, nieces, and grand-
daughters — by the conviction that their tiny feet were simply beautiful.

This conviction is hard to share if you look at the pictures of the bare   4
foot freed of its bindings that became a staple of later campaigners against the
practice. But we have to remember that this was not what most people saw.
For, once it was bound, a woman's foot was almost always covered in elegant,
colorful, embroidered shoes.

In fact, one of the attributes of a Chinese woman of good family was skill in   5
making and embroidering her own shoes, in colors appropriate for festival, for
mourning, and for every day, as well as to wear at night. Sewing a set of shoes
to take to one's husband's house was part of the preparation for marriage; and a
woman's mother-in-law would judge her, in part, by the quality of the shoes she
brought with her. Men would see their own wives' naked feet only in private.
As the Englishwoman Mrs. Archibald Little, one of the great anti-footbinding
campaigners, whom we shall be meeting again later, once put it: "Every
Chinese, when he fondles the feet of his bride, likes to imagine that they are all
that they appear — tiny, satin clad and beautifully embroidered."[14]

A woman would see her golden lotuses herself only when she took off the   6
long binding strips to change them; washing her feet, powdering them with
alum, re-binding them, and putting on her red sleeping shoes before retiring …
or donning the elegant confections for daytime wear that others would glimpse
beneath her skirt. But we should not assume that even the naked foot was the
object of repugnance. Far from it. There are many photographs from the turn
of the twentieth century of women proudly showing their golden lotuses; and
admiration of these tiny broken feet, revealed in private without their bindings,
is a regular theme of Chinese writing over the centuries....

The Pain of Binding

Footbinding was done to girls, some of them as young as three or four years old.   7
If it was done with the aim of making as small a golden lotus as possible, it was
intensely painful. The binding crushed the four smaller toes under the sole and
compressed the rear of the anklebone toward the sole too, forcing the bones
of the foot into an arch much higher than anything that occurs naturally, and
creating a sort of cleft. Often bound feet had to be cleansed of blood and pus;
occasionally they putrefied and toes dropped off. Eventually — after months
and years — the pain diminished, presumably because the sensory nerves were
permanently damaged, but walking was usually difficult for women with bound
feet. Missionary doctors in the late nineteenth century — who were grinding, no
doubt, a somewhat ethnocentric ax — reported cases where the binding caused
ulceration, gangrene, loss of one or both feet, even, in the worst case, death.[19]

It is clear that the ideal length of the three-inch lotus was rarely achieved,   8
especially outside the upper classes. Peasants and laborers often underwent a
looser form of binding, which might begin when the girl was older; and this
process was both less hobbling and less painful. The husband of one elderly
woman whose feet had been bound insisted that the less deformed five-inch
feet of some ordinary working women were no obstacle to walking or carrying
heavy loads. A three-inch foot, on the other hand, did not allow you to walk
long distances. Women with the three-inch lotus were often carried about in
sedan chairs and often supported by servants when they walked. Most women
with bound feet, however, did not need such assistance.[20]

Since the bindings were worn both day and night, the bound foot had   9
a distinctive odor — one that some found extremely unpleasant and others,
notoriously, found sexually exciting. The pseudonymous eighteenth-century
footbinding enthusiast who called himself the "Doctor of the Fragrant Lotus"
produced a monograph entitled *A Golden Garden Miscellany*, which consisted of
unconnected observations about footbinding, among which was this gem:

> *Unbearable* — painful corns; smelling the awful odor when the binding
> is suddenly removed.

There is no doubt, then, that everyone understood not only that
footbinding could limit movement and help keep women subject to their
families and to men, but also that it was extremely painful.

12. Levy, *op. cit.,* 39.

13. *Ibid.*

14. Mrs. Archibald Little, *The Land of the Blue Gown* (London: T. Fisher &
Unwin, 1902): 363.

19. Chau, MA Thesis, 13–16.

20. Levy, *op. cit.,* 283–84.

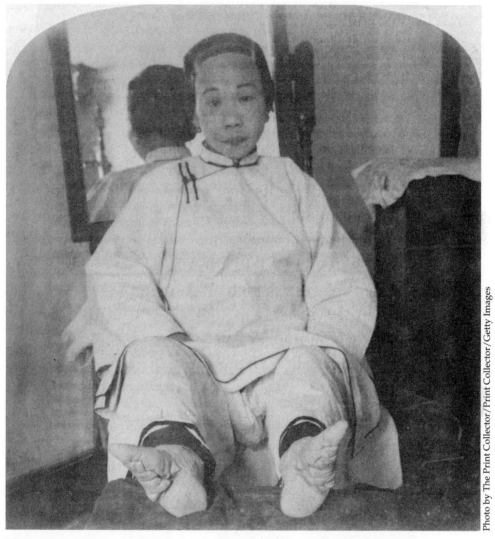

Photo by The Print Collector/Print Collector/Getty Images

Figure 9-3 A high caste lady's dainty "lily feet." Notice the deformity caused by binding the feet.

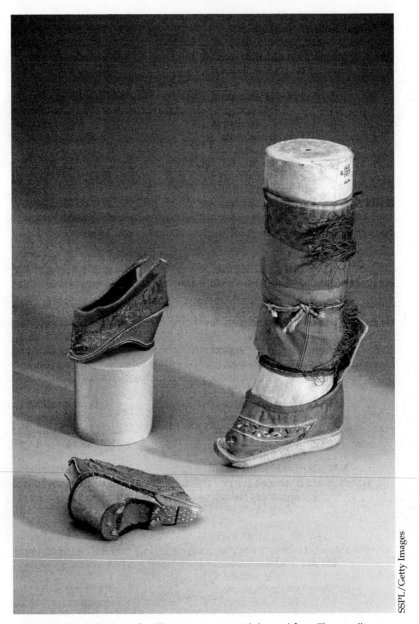

SSPL/Getty Images

Figure 9-4 Silk brocade shoes for Chinese women with bound feet. The smaller a woman's feet, the more sexually attractive she was considered. Three inches was considered ideal.

Developing a List of Topics

Once you have all your notes in a computer file (or on cards or a pad), you need to organize them into a plan for your essay. (If you've already organized your notes by topic, you can skip this stage.) The first step is to *take inventory*: you search for ideas worth developing in your essay by (1) reviewing your notes and (2) identifying and writing down all the major topics that you have learned and thought about during your research.

Here's a list of topics taken from a set of notes about the *Chicago fire of 1871*:

Mrs. O'Leary's cow kicks over the lantern: did that start the fire?
Extent of the damage
Preventing panic
Feeding the homeless
Dealing with those trapped within buildings
Drought conditions the previous summer
Preventing looting
Beginning to rebuild the city
Mobilizing manpower to fight the fire
Improvising hospital conditions
Providing shelter
How the fire spread
Crowd control
Fighting the fire
Organizing the firefighters and police
Sounding the alarm

Since the subject of this essay is an event, the items on the list are factual and brief. An essay that deals with ideas rather than events is likely to have a preliminary list of topics with longer, more abstract entries. Notice that, at this point, the sequence of the entries doesn't matter; the points are in *random order*, just as they were found in the notes. Nor do you have to include supporting evidence at this stage. That's why the list is so skinny. You are extracting what's important from the mass of your notes; you are looking for the bones of your essay.

Taking Inventory of Your Notes and Forming Paragraph Topics

- *Do write down in any order the important ideas* that you find in your notes. At this point, the items don't have to be related to each other in sequence.

- *Don't try to summarize* all your notes. At this point, you are working on organizing your topics, not summarizing your research.

- *Don't try to link the ideas that you write down to specific sources.* At this point, there is no special reason to place the names of the sources next to your new list of ideas; not every idea in your new list will necessarily be included in your essay. Later, you will decide which source to use in support of which topic sentence.

- *Do think about your own reactions* to the information that you have collected. Now you are deciding what is worth writing about.

- *Do use your own words.* At this point, even if you only jot down a phrase, it should be your own version of the source's idea. Even if the information has appeared in ten different articles and you've included it ten different times in your notes, you are now, in some sense, making it your own.

Planning a Strategy

Essays about events or people tend to have a straightforward organization based on a *time sequence*, with a beginning, middle, and end. You will have a thesis to support—"The rescue and rehabilitation efforts after the Chicago fire were competently carried out"—but the bulk of the essay will analyze what happened during and after the fire in sequential order. Abstract topics, which are often arguments, require a more complex structure.

In Chapter 1, you learned that most arguments are based on a combination of two kinds of logical reasoning:

- *Deductive reasoning:* You provide a series of linked premises, based on a general assumption that you and your reader share, that leads to a conclusion.

- *Inductive reasoning:* You provide a range of specific evidence from which you construct a conclusion.

In practice, these two basic logical tools—the use of linked premises and the use of evidence—are used together to develop the most common strategies: *cause-and-effect* and *problem-and-solution*.

Constructing an Argument: High School Dropouts

The *cause-and-effect* **essay** establishes a causal link between two circumstances. The thesis usually answers the question "Why?" Let's assume that your general subject is *high school dropouts*. Why is the high school dropout rate as high as it is today? Here are a few typical answers:

- Because class sizes are too large
- Because students are poorly prepared to handle the work
- Because many students are foreign-born and can't speak English well
- Because local governments are not providing sufficient funding
- Because family life is breaking down, leaving students without support and discipline

You may initially be inclined to write about all these causes, giving each one equal weight. But that strategy will make your essay long and unmanageable, with a thesis that pulls the reader in many contradictory directions. Yet if you focus on only one cause, you run the risk of oversimplifying your argument. You need to consider which of these causes is *most responsible* for its effect—the high dropout rate—and which ones have a *contributing influence*.

Analyzing your list should also help you to determine *which causes belong together*. For example, the problem of class size is probably linked to—caused by—the problem of inadequate funding. Here you have a smaller cause and effect embedded within the larger one:

Inadequate funding results in overly large classes, which, in turn, contribute to the dropout rate.

The links between causes—like funding and class size—form the *deductive* part of your argument. But the causes in the list above also lend themselves to *inductive* support. Comparative statistics about class size over several years and evidence of local budget cuts might (or might not) support your argument about the increasing dropout rate.

By the time you finish your research, you should be able to determine *whether your inductive evidence supports your deductive argument* about the reasons why students drop out. Assuming that it does, your essay will present factual evidence, including statistics, about class sizes, student preparedness, language difficulties, and diminished local budgets for education. The last point on your list—family breakdown—is the most abstract and so the most difficult to support. You would need to develop a series of deductive premises, along with evidence, to make a strong causal link between the decline of family life and the incidence of high school dropouts.

Let's assume that you decide on the following thesis:

> The poor educational environment, resulting from inadequate funding, makes it hard for students to learn, so they drop out.

What kinds of *counterarguments* would you have to anticipate and rebut? While much of your research supports your thesis, you have also found authorities who argue that students from strong family backgrounds perform well and stay in school even in overcrowded, poorly funded districts. You can continue to defend your preferred thesis, but you must also acknowledge your opponents' views, while pointing out their limitations.

The *problem-and-solution* essay often incorporates the cause-and-effect essay, using five stages:

1. *Establish that a problem exists.* Explain why it is a problem, and anticipate the negative consequences if nothing is done.

2. *Analyze the causes of the problem.* Here, you can include a modified version of the cause-and-effect strategy: emphasize the major causes, but remind your reader, citing evidence, that this is a complex issue, with a number of contributory influences working together.

3. *Assert the best solution.* Using the full evidence of your research, demonstrate why the preferred solution will work and indicate how you would go about implementing it.

4. *Anticipate counterarguments and answer them.* Your research has turned up authorities who have recommended different solutions. What are the advantages and disadvantages of those solutions? Is your solution better? Why?

5. *Conclude in a spirit of accommodation.* Assert your solution once again, but also consider acknowledging the complexity of the problem and making room for some of your opponents' ideas. Sometimes the arguments on either side of an issue are too evenly balanced for certainty, and you need to find a solution within common ground.

Arranging the Order of Topics: Outlining

At some point in the process of organizing your essay, your skinny list of ideas becomes an outline. An *outline* is a list of the major and minor points supporting an essay's thesis, presented in a pattern that conveys their relative importance. (See Chapter 5, pp. 195–196.)

Their major points will probably all be *parallel* or of the same kind:

- the *reasons* why **x** is true,
- or the *ways* in which **y** happens,
- or the *differences* between **x** and **y**,
- or the chief *characteristics* of **z**.

I. These major points are given the most prominent place in the outline, usually at the left-hand margin.

   A. Secondary material—the ideas, information, or examples being used as supporting evidence—appears directly under each major point and slightly to the right.

      1. You may have different kinds of evidence to support a point or a group of examples.

      2. Each should be listed on a separate line.

Traditionally, outlines are written in a standard format, with major and minor points assigned numbers and letters of the alphabet to keep them in order, as you see above. But there is absolutely no need to create a formal outline, with its letters and numbers, unless your instructor requires it or you find it useful for organizing your information. You can indicate the relationships between ideas simply by the way you place them on the page.

What is important is that, at this stage, you *revise and expand your inventory of major topics*, making new lists out of old ones, adding and deleting ideas, changing the order to correspond to your strategy. When that inventory list is as good as you can make it, you have *a sequence that will roughly correspond to the sequence of paragraphs in your essay*.

How do you decide on the best order for your topic list? Ask yourself the following questions:

- How are ideas linked together?
- Which is more important?
- What does your reader need to know first?
- What information does your reader need in order to understand a second, more complex point?
- How does one idea lead into another?

Look for an *organizing principle*. In a historical essay, the ordering principle is frequently *time*: the deployment of troops has to be described before the actual battle. In a personality profile, dominant qualities will take precedence over minor quirks. Problems get described before solutions; causes are analyzed first in order to understand their effects. One rationale for your sequence might be "most compelling" to "least compelling" reason. But an even stronger organizing principle is *"most fundamental" to "most complex"*: you start with your most basic point and demonstrate how everything else rests on that central idea.

In addition to rearranging the order of your topics, you also have to expand your inventory by *supplying supporting evidence for each major topic*. (In effect, you are filling in the secondary tiers of your outline.) Under headings like "firefighting" and "medical care," you insert factual information demonstrating that the authorities in Chicago reacted to the fire as efficiently as circumstances allowed. Similarly, having established a linked set of the causes and subcauses that encourage a higher dropout rate, you distribute the material gathered in your research—statistics, surveys, anecdotes, theories—under the appropriate topics.

Completing Your Outline

Your final organizational task is to rearrange your notes within the framework of your outline. This can be done either *directly on the computer*, working from your outline, or by *cross-referencing*. You may need to use a combination of both methods.

Using the Computer to Organize Your Essay

By Topic: Let's assume that most of your notes are contained in a file on your computer. If you originally organized your notes by topic, you simply *move your notes*, section by section, so that each portion is placed next to the appropriate topic in your outline. This is one time when cutting and pasting text is a quick and acceptable method of getting your work done. As you work, be sure to safeguard your notes. Instead of cutting and pasting, try *copying and pasting* so that your original file of notes remains intact. Keep a backup version of both your note file and your essay file. Above all, *save your work at regular and frequent intervals*.

Organizing Your Ideas

1. *Evaluate your inventory list of important ideas.*

   - Notice which ones are in the mainstream of your research, discussed by several of your sources, and which ones appear only in one or two sources.

   - Think about eliminating topics that seem minor or remote from your subject and your thesis.

   - Consider whether you have enough evidence to support all of your topics.

   - Look for and combine topics that restate the same point.

   - If you are developing an argument essay, make sure that each of the key points supporting your side, as well as your counterarguments to the opposition, is supported by your research.

2. *Think about the sequence of ideas on your final list and the possible strategies for organizing your essay.*

   - How does your list of ideas help to establish a thesis?

   - Are you working with a collection of reasons? Consequences? Problems? Dangers?

   - What kind of essay are you writing? Cause and effect? Problem and solution? Explanation of a procedure? Evaluation of reasons for an argument?

   If you are developing a historical or biographical topic:

   - Did the event fall into distinct narrative stages?

   - What aspects of the scene would an observer have noticed?

   - Which of your subject's activities best reveals his or her personality?

   If you are developing an argument:

   - Does your issue lend itself to a cause-and-effect or a problem-and-solution essay?

   - Which are your most compelling arguments?

   - Do your main reasons require deductive or inductive support?

3. *Arrange your list of topics in a sequence that has meaning for you, carries out your strategy, and develops your thesis in a clear direction.*

By Source: If you originally organized your notes by source, organizing your essay now becomes a more complex process. If your topic is straightforward and your essay is under ten pages, you can probably rearrange your notes directly on the computer, as described in the previous paragraph. You type your outline into your essay file, with wide gaps between the topics, and start to move items (copying and pasting) from one file to the other. Instead of transferring whole sections as you would if you had organized your notes by topic, you'll be pulling out a quotation or a paragraph or an example from your notes and finding the right place for it in your outline sequence. This can be tedious and painstaking work.

Be extremely careful to *make sure that the source of each piece of information is indicated next to it before you move it*. Otherwise, as you write your essay, you won't be able to document your sources. Without documentation of sources, your research efforts have no validity.

Using Cross-Referencing to Organize Your Essay

If you're working on a lengthy and complicated essay with a set of notes organized by source, or if a large portion of your notes is on paper rather than in a computer file, your best option is to use cross-referencing to complete your outline and organize your essay. Cross-referencing is used *before* physically moving material from file to file. Once again, you're working from two sets of material:

- *Your completed outline of topics.* The topics are listed either on the screen or on a long pad. Make sure to leave wide gaps between each item. Assign a number (preferably a Roman numeral), in sequence, to each topic in your outline.
- *Your notes.* It's easiest to have everything on paper, including printouts of any computer notes. Assign an identifying letter to each source (placing it at the top of each page of notes devoted to material from that source). If you have 12 sources, you'll be using A–L. Assign an Arabic numeral to each separate piece of information within the notes from a specific source.

Now, once again, slowly read through all your research notes, this time keeping your outline of topics in front of you. Every time you come across a point in your notes that should be cited in support of a topic on your outline, immediately:

1. Place the number of the outline topic (X or XI) next to the reference in your notes.
2. Place the source's identifying letter (G) and the identifying number of the item in your notes (8) under the relevant topic in your outline.

Source G

Times, October 11, "The Ruined City," p. 1

1. The fire has stopped and there has been some "blessed rain."
2. 20–30 people have died in their homes.

XI
3. Plundering everywhere — like a scene of war
   A. A thief suffocated while trying to steal jewelry from a store.
   B. People who were caught pilfering had to be released because the jail burned down.

X
4. Lake used for drinking water.
5. People dying of exposure.

IX
6. Little food: people searching the ruins

IX
7. Difficulties of transporting supplies

XI
8. Meeting of citizens at church to help protect what was left, to help homeless, and to provide water if further fires broke out

Figure 9-5 Cross-referencing: notes — step 1

For the system to work, you must complete *both* stages: notes must be keyed to the outline, and the outline must be keyed to each item in your research notes. The notes and the outline criss-cross each other; hence the term *cross-referencing*.

To illustrate cross-referencing, here is an example taken from the notes and outline for an essay on the Chicago fire. The outline was divided into three main sections: the *causes* of the fire, the *panic* during the fire, and *restoring order* after the fire. Figure 9-5 shows an excerpt from the *notes*, with Roman numerals written in the margins to indicate cross-references to three specific paragraph topics. Figure 9-6 shows a portion of the *outline*, with letters and

IX. Feeding the homeless   G6 / G7
X.   Providing basic services   G4
XI. Protecting life and property   G3 / G8

Figure 9-6 Cross-referencing: topic list — step 2

numbers indicating cross-references to specific evidence within the notes file. When you have finished cross-referencing:

- Your outline will have a precise list of sources to be cited for each major point, and

- Your research notes will have keyed numbers in most (but not necessarily all) of the margins.

Cross-referencing helps you to avoid time-consuming searches for references while you are writing the essay. When you start to work on the paragraph dealing with "Feeding the Homeless," you consult your outline and immediately go to Source G, Items 6 and 7. (Later, references to other sources will also have been placed next to Item IX on your outline.) The accumulated information will become the basis for writing that paragraph.

A few of the items in the notes for Source G have no cross-references next to them. Some will be cross-referenced to other topics in this outline, and haven't yet been given their reference numbers. Items 2 and 5, for example, would probably come under the heading of Casualties, in the section on panic during the fire. On the other hand, some items simply won't fit into the topics chosen for the outline and will be discarded.

Writing Integrated Paragraphs

Writing a research essay resembles putting together a *mosaic*. Each paragraph has a basic design, determined by its topic sentence. To carry out the design, a paragraph might contain a *group of reasons or examples* to illustrate its main idea, *or* an *extended explanation* to develop that idea in greater detail, *or a comparison* between two elements introduced in the first sentence. These are the same paragraphing designs that you use in all your writing. What makes the research essay different is the fact that the materials are assembled from many sources.

Imagine that the notes that you have taken from several different sources are boxes of tiles, each box containing a different color. You may find it easier to avoid mixing the colors and to work *only* with red tiles or *only* with blue, or to devote one corner of the mosaic to a red pattern and another to a blue. In the same way, you may find it both convenient and natural to work with only one source at a time and to avoid the decisions and the adjustments that must be made when you are combining different styles and ideas. But, of course, it is the design and only the design that dictates which colors should be used in creating the pattern of the mosaic, and *it is the design or outline of your essay that dictates which evidence should be included in each paragraph.*

When you present a topic in a given paragraph, you must work with all the relevant information that you have gathered about that topic, whether it comes

> ## Constructing Paragraphs in a Research Essay
>
> 1. *Each paragraph should possess a single main idea, usually expressed in the topic sentence, that supports the development of your essay's thesis.* That topic controls the selection and arrangement of all the information in the paragraph. Everything that is included should develop and support that single idea, without digressions.
> 2. *The body of the paragraph should contain information taken from a variety of sources.* The number of different sources that you include in any one paragraph depends on the number of authors in your research notes who have touched on that idea.
> 3. *The sentences of your completed paragraph should be easy to read, coherent, and unified.*
>   - Do integrate your material so that your reader will not be distracted by the differing sources or made aware of breaks between the various points.
>   - Don't integrate your material so completely that you forget to provide appropriate acknowledgment of your sources.

from one source or from many. Of course, you may have too much material; you may find it impossible to fit everything into the paragraph without overloading it with repetition. These rejected pieces may not fit into another part of the essay; instead, they will go back into their boxes as a backup or reserve fund of information.

Here is a paragraph from a student essay about the novelist F. Scott Fitzgerald, using MLA documentation, which presents four different accounts of an affair between Fitzgerald's wife, Zelda, and Edouard Jozan, a young Frenchman. To emphasize the variety and complexity of the research, the names of the sources and the attributing verbs and phrases have been italicized.

There is a lack of agreement about the details of the affair as well as its significance for the Fitzgeralds' marriage. *According to one of Fitzgerald's biographers,* Jozan and Zelda afterward regarded it as "nothing more than a summer flirtation" (Mayfield 97). But *Ernest Hemingway,* in his memoirs, *wrote* much later that Scott had told him "a truly sad story" about the affair, which he repeated many times in the course of their friendship (172). *Gerald and Sara Murphy,* who were present that summer and remembered the incident very well, *told* of being awakened by Scott in the middle of a September night in order to help him revive Zelda from an overdose of sleeping pills. *The Murphys were sure* that this incident was related to her affair with Jozan (Milford 111). *Nancy Milford, Zelda's biographer, believes* that the affair affected Zelda more than Scott, who, at that time, was very engrossed in his work. Indeed, *Milford's account* of the affair is the only one that *suggests* that Zelda was so deeply in love with Jozan that she asked Scott for a divorce (112). *According to an interview with Jozan,* the members of this triangle never engaged in a three-way confrontation; *Jozan told Milford* that the Fitzgeralds were "the victims of their own unsettled and a little unhealthy imagination" (112).

This paragraph gives a brief but adequate account of what is known about the events of that summer of 1924. The writer does not try to rush through the four accounts of the affair, nor does he reduce each one to a phrase, as if he expected the reader to have prior knowledge of these people and their activities. In the context of the whole essay, the paragraph provides enough information for the reader to judge whose interpretation of the affair is closest to the truth.

Accommodating Argument in Your Paragraphs

Presenting an Inductive Argument

When you write a paragraph based on *induction*, the topic sentence should clearly summarize the range of evidence being cited. Here is an example from Edward Tenner's *Why Things Bite Back*, a book about the dangers of technological progress:

topic sentence: "dangerous myth"

The startling wartime successes of penicillin created the dangerous myth of an antibiotic panacea. Even after the U.S. Food and Drug Administration began to require prescriptions in the mid-1950s, an antibiotic injection or prescription remained for many people the payoff of a medical encounter. They resisted the medical fact that antibiotics can do nothing against colds and other viral diseases. In many other countries, antibiotics are still sold legally over the counter to patients who may never get proper instructions about dosage or the importance of completing a course of treatment. Dr. Stuart B.

1st example

Levy of Boston cites an Argentinian businessman who was cured of leukemia but died of an infection by the common bacterium *E. coli*. Ten years of self-medication had produced plasmids in his body that were resistant to every antibiotic used. Governments, too, have unintentionally promoted resurgence.

transition

Indonesian authorities have literally ladled out preventive doses of tetracycline to 100,000 Muslim pilgrims for a week at a time. Since the Mecca pilgrimage has historically been one of the great mixing bowls of microorganisms, it is

2nd example

especially disturbing to learn that half of all cholera bacilli in Africa are now resistant to tetracycline.

Paragraphs presenting inductive evidence tend to be long. Tenner makes his point about the "dangerous myth" of penicillin in the topic sentence, but he doesn't immediately cite evidence. He first explains the "danger" in the second sentence, and the "myth" in the third. Only then does he introduce his first supporting point—self-medication in countries without drug regulation—with Dr. Levy's example of the antibiotic-resistant Argentinian businessman. Signaled by the transitional word "too," Tenner's second example—the Mecca pilgrimage—increases the scale of potential danger.

Presenting a Deductive Argument

In contrast to the specific examples of induction, an article on "Methods of Media Manipulation" starts in a *deductive* mode, with a series of premises:

primary premise

We are told by people in the media industry that news bias is unavoidable. Whatever distortions and inaccuracies are found in the news are caused

1st causal premise

by deadline pressures, human misjudgment, budgetary restraints, and the difficulty of reducing a complex story into a concise report. Furthermore—the

2nd causal premise

argument goes—no communication system can hope to report everything, selectivity is needed.

Parenti's alternative primary premise

I would argue that the media's misrepresentations are not at all the result of innocent error and everyday production problems, though such problems certainly do exist. True, the press has to be selective, but what principle of selectivity is involved?

causal premise

Media bias usually does not occur in random fashion; rather, it moves in the same overall direction again and again, favoring management over labor, corporations over corporate critics, affluent whites over low-income minorities, officialdom over protesters. . . . The built-in biases of the corporate mainstream media faithfully reflect the dominant ideology, seldom straying into territory that might cause discomfort to those who hold political and economic power, including those who own the media or advertise in it.

The initial presentation of Michael Parenti's argument is based on a dichotomy—contrast—between the media's view of news bias and his own. There is a disputed primary premise (bias is or is not avoidable) and a disputed secondary premise (one can't print everything vs. one prints what pleases one's corporate masters). Parenti's premises are developed in more detail, and the article goes on to support those premises through induction, by citing evidence of such manipulative tactics as "suppression by omission" and "framing."

Presenting Both Sides of an Argument

While the opening of Parenti's article presents the opposition's argument as well as his own, the tone is grudging, even hostile. He leaves no room for accommodation between the two points of view. Yet, whenever possible, *it is useful to acknowledge some merit in your opponents or in their argument.* Here are excerpts from two essays supporting opposite sides of the "wilderness preservation" issue. In the first, John Daniel is arguing that the advancement of science, if uncontrolled, can do harm to unspoiled land. He is careful, however, to distinguish between his allies and his enemies:

positive view

negative view

I don't mean to indict science in general. Many of the foremost champions of wild nature are scientists, and their work has done much to warn us of the environmental limits we are transgressing. I am arguing only against interventionist science that wants to splice genes, split atoms, or otherwise manipulate the wild—science aimed more at control than understanding, science that assumes ownership of the natural mysteries. When technological specialists come to believe that nature is answerable to their own prerogatives, they are not serving but endangering the greater community.

In William Tucker's view, society has more compelling interests, to which the wilderness movement must sometimes defer. But, before stating his argument, he pays his dues to nature:

positive view

negative view

I am not arguing against wild things, scenic beauty, pristine landscapes, and scenic preservation. What I am questioning is the argument that wilderness is a value against which every other human activity must be judged and that human beings are somehow unworthy of the landscape. The wilderness has been equated with freedom, but there are many different ideas about what constitutes freedom. . . .

Interestingly enough, Tucker then proceeds to move from his impeccably fair presentation to an argument that approaches *ad hominem*—a personal attack:

undercuts opponents

attacks by innuendo

It may seem unfair to itemize the personal idiosyncrasies of people who feel comfortable only in wilderness, but it must be remembered that the environmental movement has been shaped by many people who literally spent years of their lives living in isolation.

Citing John Muir, David Brower, and Gary Snyder, leaders of the Sierra Club who spent much time alone in the mountains, Tucker continues:

positive view

There is nothing reprehensible in this, and the literature and philosophy that emerge from such experiences are often admirable. But it

negative view   seems questionable to me that the ethic that comes out of this wilderness isolation — and the sense of ownership of natural landscapes that inevitably follows — can serve as the basis for a useful national philosophy.

Whatever his disclaimers, Tucker is rooting one of his key arguments against the wilderness movement in the personal preferences of three men. He does not, however, resort to using slanted, exaggerated, or dismissive language about his opponents. In contrast, here is Robert W. McChesney's attack on commercialism in the media:

image of attack   The commercial blitzkrieg into every nook and cranny of U.S. culture, from schools to sport to museums to movie theaters to the Internet, has lessened traditional distinctions of public service from commercialism.

The word *blitzkrieg* (literally, lightning battle) originally referred to the German army in World War II. It immediately conjures up an image of a mechanized, pitiless army rolling over everything in its path, a reference reinforced by the domestic, vulnerable image of "nook and cranny," used to describe U.S. culture, the victim. Without even articulating his point, McChesney has created a lingering association between corporations and Nazis. This is a clever use of language, but is it a fair argument? In the next example, Leslie Savan also uses emotionally charged language to attack a similar target:

image of disease   Advertising now infects just about every organ of society, and wherever advertising gains a foothold it tends to slowly take over, like a vampire or a virus.

The brutal swiftness of the blitzkrieg has been replaced by the slow insinuation of an *infection*, but both images are deadly. (The allusion to a vampire must have been tempting — advertising leaves viewers bloodless and brainwashed — but it should not be combined with the insidious, slowly creeping image of infection.) Interestingly enough, McChesney and Savan are both adopting the tactics of the commercial media that they condemn: using powerful images in an attempt to force their readers into agreement.

Presenting Arguments Fairly

Perhaps the greatest disservice that you can do your sources is to distort them so that your reader is left with a false impression of what they have said or written. Such distortion is most likely to happen when you are writing an argumentative essay.

1. **Present both sides of the argument.**

   One way of shading an argument to suit your own ends is to *misrepresent the strength of the opposition*. Let us assume that you are working with a number of articles, all of which are effectively presented and worth citing. Some clearly support your point of view; others are openly opposed; and a few avoid taking sides, emphasizing related but less controversial topics. If your essay cites only the favorable and neutral articles, and avoids any reference to the views of the opposition, you have presented the issue falsely. A one-sided presentation will make you appear to be either *biased* or *sloppy* in your research. If the sources are available and if their views are pertinent, they should be represented and, preferably, refuted in your essay.

2. **Provide a complete account of the argument.**

Sometimes, distortions occur accidentally, because you have presented only a *partial* account of a source's views. In the course of an article or a book, authors sometimes examine a variety of views before making it clear which ones they support. Or an author may have mixed opinions about the issue and see merit in more than one point of view. If you choose to quote or paraphrase material from only one section of such a work, then you must also inform your reader that these statements are not entirely representative of the writer's overall views.

3. **Make sure that you—and your reader—understand whether the source really supports the idea that you are citing.**

Ideas can get distorted because of the researcher's misunderstanding, careless note taking, or hasty reading. Review the entire section of the article or your notes before you attribute an opinion to your source. Make sure that you are not *taking a sentence out of context* or ignoring a statement in the next paragraph or on the next page that may be more typical of the writer's thinking. Writers often use an argumentative strategy that sets up a point with which they basically disagree in order to shoot it down shortly thereafter. Don't confuse a statement made for the sake of argument with a writer's real beliefs.

4. **Provide a fair presentation.**

You may be so eager to uphold your point of view that you will cite any bit of material that looks like supporting evidence. To do so, however, you may have to twist the words of the source to fit your ideas. This is one of the worst kinds of intellectual dishonesty—and one of the easiest for a suspicious reader to detect: one has only to look up the source. If your sources' evidence does not sufficiently support your side, then you should seriously consider switching sides or switching topics.

Here is a fairly clear instance of such distortion. In an essay on the need for prison reform, Garry Wills is focusing on the *deficiencies of our society's penal system*; he is not directly concerned with the arguments for or against the death penalty. But the student citing Wills in a research essay is writing specifically *in support of capital punishment*. To make Wills's argument fit into the scheme of this essay, the student must make some suspiciously selective references. Here is a paragraph from the research essay (on the left), side by side with the source:

Although the death penalty may seem very harsh and inhuman, is this not fair and just punishment for one who was able to administer death to another human being? A murderer's victim always receives the death penalty. Therefore, the death penalty for the murderer evens the score, or, as stated in the Bible, "an eye for an eye, and a tooth for a tooth." According to Garry Wills, "take a life, lose your life." Throughout the ages, society has demanded that man be allowed to right his wrongs. Revenge is our culture's oldest way of making sure that no one "gets away with" any crime. As Wills points out, according to this line of reasoning, the taking of the murderer's life can be seen as his payment to society for his misdeed.	The oldest of our culture's views on punishment is the *lex talionis*, an eye for an eye. Take a life, lose your life. It is a very basic cry—people must "pay" for their crimes, yield exact and measured recompense. No one should "get away with" any crime, like a shoplifter taking something unpaid for. The desire to make an offender suffer equivalent pain (if not compensatory excess of pain) is very deep in human nature, and rises quickly to the surface. What is lynching but an impatience with even the slightest delay in exacting this revenge? It serves our social myth to say that this impatience, if denied immediate gratification, is replaced by something entirely different—by an impersonal dedication to justice. Only lynchers want revenge, not those who wait for a verdict. That is not very likely. Look at the disappointed outcry if the verdict does not yield even delayed satisfaction of the grudge.

In the essay, the writer is citing only *part* of Wills's argument and thus makes him appear to support capital punishment. Wills is being misrepresented because (unlike the writer) he considers it fair to examine the views of the opposing side before presenting his own arguments. *The ideas that the student cites are not Wills's, but Wills's presentations of commonly accepted assumptions about punishment.* It is not entirely clear whether the writer of the research essay has merely been careless, failing to read past the first few sentences, or whether the misrepresentation is intentional.

Mistakes to Avoid When Presenting an Argument

1. Don't be one-sided; present *both* sides of an argument.
2. Don't omit crucial parts of the source's reasoning; provide a complete account of the argument.
3. Don't quote ideas out of context: make sure that you—and your reader—understand whether the source really supports the idea that you are citing.
4. Don't twist the source's ideas to fit your own purpose; provide a fair presentation.

Integrating Your Sources: Recruiting in College Athletics

To illustrate the need for careful analysis of sources before you write your paragraphs, here is a group of passages, all direct quotations, which have been gathered for a research essay on college athletics. The paragraph developed from these sources must support the writer's *thesis*:

> Colleges should, in the interests of both players and academic standards, outlaw the high-pressure tactics used by coaches when they recruit high school players for college teams.

The first three statements come from college coaches, describing recruiting methods that they have observed and carried out; the last four are taken from books that discuss corruption in athletics.

> I think in the long run, every coach must recognize this basic principle, or face the alumni firing squad. Recruiting is the crux of building a championship football team.
>
> STEVE SLOAN, Texas Tech

> Athletics is creating a monster. Recruiting is getting to be cancerous.
>
> DALE BROWN, Louisiana State University

> You don't out-coach people, you out-recruit them.
>
> PAUL "BEAR" BRYANT, University of Alabama

> It is an athletic maxim that a man with no special coaching skills can win games if he recruits well and that a tactician without talented players is a man soon without a job.
>
> KENNETH DENLINGER

> There is recruiting in various degrees in every intercollegiate sport, from crew to girls' basketball and from the Houston golf dynasty that began in the mid-50's to Southern California importing sprinters and jumpers from Jamaica.
>
> J. ROBERT EVANS

> The fundamental causes of the defects in American college athletics are too much commercialism and a negligent attitude towards the educational opportunity for which the college exists.
>
> CARNEGIE FOUNDATION, 1929

> [*Collier's* magazine, in 1905, reported that] Walter Eckersall, All-American quarterback, enrolled at Chicago three credits short of the entrance requirement and his teammate, Leo Detray, entered the school before he even graduated high school. In addition the University of Minnesota paid two players outright to play in a single game (Nebraska: 1902). A quarterback and an end also from Minnesota admitted shaving points during the 1903 Beloit game.
>
> JOSEPH DURSO

Examining the Sources

Your paragraph will focus on recruiting high school stars, as opposed to developing student athletes who enter college by the ordinary admissions procedure. Which of these ideas and observations should be included in the paragraph? And which statements should be represented by *paraphrase* or by *direct quotation*?

> I think in the long run every coach must recognize this basic principle, or face the alumni firing squad. Recruiting is the crux of building a championship football team.
>
> STEVE SLOAN

This very broad generalization seems quotable at first because it sums up the topic so well; but, in fact, it does not advance your argument any further. Therefore, you need not include Coach Sloan's statement if your topic sentence makes the same point. (In general, you should write your own topic sentences rather than letting your sources write them for you.) The phrase "alumni firing squad" might be useful to quote in a later paragraph, in a discussion of the specific influence of alumni on recruiting.

> Athletics is creating a monster. Recruiting is getting to be cancerous.
>
> DALE BROWN

Coach Brown's choice of images—"cancerous" and "monster"—is certainly vivid; but the sentence as a whole is no more than a generalized opinion about recruiting, not an *explanation* of why the situation is so monstrous. Don't quote Brown for the sake of two words.

> You don't out-coach people, you out-recruit them.
>
> PAUL "BEAR" BRYANT

This is the first statement that has advanced a specific idea: the coach may have a *choice* between building a winning team through recruiting and building a winning team through good coaching; but recruiting, not coaching, wins games. Coach Bryant, then, is not just making a rhetorical point, as the first two coaches seem to be. His seven-word sentence would make a good introduction to or summation of a point that deserves full discussion.

The remaining four statements suggest a wider range of approach and style.

> Walter Eckersall, All-American quarterback, enrolled at Chicago three credits short of the entrance requirement and his teammate, Leo Detray, entered the school before he even graduated high school. In addition, the University of Minnesota paid two players outright to play in a single game (Nebraska: 1902). A quarterback and an end also from Minnesota admitted shaving points during the 1903 Beloit game.
>
> JOSEPH DURSO

This passage emphasizes corruption more than recruiting and indicates that commercialism is nothing new in college athletics. Although the information is interesting, it is presented as a list of facts, and the language is not worth quoting. You may, however, want to summarize the example in your own words.

> The fundamental causes of the defects in American college athletics are too much commercialism and a negligent attitude towards the educational opportunity for which the college exists.
>
> CARNEGIE FOUNDATION

This extract from the 1929 Carnegie Foundation study is phrased in abstract language that is characteristic of foundation reports and academic writing in general. The foundation raises an important idea: an athlete recruited to win games (and earn fame and fortune) is likely to ignore the primary reason for going to college—to acquire an education. But there is no compelling reason to quote (rather than paraphrase) this statement. Remember that *you include quotations in your essay to enhance your presentation*; the quotation marks automatically prepare the reader for special words and phrasing. But the prose here is too colorless and abstract to justify quotation.

> There is recruiting in varying degrees in every intercollegiate sport, from crew to girls' basketball and from the Houston golf dynasty that began in the mid-50's to Southern California importing sprinters and jumpers from Jamaica.
>
> J. ROBERT EVANS

This statement presents a quite different, more detailed level of information about recruiting in several sports. Will these references be at all meaningful to the reader who is not familiar with the "Houston golf dynasty" or Jamaican track stars? To know that intensive recruitment is not limited to cash sports, such as football, is interesting, but such specifics date too quickly to be interesting to most readers.

> It is an athletic maxim that a man with no special coaching skills can win games if he recruits well and that a tactician without talented players is a man soon without a job.
>
> KENNETH DENLINGER

Largely because of parallel construction, this statement sounds both sharp and solid. In much the same way as Coach Bryant's seven words, Kenneth Denlinger sums up the contrast between coaching and recruiting, and suggests which one has the edge. Because the statement gives the reader something substantial to think about and because it is well phrased, Denlinger is probably worth quoting.

Writing the Paragraph

Should the writer include the statements by Bryant and by Denlinger, both of which say essentially the same thing? While Bryant's firsthand comment is terse and authoritative, Denlinger's is more complete and self-explanatory. A solution might be to include both, at different points in the paragraph, with Bryant cited at the end to sum up the idea that has been developed. Of course, the other five sources need not be excluded from the paragraph. Rather, if you wish, all five may be referred to, by paraphrase or brief reference, with their authors' names cited.

Here is one way of integrating this set of statements into a paragraph. Of the nine sentences, four (indicated in italics) cite no sources: the first two establish the paragraph's topic; two are used later to introduce transitional points. The other five sentences cite sources as supporting evidence. (Note that the sources are documented using MLA style; the bibliography has been omitted. MLA style is explained on pp. 452–462.)

In college athletics, what is the best way for a school to win games? Should a strong team be gradually built up by training ordinary students from scratch, or should the process be shortened and success be assured by actively recruiting players who already know how to win? The first method may be more consistent with the traditional amateurism of college athletics, but as early as 1929, the Carnegie Foundation complained that the focus of college sports had shifted from education to the material advantages of winning (Denlinger 22). Even earlier, in 1903, there were several instances of players without academic qualifications who were "hired" to guarantee victory (Durso 6). *And in recent years excellence of recruiting has become the most important skill for a coach to possess.* Kenneth Denlinger has observed, "It is an athletic maxim that a man with no special coaching skills can win games if he recruits well and that a tactician without talented players is a man soon without a job" (3). *It follows, then, that a coach who wants to keep his job is likely to concentrate on spotting and collecting talent for his team.* Coaches from LSU, Alabama, and Texas Tech all testify that good recruiting has first priority throughout college athletics (McDermott 17; Mano 41; Sloan 106). According to Bear Bryant of Alabama: "You don't out-coach people, you out-recruit them" (Mano 41).

Writing an Introduction

The introduction presents a *preview* of your essay, announcing the topic and the method(s) you are likely to use to present that topic (explanation or analysis or persuasion). Often, the introduction will include a statement of the thesis, although with some strategies (notably, problem and solution), it can be preferable to indicate the problem at the beginning and allow the argument and evidence to set the stage for a presentation of the thesis toward the end of the essay.

The introduction also has a *marketing* function. You want to encourage your reader to move past the first paragraph or two and into the body of the essay. To do so, you need to do more than set out your wares; you have to make the shop window look attractive. Using compelling or intriguing language can catch the reader's attention. Including an example or (if not too long) an anecdote can make the reader feel interested in or sympathetic to the topic that you propose to explore.

Introductions by Professional Writers

Here are the introductions of two essays by professional authors. As you read, consider whether the author tells you what he is going to write about and whether—and why—he makes you want to continue reading.

David Brooks, a writer, editor, and commentator on public affairs, wrote "People Like Us" for *Atlantic*. Michael Bérubé, who teaches English and Cultural Studies at Pennsylvania State University, published "How to End Grade Inflation" in the *Chronicle of Higher Education*.

> Maybe it's time to admit the obvious. We don't really care about diversity all that much in America, even though we talk about it a great deal. Maybe somewhere in this country there is a truly diverse neighborhood in which a black Pentecostal minister lives next to a white anti-globalization activist, who lives next to an Asian short-order cook, who lives next to a professional golfer, who lives next to a post-modern-literature professor and a cardiovascular surgeon. But I have never been to or heard of that neighborhood. Instead, what I have seen all around the country is people making strenuous efforts to group themselves with people who are basically like themselves.
>
> DAVID BROOKS, from "People Like Us"

> Last month, Princeton University announced it would combat grade inflation by proposing that A-minuses, A's and A-pluses be awarded to no more than the top 35 percent of students in any course. For those of us in higher education, the news has come as a shock, almost as if Princeton had declared that spring in central New Jersey would begin promptly on March 21, with pleasant temperatures in the 60s and 70s through the end of the semester. For until now, grade inflation was like the weather: it got worse every year, or at least everyone said so, and yet hardly anybody did anything about it.
>
> MICHAEL BÉRUBÉ, from "How to End Grade Inflation"

Brooks's introduction does everything that an introduction is supposed to do. You are quickly made aware of his *topic and its scope* (social diversity in America), his *intention* (analysis through contrast between good intentions and reality), and his *thesis* (we try to fool ourselves that we live in culturally diverse communities, but we do not). Brooks compels your attention with a striking, brief first sentence that makes you wonder what "the obvious" is going to be. Then he proceeds to attack what he regards as a national illusion, citing a string of concrete examples that, by its very length, makes you want to know what cultural type will be mentioned next. He finishes the paragraph—and his introduction—by asserting the other half of the contrast contained in his thesis: people really don't want diversity. By the end of that paragraph, Brooks's intended audience—the readers of *Atlantic*—are likely to be hooked.

In contrast, Bérubé begins his introduction much more traditionally: he tells his readers about Princeton's decision to stop grade inflation and thus provides *the context* for his essay. We know the topic and scope (grade inflation in American universities), but we don't know much as yet about his intention and his thesis. What is striking in this introduction is the use of irony: by drawing an analogy between Princeton's proposal and ideal weather conditions, Bérubé lets us know just how unsatisfactory a situation (like a rainy spring) grade inflation is and how desirable (but unlikely) it would be to find a solution to the problem. Since his audience is his fellow academics, who probably share his concerns, his readers will want to know how Bérubé proposes to solve the problem.

Introductions from Student Essays

Students introducing a research essay can provide just as comprehensive a preview of their topic, scope, intention, and thesis. What is often missing is the *vivid example* or the *compelling choice of words* to make the reader want to continue reading. Consider the following example:

> 1.   As more and more women in the United States work outside the home for longer hours, their children are often cared for by workers in day care centers or by babysitters. Some women work for economic reasons, because they are single mothers or because their families can't manage on a single salary. Many of these women would really like to stay home with their children but feel they have no choice but to go out of the home to work. Others have experienced housewife blues or have come to believe, with the feminist movement, that they can't be fulfilled without a career. In fact, psychologists have studied the children of working mothers and have concluded that being deprived of a mother's care and attention can cause lasting adverse effects on children. What can a working mother do to prevent this from happening?

Here, we have a straightforward presentation of a *problem* that, presumably, the writer will attempt to solve—or, at least, analyze and clarify—in the body of the essay. We can expect to see statistics and studies cited as well as the opinions of experts in the field. This is likely to be a solid essay that makes its point convincingly. But does the introduction make you want to read it?

> 2.   My grandparents emigrated to this country from Italy. They were eager to take advantage of the opportunities America offered and, in exchange, tried to become good citizens in the community where they settled. In a very few years, they had become completely assimilated, speaking and behaving more American than the third-generation Americans around them. For my grandparents, America was a melting

pot; for immigrants today, it is merely a host nation that provides the opportunity to have a better life without requiring or even encouraging them to give their cultural allegiance in return. Our immigration policy will never be successful, as it used to be, until there is the expectation that immigrants will leave their old cultures behind and think, speak, and act like their American neighbors.

This introduction is anchored by the *personal example* in the first few sentences, which leads into the contrast between immigration fifty years ago and immigration now, expressed as a thesis in the last sentence. Persuading readers to accept this thesis will surely require the citation of facts, statistics, and expert opinion, not just examples and anecdotal evidence. But the story of the writer's grandparents is compelling and makes the reader want to find out why—or whether—experiences like these have passed into history.

Using Visuals and Other Media as Sources

You can present ideas and cite evidence visually and aurally as well as through printed words. Some of the professional essays and articles in this book are accompanied by pictures and graphics, some of the exercises include videos, and the model research essays in Chapter 11 are accompanied by pictures and other media. Let's consider how the presence of various kinds of images and sounds can give the reader a more vivid and immediate understanding of the author's meaning.

Understanding the Impact of Visual Sources

One essential way of using visuals is to present data through *tables and figures* such as *charts, graphs, and maps.* These kinds of visuals generally compare information in separate categories at different times or in different places. In this way, visuals serve as supporting evidence, used to make a point succinctly. In "The Weight of the World" (p. 7), Don Peck finds it easier to use maps than words to raise complex issues about increasing obesity in the United States. Peck is dealing with two sets of variables: location (levels of obesity vary among the 48 states) and time (levels of obesity in each of the states varied between 1991 and 2000). By using three maps to provide snapshots over time and shading to indicate relative levels of obesity, Peck gets his point across visually.

Pictures—photographs and drawings—provide the reader with an instant impression of the author's point. Images can attract readers to the text, interest them in the topic, and encourage them to see how the thesis develops. Photographs are especially useful to authors who are writing about historical topics and want to provide readers with a sense of the period. As a context for her description of 1950s shopping centers (pp. 136–137), Lizabeth Cohen includes pictures of typical shoppers. We know that the photos are authentic because the caption cites the R.H. Macy & Co. Inc., *1957 Annual Report* and, equally important, the archival collection where Cohen found that report. You'll note that, for all the pictures used in this book, credit is given to the source—the photographer and/or the agency distributing the picture—in the caption.

Often, a picture works better than words to drive a point home. In *Glamour*, Stephen Gundle is trying to show that a "fabulous and enormous American car"—which every citizen could aspire to own—represented the "optimism and opulence" of the 1950s: "Objects took on a special exaggerated quality that expressed confidence, excitement, and even joy." But that sense of endless expansion and boundless possibility, expressed through material objects, doesn't really come across until you see the picture of the 1950 Studebaker that was featured in newspaper and magazine ads (see Figure 9-7). The design suggests a cross between a tank and a space ship, and was intended to evoke the new Age of the Airplane. In fact, inanimate objects, if they are well-photographed, can immediately capture the reader's attention. Rachelle Bergstein's account of women's love affair with "glamorous, high-quality shoes" in *Women from the Ankle Down* is encapsulated in the photo of a pair of Vivier (for Dior) shoes that epitomize the elegance of the 50s (p. 142). The ornamentation (at once blatant and subtle), the many shades of gray, and the perfectly sculpted heel justify the inclusion of these "evening boots" in the collections of the Metropolitan Museum of Art.

Visuals can also be used to enliven dull facts. In *Beyond Our Mission: America Spends While the World Saves*, Sheldon M. Garon is writing about the efforts made in Great Britain during World War II to encourage people to put their money into savings banks and war bonds. He describes the news coverage, the sound trucks and recordings, the radio broadcasts and films that were commissioned to get the message home to the nation. So far, so boring. What catches the eye is the full-page cartoon-like poster (see Figure 9-8) that the British government used to reinforce its propaganda about savings.

© Car Culture/Corbis

Figure 9-7 1950 Studebaker Commander Convertible, with its famous "bullet-nose"

Figure 9-8 Squanderbug poster, Britain, 1943

"Squanderbug, alias Hitler's Pal" made a hit in war-time London, and also adds a humorous and human note to Garon's book. An even more effective use of humor would be the inclusion of a late-eighteenth-century French cartoon (p. 167) in an essay on the history of fashion. Exaggeration to the point of absurdity makes it abundantly clear when fashion trends have become ridiculous.

Still images and moving pictures often directly appeal to the emotions, with the reader subtly encouraged to accept the author's assumptions and conclusions. A great deal depends on the *choice* of picture. Kwame Anthony Appiah's dispassionate description of foot-binding in China (pp. 402–404) may seem interesting, perhaps even amusing, as an historical curiosity. (In fact, *The Honor Code* does not provide any pictures of this process; the visuals accompanying the reading in *WFS* (pp. 405–406) were included specifically for this edition.) If the charming picture of the colorful little boot were the only image that you saw, the impression of an eccentric but basically harmless custom might be sustained. But the photograph of the unbound foot, with the toes turned downward and gnarled, warped to the point of being less than human, brings home the point that this quaint custom was actually a form of institutionalized abuse.

Similarly intense emotions are evoked by the videos of the Battle at Wounded Knee, whose URLs are included in Exercise 28 (p. 379). The still photographs of members of the tribe, the contrasting images of Big Foot in his prime and near to death, the weariness of the Indians and the hardiness of the soldiers—all suggest the inevitability of the massacre that is about to happen. The makers of the films are cleverly using these grainy historical photographs to gain sympathy and support for their cause. It is, therefore, almost jarring for the viewer when the film cuts to scenes—in color—of the battleground today, as well as interviews with descendants of the massacred tribes. What has involved the viewer was the sense of being there at the time, and moving 120 years ahead breaks the spell.

Perhaps the most effective use of still photographs in a literary text can be found in James Agee and Walker Evans's book about the Great Depression, *Let Us Now Praise Famous Men*. Evans's photograph of George Gudger (the pseudonym Evans used for sharecropper Floyd Burroughs) on the porch of a shack, with three downtrodden children and a skinny dog conveys the depths of poverty and depression that prevailed in 1930s Appalachia (Figure 9-9). But the second photograph of George Gudger, with his family (Figure 9-10), creates a more positive image: the landscape may be bare, but there's a sense of purpose about all the Gudgers which suggests that they're capable of enduring until better times arrive. Interestingly enough, the second photo was not included in *Let Us Now Praise Famous Men*. In *Believing Is Seeing: Observations on the Mysteries of Photography*, filmmaker Errol Morris interviews historian William Stott, who suggests that the publishers were determined to create and maintain an image of these sharecroppers as bitter and defeated people. In the second photo, the Gudger family "is just radiating life and virility and joy....We don't need to worry about them."

Whether for propaganda purposes or to maintain the downbeat effect of the book, the pictures were chosen for their aura of futility, even despair.

Figure 9-9 Walker Evans, "Floyd Burroughs with Tengle children"

Photo by Walker Evans/George Eastman House/ Getty Images

Figure 9-10 Walker Evans, "Burroughs Family, Hale County, Alabama"

You don't need to use images of people to make your readers comprehend the seriousness of your topic. Places and objects will do just as well. In a book entitled *Boredom*, Peter Toohey uses a picture of a prison cell to capture the futility experienced by convicts locked up in a small, bare room. Toohey's point is that confinement is counter-productive: the boredom of life in prison "benefits no one, neither the prison nor the community at large. Prison life shows the danger of enforced chronic boredom. If the boredom is not remedied it will drive a person to anger and to violence, to dangerous diversions such as narcotics, and to depression...."

AP Photo/Joel Page

Figure 9-11 A spartan prison cell in Warren, Maine

Whether prison is or isn't a suitable punishment for crime is not what the picture illustrates. Its effect is to make the viewer recoil from the meaninglessness of a life lived in these surroundings.

It's hard to pinpoint the borderline between involving and depressing your readers. If you include grim, painful images, then they must not be put in your essay just to shock the reader; they must serve as evidence to support your explanation or argument. In an article about the work of non-profit organizations (NPOs) during major disasters, should an author show pictures of victims being aided or victims deteriorating because no help has arrived? Obviously, the choice to some extent depends on the article's thesis. But the pictures should also be reasonably representative of the facts: if data indicates that NPOs used their available resources effectively in a particular relief effort, then that's what should be depicted. If you want to demonstrate that the NPOs were too under-funded or too incompetent to deliver sufficient aid—and if the facts support that view—then it would be reasonable to appeal to the reader's compassion by showing injured, untended earthquake victims or a village decimated by a tsunami.

Using Visuals and Media in Your Essay

How can pictures, videos, or music serve to support your thesis and enhance the effectiveness of your essay?

- If you were writing about the effects of plastic surgery on teenagers with facial defects, you would make the greatest impact by including "before and after" *photographs*.

- If you were explaining the connection between convicts' living conditions and the likelihood of their rehabilitation, you would want to include some *photographs or diagrams* of typical prison cells.

- If you were analyzing the effect of automobile commercials on consumer choices, you would want your reader to see several striking examples and would therefore supplement your own summaries of the action by providing *links to some filmed commercials*.

- If you were advocating limits to be set on the height of buildings in your city, you would find *photographs*—or take them yourself—of the skyline as it is now, as well as prepare *diagrams* or *computer-generated images* showing the relative heights of the proposed new buildings juxtaposed among the old ones.

- If you were describing a moment in history—the day Prohibition ended in 1933 and people could drink alcohol again, or the day Facebook first went online in 2004, you might evoke the era and draw your reader into the mood by attaching a *playlist* or *soundtrack* of music popular at that time.

For most topics, your instructor will expect you to support your thesis successfully through your text alone. Images, charts, videos, music—any nonverbal material will serve only as an extra added attraction, not the main event. And you should certainly avoid including a picture or other media simply for its own sake, rather than for its ability to illuminate your work. Still, a carefully chosen image or graphic is likely to fully engage your reader's attention and therefore increase the effectiveness of your essay. David Morgan's account of the strange occurrence at Lake Tunguska is definitely enhanced by a map of the region (p. 501) and a picture of the blast site (p. 508). Many readers will instantly recognize the stills from the films—*The Cabinet of Dr. Caligari*, *Freaks*, and *Psycho*—discussed in Bethany Dettmore's essay about horror movies. Dettmore uses these pictures (pp. 487–492) to illustrate (in the first two films) her point about the ambiguous nature of "monster" figures—half-frightening, half-sympathetic—as well as the transition, in *Psycho*, to films in which "normal" people are actually the monsters.

Some of the research topics discussed in the earlier chapters of *Writing from Sources* would benefit from the inclusion of visuals or other media:

- It's easy to find photographs of *Lawrence of Arabia*. The one shown on p. 330 would be appropriate if you were writing about Lawrence's later years, but not if you were exclusively concerned with his desert campaigns. Of course, the David Lean film is always available to cite as a reference point, and, as was indicated in Chapter 7, there are other videos to view and discuss that might provide an added dimension of interest to your essay.

- An essay about *excessive drinking at a university* could be accompanied by tables or line graphs showing instances of emergency room treatment or assaults or class attendance over time, as linked to documented consumption of alcohol. The tabulated results of any surveys or transcripts of interviews that you might conduct for this essay would certainly need to be included as an appendix (as Bethany Dettmore does in her "horror film" essay). Would you choose to include photographs or videos—your own or taken from a commercial source—of students after a hard night's drinking? Possibly, if the photographs are truly representative of the situation that you are analyzing in your essay, and if the people in the photograph have given their permission for the use of these images.

- Similar kinds of visuals—even videos—could be used in an essay about *responses to beggars*. Here you would want to consider whether the pity evoked by a picture of an unkempt, emaciated beggar would enhance or detract from the effectiveness of your essay. Again, this depends on your thesis.

- If your topic were *animal rights*, you might find it hard to resist including a picture or footage of a pathetic dog or cat to engage the reader's sympathies. But you can carry pathos too far: a laboratory specimen bristling with electrodes or twitching under torture might serve to repel rather than engage your reader's interest.

There are some *technical points* to consider when you incorporate visuals or media into your essay:

- Unless you are submitting your essay electronically, make sure that your printer can handle the *production of any photographs or graphics* that you've chosen. Don't assume that you can produce a clear copy and incorporate it into your essay at the last moment. If you are preparing your own data (such as the results of a survey), spend some time considering how to present the information, what to include and what to omit, what categories to use, and whether a table, graph, or chart is most appropriate. Then tabulate the data well in advance as you may run into difficulties formatting the information on your computer.

- Consider the *placement* of visuals. If you are integrating the pictures or graphics into your essay electronically, put each one as near as possible to the related point in your text. Make sure that the font that you use for the tables/charts is readable, but don't use such a large font that it dominates your text. Photographs should be an appropriate *size*: the details should be clear, but the pictures should not overwhelm the words.

- Visuals that include data should be explained and interpreted, either in a *caption* or in the main text. Don't assume that the reader will understand all their implications and your reasons for including them. Photos may be self-explanatory; but, at a minimum, every visual should be identified with a caption that acknowledges its source. Be aware that you may need to apply for *permission* to include a visual in your essay.

- *Using other media* presents a parallel set of technical problems. If you want your instructor to see a video or listen to a song, whether it's at the core of your essay or merely complements your research, you must make sure that you clearly indicate the place where it can be seen or heard (assuming that you've found it on the Web), preferably by *citing it in your bibliography*. (The text of your essay is probably not the best place to put a lengthy URL.) The reason for including the video or the song—its relevance to your essay—must be *explicitly conveyed in words* somewhere in your text, just as you would introduce and explain any other source. You can't expect it to speak for itself. If the lyrics are meaningful to you *in the context of your essay*, then by all means include a portion of those lyrics in your text—and explain why the lines are important.

- Other forms of media that might be incorporated into your essay include *lectures and broadcast interviews* (radio or television). In an essay about social media or about gender issues, you might want to cite a short *TED Talk* given by Johanna Blakely in 2010 on "Social Media and the End of Gender." Again, the key ideas that you take away from this lecture should be first written down and then introduced in your text so that your reader can understand their significance to the development of your essay.

- Keep in mind that *some forms of media are time-consuming to review*. Your instructor can easily scan the printed pages of your sources, or examine a graphic, or look at a picture, or even glance through the transcript of an interview. They can all be submitted with your essay and your instructor will have them at hand when your essay is read. But films and videos and playlists can take time to access and then to listen to or watch. With the best will in the world, your instructor may not have enough time to engage fully with these supplementary features of your essay, however relevant and interesting they may be. *If you have gone to the trouble of locating and using these sources, it's imperative that you write about them in the text of your essay, so your instructor will understand why they are important to you and to your work.*

ASSIGNMENT 7B: Organizing and Writing the Research Essay

A. Using the topic and preliminary bibliography that you developed for Assignment 7A, p. 350, write down a tentative list of points based on your own ideas and the information and evidence provided by your sources.

B. Develop an outline based on that list. As you do so, consider a possible thesis for the essay and a strategy that will best develop your thesis and accommodate the evidence found in your sources.

C. After you have compiled and organized a substantial list of ideas and developed a tentative thesis, reread key passages from your sources, cross-referencing the items on your list with relevant source material. While you do not have to use up everything in all your notes, you should include all relevant points.

D. Develop this outline into an eight-to-ten-page essay.

·10·
Acknowledging Sources

Research means reading, absorbing, and writing about the ideas and the words of other writers; inevitably, opportunities to plagiarize—by accident or by intention—proliferate. You must therefore understand exactly what constitutes plagiarism.

Understanding Plagiarism

> *Plagiarism is the* unacknowledged *use of another person's work, in the form of original ideas, strategies, and research, or another person's writing, in the form of sentences, phrases, and innovative terminology.*

The Moral Rationale

- Plagiarism is the equivalent of *theft*, but the stolen goods are intellectual rather than material.
- Like other acts of theft, plagiarism is against the law. The copyright law governing publications requires that authorship be acknowledged and (if the borrowed material is long enough and especially if it is used commercially) that payment be offered to the writer.
- Plagiarism violates the moral law that people should take pride in, as well as profit from, the fruits of their labor. Put yourself in the victim's place. Think about the best idea that you ever had, or the paragraph that you worked hardest on in your last paper. Now, imagine yourself finding exactly the same idea or exactly the same sentences in someone

else's essay, with no mention of your name, with no quotation marks. Would you accept the theft of your property without protest?

- Plagiarists are not only robbers, but also cheats. People who bend or break the rules of authorship, who do not do their own work, will be rightly distrusted by their instructors or future employers, who may equate a history of plagiarism with laziness, incompetence, or dishonesty. One's future rarely depends on getting a better grade on a single assignment; on the other hand, one's lifelong reputation may be damaged if one resorts to plagiarism in order to get that grade.

The Practical Rationale

Plagiarism is a bad risk for, as you observed in Exercise 14, an experienced teacher can usually detect plagiarized work. If there is any disparity in style within a student's essay, instructors can easily do a Google search to compare that material with material available on the Web. If you can't write your own essay, you are unlikely to do a good enough job of adapting someone else's work to your needs.

The excuse of "inadvertent plagiarism" is sometimes used to explain including undocumented material from the Internet in a research essay. Cutting and pasting material from Web sites may be an easy way of meeting a paper deadline, but it will inevitably invite a charge of plagiarism unless you include the sites in your bibliography. And even if you properly acknowledge your Internet sources, you must still paraphrase and/or put quotation marks around the text that you're using, rather than just pasting it in and leaving it unchanged. As Maurice Isserman suggests in the *Chronicle of Higher Education* (2 May 2003), instructors are unlikely to buy "the argument that the invention of the Internet somehow makes our old notions of intellectual property obsolete." Borrowing from an Internet source is just as much plagiarism as borrowing from a published work.

If you resort to using a paper-writing service instead of doing your own work, you are just as likely to get caught. Software that detects plagiarism—like that available at turnitin.com—enables instructors to back up their suspicions by checking a dubious paper against a vast database of previously plagiarized essays. Nor should you use the excuse that borrowing words and ideas is increasingly common practice in the world of business or government. Here is Maurice Isserman again, speaking for the vast majority of instructors: "As learning communities, colleges and universities are governed by a different set of rules than those governing the worlds of politics and commerce. What we do is teach students to develop their own voices and establish ownership of the words they use."

Finally, you will not receive greater glory by plagiarizing. On the contrary, most instructors believe that students who work hard to understand the ideas of their sources, apply them to the topic, and express them in their own words deserve high grades for their mastery of the basic skills of academic writing. There are, however, occasions when your instructor may ask you not to use secondary sources. In such cases, you would be wise to do no background reading at all, so that the temptation to borrow "inadvertently" will not arise.

When to Document Information

By acknowledging your sources, you tell your reader that someone other than yourself is the source of ideas and words in your essay. Acknowledgment—or *documentation*—usually means using *quotation marks* and *citation of the author's name*—techniques that are by now familiar to you. There are guidelines to help you decide what can and what cannot safely be used without acknowledgment, and these guidelines mostly favor complete documentation.

> *By conservative standards, you should cite a source for all facts and evidence in your essay that you did not know before you started your research.*

Knowing when to acknowledge the source of your information largely depends on common sense. For example, it is not necessary to document the fact that there are fifty states in the United States or that Shakespeare wrote *Hamlet* since these facts are *common knowledge*. On the other hand, you may be presenting more obscure information, like facts about electric railroads, which you have known since you were a child, but which may be unfamiliar to your readers. Technically, you are not obliged to document that information; but your audience will trust you more and will be better informed if you do so. In general, if the facts are not unusual, if they can be found in a number of standard sources, and if they do not vary from source to source or year to year, then they can be considered common knowledge, and the source need not be acknowledged.

Let's assume that you are preparing to document your essay about *Lawrence of Arabia*. The basic facts about the film—the year of release, the cast, the director, the technicians, the Academy Awards won by the film—might be regarded as common knowledge and not require documentation. But the cost of the film, the amount grossed in its first year, the location of the premiere, and the circumstances of production are relatively unfamiliar facts that you would almost certainly have to look up in a reference book. An authority on film who includes such facts in a study of epic films is expected to be familiar with this information and, in most cases, would not be expected to provide documentation. But a student writing on the same subject would be well advised to do so.

Similarly, if you are writing about the most recent Olympics and know who won a specific medal because you witnessed the victory on television, then it would probably not be necessary to cite a source. More complex issues surrounding the Olympics—such as the use of steroids—are less clearly in the realm of common knowledge. You may remember news broadcasts about which athletes may or may not have taken steroids before a competition, but the circumstances are hardly so memorable in their details that you would be justified in writing about them from memory. The articles that you consult to jog your memory would have to be documented.

Perhaps one of the ideas that you are writing about was firmly in your mind—the product of your own intellect—long before you started to work on your topic. Nevertheless, if you come across a version of that idea during your research, you should cite the source, indicating in the text that the idea was as much your own as the author's.

What if, while working on an essay, you develop a new idea of your own, stimulated by one of your readings? You should acknowledge the source of inspiration and, perhaps, describe how and why it affected you. (For example: "My idea for shared assignments is an extension of McKeachie's discussion of peer tutoring.") The reader should be made aware of your debt to your source as well as your independent effort.

Plagiarism: Stealing Ideas

If you present another person's ideas as your own, you are plagiarizing *even if you use your own words*. To illustrate, the paragraph on the left, by Leo Gurko, is taken from a book, *Ernest Hemingway and the Pursuit of Heroism*; the paragraph on the right comes from a student essay on Ernest Hemingway. Gurko is listed in the student's bibliography and is cited as the source of several quotations elsewhere in the essay. But the student does not mention Gurko anywhere in *this* paragraph.

Source: Leo Gurko

The Hemingways put themselves on short rations, ate, drank, and entertained as little as possible, pounced eagerly on the small checks that arrived in the mail as payment for accepted stories, and were intensely conscious of being poor. The sensation was not altogether unpleasant. Their extreme youth, the excitement of living abroad, the sense of making a fresh start, even the unexpected joy of parenthood, gave their poverty a romantic flavor.

Student Essay

Despite all the economies that they had to make and all the pleasures that they had to do without, the Hemingways rather enjoyed the experience of being poor. They knew that this was a more romantic kind of life, unlike anything they'd known before, and the feeling that everything in Paris was fresh and new, even their new baby, made them sharply aware of the glamorous aspects of being poor.

The *language* of the student paragraph does not require quotation marks, but unless Gurko is acknowledged, the student will be guilty of plagiarism. These impressions of the Hemingways, these insights into their motivation, would not have been possible without Gurko's biography—and Gurko deserves the credit for having done the research and for having formulated the interpretations. After reading extensively about Hemingway, the student may have absorbed these biographical details so thoroughly that he feels as if he had always known them. But the knowledge is still secondhand, and the source must be acknowledged.

Plagiarism: Stealing Words

Acknowledging the author by putting his or her name in a parenthetical note does not allow you to mix up your own language with that of your sources. The author's name tells your reader nothing at all about who is responsible for the choice of words. Equally important, borrowing language carelessly, perhaps in an effort to use paraphrase, often garbles the author's meaning.

Here is an excerpt from a student essay about the Norwegian playwright, Henrik Ibsen, together with the relevant passage from its source, P. F. D. Tennant's *Ibsen's Dramatic Technique*:

Source: P. F. D. Tennant	**Student Essay**
When writing [Ibsen] was sometimes under the influence of hallucinations, and was unable to distinguish between reality and the creatures of his imagination. While working on *A Doll's House* he was nervous and retiring and lived in a world alone, which gradually became peopled with his own imaginary characters. Once he suddenly remarked to his wife: "Now I have seen Nora [the heroine of *A Doll's House*]. She came right up to me and put her hand on my shoulder." "How was she dressed?" asked his wife. "She had a simple blue cotton dress," he replied without hesitation....So intimate had Ibsen become with Nora while at work on *A Doll's House* that when John	While Ibsen was still writing *A Doll's House*, his involvement with the characters led to his experiencing hallucinations that at times completely incapacitated his ability to distinguish between reality and the creations of his imagination. He was nervous, distant, and lived in a secluded world. Gradually this world became populated with his creations. One day he had the following exchange with his wife: Ibsen: Now I have seen Nora. She came right up to me and put her hand on my shoulder. Wife: How was she dressed? Ibsen: (without hesitation) She had a simple blue dress.

Paulsen asked him why she was called Nora, Ibsen replied in a matter-of-fact tone: "She was really called Leonora, you know, but everyone called her Nora since she was the spoilt child of the family."

Ibsen's involvement with his characters was so deep that when John Paulsen asked Ibsen why the heroine was named Nora, Ibsen replied in a very nonchalant tone of voice that originally she was called Leonora, but that everyone called her Nora, the way one would address the favorite child in the family (Tennant 26).

The parenthetical note at the end of the student's paragraph may give credit to Tennant's book, but it fails to indicate the debt that the student owes to Tennant's *phrasing* and *vocabulary*. Phrases like "distinguish between reality and the creatures of his imagination" must be placed in quotation marks, and so should the exchange between Ibsen and his wife. Arranging these sentences as dialogue is not adequate acknowledgment. Moreover, many of the substituted words change Tennant's meaning: "distant" does not mean "retiring"; "a secluded world" is not "a world alone"; "nonchalant" is a very different quality from "matter-of-fact." Writing like this is neither quotation nor successful paraphrase; it is doubly bad, for it both *plagiarizes* the source and *garbles* it.

Avoiding Plagiarism

- You must acknowledge a source using an appropriate form of documentation whenever you summarize, paraphrase, or quote ideas or information derived from another person or organization's work.

- You are obliged to use documentation whether the work has been published in print, has appeared on the Web, has been performed in public, has been communicated to you through an interview or e-mail, or exists as an unpublished manuscript.

- You must use two kinds of documentation when you quote a source:

  1. *You acknowledge the source of the information or ideas* through a system of documentation that provides complete publication information about the source and possibly through the citation of the author's name in your sentence.

  2. *You acknowledge the source of the exact wording* through quotation marks.

EXERCISE 32: Understanding When to Document Information

Here are some facts about the explosion of the space shuttle *Challenger*. Consider which of these facts would require documentation in a research essay—and why.

1. On January 28, 1986, the space shuttle *Challenger* exploded shortly after takeoff from Cape Canaveral.
2. It was unusually cold in Florida on the day of the launch.
3. One of the *Challenger*'s booster rockets experienced a sudden and unforeseen drop in pressure 10 seconds before the explosion.
4. The explosion was later attributed to the failure of an O-ring seal.
5. On board the *Challenger* was a $100 million communications satellite.
6. Christa McAuliffe, a high school social studies teacher in Concord, New Hampshire, was a member of the crew.
7. McAuliffe's mission duties included conducting two classroom lessons taught from the shuttle.
8. After the explosion, classes at the high school were canceled.
9. Another crew member, Judith Resnick, had a Ph.D. in electrical engineering.
10. At the time of the explosion, President Ronald Reagan was preparing to meet with network TV news correspondents to brief them on the upcoming State of the Union address.
11. The State of the Union address was postponed for a week.

EXERCISE 33: Understanding Plagiarism

In 2003, the *New York Times* reported that Brian VanDeMark, an associate professor of history at the U.S. Naval Academy (USNA), had been charged with plagiarizing the content and language of portions of books by four authors. More than 40 passages in VanDeMark's book about the origins of the atomic bomb were "identical, or nearly identical" to material published by the four authors, yet these passages contained neither acknowledgments nor quotation marks. In many instances, only a few words had been changed.

The *Chronicle of Higher Education* later reported that, as a result of these charges, the USNA had demoted VanDeMark, removed his tenure, and cut his salary. In effect, he was going to have to "re-establish his professional qualifications" as if he had just been newly hired.

Figure 10-1 shows, side by side, as published in the *Times*, parallel excerpts from VanDeMark's *Pandora's Keepers: Nine Men and the Atomic Bomb* on the left and from works by Robert S. Norris, William Lanouette, and Richard Rhodes on the right. Examine them, compare them, and determine whether, in your opinion, VanDeMark has been guilty of plagiarism.

Comparing Notes

Brian
VanDeMark
▼

Other
Authors
▼

Brian VanDeMark	Other Authors
Groves treated Oppenheimer with more respect and deference than he did any other project scientist — almost delicately, like a fine musical instrument that needed to be played just right. (Page 111)	On Groves's part he treated Oppenheimer delicately, like a fine instrument that needed to be played just right. (Robert S. Norris, *Racing for the Bomb*, Steerforth, 2002, page 243.)
The statistics were staggering: 540 buildings, more than 600 miles of roads, 158 miles of railroad track, vast quantities of water, concrete, lumber, steel, and pipe. Eventually, 132,000 workers (working 126 million man-hours) were hired... (Page 69)	The numbers at Hanford, as with most things connected to the Manhattan Project, were staggering: 540 buildings, more than 600 miles of roads, 158 miles of railroad track, vast quantities of water, concrete, lumber, steel, and pipe. Approximately 132,000 people were hired over the period (working 126 million man-hours)... (Norris, *Racing for the Bomb*, page 221.)
In a moody and rambling talk he confessed that he had failed to control the weapon he had helped create. (Page 306)	In a moody and rambling talk he confessed that he had failed to control the weapon he helped create. (William Lanouette with Bela Silard, *Genius in the Shadows: A Biography of Leo Szilard, the Man Behind the Bomb*, Scribner, 1993, page 456.)
For the next three months, both sides marshaled their forces. At Strauss' request, the FBI tapping of Oppenheimer's home and office phones continued. The FBI also followed the physicist whenever he left Princeton. (Page 259)	For the next three months, both sides marshaled their forces. The FBI tapped Oppenheimer's home and office phones at Strauss's specific request and followed the physicist whenever he left Princeton. (Richard Rhodes, *Dark Sun*, Simon & Schuster, 1995, page 539.)

Figure 10-1 Evidence of plagiarism cited in the *New York Times*

EXERCISE 34: Identifying Plagiarism

There are two ways to plagiarize the work of a source: using someone else's information or ideas without acknowledging the author's name and using language without quotation marks.

A. The following paragraph, by John Lukacs, was one of the sources used for an essay titled "Has the Credit Card Replaced the Dollar Bill?" Compare this paragraph with a paragraph taken from the student essay, and decide, sentence by sentence, whether the student has plagiarized Lukacs's work. If you find plagiarism in a specific sentence, indicate whether the plagiarism consists of:

(a) using information without acknowledging the source;

(b) using words without inserting quotation marks; or

(c) both (a) and (b).

Source

The Modern Age has been the age of money — increasingly so, perhaps reaching its peak around 1900. During the Middle Ages, there were some material assets, often land, that money could not buy; but by 1900, there was hardly any material thing that money could not buy. But during the twentieth century, the value of money diminished fast. One symptom (and cause) was inflation. By the end of the twentieth century, the inflation of stocks and of other financial instruments became even more rapid than the inflation of money, at the bottom of which phenomenon another development exists, which is the increasingly abstract character of money—due, in part, to the increasing reliance on entirely electronic transactions and on their records.

> JOHN LUKACS, "It's the End of the Modern Age,"
> *The Chronicle of Higher Education*, 26 Apr. 2002, p. B8

Student Essay

(1) For hundreds of years, we have lived in a society that worships money, believing that money can buy anything and everything. (2) A thousand years ago, during the Middle Ages, there were some things, like land, that money could not buy. (3) But by 1900, money could buy almost anything one could want. (4) That is no longer so true today. (5) John Lukacs observes that, over the last century, the value of money diminished quickly. (6) The same is true for stocks and other financial instruments. (7) In fact, our dependence on credit cards and other electronic means of transferring funds has made paper money almost irrelevant (B8).

B.   The following two paragraphs were among the sources used for an essay titled "Credentialing the College Degree." Compare these paragraphs with a paragraph taken from the student essay, and decide, sentence by sentence, whether the student has plagiarized either of these sources. If you find plagiarism in a specific sentence, indicate whether the plagiarism consists of:

(a) using information without acknowledging the source;

(b) using words without inserting quotation marks; or

(c) both (a) and (b).

Sources

Grade inflation compresses all grades at the top, making it difficult to discriminate the best from the very good, the very good from the good, the good from the mediocre. Surely a teacher wants to mark the few best students with a grade that distinguishes them from all the rest in the top quarter, but at Harvard that's not possible.

> HARVEY C. MANSFIELD, "Grade Inflation: It's Time to Face the Facts," *The Chronicle of Higher Education*, 5 Apr. 2001, p. B24

Grade inflation subverts the primary function of grades. Grades are messages. They are means of telling students—and subsequently, parents, employers, and graduate schools—how well or poorly those students have done. A grade that misrepresents a student's performance sends a false message. It tells a lie. The point of using more than one passing grade (usually D through A) is to differentiate levels of successful performance among one's students. Inflating grades to please or encourage students is confusing and ultimately self-defeating.

RICHARD KAMBER AND MARY BIGGS, "Grade Conflation:
A Question of Credibility," *The Chronicle of Higher Education*,
12 Apr. 2002, p. B14

Student Essay

(1) Some faculty are disturbed by what they regard as grade inflation. (2) They are concerned that grades will be awarded that are higher than students deserve, that will misrepresent a student's performance. (3) Kamber and Biggs, for example, believe that an inflated grade is the equivalent of a lie, for it sends a "false message." (4) Such faculty see themselves as differentiating between the different levels of successful performance, distinguishing, as Mansfield says, the best from the very good and the good from the mediocre. (5) In fact, they regard grades as a way of telling future employers how well or poorly these students have performed. (6) The emphasis is on providing students with credentials, not a successful learning experience.

C. The following two paragraphs were among the sources used for an essay entitled "Factory Work during the Industrial Revolution." Each paragraph is followed by a paragraph from a student essay. Compare each student paragraph with the source, and identify the *one* sentence in the student paragraph that does *not* contain plagiarized language.

Source A

Materially, the new factory proletariat was likely to be somewhat better off [than domestic workers who did light manufacturing work in their own homes]. On the other hand, it was unfree, under the strict control and the even stricter discipline imposed by the master or his supervisors, against whom they had virtually no legal recourse and only the very beginnings of public protection. They had to work his hours or shifts, to accept his punishments and the fines with which he imposed his rules or increased his profits.... In Continental industries with a strong paternalist tradition, the despotism of the master was at least partly balanced by the security, education, and welfare services which he sometimes provided. But for the free man entry into the factory as a mere 'hand' was entry into something little better than slavery, and all but the most famished tended to avoid it, and even when in it to resist the draconic discipline much more persistently than the women and children, whom factory owners therefore tended to prefer.

E. J. HOBSBAWM, from
The Age of Revolution: 1789–1848

Student Essay

(1) The new factory proletariat was likely to be better off materially than those who did light manufacturing in their homes, but it was unfree. (2) The factory owner and his overseers allowed no deviation from the rules that were rigorously enforced, and the workers had to do exactly what they were told. (3) They had no legal recourse and only the very start of public protection. (4) The despotism of the master was at least a little bit set off by the security, education, and welfare services that he sometimes provided. (5) But entry into the factory as a hand wasn't much better than slavery.

Source B

Most of the work in the factories was monotonously dreary, but that was also true of much of the work done in the homes. . . . The employment of women and children in the factories finally evoked an outcry from the humanitarians, but the situation was inherited from the domestic system. In the homes, however, most of the children worked under the friendly eyes of their parents and not under the direction of an overseer. That to which the laborers themselves most objected was "the tyranny of the factory bell." For the long hours during which the power kept the machines in motion, the workers had to tend them without intermission, under the discipline established by the employer and enforced by his foreman. Many domestic laborers had to maintain equally long hours in order to earn a bare subsistence, but they were free to begin, stop and rest when they pleased. The operatives in the factories felt keenly a loss of personal independence.

W. E. LUNT, from *History of England*

Student Essay

(1) Factory work was monotonous and dreary, but that was also true of work at home. (2) Humanitarians cried out against the employment of

women and children, but that was inherited from the domestic system. (3) What annoyed the laborers the most was the dictatorship of the factory bell. (4) The workers had to tend the machines without intermission, maintaining long hours to earn a bare subsistence. (5) Those who worked in their homes were free to begin, stop, and rest whenever they felt like it. (6) Factory workers keenly felt a loss of personal freedom.

Using Documentation

Documentation requires more than using quotation marks and citing the author's name in your text. You also need to provide your reader with detailed information about all your sources. This form of documentation is important for two reasons:

1. *By showing where you found your information, you are providing proof that you did your research.* Including the source's *publication history* and the *specific page* on which you found the information assures your reader that you have not made up fictitious sources and quotations. The systems of documentation that are described in this chapter and in Chapter 12 also enable your reader to distinguish your ideas from those of your sources, to know who was responsible for what, by observing the parenthetical notes or numbered notes.

2. *Documentation also enables your readers to learn more about the subject of your essay.* Methods of documentation originally developed as a way for serious scholars to share their findings with their colleagues—while making it entirely clear who had done the original research. The reader of your research essay should be given the option of going back to the library and locating the materials that you used in writing about the topic.

Throughout this book, you have seen readings followed by a list of notes that provide specific information about the sources being used in each paragraph, even in each sentence. The use of endnotes or footnotes (described in Chapter 12, pp. 533–536) is a thorough and scholarly method of acknowledging sources, but it can be cumbersome. Another widely accepted system of documentation is based on *the insertion directly into your essay of the author's name and the page on which the information can be found,* placed in parentheses and linked to a bibliography placed at the end of the essay. This style of documentation is called the *Modern Language Association (MLA)* style. It has replaced footnotes and endnotes as the most common method of documentation for undergraduates, and it will probably be the style you will use in writing general research essays, especially those in the humanities. MLA style allows your reader to see the source's name while reading the essay, instead of having to turn to a separate listing of notes at the back. Readers who want to know more about a particular source than just the author's name and a page number can still check the "Works Cited" page, which provides all the necessary details of publication.

Another frequently used kind of parenthetical documentation is the one recommended by the *American Psychological Association (APA)* for research in the social and behavioral sciences. APA style is described on pages 523–532 of Chapter 12.

Using Parenthetical Notes: MLA Style

Here is an excerpt from a biographical essay about the American novelist Ernest Hemingway, using MLA style. Notice that the parenthetical notes—often called *in-text citations*—are meaningless unless the reader can refer to an accurate and complete "Works Cited" list placed on a separate page at the end of the essay.

> Hemingway's zest for life extended to women also. His wandering heart seemed only to be exceeded by an even more appreciative eye (Hemingway 102). Hadley was aware of her husband's flirtations and of his facility with women (Sokoloff 84). Yet, she had no idea that something was going on between Hemingway and Pauline Pfeiffer, a fashion editor for *Vogue* magazine (Baker 159). She was also unaware that Hemingway delayed his return to Schruns from a business trip in New York, in February 1926, so that he might spend more time with this "new and strange girl" (Hemingway 210; also Baker 165).

Works Cited

Baker, Carlos. *Ernest Hemingway: A Life Story*. Scribner, 1969.
Hemingway, Ernest. *A Moveable Feast*. Scribner, 1964.
Sokoloff, Alice Hunt. *Hadley: The First Mrs. Hemingway*. Dodd, 1973.

Many of the basic rules for using MLA style are demonstrated in this example. Here are some points to observe.

1. Format and Punctuation

The placement of the parenthetical note within your sentence is governed by a set of very precise rules, established by conventional agreement. Like rules for quotation, these must be followed without any deviation.

a. *The parenthetical note is intended to be a part of your sentence, which should not end until the source has been cited.* For this reason, terminal punctuation (period or question mark) should be placed *after* the parenthetical note.

Incorrect

Unlike most American writers of his day, Hemingway rarely came to New York; instead, he spent most of his time on his farm near Havana. (Ross 17).

Correct

Unlike most American writers of his day, Hemingway rarely came to New York; instead, he spent most of his time on his farm near Havana (Ross 17).

b. *If the parenthetical note follows a quotation, the quotation should be closed before you open the parentheses.* Remember that the note is not part of the quotation and therefore has no reason to be inside the quotation.

Incorrect

Hemingway's farm consisted of "a domestic staff of nine, fifty-two cats, sixteen dogs, a couple of hundred pigeons, and three cows (Ross 17)."

Correct

Hemingway's farm consisted of "a domestic staff of nine, fifty-two cats, sixteen dogs, a couple of hundred pigeons, and three cows" (Ross 17).

c. *Any terminal punctuation that is part of the quotation* (like a question mark or an exclamation point) *remains inside the quotation marks.* Remember also to include a period at the end of the sentence, *after* the parenthetical note.

Incorrect

One critic reports that Hemingway said of *The Old Man and the Sea*, "Don't you think it is a strange damn story that it should affect all of us (me especially) the way it does" (Halliday 52)?

Correct

One critic reports that Hemingway said of *The Old Man and the Sea*, "Don't you think it is a strange damn story that it should affect all of us (me especially) the way it does?" (Halliday 52).

d. *When you insert the parenthetical note, leave one space before it and one space after it*—unless you are ending the sentence with terminal punctuation (period, question mark), in which case you leave no space between the closing parenthesis and the punctuation, and you leave the customary one space between the end of that sentence and the beginning of the next one.

Incorrect

Given Hemingway's intense awareness of literary tradition, style, and theory, it is strange that many critics and readers have found his work primitive(Cowley 47).

Correct

Given Hemingway's intense awareness of literary tradition, style, and theory, it is strange that many critics and readers have found his work primitive (Cowley 47).

2. Placement

The parenthetical note comes at the end of the material being documented, whether that material is quoted, paraphrased, summarized, or briefly mentioned. By convention, your reader will assume that the *parenthetical note signals the end of the material from that source.* Anything that follows is either your own idea, independently developed, or taken from a new source that will be documented by the next parenthetical note later in the text.

One critic has remarked that it has been fashionable to deride Hemingway over the past few years (Cowley 50). However, though we may criticize him, as we can criticize most authors when we subject them to close scrutiny, we should never forget his brilliance in depicting characters having grace under the pressure of a sterile, valueless, painful world (Anderson 1036).

3. Frequency

Each new point in your essay that requires documentation should have its own parenthetical note. Under no circumstances should you accumulate references to several different sources for several sentences and place them in a single note at the end of the paragraph. All the sources in the Hemingway paragraph on p. 452 cannot be covered by one parenthetical note at the end.

Incorrect

The sources of Hemingway's fiction have been variously named. One critic has said he is driven by "personal demons." Another believes that he is occupied by a desire to truly portray reality, with all its ironies and symbols. Finally, still another has stated that Hemingway is interested only in presenting "fragments of truth" (Cowley 51; Halliday 71; Levin 85).

Correct

The sources of Hemingway's fiction have been variously named. One critic has said he is driven by "personal demons" (Cowley 51). Another believes that he is occupied by a desire to truly portray reality, with all its ironies and symbols (Halliday 71). Finally, still another has stated that Hemingway is interested only in presenting "fragments of truth" (Levin 85).

4. Multiple Notes in a Single Sentence

If you are using a large number of sources and documenting your essay very thoroughly, you may need to cite two or more sources at separate points in the same sentence.

> Even at this early stage of his career, Hemingway seemed to have developed a basic philosophy of writing. His ability to perceive situations clearly and to capture the exact essence of the subject (Lawrence 93–94; O'Faolain 113) might have stemmed from a disciplined belief that each sentence had to be "true" (Hemingway 12) and that a story had to be written "as straight as you can" (Hemingway 183).

The placement of notes tells you where the writer found which information. The reference to Lawrence and O'Faolain must be inserted in midsentence because they are responsible only for the information about Hemingway's capacity to focus on his subject and capture its essence; Lawrence and O'Faolain are not responsible for the quoted material at the end of the sentence. The inclusion of each of the next two parenthetical notes tells you that a reference to "true" sentences can be found on page 12 of the Hemingway book and a reference to "straight" writing can be found on page 183.

5. Multiple Sources for the Same Point

If you have two sources to document the same point, you can demonstrate the completeness of your research by placing both in the same parenthetical note. The inclusion of Lawrence and O'Faolain in the same note—(Lawrence 93–94; O'Faolain 113)—tells you that much the same information can be found in both sources. Should you want to cite two sources but emphasize only one, you can indicate your preference by using "also."

> Hemingway's ability to perceive situations clearly and to capture the exact essence of the subject (Lawrence 93–94; also O'Faolain 113) may be his greatest asset as a writer.

There is, of course, a limit to how many sources you can cram into a single pair of parentheses; common sense will tell you what is practical and what is distracting to the reader. Usually, one or two sources will have more complete or better documented or more recent information; those are the ones to cite. If you wish to discuss the quality of information in your various sources, then you can use an explanatory endnote to do so (see pp. 468–469 on explanatory notes).

6. **Referring to the Source in the Text**

In the previous examples, the writer of the Hemingway essay has chosen not to name any sources in the text itself. That is why each parenthetical note contains a name as well as a page number. *If, however, you do refer to your source as part of your own presentation of the material, then there is no need to use the name twice; simply insert the page number in the parenthetical note.*

> During the time in Paris, Hemingway became friends with the poet Ezra Pound, who told Hemingway he would teach him how to write if the younger novelist would teach him to box. Noel Stock reports what Wyndham Lewis saw when he walked in on one of their boxing sessions:
>
> > A splendidly built young man [Hemingway] stript to the waist, and with a torso of dazzling white, was standing not far from me. He was tall, handsome, and serene, and was repelling with his boxing gloves—I thought without undue exertion—a hectic assault of Ezra's. (88)

Because Stock's name is cited in the text, it need not be placed in parentheses; the page number is enough. Stock's book would, of course, be included in the "Works Cited" list. Also notice that the parenthetical note works just as well at the end of a lengthy block quotation; but because the quotation is indented, and there are no quotation marks to signify its end, it terminates with a period placed *before* the parenthetical note, which follows separated by *one space*.

7. Including the Source's Title

Occasionally, your list of "Works Cited" will include more than one source by the same author. To avoid confusion and to specify your exact source, use an abbreviated title inside the parenthetical note. Had the author of the Hemingway essay included more than one work by Carlos Baker in the bibliography, the parenthetical note would look like this:

> Yet, she had no idea that something was going on between Hemingway and Pauline Pfeiffer, a fashion editor for *Vogue* magazine (Baker, *Life Story* 159).

If your source is a newspaper or periodical article that does not cite an author, use an abbreviation of the article's title in your parenthetical note (unless you have referred to the title in your text, in which case you need only include the page number in your note).

8. Referring to a Whole Work

Occasionally, you may refer to the overall theme of an entire work, citing the title and the author, but no specific quotation, idea, or page. If you refer to a work as a whole, no page numbers in parentheses are required.

> Hemingway's *The Sun Also Rises* focuses on the sterility and despair pervading modern culture.

9. Referring to a Source by More Than One Author

Occasionally, you will need to refer to a book that is by two, or three, or even more authors. If you refer to a text by two authors, cite their last names, joined by "and." (If you have mentioned the authors' names in your text, just include a page reference in parentheses.) If you refer to a text by three or more authors and you have not mentioned them in your text, it is acceptable (and saves space) to cite the name of the first author followed by et al., unitalicized, and then the page number, all within parentheses. *Et al.* is Latin for "and others."

Two Authors

> We may finally say of the writer Hemingway that he was able to depict the turbulent, often contradictory, emotions of modern man in a style as starkly realistic as that of the sixteenth century painter Caravaggio, who, art historians tell us, seems to say, "Here is actuality ... without deception or pretence...." (Janson and Cauman 221).

Three or More Authors

Hemingway did what no other writer of his time did: he captured the plight and total disenchantment of his age in vivid intensity (Spiller et al. 1300).

10. Referring to One of Several Volumes

You may use a single volume from a set of several volumes. If so, refer to the specific volume by using an Arabic numeral followed by a colon and a space if a page number follows. (See Chapter 12 for proper bibliographic entry of a set of volumes.)

Perhaps Hemingway's work can be best summed up by Frederick Copleston's comment concerning Camus: both writers prove that human greatness is not shown in escaping the absurdity of modern existence, but "in living in the consciousness of the absurd and yet revolting against it by…committing…[one]self and living in the fullest manner possible" (3: 393).

11. Referring to a Work of Literature

If you refer to specific passages from a well-known play, poem, or novel, then you need not cite the author; the text's name is sufficient recognition. Use Arabic numerals separated by periods for divisions such as act, scene, and line in plays and for divisions like books and lines in poems. For novels, cite the page number followed by a semicolon, "ch.," and the chapter number.

Play

Hemingway wished to show reality as truly as he could, even if he found man, as did King Lear, nothing but "a poor, bare, fork'd animal…" (3.4.106–7).

Poem

Throughout his career as a writer, Hemingway struggled to make sense of the human condition so powerfully and metaphorically presented in *The Waste Land*: "Son of man / … you know only / A heap of broken images" (2.21–23).

Novel

In *The Sun Also Rises*, toughness is an essential for living in the modern age, but even toughness has its limits in the novel; as

Jake says, "It is awfully easy to be hard-boiled about everything in the daytime, but at night it is another thing" (34; ch. iv).

12. **Referring to a Quotation from an Indirect Source**

When you quote a writer's words that you have found in a work written by someone else, you begin the citation with the abbreviation "qtd. in." This form shows the reader that you are quoting from a secondhand source, not the original.

In "Big Two-Hearted River," Hemingway metaphorically captures the pervasive atmosphere of his time in the tersest of descriptions: "There is no town, nothing ... but the burned over country" (qtd. in Anderson 1027).

13. **Referring to Sources on the Web That Don't Provide Numbered Pages**

Some sources found on the Web, whether they originally appeared in print or not, don't provide page numbers. In that case, your parenthetical note should include the author (or title) only.

Hemingway's time in Paris was enhanced by "the stimulation of his experiences with [Gertrude] Stein" (Fitch).

14. **Referring to Sources That Do Not Appear in Print or on the Web**

Sometimes you may cite information from nonprint sources such as interviews, films, or radio or television programs. If you do, be sure that the text mentions (for an interview) the name of the interviewer and/or the person being interviewed or (for a film) the name of the producer, director, and/or scriptwriter; these names should also appear in your list of "Works Cited."

Interview

In an unpublished interview conducted by the writer of this essay, the poet Phil Arnold said that a lean style like Hemingway's may be just as artificial as an elaborate one.

Preparing to Document Your Essay

- Whether you take notes or use photocopies of your sources, remember always to write down the information that you will need for your notes and bibliography.

- For print sources, look at the front of each book or periodical and jot down or photocopy the publication information on the back of the title page (for a book) or the cover, often near the "Table of Contents" (for a periodical).

- For Web sources, copy and paste all the information that you can find about the site, including the original date when the material was published and/or put online and the date of last revision (usually found at the bottom of the home page). Also copy and paste the URL and DOI (digital object identifier—a unique number assigned to digital content), if given.

- When you move notes from one file to another on your computer, make sure that the source's name goes with the relevant material.

- As you work on the first draft of your essay, include the author's name and the relevant page number in parentheses after every reference to one of your sources, to serve as a guide when you document your essay. Even in this early version, your essay will resemble the finished product, with MLA documentation.

- Material found on the Web tends to change—or disappear entirely—over time. (*Wikipedia* is an example of a source in constant flux.) Make sure that you note the date when you accessed each Web site that you use.

- Finally, when the essay is ready for final typing, read through it again, just to make sure that each reference to a source is covered by a correct and appropriate parenthetical note.

Constructing a "Works Cited" Page

None of the parenthetical notes explained above would make complete sense without a "Works Cited" page. Examples of the more detailed technical forms for "Works Cited" entries according to MLA style can be found in Chapter 12 on pages 514–522. To introduce you to the difference between the relatively simple in-text citation (or parenthetical note) and the more elaborate "Works Cited" entry, here is a sample "Works Cited" page for all of the parenthetical notes about Hemingway found earlier in this chapter.

Works Cited

inclusive page numbers for "Introduction"

Anderson, Charles R. Introduction. "Ernest Hemingway." *American Literary Masters*, edited by Anderson, Holt, 1965, pp. 1023–24.

Arnold, Philip. Personal interview, 3 Aug. 2008.

Baker, Carlos. *Ernest Hemingway: A Life Story.* Scribner, 1969.

total number of volumes placed at the end of the entry

Copleston, Frederick. *Maine de Biran to Sartre.* 1974. *A History of Philosophy,* vol. 3, Doubleday, 1946–74. 9 vols.

Cowley, Malcolm. "Nightmare and Ritual in Hemingway." Weeks, pp. 40–51.

one essay from a collection edited by Weeks (see last entry)

URL for a book accessed on the Web

Fitch, Noel Riley. *Walks in Hemingway's Paris: A Guide to Paris for the Literary Traveler.* Macmillan, 1992. *Google Books,* books.google.com /books/about/Walks_In_Hemingway_s_Paris.html?id =VcVIYdVjnJAC.

Halliday, E. M. "Hemingway's Ambiguity: Symbolism and Irony." Weeks, pp. 52–71.

Hemingway, Ernest. *A Moveable Feast.* Scribner, 1964.

second book by same author

---. *The Sun Also Rises.* 1926. Scribner, 1964.

original publication date

Janson, H. W., and Samuel Cauman. *A Basic History of Art.* Abrams, 1971.

two authors: only the first name is reversed

Lawrence, D. H. "In Our Time: A Review." Weeks, pp. 93–94.

Levin, Harry. "Observations on the Style of Ernest Hemingway." Weeks, pp. 72–85.

Ross, Lillian. "How Do You Like It Now, Gentlemen?" Weeks, pp. 39.

editor's name comes after author & title

Shakespeare, William. *King Lear. The Riverside Shakespeare.* Edited by Frank Kermode, Houghton Mifflin, 1974, pp. 1249–305.

Spiller, Robert E., et al. *Literary History of the United States.* 3rd ed., rev, Macmillan, 1963.

the date of the revised (3rd) edition is 1963

Stock, Noel. *The Life of Ezra Pound.* Pantheon, 1970.

collection editor is listed in place of author

Weeks, Robert P., editor. *Hemingway: A Collection of Critical Essays.* Prentice Hall, 1962.

MLA Style: A Sample Page

reference to
an article with
no author

reference to an
author with two
or more works
listed in the
bibliography

no source
cited

no source
cited

Orentlicher ref-
erence contains
page number
only; author
mentioned in text

reference to an
entire work; no
page citation
needed

reference to two
sources con-
taining similar
information; em-
phasis on Belkin

standard refer-
ence; author
mentioned in
the note

"Passive euthanasia" can be described as helping someone
to die by doing nothing and, according to *The Economist*,
"happens in hospitals all the time" ("Euthanasia War" 22).
It usually involves deliberate withholding of life-prolonging
measures (Keown, "Value" 6). Failing to resuscitate a patient
who has suffered a massive heart attack is one example
of passive euthanasia. Another is deciding not to feed
terminally ill patients who are unable to feed themselves.
By contrast, removing the feeding tube from a patient
who is being fed that way would be considered active
euthanasia.

The distinction between active and passive euthanasia is really about responsibility. In passive euthanasia, the
doctor or relative has done nothing directly to end the patient's life and so has less moral responsibility. An intermediate form of euthanasia—assisted suicide—is more
controversial. In assisted suicide, a doctor or other person
provides a terminally ill person with the means—pills, for
example—and the medical knowledge necessary to commit suicide. In the *Journal of the American Medical Association*,
Dr. David Orentlicher categorizes assisted suicide as a form
of passive euthanasia (1844). Derek Humphry's *Final Exit*,
which describes ways to commit suicide painlessly, and the
organization Compassion in Dying, which helps terminally
ill patients to end their lives, are both sources of instruction in assisted suicide (Belkin 50; also Elliott 27).

The professional people who care for the sick and the
dying think that there is a great difference between active
euthanasia and passive euthanasia or assisted suicide. One
panel of distinguished physicians declared themselves in
favor, by a margin of 10 to 2, of doctor-assisted suicide for
hopelessly ill patients who request it (Orentlicher 1844).

EXERCISE 35: Acknowledging Sources

Read the following passage by Charles McGrath. Then read each of the four examples taken from student essays that use McGrath as a source. Consider the following questions:

1. Has the source been misquoted or misunderstood?
2. Have the source's ideas been acknowledged with sufficient and accurate documentation, according to MLA style?
3. Have quotations from the source been indicated with quotation marks?

Source

What is it with hockey? To begin with, it is a fast, physical game that encourages players and spectators alike to burn at a much higher emotional temperature than does baseball or even football, both of which have built-in cooling-off periods. And hockey is, of course, the only game in which—on the professional level, anyway—fistfights routinely break out and in which it is customary for every team to carry on its roster an "enforcer," whose main job is to intimidate the opposition. The game has underlying it a longstanding cult of toughness. What casual fans—and apparently many parents—don't understand, though, is that a lot of hockey fighting is ritualistic. There is more pushing and posturing than there is actual punching, and the whole show—the pointing, the snarling, the chest-bumping—may actually serve as a kind of safety valve.

CHARLES MCGRATH, "Ice Sturm," *The New York Times Magazine,*
20 Jan. 2002, p. 9

Student Essay A

Hockey is one of the roughest sports there is. Because it is so fast and physical, everyone, players and spectators, gets highly emotional, and there are no cooling-off periods, as there are in sports like baseball or even football.

Student Essay B

Hockey is one of the roughest sports there is. As Charles McGrath observes, the game depends on breakneck speed and constant physical contact, with no opportunity for players or audience to catch their breath and calm down. The cult of toughness that underlies such a frenzied, belligerent sport would naturally encourage fighting in the stands and on the field. (McGrath, 9)

Student Essay C

Hockey is one of the roughest sports there is. But according to Charles McGrath, the "cult of toughness" associated with hockey, which makes the players seem so violent and dangerous, is largely "ritualistic," based upon menacing gestures and a pretense of belligerence (9).

Student Essay D

Hockey is one of the roughest sports there is. In contrast to games like baseball and football, players and spectators "burn at a high emotional level," which inevitably causes "fistfights to routinely break out." This "ritualistic pushing" and shoving is part of the "cult of toughness" that makes the game exciting (McGrath, p 9).

EXERCISE 36: Documenting Sources Correctly

Each of the following excerpts from student essays is preceded by publication information about the source cited. Each passage breaks the rules of MLA in-text citation. Consulting the following categories of possible errors, decide what is wrong with the documentation of each excerpt. More than one answer might apply.

1. The placement of the quotation marks is incorrect.
2. The source's name is not cited correctly.
3. The terminal punctuation is in the wrong place.
4. The spacing of the documentation is incorrect.
5. The form of the citation is incorrect.

Example One

Hill, Christopher. *The World Turned Upside Down*. Penguin, 1975.

John Milton was hardly able to identify with the hardships of the poor. He was "a leisure-class individual, who never knew what it was to labor under a small taskmaster's eye(Hill 400)."

Example Two

Dawkins, Richard. *The Selfish Gene*. Oxford UP, 1989.

Richard Dawkins believes that "individuals are not stable things, they are fleeting. Chromosomes too are shuffled into oblivion, like hands of cards soon after they are dealt. The genes are not destroyed by crossing over, they merely change partners and march on." (Dawkins 35)

Example Three

Butterfield, Herbert. *Napoleon*. 1939. Collier, 1962.

Napoleon once acknowledged that he was a pantheist: "If I had to have a religion I could worship the sun, which gives life to everything. The sun is the true god of the earth (Butterfield 118).

Example Four

Southwick, Ron. "Fighting for Research on Animals." *The Chronicle of Higher Education*, 12 Apr. 2002, p. A24.

The use of animals in medical research continues. According to a recent article in the *Chronicle of Higher Education*, "rodents and birds make up 95 percent of all animals used in laboratory studies, and scores of biomedical researchers are turning to mice to further their studies of cancer and other diseases" (A24).

Example Five

Kamber, Richard, and Mary Biggs. "Grade Conflation: A Question of Credibility." *The Chronicle of Higher Education*, 12 Apr. 2002, p. B14.

Most faculty believe that "inflating grades to please or encourage students is confusing and ultimately self-defeating." (Kamber B14)

Example Six

Spalter, Anne Morgan. *The Computer in the Visual Arts*. Addison-Wesley, 1999.

Anne Morgan Spalter wonders how we can still determine what is real in art: "If a virtual environment can be created that is indistinguishable from a real environment, with objects that look, feel, and behave like objects in the real world, is the viewer having a "real" experience" (Spalter, 314)?

Example Seven

Mander, Jerry. *Four Arguments for the Elimination of Television*. Morrow, 1978.

We are often told that television "changes the way humans receive information from the world . . . offer[ing] a very narrow-gauged sense experience" (Mander, p. 349).

Managing Documentation

Once you have assembled the right materials to support your ideas, you should, whenever appropriate, include your sources' names in your sentences as a way of keeping them before your reader's eye.

Putting Parenthetical Notes in the Right Place

In general, the citation of an author's name tells your reader that you are starting to use new source material; the parenthetical note signals that you are no longer using that source.

If the name is not cited at the beginning, readers may not be aware that a new source has been introduced until they reach the parenthetical note. Here is a brief passage from an essay that illustrates this kind of confusion:

no source?

The year 1946 marked the beginning of the postwar era. This meant the demobilization of the military, creating a higher unemployment rate because of the large number of returning soldiers. This also meant a slow-down in industry, so that layoffs also added to the rising rate of unemploy-

Phillips = source

ment. As Cabell Phillips put it: "Motivation [for the Employment Act of 1946] came naturally from the searing experience of the Great Depression, and fresh impetus was provided by the dread prospect of a massive new wave of unemployment following demobilization" (292–93).

The reader assumes that Cabell Phillips is responsible for the quotation and only the quotation and that the reference to Phillips covers only the material that starts with his name and ends with the page number. In this passage, then, *the first three sentences are not documented.* Although the writer apparently took all the information from Phillips, his book is not being acknowledged as the source. Phillips's name should be cited somewhere at the beginning of the paragraph (the second sentence would be a good place).

You may need to insert a parenthetical note in midsentence if that single sentence contains references to *two* different sources. Or you might want to place a note in midsentence to indicate exactly where a source's opinion leaves off and your own begins:

These examples of hiring athletes to play in college games, cited by Joseph Durso (6), suggest that recruiting tactics in 1903 were not as subtle as they are today.

If the page number were put at the end of the sentence, the reader would assume that Durso was responsible for the comparison between 1903 and the present, but he is not. Only the examples must be documented, not the conclusion drawn from these examples. In this case, the *absence* of a parenthetical note at the end of the sentence signals to the reader that this conclusion is the writer's own.

Using Parenthetical Notes to Signal Transitions

Here is a passage in which the techniques of documentation have been used to their fullest extent and the transitions between sources are clearly indicated. This example is taken from Jessie Bernard's "The Paradox of the Happy Marriage," an examination of the woman's role in American marriage. At this point, Bernard has just established that more wives than husbands acknowledge that their marriages are unhappy:

topic sentence	These findings on the wife's marriage are especially poignant because marriage in our society is more important for women's happiness than for
quotation	men's. "For almost all measures, the relation between marriage, happiness and overall well-being was stronger for women than for men," *one study reports*
paraphrase	(Bradburn 150). In fact, the strength of the relationship between marital and overall happiness was so strong for women that *the author wondered* if "most women are equating their marital happiness with their overall happiness"
quotation	(Bradburn 159). *Another study* based on a more intensive examination of the data on marriage from the same sample *notes* that "on each of the marriage
quotation	adjustment measures...the association with overall happiness is considerably stronger for women than it is for men" (Orden and Bradburn 731). *Karen Renne also found* the same strong relationship between feelings of general well-
summary	being and marital happiness: those who were happy tended not to report marital dissatisfaction; those who were not, did. "In all probability the respondent's
quotation	view of his marriage influences his general feeling of well-being or morale"
paraphrase	(64); this relationship was stronger among wives than among husbands (63).[2] A strong association between reports of general happiness and reports of
summary	marital happiness was also found a generation ago (Watson).

2. Among white couples, 71 percent of the wives and 52 percent of the husbands who were "not too happy" expressed marital dissatisfaction; 22 percent of the wives and 18 percent of the husbands who were "pretty happy" expressed marital dissatisfaction; and 4 percent of the wives and 2 percent of the husbands who were "very happy" expressed marital dissatisfaction.

This paragraph contains *six* parenthetical notes to document the contents of seven sentences. Four different works are cited, and, where the same work is cited twice consecutively (Bradburn and Renne), the reference is to a different page. The material taken from page 64 of Renne covers a sentence and a half, from the name "Karen Renne" to the parenthetical note; the remainder of the sentence comes from page 63. Finally, there is no page reference in the note citing Watson, since Bernard is referring the reader to the entire article, not to a single part of it. Notice also that:

- Bernard quotes frequently, but she never places quotations from two different sources together in the same sentence.
- She is careful to use her own voice to provide continuity between the quotations.
- The reader is never in doubt as to the source of information.

Although Bernard does not always cite the name of the author, we are immediately told in each case that there is a source—"one study reports"; "the author wondered"; "another study based on a more intensive examination of the data on marriage from the same sample"; "Karen Renne also found." These phrases not only acknowledge the source but also provide vital transitions between these loosely related points.

Using Explanatory Notes

You will have noticed that, in the excerpt from Bernard above, following the second parenthetical reference to Renne, there is a number. This calls the reader's attention to a separate note appearing at the bottom of the paragraph. (In the actual essay, the note would appear either at the bottom of the page or, together with other notes, on a *separate sheet* at the end of the essay.) Jessie Bernard is using an *explanatory note* as a way of including information that does not quite fit into the text of her essay.

If your research has been thorough, you may find yourself with excess material. It can be tempting to use up every single note in your file and cram all the available information into your essay. But if you include too much extraneous information, your reader will find it hard to concentrate on the real topic of your paragraph.

To illustrate this point, here are two paragraphs dealing with the domestic life of the English novelist, Charles Dickens: one is bulging; the other is streamlined. The first contains an analysis of Dickens's relationship with his sister-in-law; in the second, he decides to take a holiday in France.

Paragraph 1

Another good friend to Charles Dickens was his sister-in-law. Georgina had lived with the family ever since they had returned from an American tour in June 1842. She had grown attached to the children while the couple was away (Pope-Hennessy 179–80). She now functioned as an occasional secretary to Dickens, specifically when he was writing A Child's History of England, which Pope-Hennessy terms a "rather deplorable production."

Dickens treated the history of his country in a very unorthodox manner (311). Dickens must have felt close to Georgina since he chose to dictate the *History* to her; with all his other work, Dickens always worked alone, writing and correcting it by himself (Butt and Tillotson 20–21). Perhaps a different woman would have questioned the relationship of her younger sister to her husband; yet Kate Dickens accepted this friendship for what it was. Pope-Hennessy describes the way in which Georgina used to take over the running of the household whenever Kate was indisposed. Kate was regularly too pregnant to go anywhere. She had ten children and four miscarriages in a period of fifteen years (391). Kate probably found another woman to be quite a help around the house. Pope-Hennessy suggests that Kate and her sister shared Charles Dickens between them (287).

This paragraph obviously contains too much information, most of which is unrelated to this topic. Pope-Hennessy's opinion of the history of England and the history of Kate's pregnancies are topics that may be worth discussing, but not in this paragraph. This extraneous material could be shifted to other paragraphs of the essay, placed in explanatory notes, or simply omitted.

Paragraph 2

In 1853, three of Dickens's closest friends had died (Forster 124),[5] and the writer himself, having become even more popular and busy since the publication of *David Copperfield* (Maurois 70), began to complain of "hypochondriacal whisperings" and also of "too many invitations to too many parties" (Forster 125). In May of that year, a kidney ailment that had plagued Dickens since his youth grew worse (Dickens, *Letters* 350), and, against the advice of his wife, he decided to take a holiday in Boulogne (Johnson 757).[6]

5. The friends were Mr. Watson, Count d'Orsay, and Mrs. Macready.
6. Tillotson, Dickens's doctor, who had been in Boulogne the previous October, was the one to encourage him to go there.

This second, much shorter, paragraph suggests that related but less important detail can usefully be put into explanatory notes where, if wanted, it is always available. Readers of the second paragraph are being given a choice: they can absorb the essential information from the paragraph alone, or they can examine the topic in greater depth by referring also to the explanatory notes. The first research essay in Chapter 11 includes seven explanatory notes (p. 496).

Explanatory notes should be reserved for information that, in your view, is useful and to some degree relevant to the topic; if it is uninteresting and way off the point, simply omit it. If you indulge too often in explanatory notes, your notes may be longer than your essay. Remember to find out whether including explanatory notes is acceptable to your instructor.

Avoiding Excessive Documentation

Here is another paragraph from an essay about Charles Dickens, in which the writer describes the novelist's daily routine, using numerous parenthetical notes to thoroughly document all the detail.

> Dickens's regular work habits involved writing at his desk from about nine in the morning to two in the afternoon (Butt and Tillotson 19; Pope-Hennessy 248), which left a good deal of time for other activities. Some of his leisure each day was regularly spent in letter-writing, some in walking and riding in the open air (Pope-Hennessy 305, quoting Nathaniel Sharswell). Besides this regular routine, on some days he would devote time to reading manuscripts which Wills, his sub-editor on *Household Words*, would send to him for revision and comment (Forster 65; Johnson 702).

In this passage, *three parenthetical notes* are needed for *three sentences* because a different biography or pair of biographies is the source for each piece of information. To combine all the sources in a single note would confuse, rather than simplify, the acknowledgments. Having come across the same information in more than one biography, the writer of this essay is not only making it clear where the information came from, but is also providing the reader with a *choice of references*. Since the sources are given equal status in the notes (by being placed in alphabetical order and separated by a semicolon), the reader can assume that they are equally reliable. Had the writer thought that one was more thorough or more convincing than another, she would have either omitted the secondary one or indicated its status by placing it after "also" (Johnson 702; also Forster 65).

But an abundance of parenthetical notes is not always appropriate. As the following example demonstrates, excessive documentation only creates clutter.

> In contrast to the Dickenses' house in London, this setting was idyllic: the house stood in the center of a large garden complete with woods, waterfall, roses (Forster 145), and "no end of flowers" (Forster 146). For a fee, the Dickenses fed on the produce of the estate and obtained their milk fresh from the landlord's cow (Forster 146). What an asset to one's peace of mind to have such a cooperative landlord as they had (Pope-Hennessy 310; Johnson 758; Forster 147) in the portly, jolly Monsieur Beaucourt (Forster 147)!

This entire passage is taken from three pages in Forster's biography of Dickens, and a single note could document the entire paragraph. What information is provided in the last sentence that justifies a parenthetical note citing three sources? And what does the last note document? Is it only Forster who is aware that Monsieur Beaucourt is portly and jolly? To avoid tiring and irritating his readers, the writer here would have been well advised to ignore the supporting evidence in Pope-Hennessy and Johnson, and use a single reference to Forster.

Using Umbrella Notes

As in the previous example, you sometimes have to cite the same source for several sentences or even for several paragraphs at a stretch. Instead of repeating "Forster 146" again and again, you can use a single note to cover the entire sequence. These notes, often called *umbrella notes,* cover a sequence of sentences as an umbrella might cover more than one person. Umbrella notes are generally used in essays where the sources' names are not often cited in the text, and so the reader cannot easily figure out the coverage by assuming that the name and the parenthetical note mark the beginning and ending points. Using an umbrella leaves the reader in no doubt as to how much material the note is covering.

An umbrella note consists of an explanation of how much material is being covered by a source. Such a note is too long to be put in parentheses within the text and generally takes the form of *an explanatory note placed outside the body of your essay.* Here is an example:

> 2. The information in this and the previous paragraph dealing with Dickens's relationship with Wilkie Collins is entirely derived from Hutton 41–49.

Inside your essay, the superscript number 2 referring the reader to this note would follow right after the *last* sentence that uses material from Hutton to discuss Dickens and Wilkie Collins.

Of course, umbrella notes work only when you are using a single source for a reasonably long stretch. If you use two sources, you have to distinguish between them in parenthetical notes, and the whole point of the umbrella—to cut down on the number of notes—is lost.

Umbrella notes must also be used with caution when you are quoting. Because the umbrella provides the reference for a long stretch of material, the citation usually includes several pages; but how will the reader know on which page the quotation appears? Sometimes you can add this information to the note itself:

> 2. The information in this and the previous paragraph is entirely derived from Hutton 41–49. The two quotations from Dickens's letters are from pages 44 and 47, respectively.

However, if you use too many umbrella notes, or if you expect a single note to guide your reader through the intricacies of a long paragraph, you will have abused the device. Your essay will have turned into a series of summaries, with each group of paragraphs describing a single source. That is not what a research essay is supposed to be.

EXERCISE 37: Using the Right Amount of Documentation

The first four paragraphs from a student essay about the San Francisco earthquake are reproduced below. Read through each paragraph. Decide whether the writer has (a) used *enough or too much quotation;* (b) has provided *a sufficient amount of documentation;* and (c) whether the *MLA forms are used correctly.* Note: The sources are not provided here.

The Aftermath of the San Francisco Earthquake

1. San Francisco has long been plagued by earth tremors. "Severe quakes had been felt in 1864, 1898, and 1900, but it was not until 5:13 a.m. on April 18, 1906, that the rocky masses of the San Andreas Fault, the greatest fracture anywhere on the earth's crust, heaved violently and doomed San Francisco as it then existed" (Lamott 219). The quake was followed by a fire that destroyed the center of the town and burned on until April 21, when the ashes were wetted down by rain (Lamott 219).

2. The water mains broke, the gas works blew up, and the chief of the fire department perished when the chimney of his home fell on him as he slept in bed. By mid-morning the fire department resorted to dynamiting the downtown business district to stop the flaming fury which was being blown rapidly by a west wind, obliterating everything in its path.

3. In a few short hours most of San Francisco was in ruins (Conrad 30). "Four square miles, making up 512 blocks in the center of town, were gone, along with 28,000 buildings and a total property value of about $500 million" (Lamott 219). Approximately 700 people had died and approximately 250,000 people were left homeless (Lamott 219). The homeless took refuge in the Presidio, Richmond District, and Golden Gate Park. Tents were set up, then outdoor kitchens, and a makeshift operating room, where several babies were born (Conrad 30). The city was far from beaten. Henry Miller, a millionaire cattle rancher, gave out free beef to the homeless for seven days, and a merchant, Raphael Weill, imported trainloads of clothes and personally walked through the tent cities to see that everyone was clothed (Conrad 31).

4. On every side there was death and suffering. Hundreds were injured, either burned, crushed, or struck by falling pieces from the buildings (Conrad 32). San Franciscans insisted on telling everyone, "It wasn't an earthquake that destroyed us, it was the fire." Starting in the business section of Market Street, the giant flames swept towards Russian Hill, Chinatown, North Beach, and Telegraph Hill.

Preparing the Final Bibliography

The bibliography of "Works Cited" becomes especially important when you use MLA documentation, as it is the only place where your reader can find publication information about your sources. Which works you include in your final bibliography may depend on the wording and intention of your assignment. There is an important difference between a list of works that you have *consulted* or *examined* and a list of works that you have *cited* or actually used in writing your essay. Many instructors restrict the bibliography to "Works Cited," but you may be asked to submit a list of "Works Consulted." The purpose of a "Works Consulted" bibliography is to help your readers to find appropriate background information, not to overwhelm them with your extensive research. Don't present a collection of 35 titles if you actually cite only 5 sources in your essay.

> *An appropriate final bibliography of "Works Cited" for an undergraduate essay consists of all the sources that you included and documented, through parenthetical notes, in your essay.*

If you consulted a book in the hope that it contained some relevant information, and if it provided nothing useful, should you include it in your final bibliography? You might do so to prevent your readers from consulting works with misleading titles in the belief that they might be useful, but only if your bibliography is *annotated* so that the book's lack of usefulness can be pointed out. Finally, if you have been unable to locate a source and have thus never examined it yourself, you may not ordinarily include it in your final bibliography, however tempting the title may be.

Annotating Your Bibliography

Annotating your bibliography is an excellent way to demonstrate the quality of your research. But, to be of use, your brief annotations must be informative. The following phrases do not tell the reader very much: "an interesting piece"; "a good article"; "well-done"; "another source of well-documented information." What is well done? Why is it interesting? What is good about it? How much and what kind of information does it contain? A good annotated bibliography will answer some of these questions.

The bibliography on the following pages presents the basic facts about the author, title, and publication, as well as some *evaluative information.* If the annotations were omitted, these entries would still be correct, for they conform to the standard rules for MLA bibliographical format. Without the annotation, one would simply have to change the heading to "Works Consulted" (if it includes some works not cited in your essay) or "Works Cited."

HEMINGWAY IN 1924: AN ANNOTATED BIBLIOGRAPHY
OF WORKS CONSULTED

Baker, Allie. *The Hemingway Project*. www.thehemingwayproject.com/. Accessed 13 Mar. 2015. A communal blog, organized by Allie Baker, who has invited Hemingway fans to contribute new material that supplements the standard bios. Includes "The Hadley Tapes," recorded by Hadley Hemingway in 1972, plus interviews with a variety of writers and fans (whose reliability may be variable). Useful for browsing, but (except for Hadley), credentials should be checked.

Baker, Carlos. *Ernest Hemingway: A Life Story*. Scribner, 1969. 563 pages of biography, with 100 pages of footnotes. Everything seems to be here, presented in great detail.

Donaldson, Scott. *By Force of Will: The Life and Art of Ernest Hemingway*. Viking, 1977. The material isn't organized chronologically; instead, the chapters are thematic, with titles like "Money," "Sex," and "War." Episodes from Hemingway's life are presented within each chapter. The introduction calls this "a mosaic of [Hemingway's] mind and personality."

Ernest Hemingway, Paris. c. 1924. *John F. Kennedy Presidential Library and Museum*, www.jfklibrary.org/Asset-Viewer/Archives/EHPH-05738 .aspx. A wonderful photograph of Hemingway in 1924, lounging in a chair, wearing a beret, and looking smug and shy at the same time.

Fitch, Noel Riley. *Walks in Hemingway's Paris: A Guide to Paris for the Literary Traveller*. Macmillan, 1992. *Google Books*, books.google.com/books /about/Walks_In_Hemingway_s_Paris.html?id=VcVIYdVjnJAC. Useful and detailed guide to the places and streets that Hemingway frequented in 1924, with especially helpful maps.

Goodheart, Eugene. "Ernest Hemingway." *The Cambridge Companion to American Novelists*. Edited by Timothy Parrish, Cambridge UP, 2013, pp. 104–13. An anthology of short (less than 10 pages) essays by noted academics, mostly focused on the novelists' literary output. Goodheart identifies and briefly discusses some major themes of Hemingway's work: courage and heroism, and arenas where they are tested—war and the bullring.

Gopnik, Adam, editor. *Americans in Paris: A Literary Anthology*. Library of America, 2004. This anthology contains short excerpts from literary works and memoirs by contemporaries of Hemingway, such as William Faulkner, E. E. Cummings, Gertrude Stein, and John Dos Passos, providing an account of what life was like in Paris in the 1920s by people who were there at the time. The excerpt by Harry Crosby is particularly good at evoking atmosphere.

Hemingway, Ernest. *A Moveable Feast*. Scribner, 1964. This is Hemingway's own version of his life in Paris. It sounds authentic, but there's also a very strongly nostalgic tone, so it may not be trustworthy.

---. *The Letters of Ernest Hemingway, 1920–25*. Edited by Sandra Spanier, Albert J. DeFazio III, and Robert W. Trogdon, vol. 2, Cambridge UP, 2012. 3 vols. Collects all the letters that have ever been found. Authorized by the Hemingway Foundation. Most of his letters to Hadley didn't survive (but hers to him did, because Hemingway kept them). Certainly worth examining. Lots of editorial comment.

Hemingway, Leicester. *My Brother, Ernest Hemingway*. World, 1962. *Google Books*, books.google.com/books?id=JZHVCwAAQBAJ. For 1924–1925, L. H. uses information from Ernest's letters (as well as commonly known facts). The book reads like a third-hand report, very remote; but L. H. sounds honest, not as if he were making up things that he doesn't know about.

Hemingway Resource Center. *Hemingway Resource Center*, 2015, www.lostgeneration.com/. A site that is partly informative and partly commercial—they sell and auction memorabilia. The bibliography is quite comprehensive, with links to good photo collections and other Hemingway sites. The biography includes a section on "The Paris Years."

Hemingway Society. Ernest Hemingway Foundation, 2015, www.hemingwaysociety.org/. Run by and apparently for academics, the Society publishes the *Hemingway Review* and *Newsletter*, holds conferences, and gives out awards for scholarship. There is surprisingly little information about Hemingway available on the site. Not for amateurs.

Hotchner, A. E. *Papa Hemingway*. Random House, 1955. This book is called a "personal memoir." Hotchner met Hemingway in 1948, evidently hero-worshiped him, and tape-recorded his reminiscences. The book is their dialogue (mostly Hemingway's monologue). No index or bibliography. Hotchner's adoring tone is annoying, and the material resembles that of *A Moveable Feast*, which is better written.

Kennedy, J. Gerald. "Hemingway, Hadley, and Paris: The Persistence of Desire." *The Cambridge Companion to Hemingway*, edited by Scott Donaldson, Cambridge UP, 1996. *Google Books*, /books.google.com/books?id=9qFrwKJGcIIC. A brisk overview of the Hemingways' time in Paris, which sounds a bit like a gossip column. (Ernest is tiring of Hadley because she is becoming too "matronly [Kennedy's description]." Useful for its connections between the experience of the Hemingways and the characters of *The Sun Also Rises*.

Lamb, Robert Paul. "Fishing for Stories." *Modern Fiction Studies*, vol. 37, no. 2, Summer 1991, pp. 161–81. *Project Muse*, http://muse.jhu.edu/. Hemingway's experience in Paris and Pamplona as seen through the writing of his short story "Big Two-Hearted River." More about the story than about Paris.

Meyers, Jeffrey. *Hemingway: A Biography*. HarperCollins, 1999. Includes several maps and two chronologies: illnesses and accidents, and travel. Book organized chronologically, with every year accounted for, according to table of contents. Well-documented critical biography, with personal anecdotes taking a backseat to literary.

Moddelmog, Debra A., and Suzanne Del Gizzo. *Ernest Hemingway in Context*. Cambridge UP, 2013. A collection of essays, none over 10 pages long, showing how Hemingway's significance and reputation have changed over time. The "critical overview" of all the biographies would be particularly useful to read at the beginning of research. Other essays on "Masculinity," "Hunting," "Politics," "Sex and Marriage," etc. A good starter book.

O'Rourke, Sean. "Evan Shipman and Hemingway's Farm." *Journal of Modern Literature*, vol. 21, no. 1, Summer 1997, pp. 155–59. *JSTOR*, www.jstor.org/stable/3831582. Not much more than a brief account of a much-told anecdote about Hemingway and his friends purchasing a picture by Miró.

Paul. *Hemingway's Paris*, hemingwaysparis.blogspot.com/. Accessed 19 Sept. 2015. A small collection of pictures and maps of Hemingway and 1924 Paris, presented by Paul, who lists his astrological sign and his favorite movies in his blog's profile.

Reed, Shannon. "The Expatriotes [sic] in Paris and Hemingway's Reflections in *The Sun Also Rises*." *Google Books*, books.google.com /books/about/The_Expatriotes_in_Paris_and_Hemingway_s .html?id=zD3rGCbsybEC. A brief overview of Hemingway and *Sun*, which reads like an undergraduate essay.

Reynolds, Michael. *Hemingway: The Paris Years*. Blackwell, 1989. Second of three-volume biography. Includes a chronology covering December 1921 through February 1926 and five maps ("Hemingway's Europe 1922–26," "France," "Switzerland," "Italy," and "Key points for Hemingway's several trips through France and Spain").

Sindelar, Nancy W. *Influencing Hemingway: The People and Places That Shaped His Life and Work*. Rowman & Littlefield, 2014. Sindelar's purpose: to provide an understanding of Hemingway through examining the places where he lived and the people he met. Seven pages on Hemingway and Hadley in 1924 would provide a good introduction before reading longer accounts in standard bios. Good documentation and a useful short bibliography. Interesting pictures of Hemingway in front of his apartment house, and Bumby with Gertrude Stein.

Sokoloff, Alice Hunt. *Hadley, the First Mrs. Hemingway.* Dodd, 1973. This is the Paris experience from Hadley's point of view, most of it taken from her recollections and from the standard biographies. (Baker is acknowledged.) It's a very slight book—102 pages—but there's an index and footnotes, citing letters and interviews that some of the other biographers might not have been able to use.

Weeks, Robert P., editor. *Hemingway: Twentieth Century Perspectives.* Prentice Hall, 1962. Contains many important essays on Hemingway's life and art. Offers a selected annotated bibliography.

Workman, Brooke. "Twenty-Nine Things I Know about Bumby Hemingway." *The English Journal*, vol. 72, no. 2, Feb. 1983, pp. 24–26. JSTOR, doi:10.2307/816722. An extended anecdote about how Workman tried and failed to meet Hemingway's son, Bumby. More about Workman than about Bumby.

Guidelines for Bibliographical Entries

(Additional models can be found in Chapter 12)

1. The bibliography is always listed on a *separate sheet* at the *end* of your research essay. The title should be centered, one inch from the top of the page.

2. The bibliography is *double-spaced* throughout.

3. Each bibliographical entry starts with *the author's last name at the margin*; the second line of the entry (if there is one) is indented *five spaces*, approximately one-half inch. This format—called "hanging indentation"—enables the reader's eye to move quickly down the list of names at the left-hand margin.

4. The bibliography is in *alphabetical order*, according to the last name of the author.

   ■ If there are two authors, only the first has the name reversed: "Woodward, Robert, and Carl Bernstein."

(continued)

(continued)

- If an author has more than one work included on your list, do not repeat the name each time: alphabetize the works by that author; place the name at the margin preceding the first work; for the remaining titles, replace the name with three hyphens, followed by a period and one space.

  Freud, Sigmund. *Civilization and Its Discontents.* Hogarth, 1930.

  ---. *Moses and Monotheism.* Knopf, 1939.

- A work that has no author should be alphabetized within the bibliography according to the first letter of the title (excluding "A," "An," and "The"); the title is placed at the margin as the author's name would be.

5. A bibliographical entry for a *book* is read as a list of four items — *author*; *title* in italics, including subtitle, separated by a colon; *publisher*; and *date*. Separate the publisher and date with a comma. All the information should always be presented in exactly the same order that you see in the model bibliography on pages 474–477. If you read the book online, give the name of the Web site in italics (e.g., *Google Books*) followed by a comma, then the URL. If you read it as an e-book, give the e-book reader (e.g., Nook) after the date.

6. A bibliographical entry for a *periodical* article that you read in *print* starts with the author's name and the article title (in quotation marks), each followed by a period and one space. Then comes the name of the periodical, *italicized*, followed by a comma and one space. What comes next depends on the kind of periodical you are citing.

   - For *quarterly and monthly journals and magazines,* insert "vol." and the volume number, "no." and the issue number, and the season or month and year of publication. Follow each of these items with a comma.

   - For *daily, weekly, or biweekly magazines and newspapers,* include the full date — day, month, and year.

   - For Web magazines, after the article title, give the name of the Web site (italicized), followed by the day, month, and year of publication, and the URL. Separate each item with a comma.

   - End with the inclusive pages of the article followed by a period.

     Tobias, Sheila, and Carol Weissbrod. "Anxiety and Mathematics: An Update." *Harvard Educational Review*, vol. 50, no. 1, Spring 1980, pp. 61–67.

     Winkler, Karen J. "Issues of Justice and Individual's Rights Spur Revolution in Political Philosophy." *Chronicle of Higher Education* 16 Apr. 1986, pp 6–8.

(continued)

7. A bibliographical entry for a *periodical* article that you read on the Web starts in the same way as an entry for a print article: Author's name. Article title (in quotation marks). Periodical or journal title (italicized). Volume, issue, season or month and year (for a journal) or complete date (in month day year format, for a newspaper). Inclusive page numbers (if available). URL or DOI. If you accessed the article via a database, insert the name of the database (italicized) before the URL or DOI.

> Goldman, Louis. "The Betrayal of the Gatekeepers: Grade Inflation." *The Journal of General Education*, vol. 37, no. 2, 1985, pp. 97–121. *ERIC*, http://eric.ed.gov/?id=EJ340362.

> Martinez, Ruben. "The Kindness of Strangers." *The New York Times*, 24 Dec. 2004, www.nytimes.com/2004/12/24/opinion/the -kindness-of-strangers.html.

8. A bibliographical entry for a *Web site* will vary according to the site and the amount of information that you can find. Here's what you should note down for possible use, in the following order: Author's name. Title of the Web site (italicized). Organization/ library/museum/publisher of the Web site. Date (check the bottom of the page for the most recent update). URL. If there is no publication date, note the date you accessed the site. To cite a short work from the Web site, insert the title of the work in quotation marks after the author's name. If the title of the Web site is the same as the sponsoring organization, you need not repeat the information.

9. Each entry of the bibliography ends with a period.

EXERCISE 38: Preparing the Bibliography

Correct the errors of form in the following bibliography:

Becker, Howard S, Geer, Blanche, and Everett C. Hughes. Making the Grade (1968) Wiley.

Dressel, Paul L.. College and University Curriculum, McCutcheon, 1971.

(same)----Handbook of Academic Evaluation. Jossey-Bass: 1976.

J. F. Davidson, "Academic Interest Rates and Grade Inflation," Educational Record. ERIC 56, 1975, 2. 122-5. Accessed Jan. 18, 2011.

New York Times. "Job Plight of Young Blacks Tied to Despair, Skills Lack," April
     19, 1983: Section A page 14. 10 feb. 2011. New York Times.

Milton Ohmer, Howard R. Pollio and James A. Eison. GPA Tyranny,
     Education Digest 54, issue 4 Dec 1988 pp. 11-14.

Leo, John. "A for Effort". Or for Showing Up. U.S. News & World Report,
     18 Oct, 1993: ProQuest database January 30, 2011.

Kennedy, Donald. *What Grade Inflation? The New York Times* June 13,
     1994 the New York Times sponsored Web site on February 2, 2011.
          Bretz, Jr., Robert D. "College Grade Point Average as a Predictor of
Adult Success: a Meta-Analytical Review and Some Additional Evidence"
Public Personnel Management 18   (Spring 1989) pp. 11-22.

Presenting Your Essay

A well-presented research essay must conform to a few basic mechanical rules:

1. Type your essay on a computer.

2. Double-space throughout the essay.

3. If you are not submitting your essay electronically, use 8½-by-11-inch paper; leave 1-inch margins on both sides as well as at the top and bottom. Make sure that your printer makes clear copies. Use only one side of the page.

4. Number each page in the upper right corner; if you are working in MLA style, also include your last name with the number (Doe 4).

5. Proofread your essay more than once.

6. Include your full name, your instructor's name, the name of the course, and the date on the first page of the essay at the top left margin. Place the title of the essay, centered, a few lines below that information.

Check with your instructor for any other special rules that may apply to the assignment.

A Checklist for Revision

As you read and reread your essay, keep the following questions in mind:

1. Does the essay have a single focus that is clearly established and maintained throughout?

2. Does the essay have a thesis or a consistent point of view about the events or issues being described?

(continued)

3. If it is a narrative essay, does the narration have a beginning, middle, and end? If it is an argument essay, are all assumptions explained and defended, and are all obvious counterarguments accommodated or refuted?

4. Does the essay begin with an informative introduction?

5. Does the essay end on a conclusive note?

6. Does each paragraph have a clear topic sentence?

7. Does each paragraph contain one and only one topic? Should any paragraphs be merged or deleted?

8. Are the paragraphs long enough to be convincing? Is each point supported by facts and information?

9. Does the development of the essay depend entirely on a dry listing of facts and examples, or do you offer explanations and relevant commentary? Is there a good balance between generalization and detail?

10. Do you use transitions to signal the relationship between separate points?

11. Is there unnecessary repetition? Are there any sentences that lack content or add nothing to the essay?

12. Is the style appropriate for a formal essay? Do the sentences seem too conversational, as if you were sending an e-mail?

13. Does the reader get a sense of the relative importance of the sources being used?

14. Do you use enough citations? Does the text of the essay make it clear when you are using a specific source, and who that person is?

15. Do you use one source for very long stretches at a time?

16. Is there an appropriate number of parenthetical notes, rather than too many or too few?

17. Is it clear how much material is covered by each note?

18. If you are including endnotes, does each note provide important explanatory information?

19. Are the quotations well chosen?

20. Is paraphrase properly used? Is the style of the paraphrase consistent with your style?

21. In preparing your bibliography, have you followed the MLA rules exactly? Have you formatted each entry correctly?

22. Have you proofread the essay (in addition to using a spellchecker)?

23. Is the essay convincing? Will your reader accept your analysis, interpretation, and arguments?

▪11▪
Two Research Essays

The two student research papers in this chapter illustrate two different kinds of documentation.

Bethany Dettmore uses the evidence of three films, various print and Internet sources, and her own survey to develop and support a theory about why audiences enjoy horror movies. After *describing* and *interpreting* the films' narratives and *analyzing* the expectations that viewers form about their experiences in the theater, she concludes that horror films both reflect and alleviate some of our society's deepest fears. Note that Dettmore has used mostly print sources, some of which were accessed on the Web. Dettmore acknowledges her sources with MLA documentation. She summarizes, paraphrases, or quotes her sources, using brief and unobtrusive parenthetical notes, generally at the ends of sentences. Almost everything that she wants to say is said within the body of the essay, so there are only a few explanatory endnotes.

David Morgan combines *narrative and analysis* by describing the aftermath of the strange event that happened in 1908 at Lake Tunguska, Siberia, and then exploring some of the many theories that have been used to explain that event over the last one hundred years. The bibliography for this essay contains fewer sources, which are cited less frequently than the sources are in Dettmore's essay. The writer's purpose is to help his readers understand what might have happened at Lake Tunguska and to clarify the scientific explanations. He is not attempting to reconstruct the event in complete detail or trying to convince his readers, by citing authorities, that his conclusions are the right ones. Like many essays in the social sciences, this paper uses a variation of the author-year method of parenthetical note documentation. (This variation, often called APA after the American Psychological Association, is described in Chapter 12, on pp. 523–526.) Having the date, as well as the author, included within the body of the essay is especially useful when you are reading about scientific theories developed over a span of one hundred years.

Bethany Dettmore

Professor Greene

English 102

May 2009

Looking at Horror Films

introduction

In the lobby of the movie theater, the walls are lined with posters advertising what is "Coming Soon" to the cinema. Between the photos of cute couples and strapping action heroes lurk the dark forms of scream- ing women, monsters, and ghostly mansions. These images represent the genre of horror, a staple of entertainment since the beginning of cin- ema. Year after year all through the twentieth century, Hollywood has

context: the horror genre

produced movies that have no other purpose than to evoke fear in their viewers. Nor has the genre's importance diminished in the twenty-first century: in 2004, Roger Ebert reported that he had reviewed fifteen differ- ent horror films. Although the vast majority of horror films have earned a poor critical reputation over the years, they have always been an excellent investment for Hollywood studios and a surefire attraction for audiences. This paper will explore some of the reasons for the popularity of hor-

topic: is there a "legitimate social purpose"?

ror films and consider whether they exist only to provide cheap thrills or whether, in some respects, they serve a legitimate social purpose.

premise: audience participation

For any movie to be successful, the audience has to enter into the experience unfolding on the screen, almost as if each person sitting in the theater is participating in the story and feeling the emotions of some of the characters. Far from being passive observers, moviegoers help to

two sources: B.D. prefers the first

"create the experience [they] are enjoying" while the director must work to "activate the imaginations that reach out to meet his own" (Prawer 20; also Dickstein 67). In doing so, the viewer is taking a risk. Will the experience be a good one? Or will some people in the audience respond so deeply to what is happening on screen that the emotions aroused become difficult

secondary prem- ise: participation involves a sense of risk

to deal with? Viewing a horror film involves an even greater risk, for the audience is expected not just to undergo an experience, but also "to court a certain danger, to risk being disturbed, shaken up, assaulted" (Dickstein 68). It is as if, by buying a ticket for the film, the moviegoer agrees to participate in what Andrew Tudor calls a "collective nightmare" (3).

It is because seeing a horror movie can pose such a great emotional and psychological risk that moviegoers are sharply divided in their reactions to

Dettmore 2

2nd topic: what
needs do horror
films satisfy?

the genre. Some love horror movies so much that they make a point of seeing every one that opens; others refuse to enter a theater with a monster or a screaming woman on the poster. In a survey conducted for this essay with respondents from both sexes and spanning all age groups, over 46% of the respondents said that they watched horror films very often or sometimes, while the remainder did so rarely (47%) or never (6%). One respondent described horror as nothing more than "bad acting, dark sets and leaves you empty afterwards." What keeps such viewers away is apparently not so much the blood and gore (which 11% of the respondents said was what scared them most about such films) or the villains and monsters (8%), but the element of suspense—leading to fear—built into the plot (62%). Interestingly enough, that same element—suspense—is also the reason cited by 42% of the respondents for why they enjoy horror films; it captures their interest and hooks them for the remainder of the film. One respondent wrote that horror films promise "a suspenseful plot that carries you on a mysterious rollercoaster." We can only conclude that some people like to be frightened!

survey = evidence
to support
premise

crucial factor =
suspense (sense
of risk)

Why, then, do many thousands of people want to sit in a movie theater and feel the threat that something dire will happen? (Tudor 8). Here, the survey provides us with a useful distinction between creating *suspense*, the quality that two-thirds of the respondents see as the essence of a horror film, and creating *fear*, the quality chosen by the other third. It seems likely that the two-thirds focusing on suspense are people who go to see horror films regularly. They don't want or expect to experience a lot of terror and dread; instead, they anticipate a certain amount of tension and nervous anxiety that—if the film is any good—will be resolved by the final shot. Such viewers expect that "fear will be aroused, then controlled" (Giles 39). There is always a time limit: the length of the movie. Their anxiety is "neutralized" and can even become pleasurable because it is experienced in safe surroundings (Dickstein 69).

distinction be-
tween suspense
(risk is con-
trolled) and fear

quotation con-
tains keyword:
"controlled"

The secure environment of the movie theater makes it possible for us to experience another emotion—catharsis, the feeling that can occur when you have been under an intense threat and then realize that it has gone away. Janet Maslin compares the emotion that we can experience during horror films to that of people gawking at highway accidents or watching TV dramas about fatal illnesses: "The knowledge that these things have befallen others provides a grim relief for those who have been spared."

controlled
risk → relief
(or catharsis)

paraphrase intro-
duces quotation

Dettmore 3

examples (anec-
dotal evidence) of
catharsis

same pattern:
paraphrase leads
to quotation

2 notes; 2 sources;
only one quoted

Other people's misfortunes—in real life or on the screen—act as our own shield against disaster. Using the "roller coaster" image again, the critic Linda Williams recalls the experience of seeing *Psycho* for the first time, describing it as a "roller coaster sensibility of repeated tension and release, assault and escape" (163). What she carried home with her was the release and the escape, not the tension and the assault. The viewers know that, however terrifying the situation may be in the movie, someone or something will intervene and put things right (Tudor 214-15) and they can leave the theater "drained and satisfied" (Dickstein 77).

plot resolution:
danger controlled
and averted

transition to new
point: curiosity

author's name in
text because his
ideas are key

return to B.D.'s
voice

But horror films also appeal to audiences on a more intellectual level. We don't just feel anxiety and terror; we also want to know how the story is going to work out. We admire the ingenuity of the writer and director as we wait for the ending when, we anticipate, all the mysteries of the plot will be logically revealed (Solomon 254). But, in a horror film, we don't just want to know what will happen next. The very weirdness of the characters, settings, and situations excites our curiosity. According to Noel Carroll in "The General Theory of Horrific Appeal," the central theme of horror movies is a voyage of discovery; their business is "proving, disclosing, discovering and confirming the existence of something that is impossible" (3). What beings could be more "impossible" than monsters and aliens? If the film is any good, we begin to focus less on the horribleness of these creatures and more on the logic behind their story. We wonder whether such creatures can really exist, and we want to find out how.

B.D.'s extended
topic sentence(s):
overcoming
danger

supported by
quoted source

return to B.D.'s
voice

Our interest is also stimulated by the elements of myth in many horror films. Like popular epics such as *The Lord of the Rings* or *Star Wars*, a good horror movie often revolves around a group of people confronted with dire peril who must find strength that they didn't realize they possessed so that their cause will eventually triumph. Because the danger and the fear are so great, the heroism needed to overcome the danger must be equally great. R. H. W. Dillard describes the myth of the horror film in religious terms: "Like a medieval morality play, the horror film deals with the central issue of Christian life—the struggle between the spirits of good and evil for the possession of man's immortal soul" (36). Such themes are common to all societies because they speak to our deepest need to know who we are, why we are here, and what use we will make of our lives. Jonathan Crane insists that such needs go far beyond "the influence of everyday life": "When audience members engage with a horror film they are not enjoying

introduction of main ideas = 1/4 of essay

visions that respond to everyday fears; they are responding to atavistic terrors nearly as old as the reptilian brain" (24-25). To explore some of these themes, I want to focus briefly on three landmark horror films: *The Cabinet of Dr. Caligari*, *Freaks*, and *Psycho*.

no source: B.D.'s own summary of the film

Regarded as the first classic horror film, *The Cabinet of Dr. Caligari* was made in Germany as a silent movie. In 1919, Hans Janowitz, a Czech poet, and Carl Mayer, an Austrian artist, wrote a script that told the story of a bizarre murder, in a terrifying dreamlike setting, based on a legend in Janowitz's hometown. At the center of the narrative are the sinister hypnotist Dr. Caligari, who operates a fortune-telling booth at a fair, and his "creature" Cesare, a young man who, while hypnotized, looks into the future, tells fortunes, and on occasion commits brutal murders. One of the striking scenes of the film shows the entire population of the village chasing after Cesare, who has abducted and is likely to murder the heroine. As Figure 1 illustrates, this scene emphasizes what the extremely creepy appearance and behavior

building link to theme of risk from alien figures

of Dr. Caligari and Cesare—weird even by silent-movie standards—have told the audience (Prawer 172): these are not normal humans but alien beings, who pose a threat to ordinary people and must be rooted out.

At the end of the movie, it is discovered that Dr. Caligari himself has actually been under the influence of an eighteenth century homicidal hypnotist who has been inhabiting his body. But an even more upsetting revelation is that, even while he—through Cesare—has been terrorizing the village, Dr. Caligari has simultaneously held the respectable post of director of an insane asylum some distance away. In effect, the madman has been in charge of the asylum.

key sentence: 2nd half is B.D.'s own conclusion

If, as Stephen Prince describes, horror movies can be regarded as representations of our own psychic processes (118), then *The Cabinet of Dr. Caligari* is all about our fear of the alien in our midst. In *Caligari's Children*, S. S. Prawer analyzes the many roles that Dr. Caligari assumes in the audience's imagination. He is the "stranger who disrupts the normal lives of the inhabitants of a small town" (172), yet he plays a vital part in the life of the community as the person in charge of one of its important institutions (173). He

several notes from the same source

is one of the first of a long line of mad scientists to dominate the genre, and yet he is also a "mystic" who understands ancient secrets (173). He controls the actions of the unfortunate Cesare, yet he himself is the victim of "demonic possession" (171). Most interesting, we are terrified by Caligari

Photo by John Kobal Foundation/Getty Images

Figure 1 The hypnotized Cesare flees with his intended victim through a nightmarish landscape, in a still from *The Cabinet of Dr. Caligari*.

reminder of source's name

both because of and despite the fact that his odd way of walking makes him seem deformed and crippled (174). As Prawer puts it, all of these impressions of Caligari are intended "to suggest monsters arising from the subconscious" of the viewer (176), monsters that have long been sup-

we identify with the monster and his creatures

pressed by civilized society (Wood 10). We begin to believe that "we are all characters in a madman's dream" (Schneider 36).

     In the same way, Cesare is also a character on whom we can project our ambivalence about our "dark desires" (Prawer 181). He is a zombielike

reliance on a single source

figure who commits acts forbidden to the culturally inhibited audience, yet who doesn't have to take responsibility because he is being controlled by the hypnotist. Prawer points out that Cesare is the first of a long line of horror film monsters who may seem horrifying but for whom we also feel pity and even affection (178; also Dillard 39). Indeed, Dillard points out that,

> However alien these monsters might appear, they are essentially like us: The vampires and werewolves, monsters and mummies are all human at source and are all personifications of that potentiality for evil and sin which is so much a part of us all. Hero and villain are much the same—both human, both flawed unto death.... (41)

summary of source

Casper Tybjerg makes a related point when he disputes with critics who believe that the standard source of fear in horror films has to be the inhuman "monster" figure: "Although Cesare and Caligari are certainly menacing, the real danger is in the threat of madness and of reality breaking down" (16; also Soren 30).[1] What keeps the audience interested in this "ongoing nightmare" (Schneider 34) is the possibility of their own emotional or moral breakdown.

B.D.'s summary of the film's significance

     It is the ambiguity of *The Cabinet of Dr. Caligari* that makes it such a great horror film. We can recognize something of ourselves in these alien figures who should really repel us. The publicity campaign for the opening of *Caligari* in Berlin in 1920 captured the film's underlying horror: people

citation of primary source

were invited to come to see the movie with the assurance: "You must be a Caligari!" (Clarens 16-17).

transition: link between 2 films

     As the title suggests, the characters in *Freaks*, a 1932 film by Tod Browning, are abnormal in a different way from Caligari and Cesare. Here, the immediate focus of horror is the physical deformity of the freaks in a circus sideshow, which is contrasted with the beauty of Cleopatra, the trapeze artist with whom one of the midgets, Hans, falls in love. (Figure 2 captures that contrast.) Although she agrees to marry him, Cleopatra is actually plotting (with Hercules, the Strong Man) to murder Hans for his money. When the rest of the freaks discover what Cleopatra and Hercules are trying to do, they hunt down, capture, and attack the two, mutilating her until she is "one of them"[2]—a "Hen Woman" suitable for viewing in a freak show.

B.D.'s summary of plot

One of the major selling points of the film—when Browning was trying to convince MGM to produce it and when MGM was attempting to market it—was that the freak characters were played not by professional actors but by real Siamese twins, bearded ladies, pinheads, dwarves, and so on.

no source cited—common knowledge?

Photofest

Figure 2 When the "freaks" in a circus sideshow learn that the "normal" Cleopatra (standing at right) is planning to marry the midget Hans (on table) only to murder him for his money, they take a horrifying revenge (*Freaks*).

Browning went to a great deal of trouble to portray his characters sympa-
thetically, with the freaks often shown behaving like normal people. In one
scene, for example, two dwarves have a normal conversation in a setting
with miniaturized furniture and props, so that everything seems quite
familiar and ordinary to the audience—until a normal-sized person arrives
on the scene (Clarens 70).[3] As Clarens puts it, "Freaks among themselves
cease to be freaks" (71). They are also sympathetic because they make the
best of their handicaps, with the pinhead flirting, the limbless worm lighting cigarettes, the armless woman drinking from a glass (Thomas 136). At
the beginning, the freaks are very trusting of normal people, welcoming
them into their society. In all these ways, the audience is encouraged to
accept them as "normal." For example, in a key scene, when we first see
the freaks from a distance, they appear to us as monstrous, misshapen
creatures capering around in a bizarre kind of dance; but this impression
changes in the next close-up shot as the freaks "are transformed from
agents of terror to objects of compassion within moments" (Thomas 137).

Here is the crucial issue of the film. To what extent will the audience
actually sympathize with the freaks, accepting them as people like us,
living in a little world that mirrors ours? On the one hand, we tend to have
a reflex prejudice against deformity. Many in the audience will be turned
off by the initial shot of the freaks dancing; the distorted figures will make
them feel unsettled and afraid (Cantor and Oliver 55). According to Michael
Grant, we inevitably feel a sense of revulsion for what we regard as lesser
beings: "In the cruelty of our sarcasm, we look down upon them, and it
seems that there is no way for the small protagonist, a being in the process of discovering the world's bitterness, to escape his fate when he can't
even reach the door handle" (128). In this perversion of the "there but for
the grace of God . . ." response, we are eager to disassociate ourselves from
these images because they might suggest to us that freaks are humans like
us and that we might also be like them. Certainly, some audiences in 1932
felt that revulsion: at a preview in San Diego, one woman ran up the aisle
screaming; many movie theaters refused to show the film; and, in New
York, thirty minutes of footage were cut by the censors (Clarens 70).[4]

On the other hand, audiences who stay with the movie will almost
certainly sympathize with poor Hans, the victim of the greedy, unfeeling
Cleopatra. If a horror film has to have a monster, surely it is the "normal"

quotation →
2 notes needed to
the same source

unclear whether
this is B.D.'s idea
or Thomas's

key point signalled

again, identi-
fication with
"monster," now
deformed

counter-
argument:
revulsion, not
identification

B.D.'s summary
of source

practical evidence
as a change from
theory

return to
basic theme:
identification

and beautiful Cleopatra, who is shown to have no redeeming qualities at all.[5] As one reviewer on the Internet puts it, "You quickly realize who Browning intends to be the real freaks. It is the 'normal' people who display the worst human traits of deceit and greed. The 'freaks' are shown to be loyal to each other, having an unwritten code of honor" (Bright).

And yet, in the final twist, Browning seems to turn Cleopatra into the victim and the freaks into the monsters by having them take their ghastly revenge on her. The scene in which they hunt her down is easily the most terrifying in the film, as the previously rather charming freaks become grotesque and predatory before our eyes. Are we horrified by what they do to Cleopatra, or are we horrified by what the freaks have become? Or are we afraid that we might have the potential to become like freaks ourselves?

Clarens believes that, although we recognize that the freaks are entitled to their "just retribution," all along our sympathy for them has been no more than "intellectual," and we are naturally more concerned about the fate of Cleopatra and Hercules, who are more like us (71). Thomas, however, takes a broader view, recognizing the ambiguity that is so often at the center of the horror movie. He wonders whether the freaks can simultaneously "be seen both as objects of sympathy and as nightmarish incarnations of the nonhuman." Does the grotesque ending undercut everything that Browning was trying to achieve in the film? Ultimately, Thomas concludes that Browning does succeed because so much sympathy has been created for the freaks during the course of the film that we will stifle our disgust at the ending: "We are horrified, but we are simultaneously ashamed of our horror; for we remember that these are not monsters at all but people like us, and we know that we have again been betrayed by our own primal fears" (137; also Herzogenrath 195). If Thomas is right—and *Freaks* has always been a cult classic—then the horror film has once again enabled us to see the freakish monster within ourselves and—going a step further than Caligari—forgive ourselves for being human.

Psycho (1960) marks a shift from the traditional horror film in which terror is found in monster figures that are clearly alien or abnormal. According to some critics, through this one film, Alfred Hitchcock transformed the entire genre, allowing horror to be seen in the context of contemporary

Figure 3 Anthony Perkins as Norman Bates and Janet Leigh as Marian Crane (*Psycho*).

American society (Jancovich 4). On the surface, the relationships between the characters in *Psycho* are quite ordinary: two sisters, mother and son, innkeeper and customer (Brand 21). Figure 3 shows us two average people in conversation; there's nothing monstrous about them. We certainly don't anticipate that Marian Crane, someone with a rather unsavory back story whom we accept as our heroine, will be savagely killed one-third of the way through the film. So we are unprepared for the famous shower scene at the Bates Motel: "We see an old woman with white hair pull back the shower curtain and stab Marian a half dozen times. The scene is back lit and we don't get a clear picture of the face of the murderer" (Ghani). We also don't anticipate that the murderer will turn out to be the amiable Norman Bates, almost cozy in his wooly cardigan. In a way, it would be easier on the audience if the murderer were an intergalactic intruder or a time-traveling Ice Age warrior, or some sort of freak or clairvoyant from a

normalcy

why quote this?

repetition of "we don't"

return to initial theme of security

traveling circus. We know that such beings appear only in horror films, not in real life, and we can sit secure in our seats waiting for the end of the movie.

conclusion (in B.D.'s voice): controlled risk becomes fear

Once the audience understands that "the monster within" (Dickstein 74) lurks in ordinary people and in familiar social settings, and an apparently normal person can be transformed into a psychotic murderer without any warning (Tudor 221), that sense of security is gone forever from the horror film.[6] These new monsters

> do not come from outside our nebulous social networks; they
> do not arrive in our suburbs fresh from the remote Carpathian
> mountains; they are not created by . . . well-intentioned scientists
> who err as ambitious humans will. They are us, and we never

unpredictability

> know when we will act as monsters. (Crane 8; also Ebert)[7]

placement of the note → all (including quotation) taken from Tudor

Throughout the early parts of *Psycho*, we are encouraged to have sympathy for Norman Bates, and, as Tudor points out, it is possible to retain some of that sympathy even after we realize that he is Marian's murderer. But, as with our response to the ending of *Freaks*, the collision between our revulsion and our sympathy makes us ambivalent and acutely uncomfortable. The ultimate effect is a kind of audience paranoia. Our perceptions are no longer reliable, and we can no longer trust the most "normal" of our friends and relations, for they might at any time attack us: "The world in which this kind of horror makes sense, then, is one which is fundamentally unreliable" (Tudor 221; also Freeland 192).

B.D.'s summary

In recent years, for many film critics, horror has not been considered a legitimate genre. They regard post-*Psycho* horror films as worthless: imitative, predictable, sleazy, and much too concerned with blood and gore. As one writer in a college newspaper put it, such films are "dismissed by critics across the board . . . as a disgustingly stupid thing to enjoy" (Olson; also Crane 2-3). The audience is so accustomed to the trite plot devices

degeneration of the horror film genre

that they know exactly what will happen in the next scene—and announce it out loud—minutes before it occurs. Even the movie music sends clear signals to the audience (Scott). The chief attraction of the traditional horror film—suspense—is totally gone. Yet, according to the Internet Movie Database, horror films remain among Hollywood's top grossing movies (IMDb.com). Leaving aside the teenage boys who revel in

Dettmore 12

B.D. announces a key point

the blood and gore, what continues to be the attraction? In my view, removing the element of suspense from horror films has restored to the audience the sense of security that they used to feel when the movie

we no longer want suspense

was populated by monsters that you were unlikely to meet in everyday life. If the nice guy whose locker is next to yours or the waitress at the diner is going to turn into a serial murderer, you'll only be able to stay

we prefer control over risk

within your comfort zone if you can predict the appearance of the ax in advance.

In place of suspense, the modern horror film provides excess: too much blood, too much violence, too much sex. The original horror films gained their interest from exploring the nature of evil and the

unbelievable excess = distraction from possible insecurity

psychology of madness; they didn't need buckets of gore to keep the audience's attention (Crane 4). Now, however, nothing is left to the imagination:

> There is no opportunity to view the monster as the embodiment of a community's fears, or as the darker side of man's nature, or as anything other than a cryptic, single-minded creep. There's no time to identify with the characters, since they are killed off so quickly that they don't have time to impress themselves upon an audience. (Maslin)

objective = numbness

The effect of all the blood and all the violence is to desensitize the audience; the gore serves as an anesthetic to prevent us from feeling anything at all. According to Aviva Briefel, those watching the ultra-bloody *Texas Chain Saw Massacre* find it hard to identify with anyone in the film: certainly not the sadistic killers, or even the masochistic victims, who

lack of identification

allow themselves to become sitting ducks: "We may feel endangered by the images of violence on screen, but we are ultimately numb to the pain they represent" (19).

Horror films have always tended to "perfectly mirror the fears of contemporary society" (Soren 153) and have been especially popular in times

heavy reliance on sources in this paragraph

of social disruption (Dickstein 66). Their function has always been to assure their audience of "man's ability to cope with and even prevail over the evil of life which he can never hope to understand" (Dillard 37). But each generation demands a different kind of horror movie, one that is (in the words of a Hollywood producer) "'in tune with the zeitgeist'" (qtd. in Shone). The

thesis (A): pre-9/11, horror film satisfied need for controlled catharsis

9/11 = turning point

B.D.'s own voice

thesis (B): post-9/11, horror movies supply an anes-thetic against fears inherent and unstoppable in the real world

time is over for what Tudor calls "secure horror": movies in which man's ingenuity invariably triumphs over monstrous evil. Such films belonged to an age that was "confident of its own capacity to survive all manner of threats" (220). Since 9/11, our confidence, public and private, has been shaken, perhaps irretrievably. So it is not surprising that, on the one hand, horror movies continue to draw huge audiences (Blake 12). People still need to view "imaginative and plausible encounters with evil and cosmic amorality [because] they help us ponder and respond emotionally to natu-ral and deep worries about the nature of the world" (Freeland 193). But, given the enemy we face in the war on terror, an enemy that is "nebulous" and "wraith-like," that "regroups whenever you strike it" (Shone), it is no longer easy to believe that the monster will be vanquished at the end of the two-hour film. People are more on edge, more vulnerable to fear and terror. What they seek is the anesthetizing power of the contemporary horror film with all its formulaic predictability and gory special effects. Horror films can no longer compete on their own terms with the real terror existing in the world (Solomon 254).

Dettmore 14

Notes

*digression →
belongs in an
explanatory note*

1. The famous Expressionist set designs for *Caligari* carry out the theme of the breakdown of reality. David Soren points out that "the sets are distorted, often jagged and harsh, indicators of the madness in which the characters are trapped" (30; also Cook 110).

*could be inte-
grated into the
text?*

2. One of the most frightening scenes in the movie shows the wedding festivities, with the freaks dancing around Cleopatra—she and Hercules are the only normal people attending—chanting: "We accept her, we accept her, gobble gobble, one of us, one of us."

*could be inte-
grated into the
text?*

3. Given this focus on normality among the freaks, some critics conclude that *Freaks* is not actually a horror movie. Peter Hutchings argues that it "functions as a kind of anti-horror film" because it completely avoids any of the special effects typical of horror movies and derives its thrills simply from the contrast between the normal and the abnormal (27).

digression → note

4. Interestingly enough, in the United Kingdom, *Freaks* was banned for thirty years, not for fear of audience reaction, but because Browning was considered to have exploited his cast. Skal reports that some cast members did, indeed, feel degraded by its content. Olga Roderick, who played the role of the bearded lady, told reporters that the film was "an insult to all freaks everywhere" (156).

*is this note
needed?*

5. Bernd Herzogenrath concludes that Cleopatra (and Hercules, too) "reveal the extremity of American individualism and the greed of American society" (187).

digression → note

6. During screenings of *Psycho*, there was an amazing amount of screaming and dashing up the aisles as members of the audience tried to get out. In certain scenes, people could hardly hear the soundtrack (Williams 164).

digression → note

7. Tom Shone points out that when "America's bogeymen no longer smacked of the supernatural, but hailed from your neighbor's backyard," Hollywood stopped calling these movies "horror films" and instead produced "psychological thrillers" and "suspense movies."

Dettmore 15

Works Cited

"All-Time Worldwide Box Office." *IMDb*, 10 July 2005, www.imdb.com/chart /boxoffice.

Blake, Linnie. *The Wounds of Nations: Horror Cinema, Historical Trauma, and National Identity*. Manchester UP, 2008.

Brand, James. *A Study into Horror Films and Their Remakes*. Dissertation, U of Portsmouth, 2007.

Briefel, Aviva. "Monster Pains: Masochism, Menstruation, and Identification in the Horror Film." *Film Quarterly*, vol. 58, no. 3, Summer 2005, pp. 16-27, doi:10.1525/fq.2005.58.3.16.

Gerb (Gerry Bright). Comment on *Freaks*, directed by Tod Browning. *Dooyoo*, 2 Oct. 2002, www.dooyoo.co.uk/movie-dvd/freaks-dvd/#/tab/opi.

The Cabinet of Dr. Caligari. Directed by Robert Wiene. Image Entertainment, 1921.

Cantor, Joanne, and Mary Beth Oliver. "Developmental Differences in Responses to Horror." *Horror Films: Current Research on Audience Preferences and Reactions*, edited by James B. Weaver III and Ron Tamborini. Erlbaum, 1996, pp. 63-80. *Google Books*, books.google.com/books /about/Horror_Films.html?id=3Tn8AQAAQBAJ.

Carroll, Noel. "The General Theory of Horrific Appeal." Schneider and Shaw, pp. 1-9.

Clarens, Carlos. *An Illustrated History of Horror and Science-Fiction Films*. Da Capo, 1967.

Cook, David A. *A History of Narrative Film*. Norton, 1990.

Crane, Jonathan Lake. *Terror and Everyday Life*. Sage, 1994. *Google Books*, books.google.com/books?isbn=0803958498.

Dickstein, Morris. "The Aesthetics of Fright." Grant, pp. 65-78.

Dillard, R. H. W. "The Pageantry of Death." Huss and Ross, pp. 36-41.

Ebert, Roger. "Movie Reviews: *Carrie*." *RogerEbert.com*, 1 Jan. 1976, www.rogerebert.com/reviews/carrie-1976.

Freaks. Directed by Tod Browning, Warner Home Video, 1932.

Freeland, Cynthia. "Horror and Art-Dread." Prince, pp. 189-205.

Ghani, Cyrus. *My Favorite Films*. Mage, 2004.

Giles, Dennis. "Conditions of Pleasure in Horror Cinema." Grant, pp. 38-52.

Grant, Barry Keith, editor. *Planks of Reason: Essays on the Horror Film*. Scarecrow, 1984.

Grant, Michael. "On the Question of the Horror Film." Schneider and Shaw, pp. 120-37.

Herzogenrath, Bernd, editor. *The Films of Tod Browning*. Black Dog, 2006.

Dettmore 16

Huss, Roy, and T. J. Ross, editors. *Focus on the Horror Film.* Prentice, 1972. *Google Books,* books.google.com/books?id=FBMWcgAACAAJ.

Hutchings, Peter. *The Horror Film.* Pearson, 2004.

Jancovich, Mark, editor. *Horror, the Film Reader.* Routledge, 2002. *Google Books,* books.google.com/books?isbn=0415235626.

---. Introduction. Jancovich, 1-9.

Maslin, Janet. "Bloodbaths Debase Movies and Audiences." *The New York Times,* 21 Nov. 1982, www.nytimes.com/1982/11/21/movies/film -view-bloodbaths-debase-movies-and-audiences.html.

Olson, Melissa. "Horror Films Are Like Broken Records." *Daily Trojan.* University of Southern California, 8 June 2005, dailytrojan .com/2005/06/08/horror-films-are-like-broken-records/.

Prawer, S. S. *Caligari's Children.* Oxford UP, 1980.

Prince, Stephen. "Dread, Taboo, and *The Thing*: Toward a Social Theory of the Horror Film." Prince, pp. 118-30.

---, editor. *The Horror Film.* Rutgers UP, 2004. *Google Books,* books.google .com/books?isbn=0813533635.

Psycho. Directed by Alfred Hitchcock. 1960. MCA Home Video, 1998.

Schneider, Steven Jay. *100 European Horror Films.* British Film Institute, 2007. British Film Institute Film Guides.

Schneider, Steven Jay, and Daniel Shaw, editors. *Dark Thoughts: Philosophic Reflections on Cinematic Horror.* Scarecrow, 2003. *Google Books,* books .google.com/books?isbn=0810847922.

Scott, Kirsty. "Music + Chase Scenes = New Formula for Fear." *The Guardian,* 5 Aug. 2004, www.theguardian.com/uk/2004/aug/05/film.filmnews1.

Shone, Tom. "This Time It's Personal." *The Guardian,* 25 Nov. 2005, www .theguardian.com/film/2005/nov/25/1.

Skal, David J. *The Monster Show: A Cultural History of Horror.* Macmillan, 2001. *Google Books,* books.google.com/books?isbn=0571199968.

Solomon, Robert. "Real Horror." Schneider and Shaw, pp. 230-64.

Soren, David. *The Rise and Fall of the Horror Film.* Midnight Marquee, 1997.

Thomas, John. "Gobble, Gobble . . . One of Us!" Huss and Ross, pp. 135-38.

Tudor, Andrew. *Monsters and Mad Scientists: A Cultural History of the Horror Movie.* Blackwell, 1989.

Tybjerg, Casper. "Shadow-Souls and Strange Adventures: Horror and the Supernatural in European Silent Film." Prince, pp. 15-39.

Williams, Linda. "Learning to Scream." Jancovich, pp. 163-68.

Wood, Robin. Introduction. *American Nightmare: Essays on the Horror Film,* edited by Andrew Britton et al., Festival of Festivals, 1979, pp. 7-28.

The Horror Film Survey

Name_____

This survey includes four multiple-choice questions and two open-ended questions asking for short responses. Circle your answers to the multiple-choice questions, and respond to the open-ended questions in the spaces provided.

1. How often do you watch horror films?
    a. Very often 13.5%
    b. Some of the time 32.5%
    c. Not very often 47%
    d. Never 6%

2. Where do you watch horror films?
    a. In theaters 9%
    b. At home 46%
    c. Half in theaters and half at home 39%
    d. Nowhere 6%

3. What scares you most about horror films?
    a. The blood and gore 11%
    b. The suspense 62%
    c. The villains 8%
    d. Identification with the victims 18%

4. How would you best describe horror films?
    a. A cheap thrill 23.5%
    b. An art form 19%
    c. Trashy films 8.5%
    d. A legitimate genre 49%

5. What do you like/dislike about horror films?
    Like: Creates suspense 42%
    Dislike: Predictability 35%
                Scares me long after the movie 23%

6. How would you define a horror film?
    Any film that creates suspense 66%
    Any film that creates fear 33%

Explaining the Tunguskan Phenomenon

The Tunguska River Valley in Siberia has always been an area of swamps and bogs, forests and frozen tundra, sparsely populated, and remote and inaccessible to most travelers. It was at dawn on June 30, 1908, that witnesses in the Tungus observed a light glaring more brightly than anything they had ever seen. This cosmic phenomenon, they said, was bluish-white in color and gradually became cigarlike in shape. Just as terrifying to the few people inhabiting that part of Siberia was the tremendous noise that accompanied the light, a noise that was reported to have been heard 1,000 kilometers from the site (Parry, 1961). Some who were in the vicinity were deafened, while others farther away apparently became speechless and displayed other symptoms of severe trauma. The Tungus community refused to go near the site or speak of the occurrence, and some even denied that it had ever happened (Crowther, 1931). The event was so frightening to these simple peasants that many believed it had been an act of divine retribution, a punishment by a god demanding vengeance (Baxter & Atkins, 1976).

Since 1921, when the first perilous expedition to the Tungus region confirmed that a remarkable event had indeed taken place, scientists have attempted to explain what it was and why it happened. Over 100 years later, the various theories developed to explain the explosion in the Tunguska Valley have become almost as interesting a phenomenon as the original occurrence. Like doctors trying to diagnose a disease by examining the symptoms, scientists have analyzed the fragmentary evidence and published theories that supposedly account for it. However, no theory has been entirely convincing. The purpose of this essay is to provide a brief description of some of the major interpretations of the Tunguska occurrence and to suggest that, in their efforts to substantiate their theories, scientists can be fallible.

At dawn on that day in June 1908, a huge object was said to have come from space into the earth's atmosphere, breaking the sound barrier, and, at 7:17 a.m., slammed into the ground in the central Siberian plateau.

---

*Note that APA requires a separate cover page with the student's name, course title, instructor name, and date centered at the bottom of the page. The paper's title should be centered in the middle of the page. All pages have a short version of the essay's title and the page number at the top, including the cover page.

Figure 1 A map of the Tunguska region, showing the extent of the blast's impact and the region's remote location in Siberia.

Moments before the collision, a thrust of energy caused people and animals to be strewn about, structures destroyed, and trees toppled. Immediately afterward, a pillar or "tongue" of fire could be seen in the sky several hundred miles away; others called it a cylindrical pipe. A thermal air current of extremely high temperature caused forest fires to ignite and spread across 40 miles, melting metal objects scattered throughout the area. Several shock waves were felt for hundreds of miles around, breaking windows and tossing people, animals, and objects in the air. Finally, black rain fell from a menacing-looking cloud over a radius of 100 miles. It is no wonder that the peasants of the Tunguska River Valley thought that this was the end of the world (Baxter & Atkins, 1976; Krinov, 1966).

For a variety of reasons, this devastating occurrence remained almost unknown outside Russia—and even outside central Siberia—for many years. The Tungus (see Figure 1) is extremely remote, even for Russia, which is such a vast country that transportation and communication between places can be slow and difficult. The few people living in the area who actually witnessed what happened were mostly peasants and nomadic tribesmen, and did not have much opportunity or inclination to talk about what they had seen. There was little publicity, and what there was was limited to local Siberian newspapers (Krinov, 1966). During that summer, there was a lot of discussion in the newspapers of the European capitals about peculiar lights and colors seen in the northern skies, unusually radiant sunsets, some magnetic disturbances, and strange dust clouds (Cowan, Atluri, & Libby, 1965). But, since news of the events at the Tungus River had hardly yet been heard even in Moscow, there was no way for scientists in other countries to see a connection between these happenings.

It was only in 1921, when Russia was relatively stable after years of war, revolution, and economic problems, that the first expedition to investigate the event at Tunguska actually took place (Crowther, 1931). That it occurred then at all was largely because an energetic Russian scientist, Leonid Kulik, had become fascinated by meteorites. He read in an old Siberian newspaper that, in 1908, a railway train had been forced to stop because a meteorite fell in its path—a story that was quite untrue. Kulik thought that he might become the discoverer of the greatest meteorite ever found on earth and determined to search for evidence that such a meteorite existed. Authorized by the Soviet Academy, Kulik led a series of expeditions to the Tungus River. In 1921, he did not even reach the site, for the route was almost impassable. In 1927, and annually for the next few years, Kulik did, indeed, explore the devastated area and was able to study the evidence of what had happened and listen to the oral accounts of the event provided by those inhabitants who were still alive and who were willing to talk to him. Finally, in 1938–39, Kulik traveled to the Tungus for the last time, for the purpose of taking aerial photographs that might confirm his meteorite theory (Baxter & Atkins, 1976).

Kulik and his fellow investigators believed that whatever had happened at the Tungus River had been caused by a meteorite. So, what they expected to find was a single, vast crater to mark the place where the meteorite had landed. Such a crater, however, was simply not there (Cowan, Atluri, & Libby, 1965). Instead, Kulik found a vast devastated and burned area, a forest of giant trees with their tops cut off and scattered around (Crowther, 1931). In 1928, without the benefit of an aerial view of the region, Kulik concluded from his various vantage points on the ground that, around the circumference of the area where the meteorite had landed, there was a belt of upright dead trees, which he named the "telegraph pole forest." Scattered around the perimeter of the frozen swamp, which he called the "cauldron," were groups of fallen trees, with their tops all pointing away from the direction of where the blast had occurred (Cowan, Atluri, & Libby, 1965). None of this was consistent with Kulik's meteorite theory, and he could only attribute the odd pattern of upright and fallen trees to a shock wave or "hot compressed-air pockets," which had missed some trees and affected others (Baxter & Atkins, 1976). The account of his discovery in the *Literary Digest* of 1929 states that "each of the falling meteoric fragments must have worked, the Russian scientists imagine, like a gigantic piston," with compressed air knocking trees down like toothpicks ("What a Meteor," 1929, p. 34). Kulik continued to insist that the fire and the resultant effect on the trees was the result of a meteorite explosion. But the Russian scientist V. G. Fesenkov estimated that such destruction could only have been caused by an object of at least several hundred meters, and that, if anything of this size or force had hit the ground, it would have left a crater (Baxter & Atkins, 1976).

Kulik found other evidence that could not easily be explained by the meteorite theory. Although there was no trace of a single large crater (Cowan, Atluri, & Libby, 1965), there were numerous shallow cavities scattered around the frozen bog (Olivier, 1928). For several years, Kulik attempted to bore into the ground, seeking evidence that these pits and ridges were formed by lateral pressure caused by gases exploding from the meteorite's impact. Kulik described the scene as "not unlike a giant duplicate of what happens when a brick from a tall chimney-top falls into a puddle of mud. Solid ground actually must have splashed outward in every direction." In this account, the supposed meteorite became "the great swarm of meteors" that "must have traversed" the atmosphere for several hundred miles, pushing ahead of it a "giant bubble of superheated atmosphere" that was "probably responsible" for the burned countryside ("What a Meteor," 1929, p. 33). All the "must have's" and "probably's" make a good narrative, but are not scientifically convincing.

Similarly, Kulik endeavored to explain eyewitness accounts of the huge fireball in the sky that burned one observer's shirt off his back and threw him off his porch (Cowan, Atluri, & Libby, 1965). Such extreme heat waves had never before been known to have accompanied the fall of a meteorite, but Kulik decided that this meteorite was much larger than those previously recorded and that therefore it would have released much more energy upon impact and that would account for such radiant heat (Baxter & Atkins, 1976). So obsessed was Kulik with the idea that somewhere buried in the Tungus swamp was a phenomenal meteorite that he focused the efforts of all the expeditions to the area during his lifetime on digging beneath the frozen tundra and to some extent neglected the examination of other evidence that might have further threatened the theory that he was determined to prove (Parry, 1961). Initially, he was successful in convincing the scientific community that his theory was correct. It is most interesting to read excerpts from the *American Weekly* of 1929 flatly asserting that a meteorite had fallen in Siberia and that Professor Kulik had brought back photographs of the giant crater that he found, as well as small samples of meteoric materials. The article is accompanied by a photograph of Professor Kulik measuring "the main crater, where the largest mass of this celestial visitor buried itself in the earth" (as cited in "What a Meteor," p. 34).

While Kulik's expeditions were still searching for evidence of a meteorite, other scientists were hypothesizing that the Tunguska explosion might have been caused by a small comet, which would account for the absence of a crater. Comets are composed of ice, frozen gases, and dust, and as they travel around the sun, they develop a long tail. Upon impact, a comet might give off a trail of gases and dust, which would create a bright and colorful night sky similar to that observed after the explosion. This would not be true of a meteorite, which has no gaseous trail and thus leaves no trace in the atmosphere. It has also been suggested that the observed direction of the object's travel was more typical of a comet than a meteorite (Florensky, 1963). If the comet had blown up approximately two miles above the site, that would explain why some trees survived while others did not (Parry, 1961). On the other hand, there is no evidence that a comet had ever crashed on earth before, or caused a comparable change in magnetic and atmospheric phenomena, or even come so close without being sighted (Baxter & Atkins, 1976). Those scientists supporting the comet theory have suggested that, although it is unusual for any comet to come that close to earth without anyone sighting it, the one landing at Tunguska might have been small enough to go by unnoticed. But that idea is contradicted by Fesenkov's estimate that, to cause such destruction, the nucleus of the Tunguskan comet— if there was one—would have been only slightly smaller than those of well-documented comets that were visible at great distances (Cowan, Atluri, & Libby, 1965).

The next major explanation for the cosmic phenomenon at Tunguska could only have been formulated after World War II, when the scientific community had learned how to make atomic explosions and had become familiar with their aftermath. Aleksander Kazantsev, a Russian scientist and (equally important) science-fiction writer, had visited Hiroshima after the atom bomb explosion and had studied the data describing its impact and aftermath. Because of certain similarities in the blast effects—the burnt yet upright trees, the mushroom cloud, the black rain—Kazantsev and other scientists concluded that the blast of 1908 was an atomic explosion estimated at a minimum of ten times the strength of the one at Hiroshima (Parry, 1961). Witnesses had described the blinding flash and withering heat at Hiroshima in much the same way that the Siberian peasants described the frightening blast at Tunguska. The melting heat that Kulik found so inconsistent with his meteorite theory was more consistent with an atomic explosion (Baxter & Atkins, 1976). It is worth pointing out that scientists went on to develop the hypothesis that a nuclear explosion had occurred at Tunguska even though their theorizing was largely based on stories told by ignorant peasants, believers in devils and wrathful gods, who could quite easily have exaggerated what had actually happened to improve their stories. Even though these eyewitness accounts were gathered twenty or more years after the actual event, and had quite possibly entered the folklore of the countryside (Krinov, 1966), they were still regarded as the purest evidence.

To test whether a nuclear explosion might have occurred, scientists examined the trees for radioactivity and for any unusual increase in normal growth patterns, shown by greater spacing between the age lines, that might have been the result of radioactivity. What they found was that some trees at the site grew to be four times greater than what would normally have been expected. Similarly, scabs that appeared on the hides of local reindeer were explained as being the result of radioactive contamination (Baxter & Atkins, 1976). This evidence, by no means conclusive (Florensky, 1963), was cited as proof that such an atomic explosion had taken place, just as Kulik had cited the existence of shallow pits in the terrain as proof that a meteorite had exploded.

Assuming that what happened at Tunguska was the result of an atomic blast, and faced with the fact that nuclear fission was not within man's grasp before the 1940s, Kazantsev and his colleagues concluded that the phenomenon must have involved extraterrestrial beings and that the explosion was caused by a UFO, propelled by atomic energy, that crashed (Parry, 1961). The pattern of devastation on the ground, as seen from the air, suggested that the object took a zigzag path, changing its direction as it came closer and closer to earth. Advocates of the UFO theory argue such a change in direction would not have been possible with a natural object like a meteorite or comet, and that the object—a spacecraft—was driven by intelligent beings who were trying to land without hitting a more densely populated area. They hypothesize that the craft had some mechanical problem that made it necessary to land but that the initial angle of its trajectory was too shallow for landing and would only have bounced the craft back into space. So the navigators tried to maneuver and correct the angle, but swerved, came down too sharply, and exploded (Baxter & Atkins, 1976). On the other hand, it seems just as possible that a natural object swerved or that debris from a nonatomic explosion was thrown in zigzag directions than that navigators from outer space ran into mechanical troubles and crash-landed. If probability is going to be disregarded in order to support one theory, then the same suspension of the natural order of things can be used to confirm an equally unlikely theory.

In the late 1950s, an exploratory team examined the Tunguska site with an advanced magnetic detector and, in 1962, scientists magnified the soil and found an array of tiny, colored, magnetic, ball-shaped particles, made of cobalt, nickel, copper, and germanium (Baxter & Atkins, 1976). According to extraterrestrial-intelligence specialists, these could have been the elements used for electrical and technical instruments, with the copper used for communication services and the germanium used in semiconductors (Parry, 1961). However, controlled experiments would be necessary to make this atomic-extraterrestrial argument convincing.

Even though it took place over one hundred years ago in a desolate part of the world, such a photogenic event as the Tunguskan phenomenon hasn't escaped being captured in videos. One example is a History Channel production (Wegher, 2014) that uses colorful reconstructions and interviews with scientists (whose credentials are not on display) to suggest that the phenomenon was the result of the landing of a UFO and a nuclear explosion, combined. As one commentator on the program observed: "They sent a message for us to know...that they are watching us very benevolently."

Scientists who find the UFO and extraterrestrial explanations less than credible have turned to the most recent theories of physics and astronomy to explain what might have happened in the Tungus. Some (including Kazantsev) argue that such an explosion might have been caused by debris from space colliding with the earth (Morrison & Chapman, 1990), or by antimatter, which exploded as it came in contact with the atmosphere (Parry, 1961). Alternatively, the explosion might have been caused by a "black hole" hitting the earth in Siberia and passing through to emerge on the other side. Those opposing these theories point, again, to the absence of a crater and to the numerous eyewitness accounts that describe the shape of the object and the sound of the blast, all of which would be inconsistent with antimatter or black-hole theories (Baxter & Atkins, 1976). However, a 1973 article in *Nature* asserts that a black hole would not, in fact, leave a crater, but would simply enter the earth at a great velocity and that a shock wave and blast might possibly accompany its entrance (Jackson & Ryan, 1973). Comparisons have also been made with a similar but smaller incident that happened in 1930, in a stretch of Brazilian jungle as remote as Tunguska. Eyewitnesses reported the appearance of three fireballs, resulting in a one-megaton explosion and massive destruction of the forest. Coincidentally or not, the explosion occurred at the same time as the yearly Perseids meteor shower. The investigation into this phenomenon has been hampered by the unavailability of the eyewitness accounts, contained in diaries that are held by the Vatican (Stacy, 1996).

Even with the trail getting colder, scientists have not given up on finding out what occurred on June 30, 1908. In recent years, conferences have taken place almost annually, in Moscow and in Krasnoyarsk, Siberia, to exchange theories and examine on-site evidence. Andrei Ol'khovatov (2001), an independent scientist with a website devoted to Tunguska, believes that the explosion was "a manifestation of tectonic energy" related to the release of atmospheric energy in several notable earthquakes that have demonstrated some of the same electrical and fiery phenomena. In 1999, an expedition from the University of Bologna, headed by Dr. Luigi Foschini and focused on Lake Ceko, not far from Lake Tunguska, used sonar and underwater cameras before drilling for samples from the lake bed (Foschini, 1999). Shortly afterward, Dr. Robert Foot of the

Sovfoto/UGI via Getty Images

Figure 2 An aerial photograph of the blast site in 1999, showing some of the 2,200 square kilometers (800 square miles) in which 60 million trees were destroyed.

University of Melbourne claimed that the cause of the Tunguska explosion must have been "mirror matter": matter that exists in the universe to spin in the opposite direction from the normal spinning of subatomic material and so "maintain left-right symmetry in the Universe." Foot said that mirror matter is "very hard to detect," but "interaction between atoms in the air and mirror atoms" could happen and might have caused an explosion of Tunguskan dimensions (Chown, 2001).

In recent years, conflicting theories still abound. Continuing to explore the possibility of impact from a comet, Bill Napier and David Asher (2009) suggest that heavy-duty, "globally destructive impactors [that] ultimately derive from the Oort Cloud" of comets may be related to the Tunguska event (p. 121). There is also an ongoing struggle, fought in the pages of geological journals, between one group of Italian scientists, who believe that the nearby Lake Cheko might be a secondary impact crater and thus offer proof that the events at Lake Tunguska were, indeed, caused by a meteor's impact (Gasperini et al., 2007), and a second international group of scientists, who insist that the environment around Lake Cheko doesn't suggest that a meteor might have landed and that no meteorite could have been large enough to make that big a hole (Collins et al., 2008). In 2012, Vladamir Rubtsov (2013) ruled out the asteroid and comet theories and seemed to concede defeat, concluding that "there seems to exist in space another type of dangerous space objects [sic] whose nature still remains unknown."

At the same time, building on Ol'khovatov's idea of tectonic energy, Wolfgang Kundt is turning the "meteor from outer space" theory inside out, arguing that what happened at Tunguska took anywhere from two minutes to an hour—far longer than it would for a meteor to land. He points out that, according to eyewitness accounts, "one man even had time [to wash] in the bath house to meet the death clean." Partly on this basis, Kundt concludes that the outburst came from inside the earth, not the sky, and involved a "Kimberline," a tall, very thin funnel found at places where the earth conceals a fracture zone. When the natural gas within the Kimberline explodes, it vents violently upward like a big mushroom cloud (Kundt, 2007, p. 333), an image that seems to account for an earlier generation's "atomic bomb" theory.

The mystery of the Tunguskan phenomenon has recently become headline news again. First, a burst of meteorites appeared to fall in Chelyabinsk on February 13, 2013. Many months later, investigators were able to raise a huge, 1,257-pound, five-foot rock from the bottom of Cerbarkul Lake. NASA has described what landed in Chelyabinsk as "a tiny asteroid," and scientists are hopeful that their tests will confirm that the rock—which arrived with a bright flash and a monstrous noise—will be identified as a meteor similar to the one that (according to CNN) landed at Tunguska (Smith-Spark, 2013).

Less than a year later, on September 6, 2014, when inhabitants of Managua, Nicaragua, heard an enormous noise and felt the earth shuddering, the first reaction of scientists was that a Tunguskan-variety meteorite might have landed. Although there was no flash of fire in the air, the discovery of a large crater initially seemed to suggest that whatever crashed was part of an asteroid that had been scheduled to pass overhead around the same time. Subsequently, it was confirmed that the asteroid had been long gone—13 hours—by the time the impact occurred, and even the existence of the crater (first reported by *National Geographic*) was, in NASA's view, no longer certain (Dattaro, 2014). As with previous phenomena, the scientists' inability to agree on what actually happened adds greatly to the human interest of the event.

What is most fascinating about the Tunguska Valley phenomenon is that, despite all the advances in science over the past 100 years, investigators cannot now be any more certain of the cause of the blast than they were in 1921, when Kulik first came near the site. None of the theories presented is wholly convincing, for all of them rely to some extent on human observers, whose accounts of events are notoriously unreliable, or hypotheses based on ambiguous evidence, without the support of controlled tests and experiments. Even the introduction of modern, high-tech equipment has not established a convincing explanation.

Examining these hypotheses about what did or did not land and explode in Siberia does teach us that scientific theories are sometimes based on the selective interpretation of evidence and that scientists, like everyone else, tend to believe their own theories and find the evidence that they want to find. Although the language that they use is very different, the accounts of what happened at Tunguska according to Kulik, Kazantsev, and their other scientific colleagues are not so very different from what the local peasants say that they saw. Both have a closer resemblance to science fiction than science fact.

References

Baxter, J., & Atkins, T. (1976). *The fire came by: The riddle of the great Siberian explosion.* Garden City, NY: Doubleday.

Chown, M. (2001, July 28). What lies beneath. *New Scientist, 54*(2301), 17.

Collins, G. S., Artemieva, N., Wu, K., Bland, P. A., Reimold, W. U., & Koeber, C. (2008). Evidence that Lake Cheko is not an impact crater. *Terra Nova, 20,* 165–168. doi:10.1111/j.1365-3121.2008.00791.x

Cowan, C., Atluri, C. R., & Libby, W. F. (1965, May 29). Possible antimatter content of the Tunguska meteor of 1908. *Nature, 206,* 861–865.

Crowther, J. G. (1931). More about the great Siberian meteorite. *Scientific American, 144*(5), 314–317.

Dattaro, L. (2014, September 9). *Was Nicaragua crater caused by a meteorite? Unlikely, says NASA.* Retrieved from Weather Channel website: http://www.weather.com/news/science/space/was-nicaragua-crater-caused-by-a-meteorite-unlikely-says-nasa-2014090

Florensky, K. P. (1963, November). Did a comet collide with the earth in 1908? *Sky and Telescope, 26*, 268–269.

Foschini, L. (1999, July 28). *Last operations in Tunguska*. Retrieved from University of Bologna Department of Physics website: http://www-th.bo.infn.it/tunguska/press2807_en.htm

Gasperini, L., Alvisi, F., Biasini, G., Bonatti, E., Longo, G., Pipan, M., & Serra, R. (2007). A possible impact crater for the 1908 Tunguska Event. *Terra Nova, 19*, 245–251. doi:10.1111/j.1365-3121.2007.00742.x

Jackson, A. A., & Ryan, M. P. (1973, September 14). Was the Tungus event due to a black hole? *Nature, 245*, 88–89.

Krinov, E. L. (1966). *Giant meteorites*. London, England: Pergamon.

Kundt, W. (2007). What happened north of the Stony Tunguska River in the early morning of 30 June 1908? In P. T. Bobrowsky & H. Rickman (Eds.), *Comet/asteroid impacts and human society: An interdisciplinary approach* (pp. 331–332). Berlin, Germany: Springer.

Morrison, D., & Chapman, C. R. (1990, March). Target earth: It will happen. *Sky and Telescope, 79*, 261–265.

Napier, B., & Asher, D. (2009). The Tunguska impact event and beyond. *Astronomy and Geophysics, 50*(1), 1.18–1.26. doi:10.1111/j.1468-4004.2009.50118.x

Olivier, C. P. (1928). The great Siberian meteorite. *Scientific American, 139*(1), 42–44.

Ol'khovatov, A. (2001, June 28). *The tectonic interpretation of the 1908 Tunguska event*. Retrieved from http://olkhov.narod.ru/tunguska/index.html

Parry, A. (1961). The Tungus mystery: Was it a spaceship? In A. Parry (Ed.), *Russia's rockets and missiles* (pp. 248–267). London, England: Macmillan.

Rubtsov, V. (2013). *Reconstruction of the Tunguska event of 1908: Neither an asteroid, nor a comet core*. Retrieved from Cornell University Library website: http://arxiv.org/abs/1302.6273

Smith-Spark, L. (2013, October 17). *Russian divers find huge suspected meteorite chunk in Chelyabinsk*. Retrieved from CNN website: http://www.cnn.com/2013/10/17/world/europe/space-russia-chelyabinsk-meteorite/

Stacy, D. (1996). *Another Tunguska?* Retrieved from Anomalist website: http://www.anomalist.com/reports/tunguska.html

Wegher, B. (Producer). (2014). *Was the 1908 Siberian blast an early atomic bomb?* [Television film]. United States: The History Channel.

What a meteor did to Siberia. (1929, March 16). *Literary Digest*, 33–34.

·12·

Some Basic Forms
for Documentation:
MLA, APA, and Endnotes

MLA Style

The Modern Language Association (MLA) style is used primarily in the humanities. It calls for sources to be cited in the text through a signal phrase and parenthetical citation. A Works Cited page at the end of the essay provides full bibliographic information for all your sources. See p. 461 for a model Works Cited page.

You can find guidelines for preparing MLA documentation in Chapter 10, on pages 452–460. See also the list of Works Cited in the student essay "Looking at Horror Films," on pages 497–498 in Chapter 11. For more details and examples, as well as guidelines for kinds of sources not listed here, see the seventh edition of the *MLA Handbook*, 8th edition (2016).

MLA Style In-Text Citations

Provide an in-text citation for all quotations, paraphrases, summaries, or ideas or information taken from sources. Remember that in your essay, you will often include the author's name within your sentence. In such cases, your in-text citation need only include the page number. If you have not named the source via a signal phrase, list both the author's name and the page number in parentheses at the end of the sentence.

Author Named in a Signal Phrase

As Erik Larson writes, many Americans believe that the sinking of the *Lusitania* spurred Woodrow Wilson to join World War I, when in fact more than two years passed before the U.S. declared war on Germany (355).

Author Named in Parenthetical Citation

By the last few decades of the twentieth century, hospitals became the place where most Americans died, with only 17% of patients dying at home (Gawande 6).

Unknown Author

Use the work's complete title in a signal phrase or a shortened version of the title in the parenthetical citation.

Daily physical activity is an essential part of combating Type 2 diabetes ("Diabetes & Kids").

Two Authors

The Internet has enabled donors to remain connected to the recipients of their charitable giving and follow the impact of their dollars over time (Kristof and WuDunn 12).

Three or More Authors

Give only the first author's last name, followed by the abbreviation "et al." (Latin for "and others").

When patients report extreme pain, they often perceive it as "a threat to their continued existence—not merely to their lives, but to their integrity as persons" (Henderson et al. 11).

Corporate or Government Author

List the organization as you would the author.

Doctors without Borders estimates that the humanitarian crisis in Syria has displaced more than 10 million citizens, both within the country and among neighboring nations.

Two or More Works by the Same Author

Distinguish two works by the same author by including in the parenthetical citation a brief version of the title of each work, followed by the page number.

> According to McCullough, the great construction projects of the 1870s ushered in "a momentous new Age of Progress" in the nation (*Great Bridge* 81); such striving was proudly believed to be "in the American grain" (*Path* 255).

Two or More Authors with the Same Last Name

In the signal phrase or parenthetical citation, include a first initial to differentiate between authors with the same last name.

> Unlike many of their Eastern European counterparts, the Jewish and Muslim communities of Uzbekistan spoke a common language (A. Cooper 9).

Source Quoted in Another Source

Use the abbreviation "qtd. in" and cite the original source.

> Unable to distinguish the vocabulary of the natives of Tierra del Fuego, Charles Darwin pronounced that "their language does not deserve to be called articulate" (qtd. in Hawken 91).

Source Without Page Numbers

List a section or paragraph number, if given. Otherwise, list the author's name only.

> Despite the popular belief in the familial, health, and social benefits of family dinner, "the stress that cooking puts on people, particularly women, may not be worth the trade-off" (Marcotte).

MLA Works Cited

Print Sources

Start with the author's name. Then give the title (and subtitle, if any), italicized. List any containers in which the source appears, such as a periodical or anthology, and any contributors to the source. Give the version and number, if any, followed by the publisher (abbreviating "University Press" as "UP"), the publication date, and any page numbers for the source. Separate these items with commas.

Book by a Single Author

Ng, Celeste. *Everything I Never Told You.* Penguin, 2014.

Books by Two Authors

List the first author last name first; list the second author first name first.

Kristof, Nicholas, and Sheryl WuDunn. *A Path Appears: Transforming Lives, Creating Opportunity.* Knopf, 2014.

Book by Three or More Authors

List only the first author's name followed by "et al."

Spiller, Robert E., et al. *Literary History of the United States.* Macmillan, 1946.

Corporate Author

National Geographic. *National Geographic Road Atlas.* National Geographic Society, 2014.

Edited Collection of Essays Written by Different Authors

Kanna, Ahmed, editor. *The Superlative City: Dubai and the Urban Condition in the Twenty-First Century.* Harvard UP, 2013.

Essay from an Edited Collection

Mitchell, Kevin. "The Future Promise of Architecture in Dubai." *The Superlative City: Dubai and the Urban Condition in the Twenty-First Century,* edited by Ahmed Kanna, Harvard UP, 2013, pp. 149-66.

If you are citing more than one essay from the collection, do not repeat the full publication information for the collection. After the essay title, give the editor's name and the page numbers of the essay.

Mitchell, Kevin. "The Future Promise of Architecture in Dubai." Kanna, pp. 149-66.

Author with an Editor or Translator

Gavron, Assaf. *The Hilltop: A Novel.* Translated by Steven Cohen, Scribner, 2014.

Book in a Republished Edition

Orwell, George. *Animal Farm*. 1946. Signet, 1959.

Multivolume Work

Belasco, Susan, and Linck Johnson, editors. *The Bedford Anthology of
American Literature*. Bedford, 2014. 2 vols.

Introduction, Preface, Foreword, or Afterword

Dunham, Lena. Foreword. *The Liars' Club*, by Mary Karr, Penguin Classics,
2015, pp. xi-xiii.

Sacred or Classic Text

The Jerusalem Bible. Edited by Alexander Jones, Reader's Edition,
Doubleday, 1963.

Pamphlet or Brochure

Cite a brochure as you would a book.

The Legendary Sleepy Hollow Cemetery. Friends of Sleepy Hollow Cemetery,
2008.

Entry in an Encyclopedia, Dictionary, or Wiki

If no author is given, start with the title of the entry. Page numbers are not
needed because the entries are arranged alphabetically. If the work is not well-
known, provide the full publication information.

Robinson, Lisa Clayton. "Harlem Writers Guild." *Africana: The Encyclopedia
of the African and African American Experience*, 2nd ed., Oxford UP, 2005.

Government Publication

Start with the name of the government followed by the name of the department
and the agency, if there is one.

United States, Department of Education. *Helping Young Children and
Families Cope with Trauma*. Government Printing Office, 2012.

Article in a Scholarly Journal

Ramsay, Debra. "Brutal Games: *Call of Duty* and the Cultural Narrative of
World War II." *Cinema Journal*, vol. 54, no. 2, Winter 2015, pp. 94-113.

Article in a Monthly Magazine

> Bryan, Christy. "Ivory Worship." *National Geographic*, Oct. 2012, pp. 28-61.

Article in a Weekly Magazine

> Grossman, Lev. "A Star Is Born." *Time*, 2 Nov. 2015, pp. 30-39.

Article in a Newspaper

If the city is not part of the newspaper's title, include it in brackets. If sections are numbered, include the section number after the date.

> Krantz, Laura. "Remedial Math Not Always a Solution." *The Boston Globe*,
> 4 July 2015, p. A1.

Article without an Author

Start with the title, as you would for a book without an author.

> "Milestones." *Ms*, Fall 2014, p. 9.

Letter to the Editor

Insert the label "Letter" after the title, or, if there is no title, after the author's name.

> Tobler, Matthew. "Climate Geoengineering." *Scientific American*, 14 Apr.
> 2015, p. 6. Letter.

Editorial

Cite an editorial as you would cite an article with no author, inserting the label "Editorial" after the title.

> "Prosecute Torturers and Their Bosses." *The New York Times*, 22 Dec. 2014,
> p. A26. Editorial.

Book or Film Review

List the reviewer first, followed by the title of the review. Then insert "Rev. of" and the title of the work being reviewed. For a book, add the author's name after the book title. For a film or other media, use the director's name.

> Lane, Anthony. "Human Bondage." Review of *Spectre*, directed by Sam
> Mendes, *The New Yorker*, 16 Nov. 2015, pp. 96-97.

Interview

Start with the person being interviewed. You may choose to list the name of the interviewer.

> Adichie, Chimamanda Ngozi. Interview by Chinelo Okparanta, *Poets & Writers*, July-August 2013, pp. 46-47.

Letter

Include the label "Letter to" and list the recipient and the date. If the letter is not dated, use "n.d." for "no date." Treat a published letter as an entry in a collection, providing the title of the collection, editor, publication information, and medium. For a personal letter, include the label "Letter to the author." Give the medium as "MS" ("manuscript") for a handwritten letter, or "TS" ("typescript") for a typed letter.

> Bishop, Elizabeth. Letter to Marianne Moore, 5 Feb. 1940. *One Art: Letters of Elizabeth Bishop*, edited by Robert Giroux, Farrar, 1994, p. 87.
> Appel, Jonathan. Letter to the author, 14 Dec. 2011.

Unpublished Dissertation

> Werlin, Julianne. "The Impossible Probable: Modeling Utopia in Early Modern England." Dissertation, Princeton U, 2012.

Electronic Sources

Here is the general format for sources from the Web. Include as many of the following elements as you can find. Some sources may have more than one container, such as a periodical and a database. If a DOI is available, give that instead of the URL. If no publication date is given, end with the date you accessed the source. Omit the publisher of a Web site when it is the same as the Web site's title.

> Author's last name, First name. "Title of the Work." *Title of the Container*. Publisher, date, URL.

Entire Web Site

> Halsall, Paul, editor. *Internet Modern History Sourcebook*. Fordham U, 4 Nov. 2011, legacy.fordham.edu/halsall/index.asp.

Short Work on a Web Site

> Enzinna, Wes. "Syria's Unknown Revolution." *Pulitzer Center on Crisis Reporting*, 24 Nov. 2015, pulitzercenter.org/projects/middle-east -syria-enzinna-war-rojava.

Book Accessible on the Web

List the print publication information first, followed by the title of the Web site, e-reader format, or database.

> Singer, Peter. *Practical Ethics*. Cambridge UP, 1993. *Google Books*, books .google.com/books?id=lNgnV0eDtM0C.
> Doerr, Anthony. *All the Light We Cannot See*. Scribner, 2014. Nook.
> Goldsmith, Oliver. *The Vicar of Wakefield: A Tale*. Philadelphia, 1801. *America's Historical Imprints*, infoweb.newsbank.com.ezproxy.bpl.org/.

Article in an Online Journal

Format as you would an article from a scholarly print journal, but end with the URL.

> Bryson, Devin. "The Rise of a New Senegalese Cultural Philosophy?" *African Studies Quarterly*, vol. 14, no. 3, Mar. 2014, pp. 33-56, asq.africa.ufl.edu/files/Volume-14-Issue-3-Bryson.pdf.

Article in a Database

Format as you would an article from an online journal, but insert the name of the database and DOI, if available.

> Coles, Kimberly Anne. "The Matter of Belief in John Donne's Holy Sonnets." *Renaissance Quarterly*, vol. 68, no. 3, Fall 2015, pp. 899-931. *JSTOR*, doi:10.1086/683855.

Article in a Newspaper

> Crowell, Maddy. "How Computers Are Getting Better at Detecting Liars." *The Christian Science Monitor*, 12 Dec. 2015, www.csmonitor.com /Science/Science-Notebook/2015/1212/How-computers-are-getting -better-at-detecting-liars.

Article in an Online Magazine

> Leonard, Andrew. "The Surveillance State High School." *Salon*, 27 Nov. 2012, www.salon.com/2012/11/27/the_surveillance_state_high_school/.

Entire Blog

Ng, Amy. *Pikaland*. Pikaland Media, 2015, www.pikaland.com/.

Blog Post or Comment

Eakin, Emily. "*Cloud Atlas's* Theory of Everything." *NYR Daily*, NYREV,
2 Nov. 2012, www.nybooks.com/daily/2012/11/02/ken-wilber-cloud
-atlas/.

mitchellfreedman. Comment on "*Cloud Atlas's* Theory of Everything," by
Emily Eakin. *NYR Daily*, NYREV, 3 Nov. 2012, www.nybooks.com
/daily/2012/11/02/ken-wilber-cloud-atlas/.

E-mail Message

Thornbrugh, Caitlin. "Coates Lecture." Received by Rita Anderson, 20 Oct.
2015.

Posting to an Online Forum or Discussion List

Give the subject line as the title, in quotation marks.

Yen, Jessica. "Quotations within Parentheses (Study Measures)."
Copyediting-L, 18 Mar. 2016, list.indiana.edu/sympa/arc/copyediting
-l/2016-03/msg00492.html.

Tweet

In place of a title, list the entire tweet in quotation marks. List the date, time,
and URL.

YAppelbaum. "I earnestly, honestly believe that never before have
intellectuals reached such large audiences with so much fine work."
Twitter, 1 July 2015, 8:49 a.m., https://twitter.com/YAppelbaum
/status/616272425244827648.

Facebook Post

Bedford English. "Stacey Cochran explores Reflective Writing in the classroom and as a writer: http://ow.ly/YkjVB." *Facebook*, 15 Feb. 2016,
www.facebook.com/BedfordEnglish/posts/10153415001259607.

Audio, Visual, and Other Sources

Film

> *Inside Out.* Directed by Pete Docter, Pixar, 2015.

If you wish to emphasize the director, list him or her first, before the film's title.

> Linklater, Richard, director. *Boyhood.* Performances by Patricia Arquette
> and Ethan Hawke, IFC, 2014.

Television or Radio Episode

List the episode in quotation marks, then give the title of the program in italics and any contributers, such as the writer, director, performers, or narrator; the network; and the date of broadcast.

> "Free Speech on College Campuses." *Washington Journal,* narrated by Peter
> Slen, C-SPAN, 27 Nov. 2015.

If you viewed or listened to the program on the Web, end with the URL.

> "Take a Giant Step." *Prairie Home Companion,* narrated by Garrison Keillor,
> American Public Media, 27 Feb. 2016, prairiehome.publicradio.org
> /listen/full/?name=phc/2016/02/27/phc_20160227_128.

Live Performance

> *The Draft.* By Peter Snoad, directed by Diego Arciniegas, Hibernian Hall,
> Boston, 10 Sept. 2015.

Lecture or Address

> Smith, Anna Deavere. "On the Road: A Search for American Character."
> National Endowment for the Humanities, John F. Kennedy Center for
> the Performing Arts, Washington, 6 Apr. 2015. Address.

For a lecture or address viewed on the Web, italicize the name of the Web site and give the URL.

> Khosla, Raj. "Precision Agriculture and Global Food Security." *US
> Department of State: Diplomacy in Action,* 26 Mar. 2013, www.state
> .gov/e/stas/series/212172.htm. Address.

Podcast

McDougall, Christopher. "How Did Endurance Help Early Humans
Survive?" *TED Radio Hour*, National Public Radio, 20 Nov. 2015, www
.npr.org/2015/11/20/455904655/how-did-endurance-help-early
-humans-survive.

Sound Recording

You may choose to list the composer or the performer first, depending on
whom you want to emphasize.

Bizet, Georges. *Carmen*. Performances by Jennifer Larmore, Thomas Moser,
Angela Gheorghiu, and Samuel Ramey, Bavarian State Orchestra and
Chorus, conducted by Giuseppe Sinopoli, Warner, 1996.
Adele. "Hello." 25. XL, 2015.

Work of Art

For an original work of art, list the institution and city where the artwork is
found. For artworks viewed on the Web, add the URL.

Brueghel, Pieter. *The Beggars*. 1568, Louvre, Paris.
Brueghel, Pieter. *The Beggars*. 1568, Louvre, Paris, www.louvre.fr/en
/oeuvre-notices/beggars.

Map, Chart, or Table

If you accessed the visual online, give the URL.

"Number of Measles Cases by Year since 2010." *Centers for Disease Control
and Prevention*, 2 Jan. 2016, www.cdc.gov/measles/cases-outbreaks
.html.

Cartoon

Zyglis, Adam. "City of Light." *Buffalo News*, 8 Nov. 2015, adamzyglis
.buffalonews.com/2015/11/08/city-of-light/. Cartoon.

Advertisement

AT&T. *National Geographic*, Dec. 2015, p. 14. Advertisement.
Toyota. *The Root*. Slate Group, 28 Nov. 2015, www.theroot.com.
Advertisement.

APA Style

The documentation format recommended by the American Psychological Association is used primarily in the social and behavioral sciences, especially in sociology and psychology. It is also often employed in subjects like anthropology, astronomy, business, education, linguistics, and political science. Like MLA style, APA documentation is based on parenthetical references to author and page. The chief difference is that the APA system emphasizes the work's *date of publication*, placing it in parenthesis immediately after the author's name.

> Ordway (2014) noted that the efficacy of speech therapy prior to age 4 increased significantly when it occurred in conjunction with play (p. 781).

APA Style In-Text Citations

Signal phrases in APA style refer to the author by last name only, and they use past tense or present perfect tense, not present tense ("observed" or "has observed," rather than "observes"). Use the abbreviation "p." or "pp." to cite page numbers. Remember that if you include the author's name in your signal phrase, you do not need to repeat it in the parenthetical citation.

MLA

Primitive religious rituals may have been a means for deterring collective violence (Girard 1).

According to Winterowd and Williams, Brain Theory suggests two extremes of writing style, the appositional and the propositional (4).

APA

Primitive religious rituals may have been a means for deterring collective violence (Girard, 1972, p. 1).

According to Winterowd and Williams (2015), Brain Theory suggests two extremes of writing style, the appositional and the propositional (p. 4).

Single Author

As Larson (2015) observed, many Americans believe that the sinking of the *Lusitania* spurred Woodrow Wilson to join World War I, when in fact more than two years passed before the U.S. declared war on Germany (p. 355).

If the author is not named in the signal phrase, insert the author's last name and the year of publication before the page number in the parenthetical citation at the end of the sentence, separated by commas.

> By the last few decades of the twentieth century, hospitals became the place where most Americans died, with only 17% of patients dying at home (Gawande, 2015, p. 6).

Two Authors

> According to Kristof & WuDunn (2014), the Internet has enabled donors to remain connected to the recipients of their charitable giving and follow the impact of their dollars over time (p. 12).

Three, Four, or Five Authors

The first time you cite the source, list all authors in the signal phrase or in the parenthetical citation at the end of sentence. In subsequent citations, use the first author's name followed by "et al."

> Henderson, King, Strauss, Estroff, and Churchill (1997) noted that when patients reported extreme pain, they often perceived it as "a threat to their continued existence—not merely to their lives, but to their integrity as persons" (p. 11).

Six or More Authors

Use the first author's name followed by "et al." in all citations.

> According to Arthur et al. (2015), substance abuse prevention programs have a favorable effect on students' academic achievement (p. 497).

Unknown Author

Use the work's complete title in a signal phrase or a shortened version of the title in the parenthetical citation.

> Daily physical activity has proved to be an essential part of combating Type 2 diabetes ("Diabetes & Kids," 2014).

Corporate or Government Author

List the organization as you would the author, either in a signal phrase or in the parenthetical citation.

> Doctors Without Borders estimated that the humanitarian crisis in Syria has displaced more than 10 million citizens, both within the country and among neighboring nations (p. 14).

Two or More Works by the Same Author in the Same Year

Since APA style gives the year of publication right after the author's name, there is less chance of confusion when citing multiple works by the same author. If two or more works were published in the same year, add a lowercase letter after the year to indicate which work you are citing. You will use that letter in the references list as well.

> In its report *The More Effective Use of Resources*, the Carnegie Commission on Higher Education (1972c) recommended that "colleges and universities develop a 'self-renewal' fund of 1 to 3 percent each year taken from existing allocations" (p. 105).

Two or More Authors with the Same Last Name

Include the author's first initial to distinguish between authors with the same last name.

> Unlike many of their Eastern European counterparts, the Jewish and Muslim communities of Uzbekistan spoke a common language (A. Cooper, p. 9).

Source Quoted in Another Source

Use the phrase "as cited in" to indicate the source where you found the quotation.

> Unable to distinguish the vocabulary of the natives of Tierra del Fuego, Charles Darwin pronounced that "their language does not deserve to be called articulate" (as cited in Hawken, 2007, p. 91).

Source Without Page Numbers

If a Web source lacks page numbers but has paragraph numbers, use those, with the abbreviation "para." If the source lacks paragraph numbers too, give the heading of the section from which you are quoting, then the paragraph number within that section.

> In their 2015 study, Symonds & Deml revealed that male athletes used imagery more frequently during rehabilitation than female athletes (Discussion section, para. 1).

Personal Communication

E-mail messages, letters, interviews, social media posts, and other similar personal communications should be cited in the text only, not in the references list.

> A similar self-portrait painted in 1954 was destroyed in a house fire later that year (T. Meade, personal communication, January 16, 2015).

APA References

Here are some of the ways that APA style lists of references differ from style works cited pages:

- Authors' first and middle names are designated by initials only. When there are multiple authors, they are listed last name first, and an ampersand (&) is used instead of *and*.
- Multiple works by the same author are listed chronologically. Instead of using dashes to indicate the same author, as MLA style does, each entry starts with the author's full name.
- The date of publication is placed in parentheses immediately after the author's name.
- In the title of a book or article, only the first word, the first word of the subtitle, and proper nouns and adjectives are capitalized. The rest of the title should be lowercase.
- Titles of articles and sections of a longer work (e.g., a chapter of a book) are neither italicized nor put in quotation marks.
- Places of publication are included. In the United States, both cities and states are given; for non-U.S. places of publication, cities and countries are given.
- The bibliography is titled *References*, rather than *Works Cited*.

The following is a brief list of model entries for APA style. For additional examples of the use of APA style, see "Explaining the Tunguskan Phenomenon" in Chapter 11 (pp. 500–511).

Print Sources

Start with the author's name and first initial. Then give the title (and subtitle, if any), italicized; only the first word of the title and subtitle, along with any proper nouns, should be capitalized. List the city and state of publication, followed by a colon, and end with a shortened version of the publisher's name (omitting "Inc." or "Co." or initials).

Book by a Single Author

Ng, C. (2014). *Everything I never told you.* New York, NY: Penguin.

Books by Two Authors

Kristof, N. & WuDunn, S. (2014). *A path appears: Transforming lives, creating opportunity.* New York, NY: Knopf.

Book by Three to Seven Authors

List all authors up to seven, giving their last names and middle initials. Use an ampersand (&) before the name of the last author.

> Colombo, G., Cullen, R., & Lisle, B. (2013). *Rereading America: Cultural contexts for critical thinking and writing.* Boston, MA: Bedford/St. Martin's.

Book by Eight or more Authors

List the first six authors followed by three ellipsis dots and the last author's name.

> Sommer, S., Ball, B., Churchill, L., Elkins, C., Janowski, M. J., Roberts, K.,... Archer, E. (2010). *Nursing education.* Leawood, KS: ATI.

Corporate Author

If the author is also the publisher, give the word "Author" in place of the publisher.

> National Geographic Society (2014). *National Geographic Road Atlas.* Washington, DC: Author.

Edited Collection of Essays Written by Different Authors

> Kanna, A. (Ed.). (2013). *The superlative city: Dubai and the urban condition in the twenty-first century.* Cambridge, MA: Harvard University Press.

Essay from an Edited Collection

> Mitchell, K. (2013). The future promise of architecture in Dubai. In A. Kanna (Ed.), *The superlative city: Dubai and the urban condition in the twenty-first century.* (pp. 143–166). Cambridge, MA: Harvard University Press.

Author with an Editor

> Freud, S., & Strachey, J. (Ed.). (1953). *The interpretation of dreams.* New York, NY: Basic Books. (Original work published 1899)

Author with a Translator

> Gavron, A. (2014). *The hilltop: A novel.* (S. Cohen, Trans.). New York, NY: Scribner. (Original work published 2013)

Book in a Republished Edition

> Keynes, J. M. (2009). *The general theory of employment, interest, and money.* 1946. New York, NY: Signet. (Original work published 1965)

Multivolume Work

> Belasco, S., & Johnson, L. (Eds.). (2014). *The Bedford anthology of American literature*. 2 vols. Boston: Bedford/St. Martin's.

Introduction, Preface, Foreword, or Afterword

> Mortimer, I. (2015). Foreword. In K. Warner, *Edward II: The unconventional king* (pp. 9-12). Gloucestershire, England: Amberley.

Sacred or Classical Text

APA does not require listing sacred texts or classical Greek and Roman texts in your references list. Cite them internally.

Government Document

Start with the government agency or department, and put "Author" in the position of the publisher.

> U.S. Education Department. (2012). *Helping young children and families cope with trauma*. Washington, DC: Author.

Article in a Scholarly Journal

Do not use quotation marks around article titles. If each issue of the journal begins with page 1, give the issue number in parentheses directly after the volume. Do not use the abbreviation "pp." for articles in journals or magazines.

> Ramsay, D. (2015). Brutal games: "Call of duty" and the cultural narrative of World War II. *Cinema Journal, 54*(2), 94–113.

Article in a Magazine

> Yager, S. (2015, August). Prison born. *Atlantic, 316*, 62–71.

Article in a Newspaper

Page numbers for newspaper articles do use the abbreviation "p." or "pp."

> Krantz, L. (2015, July 4). Remedial math not always a solution. *The Boston Globe*, p. A1.

Article without an Author

Start with the title and format appropriately for a journal, magazine, or newspaper.

> Milestones. (2014, Fall). *Ms., 24*(3), 9.

Letter to the Editor

Insert the label "Letter to the editor" in brackets after the title. Follow the appropriate style for journals, magazines, or newspapers.

Tobler, M. (2015, April 14). Climate geoengineering. [Letter to the editor]. *Scientific American, 312*(5), 6.

Book or Film Review

After the review title, insert brackets with the label "Review of the book" or "Review of the motion picture," followed by the book or film title. Follow the appropriate style for journals, magazines, or newspapers.

Mann, C. (2015, June). What was famine? [Review of the book *Eating people is wrong, and other essays on famine, its past, and its future*, by Cormac Ó Gráda]. *Pacific Standard, 8*(3), 70–71.

Unpublished Dissertation

Werlin, J. (2012). *The impossible probable: Modeling utopia in early modern England*. (Unpublished doctoral dissertation). Princeton University, Princeton, NJ.

Electronic Sources

The *Publication Manual of the American Psychological Association*, sixth edition, advises that citations should include a digital object identifier (DOI)—a unique number assigned to content, such as a journal article—whenever possible. If a source does not have a DOI, give the URL for the home page of the periodical. If an online document has no page numbers, give paragraph numbers if they are noted onscreen, using the abbreviation "para."

Document from a Web Site

Jorgensen, J. (2015, June 11). *Digital trends in fairy-tale scholarship*. Retrieved from Digital Humanities Now website: http://digitalhumanitiesnow. org/2015/06/editors-choice-digital-trends-in-fairy-tale-scholarship/

Book Accessible on the Web

Give the URL for the home page of the Web site where you viewed the book. For an e-book, use a label to indicate the version, in brackets ("Kindle version," "Nook version").

Singer, P. (1993). *Practical ethics*. Retrieved from http://books.google.com/

Singer, P. (1993). *Practical ethics* [Nook version]. Retrieved from http://www.barnesandnoble.com/

Journal Article Accessible on the Web

Format as you would an article from a scholarly print journal, but end with the DOI. If no DOI is available, give the URL of the home page where you retrieved the article. Do not include the name of the database, if any.

Kowalik, B. (2013). Eros and pilgrimage in Chaucer's and Shakespeare's poetry. *Text Matters, 3*(3), 27-41. doi:10.2478/texmat-2013-0024

Pierce, S., & Arora, K. S. (2015). From impatience to empathy. *Narrative Inquiry in Bioethics, 5*(1), 19-20. Retrieved from http://www.nibjournal.org/

Magazine Article Accessible on the Web

Deneen, P. J. (2015, June). The power elite. *First Things*. Retrieved from http://www.firstthings.com/

Newspaper Article Accessible on the Web

Charney, N. (2011, August 20). Art theft, from the "Mona Lisa" to today. *LA Times*. Retrieved from http://www.latimes.com/

Blog Post or Comment

Start with the author's real name or screen name. For a comment, insert "Re:" before the title of the original blog post. Give the label "Blog post" or "Blog comment" in brackets after the title, followed by the URL of the post.

Gardner, T. (2015, 23 June). Ten ethical scenarios for professional writing [Blog post]. Retrieved from http://blogs.bedfordstmartins.com/bits/business-writing/ten-ethical-scenarios-for-professional-writing/tgardner/

Maryannlibrarian. (2014, April 1). Re: Mobilizing to reduce disparities in health care [Blog comment]. Retrieved from http://chronicle.com/blogs/saysomething/2014/04/01/mobilizing-to-reduce-disparities-in-health-care/

Podcast

Solomon, A. (2013, April). *Love, no matter what.* [Video podcast]. Retrieved from TED on https://www.ted.com/

E-mail Message

E-mails, like interviews and letters, are considered personal communication and are not included in the references list.

Posting to an Online Forum or Discussion List

Only include the posting in your list of references if it is archived. Otherwise, it is considered personal communication and should be cited only in the text.

Bockelman, P. (2015, April 24). School information meeting [Electronic mailing list message.] Retrieved from to https://groups.yahoo.com/neo/groups/somerville-4-schools

Tweet

Start with the author's real name, and give the screen name in brackets. If the real name is not available, use the screen name without the brackets. Give the entire tweet as the title, followed by the label "Tweet" in brackets.

Appelbaum, Y. [YAppelbaum]. (2015, 1 July). I earnestly, honestly believe that never before have intellectuals reached such large audiences with so much fine work [Tweet]. Retrieved from https://twitter.com/YAppelbaum/status/616272425244827648

Facebook Post

Use the author's name as it appears in the post. Give a short phrase from the post as the title, and follow with the label "Facebook post" in brackets. If the post is from a personal Facebook page not accessible to the public, cite it as personal communication in the body of your text only.

City of Boston. (2015, June 26). Report housing discrimination [Facebook post]. Retrieved July 12, 2015, from https://www.facebook.com/cityofboston

Audio, Visual, and Other Sources

Docter, P. (Director). (2015). *Inside out.* [Motion picture]. United States: Pixar.

Television Program or Episode

For a television broadcast, start with the producer. For an episode in a series, start with the writer and director of the episode, and list the series name after the episode title. If you retrieved the episode from the Web, end with "Retrieved from" and the URL.

Burkey, P. (Producer). (2015, July 13). *NBC nightly news with Lester Holt* [Television broadcast]. Boston, MA: WGBH.

Young, R. (Writer & Director). (2013, October 22). Hunting the nightmare bacteria [Television series episode]. In *Frontline*. Retrieved from http://www.pbs.org/

Lecture or Speech

Goldberger, P. (2015, April 20). *The generic city*. Address at University of California, Berkeley, Berkeley, CA.

Music Recording

Alexander, J. (2015). Lush life. On *My favorite things*. [CD]. New York, NY: Motéma Music.

Graph, Chart, Table, or Map

Give information about the type of source in brackets ([Data set], [Graph], etc.). If the graphic is part of a larger document, do not italicize the title.

Swanberg, S. E. (2015). *Ebola outbreak in West Africa as of Sept. 25, 2014*. [Graph]. Retrieved from http://www.scilogs.com/tenacious-telomere/ ebola-can-we-head-off-the-cdcs-dire-prediction/

Work of Art

Insert a label in brackets after the title, then give the location of the artwork, the city, and the state or country.

Brueghel, P. (1568). *The beggars* [Painting]. Louvre, Paris, France.

CSE: Numbered Bibliography

The documentation format recommended by the Council of Science Editors is used primarily in the sciences. In this method, you number each entry in your references list. Then, to cite a source in your essay, place the number of the work to which you are referring in parentheses or as a superscript.

Theorem 2 of Joel, Shier, and Stein (2) is strengthened in the following theorem:

The following would be a consequence of the conjecture of McMullen and Shepher[3]:

In the citation-name method, you arrange your references list in alphabetical order. In the citation-sequence method, your references list follows the order in which you cite the sources in your essay. A third method, the name-year method, resembles the author-date method used by APA. Consult your instructor or *Scientific Style and Format: The CSE Manual for Authors, Editors, and Publishers*, 8th edition.

Chicago: Endnote/Footnote Documentation

Many academic books document sources with *footnotes* or *endnotes*. In this system, based on *The Chicago Manual of Style*, superscript numbers in your essay correspond to notes containing publication information, which appear either at the bottom of the page (footnotes) or on a separate page at the end of the essay (endnotes). A bibliography is often included at the end of the essay.

This brief excerpt from a biographical essay about Ernest Hemingway shows you what the endnote/footnote system looks like.

> Hemingway's zest for life extended to women also. His wandering heart seemed only to be exceeded by an even more appreciative eye.[6] Hadley was aware of her husband's flirtations and of his facility with women.[7] Yet, she had no idea that something was going on between Hemingway and Pauline Pfeiffer, a fashion editor for *Vogue* magazine.[8] She was also unaware that Hemingway delayed his return to Schruns from a business trip to New York, in February 1926, so that he might spend some more time with this "new and strange girl."[9]
>
> 6. Ernest Hemingway, *A Moveable Feast* (New York: Scribner, 1964), 102.
>
> 7. Alice Hunt Sokoloff, *Hadley: The First Mrs. Hemingway* (New York: Dodd, Mead, 1973), 84.
>
> 8. Carlos Baker, *Ernest Hemingway: A Life Story* (New York: Scribner, 1969), 159.
>
> 9. Hemingway, 210. Also Baker, 165.

If your instructor asks you to use endnotes or footnotes, do not put parenthetical citations, as in MLA or APA style, anywhere within the text of the essay. Instead, at each place where you would insert a parenthetical reference, put a number to indicate to your reader that there is a corresponding footnote or endnote.

When inserting the numbers, follow these rules:

- The note number is raised slightly above the line of your essay (superscript).

- The notes are numbered consecutively: if you insert a note somewhere, renumber the rest.

- Every note should contain at least one separate piece of information. Never write a note that states only, "See footnote 3." The reader should be told enough to make it unnecessary to consult footnote 3.

▪ While a note may contain more than one piece of information (for example, the source reference as well as some additional explanation of the point that is being documented), the note should have only one number. Do not place two note numbers together, like this: [6,7].

Unless your instructor specifies otherwise, use endnotes rather than footnotes and include a bibliography.

The *format of the notes* is the reverse of the standard bibliography format: the first line of the note is indented five spaces, with the second and subsequent lines flush with the left margin. The note begins with a number, corresponding to the number in the text of the essay; the number is followed by a period. The author's name is in first-name/last-name order; author and title are separated by commas, not periods; publication information is placed in parentheses; and the note ends with the page reference and a period.

Start the list of endnotes on a new page after the text of the essay, numbering it (and any subsequent pages) in sequence with the rest of the pages. Center the title *Notes* one inch from the top of the page, double-space, and begin the first entry. Double-space the entire thing.

The *format of the bibliography* is the same as the "Works Cited" format for parenthetical documentation that was described in Chapter 7 and Chapter 10: the sources are alphabetized by last name, with the second and subsequent lines of each entry indented. The bibliography starts on a new page following the list of endnotes, or following the essay if you are using footnotes.

Here is a list of seven notes, illustrating some of the most common forms, followed by a bibliography consisting of the same seven sources:

Notes

1. Helen Block Lewis, *Psychic War in Men and Women* (New York: New York University Press, 1976), 43.

2. Gertrude Himmelfarb, "Observations on Humanism and History," in *The Philosophy of the Curriculum*, ed. Sidney Hook, 85 (Buffalo: Prometheus, 1975).

3. Harvey G. Cox, "Moral Reasoning and the Humanities," *Liberal Education* 71, no. 3 (1985): 196.

4. Lauro Martines, "Mastering the Matriarch," *Times Literary Supplement*, February 1, 1985, 113.

5. Carolyn See, "Collaboration with a Daughter: The Rewards and Cost," *New York Times* June 19, 1986, late edition, C2.

6. Andrew R. Heinze, "Jews and American Popular Psychology: Reconsidering the Protestant Paradigm of Popular Thought," *The Journal of American History* 88, no. 3 (2001), http://www.historycooperative.org/journals/jah/88.3/heinze.html.

7. Gwen Sharp, "The Geography of a Restaurant Menu," *Sociological Images*, May 1, 2015, http://thesocietypages.org.

Bibliography

Cox, Harvey G. "Moral Reasoning and the Humanities." *Liberal Education* 71, no. 3 (1985): 195–204.

Heinze, Andrew R. "Jews and American Popular Psychology: Reconsidering the Protestant Paradigm of Popular Thought." *The Journal of American History* 88, no. 3 (2001). http://www.historycooperative.org/journals/jah/88.3/heinze.html.

Himmelfarb, Gertrude. "Observations on Humanism and History." In *The Philosophy of the Curriculum*, edited by Sidney Hook, 81–88. Buffalo: Prometheus, 1975.

Lewis, Helen Block. *Psychic War in Men and Women*. New York: New York University Press, 1976.

Martines, Lauro. "Mastering the Matriarch." *Times Literary Supplement*, February 1, 1985, 113.

See, Carolyn. "Collaboration with a Daughter: The Rewards and Cost." *New York Times*, June 19, 1986, late edition, C2.

Sharp, Gwen. "The Geography of a Restaurant Menu." Sociological Images, May 1, 2015. http://thesocietypages.org.

The first time you cite a new source, the note should contain detailed information about publication history. The second time you cite the same source, and all subsequent times, use a *short form*, consisting of the author's last name, a shortened title, and a page number:

8. Lewis, *Psychic War*, 74.

The short form makes it unnecessary to use any Latin abbreviations, like *ibid.* or *op. cit.*, in your notes.

For advice about using footnotes rather than endnotes, and for more examples and guidelines for kinds of sources not illustrated here, see *The Chicago Manual of Style*, 16th edition (2010).

Notes Plus Page Numbers in the Text

If you are using only one source in your essay, it is a good idea to include a footnote at the first reference and, thereafter, cite the page number of the source in the text of your essay.

For example, if your essay is exclusively about Sigmund Freud's *Civilization and Its Discontents*, document your first reference to the work with a complete note, citing the edition that you are using:

*Sigmund Freud, *Civilization and Its Discontents* (Garden City, NY: Doubleday, 1958), 72. All further citations refer to this edition.

This single note explains to your reader that you are intending to use the same edition whenever you cite this source. All subsequent references to this book will be followed by the page reference, in parentheses, usually at the end of your sentence.

> Freud has asserted that "the greatest obstacle to civilization [is] the constitutional tendency in men to aggression against one another..." (101).

This method is most useful in essays on literary topics when you are focusing on a single author, without citing secondary sources. Ask your instructor if you are unsure whether this method is appropriate for your essay.

Acknowledgments

Chapter 1

Donna Freitas, Excerpt from THE END OF SEX by Donna Freitas. Copyright © Apr 2, 2013 by Donna Freitas. Reprinted by permission of Basic Books, a member of the Perseus Book Group.

Thane Rosenbaum, "Eye for an Eye: The Case for Revenge," *The Chronicle of Higher Education*, March 26, 2013. Copyright © 2013 by The Chronicle of Higher Education. Reprinted by permission of The Chronicle of Higher Education. All rights reserved.

Chapter 2

Bridget Anderson, "Just Another Job? The Commodification of Domestic Labor," from GLOBAL WOMAN, edited by Barbara Ehrenreich and Arlie Russell Hochschild. Copyright © 2002. Reprinted by permission of the author.

Yochai Benkler, Excerpt from THE PENGUIN AND THE LEVIATHAN by Yochai Benkler. Copyright © 2011 by Yochai Benhler. Reprinted by permission of Crown Business, an imprint of the Crown Publishing Group, a division of Penguin Random House LLC. All rights reserved.

Marcus Boon, Excerpt from IN PRAISE OF COPYING by Marcus Boon, p. 5, Cambridge, Mass.: Harvard University Press. Copyright © 2010 by the President and Fellows of Harvard College. Reprinted by permission of the publisher.

Sheldon M. Garon, Excerpt from BEYOND OUR MEANS by Sheldon M. Garon. Copyright © 2013. Reprinted with permission of Princeton University Press. Permission conveyed through Copyright Clearance Center, Inc.

Sherry Turkle, Excerpt from ALONE TOGETHER. Copyright © 2012 by Sherry Turkle. Reprinted by permission of Basic Books, a member of the Perseus Books Group.

Paul Tough, Excerpt from HOW CHILDREN SUCCEED by Paul Tough. Copyright © 2012 by Paul Tough. Reprinted by permission of Houghton Mifflin Harcourt Publishing Company. All Rights Reserved.

Jessica Higgins, "Is a Picture Worth a Thousand Notes?" *The Chronicle of Higher Education*, January 24, 2014. Copyright © 2014 by The Chronicle of Higher Education. Reprinted by permission of The Chronicle of Higher Education. All rights reserved.

Bertrand Russell, "The Social Responsibility of Scientists," from FACT AND FICTION. Copyright © 2009. Reprinted by permission of the Taylor & Francis Books UK and the Bertrand Russell Peace Foundation.

Mike Rose, "Making Sparks Fly," *The American Scholar*, Volume 80, No. 3, Summer 2011. Copyright © 2011 by Mike Rose. Reprinted by permission of the publisher.

Stephen Marche, "Is Facebook Making Us Lonely?" as first published in *The Atlantic Magazine*. Copyright © 2012 The Atlantic Media Co. Distributed by Tribune Content Agency, LLC. All rights reserved.

Chapter 3

John Lahr, "Petrified," as first published in *The New Yorker*, August 28, 2008. Copyright © 2008 by John Lahr. Reprinted by permission of Georges Borchardt, Inc., on behalf of the author.

Lizabeth Cohen, Excerpt from A CONSUMER'S REPUBLIC by Lizabeth Cohen, Copyright © 2003 by Lizabeth Cohen. Reprinted by permission of Alfred A. Knopf, an imprint of the Knopf Doubleday Publishing Group, a division of Penguin Random House LLC. All rights reserved.

Hanna Rosin, Excerpt from THE END OF MEN: AND THE RISE OF WOMEN by Hanna Rosin. Copyright © 2012 by Hanna Rosin. Reprinted by permission of Riverhead, an imprint of Penguin Publishing Group, a division of Penguin Random House LLC.

Rachelle Bergstein, Excerpt from pp. xii–xiii [370 words] from WOMEN FROM THE ANKLE DOWN by Rachelle Bergstein. Copyright © 2012 by Rachelle Bergstein. Reprinted by permission of HarperCollins Publishers.

Rachel Shteir, Excerpt from THE STEAL: A CULTURAL HISTORY OF SHOPLIFTING by Rachel Shteir. Copyright © 2011 by Rachel Shteir. Reprinted by permission of Penguin Press, an imprint of Penguin Publishing Group, a division of Penguin Random House LLC.

Chris Rojek, Excerpt from FAME ATTACK. Copyright © 2012 by Chris Rojek. Reprinted by permission of Bloomsbury Academic, an imprint of Bloomsbury Publishing Plc.

Chapter 4

Niccolo Machiavelli, Excerpt from THE PRINCE by Niccolo Machiavelli, translated by Tim Parks. Translation Copyright © 2009 by Tim Parks. Reprinted by permission of Penguin Books, an imprint of Penguin Publishing Group, a division of Penguin Random House LLC.

Tom Lutz, Excerpt from CRYING: THE NATURAL AND CULTURAL HISTORY OF TEARS by Tom Lutz. Copyright © 1999 by Tom Lutz. Reprinted by permission of W. W. Norton & Company, Inc.

Giles Slade, Excerpt from THE BIG DISCONNECT by Giles Slade, Amherst, NY: Prometheus Books, 2012, pp. 30–31, 237–239, 285. Copyright © 2012 by Giles Slade. All rights reserved. Used with permission of the publisher; www.prometheusbooks.com.

Martha C. Nussbaum, Excerpt from CULTIVATING HUMANITY by Martha C. Nussbaum, p. 294, Cambridge, Mass.: Harvard University Press. Copyright © 1997 by the President and Fellows of Harvard College. Reprinted by permission of the publisher.

Pamela Haag, "Death by Treacle," *The American Scholar*, Volume 81, No. 2, Spring 2012. Copyright © 2012 by Pamela Haag. Reprinted by permission of the publisher.

Chapter 5

Chapter 6

Chapter 8

Index

Thematic Reading Clusters

The College Experience

Men and Women

Social Media